Lecture Notes in Computer Science 8813

Commenced Publication in 1973
Founding and Former Series Editors:
Gerhard Goos, Juris Hartmanis, and Jan van Leeuwen

Dimitris Gritzalis   Aggelos Kiayias
Ioannis Askoxylakis (Eds.)

Cryptology and Network Security

13th International Conference, CANS 2014
Heraklion, Crete, Greece, October 22-24, 2014
Proceedings

 Springer

Volume Editors

Dimitris Gritzalis
Athens University of Economics & Business
Department of Informatics
76, Patission Str., 10434 Athens, Greece
E-mail: dgrit@aueb.gr

Aggelos Kiayias
National and Kapodistrian University of Athens
Department of Informatics and Telecommunications
Panepistimiopolis, 15784 Athens, Greece
E-mail: aggelos@di.uoa.gr

Ioannis Askoxylakis
FORTH-ICS
Vassilika Vouton
P.O. Box 1385, 711 10 Heraklion, Crete, Greece
E-mail: asko@ics.forth.gr

ISSN 0302-9743   e-ISSN 1611-3349
ISBN 978-3-319-12279-3   e-ISBN 978-3-319-12280-9
DOI 10.1007/978-3-319-12280-9
Springer Cham Heidelberg New York Dordrecht London

Library of Congress Control Number: 2014950927

LNCS Sublibrary: SL 4 – Security and Cryptology

Typesetting: Camera-ready by author, data conversion by Scientific Publishing Services, Chennai, India

Printed on acid-free paper

Springer is part of Springer Science+Business Media (www.springer.com)

Preface

The 13th International Conference on Cryptology and Network Security (CANS) took place on Heraklion, on the island of Crete, Greece, during October 20–22, 2014, and was organized by the Institute of Computer Science of the Foundation for Research and Technology - Hellas (FORTH-ICS).

The conference received 86 submissions, four of which were withdrawn. The Program Committee (PC) decided to accept 25 papers for presentation at the conference. Most submitted papers were reviewed by at least three PC members, while submissions co-authored by a PC member received at least one additional review. In addition to the PC members, a number of external reviewers joined the review process in their particular areas of expertise. The initial reviewing period was followed by a lively discussion phase that enabled the committee to converge on the final program. There were six papers that were conditionally accepted and shepherded by assigned PC members in a second round of reviewing. All conditionally accepted papers were included in the program. The paper submission, reviewing, discussion, and the preparation of proceedings were facilitated by the Web-based system EasyChair.

The objective of the CANS conference is to support excellent research in cryptology and network security and promote the interaction between researchers working in these areas. The PC strived to broaden the program and include papers covering diverse areas such as encryption, cryptanalysis, malware analysis, privacy and identification systems as well as various types of network protocol design and analysis work. The program also featured three keynote speakers, Sotiris Ioannidis from FORTH, Moni Naor from Weizmann Institute of Science, and Dawn Song from the University of California, Berkeley, who gave lectures on cutting-edge research on cryptology and network security. The titles and abstracts of their talks can be found in this proceedings volume.

Finally, we would like to thank all the authors who submitted their research work to the conference, the members of the Organizing Committee, who worked very hard for the success and smooth operation of the event, and the members of the Steering Committee and particularly Yvo Desmedt whose guidance during various stages of the PC work was invaluable. Last but not least, we thank all the attendees who participated and contributed to the stimulating discussions after the talks and during the breaks and social events that took place as part of the conference program.

October 2014

Dimitris Gritzalis
Aggelos Kiayias
Ioannis Askoxylakis

Organization

Program Committee

Isaac Agudo	University of Malaga, Spain
Giuseppe Ateniese	University of Rome, Italy
Mike Burmester	Florida State University, USA
Dario Catalano	University of Catania, Italy
George Danezis	Microsoft Research, UK
Ed Dawson	University of Queensland, Australia
Sabrina De Capitani	
Di Vimercati	Università degli Studi di Milano, Italy
Roberto Di Pietro	University of Rome Tre, Italy
Itai Dinur	ENS, France
Sara Foresti	Università degli Studi di Milano, Italy
Joaquin Garcia-Alfaro	TELECOM SudParis, France
Dieter Gollmann	TU Hamburg, Germany
Sushil Jajodia	George Mason University, USA
Stanislaw Jarecki	University of California Irvine, USA
Vassilios Katos	Democritus University of Thrace, Greece
Panos Kotzanikolaou	University of Piraeus, Greece
Helger Lipmaa	University of Tartu, Estonia
Javier Lopez	University of Malaga, Spain
Evangelos Markatos	University of Crete, Greece
Adam O'Neil	Georgetown University, USA
Kenny Paterson	RH - University of London, UK
Siani Pearson	HP Laboratories
Rene Peralta	NIST, USA
Christian Rechberger	DTU, Denmark
Kui Ren	SUNY Buffalo, USA
Panagiotis Rizomiliotis	University of the Aegean, Greece
Ahmad-Reza Sadeghi	University of Darmstadt, Germany
Reihaneh Safavi-Naini	University of Calgary, Canada
Pierangela Samarati	Università degli Studi di Milano, Italy
Nitesh Saxena	University of Alabama, USA
George Spanoudakis	City University, UK
Ioannis Stamatiou	University of Patras, Greece
Francois-Xavier Standaert	University of Louvain, Belgium
Willie Susilo	University of Wollongong, Australia

Katsuyuki Takashima   Mitsubishi Electric
Marianthi Theoharidou   Joint Research Center, Italy
Nikos Triandopoulos   EMC RSA Labs, USA
Huaxiong Wang   NTU, Singapore
Moti Yung   Google
Hong-Sheng Zhou   VCU, USA
Vasilis Zikas   UCLA, USA

Additional Reviewers

Alderman, James   Moody, Dustin
Anand, S Abhishek   Moyano, Francisco
Baldimtsi, Foteini   Mukhopadhyay, Dibya
Bartlett, Harry   Nieto, Ana
Blanc, Gregory   Nishide, Takashi
D'Errico, Michela   Onete, Cristina
Di Raimondo, Mario   Pan, Jiaxin
Dmitrienko, Alexandra   Papadopoulos, Dimitrios
Donida Labati, Ruggero   Perlner, Ray
Fernandez, Carmen   Peters, Thomas
Garg, Sanjam   Poettering, Bertram
Gaspar, Lubos   Procter, Gordon
Gentry, Craig   Puglisi, Orazio
Guo, Fuchun   Rios, Ruben
Han, Jinguang   Schmidt, Desmond
Heuser, Stephan   Shahandashti, Siamak
Huang, Qiong   Shirvanian, Maliheh
Jhawar, Mahavir   Shrestha, Babins
Jiang, Shaoquan   Smart, Nigel
Jost, Daniel   Sugawara, Takeshi
Koelbl, Stefan   Tackmann, Björn
Koeune, François   Tang, Qiang
Krotofil, Marina   Tiessen, Tyge
Latsiou, Aikaterina   Xiao, Weijun
Lauridsen, Martin M.   Yang, Guomin
Liang, Kaitai   Yasuda, Takanori
Matsuda, Takahiro   Zhang, Bingsheng
Mitelbach, Arno   Zhang, Liangfeng
Mohamed, Manar

Invited Talks

Invited Talk 1: Primary-Secondary-Resolvers Membership Proof Systems and their Application to DNSSEC

Moni Naor

Weizmann Institute of Science
Rehovot, Israel
moni.naor@weizmann.ac.il

Abstract. We consider Primary-Secondary-Resolver Membership Proof Systems (PSR for short) that enable a secondary to convince a resolver whether or not a given a element is in a set defined by the primary without revealing more information about the set.

The main motivation is studying the problem of zone enumeration in DNSSEC. DNSSEC is designed to prevent network attackers from tampering with domain name system (DNS) messages. The cryptographic machinery used in DNSSEC, however, also creates a new vulnerability - Zone Enumeration, where an adversary launches a small number of online DNSSEC queries and then uses offline dictionary attacks to learn which domain names are present or absent in a DNS zone.

We explain why current DNSSEC (NSEC3) suffers from the problem of zone enumeration: we use cryptographic lower bounds to prove that in a PSR system the secondary must perform non trivial online computation and in particular under certain circumstances signatures. This implies that the three design goals of DNSSEC — high performance, security against network attackers, and privacy against zone enumeration — cannot be satisfied simultaneously.

We provide PSR constructions matching our lower bound and in particular suggest NSEC5, a protocol that solves the problem of DNSSEC zone enumeration while remaining faithful to the operational realities of DNSSEC. The scheme can be seen as a variant of NSEC3, where the hash function is replaced with an RSA based hashing scheme. Other constructions we have are based on the BonehLynnShacham signature scheme, Verifiable Random and Unpredictable Functions and Hierarchical Identity Based Encryption.

The talk is based on the papers "NSEC5: Provably Preventing DNSSEC Zone Enumeration" by Sharon Goldberg, Moni Naor, Dimitrios Papadopoulos, Leonid Reyzin, Sachin Vasant and Asaf Ziv and "PSR Membership Proof Systems" by Moni Naor and Asaf Ziv.

Invited Talk 2: Ask Us before you download: Lessons from Analyzing 3 Million Android Apps

Dawn Song

University of California, Berkeley
Berekely, CA, USA
dawnsong@cs.berkeley.edu

Abstract. Android is the most popular mobile platform currently, with over 1 billion devices activated. Millions of Android Apps have been downloaded billions of times. What are the security and privacy issues in these millions of apps? What lessons can we learn to ensure better app security and mobile security? In this talk, I will share our insights and lessons learned from analyzing over 3 million apps.

Invited Talk 3: Security applications of GPUs

Sotiris Ioannidis

Institute of Computer Science
Foundation for Research & Technology Hellas, Greece
sotiris@ics.forth.gr

Abstract. Modern graphics processors have been traditionally used for gaming, but in the last few years they have been used more and more in the area of high performance computing. In this talk we will explore alternate uses of graphics processors, in the area of security. We will discuss how a defender can use graphics hardware to bolster system defenses, and how miscreants can exploit them to build better and stealthier malware.

Table of Contents

Bootstrappable Identity-Based Fully Homomorphic Encryption

Michael Clear and Ciarán McGoldrick

School of Computer Science and Statistics,
Trinity College Dublin, Ireland

Abstract. It has been an open problem for a number of years to construct an identity-based fully homomorphic encryption (IBFHE) scheme (first mentioned by Naccache at CHES/CRYPTO 2010). At CRYPTO 2013, Gentry, Sahai and Waters largely settled the problem by presenting leveled IBFHE constructions based on the Learning With Errors problem. However their constructions are not bootstrappable, and as a result, are not "pure" IBFHE schemes. The major challenge with bootstrapping in the identity-based setting is that it must be possible to noninteractively derive from the public parameters an "encryption" of the secret key for an arbitrary identity. All presently-known leveled IBFHE schemes only allow bootstrapping if such an "encryption" of the secret key is supplied out-of-band. In this work, we present a "pure" IBFHE scheme from indistinguishability obfuscation, and extend the result to the attribute-based setting. Our attribute-based scheme is the first to support homomorphic evaluation on ciphertexts with different attributes. Finally, we characterize presently-known leveled IBFHE schemes with a view to developing a "compiler" from a leveled IBFHE scheme to a bootstrappable IBFHE scheme, and sufficient conditions are identified.

1 Introduction

Fully homomorphic encryption (FHE) is a cryptographic primitive that facilitates arbitrary computation on encrypted data. Since Gentry's breakthrough realization of FHE in 2009 [1], many improved variants have appeared in the literature [2–6]. Leveled FHE is a relaxation that supports evaluation of circuits of limited (multiplicative) depth. Such a limit L is specified in advance of generating the parameters of the scheme. The size of the parameters along with the size of keys and ciphertexts are allowed to depend on L. In the public-key setting, a leveled FHE scheme can be transformed into a "pure" FHE scheme (i.e. a scheme supporting evaluation of circuits of unlimited depth) via Gentry's *bootstrapping* theorem [1].

In brief, the process of *bootstrapping* entails using the scheme to homomorphically evaluate its own decryption circuit. More precisely, ciphertexts in existing FHE schemes contain a level of "noise". As long as this "noise" remains below a certain threshold, decryption can be performed correctly. The goal of bootstrapping is to return the noise to a reduced level, so homomorphic operations

D. Gritzalis et al. (Eds.): CANS 2014, LNCS 8813, pp. 1–19, 2014.

can continue to be performed. This is achieved by publishing encryptions of the secret key bits, and homomorphically evaluating the scheme's decryption circuit on a "noisy" ciphertext to produce a ciphertext with less noise.

Identity-Based Encryption (IBE) is centered around the notion that a user's public key can be efficiently derived from an identity string and system-wide public parameters / master public key. The public parameters are chosen by a trusted authority along with a secret trapdoor (master secret key), which is used to extract secret keys for user identities. The first secure IBE schemes were presented in 2001 by Boneh and Franklin [7] (based on bilinear pairings), and Cocks [8] (based on the quadratic residuosity problem).

At his talk at CHES/Crypto 2010, Naccache [9] mentioned "identity-based fully homomorphic encryption" as an open problem. At Crypto 2013, Gentry, Sahai and Waters presented the first identity-based (leveled) fully homomorphic encryption scheme [6], largely settling the problem raised by Naccache, which had been further explored in [10,11].

Achieving fully homomorphic encryption (FHE) in the identity-based setting turned out to be quite a tricky problem, for a variety of reasons. Prior to [6], there were two paradigms for constructing leveled FHE:

1. Gentry's original paradigm based on ideals, which was introduced in [1] (works which built on this include [2,3]); and
2. Brakersi and Vaikuntanathan's paradigm based on the learning with errors (LWE) problem [4,5] entailing techniques such as relinearization, modulus switching and dimension reduction.

It appeared like there was limited potential for obtaining identity-based FHE from the first paradigm because no secure IBE schemes had been constructed with this structure; that is, roughly speaking no IBE scheme associated an identity with an ideal, and a secret key with a "short" generator for that ideal.

The second paradigm appeared more fruitful. Starting with the work of Gentry, Peikert and Vaikuntanathan (GPV) [12], constructions of IBE from LWE had emerged [13–15]. But it was not straightforward to adapt Brakersi and Vaikuntanathan's (BV) ideas to the identity-based setting. The main reason for this is that BV-type FHE relies on having "encryptions" of some secret key information, termed an *evaluation key*. If a user directly supplies this information to an evaluator out-of-band, then evaluation can be accomplished as in BV. IBE schemes where the evaluation key can be generated by the key holder, but cannot be derived non-interactively, have been termed "weak" [10,11]. Due to the difficulty of non-interactively deriving an "encryption" of secret key information for a given identity (based on public information alone) meant that the BV paradigm also seemed inhospitable to IBE.

Recently Gentry, Sahai and Waters (GSW) [6] developed a new paradigm from LWE where the secret key is an *approximate* eigenvector of a ciphertext. Their construction is both elegant and asymptotically faster than existing FHE schemes. Furthermore, it does not rely on an evaluation key, which means that it can be adapted to support IBE. In fact, a "compiler" was proposed in [6] to transform an LWE-based IBE satisfying certain properties into an identity-based (leveled) fully homomorphic encryption (IBFHE) scheme, and it was noted that several existing LWE-based IBE schemes satisfy the required properties. The resulting IBFHE constructions are leveled i.e. they can evaluate circuits of bounded multiplicative depth (polynomial in the security parameter, and fixed prior to generation of the public parameters). However unlike their public-key counterparts, these constructions are not bootstrappable, since bootstrapping relies on "encryptions" of secret key information, akin to an evaluation key. As such, to the best of our knowledge, there are no known "pure" IBFHE schemes in the literature, since Gentry's bootstrapping theorem from [1] is the only known way of converting a leveled FHE scheme to a "pure" FHE scheme.

In this paper, we identify sufficient conditions for these leveled IBFHE constructions to be bootstrappable, and we construct the first "pure" IBFHE scheme, which we believe finally resolves the question raised by Naccache [9].

1.1 Contributions

Construction of "Pure" IBFHE. we construct the first "pure" ibfhe scheme using the technique of "punctured programming" [16], a powerful tool combining an indistinguishability obfuscator [17] with a puncturable pesudorandom function (prf) [18–20],

A Compiler from leveled IBFHE to "Pure" IBFHE. We exploit indistinguishability obfuscation in constructing a compiler from a leveled IBFHE satisfying certain properties to a bootstrappable, and hence "pure", IBFHE. Our main idea is to include in the public parameters an obfuscation of a program (with the master secret key embedded) so that the evaluator can non-interactively derive an "evaluation key" for any identity. Although our compiler falls short of working with arbitrary leveled IBFHE schemes, we establish sufficient conditions for a leveled IBFHE to satisfy in order for it to be bootstrappable. This leads us to an interesting characterization of compatible schemes, which also encompasses our positive result above.

Attribute-Based Fully Homomorphic Encryption (ABFHE) in the Multi-Attribute Setting. Sahai and Waters [21] introduced a generalization of IBE known as Attribute-Based Encryption (ABE). In a (key-policy)* ABE scheme, a user Alice encrypts her message with a descriptive tag or *attribute*. The trusted authority issues secret keys for *access policies* to users depending on their credentials. Hence, if a user Bob is given a secret key for a policy f, he can decrypt messages with attributes that satisfy f. More precisely, let c_a be a ciphertext that encrypts the message m with some attribute a. Then Bob can recover the message m if and only if a satisfies his policy f; that is, $f(a) = 1$ (note that policies can be viewed as predicates).

---

* There are other variants such as ciphertext-policy ABE [22], but we focus on key-policy ABE here.

Gentry, Sahai and Waters [6] constructed the first leveled Attribute-Based Fully Homomorphic Encryption scheme (ABFHE). However, their scheme only works in the single-attribute setting. In other words, homomorphic evaluation is supported only for ciphertexts with the same attribute.

We present the first ABFHE that supports evaluation on ciphertexts with different attributes. We formalize the notion of multi-attribute ABFHE, which can be viewed as an attribute-based analog to the notion of multi-key FHE [23].

Example Scenario

To further illustrate the usefulness of multi-attribute ABFHE, we provide a sketch of an application scenario. Consider a hospital H that avails of the computational facilities of a cloud provider E. Data protection legislation requires the hospital to encrypt all sensitive data stored on third party servers. The hospital deploys attribute-based encryption to manage access to potentially sensitive data. Therefore it manages a "trusted authority" that issues secret keys for access policies to staff in accordance with their roles / credentials. Beyond deploying standard attribute-based encryption, H elects to adopt multi-attribute ABFHE because this allows computation to be performed on encrypted data stored at a third party facility such as E.

Parties such as outside researchers, medical practitioners and internal staff in H are able to encrypt sensitive data with appropriate attributes in order to limit access to authorized staff. For example, a doctor in the maternity unit might encrypt medical data with the attribute "MATERNITY" and a researcher in the cardiology unit might encrypt her data with the attribute "CARDIOLOGY". Suppose both encrypted data sets are sent to the cloud provider E to carry out computational processing on the data (while remaining encrypted). A multi-attribute ABFHE allows E to perform the desired computation homomorphically on both data sets irrespective of the fact that the data sets were encrypted with different attributes.

Suppose a staff member at H has an access policy f defined by

$$f(x) \triangleq x = \text{"MATERNITY" OR } x = \text{"CARDIOLOGY".}$$

Then this staff member is able to decrypt the result of the computation. This matches our intuition because her policy permits her access to both the data sets used in the computation. However, a member of staff whose access policy permits access to either "MATERNITY" or "CARDIOLOGY" (but not both) should not be able to decrypt the result.

2 Preliminaries

2.1 Notation

A quantity is said to be negligible with respect to some parameter κ, written $\mathsf{negl}(\kappa)$, if it is asymptotically bounded from above by the reciprocal of all polynomials in κ.

For a probability distribution $\mathcal{D}$, we denote by $x \xleftarrow{\$} \mathcal{D}$ the fact that x is sampled according to $\mathcal{D}$. We overload the notation for a set S i.e. $y \xleftarrow{\$} S$ denotes that y is sampled uniformly from S. Let $\mathcal{D}_0$ and $\mathcal{D}_1$ be distributions. We denote by $\mathcal{D}_0 \underset{C}{\approx} \mathcal{D}_1$ and the $\mathcal{D}_0 \underset{S}{\approx} \mathcal{D}_1$ the facts that $\mathcal{D}_0$ and $\mathcal{D}_1$ are computationally indistinguishable and statistically indistinguishable respectively.

We use the notation $[k]$ for an integer k to denote the set $\{1, \ldots, k\}$.

2.2   Identity Based Encryption

An Identity Based Encryption (IBE) scheme is a tuple of probabilistic polynomial time (PPT) algorithms (Setup, KeyGen, Encrypt, Decrypt) defined with respect a message space $\mathcal{M}$, an identity space $\mathcal{I}$ and a ciphertext space $\mathcal{C}$ as follows:

- Setup(1^κ):
  On input (in unary) a security parameter κ, generate public parameters PP and a master secret key MSK. Output (PP, MSK).

- KeyGen(MSK, id):
  On input master secret key MSK and an identity id: derive and output a secret key $\mathsf{sk_{id}}$ for identity id.

- Encrypt(PP, id, m):
  On input public parameters PP, an identity id, and a message $m \in \mathcal{M}$, output a ciphertext $c \in \mathcal{C}$ that encrypts m under identity id.

- Decrypt($\mathsf{sk_{id}}, c$):
  On input a secret key $\mathsf{sk_{id}}$ for identity id and a ciphertext $c \in \mathcal{C}$, output m' if c is a valid encryption under id; output a failure symbol $\bot$ otherwise.

Indistinguishability under a chosen plaintext attack (IND-CPA) for IBE comes in two flavors - *selective* (denoted by IND-sID-CPA) and *full/adaptive* (denoted by IND-ID-CPA). In the former, the adversary has to choose an identity to attack prior to receiving the public parameters, whereas in the latter, the adversary can make arbitrary secret key queries before choosing a target identity. Formally, the security notions are defined by an adversary $\mathcal{A}$'s success in the following game(s).

- Set $\mathsf{id}^* \leftarrow \bot$.
- (**Selective-security only**): $\mathcal{A}$ chooses an identity $\mathsf{id}^* \leftarrow \mathcal{I}$ to attack.
- The challenger generates (PP, MSK) $\leftarrow$ Setup(1^κ), and gives PP to $\mathcal{A}$.
- **Key Queries (1)**: $\mathcal{A}$ can make queries to an oracle $\mathcal{O}$ defined by

$$\mathcal{O}(\mathsf{id}) = \begin{cases} \mathsf{KeyGen}(\mathsf{MSK}, \mathsf{id}) & \text{if } \mathsf{id} \neq \mathsf{id}^* \\ \bot & \text{otherwise} \end{cases}.$$

- (**Full-security only**): $\mathcal{A}$ chooses its target identity $\mathsf{id}^* \leftarrow \mathcal{I}$ now.
- **Challenge Phase**: $\mathcal{A}$ chooses two messages $m_0, m_1 \in \mathcal{M}$ and sends them to the challenger.

- The challenger uniformly samples a bit $b \xleftarrow{\$} \{0, 1\}$, and returns $c^* \leftarrow$ Encrypt($\mathsf{PP}, \mathsf{id}^*, m_b$).
- **Key Queries (2)**: $\mathcal{A}$ makes additional queries to $\mathcal{O}$.
- **Guess**: $\mathcal{A}$ outputs a guess bit b'.

The adversary is said to win the above game if $b = b'$.

2.3   Identity-Based Fully Homomorphic Encryption (IBFHE)

We first define Leveled IBFHE. This definition is for the single-identity setting, which we consider in this paper. This means that evaluation is supported only for ciphertexts with the same identity.

Definition 1. *A Leveled IBFHE scheme with message space $\mathcal{M}$, identity space $\mathcal{I}$, a class of circuits $\mathbb{C} \subseteq \mathcal{M}^* \to \mathcal{M}$ and ciphertext space $\mathcal{C}$ is a tuple of PPT algorithms* (Setup, KeyGen, Encrypt, Decrypt, Eval) *defined as follows:*

- Setup($1^\kappa, 1^L$):
  On input (in unary) a security parameter κ, and a number of levels L (maximum circuit depth to support) generate public parameters PP *and a master secret key* MSK. *Output* (PP, MSK).
- KeyGen, Encrypt *and* Decrypt *are defined the same as IBE.*
- Eval($\mathsf{PP}, C, c_1, \ldots, c_\ell$): *On input public parameters* PP, *a circuit $C \in \mathbb{C}$ and ciphertexts $c_1, \ldots, c_\ell \in \mathcal{C}$, output an evaluated ciphertext $c' \in \mathcal{C}$.*

More precisely, the scheme is required to satisfy the following properties:

- *Over all choices of* (PP, MSK) $\leftarrow$ Setup(1^κ), $\mathsf{id} \in \mathcal{I}$, $C : \mathcal{M}^\ell \to \mathcal{M} \in \{C \in \mathbb{C} : \mathsf{depth}(C) \leq L\}$, $\mu_1, \ldots, \mu_\ell \in \mathcal{M}$, $c_i \leftarrow$ Encrypt($\mathsf{PP}, \mathsf{id}, \mu_i$) *for $i \in [\ell]$, and $c' \leftarrow$ Eval($\mathsf{PP}, C, c_1, \ldots, c_\ell$):*
  - *Correctness*
    $$\mathsf{Decrypt}(\mathsf{sk}, c') = C(\mu_1, \ldots, \mu_\ell) \tag{2.1}$$
    for any sk $\leftarrow$ KeyGen(MSK, id).
  - *Compactness*
    $$|c'| = \mathsf{poly}(\kappa) \tag{2.2}$$

In a leveled fully homomorphic encryption scheme, the size of the public parameters along with the size of keys are allowed to depend on L.

There are different ways to define bootstrapping; the formulation here was chosen to best fit with the results in this paper. We assume without loss of generality that the class of circuits $\mathbb{C}$ supported by the scheme is built from a set of binary operations e.g: $\{\oplus, \odot\}$ i.e. $\oplus : \mathcal{M} \times \mathcal{M} \to \mathcal{M}$ and $\odot : \mathcal{M} \times \mathcal{M} \to \mathcal{M}$.

Definition 2. *A leveled IBFHE is said to be bootstrappable if there exists a pair of PPT algorithms*
(GenBootstrapKey, Bootstrap) *defined as follows:*

- GenBootstrapKey(PP, id) : *takes as input public parameters* PP *and an identity* id, *and outputs a* bootstrapping key $\mathsf{bk_{id}}$.
- Bootstrap(PP, $\mathsf{bk_{id}}$, c) *takes as input public parameters* PP, *a* bootstrapping key $\mathsf{bk_{id}}$ *for identity* id, *and a ciphertext* $c \in \mathcal{C}$, *and outputs a ciphertext* $c' \in \mathcal{C}$.

Over all (PP, MSK): *for every pair of ciphertexts* $c_1, c_2 \in \mathcal{C}$, *all identities* id *and all secret keys* $\mathsf{sk_{id}}$ *and for all* $\circ \in \{\oplus, \odot\}$:

$$\mathsf{Decrypt}(\mathsf{sk_{id}}, \mathsf{Eval}(\circ, \mathsf{Bootstrap}(\mathsf{PP}, \mathsf{id}, c_1), \mathsf{Bootstrap}(\mathsf{PP}, \mathsf{id}, c_2))$$
$$= \mathsf{Decrypt}(\mathsf{sk_{id}}, c_1) \circ \mathsf{Decrypt}(\mathsf{sk_{id}}, c_2).$$

Informally, what the above definition says is that at least one additional homomorphic operation (either $\oplus$ or $\odot$) can be applied to a pair of "refreshed" (i.e. bootstrapped) ciphertexts before bootstrapping is needed again. For a more thorough discussion on bootstrapping, we refer the reader to [1].

2.4 Indistinguishability Obfuscation

Garg et al. [?] recently introduced a candidate construction of an indistinguishability obfuscator based on multi-linear maps. Many of our constructions in this work depend on the notion of indistinguishability obfuscation. Here we give a brief overview of its syntax and security definition.

Definition 3 (Indistinguishability Obfuscation (Based on Definition 7 from [24])). *A uniform PPT machine* $i\mathcal{O}$ *is called an indistinguishability obfuscator for every circuit class* $\{\mathcal{C}_\kappa\}$ *if the following two conditions are met:*

- **Correctness:** *For every* $\kappa \in \mathbb{N}$, *for every* $C \in \mathcal{C}_\kappa$, *for every* x *in the domain of* C, *we have that*

$$\Pr[C'(x) = C(x) : C' \leftarrow i\mathcal{O}(C)] = 1.$$

- **Indistinguishability:** *For every* $\kappa \in \mathbb{N}$, *for all pairs of circuits* $C_0, C_1 \in \mathcal{C}_\kappa$, *if* $C_0(x) = C_1(x)$ *for all inputs* x, *then for all PPT adversaries* $\mathcal{A}$, *we have:*

$$|\Pr[\mathcal{A}(i\mathcal{O}(C_0)) = 1]| - |\Pr[\mathcal{A}(i\mathcal{O}(C_1)) = 1]| \leq \mathsf{negl}(\kappa).$$

2.5 Puncturable Pseudorandom Functions

A puncturable pseudorandom function (PRF) is a constrained PRF (Key, Eval) with an additional PPT algorithm Puncture. Let $n(\cdot)$ and $m(\cdot)$ be polynomials. Our definition here is based on [24] (Definition 3.2). A PRF key K is generated with the PPT algorithm Key which takes as input a security parameter κ. The Eval algorithm is deterministic, and on input a key K and an input string $x \in \{0,1\}^{n(\kappa)}$, outputs a string $y \in \{0,1\}^{m(\kappa)}$.

A puncturable PRF allows one to obtain a "punctured" key $K' \leftarrow$ Puncture (K, S) with respect to a subset of input strings $S \subset \{0,1\}^{n(\kappa)}$ with $|S| = \mathsf{poly}(\kappa)$.

It is required that $\mathsf{Eval}(K, x) = \mathsf{Eval}(K', x) \quad \forall x \in \{0,1\}^{n(\kappa)} \backslash S$, and for any poly-bounded adversary $(\mathcal{A}_1, \mathcal{A}_2)$ with $S \leftarrow \mathcal{A}_1(1^\kappa) \subset \{0,1\}^{n(\kappa)}$ and $|S| = \mathsf{poly}(\kappa)$, any key $K \leftarrow \mathsf{Key}(1^\kappa)$, any $K' \leftarrow \mathsf{Puncture}(K, S)$, and any $x \in S$, it holds that

$$\Pr[\mathcal{A}_2(K', x, \mathsf{Eval}(K, x)) = 1] - \Pr[\mathcal{A}_2(K', x, u) = 1] \leq \mathsf{negl}(\kappa)$$

where $u \xleftarrow{\$} \{0,1\}^{m(\kappa)}$.

3   Construction of "Pure" IBFHE

We now construct a "pure" IBFHE from indistinguishability obfuscation. The main idea is to use the technique of punctured programming, which involves using indistinguishability obfuscation together with a puncturable PRF. In our case, we use the puncturable PRF for the derivation of a user's public key from her identity. Moreover, a unique key pair for a public-key encryption (PKE) scheme can be associated with every identity. If the PKE scheme is also "pure" fully-homomorphic, then we obtain a "pure" IBFHE scheme. Let $\mathcal{E}_{\mathsf{FHE}} := (\mathsf{Gen}, \mathsf{Encrypt}, \mathsf{Decrypt}, \mathsf{Eval})$ be a public-key FHE. We denote by $\mathcal{PK}_{\mathsf{FHE}}$ and $\mathcal{SK}_{\mathsf{FHE}}$ its public-key and private-key space respectively. Consider the following function $F_{\mathsf{MapPK}} \colon \mathcal{I} \to \mathcal{PK}_{\mathsf{FHE}}$ that maps an identity $\mathsf{id} \in \mathcal{I}$ to a public key for $\mathcal{E}_{\mathsf{FHE}}$:

Program $F_{\mathsf{MapPK}}(\mathsf{id})$:

1. Compute $r_{\mathsf{id}} \leftarrow \mathsf{PRF.Eval}(K, \mathsf{id})$.
2. Compute $(\mathsf{pk}_{\mathsf{id}}, \mathsf{sk}_{\mathsf{id}}) \leftarrow \mathcal{E}_{\mathsf{FHE}}.\mathsf{Gen}(1^\kappa; r_{\mathsf{id}})$.
3. **Output** $\mathsf{pk}_{\mathsf{id}}$

A formal description of a scheme $\hat{\mathcal{E}}_*$ that uses an obfuscation of F_{MapPK} is as follows.

- $\hat{\mathcal{E}}_*.\mathsf{Setup}(1^\kappa)$: Compute $K \leftarrow \mathsf{PRF.Key}(1^\kappa)$, compute obfuscation $H \leftarrow i\mathcal{O}(F_{\mathsf{MapPK}})$ of F_{MapPK} with K embedded. Output (H, K) (note that H constitutes the public parameters and K constitutes the master secret key).
- $\hat{\mathcal{E}}_*.\mathsf{KeyGen}(K, \mathsf{id})$: Compute $r_{\mathsf{id}} \leftarrow \mathsf{PRF.Eval}(K, \mathsf{id})$, compute $(\mathsf{pk}_{\mathsf{id}}, \mathsf{sk}_{\mathsf{id}}) \leftarrow \mathcal{E}_{\mathsf{FHE}}.\mathsf{Gen}(1^\kappa; r_{\mathsf{id}})$, and output $\mathsf{sk}_{\mathsf{id}}$.
- $\hat{\mathcal{E}}_*.\mathsf{Encrypt}(H, \mathsf{id}, m)$: Compute $\mathsf{pk}_{\mathsf{id}} \leftarrow H(\mathsf{id})$ and output $\mathcal{E}_{\mathsf{FHE}}.\mathsf{Encrypt}(\mathsf{pk}_{\mathsf{id}}, m)$.
- $\hat{\mathcal{E}}_*.\mathsf{Decrypt}(\mathsf{sk}_{\mathsf{id}}, c)$: Output $\mathcal{E}_{\mathsf{FHE}}.\mathsf{Decrypt}(\mathsf{sk}_{\mathsf{id}}, c)$.
- $\hat{\mathcal{E}}_*.\mathsf{Eval}(H, C, c_1, \ldots, c_\ell)$: Compute $\mathsf{pk}_{\mathsf{id}} \leftarrow H(\mathsf{id})$ and output $\mathcal{E}_{\mathsf{FHE}}.\mathsf{Eval}(\mathsf{pk}_{\mathsf{id}}, C, c_1, \ldots, c_\ell)$.

Lemma 1. *Assuming indistinguishability obfuscation, a secure puncturable PRF and an* IND-CPA-*secure public-key FHE scheme* $\mathcal{E}_{\mathsf{FHE}}$, *the scheme* $\hat{\mathcal{E}}_*$ *is* IND-sID-CPA *secure.*

The proof of Lemma 1 is given in Appendix A.

Theorem 1. *Assuming indistinguishability obfuscation, one-way functions and fully homomorphic encryption, there exists an* IND-sID-CPA*-secure "pure" IBFHE scheme i.e. an identity-based scheme that can homomorphically evaluate all circuits.*

Proof. The construction $\hat{\mathcal{E}}_*$ is fully homomorphic if the underlying PKE scheme $\mathcal{E}_{\mathsf{FHE}}$ is fully homomorphic. Lemma 1 shows that $\hat{\mathcal{E}}_*$ is IND-sID-CPA secure assuming indistinguishability obfuscation, one-way functions and the IND-CPA security of $\mathcal{E}_{\mathsf{FHE}}$. The result follows.   □

Note that because our IBFHE relies on (public-key) "pure" FHE and because all constructions of "pure" FHE that we know of require a circular security assumption, it naturally follows that our IBFHE also requires a circular security assumption. Furthermore, our IBFHE is only shown to be selectively secure. While there is a generic transformation from a selectively-secure IBE to a fully-secure IBE [25], this transformation incurs a degradation in security by a factor of 2^s where $s = |\mathcal{I}|$ is the size of the identity space. Obtaining a fully secure "pure" IBFHE "directly" remains an open problem. These remarks also apply to our attribute-based constructions, which are presented next.

3.1   Extension to Attribute Based Encryption

The scheme $\hat{\mathcal{E}}_*$ can be extended to an Attribute Based Encryption (ABE) scheme. Recall that in a (key-policy) ABE scheme, an encryptor associates an attribute $a \in \mathbb{A}$ with her message, whereas a decryptor can only successfully decrypt a ciphertext with attribute $a \in \mathbb{A}$ if he holds a secret key for a policy (i.e. a predicate) $f \colon \mathbb{A} \to \{0,1\}$ with $f(a) = 1$. We denote by $\mathbb{F}$ the class of supported policies. Therefore, in an ABE scheme, the trusted authority issues secret keys for policies instead of identities as in IBE. The fundamental difference is that there is no longer a one-to-one correspondence between attributes and policies (which is the case in IBE).

Beyond notationally replacing the set of identities $\mathcal{I}$ with a set of attributes $\mathbb{A}$ in $\hat{\mathcal{E}}_*$, nothing changes for setup, encryption and evaluation. The primary change takes place with respect to key generation. In KeyGen, given a punctured PRF key K' and a policy $f \in \mathbb{F}$, we return as the secret key for f an obfuscation $d_f \leftarrow i\mathcal{O}(F_{\mathsf{MapSK}_f})$, where F_{MapSK_f} is defined as follows with respect to f:

Program $F_{\mathsf{MapSK}_f}(\mathsf{a})$:

1. If $f(a) = 0$, **Output** $\perp$.
2. Compute $r_a \leftarrow \mathsf{PRF.Eval}(K, a)$.
3. Compute $(\mathsf{pk}_a, \mathsf{sk}_a) \leftarrow \mathcal{E}_{\mathsf{FHE}}.\mathsf{Gen}(1^\kappa; r_a)$.
4. **Output** sk_a.

Decryption is straightforward: given a secret key for f, namely the obfuscation d_f, a decryptor simply computes $\mathsf{sk}_a \leftarrow d_f(a)$ (she can store sk_a for future use to avoid re-evaluating d_f) where a is the attribute associated with ciphertext c, and then computes the plaintext $m \leftarrow \mathcal{E}_{\mathsf{FHE}}.\mathsf{Decrypt}(\mathsf{sk}_a, c)$. Hence, we obtain an ABFHE for general-purpose policies f.

3.2   Multi-attribute ABFHE

One of the limitations of our ABFHE construction is that homomorphic evaluation is restricted to the single-attribute setting. In other words, homomorphic evaluation is only supported for ciphertexts with the same attribute. In fact, this is the case for the only known leveled ABFHE in the literature [6].

A related notion to multi-attribute ABFHE was formalized in [26], although we will use a simpler definition here. Recall our illustrated example from the introduction, where a computation was performed on data encrypted under the attribute "MATERNITY" along with data encrypted under the attribute "CARDIOLOGY". In this case, the number of *distinct attributes* was 2.

Let M be an upper bound on the number of distinct attributes supported when homomorphically evaluating a circuit. In multi-attribute ABFHE, the main syntactic change is that the size of an evaluated ciphertext is allowed to depend on M. Also, M is a parameter that is specified in advance of generating the public parameters.

To be more precise, consider ciphertexts $c_1, \ldots, c_\ell$ passed to the Eval algorithm. Each of the ℓ ciphertexts may have a different attribute. Thus there is at most $k \leq \ell$ distinct attributes in this set. As long as $k \leq M$, the scheme can handle the evaluation of a circuit. Let $c' \leftarrow \mathsf{Eval}(\mathsf{PP}, C, c_1, \ldots, c_\ell)$ be an evaluated ciphertext, where PP is the public parameters and C is a circuit. It is required that $|c'| = \mathsf{poly}(\kappa, M)$.

The main idea in [26] is to use multi-key FHE, as introduced by López-Alt, Tromer and Vaikuntanathan [23], to construct a scheme with similar properties to a multi-attribute ABFHE, but with a few limitations. One of these limitations is that only a bounded number of ciphertexts N can be evaluated (where N is fixed a priori), regardless of whether there are less than N distinct attributes. So basically, the scheme from [26] places a limit on the number of independent senders. In contrast, multi-attribute ABFHE permits an unbounded number of independent senders provided the total number of distinct attributes is at most M.

Multi-Attribute ABFHE can be viewed as an attribute-based analog to multi-key FHE from [23]. In multi-key FHE, the size of evaluated ciphertexts depends on an a priori fixed parameter M, which represents the number of independent keys tolerated by the scheme. Hence data encrypted under at most M distinct public keys $\mathsf{pk}_1, \ldots, \mathsf{pk}_M$ can be used together in an evaluation.

We exploit multi-key FHE to construct a multi-attribute ABFHE. Our scheme is very similar to our (single-attribute) ABFHE scheme described above in Section 3.1. The main change is that $\mathcal{E}_{\mathsf{FHE}}$ is replaced with a multi-key FHE scheme $\mathcal{E}_{\mathsf{MKFHE}}$ (such as the NTRU-based scheme from [23]). The latter is instantiated with parameter M supplied when generating the public parameters. Suppose a collection of input ciphertexts $c_1, \ldots, c_\ell$ are associated with a set of $k \leq M$

distinct attributes $a_1, \ldots, a_k \in \mathbb{A}$. Hence, an evaluated ciphertext c' is associated with a *set* $A = \{a_1, \ldots, a_k\}$.

Decryption depends on the intended semantics. One may wish that the decryption process is collaborative i.e. there may not be a single f that satisfies all k attributes, but users may share secret keys for a set of policies $\{f\}$ that "covers all" k attributes. Alternatively, and this is the approach taken in [26], it may be desired that a user can only decrypt c' if she has a secret key for a policy f that satisfies *all* k attributes. We take the former approach here.

In our scheme, secret keys are the same as those in the single-attribute scheme from the previous section; that is, a secret key for f is on obfuscation $d_f \leftarrow i\mathcal{O}(F_{\mathsf{MapSK}_f})$ of the program F_{MapSK_f}. Let c' be a ciphertext associated with k distinct attributes $a_1, \ldots, a_k$. To decrypt c' with a secret key d_f for policy f, a decryptor does the following: if $f(a_i) = 1$ for every $i \in [k]$, compute $\mathsf{sk}_{a_i} \leftarrow d_f(a_i)$, and output $m \leftarrow \mathcal{E}_{\mathsf{MKFHE}}.\mathsf{Decrypt}(\{\mathsf{sk}_{a_1}, \ldots, \mathsf{sk}_{a_k}\}, c')$; otherwise output $\perp$. Suppose a user has secret keys for t different policies $f_1, \ldots, f_t$. As long as every attribute a_i satisfies at least one of these policies, the user can obtain the corresponding sk_{a_i} and decrypt the $\mathcal{E}_{\mathsf{MKFHE}}$ ciphertext c in the same manner as above.

4 A Compiler to Transform a Leveled IBFHE into a "Pure" IBFHE

So far we have obtained "pure" IBFHE, ABFHE and multi-attribute ABFHE schemes. Although these constructions are impractical, they serve as possibility results for these primitives. Next we turn our attention to obtaining a "compiler" to transform an arbitrary leveled IBFHE into a bootstrappable IBFHE, and as a consequence, a "pure" IBFHE. One of the primary reasons for this is efficiency. One of the reasons our previous constructions are impractical is that they rely on indistinguishability obfuscation for the frequently used process of deriving a public-key for a user's identity. With appropriate parameters, bootstrapping is a process that might be carried out infrequently - or needed only in especially rare occasions. Therefore, preserving the performance of existing leveled IBFHEs for encryption, decryption and evaluation of "not-too-deep" circuits is desirable. But having the capability to bootstrap, even if expensive, is useful in those cases where evaluation of a deep circuit is needed. This is particularly true in the identity-based setting because keys cannot be generated on a once-off basis as they might be in many applications** of public-key FHE, nor can they be changed as frequently, since all users of the identity-based infrastructure are affected.

Intuitively, the central idea to make a leveled IBFHE scheme bootstrappable is as follows. Firstly, we include an obfuscation of a program in the public parameters. This program "hides" the master secret key (trapdoor) of the scheme. Such

---

** For many applications of public-key FHE, leveled FHE is usually adequate because a new key pair can be generated on a once-off basis for a particular circuit, whose depth is known, and a leveled FHE can be parameterized accordingly.

a program can use the trapdoor to generate a secret key for an identity, and then use that secret key to output a bootstrapping key that is derived from the secret key. Hence, an evaluator can run the obfuscated program to non-interactively accomplish bootstrapping.

However in order to prove selective security of such a scheme, we need to remove all secret key information for the adversary's target identity. The reason for this is that our obfuscator is not a virtual black-box obfuscator i.e. we cannot argue that the obfuscated program leaks no information about the trapdoor to the adversary. Therefore, certain properties are needed of a leveled IBFHE scheme $\mathcal{E}$ before it is admissible for our "compiler".

4.1   Weakly-Bootstrappable IBFHE

Our starting point is leveled IBFHE schemes, such as those constructed via the GSW compiler from [6], that support bootstrapping when given "encryptions" of secret key bits. We refer to such "encryptions" of secret key bits as a *bootstrapping key*. As mentioned in the introduction, there is no known way (in current schemes) to non-interactively derive a bootstrapping key for a given identity from the public parameters alone. The only way bootstrapping can be achieved in such schemes is when a bootstrapping key is passed to the evaluator out-of-band, which breaks an attractive property of IBE, namely that all keys are derivable from the public parameters and a user's identity alone.

We now give a formal definition for a leveled IBFHE that supports bootstrapping when supplied with a bootstrapping key, and we say such a scheme is *weakly bootstrappable*. The main difference between *weakly bootstrappable* and *bootstrappable* (see Definition 2) is that the former requires a secret key for an identity in order to generate a bootstrapping key, whereas the latter only needs an identity. Note that the leveled IBFHEs from [6] are weakly bootstrappable.

Definition 4. *A leveled IBFHE scheme $\mathcal{E}$ is said to be weakly bootstrappable if there exists a pair of PPT algorithms* (WGenBootstrapKey, Bootstrap) *where* Bootstrap *is defined as in Definition 2 and* WGenBootstrapKey *is defined as follows:*

- WGenBootstrapKey(PP, $\mathsf{sk_{id}}$) : *takes as input public parameters* PP *and a secret key* $\mathsf{sk_{id}}$ *for identity* id, *and outputs a* bootstrapping key $\mathsf{bk_{id}}$.

Like a bootstrappable leveled IBFHE, a weakly-bootstrappable leveled IBFHE requires a circular security assumption to be made to prove IND-sID-CPA security. This is because an adversary is given $\mathsf{bk_{id^*}}$ for her target identity $\mathsf{id^*}$, which consists of encryptions of secret key bits.

4.2   Single-Point Trapdoor Puncturability

The next requirement we place on a leveled IBFHE to work with our compiler is called single-point trapdoor puncturability. Intuitively, this means that there is a way to "puncture" the master secret key (aka trapdoor) T to yield a *proper subset* $T' \subset T$ that is missing information needed to derive a secret key for a given identity id*. Furthermore, for all other identities id $\neq$ id*, the punctured trapdoor contains enough information to efficiently derive the *same* secret key for id as one would derive with the original trapdoor T, assuming we are given the same randomness. A formal definition will help to elucidate this notion.

Definition 5. *An IBE scheme $\mathcal{E}$ is single-point trapdoor-puncturable if there exists PPT algorithms* TrapPuncture *and* SimKeyGen *with*

- TrapPuncture(T, id^*): *On input trapdoor T and identity* id*, *output a "punctured trapdoor" $T' \subset T$ with respect to* id*.
- SimKeyGen(T', id): *On input a "punctured trapdoor" T' with respect to some identity* id*, *and an identity* id, *output a secret key for* id *if* id $\neq$ id*, *and* $\perp$ *otherwise.*

and these algorithms satisfy the following conditions for any $(\text{PP}, T) \leftarrow \mathcal{E}.\text{Setup}(1^\kappa)$, id* $\in \mathcal{I}$ *and* $T' \leftarrow$ TrapPuncture$(T, \text{id}^*) \subset T$:

$$\mathcal{E}.\text{KeyGen}(T, \text{id}) = \text{SimKeyGen}(T', \text{id}) \quad \forall \text{id} \in \mathcal{I} \setminus \{\text{id}^*\}. \tag{4.1}$$

4.3 Our Compiler

Let $\mathcal{E}$ be a *leveled* IBFHE scheme. The required properties that $\mathcal{E}$ must satisfy for compatibility with our compiler are:

Property 1: (Weakly-Bootstrappable) $\mathcal{E}$ is weakly-bootstrappable i.e. there exists a pair of PPT algorithms (WGenBootstrapKey, Bootstrap) satisfying Definition 4.

Property 2: (Single-Point Trapdoor-Puncturable) $\mathcal{E}$ is single-point trapdoor-puncturable i.e. there exists a pair of PPT algorithms (TrapPuncture, SimKeyGen) satisfying Definition 5.

Property 3: (Indistinguishability given punctured trapdoor) For all id $\in \mathcal{I}$ and $m \in \mathcal{M}$: for every $\text{sk}_{\text{id}^*} \leftarrow \mathcal{E}.\text{KeyGen}(T, \text{id}^*)$, and $\text{bk}_{\text{id}^*} \leftarrow$ WGenBootstrapKey$(\text{PP}, \text{sk}_{\text{id}^*})$, the distributions

$$\{(\text{PP}, T', \text{bk}_{\text{id}^*}, \mathcal{E}.\mathcal{E}.\text{Encrypt}(\text{PP}, \text{id}^*, m)\} \underset{C}{\approx} \{(\text{PP}, T', \text{bk}_{\text{id}^*}, \mathcal{E}.\mathcal{E}.\text{Encrypt}(\text{PP}, \text{id}^*, m')) : m' \overset{\$}{\leftarrow} \mathcal{M}\}$$

are computationally indistinguishable.

There are concrete schemes that *almost* meet all three properties. One such example is the leveled IBFHE from Appendix A of [6]. This scheme admits algorithms (TrapPuncture, SimKeyGen) that satisfy a relaxation of Equation 4.1 in Definition 5, namely the requirement of equality is relaxed to statistical indistinguishability; more precisely it holds that

$$\mathcal{E}.\text{KeyGen}(T, \text{id}) \underset{S}{\approx} \text{SimKeyGen}(T', \text{id}) \quad \forall \text{id} \in \mathcal{I} \setminus \{\text{id}^*\}$$

for any id $\in \mathcal{I}$. However, we have been unable to find a leveled IBFHE scheme (from the GSW compiler) that meets the stronger condition of Equation 4.1.

Note that it is only necessary that SimKeyGen run in polynomial time - the essential challenge is to derive some "canonical" secret key for an identity given *less* trapdoor information (but the same randomness). A discussion of the failure of single-point trapdoor-punturability in current LWE-based leveled IBFHE schemes can be found in the full version of this work [27].

Formal Description. We now proceed with a formal description of a bootstrappable scheme $\hat{\mathcal{E}}_1$ that is constructed using a scheme $\mathcal{E}$ satisfying the above properties. Let (WGenBootstrapKey, Bootstrap) be a pair of PPT algorithms meeting Property 1.

Consider the following program F_{GenBK} to generate a bootstrapping key:

Program $F_{\mathsf{GenBK}}(\mathsf{id})$:

1. Compute $r_1 \parallel r_2 \leftarrow \mathsf{PRF.Eval}(K, \mathsf{id})$.
2. Compute $\mathsf{sk_{id}} \leftarrow \mathsf{KeyGen}(T, \mathsf{id}; r_1)$.
3. **Output** $\mathsf{WGenBootstrapKey}(\mathsf{PP}_{\mathcal{E}}, \mathsf{sk_{id}}; r_2)$.

The scheme $\hat{\mathcal{E}}_1$ includes an obfuscation of this program (with key K and trapdoor T) for the purpose of bootstrapping:

- $\hat{\mathcal{E}}_1.\mathbf{Setup}(1^\kappa)$: Set $(\mathsf{PP}_{\mathcal{E}}, T) \leftarrow \mathcal{E}.\mathsf{Setup}(1^\kappa)$. Compute $K \leftarrow \mathsf{PRF.Key}(1^\kappa)$. Compute $\beta \leftarrow i\mathcal{O}(F_{\mathsf{GenBK}})$. Output $(\mathsf{PP} := (\mathsf{PP}_{\mathcal{E}}, \beta), \mathsf{MSK} := T)$.
- $\hat{\mathcal{E}}_1.\mathbf{KeyGen} = \mathcal{E}.\mathsf{KeyGen}$; $\hat{\mathcal{E}}_1.\mathbf{Encrypt} = \mathcal{E}.\mathsf{Encrypt}$; $\hat{\mathcal{E}}_1.\mathbf{Decrypt} = \mathcal{E}.\mathsf{Decrypt}$.
- $\hat{\mathcal{E}}_1.\mathbf{Bootstrap}(\mathsf{PP}, \mathsf{id}, c)$: Parse PP as $(\mathsf{PP}_{\mathcal{E}}, \beta)$. Set $\mathsf{bk_{id}} \leftarrow \beta(\mathsf{id})$. Output $\mathsf{Bootstrap}(\mathsf{PP}_{\mathcal{E}}, \mathsf{bk_{id}}, c)$.

The main idea is that $\hat{\mathcal{E}}_1$ includes an obfuscation $\beta \leftarrow i\mathcal{O}(F_{\mathsf{GenBK}})$ in its public parameters so an evaluator can derive a bootstrapping key $\mathsf{bk_{id}}$ for a given identity id and then invoke Bootstrap.

Theorem 2. *Assuming indistinguishability obfuscation, one-way functions, $\hat{\mathcal{E}}_1$ is* IND-sID-CPA *secure if $\mathcal{E}$ satisfies Property 1 - Property 3.*

The theorem is proved in Appendix B.

Note that the construction $\hat{\mathcal{E}}_*$ from Section 3 satisfies Property 1 - Property 3. We discuss this in more detail in the full version [27].

Alternative Approach. There is an alternative approach to constructing our compiler which relies on a different requirement to single-point puncturability. However, the bootstrappable schemes that are produced are less efficient. An overview of this approach is given in the full version.

Acknowledgments. We would like to thank the anonymous reviewers of CANS 2014 for their helpful comments. We would like to especially thank one of the reviewers for suggesting an improvement to the attribute-based construction in Section 3.1 (the secret keys in our original construction were obfuscations of the decryption function, which is less efficient), in addition to suggesting interesting directions for future work.

References

1. Gentry, C.: Fully homomorphic encryption using ideal lattices. In: Proceedings of the 41st annual ACM Symposium on Theory of Computing STOC 2009, p. 169 (September 2009)
2. Smart, N., Vercauteren, F.: Fully homomorphic encryption with relatively small key and ciphertext sizes. In: Nguyen, P.Q., Pointcheval, D. (eds.) PKC 2010. LNCS, vol. 6056, pp. 420–443. Springer, Heidelberg (2010)
3. van Dijk, M., Gentry, C., Halevi, S., Vaikuntanathan, V.: Fully homomorphic encryption over the integers. In: Gilbert, H. (ed.) EUROCRYPT 2010. LNCS, vol. 6110, pp. 24–43. Springer, Heidelberg (2010)
4. Brakerski, Z., Vaikuntanathan, V.: Fully homomorphic encryption from ring-LWE and security for key dependent messages. In: Rogaway, P. (ed.) CRYPTO 2011. LNCS, vol. 6841, pp. 505–524. Springer, Heidelberg (2011)
5. Brakerski, Z., Vaikuntanathan, V.: Efficient Fully Homomorphic Encryption from (Standard) LWE. Cryptology ePrint Archive, Report 2011/344 (2011), http://eprint.iacr.org/
6. Gentry, C., Sahai, A., Waters, B.: Homomorphic encryption from learning with errors: Conceptually-simpler, asymptotically-faster, attribute-based. In: Canetti, R., Garay, J.A. (eds.) CRYPTO 2013, Part I. LNCS, vol. 8042, pp. 75–92. Springer, Heidelberg (2013)
7. Boneh, D., Franklin, M.K.: Identity-based encryption from the weil pairing. In: Kilian, J. (ed.) CRYPTO 2001. LNCS, vol. 2139, pp. 213–229. Springer, Heidelberg (2001)
8. Cocks, C.: An identity based encryption scheme based on quadratic residues. In: Honary, B. (ed.) Cryptography and Coding 2001. LNCS, vol. 2260, pp. 360–363. Springer, Heidelberg (2001)
9. Naccache, D.: Is theoretical cryptography any good in practice (2010); Talk given at CHES 2010 and Crypto 2010
10. Brakerski, Z., Vaikuntanathan, V.: Efficient Fully Homomorphic Encryption from (Standard) LWE. Cryptology ePrint Archive, Report 2011/344 Version: 20110627:080002 (2011), http://eprint.iacr.org/
11. Clear, M., Hughes, A., Tewari, H.: Homomorphic encryption with access policies: Characterization and new constructions. In: Youssef, A., Nitaj, A., Hassanien, A.E. (eds.) AFRICACRYPT 2013. LNCS, vol. 7918, pp. 61–87. Springer, Heidelberg (2013)
12. Gentry, C., Peikert, C., Vaikuntanathan, V.: Trapdoors for hard lattices and new cryptographic constructions. In: STOC 2008: Proceedings of the 40th Annual ACM Symposium on Theory of Computing, pp. 197–206. ACM, New York (2008)
13. Agrawal, S., Boneh, D., Boyen, X.: Efficient lattice (H)IBE in the standard model. In: Gilbert, H. (ed.) EUROCRYPT 2010. LNCS, vol. 6110, pp. 553–572. Springer, Heidelberg (2010)
14. Agrawal, S., Boneh, D., Boyen, X.: Lattice basis delegation in fixed dimension and shorter-ciphertext hierarchical ibe. In: Rabin, T. (ed.) CRYPTO 2010. LNCS, vol. 6223, pp. 98–115. Springer, Heidelberg (2010)
15. Cash, D., Hofheinz, D., Kiltz, E., Peikert, C.: Bonsai trees, or how to delegate a lattice basis. In: Gilbert, H. (ed.) EUROCRYPT 2010. LNCS, vol. 6110, pp. 523–552. Springer, Heidelberg (2010)
16. Sahai, A., Waters, B.: How to use indistinguishability obfuscation: Deniable encryption, and more. IACR Cryptology ePrint Archive 2013, 454 (2013)

17. Garg, S., Gentry, C., Halevi, S., Raykova, M., Sahai, A., Waters, B.: Candidate indistinguishability obfuscation and functional encryption for all circuits. In: FOCS, pp. 40–49. IEEE Computer Society (2013)
18. Boneh, D., Waters, B.: Constrained pseudorandom functions and their applications. In: Sako, K., Sarkar, P. (eds.) ASIACRYPT 2013, Part II. LNCS, vol. 8270, pp. 280–300. Springer, Heidelberg (2013)
19. Boyle, E., Goldwasser, S., Ivan, I.: Functional signatures and pseudorandom functions. In: Krawczyk, H. (ed.) PKC 2014. LNCS, vol. 8383, pp. 501–519. Springer, Heidelberg (2014)
20. Kiayias, A., Papadopoulos, S., Triandopoulos, N., Zacharias, T.: Delegatable pseudorandom functions and applications. In: ACM Conference on Computer and Communications Security, pp. 669–684. ACM (2013)
21. Sahai, A., Waters, B.: Fuzzy identity-based encryption. In: Cramer, R. (ed.) EUROCRYPT 2005. LNCS, vol. 3494, pp. 457–473. Springer, Heidelberg (2005)
22. Bethencourt, J., Sahai, A., Waters, B.: Ciphertext-policy attribute-based encryption. In: Proceedings of the 2007 IEEE Symposium on Security and Privacy, SP 2007, pp. 321–334. IEEE Computer Society, Washington, DC (2007)
23. López-Alt, A., Tromer, E., Vaikuntanathan, V.: On-the-fly multiparty computation on the cloud via multikey fully homomorphic encryption. In: Proceedings of the 44th Symposium on Theory of Computing, STOC 2012, pp. 1219–1234. ACM Press, New York (2012)
24. Goldwasser, S., Goyal, V., Jain, A., Sahai, A.: Multi-input functional encryption. Cryptology ePrint Archive, Report 2013/727 (2013), http://eprint.iacr.org/
25. Boneh, D., Boyen, X.: Efficient selective-id secure identity based encryption without random oracles. IACR Cryptology ePrint Archive 2004, 172 (2004)
26. Clear, M., McGoldrick, C.: Policy-Based Non-interactive Outsourcing of Computation using multikey FHE and CP-ABE. In: Proceedings of the 10th Internation Conference on Security and Cryptography, SECRYPT 2013 (2013)
27. Clear, M., McGoldrick, C.: Bootstrappable identity-based fully homomorphic encryption. Cryptology ePrint Archive, Report 2014/491 (2014), http://eprint.iacr.org/

A   Proof of Lemma 1

Lemma 1. *Assuming indistinguishability obfuscation, a secure puncturable PRF and an* IND-CPA-*secure public-key FHE scheme* $\mathcal{E}_{\mathsf{FHE}}$, *the scheme* $\hat{\mathcal{E}}_*$ *is* IND-sID-CPA *secure.*

Proof. We prove the lemma via a hybrid argument.

Game 0: This is the real system.

Game 1: This is the same as Game 0 except for the following changes. Suppose the adversary chooses id^* as the identity to attack. We compute $K' \leftarrow$ PRF.Puncture(K, id^*) and answer secret key requests using K' instead of K.

The adversary cannot detect any difference between the games since for all $\mathsf{id} \neq \mathsf{id}^*$, it holds that PRF.Eval$(K, \mathsf{id}) =$ PRF.Eval(k', id).

Game 2: This is the same as Game 1 except that we make the following changes to F_{MapPK}:

- Add before step 1: if $\mathsf{id} = \mathsf{id}^*$, then output $\mathsf{pk}_{\mathsf{id}^*}$ (defined below). Else run steps 1 - 3.
- Replace K with K'.

where $(\mathsf{pk}_{\mathsf{id}^*}, \mathsf{sk}_{\mathsf{id}}) \leftarrow \mathcal{E}_{\mathsf{FHE}}.\mathsf{Gen}(1^\kappa; r_{\mathsf{id}^*})$ and $r_{\mathsf{id}^*} \leftarrow \mathsf{PRF}.\mathsf{Eval}(K, \mathsf{id}^*)$.

Observe that the modified function is identical to F_{MapPK}, and due to the security of indistinguishability obfuscation, their respective obfuscations are thus computationally indistinguishable.

Game 3: This is the same as Game 2 except that we change how $\mathsf{pk}_{\mathsf{id}^*}$ is computed. We do this indirectly by changing how r_{id^*} is computed instead. More precisely, we choose a uniformly random string $r_{\mathsf{id}^*} \xleftarrow{\$} \{0,1\}^m$ where m is the length of the pseudorandom outputs of $\mathsf{PRF}.\mathsf{Eval}$ i.e. $m = |\mathsf{PRF}.\mathsf{Eval}(K, \mathsf{id}^*)|$.

By the security of the puncturable PRF, we have that

$$\{(K', \mathsf{id}^*, \mathsf{PRF}.\mathsf{Eval}(K, \mathsf{id}^*))\} \underset{C}{\approx} \{(K', \mathsf{id}^*, r) : r \xleftarrow{\$} \{0,1\}^m)\}.$$

It follows that Game 2 and Game 3 are computationally indistinguishable.

Game 4: This is the same as Game 3 except that we replace the challenge ciphertext with an encryption of a random message. The adversary has a zero advantage in this game.

If a PPT adversary $\mathcal{A}$ can distinguish between Game 3 and Game 4, then there exists a PPT adversary $\mathcal{B}$ that can use $\mathcal{A}$ to attack the IND-sID-CPA security of $\mathcal{E}_{\mathsf{FHE}}$. When $\mathcal{B}$ receives the challenger's public key pk, it sets $\mathsf{pk}_{\mathsf{id}^*} \leftarrow \mathsf{pk}$ where id^* is the target identity chosen by $\mathcal{A}$. Note that $\mathsf{pk}_{\mathsf{id}^*}$ has the same distribution as that from Game 3. Suppose m_0 and m_1 are the messages chosen by $\mathcal{A}$. $\mathcal{B}$ samples a random bit b, and also samples a random message $m' \xleftarrow{\$} \mathcal{M}$, and sends (m_b, m') to the IND-CPA challenger, who responds with a challenge ciphertext c^*. Then $\mathcal{B}$ relays c^* to $\mathcal{A}$ as the challenge ciphertext. Let b' denote the random bit chosen by the challenger. If $b' = 0$, then the game is distributed identically to Game 3; otherwise if $b' = 1$ it is distributed identically to Game 4. It follows that any $\mathcal{A}$ with a non-negligible advantage distinguishing between the games contradicts the hypothesized IND-CPA security of $\mathcal{E}_{\mathsf{FHE}}$. $\qquad\square$

B   Proof of Theorem 2

Theorem 2. *Assuming indistinguishability obfuscation, one-way functions, $\hat{\mathcal{E}}_1$ is IND-sID-CPA secure if $\mathcal{E}$ satisfies Property 1 - Property 3.*

Proof. We prove the theorem via a hybrid argument.

Game 0: This is the real system.

Game 1: This is the same as Game 0 except for the following changes. Suppose the adversary chooses id^* as the identity to attack. Compute $r_1 \parallel r_2 \leftarrow \mathsf{PRF}.\mathsf{Eval}(K, \mathsf{id}^*)$ and compute $\mathsf{bk}_{\mathsf{id}^*} \leftarrow \mathsf{WGenBootstrapKey}(\mathsf{PP}_{\mathcal{E}}, \mathsf{sk}_{\mathsf{id}^*}; r_2)$ where

$\mathsf{sk_{id^*}} \leftarrow \mathsf{KeyGen}(T, \mathsf{id^*}; r_1)$. Make the following changes to F_{GenBK}, which we call F'_{GenBK}, and set $\beta \leftarrow i\mathcal{O}(F'_{\mathsf{GenBK}})$

1. if $\mathsf{id} = \mathsf{id^*}$, then output $\mathsf{bk_{id^*}}$.
2. Else: Run Step 1 - 3 of F_{GenBK}.

Observe that F_{GenBK} is identical to F'_{GenBK} since $\mathsf{bk_{id^*}}$ is computed above in the same manner as F_{GenBK}. The games are indistinguishable due to the security of indistinguishability obfuscation.

Game 2: This is the same as Game 1 except with the following changes. Compute a punctured PRF key $K' \leftarrow \mathsf{PRF.Puncture}(K, \mathsf{id^*})$ that is defined for all strings except the input string $\mathsf{id^*}$, where $\mathsf{id^*}$ is the "target" identity chosen by the adversary. Replace all occurrences of K in F'_{GenBK} with K'. We call the modified function F''_{GenBK}.

Observe that $F'_{\mathsf{GenBK}} = F''_{\mathsf{GenBK}}$ because $\mathsf{PRF.Eval}(K, \mathsf{id}) = \mathsf{PRF.Eval}(k', \mathsf{id})$ for all $\mathsf{id} \neq \mathsf{id^*}$. Therefore, the games are indistinguishable due to the security of indistinguishability obfuscation.

Game 3: This is the same as Game 2 except that we change how $\mathsf{bk_{id^*}}$ is computed. We do this indirectly by changing how $r_1 \parallel r_2 \leftarrow \mathsf{PRF.Eval}(K, \mathsf{id^*})$ is computed instead. More precisely, we choose a uniformly random string $r'_1 \parallel r'_2 \overset{\$}{\leftarrow} \{0,1\}^m$ where m is the length of the pseudorandom outputs of $\mathsf{PRF.Eval}$ i.e. $m = |\mathsf{PRF.Eval}(K, \mathsf{id^*})|$.

By the security of the puncturable PRF, we have that

$$\{(K', \mathsf{id^*}, \mathsf{PRF.Eval}(K, \mathsf{id^*}))\} \underset{C}{\approx} \{(K', \mathsf{id^*}, r) : r \overset{\$}{\leftarrow} \{0,1\}^m)\}.$$

It follows that Game 2 and Game 3 are computationally indistinguishable.

Game 4: This is the same as Game 3 except that we make the following changes. We compute a punctured trapdoor $T' \subset T$ using the $\mathsf{TrapPuncture}$ algorithm (which exists by Property 2) i.e. $T' \leftarrow \mathsf{TrapPuncture}(T, \mathsf{id^*})$. We answer secret key queries with $\mathsf{SimKeyGen}(T', \cdot)$. The games cannot be distinguished by an adversary as a result of Equation 4.1 in Definition 5 (single-point trapdoor puncturability).

Game 5: The only change in this game is that we set $\beta \leftarrow i\mathcal{O}(F'''_{\mathsf{GenBK}})$ where F'''_{GenBK} is the same as F''_{GenBK} except $\mathsf{sk_{id}}$ is computed as

$$\mathsf{sk_{id}} \leftarrow \mathsf{SimKeyGen}(T', \mathsf{id}; r_1).$$

As a result of Equation 4.1 in Definition 5 (single-point trapdoor puncturability), we have that $F'''_{\mathsf{GenBK}} = F''_{\mathsf{GenBK}}$ and hence their obfuscations are indistinguishable to a PPT adversary by the security of indistinguishability obfuscation.

Game 6: Note that Game 5 removes all references to T. In this game, we produce the challenge ciphertext given to the adversary as an encryption of a uniformly random message $m' \overset{\$}{\leftarrow} \mathcal{M}$. The adversary has a zero advantage in this game.

An efficient distinguisher $\mathcal{D}$ that can distinguish between Game 5 and Game 6 can be used to violate Property 3. Let b be the challenger's random bit. Let

m_0 and m_1 be the messages chosen by the adversary. Given a challenge instance of Property 3 of the form $(\mathsf{PP}, T', \mathsf{bk}_{\mathsf{id}^*}, c^*)$ where id^* is the adversary's target identity, and c^* is an encryption of either m_b or a uniformly random element in $\mathcal{M}$. Note that PP, T' and $\mathsf{bk}_{\mathsf{id}^*}$ are distributed identically to both Game 5 and Game 6. Hence, we can construct an algorithm to perfectly simulate $\mathcal{D}$'s view, and give c^* to $\mathcal{D}$ as the challenge ciphertext. If c^* encrypts m_b, Game 5 is perfectly simulated; otherwise if c^* encrypts a random message, Game 6 is perfectly simulated. It follows that a non-negligible advantage distinguishing between Game 5 and Game 6 implies a non-negligible advantage distinguishing the LHS and RHS distributions of Property 3.   □

Proxy Re-encryption
with Unforgeable Re-encryption Keys*

Hui Guo, Zhenfeng Zhang, and Jiang Zhang

Trusted Computing and Information Assurance Laboratory, Institute of Software, Chinese
Academy of Sciences, Beijing, China
{guohui,zfzhang,zhangjiang}@tca.iscas.ac.cn

Abstract. Proxy re-encryption (PRE) provides nice solutions to the delegation
of decryption rights. In proxy re-encryption, the delegator Alice generates re-
encryption keys for a semi-trusted proxy, with which the proxy can translate a
ciphertext intended for Alice into a ciphertext for the delegatee Bob of the same
plaintext. Existing PRE schemes have considered the security that the collusion
attacks among the proxy and the delegatees cannot expose the delegator's secret
key. But almost all the schemes, as far as we know, failed to provide the security
that the proxy and the delegatees cannot collude to generate new re-encryption
keys from the delegator to any other user who has not been authorized by the
delegator. In this paper, we first define the notion of the unforgeability of re-
encryption keys to capture the above attacks. Then, we present a non-interactive
CPA secure PRE scheme, which is resistant to collusion attacks in forging re-
encryption keys. Both the size of the ciphertext and the re-encryption key are
constant. Finally, we extend the CPA construction to a CCA secure scheme.

1 Introduction

Proxy re-encryption was first proposed by Blaze, Bleumer and Strauss [3] in 1998,
which allows the proxy to transform a ciphertext for Alice into a ciphertext of the same
message for Bob. During the transformation, the proxy learns nothing about the underlying message. Proxy re-encryption has many applications, such as email forwarding
[6], distributed files systems [1] and revocation systems [22].

There are several desired properties for PRE schemes [1]:

1. Unidirectional, the proxy can only transform the ciphertext from Alice to Bob;
2. Non-interactive, Alice generates re-encryption keys using Bob's public key; no
   trusted third party or interaction is needed;
3. Proxy invisibility, both sender and recipient do not know whether the proxy is active;
4. Key optimal, the size of Bob's secret key is constant, no matter how many delegations he accepts;

---

* The work is supported by the National Basic Research Program of China (No.
2013CB338003), and the National Natural Science Foundation of China (No.61170278,
91118006).

D. Gritzalis et al. (Eds.): CANS 2014, LNCS 8813, pp. 20–33, 2014.

5. Collusion-safe (or master secret secure), the proxy and a set of colluding delegatees cannot recover Alice's secret key;
6. Non-transferable, the proxy with a set of colluding delegatees cannot re-delegate decryption rights.

Many PRE schemes [1][6][18][10][23] have achieved the first five properties. But, as far as we know, there is no (non-interactive) schemes that achieved the sixth property. In other words, if Bob and a malicious proxy collude, they might derive new re-encryption keys without Alice's authorization. Our work is making efforts to address this issue.

1.1 Related Work

Libert and Vergnaud [17] proposed traceable proxy re-encryption. A PRE scheme is traceable if any set of proxies colluding with delegatees is unable to generate a new re-encryption key that cannot be traced back to one of them. They also presented a traceable PRE scheme of which the size of both the public/secret key and the ciphertext depend on the number of the delegatees. Hayashi et al. [13] introduced the strong unforgeability of re-encryption keys against collusion attacks (sUFReKey-CA) and proposed PRE constructions aiming at achieving sUFReKey-CA under two variants of the Diffie-Hellman inversion assumption. Unfortunately, Isshiki et al. [15] gave concrete attacks to both the sUFReKey-CA property and the underlying assumptions of their scheme. Moreover, the definition of sUFReKey-CA seems too strong to be satisfied. In their definition, an adversary $\mathcal{A}$ colludes with proxies and delegatees, and obtains a set of re-encryption keys and a set of secret keys. $\mathcal{A}$ is said to be successful if she outputs a new "re-encryption key" in any form. In such a case, there exists an adversary who simply outputs $R^{\dagger}_{*\rightarrow j} = (R_{*\rightarrow\beta}, sk_{\beta})$, where $R_{*\rightarrow\beta}$ denotes a re-encryption key and β denotes a delegatee in collusion. $\mathcal{A}$ is a successful attacker since she could re-encrypt the target user's ciphertext to anyone as follows. $\mathcal{A}$ re-encrypts the ciphertext to delegatee β and then decrypts it with sk_{β}. Finally, $\mathcal{A}$ encrypts the message to anyone she wants.

All the works mentioned above cannot prevent delegatees and proxies from pooling their secrets to forge dummy re-encryption keys without the delegator's consent.[1] These special dummy re-encryption keys can be used to re-encrypt ciphertexts to a dummy user whose secret key is known by everyone. To the best of our knowledge, all the existing non-interactive PRE schemes are vulnerable to the above attack, including certificate-based PRE [3][1][14][10][20][8][23], identity-based PRE [12][9][21][7] and attribute-based PRE [19][16].

1.2 Our Contribution

First, we define unforgeability of re-encryption keys against collusion attack to capture illegal transference of delegation. In our security model, an adversary adaptively corrupts delegatees and delegations after she sees the target delegator, and is still infeasible

---

[1] For an example, In [1], a proxy with $rk = g^{\frac{b}{a}}$ and a delegatee with a secret exponent b are able to derive a dummy re-encryption key $g^{\frac{1}{a}}$. This dummy re-encryption key could be used to transform ciphertexts intended for the delegator to a dummy user with public key $pk' = g$ that everyone has its "secret" exponent.

to generate some "valid" re-encryption keys without the permission of the delegator. We clarify that our security model only aims at capturing the illegal generations of new re-encryption keys, which to some extent captures the most "direct" way of re-delegating decryption rights. But due to the inherited feature of PRE schemes (i.e., delegation of decryption rights), there might be other (trivial) ways of transferring decryption rights that cannot be covered by our security model, which will be discussed later. Since unforgeability of re-encryption keys prevents the proxy colluding with delegatees to generate a new re-encryption key, we need not consider the traceablity proposed in [17].

Then, we present a CPA secure scheme with unforgeable re-encryption keys, which is non-interactive and key optimal. Basically, we build upon the BBS+ signature [2], and construct a PRE scheme with re-encryption keys performed as "a signature on the delegatee's public key". Namely, the unforgeability against adaptively chosen message attack of the underlying signature implies the unforgeability of re-encryption keys. The security is proven under the q-SDH assumption in the standard model.

Finally, we give some extensions and discussions on our construction. The CPA construction could be easily extended into a CCA secure PRE scheme. We present the CCA security model and its proof in the full version. Then, we give detailed comparisons of some representative unidirectional PRE schemes in efficiency and security. The results demonstrate that our scheme achieves better security at a slight efficiency loss.

2   Proxy Re-encryption with Unforgeable Re-encryption Keys

In this section, we first introduce the definitions of PRE. Then, we give the CPA security definition and the security definition for the unforgeability of re-encryption keys against collusion attacks.

2.1   Proxy Re-encryption

We describe the definition of unidirectional PRE scheme in [17]. A single hop unidirectional PRE scheme is a tuple of algorithms [1][18][17]:

- Setup(λ) : On input the security parameter λ, this algorithm outputs the public parameter param which specifies the plaintext space $\mathcal{M}$, the ciphertext space $\mathcal{C}$ and the randomness space $\mathcal{R}$.

- KeyGen(param) : This algorithm outputs the user's public key and secret key (pk_i, sk_i). We omit param in the following algorithms' inputs.

- ReKeyGen(sk_i, pk_j) : This algorithm outputs a re-encryption key $rk_{i\to j}$.

- CheckKey($pk_i, pk_j, rk_{i\to j}$) : This algorithm outputs $b \in \{0, 1\}$, indicating whether the re-encryption key $rk_{i\to j}$ from user i to user j is valid.

- Enc$_1$(pk_j, m) : This algorithm takes pk_j and $m \in \mathcal{M}$ as inputs, and outputs a first level ciphertext C'_j, which cannot be re-encrypted.

- Enc$_2$(pk_i, m) : This algorithm takes pk_i and $m \in \mathcal{M}$ as inputs, and outputs a second level ciphertext C_i, which can be re-encrypted.

– $\text{ReEnc}(rk_{i \to j}, C_i)$: C_i is a ciphertext under pk_i. This algorithm outputs a first level ciphertext C'_j or an error symbol $\perp$.

– $\text{Dec}_1(sk_j, C'_j)$: This algorithm outputs a message $m \in \mathcal{M}$ or an error symbol $\perp$.

– $\text{Dec}_2(sk_i, C_i)$: This algorithm outputs a message $m \in \mathcal{M}$ or an error symbol $\perp$.

Correctness. For any key pairs $(pk_i, sk_i), (pk_j, sk_j) \leftarrow \text{KeyGen}(\text{param})$, any re-encryption key $rk_{i \to j}$ satisfying $\text{CheckKey}(pk_i, pk_j, rk_{i \to j}) = 1$ and any message $m \in \mathcal{M}$, the following conditions hold:

$$\text{Dec}_1(sk_j, \text{Enc}_1(pk_j, m)) = m; \quad \text{Dec}_2(sk_i, \text{Enc}_2(pk_i, m)) = m;$$

$$\text{CheckKey}(pk_i, pk_j, \text{ReKeyGen}(sk_i, pk_j)) = 1;$$

$$\text{Dec}_1(sk_j, \text{ReEnc}(rk_{i \to j}, \text{Enc}_2(pk_i, m))) = m.$$

Similar to [17], we resort to an additional algorithm CheckKey, to define the unforgeability of re-encryption keys. However, unlike in [17] where the CheckKey algorithm needs to take the secret key of user i as input, the CheckKey algorithm here only needs the public key pk_i of user i. Therefore, the validity check is public. Another difference is that the CheckKey algorithm should satisfy two correctness requirements: First, re-encryption keys output by ReKeyGen should pass the the CheckKey algorithm; Second, any re-encryption key that passes the CheckKey algorithm should re-encrypt ciphertexts correctly with respect to the 1st level decryption algorithm.

2.2 Security Model

We adopt the Knowledge of Secret Key model, where all users should prove knowledge of their secret keys before registering public keys. We also assume a static model where adversaries are not allowed to adaptively corrupt users. We provide the following oracles to a CPA adversary:

– Uncorrupted Key generation $\mathcal{O}_{\text{hkg}}(i)$: Compute $(pk_i, sk_i) \leftarrow \text{KeyGen}(i)$, return pk_i.

– Corrupted Key generation $\mathcal{O}_{\text{ckg}}(i)$: Compute $(pk_i, sk_i) \leftarrow \text{KeyGen}(i)$, return (sk_i, pk_i).

– Re-encryption key generation $\mathcal{O}_{\text{rkg}}(pk_i, pk_j)$: On input of (pk_i, pk_j), where pk_i, pk_j were generated before by KeyGen, return a re-encryption key $rk_{i \to j} \leftarrow \text{ReKeyGen}(sk_i, pk_j)$.

To capture the CPA security notion for single-hop unidirectional PRE schemes, we associate a CPA adversary $\mathcal{A}$ with the following template security experiment:

Experiment $\text{Exp}^{\text{pre}}_{\Pi, \mathcal{A}}(\lambda)$
param $\leftarrow \text{Setup}(\lambda)$;
$(pk^*, m_0, m_1) \leftarrow \mathcal{A}^{\mathcal{O}'}(\text{param})$;
$d^* \leftarrow \{0, 1\}$;
$C^* = \text{Enc}_\delta(pk^*, m_{d^*})$;
$d' \leftarrow \mathcal{A}^{\mathcal{O}'}(\text{param}, C^*)$;
If $d' = d^*$ return 1;
else return 0.

In the above experiment, $\mathcal{O}' = \{\mathcal{O}_{hkg}, \mathcal{O}_{ckg}, \mathcal{O}_{rkg}\}$ and $\delta \in \{1, 2\}$ specifies which level ciphertext that $\mathcal{A}$ attacks. The advantage of $\mathcal{A}$ is defined as

$$\mathrm{Adv}^{pre}_{\Pi,\mathcal{A}}(\lambda) = |\Pr[\mathrm{Exp}^{pre}_{\Pi,\mathcal{A}}(\lambda) = 1] - \frac{1}{2}|.$$

Definition 1 (CPA Security at the 2nd Level Ciphertext). *For any PRE scheme Π_s, we instantiate the experiment with a CPA adversary $\mathcal{A}$ and $\delta = 2$. It is required that pk^* is uncorrupted and $|m_0| = |m_1|$. If C^* denotes the challenge ciphertext, $\mathcal{A}$ can never make re-encryption key generation $\mathcal{O}_{rkg}(pk^*, pk_j)$, where pk_j is corrupted.*

Π_s is said to be secure against chosen plaintext attacks at the 2nd level ciphertext if for any polynomial time adversary $\mathcal{A}$, the advantage function $\mathrm{Adv}^{pre}_{\Pi_s,\mathcal{A}}(\lambda)$ is negligible in λ.

Definition 2 (CPA Security at the 1st Level Ciphertext). *For any PRE scheme Π_s, we instantiate the experiment with a CPA adversary $\mathcal{A}$ and $\delta = 1$. It is required that pk^* is uncorrupted and $|m_0| = |m_1|$.*

Π_s is said to be secure against chosen plaintext attacks at the 1st level ciphertext if for any polynomial time adversary $\mathcal{A}$, the advantage function $\mathrm{Adv}^{pre}_{\Pi_s,\mathcal{A}}(\lambda)$ is negligible in λ.

Now, let's consider the unforgeability of re-encryption keys against collusion attacks. To formulate this security definition, we define the experiment:

Experiment $\mathrm{Exp}^{pre,uf}_{\Pi,\mathcal{A}}(\lambda)$
    $(param, pk^*) \leftarrow \mathrm{Setup}(\lambda);$
    $(rk_{*\to j'}, (sk_{j'}, pk_{j'})) \leftarrow \mathcal{A}^{\mathcal{O}_{ckg}, \mathcal{O}_{rkg}}(param, pk^*);$
    If $\mathrm{CheckKey}(pk^*, pk_{j'}, rk_{*\to j'}) = 1 \wedge$
      $\mathcal{A}$ has not queried $rk_{*\to j'} \leftarrow \mathcal{O}_{rkg}(pk^*, pk_{j'}) \wedge$
      $(sk_{j'}, pk_{j'})$ is a valid key pair in key space
    return 1;
    else return 0.

In the above experiment, the adversary is given the secret keys of all the users except the target user, and aims at forging a new re-encryption key from the target user to any other users without the permission of the target user (i.e., the forged re-encryption key is not output by the re-encryption key generation oracle). Since the CheckKey algorithm only needs the public key pk_i of user i, the validity check is public.

The advantage of $\mathcal{A}$ is defined as

$$\mathrm{Adv}^{pre,uf}_{\Pi,\mathcal{A}}(\lambda) = |\Pr[\mathrm{Exp}^{pre,uf}_{\Pi,\mathcal{A}}(\lambda) = 1]|.$$

Definition 3 (Unforgeability of Re-Encryption Keys). *A unidirectional PRE scheme Π_s satisfies the property of unforgeability of re-encryption keys if for any polynomial time adversary $\mathcal{A}$, the advantage function $\mathrm{Adv}^{pre,uf}_{\Pi_s,\mathcal{A}}(\lambda)$ is negligible in λ.*

In the security experiment, the adversary is required to output the secret key of the delegatee (either a corrupted party or a fake user generated by adversary). Note that if someone receives only the re-encryption key from the adversary and he does not hold the related secret key, he wouldn't threaten the security of the delegator. That is guaranteed by the CPA security of the 2nd level ciphertext.

For a strong security notion, in the unforgeability experiment we provide the adversary with an $\mathcal{O}_{ckg}$ oracle such that it can obtain all the secret keys of other users. In addition, we allow the adversary to choose any public key $pk_{j'}$ as its target with only a restriction that it must know the associated secret key $sk_{j'}$. We note that the requirement of outputting $sk_{j'}$ is reasonable, which can usually help to check the validity of the public key $pk_{j'}$ such as in our case.

We remark that our definition cannot cover all the cases of transference of decryption rights inherited from PRE schemes. Consider the following attack. An adversary obtains the re-encryption key $rk_{A\rightarrow B}$ and the secret key sk_B from the challenger, and aims at re-delegating decryption rights to Charlie with the public key pk_C. She simply outputs an obfuscation of the following program: 1) Decrypt the input ciphertext by first re-encrypting it using $rk_{A\rightarrow B}$; 2) Encrypt the resulting message by using Charlies's public key, and outputs the ciphertext.

3   A CPA Secure PRE Scheme

In our paper, we use λ to denote the security parameter. We recall the definitions of the bilinear groups [4,5]. We write $\mathbb{G} = \langle g \rangle$ to denote that g generates the group $\mathbb{G}$. Let $\mathbb{G}$ and $\mathbb{G}_T$ be two cyclic groups of prime order p, a map $e: \mathbb{G} \times \mathbb{G} \rightarrow \mathbb{G}_T$ is said to be a bilinear map if it satisfies the following conditions:

1. for all $u, v \in \mathbb{G}$ and $a, b \in \mathbb{Z}_p$, we have $e(u^a, v^b) = e(u, v)^{ab}$.
2. e is non-degenerate (i.e. if $\mathbb{G} = \langle g \rangle$, then $\mathbb{G}_T = \langle e(g, g) \rangle$).
3. e is efficiently computable.

We denote the following PRE scheme by SI.

Setup(λ) : Let λ be the security parameter, $\mathbb{G}$ and $\mathbb{G}_T$ be groups of prime order p, and $e: \mathbb{G} \times \mathbb{G} \rightarrow \mathbb{G}_T$ be a bilinear map. Randomly choose $g_1, g_2, h_1, h_2 \leftarrow \mathbb{G}$ and compute $L = e(h_1, h_2)$. The system parameters are param $= (g_1, g_2, h_1, h_2, L)$.

KeyGen(param) : User i uniformly picks $x_i, y_i, z_i \leftarrow \mathbb{Z}_p^*$ at random, set $sk_i = (x_i, y_i, z_i)$ as the secret key and compute the public key $pk_i = (X_i, Y_i, Z_i) = (h_1^{x_i}, h_1^{y_i}, g_1^{z_i})$. Return key pair (sk_i, pk_i).

ReKeyGen(sk_i, pk_j) : Given $sk_i = (x_i, y_i, z_i)$ and $pk_j = (X_j, Y_j, Z_j)$ as inputs, user i picks $s, t \leftarrow \mathbb{Z}_p$ at random, computes the re-encryption key $rk_{i\rightarrow j} = (W, s, t) = ((g_2^s h_2 Z_j)^{1/(x_i + t y_i)}, s, t)$. Return $rk_{i\rightarrow j}$.

CheckKey($pk_i, pk_j, rk_{i\rightarrow j}$) : Given $pk_i = (X_i, Y_i, Z_i)$, $pk_j = (X_j, Y_j, Z_j)$ and $rk_{i\rightarrow j} = (W, s, t)$ as inputs, return 1 if $e(X_i Y_i^t, W) = e(h_1, g_2^s) \cdot e(h_1, h_2) \cdot e(h_1, Z_j)$ and 0 otherwise.

$\text{Enc}_1(pk_j, m)$: Given a public key pk_j and a message $m \in \mathbb{G}_T$, pick $r \leftarrow \mathbb{Z}_p$ randomly, compute $c'_0 = L^r \cdot m, c'_1 = g_1^r, c'_2 = L^r \cdot e(h_1^r, Z_j)$ and return a 1st level ciphertext $C'_j = (c'_0, c'_1, c'_2)$.

$\text{Enc}_2(pk_i, m)$: Given a public key pk_i and a message $m \in \mathbb{G}_T$, pick $r \leftarrow \mathbb{Z}_p$ randomly, compute $c_0 = L^r \cdot m, c_1 = g_1^r, c_2 = g_2^r, c_3 = X_i^r, c_4 = Y_i^r$ and return a 2nd level ciphertext $C_i = (c_0, c_1, c_2, c_3, c_4)$.

$\text{ReEnc}(rk_{i \to j}, C_i)$: Given a re-encryption key $rk_{i \to j} = (W, s, t)$ and a 2nd level ciphertext $C_i = (c_0, c_1, c_2, c_3, c_4)$, compute $c'_0 = c_0, c'_1 = c_1, c'_2 = e(c_3 c_4^t, W)/e(c_2, h_1^s)$ and return a 1st level ciphertext $C'_j = (c'_0, c'_1, c'_2)$.

$\text{Dec}_1(sk_j, C'_j)$: Given secret key $sk_j = (x_j, y_j, z_j)$ and a 1st level ciphertext C'_j, compute $m = c'_0 \cdot e(h_1, {c'_1}^{z_j})/c'_2$ and return m.

$\text{Dec}_2(sk_i, C_i)$: Given secret key $sk_i = (x_i, y_i, z_i)$ and a 2nd level ciphertext C_i, compute $m = c_0/e(c_3^{1/x_i}, h_2)$ and return m.

The correctness of SI is not complicated and we omit it here.

Remark 1. It is easy to check that our scheme is unidirectional, non-interactive, proxy-invisible, key optimal and master secret secure. Here, we only give a brief discussion for proxy invisible property.

Let $C'_j = (c'_0, c'_1, c'_2)$ denote a re-encrypted ciphertext of $C_i = (c_0, c_1, c_2, c_3, c_4)$ and $rk_{i \to j} = (W, s, t)$ denote a re-encryption key that passes the CheckKey algorithm, we obtain $c'_0 = c_0 = L^r \cdot m, c'_1 = c_1 = g_1^r, c'_2 = e(c_3 c_4^t, W)/e(c_2, h_1^s) = L^r \cdot e(h_1^r, Z_j)$. $C'_j = (c'_0, c'_1, c'_2)$ is just in the same distribution as the 1st level ciphertext output by the Enc_1 algorithm. Therefore, SI is proxy-invisible.

3.1   Security

Let $\mathbb{G}$, $\mathbb{G}_T$ and e be bilinear groups defined before, we first recall the hardness assumptions required in our scheme:

DBDH Assumption. For an algorithm $\mathcal{B}$, define its advantage as

$$\text{Adv}_{\mathcal{B}}^{\text{DBDH}}(\lambda) = | \Pr[\mathcal{B}(g, g^a, g^b, g^c, e(g, g)^{abc}) = 1] -$$

$$\Pr[\mathcal{B}(g, g^a, g^b, g^c, e(g, g)^z) = 1]|$$

where $a, b, c, z \leftarrow \mathbb{Z}_p$ are randomly chosen. We say that the DBDH (Decisional Bilinear Diffie-Hellman) assumption holds, if for any probabilistic polynomial time (PPT) algorithm $\mathcal{B}$, its advantage $\text{Adv}_{\mathcal{B}}^{\text{DBDH}}(\lambda)$ is negligible in λ.

q-SDH Assumption. For an algorithm $\mathcal{B}$, define its advantage as

$$\text{Adv}_{\mathcal{B}}^{q\text{-SDH}}(\lambda) = \Pr[\mathcal{B}(g, g^a, g^{a^2} \ldots, g^{a^q}) = (g^{\frac{1}{a+c}}, c)]$$

where $a \in \mathbb{Z}_p^*$. We say that the q-SDH (q-Strong Diffie-Hellman) assumption holds, if for any PPT algorithm $\mathcal{B}$, its advantage $\text{Adv}_{\mathcal{B}}^{q\text{-SDH}}(\lambda)$ is negligible in λ.

Now, let's consider the security of scheme SI.

Theorem 1. *Scheme SI is CPA secure at both the 2nd level and the 1st level ciphertexts under the DBDH assumption.*

The theorem is obtained by combining Lemma 1 and Lemma 2 as follows.

Lemma 1. *Scheme SI is CPA secure at the 2nd level ciphertexts under the DBDH assumption.*

Proof. Let $\mathcal{A}$ be a CPA adversary attacking our scheme at level 2 with advantage ϵ. We construct an algorithm $\mathcal{B}$ to solve the DBDH problem by interacting with $\mathcal{A}$. The algorithm $\mathcal{B}$ takes a random challenge $(g, A = g^a, B = g^b, C = g^c, T)$ as input. $\mathcal{B}$'s goal is to decide whether $T = e(g,g)^{abc}$ or random. The algorithm $\mathcal{B}$ proceeds as follows.

Setup(λ): Randomly choose $\delta \leftarrow \mathbb{Z}_p^*$, set $g_1 = g, g_2 = g^\delta, h_1 = g^a, h_2 = g^b, L = e(g^a, g^b)$. The system parameter is param $= (g_1, g_2, h_1, h_2, L)$.

Phase 1 : $\mathcal{B}$ answers $\mathcal{A}$'s queries as follows.

- $\mathcal{O}_{\text{hkg}}(i)$: Randomly choose $x_i, y_i, z_i \leftarrow \mathbb{Z}_p^*$. If it is the k-th key generation query (that $\mathcal{B}$ guesses it will be the target user), let $i^* = i$, compute $pk_{i^*} = (X_i = g^{x_{i^*}}, Y_i = g^{y_{i^*}}, Z_i = g^{z_{i^*}})$, implicitly setting $sk_{i^*} = (\frac{x_{i^*}}{a}, \frac{y_{i^*}}{a}, z_{i^*})$. Otherwise, compute $pk_i = (X_i = h_1^{x_i}, Y_i = h_1^{y_i}, Z_i = h_2^{-1}g^{z_i})$, implicitly setting $sk_i = (x_i, y_i, z_i - b)$. Return pk_i.

- $\mathcal{O}_{\text{ckg}}(i)$: Randomly choose $x_i, y_i, z_i \leftarrow \mathbb{Z}_p^*$, and set $sk_i = (x_i, y_i, z_i)$. Compute $pk_i = (X_i = h_1^{x_i}, Y_i = h_1^{y_i}, Z_i = g_1^{z_i})$. Return (sk_i, pk_i).

- $\mathcal{O}_{\text{rkg}}(pk_i, pk_j)$: Given (pk_i, pk_j) where pk_i and pk_j were generated by $\mathcal{O}_{\text{hkg}}$ or $\mathcal{O}_{\text{ckg}}$, $\mathcal{B}$ distinguishes the following cases:

   • If $pk_i \neq pk_{i^*}$, run ReKeyGen(sk_i, pk_j), and return whatever it outputs;
   • If $pk_i = pk_{i^*}$, pk_j is uncorrupted, pick $s, t \leftarrow \mathbb{Z}_p$, compute
   $$W = (g_2^s h_2 Z_j)^{(\frac{x_{i^*}}{a} + t \cdot \frac{y_{i^*}}{a})^{-1}} = (g^a)^{\frac{s \cdot \delta + z_j}{x_{i^*} + t y_{i^*}}}. \text{ Return } rk_{i \to j} = (W, s, t).$$
   • If $pk_i = pk_{i^*}$, pk_j is corrupted, return $\perp$.

Challenge : When $\mathcal{A}$ decides to finish Phase 1, it outputs m_0, m_1 and a target public key pk^*. If $pk_{i^*} \neq pk^*$, $\mathcal{B}$ outputs a random bit and aborts. Otherwise, $\mathcal{B}$ picks a random coin $b \in \{0, 1\}$, and computes $c_0 = T \cdot m_b, c_1 = g_1^r = g^c, c_2 = g_2^r = (g^c)^\delta$, $c_3 = X_i^r = (g^c)^{x_{i^*}}, c_4 = Y_i^r = (g^c)^{y_{i^*}}$. Suppose $\mathcal{A}$ makes $\mathcal{O}_{\text{hkg}}$ queries at most q_{hkg} times. Then, the probability that $\mathcal{B}$ guesses right i^* in Challenge phase is at least $1/q_{\text{hkg}}$.

Phase 2 : $\mathcal{B}$ answers $\mathcal{A}$'s queries as Phase 1.

Finally, $\mathcal{A}$ outputs a guess $b' \in \{0, 1\}$. If $b = b'$, $\mathcal{B}$ outputs 1, else outputs 0. The advantage that $\mathcal{B}$ solves the DBDH problem is at least $1/q_{\text{hkg}} \cdot \epsilon$, which completes the proof.   ∎

Lemma 2. *Scheme* SI *is CPA secure at the 1st level ciphertexts under the DBDH assumption.*

Proof. Let $\mathcal{A}$ be a CPA adversary attacking our scheme at level 1 with advantage ϵ. We construct an algorithm $\mathcal{B}$ to solve the DBDH problem by interacting with $\mathcal{A}$. The algorithm $\mathcal{B}$ takes a random challenge $(g, A = g^a, B = g^b, C = g^c, T)$ as input. $\mathcal{B}$'s goal is to decide whether $T = e(g, g)^{abc}$ or random. The algorithm $\mathcal{B}$ proceeds as follows.

Setup(λ): Randomly choose $\delta \leftarrow \mathbb{Z}_p^*$, set $g_1 = g, g_2 = g^\delta, h_1 = g^a, h_2 = g^b, L = e(g^a, g^b)$. The system parameter is param $= (g_1, g_2, h_1, h_2, L)$.

Phase 1 : $\mathcal{B}$ answers $\mathcal{A}$'s queries as follows.

 - $\mathcal{O}_{hkg}(i)$: Randomly choose $x_i, y_i, z_i \leftarrow \mathbb{Z}_p^*$. If it is the k-th key generation query (that $\mathcal{B}$ guesses it will be the target user), let $i^* = i$, compute $pk_{i^*} = (X_i = h_1^{x_{i^*}}, Y_i = h_1^{y_{i^*}}, Z_i = h_2^{-1} g^{z_{i^*}})$, implicitly setting $sk_{i^*} = (x_{i^*}, y_{i^*}, z_{i^*} - b)$. Otherwise, compute $pk_i = (X_i = h_1^{x_i}, Y_i = h_1^{y_i}, Z_i = g_1^{z_i})$, implicitly setting $sk_i = (x_i, y_i, z_i)$. Return pk_i.

 - $\mathcal{O}_{ckg}(i)$: Randomly choose $x_i, y_i, z_i \leftarrow \mathbb{Z}_p^*$, and set $sk_i = (x_i, y_i, z_i)$. Compute $pk_i = (X_i = h_1^{x_i}, Y_i = h_1^{y_i}, Z_i = g_1^{z_i})$. Return (sk_i, pk_i).

 - $\mathcal{O}_{rkg}(pk_i, pk_j)$: Given (pk_i, pk_j) where pk_i and pk_j were generated by $\mathcal{O}_{hkg}$ or $\mathcal{O}_{ckg}$, $\mathcal{B}$ runs ReKeyGen (sk_i, pk_j), and return whatever it outputs.

Challenge : When $\mathcal{A}$ decides to finish Phase 1, it outputs m_0, m_1 and a target public key pk^*. If $pk_{i^*} \neq pk^*$, $\mathcal{B}$ outputs a random bit and aborts. Otherwise, $\mathcal{B}$ picks a random coin $b \in \{0, 1\}$, and computes $c_0' = T \cdot m_b, c_1' = g_1^r = g^c, c_2' = L^r \cdot e(h_1^r, Z_{i^*}) = e(g^a, g^c)^{z_{i^*}}$. Suppose $\mathcal{A}$ makes $\mathcal{O}_{hkg}$ queries at most q_{hkg} times. Then, the probability that $\mathcal{B}$ guesses right i^* in Challenge phase is at least $1/q_{hkg}$.

Phase 2 : $\mathcal{B}$ answers $\mathcal{A}$'s queries as Phase 1.

Finally, $\mathcal{A}$ outputs a guess $b' \in \{0, 1\}$. If $b = b'$, $\mathcal{B}$ outputs 1, else outputs 0. The advantage that $\mathcal{B}$ solves the DBDH problem is at least $1/q_{hkg} \cdot \epsilon$, which completes the proof. ∎

Theorem 2. *The re-encryption keys of our scheme are unforgeable under the q-SDH assumption.*

Proof. Assume an adversary $\mathcal{A}$ succeeds in generating fake re-encryption keys. Suppose it makes at most q re-encryption key queries from the target user to others. We construct an algorithm $\mathcal{B}$ which solves the q-SDH problem.

Given an instance of the q-SDH problem $(g, A_1 = g^a, A_2 = g^{a^2} \dots, A_q = g^{a^q})$, $\mathcal{B}$ obtains a generator $\hat{g}, \hat{g}^a$ and $q - 1$ SDH pairs $\{(B_l, e_l)\}_{l=1}^q$ such that $e(B_l, \hat{g}^a \hat{g}^{e_l}) =$

$e(\hat{g}, \hat{g})$ for each i by applying the technique of Boneh and Boyen in the proof of Theorem 2 in [4].[2] Any new pairs (B_{l^*}, e_{l^*}) besides these pairs lead to the solution of the original q-SDH problem. $\mathcal{B}$ invokes $\mathcal{A}$ as follows.

Setup(λ) : Randomly choose $\delta, \gamma, k, \tau \leftarrow \mathbb{Z}_p^*$, set $g_1 = \hat{g}, g_2 = \hat{g}^\delta, h_1 = \hat{g}^\gamma, h_2 = \hat{g}^{ak} \cdot \hat{g}^\tau, L = e(h_1, h_2)$. The system parameter is param $= (g_1, g_2, h_1, h_2, L)$. For the target user, randomly choose $x_{i^*}, y_{i^*}, z_{i^*} \leftarrow \mathbb{Z}_p^*$, compute $pk^* = pk_{i^*} = (X_{i^*} = h_1^{ax_{i^*}}, Y_{i^*} = h_1^{y_{i^*}}, Z_{i^*} = g_1^{z_{i^*}})$, implicitly setting $sk_{i^*} = (ax_{i^*}, y_{i^*}, z_{i^*})$. Return (param, pk_{i^*}).

$\mathcal{O}_{ckg}(i)$: Randomly choose $x_i, y_i, z_i \leftarrow \mathbb{Z}_p^*$, set $sk_i = (x_i, y_i, z_i)$. $\mathcal{B}$ compute $pk_i = (X_i = h_1^{x_i}, Y_i = h_1^{y_i}, Z_i = g_1^{z_i})$. Return (sk_i, pk_i).

$\mathcal{O}_{rkg}(i)$: Queried by a pair of keys (pk_i, pk_j) where pk_i and pk_j were generated by $\mathcal{O}_{ckg}$ or in the Setup Phase, $\mathcal{B}$ distinguishes the following cases:

- $pk_i \neq pk_{i^*}$: Run ReKeyGen(sk_i, pk_j), and return whatever it outputs.

- $pk_i = pk_{i^*}$: In all the q queries, $\mathcal{B}$ randomly chooses l^*-th query ($l^* \in \{1, \cdots, q\}$). If it is the l-th query and $l = l^*$, choose $t_l \in \mathbb{Z}_p$ at random and set $s_l = (t_l y_{i^*} k - (\tau + z_j) x_{i^*})/(\delta x_{i^*})$, then we obtain $W_l = (g_2^{s_l} h_2 Z_j)^{\frac{1}{ax_{i^*} + t_l y_{i^*}}} = (\hat{g}^{\delta(t_l y_{i^*} k - (\tau + z_j) x_{i^*})/(\delta x_{i^*})} (\hat{g}^{ak} \hat{g}^\tau) \hat{g}^{z_j})^{\frac{1}{ax_{i^*} + t_l y_{i^*}}} = \hat{g}^{k/x_{i^*}}$. Otherwise, choose a fresh q-SDH pair $(B_l, e_l) \leftarrow \mathbb{Z}_p$ and $s_l \leftarrow \mathbb{Z}_p$ randomly, set $t_l = x_{i^*} e_l / y_{i^*}$, then we obtain $W_l = (g_2^{s_l} h_2 Z_j)^{\frac{1}{ax_{i^*} + t_l y_{i^*}}} = (\hat{g}^{\delta s_l} (\hat{g}^{ak} \hat{g}^\tau) \hat{g}^{z_j})^{\frac{1}{ax_{i^*} + t_l y_{i^*}}} = \hat{g}^{\frac{k}{x_{i^*}}} \hat{g}^{\frac{-e_l k + \delta s_l + \tau + z_j}{x_{i^*}(a + e_l)}} = \hat{g}^{\frac{k}{x_{i^*}}} B_l^{\frac{-e_l k + \delta s_l + \tau + z_j}{x_{i^*}}}$. Return (W_l, s_l, t_l).

Finally, $\mathcal{A}$ outputs $(sk_{j'}, pk_{j'})$ and $rk_{i^* \to j'} = (W', s', t')$ such that CheckKey $(pk_{i^*}, pk_{j'}, rk_{i^* \to j'}) = 1$, where $(sk_{j'}, pk_{j'})$ belongs to key space and $\mathcal{A}$ has not queried $rk_{i^* \to j'} \leftarrow \mathcal{O}_{rkg}(pk_{i^*}, pk_{j'})$. Distinguish the following three cases:

1. $t' \notin \{t_l\}$, denote $v = \delta s' + \tau + z_{j'}$ and $e' = t' y_{i^*} / x_{i^*}$, then $e' \notin \{e_l\}$. Observe that $W' = (g_2^s h_2 Z_j)^{\frac{1}{ax_{i^*} + t' y_{i^*}}} = (\hat{g}^{\delta \cdot s'} (\hat{g}^{ak} \cdot \hat{g}^\tau) \hat{g}^{z_{j'}})^{\frac{1}{ax_{i^*} + t' y_{i^*}}} = \hat{g}^{\frac{k}{x_{i^*}}} \cdot \hat{g}^{\frac{-ke' + v}{x_{i^*}(a + e')}}, B' = (W' \hat{g}^{-\frac{k}{x_{i^*}}})^{\frac{x_{i^*}}{-ke' + v}}$. Using this new SDH pair (B', e'), $\mathcal{B}$ can solve the original q-SDH problem.

2. $t' = t_l, W' = W_l$ for some $l \in [1, q]$. This happens with negligible probability unless $\mathcal{A}$ solves the relative discrete logarithm between g_1 and g_2.

3. $t' = t_l, W' \neq W_l$ for some $l \in [1, q]$. With probability $1/q$, $l = l^*$. We obtain $W'/W_l = (g_2^{s' - s_l} \hat{g}^{z_{j'} - z_j})^{\frac{1}{ax_i + t' y_i}} = (\hat{g}^{\delta \cdot (s' - s_l) + z_{j'} - z_j})^{\frac{1}{x_i a + t' y_i}}$. Since $(s', z_{j'}) \neq$

---

[2] In brief, $\mathcal{B}$ generates a generator $\hat{g} = g^{\prod_{k=1}^{q-1}(a + e_k)} \in \mathbb{G}$ for random $e_1, \ldots, e_{q-1} \in \mathbb{Z}_p^*$. Then, it prepares $q - 1$ pairs $\{(B_l, e_l)\}_{l=1}^{q-1}$ where $B_l = \hat{g}^{\frac{1}{a + e_l}} = g^{\prod_{k=1, k \neq l}^{q-1}(a + e_k)}$.

(s_j, z_j), we compute $B_{l^*} = (W'/W)^{\frac{1}{(s'-s)\delta + z_{j'} - z_j}}, e_{l^*} = t'y_{i^*}/x_{i^*}$. $\mathcal{B}$ can solve the original q-SDH problem with this new SDH pair (B_{l^*}, e_{l^*}).

If the success probability of $\mathcal{A}$ is ϵ, success probability of $\mathcal{B}$ is ϵ/q at least, which completes the proof.   ∎

4   Discussion and Comparison

In this section, first we extend our scheme to a CCA secure construction. Then, we compare our constructions with several single-hop unidirectional PRE schemes in the literature.

4.1   A CCA Secure Extension

We extend the SI scheme to a CCA secure construction using the technique of Zhang et al. [23]. We denote the following PRE scheme by SII.

Setup(λ) : Let λ be the security parameter, $\mathbb{G}$ and $\mathbb{G}_T$ be groups of prime order p, and $e: \mathbb{G} \times \mathbb{G} \to \mathbb{G}_T$ be a bilinear map. Randomly choose $g_1, g_2, h_1, h_2 \leftarrow \mathbb{G}$ and compute $L = e(h_1, h_2)$. Let $H_0 : \{0,1\}^l \times \mathbb{G} \to \mathbb{Z}_p^*$ be a collision-resistant hash function, $H_1 : \mathbb{G}_T \to \{0,1\}^{l_1}$ be a collision-resistant and one-way hash function and $H_2 : \mathbb{G}_T \to \{0,1\}^{l_2}$ be a universal hash function, where $l = l_1 + l_2$ and $l < \log p$ such that the generalized leftover hash lemma holds [11] in respect to negl(λ) for security. For simplicity, we let the message space $\mathcal{M} = \{0,1\}^{l_2}$. The system parameters are param $= (g_1, g_2, h_1, h_2, L, H_0, H_1, H_2)$.

KeyGen($param$), ReKeyGen(sk_i, pk_j) and CheckKey($pk_i, pk_j, rk_{i \to j}$) : The same as in SI.

Enc$_1$(pk_j, m) : Given a public key pk_j and a message m, pick $r, \gamma \leftarrow \mathbb{Z}_p$ randomly, compute $c_0' = H_1(L^r) \| H_2(L^r) \oplus m$, $c_1' = g_1^r$, $c_2' = L^r \cdot e(h_1^r, Z_j)$, $c_3' = (u^\psi v^\gamma w)^r$ where $\psi = H_0(c_0', c_1')$. Return a 1st level ciphertext $C_j' = (\gamma, c_0', c_1', c_2', c_3')$.

Enc$_2$(pk_i, m) : Given a public key pk_i and a message m, pick $r, \gamma \leftarrow \mathbb{Z}_p$ randomly, compute $c_0 = H_1(L^r) \| H_2(L^r) \oplus m$, $c_1 = g_1^r$, $c_2 = g_2^r$, $c_3 = X_i^r$, $c_4 = Y_i^r$, $c_5 = (u^\psi v^\gamma w)^r$ where $\psi = H_0(c_0, c_1)$. Return a 2nd level ciphertext $C_i = (\gamma, c_0, c_1, c_2, c_3, c_4, c_5)$.

ReEnc($rk_{i \to j}, C_i$) : Given a re-encryption key $rk_{i \to j} = (W, s, t)$ and a 2nd level ciphertext $C_i = (\gamma, c_0, c_1, c_2, c_3, c_4, c_5)$, compute $\psi = H_0(c_0, c_1)$ and check the following relations:

$$e(c_1, g_2) = e(g_1, c_2), e(c_1, X_i) = e(g_1, c_3),$$

$$e(c_1, Y_i) = e(g_1, c_4), e(c_1, u^\psi v^\gamma w) = e(g_1, c_5). \tag{1}$$

If the above relations hold, compute $c_0' = c_0$, $c_1' = c_1$, $c_2' = e(c_3 c_4^t, W)/e(c_2, h_1^s)$, $c_3' = c_5$ and return a 1st level ciphertext $C_j' = (\gamma, c_0', c_1', c_2', c_3')$. Otherwise, return "$\perp$".

$Dec_1(sk_j, C'_j)$: Given a secret key sk_j and a 1st level ciphertext C'_j, compute $\psi = H_0(c_0, c_1)$ and check the following relation

$$e(c'_1, u^\psi v^\gamma w) = e(g_1, c'_3). \tag{2}$$

If the above relation does not hold, return "$\perp$". Otherwise, parse $c'_0 = \tau_1 || \tau_2$, compute $K = c'_2 / e(h_1, c'_1{}^{z_j})$. If $\tau_1 = H_1(K)$, return $m = \tau_2 \oplus H_2(K)$, else return "$\perp$".

$Dec_2(sk_i, C_i)$: Given a secret key sk_i and a 2nd level ciphertext C_i, compute $\psi = H_0(c_0, c_1)$ and check the relations (1). If the relations do not hold, return "$\perp$". Otherwise, parse $c_0 = \tau_1 || \tau_2$ and compute $K = e(c_3^{1/x_i}, h_2)$. If $\tau_1 = H_1(K)$, return $m = \tau_2 \oplus H_2(K)$, else return "$\perp$".

We omit the correctness of SII due to the space limit.

Theorem 3. *Assume H_0 is a collision-resistant hash function, H_1 is a collision-resistant and one-way hash function and H_2 is a universal hash function, scheme SII is CCA secure at both the 2nd level and the 1st level ciphertexts under the DBDH assumption.*

The CCA security definition and proof are in the full version.

4.2   Comparison

We compare our scheme with single-hop unidirectional PRE schemes in the literature. These schemes are representative because of their better efficiency and security. In Table 1, t_p, t_m, t'_e, t_e, t_s and t_v denote the time for computing a bilinear pairing, a multi-exponentiation in group $\mathbb{G}$, an exponentiation in group $\mathbb{G}_T$, an exponentiation in group $\mathbb{G}$, a signing algorithm and a verification algorithm, respectively. $|svk|$, $|\sigma|$, $|\mathbb{Z}_p|$, $|\mathbb{G}|$ and $|\mathbb{G}_T|$ denote the bit-length of a verification key, a signature for a ciphertext, an integer in $\mathbb{Z}_p$, an element in $\mathbb{G}$ and an element in $\mathbb{G}_T$, respectively.

We use optimizations in our construction SII, which is also used in [23]. First, we replace the relations check (1) with $e(c_1, g_2^{r_1} X_i^{r_2} Y_i^{r_3} (u^\psi v^\gamma w)^{r_4}) = e(g_1, c_2^{r_1} c_3^{r_2} c_4^{r_3} c_5^{r_4})$ by randomly choosing $r_1, r_2, r_3, r_4 \in \mathbb{Z}_p^*$. Second, we pre-compute the value $e(h_1, Z_j)$ in algorithm Enc_1 and h_1^s in ReEnc. Third, by the collision resistance of H_1, we omit checking the relation (2) and compute $K = \frac{c'_2 \cdot e(c'_3, g_1^{r_1})}{e((u^\psi v^\gamma w)^{r_1} h_1^{z_j}, c'_1)}$ by randomly choosing $r_1 \in \mathbb{Z}_p^*$.

Table 1 and Table 2 are efficiency and security comparisons among the well-known and relative schemes. Since both the schemes in [18] and [23] can be optimized by using the same techniques as ours, we choose to compare these schemes after taking similar optimizations.

In Table 1, as [18] and [23], the sizes of the public key and the ciphertexts of our scheme SI and scheme SII are constant. The computational costs of decryption algorithms of the scheme SII are as low as those in [23]. In Table 2, we see the construction SII is the only scheme that has both CCA security and unforgeability of re-encryption keys. The result indicates that our scheme SII achieves better security at a slight efficiency loss.

Table 1. Efficiency comparisons among unidirectional PRE schemes. $O(n) = O(\log N)$, where N denotes the maximum number of delegatees for each delegator

Schemes	Public Key and Ciphertext Size			Computational Cost				
	PK	1st level	2nd level	Enc		ReEnc	Dec	
				1st level	2nd level		1st level	2nd level
LV08a [18]	$\|G\|$	$4\|G\|+\|G_T\|+$ $\|svk\|+\|\sigma\|$	$2\|G\|+\|G_T\|+$ $\|svk\|+\|\sigma\|$	t_m+4t_e+ t_s	t_m+2t_e+ t_s	$2t_p+$ $4t_e+t_v$	$3t_p+$ $3t_e+t_v$	$3t_p+$ $2t_e+t_v$
LV08b [17]	$(n+2)\|G\|+$ $\|G_T\|$	$2\|G_T\|$	$\|G_T\|+(n+$ $2)\|G\|$	$2t_p+t_e$	$t'_e+(n+$ $2)t_e$	$2t_p$	t'_e	t_p+t_e
ZZC14 [23]	$2\|G\|$	$\|G_T\|+2\|G\|+$ $l+\|\mathbb{Z}_p\|$	$3\|G\|+l+\|\mathbb{Z}_p\|$	t_p+t_m+ t'_e+2t_e	$t_m+t'_e+$ $2t_e$	$3t_p+2t_m$	$2t_p+t_m+$ t_e	$3t_p+$ $2t_m+t_e$
Scheme SI	$3\|G\|$	$2\|G_T\|+\|G\|$	$\|G_T\|+4\|G\|$	t'_e+t_e	t'_e+4t_e	$2t_p+t_e$	t_p+t_e	t_p+t_e
Scheme SII	$3\|G\|$	$\|G_T\|+2\|G\|+$ $l+\|\mathbb{Z}_p\|$	$5\|G\|+l+\|\mathbb{Z}_p\|$	t_p+t_m+ t'_e+2t_e	$t_m+t'_e+$ $4t_e$	$4t_p+$ $2t_m+t_e$	$2t_p+t_m+$ t_e	$3t_p+$ $2t_m+t_e$

Table 2. Security comparisons among unidirectional schemes

Schemes	Security of Ciphertext	Security Assumption	Unforgeability of Re-Encryption Keys	Unforgeability of Re-Encryption Keys Assumption
LV08a [18]	RCCA	3-wDBDHI	×	-
LV08b [17]	CPA	Augmented DBDH	×	-
ZZC14[23]	CCA	DBDH	×	-
Scheme SI	CPA	DBDH	√	q-SDH
Scheme SII	CCA	DBDH	√	q-SDH

5 Conclusion

In this paper, the notion of unforgeable re-encryption keys against collusion attacks is formulated. This definition could be seen as a definition of non-transferable property to some extent. Then, a non-interactive CPA secure PRE scheme is presented and its re-encryption keys are proven to be unforgeable against collusion attacks. The length of the re-encryption key is constant. Finally, the CPA secure PRE scheme is extended to a CCA secure one.

Acknowledgement. We would like to thank the anonymous CANS reviewers for their helpful comments.

References

1. Ateniese, G., Fu, K., Green, M., Hohenberger, S.: Improved Proxy Re-Encryption Schemes with Applications to Secure Distributed Storage. ACM Transactions on Information and System Security (TISSEC) 9(1), 1–30 (2006)
2. Au, M.H., Susilo, W., Mu, Y.: Constant-Size Dynamic k-TAA. In: De Prisco, R., Yung, M. (eds.) SCN 2006. LNCS, vol. 4116, pp. 111–125. Springer, Heidelberg (2006)
3. Blaze, M., Bleumer, G., Strauss, M.J.: Divertible Protocols and Atomic Proxy Cryptography. In: Nyberg, K. (ed.) EUROCRYPT 1998. LNCS, vol. 1403, pp. 127–144. Springer, Heidelberg (1998)
4. Boneh, D., Boyen, X.: Efficient Selective-ID Secure Identity-Based Encryption Without Random Oracles. In: Cachin, C., Camenisch, J.L. (eds.) EUROCRYPT 2004. LNCS, vol. 3027, pp. 223–238. Springer, Heidelberg (2004)

5. Boneh, D., Franklin, M.: Identity-Based Encryption from the Weil Pairing. In: Kilian, J. (ed.) CRYPTO 2001. LNCS, vol. 2139, pp. 213–229. Springer, Heidelberg (2001)

6. Canetti, R., Hohenberger, S.: Chosen-Ciphertext Secure Proxy Re-Encryption. In: Proceedings of the 14th ACM Conference on Computer and Communications security, pp. 185–194. ACM (2007)

7. Chandran, N., Chase, M., Vaikuntanathan, V.: Functional Re-encryption and Collusion-Resistant Obfuscation. In: Cramer, R. (ed.) TCC 2012. LNCS, vol. 7194, pp. 404–421. Springer, Heidelberg (2012)

8. Chow, S.S.M., Weng, J., Yang, Y., Deng, R.H.: Efficient Unidirectional Proxy Re-Encryption. In: Bernstein, D.J., Lange, T. (eds.) AFRICACRYPT 2010. LNCS, vol. 6055, pp. 316–332. Springer, Heidelberg (2010)

9. Chu, C.-K., Tzeng, W.-G.: Identity-Based Proxy Re-encryption Without Random Oracles. In: Garay, J.A., Lenstra, A.K., Mambo, M., Peralta, R. (eds.) ISC 2007. LNCS, vol. 4779, pp. 189–202. Springer, Heidelberg (2007)

10. Deng, R.H., Weng, J., Liu, S., Chen, K.: Chosen-Ciphertext Secure Proxy Re-encryption without Pairings. In: Franklin, M.K., Hui, L.C.K., Wong, D.S. (eds.) CANS 2008. LNCS, vol. 5339, pp. 1–17. Springer, Heidelberg (2008)

11. Dodis, Y., Ostrovsky, R., Reyzin, L., Smith, A.: Fuzzy Extractors: How to Generate Strong Keys from Biometrics and Other Noisy Data. SIAM Journal on Computing 38(1), 97–139 (2008)

12. Green, M., Ateniese, G.: Identity-Based Proxy Re-encryption. In: Katz, J., Yung, M. (eds.) ACNS 2007. LNCS, vol. 4521, pp. 288–306. Springer, Heidelberg (2007)

13. Hayashi, R., Matsushita, T., Yoshida, T., Fujii, Y., Okada, K.: Unforgeability of Re-Encryption Keys against Collusion Attack in Proxy Re-Encryption. In: Iwata, T., Nishigaki, M. (eds.) IWSEC 2011. LNCS, vol. 7038, pp. 210–229. Springer, Heidelberg (2011)

14. Hohenberger, S., Rothblum, G.N., Shelat, A., Vaikuntanathan, V.: Securely Obfuscating Re-encryption. In: Vadhan, S.P. (ed.) TCC 2007. LNCS, vol. 4392, pp. 233–252. Springer, Heidelberg (2007)

15. Isshiki, T., Nguyen, M.H., Tanaka, K.: Attacks to the Proxy Re-Encryption Schemes from IWSEC2011. In: Sakiyama, K., Terada, M. (eds.) IWSEC 2013. LNCS, vol. 8231, pp. 290–302. Springer, Heidelberg (2013)

16. Liang, K., Fang, L., Susilo, W., Wong, D.S.: A Ciphertext-Policy Attribute-Based Proxy Re-Encryption with Chosen-Ciphertext Security. In: 2013 5th International Conference on Intelligent Networking and Collaborative Systems (INCoS), pp. 552–559. IEEE (2013)

17. Libert, B., Vergnaud, D.: Tracing Malicious Proxies in Proxy Re-Encryption. In: Galbraith, S.D., Paterson, K.G. (eds.) Pairing 2008. LNCS, vol. 5209, pp. 332–353. Springer, Heidelberg (2008)

18. Libert, B., Vergnaud, D.: Unidirectional Chosen-Ciphertext Secure Proxy Re-encryption. In: Cramer, R. (ed.) PKC 2008. LNCS, vol. 4939, pp. 360–379. Springer, Heidelberg (2008)

19. Luo, S., Hu, J., Chen, Z.: Ciphertext Policy Attribute-Based Proxy Re-encryption. In: Soriano, M., Qing, S., López, J. (eds.) ICICS 2010. LNCS, vol. 6476, pp. 401–415. Springer, Heidelberg (2010)

20. Shao, J., Cao, Z.: CCA-Secure Proxy Re-encryption without Pairings. In: Jarecki, S., Tsudik, G. (eds.) PKC 2009. LNCS, vol. 5443, pp. 357–376. Springer, Heidelberg (2009)

21. Wang, H., Cao, Z., Wang, L.: Multi-Use and Unidirectional Identity-Based Proxy Re-Encryption Schemes. Information Sciences 180(20), 4042–4059 (2010)

22. Yu, S., Wang, C., Ren, K., Lou, W.: Attribute Based Data Sharing with Attribute Revocation. In: Proceedings of the 5th ACM Symposium on Information, Computer and Communications Security, pp. 261–270. ACM (2010)

23. Zhang, J., Zhang, Z., Chen, Y.: PRE: Stronger Security Notions and Efficient Construction with Non-Interactive Opening. In: Theoretical Computer Science (2014)

On the Lossiness of 2^k-th Power and the Instantiability of Rabin-OAEP [*]

Haiyang Xue[1,2,3], Bao Li[1,2], Xianhui Lu[1,2],
Kunpeng Wang[1,2], and Yamin Liu[1,2]

Data Assurance and Communication Security Research Center,
Chinese Academy of Sciences, Beijing, China
State Key Laboratory of Information Security, Institute of Information Engineering,
Chinese Academy of Sciences, Beijing, China
University of Chinese Academy of Sciences, Beijing, China
{hyxue12,lb,xhlu,kpwang,ymliu}@is.ac.cn

Abstract. Seurin (PKC 2014) proposed the 2-Φ/4-hiding assumption which asserts the indistinguishability of Blum Numbers from pseudo Blum Numbers. In this paper, we investigate the lossiness of 2^k-th power based on the 2^k-Φ/4-hiding assumption, which is an extension of the 2-Φ/4-hiding assumption. And we prove that 2^k-th power function is a lossy trapdoor permutation over Quadratic Residuosity group. This new lossy trapdoor function has $2k$-bits lossiness for k-bits exponent, while the RSA lossy trapdoor function given by Kiltz et al. (Crypto 2010) has k-bits lossiness for k-bits exponent under Φ-hiding assumption in lossy mode. We modify the square function in Rabin-OAEP by 2^k-th power and show the instantiability of this Modified Rabin-OAEP by the technique of Kiltz et al. (Crypto 2010). The Modified Rabin-OAEP is more efficient than the RSA-OAEP scheme for the same secure bits. With the secure parameter being 80 bits and the modulus being 2048 bits, Modified Rabin-OAEP can encrypt roughly 454 bits of message, while RSA-OAEP can roughly encrypt 274 bits.

Keywords: Rabin, OAEP, Lossy trapdoor function, Φ-hiding.

1 Introduction

Lossy Trapdoor Function. Peikert and Waters [25] proposed the notion of lossy trapdoor function (LTDF) in STOC 2008. LTDF implies cryptographic primitives such as classic one-way trapdoor function [8], collision resistant hash function [13], oblivious transfer protocol [14], chosen ciphertext secure public key encryption scheme [25], deterministic public key encryption scheme [3], and selective opening secure public key encryption scheme [17]. LTDFs can be constructed based on many assumptions, such as DDH[25], DCR[11], LWE[25], etc.

---

[*] Supported by the National Basic Research Program of China (973 project)(No.2013CB338002), the National Nature Science Foundation of China (No.61070171, No.61272534).

D. Gritzalis et al. (Eds.): CANS 2014, LNCS 8813, pp. 34–49, 2014.

Kiltz *et al.* [22] showed that the RSA function $f : x \rightarrow x^e \mod N$ is a $\log e$ lossy trapdoor permutation (LTDP) under the Φ-hiding assumption. The Φ-hiding assumption was firstly proposed by Cachin, Micali and Stadler [5]. Intuitively, this assumption states that given an RSA modulus $N = pq$, it is hard to distinguish primes that divide $\phi(N)$ from those that do not, where ϕ is the Euler function. Kiltz *et al.* [22] then showed that the lossiness of RSA implies that the RSA-OAEP is indistinguishable against chosen plaintext attack (IND-CPA) in the standard model by instantiating the hash with t-wise independent hash. Subsequently, Kakvi and Kiltz [21] gave a tight proof of the security of RSA-FDH using the lossiness of RSA function.

Recently, Seurin [26] extended the Φ-hiding assumption to the 2-Φ/4-hiding assumption and showed that the Rabin function is lossy with two bits over the Quadratic Residuosity subgroup and 1 bit over the integers $1 \leq x \leq (N-1)/2$ with Jacobi symbol 1. The 2-Φ/4-hiding assumption is the indistinguishability of Blum Numbers, *i.e.* $p, q \equiv 3 \mod 4$, from pseudo Blum Numbers *i.e.* $p, q \equiv 1 \mod 4$. They also investigated the Rabin Williams signature and gave a tight proof of the Rabin-FDH by following the steps of Kakvi and Kiltz [21].

On the other line, Joye and Libert [19] investigated the Extended pseudo Blum Number and the Gap-2^k-Res assumption. They proposed an efficient LTDF based on the Gap-2^k-Res assumption and DDH assumption over 2^k-th Residuosity.

Optimal Asymmetric Encryption Padding. Bellare and Rogaway [2] introduced Optimal asymmetric encryption padding (OAEP) as a replacement of they widely used RSA PKCS #1 v1.5 [1]. And they proved that OAEP is secure in the random oracle model. When implementing this scheme in practice, the random oracle is replaced by a cryptographic hash function which is not random. Canetti [6] *et al.* showed that there are schemes which are secure in the random oracle model but not secure in the standard model. Two mostly studied OAEP schemes are the RSA-OAEP and Rabin-OAEP. The first evidence that RSA-OAEP could achieve a standard security notion in the standard model was proposed by Kiltz *et al.* [22] stating that the RSA-OAEP is IND-CPA secure under the Φ-hiding assumption. They proved that OAEP is a randomness extractor, that fools distinguishers with small range output. They also investigated the Multi-prime Φ-hiding assumption in order to improve the lossiness of RSA function. Some subsequent works [16][24] improved the security bound and investigated the regularity over subdomain. In terms of practice, the Rabin-OAEP is a competent substitution of RSA-OAEP. But the security of Rabin-OAEP has not been proven in the standard model under better-understood assumptions. One research direction is using the technique of Kiltz *et al.* [22] with the combination of LTDF and OAEP. But this method requires that the LTDF has enough lossiness. Seurin [26] noticed that one first step in this direction is to consider the multi prime pseudo Blum Numbers, but in order to get m bits lossiness, product of $m/2$ secure primes are required. This method reduces the security level and the computational efficiency.

The instantiability of Rabin-OAEP and concrete analysis of the security are interesting questions. The problem is to find a well-understood assumption, construct LTDF with enough lossiness and reduce the security to this assumption in the standard model. As shown above, Seurin [26] investigated the 2-$\Phi/4$-hiding assumption and showed that Rabin fucntion loses 2 bits over QR group. The 2-$\Phi/4$-hiding assumption asserts that it is hard to tell if $N = (2^2 s' + 2^2 - 1)(2^2 t' + 2^2 - 1)$ or $N = (2^2 p' + 1)(2^2 q' + 1)$ for some s', t', p' and q'. Inspired by Joye and Libert' scheme [19], a natural extension is the 2^k-$\Phi/4$-hiding assumption and the 2^k-th power function. The 2^k-th power function loses about $2k$ bits which is enough for the instantiability of OAEP given by Kiltz et al.[22].

1.1 Our Contributions

In this paper, we consider the problem of reducing the security of Rabin-OAEP to a well-understood assumption. Inspired by Joye and Libert' scheme [19], we first extend the 2-$\Phi/4$-hiding assumption to 2^k-$\Phi/4$-hiding assumption. Then we show that the 2^k-th power is lossy over the Quadratic Residuosity (QR) group under the 2^k-$\Phi/4$-hiding assumption. We also modify the classic Rabin-OAEP with 2^k-th power and prove that it is IND-CPA secure in the standard model using the lossiness of 2^k-th power. In the following, we explain our result with more details.

Lossiness of 2^k-th Power. In order to prove the lossiness of 2^k-th power, we firstly proposed the 2^k-$\Phi/4$-hiding assumption. Intuitively, this assumption is that, given k, it is hard to distinguish RSA modulus N which is the product of two primes with the least significant $k + 1$ bits being all 1 from those which is the product of two primes with the least significant $k + 1$ bits being all 0 except the last one. The 2^k-$\Phi/4$-hiding assumption asserts that, given (N, k) where N is product of two primes and $k \leq (\frac{1}{4} - \varepsilon) \log N$, it is hard to tell if $N = (2^{k+1} s' + 2^{k+1} - 1)(2^{k+1} t' + 2^{k+1} - 1)$ or $N = (2^{k+1} p' + 1)(2^{k+1} q' + 1)$ for some s', t', p' and q'. We call the numbers of the first kind the Extended Blum Numbers and those of the second kind the Extended pseudo Blum Numbers. Note that it is actually the 2-$\Phi/4$-hiding assumption when $k = 1$. For an Extended Blum Number N, the 2^k-th power is a trapdoor permutation over QR group. For Extended pseudo Blum Number N, the 2^k-th power is a 2^{2k}-to-1 map over QR. Thus we attain new efficient lossy trapdoor permutation. One problem of the QR group is that it is not efficiently recognizable, but the Signed QR subgroup can be recognized efficiently according to [10][26]. We also investigate the 2^k-th power over Signed QR group in the Appendix.

Modified Rabin-OAEP. We modify the Rabin-OAEP and call it Modified Rabin-OAEP. The one way function after OAEP is the 2^{k+1}-th power function. The security proof of our Modified Rabin-OAEP follows by extending Kiltz et al.'s proof of RSA-OAEP. Under the same security bits, the 2^k-th power loses about 2 times of the RSA function, and hence the Modified Rabin-OAEP can encrypt longer message. Precisely, for 80 bits security, let $n = 2048$, then $k = 432$.

Our Modified Rabin-OAEP can encrypt 454 bits at once while the RSA-OAEP for the same security bits can encrypt 274 bits only. Assuming the regularity of 2^{k+1}-th power on certain subdomains, message of 534 bits can be encrypted.

1.2 Outline

This paper is organized as follows. In Sect. 2, we introduce the notations and recall the definition of lossy trapdoor function and OAEP. In Sect. 3, we present 2^k-Φ/4-hiding assumption and analyse the lossiness of 2^k-th power. In Sect. 4, we present a construction of LTDF based on the 2^k-Φ/4-hiding assumption and compare it with previous LTDFs. In Sect. 5, we propose the Modified Rabin-OAEP scheme and show the instantiability of this encryption scheme. In Sect. 6, we conclude this paper.

2 Preliminaries

2.1 Notations

If S is a set, we denote by $|S|$ the cardinality of S, and denote by $x \leftarrow S$ the process of sampling x uniformly from S. If A is an algorithm, we denote by $z \leftarrow A(x, y, \cdots)$ the process of running A with input $x, y, \cdots$ and output z. For an integer n, we denote by $[n]$ the set of $\{0, 1, \cdots, n-1\}$. A function is *negligible* if for every $c > 0$ there exists a λ_c such that $f(\lambda) < 1/\lambda^c$ for all $\lambda > \lambda_c$.

2.2 Definitions

Definition 1 (Lossy Trapdoor Functions). *A collection of (m, l)-lossy trapdoor functions are 4-tuple of probabilistic polynomial time (PPT) algorithms $(S_{inj}, S_{loss}, F_{ltdf}, F_{ltdf}^{-1})$ such that:*

1. Sample Lossy Function $S_{loss}(1^n)$. *Output a function index $\sigma \in \{0, 1\}^*$ with implicitly understood domain $\mathcal{D}$ of size 2^m.*
2. Sample Injective Function $S_{inj}(1^n)$. *Output a pair $(\sigma, \tau) \in \{0, 1\}^* \times \{0, 1\}^*$ where σ is a function index with domain $\mathcal{D}$ of size 2^k and τ is a trapdoor.*
3. Evaluation algorithm F_{ltdf}. *For every function index σ produced by either S_{loss} or S_{inj}, the algorithm $F_{ltdf}(\sigma, \cdot)$ computes a function $f_\sigma : \mathcal{D} \to \{0, 1\}^*$ with one of the two following properties:*
   - *Lossy: If σ is produced by S_{loss}, then the image of f_σ has size at most 2^{m-l}.*
   - *Injective: If σ is produced by S_{inj}, then the function f_σ is injective.*
4. Inversion algorithm F_{ltdf}^{-1}. *For every pair (σ, τ) produced by S_{inj} and every $x \in \{0, 1\}^m$, we have $F_{ltdf}^{-1}(\tau, F_{ltdf}(\sigma, x)) = x$.*

In the above algorithms, the two ensembles $\{\sigma, \sigma \leftarrow S_{loss}(1^n)\}$ and $\{\sigma, (\sigma, \tau) \leftarrow S_{inj}(1^n)\}$ are computationally indistinguishable.

- *We call this lossy trapdoor permutation (LTDP) if the functions in the injective mode are permutations.*
- *We call the functions regular if the functions in the lossy mode are k to 1 for some k.*

Definition 2 (*t*-wise independent hash function). *Let $H : K \times D \to R$ be a hash function. We say that H is t-wise independent if for all distinct $x_1, \cdots x_t \in D$ and all $y_1, \cdots y_t \in R$*

$$Pr[H(k, x_1) = y_1 \wedge \cdots \wedge H(k, x_t) = y_t : k \leftarrow K] = \frac{1}{|R|^t}.$$

In other words, $H(k, x_1), \ldots, H(k, x_t)$ are all uniformly and independently random.

3   The 2^k-$\Phi/4$-Hiding Assumption and 2^k-th Power

In this section, we first propose the 2^k-$\Phi/4$ assumption, then analyze the properties of 2^k-th power function over QR.

3.1   The 2^k-$\Phi/4$-Hiding Assumption

Intuitively, the assumption is that, given secure parameters n and $k < n/4 - 1$ it is hard to distinguish RSA modulus N which are product of two primes with the least significant $k + 1$ bits being all 1 from those which are product of two primes with the least significant $k + 1$ bits being all 0 except the last one. In both cases, the least significant $k + 1$ bits of the modulus N are all zero except the last one. Formally, we define two distributions:

$$R = \{N : N = pq \text{ with } \log p \approx \log q \approx \lfloor \frac{n}{2} \rfloor \text{ and } p, q \equiv 2^{k+1} - 1 \mod 2^{k+1}\},$$

$$L = \{N : N = pq \text{ with } \log p \approx \log q \approx \lfloor \frac{n}{2} \rfloor \text{ and } p, q \equiv 1 \mod 2^{k+1}\}.$$

The 2^k-$\Phi/4$ assumption asserts that, for a probability polynomial time (PPT) distinguisher D the following advantage is negligible:

$$\mathbf{Adv}_D(n) = Pr[D(R) = 1] - Pr[D(L) = 1].$$

In order to enhance the strength of this assumption, we add requirements for p and q. In distribution R, we require that $p = 2^{k+1}s' + 2^{k+1} - 1$ (resp. $q = 2^{k+1}t' + 2^{k+1} - 1$) for odd number s' (resp. t'), we also require that $2^k s' + 2^k - 1$ and $2^k t' + 2^k - 1$ are primes (p, q are strong primes); in distribution L, we require that $p = 2^{k+1}p' + 1$ (resp. $q = 2^{k+1}q' + 1$) for prime number p' (resp. q')

This assumption is an extension of the 2-$\Phi/4$-hiding assumption [26] for $k = 1$. We call the numbers in distribution R the Extended Blum Numbers and those in L the Extended pseudo Blum Numbers. Joye and Libert [19] investigated the

Extended pseudo Blum Number. In their paper, they generalized the Goldwasser-Micali cryptosystem [15] to encrypt many bits at once by using the Extended pseudo Blum Number. The underlying assumption is the Gap-2^k-Res assumption which is implied by the original QR assumption. There is an efficient algorithm [20] for generating Extended pseudo Blum Numbers. We can modify this algorithm to get an efficient algorithm for generating Extended Blum Numbers. The distribution R and L can be chosen efficiently.

Analysis of the 2^k-$\Phi/4$-Hiding Assumption. It is easy to break the 2^k-$\Phi/4$-hiding problem with the factorization of modulus N. However, it seems that there is no known algorithm to break this problem without factoring the modulus N. [27] and [28] investigated the RSA modulus with primes sharing least significant bits. If given the modulus primes p and q sharing the least $k+1$ significant bits (denote it by l), at most 4 candidates l can be computed by solving the equation $x^2 = N \mod 2^{k+1}$. In our case, the equation is $x^2 = 1 \mod 2^{k+1}$, and 1, $2^{k+1} - 1$ are the two candidates of l. It is still difficult to decide which distribution the modulus N belongs to. Joye and Libert [19] have investigated the security parameters for the Extended pseudo Blum Numbers. When k is too large, by Coppersmith's method [7] with LLL algorithm [23], N can be factored in time $poly(n)$ with advantage $O(N^\varepsilon)$ if $k = n/4 - \varepsilon n - 1$. We have εn bits security here. We now consider Extended Blum Numbers. Pollard's $p - 1$ method dose not work. The powerful Coppersmith's method bounds the size of k to $n/4 - \varepsilon n - 1$ for the Extended Blum Numbers too. So we end up with the same upper bound:

$$k \leq \frac{1}{4}n - \varepsilon n - 1,$$

for εn bits security. For example, if $n = 2048$, we set $\varepsilon = 0.04$ (about 80 bits security), k can be about 430.

3.2 2^k-th Power over QR Group

Let $N = pq$ be a product of two distinct $n/2$ bits primes. The group Z_N^* consists of all elements of Z_N that are invertible modulo N. Then Z_N^* has order $\phi(N) = (p - 1)(q - 1)$. Denote QR the subgroup of Z_N^* of quadratic residues modulo N. Note that QR has order $\phi(N)/4$. We now consider the 2^k-th power over the subgroup QR.

Let N be an Extended Blum Number, then we have that the order of QR is an odd number. In fact the Extended Blum Number is a special case of the Blum Number. The Extended Blum Number has all the properties of the Blum Numbers. The square map is a permutation over QR, thus the 2^k-th power is a permutation over QR.

We now consider the Extended pseudo Blum Number $N = pq$ with $p, q \equiv 1 \mod 2^{k+1}$. We recall the definition of the m-th power residue symbol for a divisor m of $p - 1$ presented in [19] and [31]. Here we consider the case for $m = 2^i$ for $1 \leq i \leq k + 1$.

Definition 3. *Let p be an odd prime and $p \equiv 1 \mod 2^{k+1}$. For $1 \leq i \leq k+1$, the symbol*

$$\left(\frac{a}{p}\right)_{2^i} := a^{\frac{p-1}{2^i}} \mod p,$$

is the 2^i-th power residue symbol modulo p, where $a^{\frac{p-1}{2^i}} \mod p$ is in $[-(p-1)/2, (p-1)/2]$.

Let a and b be two integers coprime to p,

$$\left(\frac{ab}{p}\right)_{2^i} = \left(\frac{a}{p}\right)_{2^i} \left(\frac{b}{p}\right)_{2^i}. \tag{1}$$

Thus, we have

$$\left(\frac{a^2}{p}\right)_{2^i} = \left[\left(\frac{a}{p}\right)_{2^i}\right]^2 = \left(\frac{a}{p}\right)_{2^{i-1}}. \tag{2}$$

For any integer a and any Extended pseudo Blum Number N, we generalize the Jacobi symbol as the product of the m-th power residue Legendre symbol

$$\left(\frac{a}{N}\right)_{2^i} = \left(\frac{a}{p}\right)_{2^i} \left(\frac{a}{q}\right)_{2^i}. \tag{3}$$

Lemma 1. *Let N be the Extended pseudo Blum Number associated with k, then the 2^k-th power map $g : x \to x^{2^k}$ $(x \in QR)$ is a 2^{2k}-to-1 map and the 2^{k+1}-th power map $h : x \to x^{2^k}$ $(x \in Z_N^*)$ is a $2^{2(k+1)}$-to-1 map.*

Proof. To prove this result, we investigate a sequence of subgroups and square maps on them. Precisely, for $0 \leq s \leq k+1$, we consider the subgroups of Z_N^* denoted by

$$R^s := \{x^{2^s} | x \in Z_N^*\},$$

and define the square map $f_i : y \to y^2$ from R^i to R^{i+1} for $0 \leq i \leq k$. Note that here R^0 is Z_N^* itself. We also define here and in the followings that

$$J^s_{(+,+)} := \left\{ x | x \in R^s, \left(\frac{x}{p}\right)_{2^{s+1}} = 1, \left(\frac{x}{q}\right)_{2^{s+1}} = 1 \right\},$$

$$J^s_{(-,-)} := \left\{ x | x \in R^s, \left(\frac{x}{p}\right)_{2^{s+1}} = -1, \left(\frac{x}{q}\right)_{2^{s+1}} = -1 \right\},$$

$$J^s_{(+,-)} := \left\{ x | x \in R^s, \left(\frac{x}{p}\right)_{2^{s+1}} = 1, \left(\frac{x}{q}\right)_{2^{s+1}} = -1 \right\},$$

$$J^s_{(-,+)} := \left\{ x | x \in R^s, \left(\frac{x}{p}\right)_{2^{s+1}} = -1, \left(\frac{x}{q}\right)_{2^{s+1}} = 1 \right\}.$$

Note that the above sets divide R_s into four parts of the same size. And $J^s_{(+,+)}$ is actually the subgroup R_{s+1}.

We need only to prove that the map f_i is a 4-to-1 map. The map $g = f_k \circ f_{k-2} \cdots \circ f_1$ is 2^{2k}-to-1 naturally. For any element $a \in R_s$, by equation 2,

$$\left(\frac{f_i(a)}{p}\right)_{2^{i+2}} = \left(\frac{a}{p}\right)_{2^{i+1}} \equiv \pm 1 \mod p.$$

It also holds for modulus q. The four preimages of $f_i(a)$ fall into one of $J^i_{\pm 1, \pm 1}$. We have that f_i is a 4-to-1 map. Then we have that 2^k-th power over QR is a 2^{2k}-to-1 map and 2^{k+1}-th power over Z^*_N is a $2^{2(k+1)}$-to-1 map.   □

We illustrate the result of Lemma 1 and Lemma 3 in Figure 1.

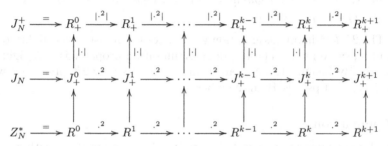

Here, R^s is the subgroup of Z^*_N with 2^s-th residuocity. J^s_+ is the subset of R^s with Legendre symbol 1. J^+_N is the subset of J^s_+ greater than 0. $\cdot^2$ represents the square map. $|\cdot|$ represents the absolute value and $|\cdot^2|$ is the square map over signed group. R^0 is actually Z^*_N and J^0_+ is J^+_N. It satisfies that $R^0 \supset R^1 \cdots \supset R^{k+1}$, $J^0_+ \supset J^1_+ \cdots \supset J^{k+1}_+$ and $R^0_+ \supset R^1_+ \cdots \supset R^{k+1}_+$. The 2^k-th power over QR is the combination of square maps from R^1 to R^{k+1}. The 2^k-th power over Signed QR is the combination of square maps from R^0_+ to R^k_+. See Appendix for more information about Signed QR group.

Fig. 1. Square map step by step for Extended Blum Number N with associated k

4   LTDP Based on the 2^k-Φ/4-Hiding Assumption

We now give a constructions of 2^{2k}-to-1 lossy trapdoor permutation over the QR group based on the 2^k-Φ/4-hiding assumption. The modulus N is an Extended Blum Number in the injective mode and is an Extended pseudo Blum Number in the lossy mode.

4.1   LTDP over QR

We define $LTDP_{QR} = (S_{inj}, S_{loss}, f_{QR}, f^{-1}_{QR})$ as follows:

1. *Sample Injective Function S_{inj}.* On input 1^n, S_{inj} chooses a proper k and random N in distribution R and the function index is $\sigma = \{N, k\}$. The trapdoor is $t = (p, q)$.

2. *Sample Lossy Function S_{loss}.* On input 1^n, S_{loss} chooses a proper k and random N in distribution L and the function index is $\sigma = \{N, k\}$.
3. *Evaluation algorithm f_{QR}.* Given a function index $\sigma = \{N, k\}$ and input $x \in QR$ the algorithm outputs $z = x^{2^k} \mod N$.
4. *Inversion algorithm f_{QR}^{-1}.* Given $z \in QR$ compute the 2^k root over Signed QR with the trapdoor p, q.

Remark 1. For Extended Blum Numbers, the order of the QR group is an odd number, we can compute the square root over QR k times to get the root in the injective mode. The trapdoor can be set as the inverse of $2^k \mod \frac{\phi(N)}{4}$. Then, given $z \in QR$, the 2^k root is in fact $z^t \mod N$.

Theorem 1. *If the 2^k-$\Phi/4$-hiding assumption holds, then $LTDP_{QR}$ is an 2^{2k}-to-1 lossy trapdoor permutation.*

Proof. The 2^k-$\Phi/4$-hiding assumption guarantees the indistinguishability of the lossy and injective mode. The trapdoor permutation property is a straight forward result. By Lemma 1, any element in f_{QR} has exactly 2^{2k} preimages when N is an Extended pseudo Blum Number. $\square$

4.2 Comparison

In Table 1, we compare the above two lossy trapdoor permutations with previous LTDFs. The second column lists the basic number-theoretic assumptions used for guaranteeing the security. The third and fourth columns show the size of an input message in bits and that of the function index respectively. The fifth column lists the size of lossiness. The sixth column shows the computational complexity of the corresponding function. According to [29], the complexity of multiplication is $O(n)$ here. The last column is the computational complexity for one bit lossiness.

5   Modified Rabin-OAEP

LTDF over Z_N^* can be used to instantiate the Rabin-OAEP. In [22], Kiltz *et al.* gave a generic result of building IND-CPA secure padding based encryption by combining a lossy TDP and a fooling extractor, and they proved that the OAEP is an adaptive fooling extractor with well chosen parameters. Then, they showed the instantitation of RSA-OAEP based on the Φ-hiding assumption. By the technique of Kiltz *et al.*, we prove that the Rabin-OAEP with a slight modification over Z_N^* is IND-CPA in the standard model based on the 2^k-$\Phi/4$-hiding assumption.

We recall a theorem in [22] here. For more details of padding based encryption please refer to [22].

Theorem 2 (Theorem 1 in [22]). *Let $\mathcal{F}$ be a lossy trapdoor permutation with residual leakage s and the padding transform $(\pi, \hat{\pi})$ is a (s, ε) adaptive fooling extractor, The padding based encryption by combination of $\mathcal{F}$ and $(\pi, \hat{\pi})$ is IND-CPA secure.*

Table 1. Comparison with existing LTDFs

	Assumption	Input size	Index size	Lossiness	Complexity	Comp/Loss
[25]	DDH	n	$n^2 \log p$	$n - \log p$	$n^2 \log p$	$n \log p$
[11]	d-linear	n	$n^2 \log p$	$n - d \log p$	$n^2 \log p$	$n \log p$
[25]	LWE	n	$n(d+w) \log q$	cn	$n(d+w) \log q$	$\frac{(d+w) \log q}{c}$
[11]	DCR	$2 \log N$	$2 \log N$	$\log N$	$4 \log^2 N$	$4 \log N$
[11]	QR	$\log N$	$\log N$	1	$3 \log N$	$3 \log N$
[19]	DDH& QR	n	$(\frac{n}{k})^2 \log N$	$n - \log N$	$(\frac{n^2}{k}) \log N$	$\frac{n^2 \log N}{n - \log N}$
[30]	DCR& QR	$\log N + k$	$2 \log N$	$3k$	$2 \log N(\log N + k)$	$\frac{2 \log N(\log N + k)}{3k}$
[22]	Φ-hiding	$\log N$	$\log N$	$\log e$	$\log e \log N$	$\log N$
[26]	2-Φ/4-hiding	$\log N$	$\log N$	2	$\log N$	$(\log N)/2$
4.1	2^k-Φ/4-hiding	$\log N$	$\log N$	$2k$	$k \log N$	$(\log N)/2$

In the first, second and sixth rows, n is the number of rows used in the matrix. In the first and second rows, p is the order of the underlying group. In the third row, $0 < c < 1$, n is the rows used in the matrix, $w = \frac{n}{\log p}$ with $p^2 \geq q$ and $d < w$. In this table, k and e are less than $\frac{1}{4} \log N - \kappa$ where κ is the security parameter.

We recall the description of OAEP for Rabin given by Boneh [4] with keyed hash function and give a full version of the Modified Rabin-OAEP encryption scheme. The OAEP for Rabin is different with the OAEP for RSA since that $x^2 \mod N$ is not a permutation on Z_N^*. Let N be an $n + 1$ bits Extended Blum Number, μ, s_0, ρ be security parameters such that $n = \mu + s_0 + \rho$. Let $G : K_G \times \{0,1\}^\rho \to \{0,1\}^{\mu+s_0}$ and $H : K_H \times \{0,1\}^{\mu+s_0} \to \{0,1\}^\rho$ be keyed hash functions.

OAEP for Rabin

The associated padding transform is $(\pi_{K_G,K_H}, \hat{\pi}_{K_G,K_H})$ defined by

Algorithm $\pi_{K_G,K_H}(m)$	**Algorithm** $\hat{\pi}_{K_G,K_H}(x)$
$Step1 : r \leftarrow \{0,1\}^\rho$	$Step1 : s \parallel t \leftarrow x$
$Step2 : s \leftarrow m \parallel 0^{s_0} \oplus G_{K_G}(r)$	$Step2 : r \leftarrow t \oplus H_{K_H}(s)$
$Step3 : t \leftarrow r \oplus H_{K_H}(s)$	$Step3 : m \parallel v \leftarrow s \oplus G_{K_G}(r)$
$Step4 : x \leftarrow s \parallel t$	$Step4 :$ If $v = 0^{s_0}$ return m
$Step5 :$ Return x	else return$\perp$.

Remark 2. Kiltz et al. [22] noted that their result also applies to Simplified OAEP given by Boneh[4] since hash function H_{K_H} in OAEP can be anything in their analysis. We remove the hash function H_{K_H} and use the Simplified OAEP for Rabin in the following. This does not affect the secure proof and parameter bound.

The Modified Rabin-OAEP

KeyGen: On input a security parameters n, choose a k and $n + 1$ bits Extended Blum Number $N = pq$ associated with k. Choose a random t-wise independent hash function G_{K_G} and a hash function H_{K_H}. Compute the inversion of $2^k \mod \frac{\phi(N)}{4}$ and denote it as d. Let $A \equiv 1 \mod p$ and $A \equiv 0 \mod q$, and $B \equiv 0 \mod p$ and $B \equiv 1 \mod q$, set

$$pk = (N, k, G_{K_G}, H_{K_H}), \quad sk = (p, q, d, A, B).$$

Encryption: On input a massage $m \in \{0, 1\}^\mu$,
    Step 1: Pick a random $r \in \{0, 1\}^\rho$ and compute $\pi_{K_G, K_H}(m)$.
    Step 2: Set the ciphertext as $c = y^{2^{k+1}} \mod N$.
Decryption: On input a ciphertext c,
    Step 1: Compute $z = c^d \mod N$.
    Step 2: Compute $z_p = z^{\frac{p+1}{4}} \mod p$ and $z_q = z^{\frac{q+1}{4}} \mod q$.
    Step 3: Set $y_1 = Az_p + Bz_q$ and $y_2 = Az_p - Bz_q$. Four square roots of z $\mod N$ is $\pm y_1, \pm y_2$. Two of them are less than $N/2$ and denote them by y_1, y_2.
    Step 4: Compute $\hat{\pi}_{K_G, K_H}(y_1)$ and $\hat{\pi}_{K_G, K_H}(y_2)$. If one of them outputs a message m and the other outputs $\perp$, then return m.

Remark 3. Note that in Step 4, if both $v = 0^{s_0}$ for y_1, y_2, the decryption can not choose between them. Boneh [4] showed that this happens with low probability, namely 2^{s_0} and s_0 is typically chosen to be greater than 128.

Theorem 3. *If G_{K_G} is a t-wise independent hash function and the 2^k-$\Phi/4$-hiding assumption holds, then the Modified Rabin-OAEP is IND-CPA secure*

1. *with advantage $\varepsilon = 2^{-u}$ for $u = \frac{t}{3t+2}(\rho - s - \log t) - \frac{2(\mu + s_0 + s)}{3t+2} - 1$.*
2. *with advantage $\varepsilon = 2^{-u}$ for $u = \frac{t}{2t+2}(\rho - s - \log t) - \frac{\mu + s_0 + s + 2}{t+1} - 1$, if it is regular on OAEP domain.*

This is almost a direct result of the combination of Theorem 1 and Theorem 2 in [22]. We omit the proof here and just point out the different part. The OAEP for Rabin is different with the OAEP for RSA since that $x^2 \mod N$ is not a permutation on Z_N^*. The least significant s_0 bits of message is padded by zero in order to choose the right plaintext from four square roots. There is 2^μ possible $(\mu + s_0, \rho)$-sources $X = (m\|0^{s_0}, R)$ here while there is $2^{\mu + s_0}$ possible $(\mu + s_0, \rho)$-sources in RSA-OAEP. This just affects the security bound of ε.

5.1   Efficiency of the Modified Rabin-OAEP

Regularity. We have analyzed the regularity of 2^{k+1}-th power over Z_N^* for Extended pseudo Blum Number. Unfortunately, in practice, the domain of Rabin-OAEP is $\{0, 1\}^{\mu + s_0 + \rho}$ (as integer) where $\mu + s_0 + \rho = n - 16$ (i.e. the most significant two bytes of the output are zeroed out). The 2^{k+1}-th power may not be regular over the subdomain $\{0, 1, \cdots, 2^{\mu + s_0 + \rho} - 1\}$. Lewko *et al.* [24] proved the regularity of RSA function over this subdomain. We assume that the 2^{k+1}-th power over this subdomain is regular and leave it as an open problem.

Concrete Parameters. If we do not assume the regularity of 2^k-th power over subdomain, from part 1 in Theorem 3, for $u = 80$ bits of security, messages of roughly $\mu = n - s - s_0 - 3 \cdot 80$ bits can be encrypted for sufficiently large t. For $n = 2048$, then $k = 432$, $s \approx 1184$, and the lossiness is 864 bits. Set $s_0 = 130$, 454 bits message ($t \approx 2000$) can be encrypted at once. Kiltz et $al.$ [22] instantiated the RSA-OAEP under the Φ-hiding assumption. 160 bits can be encrypted at once in the RSA-OAEP ($t \approx 400$). Under the investigation of Lewko et $al.$ [24] that the RSA function is regular over subdomain, 274 bits can be encrypted at once ($t \approx 2000$).

If we assume the regularity of 2^k-th power over subdomain, from part 2 in Theorem 3, for $u = 80$ bits of security, messages of roughly $\mu = n - s - s_0 - 2 \cdot 80$ bits can be encrypted For $n = 2048$, then $k = 432$, 534 bits message ($t \approx 2000$) can be encrypted at once. But this conjecture is not proved.

In Table 2, we compare the efficiency of the Modified Rabin-OAEP above with RSA-OAEP. The second column lists the basic number-theoretic assumptions used for guaranteeing the security. The following columns show the size of modulus, k or length of e, length of lossiness and encrypted message in bits, respectively. The first row is the RSA-OAEP. The second row is the Rabin-OAEP without the regular assumption ($t \approx 2000$). The last row is the Rabin-OAEP with the regular assumption ($t \approx 2000$).

Table 2. Comparison with RSA-OAEP

Scheme	Assumption	$\lfloor \log N \rfloor$	k or $\log e$	Lossiness	Message
RSA-OAEP [22][24]	Φ-hiding	2048	432	432	274
Rabin-OAEP	2^k-$\Phi/4$-hiding	2048	432	864	454
Rabin-OAEP	2^k-$\Phi/4$-hiding, Regular	2048	432	864	534

6 Conclusion

In this paper, we investigate the lossiness of 2^k-th power based on the 2^k-$\Phi/4$-hiding assumption, which is an extension of the 2-$\Phi/4$-hiding assumption. And we prove that 2^k-th power function is a lossy trapdoor permutation over Quadratic Residuosity group. We instantiate Modified Rabin-OAEP by the technique of Kiltz et $al.$. Our Modified Rabin-OAEP is more efficient than the RSA-OAEP scheme for the same secure bits.

References

1. RSA public-key cryptography standards,
   ftp://ftp.rsasecurity.com/pub/pkcs/pkcs-1
2. Bellare, M., Rogaway, P.: Optimal asymmetric encryption. In: De Santis, A. (ed.) EUROCRYPT 1994. LNCS, vol. 950, pp. 92–111. Springer, Heidelberg (1995)

3. Boldyreva, A., Fehr, S., O'Neill, A.: On notions of security for deterministic encryption, and efficient constructions without random oracles. In: Wagner, D. (ed.) CRYPTO 2008. LNCS, vol. 5157, pp. 335–359. Springer, Heidelberg (2008)
4. Boneh, D.: Simplified OAEP for the RSA and Rabin Functions. In: Kilian, J. (ed.) CRYPTO 2001. LNCS, vol. 2139, pp. 275–291. Springer, Heidelberg (2001)
5. Cachin, C., Micali, S., Stadler, M.: Computationally private information retrieval with polylogarithmic communication. In: Stern, J. (ed.) EUROCRYPT 1999. LNCS, vol. 1592, pp. 402–414. Springer, Heidelberg (1999)
6. Canetti, R., Goldreich, O., Halevi, S.: The random oracle methodology, revisited. J. ACM 51(4), 557–594 (2004)
7. Coppersmith, D.: Small solutions to polynomial equations, and low exponent rsa vulnerabilities. J. Cryptology 10(4), 233–260 (1997)
8. Diffie, W., Hellman, M.E.: New directions in cryptography. IEEE Transactions on Information Theory 22(6), 644–654 (1976)
9. Dodis, Y., Reyzin, L., Smith, A.: Fuzzy extractors: How to generate strong keys from biometrics and other noisy data. In: Cachin, C., Camenisch, J.L. (eds.) EUROCRYPT 2004. LNCS, vol. 3027, pp. 523–540. Springer, Heidelberg (2004)
10. Fischlin, R., Schnorr, C.P.: Stronger security proofs for rsa and rabin bits. J. Cryptology 13(2), 221–244 (2000)
11. Freeman, D.M., Goldreich, O., Kiltz, E., Rosen, A., Segev, G.: More constructions of lossy and correlation-secure trapdoor functions. In: Nguyen, P.Q., Pointcheval, D. (eds.) PKC 2010. LNCS, vol. 6056, pp. 279–295. Springer, Heidelberg (2010)
12. Freeman, D.M., Goldreich, O., Kiltz, E., Rosen, A., Segev, G.: More constructions of lossy and correlation-secure trapdoor functions. J. Cryptology 26(1), 39–74 (2013)
13. Goldreich, O.: The Foundations of Cryptography. Basic Techniques, vol. 1. Cambridge University Press (2001)
14. Goldreich, O.: The Foundations of Cryptography. Basic Applications, vol. 2. Cambridge University Press (2004)
15. Goldwasser, S., Micali, S.: Probabilistic encryption. J. Comput. Syst. Sci. 28(2), 270–299 (1984)
16. Herrmann, M.: Improved cryptanalysis of the multi-prime ϕ - hiding assumption. In: Nitaj, A., Pointcheval, D. (eds.) AFRICACRYPT 2011. LNCS, vol. 6737, pp. 92–99. Springer, Heidelberg (2011)
17. Hofheinz, D.: Possibility and impossibility results for selective decommitments. J. Cryptology 24(3), 470–516 (2011)
18. Hofheinz, D., Kiltz, E.: The group of signed quadratic residues and applications. In: Halevi, S. (ed.) CRYPTO 2009. LNCS, vol. 5677, pp. 637–653. Springer, Heidelberg (2009)
19. Joye, M., Libert, B.: Efficient cryptosystems from 2^k-th power residue symbols. In: Johansson, T., Nguyen, P.Q. (eds.) EUROCRYPT 2013. LNCS, vol. 7881, pp. 76–92. Springer, Heidelberg (2013)
20. Joye, M., Paillier, P.: Fast generation of prime numbers on portable devices: An update. In: Goubin, L., Matsui, M. (eds.) CHES 2006. LNCS, vol. 4249, pp. 160–173. Springer, Heidelberg (2006)
21. Kakvi, S.A., Kiltz, E.: Optimal security proofs for full domain hash, revisited. In: Pointcheval, D., Johansson, T. (eds.) EUROCRYPT 2012. LNCS, vol. 7237, pp. 537–553. Springer, Heidelberg (2012)
22. Kiltz, E., O'Neill, A., Smith, A.: Instantiability of rsa-oaep under chosen-plaintext attack. In: Rabin, T. (ed.) CRYPTO 2010. LNCS, vol. 6223, pp. 295–313. Springer, Heidelberg (2010)

23. Lenstra, A.K., Lenstra, H.W., Lovász, L.: Factoring polynomials with rational co-efficients. Mathematische Annalen 261, 515–534 (1982)
24. Lewko, M., O'Neill, A., Smith, A.: Regularity of lossy rsa on subdomains and its applications. In: Johansson, T., Nguyen, P.Q. (eds.) EUROCRYPT 2013. LNCS, vol. 7881, pp. 55–75. Springer, Heidelberg (2013)
25. Peikert, C., Waters, B.: Lossy trapdoor functions and their applications. In: STOC, pp. 187–196 (2008)
26. Seurin, Y.: On the lossiness of the rabin trapdoor function. In: Krawczyk, H. (ed.) PKC 2014. LNCS, vol. 8383, pp. 380–398. Springer, Heidelberg (2014)
27. Steinfeld, R., Zheng, Y.: On the security of rsa with primes sharing least-significant bits. Appl. Algebra Eng. Commun. Comput. 15(3-4), 179–200 (2004)
28. Sun, H.M., Wu, M.E., Steinfeld, R., Guo, J., Wang, H.: Cryptanalysis of short exponent rsa with primes sharing least significant bits. IACR Cryptology ePrint Archive 2008, 296 (2008)
29. von zur Gathen, J., Gerhard, J.: Modern Computer Algebra, 3rd edn. Cambridge University Press (2013)
30. Xue, H., Li, B., Lu, X., Jia, D., Liu, Y.: Efficient lossy trapdoor functions based on subgroup membership assumptions. In: Abdalla, M., Nita-Rotaru, C., Dahab, R. (eds.) CANS 2013. LNCS, vol. 8257, pp. 235–250. Springer, Heidelberg (2013)
31. Yan, S.Y.: Number Theory for Computing, 2nd edn. Springer (2002)

Appendix: Signed QR Group

In this appendix, we investigate the 2^k-th power over Signed QR group, and propose another version of Rabin-OAEP. This version of OAEP is not used in practice, but this is one solution of constructing OAEP-like CPA secure encryption.

2^k-th Power over Signed QR Group

We first recall the definition of Signed QR group and the group operation. Let N be an integer, we represent Z_N^* in $[-(N-1)/2, (N-1)/2]$. For $x \in Z_N^*$, define $|x|$ as the absolute value of x. we denote J_N the subgroup of Z_N^* with Jacobi symbol 1, and QR the group of quadratic residue. The signed quadratic residues is defined as the group $QR_N^+ = \{|x| : x \in QR_N\}$, and $J_N^+ := \{|x| : x \in J_N\}$. For elements g, h and the integer x, the group operation is defined by

$$g \circ h = |g \cdot h \mod N|, \quad g^{\underline{x}} = |\underbrace{g \cdot g \cdots g}_{x \text{ times}}| = |g^x \mod N|.$$

In fact, the Extended Blum Number is over a subset of Blum Numbers $N = pq$, ($p \equiv q \equiv 3 \mod 4$). They have all the properties of Blum Numbers.

Lemma 2 (Lemma 1 in [18]). *Let N be an Extended Blum Number, then*

1. $(QR_N^+, \circ)$ *is a group of order $\phi(N)/4$.*
2. $QR_N^+ = J_N^+$, *and QR_N^+ is efficiently recognizable.*
3. *The map $QR_N \mapsto QR_N^+$ is a group isomorphism.*

The order of the Signed QR is odd, the 2^k-th power is a permutation. If the factorization of N or the inverse of 2^k modulo $\phi(N)/4$ is given, the preimage of 2^k-th power is computable. The 2^k-th power is a trapdoor permutation.

Lemma 3. *Let N be an Extended pseudo Blum Number associated with k, then*

1. *$(J_N^+, \circ)$ is a group of order $\phi(N)/4$.*
2. *$\left(\frac{-1}{p}\right)_{2^k} = 1, \left(\frac{-1}{q}\right)_{2^k} = 1$.*
3. *The 2^k-th power map over J_N^+ is 2^{2k} or 2^{2k-1}-to-1.*

Proof. The map $|\cdot|$ from J_N to J_N^+ has kernel $\{\pm 1\}$, so ord $(J_N^+) = \phi(N)/4$. By the definition of 2^k residue symbol. Items 2 holds. Item 2 implies that -1 belongs to

$$J_{(-,-)}^{k-1}$$

. We define $J_+^s = J_{+,+}^s \cup J_{-,-}^s$ to be the subset of R^s with Legendre symbol 1. To prove the third item, we investigate a sequence of subgroups and square maps on them. Precisely, for $0 \leq s \leq k+1$, we consider the subgroups of Z_N^* denoted by

$$R_+^s := \{x^{2^s} | x \in J_N^+\},$$

and for $0 \leq i \leq k$ define the square map $f_i : y \to y^2$ from R_+^{i-1} to R_+^i. Note that R_+^0 is J_N^+ itself. We first prove that the map f_i is a regular 4-to-1 map for $0 \leq i \leq k-1$. Then we show that the map f_k is regularly 4-to-1 or 2-to-1 depending on whether $-1 \in J_+^k$ or not. The combination map $g = f_k \circ f_{k-1} \cdots \circ f_1$ is regularly 2^{2k} or 2^{2k-1}-to-1 naturally. We divide the map f_i into two parts. The first part is the square map and the second part is the absolute map. From part two, -1 belongs to J_+^{k-1}, the surjective map from subset R_+^{i-1} to J_+^i is a 2-to-1 map $(1 \leq i \leq k)$, and the map from J_+^j to R_+^j is a 2 tot 1 map $(1 \leq j \leq k-1)$. The absolute value is a surjective homomorphism from J_+^k to R_+^k with kernel $\{1\}$ if $-1 \notin J_+^k$ and with kernel $\{\pm 1\}$ if $-1 \in J_+^k$.   □

LTDP over Signed QR

We define $LTDP_{SQR} = (S_{inj}, S_{loss}, f_{SQR}, f_{SQR}^{-1})$ as follows:

1. *Sample Injective Function S_{inj}.* On input 1^n, S_{inj} chooses a proper k and random N in distribution R and the function index is $\sigma = \{N, k\}$. The trapdoor is $t = (2^k)^{-1} \mod \frac{\phi(N)}{4}$.
2. *Sample Lossy Function S_{loss}.* On input 1^n, S_{loss} chooses a proper k and random N in distribution L and the function index is $\sigma = \{N, k\}$.
3. *Evaluation algorithm f_{SQR}.* Given a function index $\sigma = \{N, k\}$ and input $x \in J_N^+$, the algorithm outputs $z = x^{2^k} \mod N$.
4. *Inversion algorithm f_{SQR}^{-1}.* Given $z \in J_N^+$ and trapdoor t, compute and output $z^t \mod N$.

Theorem 4. *If the 2^k-$\Phi/4$-hiding assumption holds, then $LTDP_{SQR}$ is an 2^{2k} or 2^{2k-1}-to-1 lossy trapdoor permutation.*

Another Modified Rabin-OAEP

The following scheme is another modification of Rabin-OAEP. The 2^k-th power is computed over Signed QR group. In this scheme, one needs to resample the output of OAEP until it falls into Signed QR group. The Leftover hash lemma guarantees that OAEP falls into Signed QR with probability about $\frac{1}{4}$. However, we have to admit that this is NOT done in practice.

KeyGen: On input a security parameters n, choose a k and n bits Extended Blum Number N associated with k. Choose a random t-wise independent hash function G_{K_G} and a hash function H_{K_H}. Compute the inversion of 2^k mod $\frac{\phi(N)}{4}$ and denote it as d.

$$pk = (N, k, G_{K_G}, H_{K_H}), \quad sk = d.$$

Encryption: On input a massage $m \in \{0,1\}^\mu$,
  Step 1: Pick a random $r \in \{0,1\}^\rho$ for $\rho = n - \mu$.
  Step 2: Set $s = m \parallel G_{K_G}(r)$.
  Step 3: set $t = r \parallel H_{K_H}(s)$.
  Step 4: Set $y = s \parallel t$ and view y as an integer. If $y \notin J_N^+$ goto step 1, otherwise set the ciphertext as $c = y^{2^k} \bmod N$.
Decryption: On input a ciphertext c,
  Step 1: If $c \notin J_N^+$ output $\perp$, otherwise $y = c^d \bmod N$.
  Step 2: For $y = s \parallel t$, set $r = t \oplus H_{K_H}(s)$.
  Step 3: Compute and output $m = s \oplus G_{G_K}(r)$.

Breaking and Fixing
Cryptophia's Short Combiner

Bart Mennink and Bart Preneel

Dept. Electrical Engineering, ESAT/COSIC, KU Leuven, and iMinds, Belgium
firstname.lastname@esat.kuleuven.be

Abstract. A combiner is a construction formed out of two hash functions that is secure if one of the underlying functions is. Conventional combiners are known not to support short outputs: if the hash functions have n-bit outputs the combiner should have at least almost $2n$ bits of output in order to be robust for collision resistance (Pietrzak, CRYPTO 2008). Mittelbach (ACNS 2013) introduced a relaxed security model for combiners and presented "Cryptophia's short combiner," a rather delicate construction of an n-bit combiner that achieves optimal collision, preimage, and second preimage security. We re-analyze Cryptophia's combiner and show that a collision can be found in two queries and a second preimage in one query, invalidating the claimed results. We additionally propose a way to fix the design in order to re-establish the original security results.

Keywords: hash functions, combiner, short, attack, collision resistance, preimage resistance.

1 Introduction

A hash function combiner is a construction with access to two or more hash functions, and which achieves certain security properties as long as sufficiently many underlying hash functions satisfy these security properties. The first to formally consider the principle of combiners were Herzberg [18] and Harnik et al. [17]. Two classical examples are the concatenation combiner $C_{\text{concat}}^{H_1,H_2}(M) = H_1(M) \parallel H_2(M)$ and xor combiner $C_{\text{xor}}^{H_1,H_2}(M) = H_1(M) \oplus H_2(M)$. Combiners function as an extra security barrier, still offering the desired security even if one of the hash functions gets badly broken. As such, combiners find a wide range of applications, including TLS [6–8] and SSL [15] for which the combiner security was analyzed by Fischlin et al. [14]. We refer to Lehmann's PhD thesis [22] for a comprehensive exposition of combiners.

A combiner is called *robust* for some security property if this property holds as long as at least one of the underlying hash functions does. For instance, a combiner C^{H_1,H_2} based on hash functions H_1, H_2 is called robust for collision resistance if a collision attack on the combiner implies an attack on H_1 and H_2. Note that $C_{\text{concat}}^{H_1,H_2}$ is clearly robust for collision resistance, but $C_{\text{xor}}^{H_1,H_2}$ is not. On the other hand, $C_{\text{xor}}^{H_1,H_2}$ is robust for pseudorandomness [14], while $C_{\text{concat}}^{H_1,H_2}$

D. Gritzalis et al. (Eds.): CANS 2014, LNCS 8813, pp. 50–63, 2014.

is not. Similar results can be obtained for other security properties such as (second) preimage resistance and MAC security [14, 18]. Various multi-property robust combiners have been designed by Fischlin et al. [11–13]. (Without going into detail, we refer to interesting results on the security of $C_{\text{concat}}^{H_1, H_2}$ beyond robustness, by Joux [21], Nandi and Stinson [27], Hoch and Shamir [19, 20], Fischlin and Lehmann [10], and Mendel et al. [24].)

The concatenation combiner is robust for collision resistance, but its output size is the sum of the output sizes of the underlying hash functions. At CRYPTO 2006, Boneh and Boyen [3] analyzed the question of designing a collision robust combiner with a shorter output size. This question got subsequently answered negatively by Canetti et al. [4] and Pietrzak [28, 29]. In detail, Pietrzak [29] demonstrated that no collision robust combiner from two n-bit hash functions exists with output length shorter than $2n - \Theta(\log n)$. A similar observation was recently made for (second) preimage resistance by Rjaško [31] and Mittelbach [25].

These negative results are in part credited to the rather stringent requirements the model of robustness puts on the construction, being the explicit existence of a reduction. At ACNS 2013, Mittelbach [26] introduced a relaxed model where the combiner is based on ideal hash functions and no explicit reduction is needed. Throughout, we will refer to this model as the ideal combiner model, as opposed to the standard reduction-based robust combiner model. Intuitively, the model captures the case of security of the combiner if one of the underlying hash functions is ideal but the other one is under full control of the adversary. While the ideal combiner model puts stronger requirements on the underlying primitives, it allows to bypass the limitations of the robust combiner model. Particularly, it enables analysis of more complex designs and combines well with the indifferentiability framework of Maurer et al. [23] and its application to hash functions by Coron et al. [5].

Yet, it turns out to still be highly non-trivial to construct a secure combiner in the ideal combiner model. For instance, the above-mentioned xor combiner is not secure: if $H_1 = \mathcal{R}$ is an ideal hash function, the adversary can simply define $H_2 = \mathcal{R}$. Also, ideal combiner security is not immediately achieved for straightforward generalizations of this xor combiner. As expected, the concatenation combiner is secure in the ideal combiner model, but recall that it has an output size of $2n$ bits.

Mittelbach [26] also introduced an ingenious n-bit combiner $C_{\text{mit}}^{H_1, H_2}$ from n-bit hash functions that – in the ideal combiner model – achieves optimal $2^{n/2}$ collision security and 2^n preimage and second preimage security. Mittelbach's combiner is also known as "Cryptophia's short combiner." The design circumvents the impossibility results of [3, 4, 28, 29] on the existence of short combiners in the standard combiner model. $C_{\text{mit}}^{H_1, H_2}$ is additionally proven to be a secure pseudorandom function and MAC in the robust combiner model. This result has been awarded as the best student paper of ACNS 2013.

At a high level, Mittelbach's combiner is a keyed combiner defined as

$$C_{\text{mit}}^{H_1, H_2}(k, M) = H_1(\text{prep}_1(k_1, k_2, k_3, M)) \oplus H_2(\text{prep}_2(k_4, k_5, k_6, M)),$$

where $k = (k_1, \ldots, k_6)$ is a fixed key, and prep_1 and prep_2 are two well-thought preprocessing functions discarded from this introduction (cf. Sect. 4).

Our Contribution

We re-analyze the short combiner of Mittelbach, and show the existence of an adversary that generates collisions for $C_{\mathrm{mit}}^{H_1,H_2}$ in 2 queries and second preimages in 1 query. The adversary is in line with Mittelbach's ideal combiner model, where H_1 is a random oracle $\mathcal{R}$ and H_2 is pre-defined by the adversary. The crux of the attack lies in the observation that the two preprocessing functions may not be injective, depending on the adversarial choice of H_2, an oversight in the proof.

We additionally present a solution to fix Mittelbach's combiner, which requires a more balanced usage of the keys in each of the preprocessing functions. We also prove that this fix does the job, i.e., restores the claimed security bounds up to a constant factor.

Outline

The remainder of the paper is organized as follows. We introduce some preliminaries in Sect. 2. The ideal combiner model as outlined by Mittelbach is summarized in Sect. 3. Section 4 describes Mittelbach's short combiner $C_{\mathrm{mit}}^{H_1,H_2}$ in detail. Our attacks on $C_{\mathrm{mit}}^{H_1,H_2}$ are given in Sect. 5 and we discuss how it can be fixed in Sect. 6.

2   Preliminaries

For $n \in \mathbb{N}$, we denote by $\{0,1\}^n$ the set of bit strings of size n. By $\{0,1\}^*$ we denote the set of bit strings of arbitrary length. For two bit strings x, y, their concatenation is denoted $x \| y$ and their bitwise exclusive or (xor) as $x \oplus y$ (for which x and y are presumed to be equally long). The size of x is denoted $|x|$. For $b \in \{1,2\}$, we denote by $\bar{b} = 3 - b \in \{2,1\}$. If $\mathcal{X}$ is a set, we denote by $x \xleftarrow{\$} \mathcal{X}$ the uniformly randomly sampling of an element from $\mathcal{X}$. If $\mathcal{X}$ is, on the other hand, a distribution, we use the same notation to say that x is chosen according to the distribution.

A hash function family is defined as $H : \{0,1\}^\kappa \times \{0,1\}^* \rightarrow \{0,1\}^n$ for $\kappa, n \in \mathbb{N}$, where for every $k \in \{0,1\}^\kappa$, H_k is a deterministic function that maps messages M of arbitrary length to digests of fixed length n. In security games, the key will conventionally be randomly drawn and disclosed at the beginning of the security experiment; it is simply used to select a function H_k randomly from the entire family of functions. The key input to H_k is left implicit if it is clear from the context. A random oracle on n bits is a function $\mathcal{R}$ which provides a random output of size n for each new query [2].

We model adversaries $\mathcal{A}$ as probabilistic algorithms with black-box access to zero or more oracles $\mathcal{O}_1, \ldots, \mathcal{O}_n$, written as $\mathcal{A}^{\mathcal{O}_1, \ldots, \mathcal{O}_n}$. We assume the adversary always knows the security parameters (often the input and output sizes of the combiner and underlying hash functions) and refrain from explicitly mentioning these as input to $\mathcal{A}$. We consider computationally unbounded adversaries whose complexities are measured by the number of queries made to their oracles. We assume that the adversary never makes queries to which it knows the answer in advance.

If X is a random variable, the min-entropy of X is defined as

$$\mathrm{H}_\infty(X) = -\log(\max_x \mathbf{Pr}\,(X = x)).$$

Note that we can equivalently define $\mathrm{H}_\infty(X)$ in terms of a predictor $\mathcal{A}$ that aims to guess X, denoted $\mathrm{H}_\infty(X) = -\log(\max_{\mathcal{A}} \mathbf{Pr}\,(X = \mathcal{A}))$ [1]. Following [1,9,26], we define the (average) conditional min-entropy of X conditioned on random variable Z as

$$\widetilde{\mathrm{H}}_\infty(X \mid Z) = -\log(\max_{\mathcal{A}} \mathbf{Pr}\,(X = \mathcal{A}^Z)),$$

where $\mathcal{A}$ is a predictor that participates in random experiment Z. It has been demonstrated that $\widetilde{\mathrm{H}}_\infty(X \mid Z) \geq \mathrm{H}_\infty(X, Z) - b$, where Z may take 2^b values [9,30].

3   Ideal Combiner Model

A (k, l)-combiner for security property prop is a construction based on l hash functions, that achieves prop security as long as k out of l hash functions satisfy this property. Most combiners known in literature are $(1, 2)$-combiners, considering a construction C^{H_1, H_2} from two hash functions H_1, H_2. We focus on this type of combiners. A robust black-box combiner for security property prop is a combiner C^{H_1, H_2} for which an attack under prop can be reduced to an attack on H_1 and H_2. Various results on robustness of combiners have been presented [11–14,17,18]. Pietrzak [29] proved that the output length of a collision secure black-box combiner is at least the sum of the output lengths of H_1 and H_2 (minus a logarithmic term in the output size of H_1, H_2). A similar observation was recently made for second preimage and preimage resistance by Rjaško [31] and Mittelbach [25].

At ACNS 2013, Mittelbach elegantly lifted the security of combiners to the ideal model. That is, the hash functions underpinning C^{H_1, H_2} are based on a random oracle. The model discards the explicit need of a reduction, and combines well with the indifferentiability framework of Maurer et al. [23] and its application to hash functions by Coron et al. [5]. Nevertheless, this model, and particularly capturing the fact that one of the hash functions may be non-ideal, is not at all straightforward. We paraphrase the model in our own terminology.

The prop security of a combiner $C^{H_1, H_2} : \{0, 1\}^\kappa \times \{0, 1\}^* \to \{0, 1\}^n$ based on two hash functions $H_1, H_2 : \{0, 1\}^{\kappa_h} \times \{0, 1\}^* \to \{0, 1\}^n$ is captured as follows (the model generalizes straightforwardly to other domains and ranges). Let $\mathcal{R}$ be a random oracle and $k \xleftarrow{\$} \{0,1\}^\kappa$. Consider a two-stage adversary $\mathcal{A} = (\mathcal{A}_1, \mathcal{A}_2)$ with unbounded computational power. $\mathcal{A}_1$ gets no input and outputs $b \in \{1,2\}$ and a description of an efficient stateless function $H^{\mathcal{R}} : \{0,1\}^{\kappa_h} \times \{0,1\}^* \to \{0,1\}^n$ which may make calls to $\mathcal{R}$. Then, $\mathcal{A}_2$, with oracle access to $(\mathcal{R}, H^{\mathcal{R}})$ and knowledge of the key k, aims to break security property prop for $C^{H^{\mathcal{R}}, \mathcal{R}}$ (if $b = 1$) or $C^{\mathcal{R}, H^{\mathcal{R}}}$ (if $b = 2$). Formally, the advantage of $\mathcal{A}$ is defined as follows:

$$\mathbf{Adv}_C^{\mathsf{prop}}(\mathcal{A}) = \mathbf{Pr}_{\mathcal{R},k} \begin{pmatrix} (b, H^{\mathcal{R}}, st) \xleftarrow{\$} \mathcal{A}_1, & \mathcal{A}_2^{H_1, H_2}(k, st) \text{ breaks} \\ (H_b, H_{\bar{b}}) \leftarrow (H^{\mathcal{R}}, \mathcal{R}) & : & \mathsf{prop} \text{ for } C^{H_1, H_2} \end{pmatrix},$$

where the randomness is taken over the choice of random oracle $\mathcal{R}$, random key $k \in \{0,1\}^\kappa$, and coins of $\mathcal{A}$.

The formal descriptions of the security advantages slightly differ for various types of security properties. In general, for collision, preimage, and second preimage resistance the definitions show resemblances with, but are more complex than, the formalization of Rogaway and Shrimpton [32]. For collision security of C^{H_1, H_2}, the advantage of $\mathcal{A}$ is defined as

$$\mathbf{Adv}_C^{\mathsf{coll}}(\mathcal{A}) = \mathbf{Pr}_{\mathcal{R},k} \begin{pmatrix} (b, H^{\mathcal{R}}, st) \xleftarrow{\$} \mathcal{A}_1, & M \neq M' \wedge \\ (H_b, H_{\bar{b}}) \leftarrow (H^{\mathcal{R}}, \mathcal{R}), & : & C^{H_1, H_2}(M) = \\ (M, M') \xleftarrow{\$} \mathcal{A}_2^{H_1, H_2}(k, st) & & C^{H_1, H_2}(M') \end{pmatrix}.$$

For (second) preimage resistance, we focus on everywhere (second) preimage resistance. In everywhere preimage resistance, $\mathcal{A}_1$ selects an image $Y \in \{0,1\}^n$ at the start of the experiment. In everywhere second preimage resistance, $\mathcal{A}_1$ selects a first preimage $M \in \{0,1\}^\lambda$ at the start of the experiment, for some $\lambda < \infty$. The advantages of $\mathcal{A}$ are as follows:

$$\mathbf{Adv}_C^{\mathsf{epre}}(\mathcal{A}) = \mathbf{Pr}_{\mathcal{R},k} \begin{pmatrix} (b, H^{\mathcal{R}}, Y, st) \xleftarrow{\$} \mathcal{A}_1, \\ (H_b, H_{\bar{b}}) \leftarrow (H^{\mathcal{R}}, \mathcal{R}), & : & C^{H_1, H_2}(M) = Y \\ M \xleftarrow{\$} \mathcal{A}_2^{H_1, H_2}(k, st) \end{pmatrix},$$

$$\mathbf{Adv}_C^{\mathsf{esec}[\lambda]}(\mathcal{A}) = \mathbf{Pr}_{\mathcal{R},k} \begin{pmatrix} (b, H^{\mathcal{R}}, M, st) \xleftarrow{\$} \mathcal{A}_1, & M \neq M' \wedge \\ (H_b, H_{\bar{b}}) \leftarrow (H^{\mathcal{R}}, \mathcal{R}), & : & C^{H_1, H_2}(M) = \\ M' \xleftarrow{\$} \mathcal{A}_2^{H_1, H_2}(k, st) & & C^{H_1, H_2}(M') \end{pmatrix}.$$

The notion of everywhere second preimage resistance is also known as target collision resistance [16] and implies conventional second preimage resistance where M is randomly drawn. (We note that Mittelbach [26] considered target collision resistance and conventional second preimage resistance separately. Additionally, we slightly simplified the notion of preimage resistance, considering the case $\mathcal{A}_1$ selects the image rather than a set $\mathcal{X}$ from which the first preimage is secretly and randomly drawn.)

4   Mittelbach's Combiner

We consider Cryptophia's combiner $C_{\mathrm{mit}}^{H_1,H_2} : \{0,1\}^\kappa \times \{0,1\}^* \rightarrow \{0,1\}^n$ from Mittelbach [26], where $\kappa = 6n$. Let $k_i \in \{0,1\}^n$ for $i = 1,\ldots,6$ be independently chosen keys, and write $k = (k_1,\ldots,k_6)$. Let $H_1, H_2 : \{0,1\}^* \rightarrow \{0,1\}^n$ be two hash functions. The combiner is given by

$$C_{\mathrm{mit}}^{H_1,H_2}(k, M) = H_1\left(\tilde{m}_1^1\|\cdots\|\tilde{m}_\ell^1\right) \oplus H_2\left(\tilde{m}_1^2\|\cdots\|\tilde{m}_\ell^2\right),$$

where the message $M \in \{0,1\}^*$ is first injectively padded into n-bit message blocks $m_1\|\cdots\|m_\ell = M\|\mathsf{pad}(M)$ using some padding function pad, which are subsequently preprocessed as

$$\begin{aligned}
\tilde{m}_j^1 &= H_1(1 \parallel m_j \oplus k_1) \oplus m_j \oplus k_2 \oplus H_2(1 \parallel m_j \oplus k_3), \\
\tilde{m}_j^2 &= H_2(0 \parallel m_j \oplus k_4) \oplus m_j \oplus k_5 \oplus H_1(0 \parallel m_j \oplus k_6),
\end{aligned} \tag{1}$$

for $j = 1,\ldots,\ell$. We remark that we swapped k_1 with k_3 and k_4 with k_6 compared to the original specification [26].

5   Attack

In the security model we recaptured in Sect. 3, Mittelbach proved that $C_{\mathrm{mit}}^{H_1,H_2}$ achieves collision security up to $2^{(n+1)/2}$ queries and preimage and second preimage security up to 2^n queries.[1] In the next proposition, we show that the collision result is incorrect. After the result, we also explain why the attack directly implies a second preimage attack. The work of [26] as well as its full version do not state any properties of the padding function $\mathsf{pad}(M)$. We assume a 10*-padding concatenated with length strengthening. For simplicity and without loss of generality, we assume that $|\mathsf{pad}(M)| \leq n$, which is the case if the message length is encoded with at most $n-1$ bits.

Proposition 1. *There exists an adversary $\mathcal{A}$ making 2 queries, such that* $\mathbf{Adv}_{C_{\mathrm{mit}}}^{\mathsf{coll}}(\mathcal{A}) = 1$.

Proof. Let $\mathcal{R}$ be a random oracle and $k_1,\ldots,k_6 \xleftarrow{\$} \{0,1\}^n$. We focus on an adversary $\mathcal{A} = (\mathcal{A}_1, \mathcal{A}_2)$ that finds a collision for $C_{\mathrm{mit}}^{\mathcal{R},H^{\mathcal{R}}}$, where $H^{\mathcal{R}}$ is the hash function defined by $\mathcal{A}_1$. Our adversary proceeds as follows. $\mathcal{A}_1$ outputs $b = 2$ and the following hash function $H^{\mathcal{R}}$:

$$H^{\mathcal{R}}(x) = \begin{cases} \mathcal{R}(x) \oplus y, & \text{if } x = 1\|y \text{ for some } y \in \{0,1\}^n, \\ 0, & \text{otherwise.} \end{cases}$$

---

[1] The formal preimage result is slightly different, claiming security up to $2^{\mathrm{H}_\infty(\mathcal{X})}$ queries, where the first preimage is secretly and randomly drawn from an adversarially chosen set $\mathcal{X}$.

This simplifies the combiner to $C_{\text{mit}}^{\mathcal{R},H^{\mathcal{R}}}(k,M) = \mathcal{R}\left(\tilde{m}_1^1\|\cdots\|\tilde{m}_\ell^1\right)$, where

$$\tilde{m}_j^1 = \mathcal{R}(1 \parallel m_j \oplus k_1) \oplus k_2 \oplus k_3 \oplus \mathcal{R}(1 \parallel m_j \oplus k_3),$$

for $j = 1,\ldots,\ell$. Next, the adversary $\mathcal{A}_2$ gets as input $(k_1,\ldots,k_6)$ and outputs colliding pair M and $M' = M \oplus k_1 \oplus k_3$ for some $M \in \{0,1\}^n$.

We proceed with showing that the colliding pair is valid. As $|M| = |M'| = n$, the messages are padded as $m_1\|m_2 = M\|\mathsf{pad}(M)$ and $m_1'\|m_2' = M'\|\mathsf{pad}(M')$, where $m_1 = M$, $m_1' = M'$, and $m_2 = m_2'$. The latter implies $\tilde{m}_2^1 = \tilde{m}_2'^1$. The preprocessed $\tilde{m}_1^1$ and $\tilde{m}_1'^1$ satisfy

$$\begin{aligned}
\tilde{m}_1^1 &= \mathcal{R}(1 \parallel M \oplus k_1) \oplus k_2 \oplus k_3 \oplus \mathcal{R}(1 \parallel M \oplus k_3) \\
&= \mathcal{R}(1 \parallel M \oplus k_3) \oplus k_2 \oplus k_3 \oplus \mathcal{R}(1 \parallel M \oplus k_1) = \tilde{m}_1'^1.
\end{aligned}$$

Concluding, $\tilde{m}_1^1\|\tilde{m}_2^1 = \tilde{m}_1'^1\|\tilde{m}_2'^1$ and thus

$$C_{\text{mit}}^{\mathcal{R},H^{\mathcal{R}}}(k,M) = \mathcal{R}\left(\tilde{m}_1^1\|\tilde{m}_2^1\right) = \mathcal{R}\left(\tilde{m}_1'^1\|\tilde{m}_2'^1\right) = C_{\text{mit}}^{\mathcal{R},H^{\mathcal{R}}}(k,M'). \qquad \square$$

Proposition 2. *Let $\lambda < \infty$. There exists an adversary $\mathcal{A}$ making 1 query, such that $\mathbf{Adv}_{C_{\text{mit}}}^{\mathsf{esec}[\lambda]}(\mathcal{A}) = 1$.*

Proof. In the attack of Prop. 1 the choice of M is independent of $(k_1,\ldots,k_6)$. Therefore, the attack also works if M is chosen by $\mathcal{A}_1$ at the beginning of the game. $\qquad \square$

The flaw in the security analysis of [26] lies in the fact that it only considers distributions of $\tilde{m}_j^c$ computed from $m_j, k_{3c-2}, k_{3c-1}, k_{3c}$ via (1) for $c \in \{1,2\}$, but never joint distributions of $\tilde{m}_j^c, \tilde{m}_j'^c$ given two messages m, m'. In more detail, Prop. 4.5 of the full version of [26] inadvertently assumes that $\tilde{m}^c$ and $\tilde{m}'^c$ are mutually distinct whenever $m \neq m'$. The preimage bound derived in [26] is nevertheless correct, and so are the analyses of $C_{\text{mit}}^{H_1,H_2}$ as a pseudorandom function and MAC.

6   Fix

To fix Mittelbach's combiner $C_{\text{mit}}^{H_1,H_2}$, we suggest to use an additional set of keys $l_1, l_2 \in \{0,1\}^n$ as separate input to H_1, H_2 in the preprocessing functions of (1). Consequently, we can leave out $m_j \oplus k_2$ and $m_j \oplus k_5$ from these functions as they have become redundant, and we can simply set $(k_4, k_6) = (k_1, k_2)$. (For the original $C_{\text{mit}}^{H_1,H_2}$ these keys k_2, k_4, k_5, k_6 are necessary to guarantee preimage resistance.)

More formally, we suggest combiner $C^{H_1,H_2} : \{0,1\}^\kappa \times \{0,1\}^* \to \{0,1\}^n$, where $\kappa = 4n$. Let $k_1, k_2, l_1, l_2 \in \{0,1\}^n$ be independently chosen keys, and write $kl = (k_1, k_2, l_1, l_2)$. Let $H_1, H_2 : \{0,1\}^* \to \{0,1\}^n$ be two hash functions. The combiner is given by

$$C^{H_1,H_2}(kl,M) = H_1\left(\tilde{m}_1^1\|\cdots\|\tilde{m}_\ell^1\right) \oplus H_2\left(\tilde{m}_1^2\|\cdots\|\tilde{m}_\ell^2\right),$$

where the message $M \in \{0,1\}^*$ is first injectively padded into n-bit message blocks $m_1 \| \cdots \| m_\ell = M \| \mathsf{pad}(M)$ using some padding function pad, which are subsequently preprocessed as

$$
\begin{aligned}
\tilde{m}_j^1 &= H_1(0 \parallel l_1 \parallel m_j \oplus k_1) \oplus H_2(0 \parallel l_2 \parallel m_j \oplus k_2)\,, \\
\tilde{m}_j^2 &= H_1(1 \parallel l_1 \parallel m_j \oplus k_1) \oplus H_2(1 \parallel l_2 \parallel m_j \oplus k_2)\,,
\end{aligned}
\tag{2}
$$

for $j = 1, \ldots, \ell$.

This fix, indeed, guarantees that $\tilde{m}^c$ and $\tilde{m}'^c$ are mutually different whenever m, m' are, except with small probability. In the remainder of this section, we will prove that C^{H_1,H_2} indeed achieves the originally claimed security bounds for collision, preimage, and second preimage resistance up to an inevitable constant factor. For a proof on the robustness for pseudorandomness and MAC security we refer to [26].

Before we proceed, we remark explicitly that we require $H^\mathcal{R}$ to be a stateless hash function. In the artificial case in which $H^\mathcal{R}$ is allowed to hold state, C^{H_1,H_2} is insecure. An attack is given in App. A.

Security Proofs

For $c \in \{1,2\}$ we define preprocessing function $\tilde{m}^c(kl, m)$ on input of $kl = (k_1, k_2, l_1, l_2) \in \{0,1\}^{4n}$ and $m \in \{0,1\}^n$ as

$$
\tilde{m}^c(kl, m) = H_1(c - 1 \parallel l_1 \parallel m \oplus k_1) \oplus H_2(c - 1 \parallel l_2 \parallel m \oplus k_2)\,.
$$

These preprocessing functions correspond to the two equations of (2) for $c = 1, 2$. The remainder of the proof is as follows. In Lem. 1 we compute the (conditioned) min-entropies of the values $\tilde{m}^c$. This lemma is a direct generalization of Lems. 1 and 2 of [26]. Then, preimage security is proven in Thm. 1, collision security in Thm. 2, and second preimage security in Thm. 3.

Lemma 1. *Let $\mathcal{R}$ be an n-bit random oracle and let $kl \xleftarrow{\$} \{0,1\}^{4n}$. Let $H^\mathcal{R}$ be a hash function with access to $\mathcal{R}$ (but not using kl). Then, for all $c \in \{1,2\}$ and distinct $m, m' \in \{0,1\}^n$,*

$$
\widetilde{\mathrm{H}}_\infty \left(\tilde{m}^c(kl, m) \mid kl, m \right) \geq n - \log(q_H)\,,
\tag{3}
$$

$$
\widetilde{\mathrm{H}}_\infty \left(\tilde{m}^c(kl, m) \mid \tilde{m}^c(kl, m'), kl, m, m' \right) \geq n - 2\log(q_H)\,,
\tag{4}
$$

$$
\widetilde{\mathrm{H}}_\infty \left(\tilde{m}^c(kl, m) \mid \tilde{m}^{\bar{c}}(kl, m'), kl, m, m' \right) \geq n - 2\log(q_H)\,,
\tag{5}
$$

$$
\widetilde{\mathrm{H}}_\infty \left(\tilde{m}^c(kl, m) \mid \tilde{m}^{\bar{c}}(kl, m), kl, m \right) \geq n - 2\log(q_H)\,,
\tag{6}
$$

where q_H is the number of calls to $\mathcal{R}$ in one evaluation to $H^\mathcal{R}$. (We note that conditioning in (5-6) is done on $\tilde{m}^{\bar{c}}$, as opposed to $\tilde{m}^c$ in (4).)

Proof. The combiner C is symmetric, and without loss of generality we assume $b = 2$, hence $(H_1, H_2) = (\mathcal{R}, H^\mathcal{R})$, where $\mathcal{R}$ is an n-bit random oracle and $H^\mathcal{R}$ is defined by adversary $\mathcal{A}_1$. Also, $c = 1$ without loss of generality.

The min-entropy of (3) reads

$$
\begin{aligned}
& \widetilde{H}_\infty \left(\tilde{m}^1(kl, m) \mid kl, m \right) \\
&= \widetilde{H}_\infty \left(\mathcal{R}(0 \parallel l_1 \parallel m \oplus k_1) \oplus H^\mathcal{R}(0 \parallel l_2 \parallel m \oplus k_2) \mid kl, m \right) \\
&= \widetilde{H}_\infty \left(\mathcal{R}(0 \parallel l_1 \parallel \hat{m} \oplus \hat{k}_1) \oplus H^\mathcal{R}(0 \parallel l_2 \parallel \hat{m}) \mid \hat{k}_1, l_1, l_2, \hat{m} \right),
\end{aligned}
$$

where the second step is by substitution of $(\hat{k}_1, \hat{m}) = (k_1 \oplus k_2, m \oplus k_2)$ and by leaving out the redundant k_2 in the condition. Note that the evaluation of $\mathcal{R}$ is independent of the evaluation of $H^\mathcal{R}$, *unless* $H^\mathcal{R}(0 \parallel l_2 \parallel \hat{m})$ evaluates $\mathcal{R}(0 \parallel l_1 \parallel \hat{m} \oplus \hat{k}_1)$. Here, we recall that $\hat{k}_1, l_1, l_2$ are mutually independently and randomly drawn, but $\hat{m}$ is chosen by $\mathcal{A}_2$ and may depend on $(\hat{k}_1, l_1, l_2)$. The hash function $H^\mathcal{R}$ chosen by $\mathcal{A}_1$ makes q_H evaluations of $\mathcal{R}$, which can decrease the entropy by at most $\log(q_H)$ bits in any experiment. Thus, we find:

$$
\begin{aligned}
& \widetilde{H}_\infty \left(\tilde{m}^1(kl, m) \mid kl, m \right) \\
&\geq \widetilde{H}_\infty \left(l_1, \hat{m}(\hat{k}_1, l_1, l_2) \oplus \hat{k}_1 \mid l_2, \hat{m}(\hat{k}_1, l_1, l_2) \right) - \log(q_H) \\
&\geq n - \log(q_H).
\end{aligned}
$$

We proceed with the min-entropy of (4):

$$
\begin{aligned}
& \widetilde{H}_\infty \left(\tilde{m}^1(kl, m) \mid \tilde{m}^1(kl, m'), kl, m, m' \right) \\
&= \widetilde{H}_\infty \left(\begin{matrix} \mathcal{R}(0 \parallel l_1 \parallel m \oplus k_1) \oplus H^\mathcal{R}(0 \parallel l_2 \parallel m \oplus k_2) \mid \\ \mathcal{R}(0 \parallel l_1 \parallel m' \oplus k_1) \oplus H^\mathcal{R}(0 \parallel l_2 \parallel m' \oplus k_2), kl, m, m' \end{matrix} \right) \\
&\geq \widetilde{H}_\infty \left(\begin{matrix} \mathcal{R}(0 \parallel l_1 \parallel \hat{m} \oplus \hat{k}_1) \oplus H^\mathcal{R}(0 \parallel l_2 \parallel \hat{m}), \\ \mathcal{R}(0 \parallel l_1 \parallel \hat{m}' \oplus \hat{k}_1) \oplus H^\mathcal{R}(0 \parallel l_2 \parallel \hat{m}') \end{matrix} \middle| \hat{k}_1, l_1, l_2, \hat{m}, \hat{m}' \right) - n, \quad (7)
\end{aligned}
$$

where we substituted $(\hat{k}_1, \hat{m}, \hat{m}') = (k_1 \oplus k_2, m \oplus k_2, m' \oplus k_2)$ and left out redundant k_2. Here, we recall that $\hat{m} \neq \hat{m}'$, but both message blocks may depend on $\hat{k}_1, l_1, l_2$. Before proceeding, we pause to see what happens if we were considering the original combiner $C_{\text{mit}}^{\mathcal{R}, H^\mathcal{R}}$ of Sect. 4. In this case, l_1 and l_2 are absent. The entropy term in (7) then equals at most n if $\hat{m}' = \hat{m} \oplus \hat{k}_1$ (in case $H^\mathcal{R} = \mathcal{R}$), leading to a lower bound ≥ 0. Note that the attack of Sect. 5 takes the message blocks this way.

Returning to (7), as $\hat{k}_1, l_1, l_2$ are independently and randomly drawn and $\hat{m} \neq \hat{m}'$, the two terms in the min-entropy are independent, both achieve a min-entropy of at least $n - \log(q_H)$ (by (3)), and hence

$$
\widetilde{H}_\infty \left(\tilde{m}^1(kl, m) \mid \tilde{m}^1(kl, m'), kl, m, m' \right) \geq 2(n - \log(q_H)) - n \geq n - 2\log(q_H).
$$

The same reasoning applies to the min-entropies of (5) and (6), where for the latter we particularly use that the two evaluations of $\mathcal{R}$ are mutually independent due to the domain separation $1/0$.   □

Theorem 1. *For any adversary $\mathcal{A}$, where $\mathcal{A}_2$ makes $q_{\mathcal{A}}$ queries and where every evaluation of $H^{\mathcal{R}}$ makes at most q_H calls to $\mathcal{R}$, we have $\mathbf{Adv}_C^{\mathsf{epre}}(\mathcal{A}) \le (q_H^3 + 1)q_{\mathcal{A}}/2^n$.*

Proof. Let $(H_b, H_{\bar{b}}) = (H^{\mathcal{R}}, \mathcal{R})$, where $\mathcal{R}$ is an n-bit random oracle and b and $H^{\mathcal{R}}$ are defined by adversary $\mathcal{A}_1$. Let Y be the target image. Consider an evaluation $C^{H_1, H_2}(kl, M)$, where M has not been evaluated so far. The evaluation constitutes a preimage if

$$C^{H_1, H_2}(kl, M) = \mathcal{R}(U^{\bar{b}}(M)) \oplus H^{\mathcal{R}}(U^b(M)) = Y, \tag{8}$$

for some random distributions $U^{\bar{b}}, U^b$ corresponding to (2). If this happens, at least one of the following two events occurred:

$$\mathsf{E}_1: \ H^{\mathcal{R}}(U^b(M)) \text{ evaluates } \mathcal{R}(U^{\bar{b}}(M)),$$
$$\mathsf{E}_2: \ \neg\mathsf{E}_1 \wedge (8).$$

By Lem. 1 equation (6) (or in fact a slight variation to ℓ blocks, which gives the same lower bound), $U^{\bar{b}}(M)$ given $U^b(M)$ has min-entropy at least $n - 2\log(q_H)$. In other words, any call to $\mathcal{R}$ by $H^{\mathcal{R}}$ evaluates $U^{\bar{b}}(M)$ with probability at most $2^{-(n-2\log(q_H))} = q_H^2/2^n$. As $H^{\mathcal{R}}$ makes q_H evaluations, E_1 happens with probability at most $q_H^3/2^n$. Regarding E_2, by $\neg\mathsf{E}_1$ the call to $\mathcal{R}$ is independent of $H^{\mathcal{R}}(U^b(M))$ and (8) holds with probability $1/2^n$.

As $\mathcal{A}$ has $q_{\mathcal{A}}$ attempts, it finds a preimage with probability at most $(q_H^3 + 1)q_{\mathcal{A}}/2^n$. □

Theorem 2. *For any adversary $\mathcal{A}$, where $\mathcal{A}_2$ makes $q_{\mathcal{A}}$ queries and where every evaluation of $H^{\mathcal{R}}$ makes at most q_H calls to $\mathcal{R}$, we have $\mathbf{Adv}_C^{\mathsf{coll}}(\mathcal{A}) \le (3q_H^3 + 1)q_{\mathcal{A}}^2/2^{n+1}$.*

Proof. Let $(H_b, H_{\bar{b}}) = (H^{\mathcal{R}}, \mathcal{R})$, where $\mathcal{R}$ is an n-bit random oracle and b and $H^{\mathcal{R}}$ are defined by adversary $\mathcal{A}_1$. Consider two evaluations C^{H_1, H_2} of two distinct M, M'. The two evaluations constitute a collision if

$$\mathcal{R}(U^{\bar{b}}(M)) \oplus \mathcal{R}(U^{\bar{b}}(M')) = H^{\mathcal{R}}(U^b(M)) \oplus H^{\mathcal{R}}(U^b(M')), \tag{9}$$

for some random distributions $U^{\bar{b}}, U^b$ corresponding to (2). If this happens, at least one of the following four events occurred:

$$\mathsf{E}_1: \ U^{\bar{b}}(M) = U^{\bar{b}}(M'),$$
$$\mathsf{E}_2: \ H^{\mathcal{R}}(U^b(M)) \text{ evaluates } \mathcal{R}(U^{\bar{b}}(M)),$$
$$\mathsf{E}_3: \ H^{\mathcal{R}}(U^b(M')) \text{ evaluates } \mathcal{R}(U^{\bar{b}}(M)),$$
$$\mathsf{E}_4: \ \neg(\mathsf{E}_1 \vee \mathsf{E}_2 \vee \mathsf{E}_3) \wedge (9).$$

By Lem. 1 equation (4), E_1 holds with probability at most $q_H^2/2^n$. Similar to the proof of Thm. 1, E_2 and E_3 happen with probability at most $q_H^3/2^n$ (by Lem. 1

equations (5) and (6)). Regarding E_4, by $\neg(\mathsf{E}_1 \vee \mathsf{E}_2 \vee \mathsf{E}_3)$ the call to $\mathcal{R}(U^{\bar{b}}(M))$ is independent of the other terms and (9) holds with probability $1/2^n$.

As $\mathcal{A}$ has $q_{\mathcal{A}}$ attempts, it finds a collision with probability at most $(2q_H^3 + q_H^2 + 1)\binom{q_{\mathcal{A}}}{2}/2^n \leq (3q_H^3 + 1)q_{\mathcal{A}}^2/2^{n+1}$. $\square$

Theorem 3. *For any adversary* $\mathcal{A}$, *where* $\mathcal{A}_2$ *makes* $q_{\mathcal{A}}$ *queries and where every evaluation of* $H^{\mathcal{R}}$ *makes at most* q_H *calls to* $\mathcal{R}$, *we have* $\mathbf{Adv}_C^{\mathsf{esec}[\lambda]}(\mathcal{A}) \leq (3q_H^3 + 1)q_{\mathcal{A}}/2^n$.

Proof. The proof follows from the proof of Thm. 2 with the difference that the first message M is fixed in advance. $\square$

Remark 1. We remark that the terms q_H^3 in fact also appear in the bounds of Mittelbach [26], though accidentally dropped out. (Lem. 2 of [26] considers $q = \max\{q_H, q_{\mathcal{A}}\}$, while Prop. 2 treats q as being $q_{\mathcal{A}}$.) That said, as $H^{\mathcal{R}}$ should be an efficient hash function, it is fair to assume that it makes a limited amount of evaluations of $\mathcal{R}$. Particularly, if $q_H = \mathcal{O}(1)$, we retain the original security bounds.

Remark 2. The results hold with the same bounds if the messages were padded into n'-bit message blocks for $n' < n$, and if $k_1, k_2 \in \{0,1\}^{n'}$. Changing the size of l_1, l_2 would, on the other hand, directly affect the security bounds.

Acknowledgments. This work was supported in part by the Research Fund KU Leuven, OT/13/071, and in part by the Research Council KU Leuven: GOA TENSE (GOA/11/007). Bart Mennink is a Postdoctoral Fellow of the Research Foundation – Flanders (FWO). The authors would like to sincerely thank the anonymous reviewers of CANS 2014, as well as Atul Luykx, Gregory Maxwell, and Arno Mittelbach, for their comments and suggestions.

References

1. Alwen, J., Dodis, Y., Wichs, D.: Leakage-resilient public-key cryptography in the bounded-retrieval model. In: Halevi, S. (ed.) CRYPTO 2009. LNCS, vol. 5677, pp. 36–54. Springer, Heidelberg (2009)
2. Bellare, M., Rogaway, P.: Random oracles are practical: A paradigm for designing efficient protocols. In: ACM Conference on Computer and Communications Security, pp. 62–73. ACM, New York (1993)
3. Boneh, D., Boyen, X.: On the impossibility of efficiently combining collision resistant hash functions. In: Dwork, C. (ed.) CRYPTO 2006. LNCS, vol. 4117, pp. 570–583. Springer, Heidelberg (2006)
4. Canetti, R., Rivest, R., Sudan, M., Trevisan, L., Vadhan, S.P., Wee, H.M.: Amplifying collision resistance: A complexity-theoretic treatment. In: Menezes, A. (ed.) CRYPTO 2007. LNCS, vol. 4622, pp. 264–283. Springer, Heidelberg (2007)
5. Coron, J.-S., Dodis, Y., Malinaud, C., Puniya, P.: Merkle-Damgård revisited: How to construct a hash function. In: Shoup, V. (ed.) CRYPTO 2005. LNCS, vol. 3621, pp. 430–448. Springer, Heidelberg (2005)

6. Dierks, T., Allen, C.: The TLS protocol version 1.0. Request for Comments (RFC) 2246 (January 1999), http://tools.ietf.org/html/rfc2246

7. Dierks, T., Rescorla, E.: The transport layer security (TLS) protocol version 1.1. Request for Comments (RFC) 4346 (April 2006), http://tools.ietf.org/html/rfc4346

8. Dierks, T., Rescorla, E.: The transport layer security (TLS) protocol version 1.2. Request for Comments (RFC) 5246 (August 2008), http://tools.ietf.org/html/rfc5246

9. Dodis, Y., Ostrovsky, R., Reyzin, L., Smith, A.: Fuzzy extractors: How to generate strong keys from biometrics and other noisy data. SIAM Journal of Computing 38(1), 97–139 (2008)

10. Fischlin, M., Lehmann, A.: Security-amplifying combiners for collision-resistant hash functions. In: Menezes, A. (ed.) CRYPTO 2007. LNCS, vol. 4622, pp. 224–243. Springer, Heidelberg (2007)

11. Fischlin, M., Lehmann, A.: Multi-property preserving combiners for hash functions. In: Canetti, R. (ed.) TCC 2008. LNCS, vol. 4948, pp. 375–392. Springer, Heidelberg (2008)

12. Fischlin, M., Lehmann, A., Pietrzak, K.: Robust multi-property combiners for hash functions revisited. In: Aceto, L., Damgård, I., Goldberg, L.A., Halldórsson, M.M., Ingólfsdóttir, A., Walukiewicz, I. (eds.) ICALP 2008, Part II. LNCS, vol. 5126, pp. 655–666. Springer, Heidelberg (2008)

13. Fischlin, M., Lehmann, A., Pietrzak, K.: Robust multi-property combiners for hash functions. Journal of Cryptology 27(3), 397–428 (2014)

14. Fischlin, M., Lehmann, A., Wagner, D.: Hash function combiners in TLS and SSL. In: Pieprzyk, J. (ed.) CT-RSA 2010. LNCS, vol. 5985, pp. 268–283. Springer, Heidelberg (2010)

15. Freier, A., Karlton, P., Kocher, P.: The secure sockets layer (SSL) protocol version 3.0. Request for Comments (RFC) 6101 (August 2011), http://tools.ietf.org/html/rfc6101

16. Halevi, S., Krawczyk, H.: Strengthening digital signatures via randomized hashing. In: Dwork, C. (ed.) CRYPTO 2006. LNCS, vol. 4117, pp. 41–59. Springer, Heidelberg (2006)

17. Harnik, D., Kilian, J., Naor, M., Reingold, O., Rosen, A.: On robust combiners for oblivious transfer and other primitives. In: Cramer, R. (ed.) EUROCRYPT 2005. LNCS, vol. 3494, pp. 96–113. Springer, Heidelberg (2005)

18. Herzberg, A.: On tolerant cryptographic constructions. In: Menezes, A. (ed.) CT-RSA 2005. LNCS, vol. 3376, pp. 172–190. Springer, Heidelberg (2005)

19. Hoch, J.J., Shamir, A.: Breaking the ICE - finding multicollisions in iterated concatenated and expanded (ICE) hash functions. In: Robshaw, M. (ed.) FSE 2006. LNCS, vol. 4047, pp. 179–194. Springer, Heidelberg (2006)

20. Hoch, J., Shamir, A.: On the strength of the concatenated hash combiner when all the hash functions are weak. In: Aceto, L., Damgård, I., Goldberg, L.A., Halldórsson, M.M., Ingólfsdóttir, A., Walukiewicz, I. (eds.) ICALP 2008, Part II. LNCS, vol. 5126, pp. 616–630. Springer, Heidelberg (2008)

21. Joux, A.: Multicollisions in iterated hash functions. application to cascaded constructions. In: Franklin, M. (ed.) CRYPTO 2004. LNCS, vol. 3152, pp. 306–316. Springer, Heidelberg (2004)

22. Lehmann, A.: On the Security of Hash Function Combiners. Ph.D. thesis, Technischen Universität Darmstadt, Darmstadt (2010)

23. Maurer, U.M., Renner, R., Holenstein, C.: Indifferentiability, impossibility results on reductions, and applications to the random oracle methodology. In: Naor, M. (ed.) TCC 2004. LNCS, vol. 2951, pp. 21–39. Springer, Heidelberg (2004)
24. Mendel, F., Rechberger, C., Schläffer, M.: MD5 is weaker than weak: Attacks on concatenated combiners. In: Matsui, M. (ed.) ASIACRYPT 2009. LNCS, vol. 5912, pp. 144–161. Springer, Heidelberg (2009)
25. Mittelbach, A.: Hash combiners for second pre-image resistance, target collision resistance and pre-image resistance have long output. In: Visconti, I., De Prisco, R. (eds.) SCN 2012. LNCS, vol. 7485, pp. 522–539. Springer, Heidelberg (2012)
26. Mittelbach, A.: Cryptophia's short combiner for collision-resistant hash functions. In: Jacobson, M., Locasto, M., Mohassel, P., Safavi-Naini, R. (eds.) ACNS 2013. LNCS, vol. 7954, pp. 136–153. Springer, Heidelberg (2013), Full version: Cryptology ePrint Archive, Report 2013/210
27. Nandi, M., Stinson, D.: Multicollision attacks on generalized hash functions. Cryptology ePrint Archive, Report 2004/330 (2004)
28. Pietrzak, K.: Non-trivial black-box combiners for collision-resistant hash-functions don't exist. In: Naor, M. (ed.) EUROCRYPT 2007. LNCS, vol. 4515, pp. 23–33. Springer, Heidelberg (2007)
29. Pietrzak, K.: Compression from collisions, or why CRHF combiners have a long output. In: Wagner, D. (ed.) CRYPTO 2008. LNCS, vol. 5157, pp. 413–432. Springer, Heidelberg (2008)
30. Reyzin, L.: Some notions of entropy for cryptography - (invited talk). In: Fehr, S. (ed.) ICITS 2011. LNCS, vol. 6673, pp. 138–142. Springer, Heidelberg (2011)
31. Rjaško, M.: On existence of robust combiners for cryptographic hash functions. In: Conference on Theory and Practice of Information Technologies - ITAT 2009. CEUR Workshop Proceedings, vol. 584, pp. 71–76 (2009)
32. Rogaway, P., Shrimpton, T.: Cryptographic hash-function basics: Definitions, implications, and separations for preimage resistance, second-preimage resistance, and collision resistance. In: Roy, B., Meier, W. (eds.) FSE 2004. LNCS, vol. 3017, pp. 371–388. Springer, Heidelberg (2004)

A   Breaking the Fix with Stateful $H^{\mathcal{R}}$

We present an attack on C^{H_1,H_2} of Sect. 6 in the artificial case that $H^{\mathcal{R}}$ is allowed to maintain state. We note that this attack does not invalidate the security proofs of Sect. 6, and it is solely presented for theoretical interest. In more detail, in the next proposition we show how to extend the attack of Prop. 1. The attack is more advanced, as $\mathcal{A}_2$ (who knows the l_i's) needs to pass those on to $H^{\mathcal{R}}$ (which does not know these). Note that $H^{\mathcal{R}}$ is, indeed, defined by $\mathcal{A}_1$ without a priori knowledge of the keys, but we assume $H^{\mathcal{R}}$ can hold state.

Proposition 3. *There exists an adversary $\mathcal{A}$ making 3 queries, such that* $\mathbf{Adv}_C^{\mathsf{coll}}(\mathcal{A}) = 1$.

Proof. Let $\mathcal{R}$ be a random oracle and $k_1, k_2, l_1, l_2 \xleftarrow{\$} \{0,1\}^n$. We focus on an adversary $\mathcal{A} = (\mathcal{A}_1, \mathcal{A}_2)$ that finds a collision for $C^{\mathcal{R},H^{\mathcal{R}}}$, where $H^{\mathcal{R}}$ is the hash function defined by $\mathcal{A}_1$. Our adversary proceeds as follows. $\mathcal{A}_1$ outputs $b = 2$ and the following hash function $H^{\mathcal{R}}$. The function simply outputs $H^{\mathcal{R}}(x) = \mathcal{R}(x)$ until and including *the first time* it gets evaluated on $H^{\mathcal{R}}(x)$ for $x = 1\|y\|z$ for some $y, z \in \{0,1\}^n$. At this point, define $(l_2^\star, l_1^\star) = (y, z)$, and respond all *subsequent* queries as follows:

$$H^{\mathcal{R}}(x) = \begin{cases} \mathcal{R}(1\|l_1^\star\|z), \text{ if } x = 1\|l_2^\star\|z \text{ for some } z \in \{0,1\}^n, \\ 0, \text{ otherwise.} \end{cases} \tag{10}$$

Next, $\mathcal{A}_2$ gets as input (k_1, k_2, l_1, l_2). The first query $\mathcal{A}_2$ makes is $M = l_1$, which gets padded to $l_1\|\mathsf{pad}(l_1)$. Note that in this evaluation of $C^{\mathcal{R}, H^{\mathcal{R}}}$, the first query to $H^{\mathcal{R}}$ is on input of $1\|l_2\|l_1$. The adversarial hash function is programmed in such a way that it defines $l_2^\star = l_2$ and $l_1^\star = l_1$. The adversary $\mathcal{A}_2$ ignores the outcome of the combiner evaluation.

For the remaining evaluations $H^{\mathcal{R}}$ operates as (10), and we can simplify the combiner to $C^{\mathcal{R}, H^{\mathcal{R}}}(kl, M) = \mathcal{R}\left(\tilde{m}_1^1\| \cdots \|\tilde{m}_\ell^1\right)$, where

$$\tilde{m}_j^1 = \mathcal{R}(1 \| l_1 \| m_j \oplus k_1) \oplus \mathcal{R}(1 \| l_1^\star \| m_j \oplus k_2),$$

for $j = 1, \ldots, \ell$. Next, the adversary $\mathcal{A}_2$ outputs colliding pair M and $M' = M \oplus k_1 \oplus k_2$ for some $M \in \{0,1\}^n$. The remainder of the proof follows Prop. 1, using $l_1^\star = l_1$. □

The second preimage attack of Prop. 2 generalizes similarly. A technicality occurs in the above attack as we assume the $H^{\mathcal{R}}$'s are evaluated in a sequential order. In other words, the attack may fail if $H^{\mathcal{R}}$ gets first evaluated for message block $\mathsf{pad}(l_1)$. A way to address this is to create a buffer. I.e., to make the first combiner evaluation on a concatenation of α l_1's, hence $M = l_1\| \cdots \|l_1$, and program $H^{\mathcal{R}}$ to define $l_1^\star$ as soon as it is "seen" α times.

We remark that the attacks suggest that there does not exist any combiner that achieves security against adversaries with state-maintaining $H^{\mathcal{R}}$: $\mathcal{A}_2$ can always pass on the secret keys to $H^{\mathcal{R}}$, be it in more complicated and elaborated ways than described in Prop. 3.

FFT Key Recovery for Integral Attack

Yosuke Todo and Kazumaro Aoki

NTT Secure Platform Laboratories, Tokyo, Japan

Abstract. An integral attack is one of the most powerful attacks against block ciphers. We propose a new technique for the integral attack called the Fast Fourier Transform (FFT) key recovery. When the integral distinguisher uses N chosen plaintexts and the guessed key is k bits, a straightforward key recovery requires the time complexity of $O(N2^k)$. However, the FFT key recovery method requires only the time complexity of $O(N + k2^k)$. As a previous result using FFT, at ICISC 2007, Collard *et al.* proposed that FFT can reduce the time complexity of a linear attack. We show that FFT can also reduce the complexity of the integral attack. Moreover, the estimation of the complexity is very simple. We first show the complexity of the FFT key recovery against three structures, the Even-Mansour scheme, a key-alternating cipher, and the Feistel cipher. As examples of these structures, we show integral attacks against PRØST, CLEFIA, and AES. As a result, 8-round PRØST $\tilde{P}_{128,K}$ can be attacked with about an approximate time complexity of 2^{80}. Moreover, a 6-round AES and 12-round CLEFIA can be attacked with approximate time complexities of $2^{52.6}$ and $2^{87.5}$, respectively.

Keywords: Block cipher, Integral attack, Fast Fourier Transform, Fast Walsh-Hadamard Transform, PRØST, CLEFIA, AES.

1 Introduction

An integral attack is one of the most powerful attacks against block ciphers. The integral attack was first proposed by Daemen *et al.* to evaluate the security of SQUARE [7], and then Knudsen and Wagner formalized this attack as an integral attack [14]. This attack uses N chosen plaintexts (CPs) and the corresponding ciphertexts. Generally, an integral attack consists of a distinguisher and key recovery. In the distinguisher, plaintexts are prepared in which the XOR of the R-th round output is 0. In the key recovery, R-th round outputs are recovered from ciphertexts by guessing round keys used in the last several rounds. If the guessed key is incorrect, the recovered texts are assumed to behave as random texts. On the other hand, if the guessed key is correct, the XOR of the recovered texts is 0.

We focus on the key recovery of the integral attack. Several techniques to improve the key recovery were proposed, *e.g.*, the partial-sum technique [11] and the meet-in-the-middle (MITM) technique [21]. The partial-sum technique was proposed by Ferguson *et al.* in 2000. When the integral attack uses N chosen

D. Gritzalis et al. (Eds.): CANS 2014, LNCS 8813, pp. 64–81, 2014.

Table 1. Summary of FFT key recovery, where k, k_1, and k_2 are defined in Sect. 1.1

Target cipher	Time
Even-Mansour scheme	$O(k2^k)$
Key-alternating cipher	$O(k_2 2^k)$
Feistel cipher	$O(k_1 2^{k_1} + k_2 2^{k_2})$

Table 2. Comparison of attack results. Time column only includes the time complexity of the key recovery step, and it does not include the time complexity to count the frequency of the partial bit-string of ciphertexts corresponding to the chosen plaintexts (CPs).

Target cipher	#Round	Data (CP)	Time	Technique	Reference
PRØST $\tilde{P}_{128,K}$	8	2^{64}	2^{80}	FFT	Sect. 3
PRØST $\tilde{P}_{256,K}$	9	2×2^{64}	$2^{80.9}$	FFT	Appendix D
AES	6	6×2^{32}	6×2^{50}	Partial-sum	[11]
AES	6	6×2^{32}	6×2^{50}	FFT	Sect. 4
CLEFIA	12	13×2^{112}	13×2^{106}	MITM, Partial-sum	[21]
CLEFIA	12	5×2^{112}	$2^{87.5}$	MITM, FFT	Sect. 5

plaintexts and guesses a k-bit round key, a straightforward key recovery approach requires the time complexity of $O(N2^k)$. Therefore, if enormous number of chosen plaintexts is used, the complexity of the attack increases to a very high level. The partial-sum technique can reduce the complexity, where we partially compute the sum by guessing each key one after another and reuse the partial sums. Ferguson et al. applied this technique to AES [17], and showed that a 6-round AES can be attacked with 6×2^{50} S-box lookups. The MITM technique was proposed by Sasaki et al. in 2012. This technique can reduce the complexity of the integral attack against several Feistel ciphers. In the key recovery against several Feistel ciphers, $\bigoplus(x \oplus y) = 0$ is often evaluated, where x and y are calculated from ciphertexts by guessing keys. The MITM technique first calculates $\bigoplus x$ and $\bigoplus y$ independently, and then searches keys that satisfy $\bigoplus x = \bigoplus y$ by using analysis such as the MITM attack [8]. As a result, Sasaki et al. improved integral attacks against LBlock [23], HIGHT [12], and CLEFIA [22].

Several key recovery techniques using the Fast Fourier Transform (FFT) have recently been proposed. In 2007, Collard et al. first proposed a linear attack using the FFT [6], and then Nguyen et al. extended it to a multi-dimensional linear attack [18,19]. Moreover, Bogdanov et al. proposed a zero correlation attack using the FFT in 2013 [4]. We now point out that the FFT can also be applied to the integral attack.

1.1 Our Contribution

We propose a new improved technique for the integral attack called the FFT key recovery. Table 1 shows results of the FFT key recovery, and Table 2 summarizes results of integral attacks against specific ciphers.

The FFT key recovery is useful for an integral attack with an enormous number of chosen plaintexts because the time complexity of the FFT key recovery does not depend on the number of chosen plaintexts. Therefore, the motivation to introduce this technique is similar to the reason to introduce the partial-sum technique. However, the way that the two techniques are applied is a little different, and we discuss the differences between them in Sect. 6. Another important reason to introduce the FFT key recovery is that it enables easy estimation of the time complexity of the integral attack. The partial-sum technique effectively reduces the complexity, but the attack procedure is often complicated. On the other hand, the complexity of the FFT key recovery only depends on k, where k denotes the bit length of the keys that are required to call a distinguisher on the ciphertext side.

We focus on structures for block ciphers, and estimate the security against the integral attack. Here, we focus on three structures, the Even-Mansour scheme [10] in Sect. 3, the key-alternating cipher [5] in Sect. 4, and the (generalized) Feistel cipher in Sect. 5.

The Even-Mansour scheme is a famous scheme used to construct a block cipher from a permutation, and has recently been a popular discussion topic [9,5]. When FFT key recovery is used, the time complexity of the integral attack is estimated as $O(k2^k)$. As an example of the Even-Mansour scheme, we consider PRØST [13] and show integral attacks of the scheme. PRØST is an authenticated encryption scheme, which was submitted to the CAESAR competition. The core function is called the PRØST permutation, which is extended to a block cipher by the Even-Mansour scheme. Results show that 8-round PRØST $\tilde{P}_{128,K}$ and 9-round PRØST $\tilde{P}_{256,K}$ can be attacked with the time complexity of approximately 2^{80} and $2^{80.9}$, respectively.

The key-alternating cipher is a common type of block cipher, and AES is viewed as a 10-round key-alternating cipher [3]. The time complexity of the integral attack is at least $O(k2^k)$, but we can optimize it slightly. We assume that only k_2 bits of ciphertexts are required for the distinguisher, where k_2 is always less than or equal to k. In this case, the complexity is reduced to $O(k_2 2^k)$. As an example of the key-alternating cipher, we consider AES and show an integral attack against it. Results show that a 6-round AES can be attacked with a time complexity of approximately 6×2^{50}.

The Feistel cipher is also commonly used to construct a block cipher. The MITM technique is useful in reducing the time complexity, and works well in combination with the FFT key recovery. The MITM technique evaluates $\bigoplus x$ and $\bigoplus y$ instead of $\bigoplus(x \oplus y)$. We assume that k_1 and k_2 bits are required to evaluate $\bigoplus x$ and $\bigoplus y$, respectively. In this case, the complexity of the integral attack is $O(k_1 2^{k_1} + k_2 2^{k_2})$. As an example of the Feistel cipher, we show an integral attack against CLEFIA, which is a 4-branch generalized Feistel cipher and is adopted by the ISO/IEC standard [1]. Results show that a 12-round CLEFIA can be attacked with the time complexity of approximately $2^{87.5}$ [1].

---

[1] Since this attack uses 5×2^{112} chosen plaintexts, the dominant factor in determining the time complexity is the number of chosen plaintexts. The FFT key recovery can reduce the time complexity of the key recovery step.

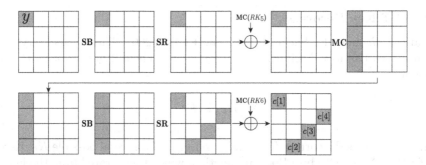

Fig. 1. Integral attack against 6-round AES

2   Related Work

2.1   Integral Attack

Integral Distinguisher. An integral distinguisher is constructed based on the following integral properties.

- All ($\mathcal{A}$) : All values appear and with exactly the same frequency in the (multi-)set of texts.
- Balance ($\mathcal{B}$) : The XOR of all texts in the set is 0.
- Constant ($\mathcal{C}$) : The bit-strings in a set are fixed to the same value.

For instance, we show the 4-round integral distinguisher of AES in Appendix A.

Key Recovery. In key recovery, the R-th round output is recovered from ciphertexts by guessing round keys used in the last several rounds. If the guessed key is incorrect, the recovered texts are expected to behave as random texts. On the other hand, if the guessed key is correct, the XOR of the recovered texts is always 0.

For instance, Fig. 1 shows the key recovery of the integral attack against a 6-round AES. Here we now have 2^{32} ciphertexts for the 6-round AES, and know that value y satisfies $\mathcal{B}$. Let $c[i]$ be bytes in the ciphertexts as shown in Fig. 1, and c_n denotes the n-th ciphertext. In this case, the XOR of y is calculated from 2^{32} ciphertexts as

$$\bigoplus_{n=1}^{2^{32}} S_5(S_1(c_n[1] \oplus K_1) \oplus S_2(c_n[2] \oplus K_2) \oplus S_3(c_n[3] \oplus K_3)$$

$$\oplus S_4(c_n[4] \oplus K_4) \oplus K_5) = 0, \tag{1}$$

where $S_1, S_2, \ldots, S_5$ are S-boxes, each of which consists of the inverse of the AES S-box and a multiplication by a field element from the inverse of the AES MDS matrix. Moreover, K_1, K_2, K_3, and K_4 are calculated from RK_6, and K_5 is calculated from RK_5. Therefore, the total bit length of the guessed keys is 40 bits. Analysis using a straightforward method incurs the approximate time complexity of $2^{32+40} = 2^{70}$. However, the partial-sum technique can reduce the complexity. Ferguson *et al.* showed that this analysis takes only 2^{50} S-box lookups [11].

2.2   FFT Key Recovery

Collard *et al.* showed a linear attack using FFT in 2007. The key recovery of a linear attack [16] uses N ciphertexts $c_1, c_2 \ldots, c_N$. Then, it guesses keys K and calculates

$$\sum_{n=1}^{N} f(c_n \oplus K). \tag{2}$$

It finally recovers the correct K to evaluate Eq. (2) for several possible Ks. Here, let $f : \{0,1\}^k \to \{0,1\}$ be a Boolean function, which is generated from the linear approximate equation. The evaluation of Eq. (2) requires the time complexity of $O(N2^k)$ using a straightforward method, and the size of N is generally enormous, e.g., $N \approx 2^k$. Collard *et al.* showed that the evaluation of Eq. (2) requires the time complexity of approximately $O(k2^k)$. Nguyen *et al.* then noticed that the Fast Walsh-Hadamard Transform (FWHT) can be used instead of the FFT [18]. Hereinafter, we show the calculation method using the FWHT.

Two k-dimensional vectors v and w are first created, where v is generated from Boolean function f and w is generated from the set of ciphertexts as indicated below.

$$v_i = f(i),$$
$$w_i = \#\{1 \leq n \leq N | c_n = i\}.$$

A k-dimensional vector, u, is calculated from v and w as

$$\begin{bmatrix} u_0 \\ u_1 \\ u_2 \\ \vdots \\ u_{2^k-1} \end{bmatrix} = \begin{bmatrix} v_0 & v_1 & v_2 & \cdots & v_{2^k-1} \\ v_1 & v_0 & v_3 & \cdots & v_{2^k-2} \\ v_2 & v_3 & v_0 & \cdots & v_{2^k-3} \\ \vdots & \vdots & \vdots & \ddots & \vdots \\ v_{2^k-1} & v_{2^k-2} & v_{2^k-3} & \cdots & v_0 \end{bmatrix} \begin{bmatrix} w_0 \\ w_1 \\ w_2 \\ \vdots \\ w_{2^k-1} \end{bmatrix}. \tag{3}$$

In this case, u_K is equal to the results of Eq. (2). Therefore, if Eq. (3) can be calculated quickly, the time complexity is reduced. Equation (3) is simply expressed as $u = V \times w$. Here, matrix V consists of four 2^{k-1}-dimensional block matrices, V_1 and V_2, as

$$V = \begin{bmatrix} V_1 & V_2 \\ V_2 & V_1 \end{bmatrix}.$$

From the diagonalization of V, we have

$$V = \begin{bmatrix} V_1 & V_2 \\ V_2 & V_1 \end{bmatrix} = \frac{1}{2} \begin{bmatrix} I & I \\ I & -I \end{bmatrix} \begin{bmatrix} V_1 + V_2 & 0 \\ 0 & V_1 - V_2 \end{bmatrix} \begin{bmatrix} I & I \\ I & -I \end{bmatrix},$$

where I is an identity matrix. Since $V_1 + V_2$ and $V_1 - V_2$ have the same structure as V, we obtain

$$V = \frac{1}{2^k} \times H_{2^k} \times \operatorname{diag}(H_{2^k} v) \times H_{2^k},$$

where $\boldsymbol{H}_{2^k}$ is the 2^k-dimensional Walsh matrix[2], and $\mathrm{diag}(\boldsymbol{H}_{2^k}v)$ is a diagonal matrix whose element in the i-th row and i-th column is the i-th element of $\boldsymbol{H}_{2^k}v$. Therefore, Eq. (3) is expressed as

$$u = \boldsymbol{V} \times w = \frac{1}{2^k}\boldsymbol{H}_{2^k} \times \mathrm{diag}(\boldsymbol{H}_{2^k}v) \times \boldsymbol{H}_{2^k}w.$$

The procedure to calculate u is given below.

1. Let us calculate $\hat{v} = \boldsymbol{H}_{2^k}v$. Then, Eq. (3) is expressed as $u = \frac{1}{2^k}\boldsymbol{H}_{2^k} \times \mathrm{diag}(\hat{v}) \times \boldsymbol{H}_{2^k}w$.
2. Let us calculate $\hat{w} = \boldsymbol{H}_{2^k}w$. Then, Eq. (3) is expressed as $u = \frac{1}{2^k}\boldsymbol{H}_{2^k} \times \mathrm{diag}(\hat{v})\hat{w}$.
3. Let us calculate $\hat{u}$ whose $\hat{u}_i$ is calculated from $\hat{v}_i \times \hat{w}_i$, and then calculate $u = \frac{1}{2^k}\boldsymbol{H}_{2^k}\hat{u}$.

In the first and second steps, we calculate the multiplication of the Walsh matrix using the FWHT, and time complexity for each is approximately the time of $k2^k$ additions. In the third step, we first calculate 2^k multiplications of the k-bit integers, where we regard that the complexity of one multiplication is equal to that for k additions. We next calculate the FWHT, and the time complexity is approximately the time of $k2^k$ additions. We finally calculate the division by 2^k, but the time complexity is negligible because it can be computed by a k-bit shift. Therefore, the time complexity of the third step is approximately $2k2^k$. Thus, the total time complexity is approximately the time of $4k2^k$ additions.

3   Integral Attack against Even-Mansour Scheme and Application to PRØST

3.1   Even-Mansour Scheme and FFT Key Recovery

The Even-Mansour scheme constructs an n-bit block cipher from an n-bit permutation, P, using two n-bit keys K_1 and K_2 as

$$c = K_2 \oplus P(p \oplus K_1),$$

where p and c denote a plaintext and a ciphertext, respectively [10]. The Even-Mansour scheme has recently been a popular topic of discussion [9,5]. When the FFT key recovery is used, we can easily evaluate the time complexity of the integral attack.

We first split permutation P into two permutations, P_1 and P_2, as $P = P_2 \circ P_1$ (see Fig. 2). We assume that P_1 has an integral distinguisher with N

---

[2]   The Walsh matrix is defined as the following recursive formulae.

$$\boldsymbol{H}_{2^1} = \begin{bmatrix} 1 & 1 \\ 1 & -1 \end{bmatrix}, \quad \boldsymbol{H}_{2^k} = \begin{bmatrix} \boldsymbol{H}_{2^{k-1}} & \boldsymbol{H}_{2^{k-1}} \\ \boldsymbol{H}_{2^{k-1}} & -\boldsymbol{H}_{2^{k-1}} \end{bmatrix} \quad (k \geq 2).$$

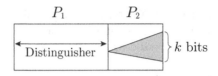

Fig. 2. Even-Mansour scheme and FFT key recovery

chosen plaintexts. Moreover, any one bit is diffused to k bits by P_2 at most. Let f be a Boolean function. Here, the input is k bits of the output of P_2, and the output is any one bit of the input of P_2. In this case, the key recovery can be expressed as

$$\bigoplus_{i=1}^{N} f(c'_i \oplus K'_2) = 0,$$

where c'_i and K'_2 are truncated to k bits from c_i and K_2, respectively. The FFT key recovery calculates the summation on the ring of integers, and we have

$$\sum_{i=1}^{N} f(c'_i \oplus K'_2) = 0 \bmod 2.$$

We can efficiently evaluate this equation using the FWHT, and the time complexity is $O(k2^k)$.

3.2   FFT Key Recovery against PRØST

PRØST is an authenticated encryption scheme, which was submitted to the CAESAR competition. The core function of PRØST $\tilde{P}_{n,K}(x)$ is the block cipher based on the single-key Even-Mansour scheme with key K, and it is defined as

$$\tilde{P}_{n,K}(x) := K \oplus P_n(x \oplus K) \quad \text{in } \{0,1\}^{2n},$$

where x and P_n denote the input and the PRØST permutation, respectively. We show the specification in Appendix B.

PRØST $\tilde{P}_{128,K}$ has a 6-round integral distinguisher with 2^{64} chosen plaintexts. We show the integral characteristics in Appendix C. Moreover, any one bit is diffused to 64 bits in 2 rounds. Let c'_i be the 64-bit truncation of ciphertexts c_i. Let f be a Boolean function that is generated from the last two-round permutation. The input is the 64-bit truncation of the output of the last 2-round permutation. The output is any one bit of the input of the last 2-round permutation. In this case, the key recovery can be expressed as

$$\bigoplus_{i=1}^{2^{64}} f(c'_i \oplus K') = 0,$$

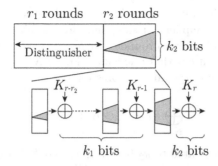

Fig. 3. Key-alternating cipher and FFT key recovery

where K' is truncated to 64 bits from K. The FFT key recovery calculates the summation on the ring of integers, and we calculate

$$\sum_{i=1}^{2^{64}} f(c_i' \oplus K').$$

From the description in Sect. 2.2, we evaluate this equation for all possible K' with $4 \times 64 \times 2^{64} = 2^{72}$ additions. The probability that this value is even for incorrect keys is expected to be 2^{-1}, but this value is always even for the correct key.

All the bits of the output of the 6-round integral characteristic satisfy $\mathcal{B}$. Therefore, we repeat this analysis for 256 bits. Since the probability that all 256 bits satisfy $\mathcal{B}$ for incorrect key K is 2^{-256}, we can recover the 256-bit key K. Thus, the total complexity is approximately $256 \times 2^{72} = 2^{80}$ additions.

We show an integral attack on 9-round PRØST $\tilde{P}_{256,K}$ in Appendix D. The time complexity is approximately $2^{80.9}$ additions.

4 Integral Attack against Key-Alternating Cipher and Application to AES

4.1 Key-Alternating Cipher and FFT Key Recovery

The key-alternating cipher [5] is one of the most popular block cipher structures. Let P_i be an n-bit permutation, and the key-alternating cipher is expressed as

$$c = K_r \oplus P_r(\cdots \oplus P_3(K_2 \oplus P_2(K_1 \oplus P_1(K_0 \oplus p)))),$$

where $K_0, K_1, \ldots, K_r$ are round keys that are calculated from the master key. Let p and c be a plaintext and a ciphertext, respectively. Similar to the case with the Even-Mansour scheme, the FFT key recovery is useful in evaluating the complexity on the integral attack.

We first split r rounds into r_1 and r_2 rounds as $r = r_1 + r_2$ (see Fig. 3). We assume that a key-alternating cipher has an r_1-round integral distinguisher with

N chosen plaintexts. Moreover, we need to guess a k-bit key which is required for this distinguisher for the ciphertext side, and any one bit of output from the r_1 rounds is diffused to k_2 bits by r_2 rounds. Let $F_{2,K'}$ be a function from k_2 bits to one bit, where K' is k_1-bit key that is calculated from $K_{r-r_2}, K_{r-r_2+1}, \ldots, K_{r-1}$. In this case, the key recovery can be expressed as

$$\bigoplus_{i=1}^{N} F_{2,K'}(c_i' \oplus K_r') = 0,$$

where c_i' and K_r' are truncated to k_2 bits from c_i and K_r, respectively. To apply the FFT key recovery, we first guess correct K', and we have

$$\sum_{i=1}^{N} F_{2,K'}(c_i' \oplus K_r') = 0 \mod 2.$$

We can efficiently evaluate this equation using the FWHT. Thus, the time complexity is $O(2^{k_1} \times k_2 2^{k_2})$.

4.2   FFT Key Recovery against AES

We show the FFT key recovery for the integral attack against a 6-round AES (see Fig. 1). Since the FFT key recovery only calculates the summation on the ring of integers, we transform Eq. (1) to

$$\sum_{n=1}^{2^{32}} S_5^{(i)}(S_1(c_n[1] \oplus K_1) \oplus S_2(c_n[2] \oplus K_2) \oplus S_3(c_n[3] \oplus K_3)$$

$$\oplus S_4(c_n[4] \oplus K_4) \oplus K_5)$$

$$= \sum_{n=1}^{2^{32}} f_{K_5}^{(i)}(F(c_n \oplus (K_1\|K_2\|K_3\|K_4))), \tag{4}$$

where F is a function from $\{0,1\}^{32}$ to $\{0,1\}^{32}$. Moreover, $f_{K_5}^{(i)}$ is a Boolean function whose output is the i-th bit of the output of S_5. We first guess K_5, and then calculate this summation using the FWHT. According to the description in Sect. 2.2, the time complexity is $4 \times 32 \times 2^{32} = 2^{39}$ additions for every K_5. Moreover, since K_5 is 8 bits, the time complexity is $2^8 \times 2^{39} = 2^{47}$ additions. The probability that this value is even for incorrect keys is expected to be 2^{-1}, but this value is always even for the correct key.

We estimate the time complexity to recover 5 keys $K_1, K_2, \ldots, K_5$ because Ferguson et al. estimated it in [11]. Since the output of S_5 is 8 bits, we repeat this analysis using the 8 bits. The probability that all 8 bits satisfy $\mathcal{B}$ for incorrect key is 2^{-8}. Since the total bit length of $K_1, K_2, \ldots, K_5$ is 40 bits, we repeat the above attack using 6 different sets. Thus, the total complexity is approximately the time of $6 \times 8 \times 2^{47} = 6 \times 2^{50}$ additions. When we use the partial-sum technique, the total time complexity is approximately the time of 6×2^{50} S-box lookups. We discuss the differences between them in Sect. 6.

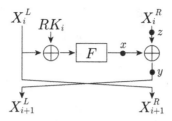

Fig. 4. Round function of Feistel cipher

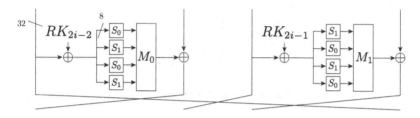

Fig. 5. Round function of CLEFIA

5 Integral Attack against Feistel Cipher and Application to CLEFIA

5.1 Feistel Cipher and FFT Key Recovery with MITM Technique

The Feistel cipher is commonly used to construct block ciphers. State X_i is separated into the left half, X_i^L, and the right half, X_i^R, and each half is updated as shown in Fig. 4. In 2012, Sasaki *et al.* proposed the MITM technique for the integral attack. Generally, the integral characteristics of the Feistel cipher satisfy $\mathcal{B}$ in the right half, namely $\bigoplus z$ becomes 0. In the MITM technique, we evaluate $\bigoplus x$ and $\bigoplus y$ independently instead of $\bigoplus z$. Then, we search for keys satisfying $\bigoplus x = \bigoplus y$ through analysis such as the MITM attack [8]. In [21], the partial-sum technique is used to evaluate $\bigoplus x$ and $\bigoplus y$, but the FFT can also be used to evaluate them.

We assume that we need to guess k_1 and k_2 bits to evaluate $\bigoplus x$ and $\bigoplus y$, respectively. If the round key is XORed with input from function F, the FFT key recovery can evaluate $\bigoplus x$ and $\bigoplus y$ with $O(k_1 2^{k_1})$ and $O(k_2 2^{k_2})$, respectively. Since the matching step of MITM analysis requires the time complexity of $O(\max\{2^{k_1}, 2^{k_2}\})$, the total time complexity of the integral attack is $O(k_1 2^{k_1} + k_2 2^{k_2})$.

5.2 CLEFIA

CLEFIA is a 128-bit block cipher, which was proposed by Shirai *et al.* in 2007. It has a 4-branch generalized Feistel network, and is adopted as an ISO/IEC standard. The round function is defined as in Fig. 5, and the i-th round output

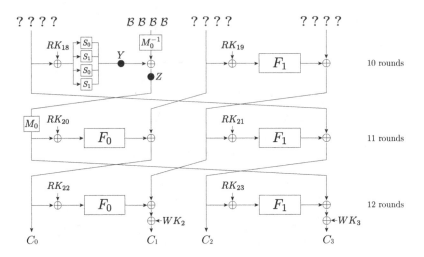

Fig. 6. Key recovery of 12-round CLEFIA

is calculated from the $(i-1)$-th round output, RK_{2i-2} and RK_{2i-1}. Moreover, the whitening keys, WK_0 and WK_1, are used in the first round, and WK_2 and WK_3 are used in the last round. For the 128-bit security version, the number of rounds is 18.

Shirai et $al.$ showed that CLEFIA has an 8-round integral distinguisher in the proposal of CLEFIA [2], and then Li et $al.$ showed that it has a 9-round integral distinguisher with 2^{112} chosen plaintexts [15]. Moreover, Sasaki and Wang showed that the complexity of the integral attack against a 12-round CLEFIA is 13×2^{106} S-box lookups using the MITM technique.

5.3   FFT Key Recovery against CLEFIA

We show the FFT key recovery against a 12-round CLEFIA. We first define some notations. Let C_1, C_2, C_3, and C_4 be ciphertexts and each value is 32 bits (see Fig. 6). Let X be any 32-bit value, and $X[i]$ denotes the i-th byte of X, namely $X = X[1]\|X[2]\|X[3]\|X[4]$. We define function $f_i : \{0,1\}^{32} \rightarrow \{0,1\}^8$ as

$$f_1(X)\|f_2(X)\|f_3(X)\|f_4(X) = F_1(X).$$

We first use the same method as the MITM technique [21], which applies the MITM attack [8] in the key recovery of the integral attack. It uses a 9-round integral distinguisher [15], where the second branch of the ninth round output satisfies $\mathcal{B}$. To optimize the MITM technique, we equivalently move the position of M_0 in the tenth round as shown in Fig. 6. As a result, we have $\bigoplus Y = \bigoplus Z$. Therefore, if $\bigoplus Y$ and $\bigoplus Z$ can be calculated with the guessed round keys, we can recover the secret key from the MITM technique. Let $\bigoplus Y$ and $\bigoplus Z$ be calculated as

$$\bigoplus Y = \bigoplus S(F_1(F_0(C_0 \oplus RK_{22}) \oplus C_1 \oplus RK_{21} \oplus WK_2) \oplus C_2 \oplus RK_{18}),$$

$$\bigoplus Z = \bigoplus M_0^{-1}(F_1(C_2 \oplus RK_{23}) \oplus C_3 \oplus WK_3),$$

where S denotes the concatenation of 4 S-boxes S_0, S_1, S_0, and S_1. In [21], each value is calculated using the partial-sum technique.

Hereinafter, we use the FFT key recovery. We need to guess 96 bits to evaluate $\bigoplus Y$. Since WK_3 does not affect $\bigoplus Z$, we need to guess 32 bits to evaluate $\bigoplus Z$. Clearly, the time complexity to evaluate $\bigoplus Z$ is negligible compared to that to evaluate $\bigoplus Y$. Therefore, we show the complexity required to evaluate $\bigoplus Y$. For instance, the first byte of $\bigoplus Y$ is calculated as

$$\bigoplus Y[1]$$
$$= \bigoplus S_0(f_1(F_0(C_0 \oplus RK_{22}) \oplus C_1 \oplus RK_{21} \oplus WK_2) \oplus C_2[1] \oplus RK_{18}[1]).$$

To execute the FFT key recovery, we transform the above equation to

$$\sum Y[1]^{(i)}$$
$$= \sum S_0^{(i)}(f_1(F_0(C_0 \oplus RK_{22}) \oplus C_1 \oplus RK_{21} \oplus WK_2) \oplus C_2[1] \oplus RK_{18}[1]),$$

where $Y[1]^{(i)}$ denotes the i-th bit of $Y[1]$ and the output of $S_0^{(i)}$ is the i-th bit of the output of S_0. Moreover, this equation is transformed by defining function f as

$$\sum Y[1]^{(i)} = \sum f\left((C_0\|C_1\|C_2[1]) \oplus (RK_{22}\|(RK_{21} \oplus WK_2)\|RK_{18}[1])\right).$$

From the description in Sect. 2.2, we can evaluate this equation for all possible $(RK_{22}\|(RK_{21}\oplus WK_2)\|RK_{18}[1])$ with $4\times72\times2^{72} \approx 2^{80.2}$ additions. Similarly, we evaluate $\sum Z[1]^{(i)}$ using the FFT key recovery, but the time complexity is negligible. Finally, we search for round keys satisfying $\sum Y[1]^{(i)} = \sum Z[1]^{(i)}$ mod 2 using analysis such as the MITM attack. Since the complexity is approximately 2^{72}, it is also negligible.

Since the output of S_0 is 8 bits, we repeat this analysis for the eight bits. Moreover, we similarly calculate the second, third, and fourth bytes of $\bigoplus Y$ and $\bigoplus Z$. Therefore, the time complexity is approximately $4 \times 8 \times 2^{80.2} = 2^{85.2}$ additions. The probability that all 32 bits satisfy $\mathcal{B}$ for incorrect keys is expected to be 2^{-32}. Since the total bit length of RK_{18}, $RK_{21} \oplus WK_2$, RK_{22}, and RK_{23} is 128 bits, we repeat above analysis using 5 different sets. Thus, the total complexity is approximately $5 \times 2^{85.2} = 2^{87.5}$ additions.

6   Discussion

We compare the FFT key recovery and the partial-sum technique. We first compare them based on their units of complexity. The complexity of the partial-sum technique is estimated from the number of S-box lookups. On the other hand, that of the FFT key recovery is estimated from the number of additions. Since the two processing speeds depend on the environment, we cannot directly compare them. However, we can roughly compare them. In the partial-sum technique, we need at least the time complexity of $O(2^{k+\ell})$, where ℓ denotes the bit length of guessed key when we partially compute the sum, *e.g.*, $\ell = 8$ for AES and $\ell = 32$ for CLEFIA. We expect that the FFT key recovery is superior to the partial-sum technique when ℓ is greater than 8. Second, we compare them based on another aspect. We compare them based on memory access. The partial-sum technique randomly accesses memories. On the other hand, the FFT key recovery sequentially accesses memories. Generally, sequential access is more efficient than the random access.

We can further optimize the FFT key recovery against specific block ciphers. For instance, if we repeat the attack for different chosen plaintext sets, we do not need to calculate $\hat{v}$ every time. We can use the same $\hat{v}$ several times. Moreover, if we use the same set of ciphertexts, we do not need to calculate $\hat{w}$ every time. Namely, we can use the same $\hat{w}$ several times. Thus, the complexity of the FFT key recovery can be reduced using these properties.

We have an open problem regarding the FFT key recovery. Since round keys of block ciphers are calculated from the secret key, some bits of round keys are automatically recovered if some bits of the secret key are recovered. The partial-sum technique can utilize this property and efficiently reduce the complexity. For instance, the integral attack against a 22-round LBlock utilizes this property [20]. However, in the FFT key recovery, we do not yet know how to utilize this property.

7   Conclusion

We proposed a new technique for the integral attack called the FFT key recovery. This technique is useful in an integral attack with an enormous number of chosen texts. Moreover, the time complexity only depends on the bit length of keys that are required for a distinguisher from the ciphertext side. Therefore, we can easily estimate the time complexity. We focus on three structures, the Even-Mansour scheme where the block size is k bits; the key-alternating cipher where the block size is k bits, and k_2 bits are required to evaluate the integral distinguisher; and the Feistel cipher where k_1 and k_2 bits are used to evaluate the MITM integral key recovery. The time complexity is $O(k2^k)$, $O(k_2 2^k)$, and $O(k_1 2^{k_1} + k_2 2^{k_2})$, respectively. As applications of the three structures, we show that 8-round PRØST $\tilde{P}_{128,K}$, a 6-round AES, and a 12-round CLEFIA can be attacked with 2^{80}, $2^{52.6}$, and $2^{87.5}$ additions, respectively.

References

1. ISO/IEC 29192-2. Information technology - Security techniques - Lightweight cryptography - Part 2: Block ciphers,
   http://www.iso.org/iso/iso_catalogue/
   catalogue_tc/catalogue_detail.htm?csnumber=56552

2. The 128-bit Blockcipher CLEFIA Security and Performance Evaluations. Sony Corporation (2007)

3. Andreeva, E., Bogdanov, A., Dodis, Y., Mennink, B., Steinberger, J.P.: On the Indifferentiability of Key-Alternating Ciphers. In: Canetti, R., Garay, J.A. (eds.) CRYPTO 2013, Part I. LNCS, vol. 8042, pp. 531–550. Springer, Heidelberg (2013)

4. Bogdanov, A., Geng, H., Wang, M., Wen, L., Collard, B.: Zero-Correlation Linear Cryptanalysis with FFT and Improved Attacks on ISO Standards Camellia and CLEFIA. In: Lange, T., Lauter, K., Lisoněk, P. (eds.) SAC 2013. LNCS, vol. 8282, pp. 306–323. Springer, Heidelberg (2013)

5. Bogdanov, A., Knudsen, L.R., Leander, G., Standaert, F.-X., Steinberger, J., Tischhauser, E.: Key-Alternating Ciphers in a Provable Setting: Encryption Using a Small Number of Public Permutations. In: Pointcheval, D., Johansson, T. (eds.) EUROCRYPT 2012. LNCS, vol. 7237, pp. 45–62. Springer, Heidelberg (2012)

6. Collard, B., Standaert, F.-X., Quisquater, J.-J.: Improving the Time Complexity of Matsui's Linear Cryptanalysis. In: Nam, K.-H., Rhee, G. (eds.) ICISC 2007. LNCS, vol. 4817, pp. 77–88. Springer, Heidelberg (2007)

7. Daemen, J., Knudsen, L.R., Rijmen, V.: The Block Cipher SQUARE. In: Biham, E. (ed.) FSE 1997. LNCS, vol. 1267, pp. 149–165. Springer, Heidelberg (1997)

8. Diffie, W., Hellman, M.E.: Exhaustive cryptanalysis of the NBS Data Encryption Standard. Computer 10, 74–84 (1977)

9. Dunkelman, O., Keller, N., Shamir, A.: Minimalism in Cryptography: The Even-Mansour Scheme Revisited. In: Pointcheval, D., Johansson, T. (eds.) EURO-CRYPT 2012. LNCS, vol. 7237, pp. 336–354. Springer, Heidelberg (2012)

10. Even, S., Mansour, Y.: A Construction of a Cipher from a Single Pseudorandom Permutation. J. Cryptology 10(3), 151–162 (1997)

11. Ferguson, N., Kelsey, J., Lucks, S., Schneier, B., Stay, M., Wagner, D., Whiting, D.: Improved Cryptanalysis of Rijndael. In: Schneier, B. (ed.) FSE 2000. LNCS, vol. 1978, pp. 213–230. Springer, Heidelberg (2001)

12. Hong, D., et al.: HIGHT: A New Block Cipher Suitable for Low-Resource Device. In: Goubin, L., Matsui, M. (eds.) CHES 2006. LNCS, vol. 4249, pp. 46–59. Springer, Heidelberg (2006)

13. Kavun, E.B., Lauridsen, M.M., Leander, G., Rechberger, C., Schwabe, P., Yalçin, T.: PRØST v1 (2014), Submission to CAESAR competition

14. Knudsen, L.R., Wagner, D.: Integral Cryptanalysis. In: Daemen, J., Rijmen, V. (eds.) FSE 2002. LNCS, vol. 2365, pp. 112–127. Springer, Heidelberg (2002)

15. Li, Y., Wu, W., Zhang, L.: Improved Integral Attacks on Reduced-Round CLEFIA Block Cipher. In: Jung, S., Yung, M. (eds.) WISA 2011. LNCS, vol. 7115, pp. 28–39. Springer, Heidelberg (2012)

16. Matsui, M.: Linear Cryptanalysis Method for DES Cipher. In: Helleseth, T. (ed.) EUROCRYPT 1993. LNCS, vol. 765, pp. 386–397. Springer, Heidelberg (1994)

17. National Institute of Standards and Technology: Specification for the ADVANCED ENCRYPTION STANDARD (AES). Federal Information Processing Standards Publication 197 (2001)

18. Nguyen, P.H., Wei, L., Wang, H., Ling, S.: On Multidimensional Linear Cryptanalysis. In: Steinfeld, R., Hawkes, P. (eds.) ACISP 2010. LNCS, vol. 6168, pp. 37–52. Springer, Heidelberg (2010)

19. Nguyen, P.H., Wu, H., Wang, H.: Improving the Algorithm 2 in Multidimensional Linear Cryptanalysis. In: Parampalli, U., Hawkes, P. (eds.) ACISP 2011. LNCS, vol. 6812, pp. 61–74. Springer, Heidelberg (2011)

20. Sasaki, Y., Wang, L.: Comprehensive Study of Integral Analysis on 22-Round LBlock. In: Kwon, T., Lee, M.-K., Kwon, D. (eds.) ICISC 2012. LNCS, vol. 7839, pp. 156–169. Springer, Heidelberg (2013)

21. Sasaki, Y., Wang, L.: Meet-in-the-Middle Technique for Integral Attacks against Feistel Ciphers. In: Knudsen, L.R., Wu, H. (eds.) SAC 2012. LNCS, vol. 7707, pp. 234–251. Springer, Heidelberg (2013)

22. Shirai, T., Shibutani, K., Akishita, T., Moriai, S., Iwata, T.: The 128-Bit Block-cipher CLEFIA (Extended Abstract). In: Biryukov, A. (ed.) FSE 2007. LNCS, vol. 4593, pp. 181–195. Springer, Heidelberg (2007)

23. Wu, W., Zhang, L.: LBlock: A Lightweight Block Cipher. In: Lopez, J., Tsudik, G. (eds.) ACNS 2011. LNCS, vol. 6715, pp. 327–344. Springer, Heidelberg (2011)

Appendix A: 4-round Integral Distinguisher of AES

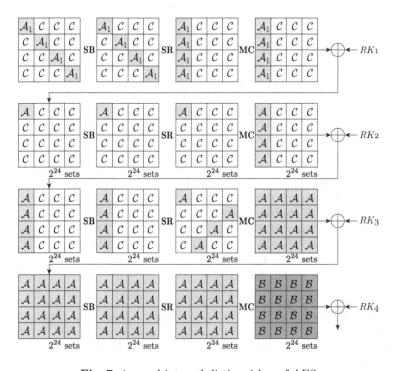

Fig. 7. 4-round integral distinguisher of AES

Figure 7 shows the 4-round integral distinguisher of AES. In the first round, 4 values satisfy $\mathcal{A}_1$, where the concatenation of their values also satisfies $\mathcal{A}$. This distinguisher uses 2^{32} chosen plaintexts, and each byte after encrypting 4 rounds satisfies $\mathcal{B}$.

Appendix B: Specification of PRØST

PRØST is an authenticated encryption scheme, which was submitted to the CAE-SAR competition. Refer to the original specification [13] and the reference implementation[3] for details.

PRØST permutation P_n ($n = 128$ or 256) adopts a substitution-permutation network, and inputs $2n$ bits and outputs $2n$ bits. We call a $2n$-bit string a state, and a 4-bit string a nibble. A state is represented as $4 \times d$ nibbles, where $d = 16$ and 32 for $n = 128$ and 256, respectively. We also refer to a four-nibble column as a slice. Figure 8 shows the state of PRØST, where the figure on the left shows the state of PRØST in [13] and the figure on the right shows our 2-dimensional representation, whose top-left square marked in light-gray is the origin of the columns and rows.

PRØST permutation consists of T rounds, where $T = 16$ and 18 for $n = 128$ and 256, respectively. The i-th round function is defined as

$$R_i := \texttt{AddConstant} \circ \texttt{ShiftPlanes} \circ \texttt{SubSlices} \quad \text{for } i = 1, 2, \ldots, T$$

SubSlices substitutes each slice using a super S-box. A super S-box replaces 16 bits, and it consists of 4 S-boxes and a multiplication by 16×16-bit matrix M. ShiftPlanes cyclically shifts the j-th row by $\pi_{2-(i \bmod 2)}(j)$ nibbles to the left for the i-th round, where π_i is defined in Table 3.

AddConstant XORs a round constant.

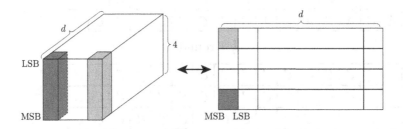

Fig. 8. Two different representations for the state of PRØST

Table 3. Definition of π_1 and π_2

	$n = 128$				$n = 256$			
	1	2	3	4	1	2	3	4
π_1	0	2	4	6	0	4	12	26
π_2	0	1	8	9	1	24	26	31

---

[3] The reference implementation can be obtained from the `crypto_aead/proest*` directory in the SUPERCOP package which is available at
`http://bench.cr.yp.to/supercop.html`.

Appendix C: Integral Distinguisher of PRØST

We experimentally search for integral distinguishers of PRØST. We set a slice of the second round input as $\mathcal{A}$ and observe the sixth round output. The XOR of the output depends on the value of the constant nibbles of the second round input. However, we can expect that bit positions whose XOR values are always zero are $\mathcal{B}$ by changing the value of the constant nibbles of the second round input. We try 1024 randomly chosen values for the constant nibbles, and the number of trials is sufficient to determine that the output bits satisfy $\mathcal{B}$ by assuming that the non-$\mathcal{B}$ bits uniformly take 0 and 1.

Through the experiment, we obtain the 5-round integral distinguisher of $\tilde{P}_{128,K}(x)$ with 2^{16} chosen plaintexts (see Fig. 9). This distinguisher is extended to the 6-round distinguisher as shown in Fig. 9, and it uses 2^{64} chosen plaintexts.

Similarly, we show the integral distinguisher of $\tilde{P}_{256,K}(x)$. We first prepare chosen plaintexts where each slice satisfies $\mathcal{A}$, and this distinguisher is extended to the 7-round distinguisher with 2^{64} chosen plaintexts. When the first slice (16 bits) satisfies $\mathcal{A}$, the seventh round output satisfy the following integral characteristic.

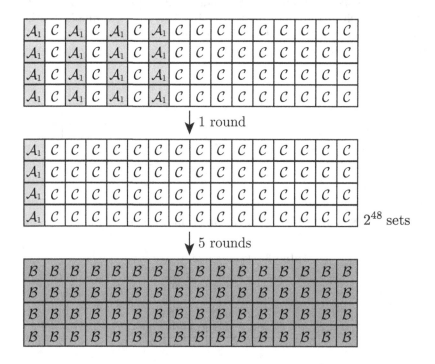

Fig. 9. 6-round integral distinguisher of $\tilde{P}_{128,K}$

> 0x30f0c00d3dc930cd090f0d0000d09000
> 0xd00c9fd390dc030d0f0000c0300090d0
> 0xd0930c0f0d000030c000d0d09003df9c
> 0x90d000c0f03009cd3dc0390d0d0f0000

Here, if the hexadecimal value in the i-th row and j-th slice is 0x3, the upper two bits satisfy $\mathcal{B}$ and the lower two bits do not satisfy $\mathcal{B}$. As another example, when the seventeenth slice (16 bits) satisfies $\mathcal{A}$, the seventh round output satisfy the following integral characteristic.

> 0x090f0d0000d0900030f0c00d3dc930cd
> 0x0f0000c0300090d0d00c9fd390dc030d
> 0xc000d0d09003df9cd0930c0f0d000030
> 0x3dc0390d0d0f000090d000c0f03009cd

In both integral characteristics, 348 bits of the seventh round output satisfy $\mathcal{B}$.

Appendix D: FFT Key Recovery against PRØST $\tilde{P}_{256,K}$

In Appendix C, we show two 7-round integral distinguishers with 2^{64} chosen plaintexts. In each distinguisher, only 348 bits of the seventh round output satisfy $\mathcal{B}$. We show the FFT key recovery using these two distinguishers. The sum of the number of bits that the two distinguishers do not satisfy $\mathcal{B}$ is 24 bits. Therefore, 488 bits of the output of the 7-round integral characteristic satisfy $\mathcal{B}$. We repeat the FFT key recovery 488 times. The time complexity is the time of $488 \times 2^{72} = 2^{80.9}$ additions. Since the probability that all 488 bits satisfy $\mathcal{B}$ for incorrect key K is 2^{-488} at most, and 2^{24} incorrect keys are expected to remain. Therefore, we exhaustively search for the remaining keys. The time complexity is 2^{24}, and it is negligible compared to the time complexity for the two FFT key recoveries.

Message Extension Attack against Authenticated Encryptions: Application to PANDA

Yu Sasaki[1] and Lei Wang[2]

[1] NTT Secure Platform Laboratories, Tokyo, Japan
sasaki.yu@lab.ntt.co.jp
[2] Nanyang Technological University, Singapore, Singapore
wang.lei@ntu.edu.sg

Abstract. In this paper, a new cryptanalysis approach for a class of authenticated encryption schemes is presented, which is inspired by the previous length extension attack against hash function based MACs. The approach is called message extension attack. The target class is the schemes that initialize the internal state with nonce and key, update the state by associated data and message, extract key stream from the state, and finally generate a tag from the updated state. A forgery attack can be mounted in the nonce-repeating model in the chosen-plaintext scenario when a function to update the internal state is shared for processing the message and generating the tag. The message extension attack is then applied to PANDA, which is a dedicated authenticated encryption design submitted to CAESAR. An existential forgery attack is mounted with 2^5 chosen plaintexts, 2^{64} computations, and a negligible memory, which breaks the claimed 128-bit security for the nonce-repeating model. This is the first result that breaks the security claim of PANDA.[1]

Keywords: message extension attack, internal state recovery, existential forgery, nonce misuse, CAESAR, PANDA.

1 Introduction

Authenticated encryption is a symmetric-key primitive which provides both of the confidentiality and the integrity of a message at the same time. The all-in-one approach of the authenticated encryption has several advantages compared to the previous one that combines independently designed encryption schemes and authentication schemes. For example, 1) the security discussion can be closed inside one scheme, which also simplifies the proper implementation of the scheme and 2) the better performance can be achieved by sharing a part of computations for encryption and authentication. Due to its generic purpose and complicated security goal, there are various methods to design authenticated encryptions.

Currently, the competition to determine new portfolio of the authenticated encryption, CAESAR, is conducted [1]. 58 algorithms were submitted in March

---

[1] Recent updates about the research on PANDA are summarized in Introduction.

D. Gritzalis et al. (Eds.): CANS 2014, LNCS 8813, pp. 82–97, 2014.
© Springer International Publishing Switzerland 2014

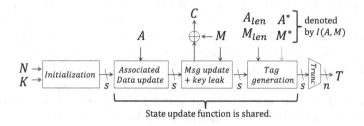

Fig. 1. Generic Computation Class of Our Target

2014, and the final portfolio will be selected in about 4 years through elaborative discussion from various points of view.

Security is one of the most important aspects of authenticated encryptions. While some of the designs submitted to CAESAR especially of mode-of-operation proposals have the security proof, others of the designs especially of dedicated construction proposals do not have the proof, and claim a certain number of bits of security based on the designers' intuition. Such claims might be later proved to be correct or broken with cryptanalysis. At the present time, cryptanalytic techniques and proving techniques for authenticated encryptions do not seem to be sophisticated enough. More generic approaches need to be discussed.

Another important security issue is the *misuse resistance*, which provides a fail safe mechanism for incorrect implementations. Many authenticated encryptions require that the same nonce value must not be repeated under the same key. Nonce-misuse resistant schemes provide a certain level of security even if the nonce value is incorrectly repeated. Considering the recent incidents such as Lucky Thirteen [2], cryptographers cannot always expect the perfect implementation with very careful security analysis, and thus providing the fail safe mechanism from the primitive level is important.

One popular design approach for authenticated encryptions is having a large state and extracting several bits from the state as a key stream. Then, the ciphertext is generated by XORing the key stream and the message, and the tag value is generated from the updated state value. The design approach is depicted in Fig. 1. The encryption method of this approach is similar to stream ciphers. The state is firstly initialized by the key K and nonce N. After updating the state by associated data A, the key stream generation will start. The tag generation function processes the length of the associated data, A_{len}, and the length of the message, M_{len}. Additionally, it may take as input some values computed from A and M denoted by A^* and M^*, e.g. the checksum of A or M. Using the empty message or a pre-specified fixed message to update the state can be regarded as M^*. In order to optimize the implementation cost, a function to update the state can be shared among the associated data processing part, the message processing part, and the tag generation part.

The class in Fig. 1 reuses the updated state value by the encryption for the authentication, and is thus very efficient. Besides, the class can achieve the *length optimality*, i.e. the ciphertext length can be exactly the same as the input message length. This class is useful and deserves careful analysis. Indeed, many designs presented so far belong to this class. The duplex sponge mode [3] is an example, and thus all the designs following the duplex sponge mode also belong to this class. Several dedicated designs submitted to CAESAR also belong to this class, e.g. AEGIS [4,5], LAC [6], PAES [7] and PANDA[8]. Besides, several designs outside CAESAR belong to it as well, e.g. ASC-1 [9], ALE [10], and FIDES [11].[2]

Let us consider the nonce-misuse resistance of this class. On one hand, the confidentiality of the ciphertext is trivially broken by repeating the same K, N, A. Because the first key stream stays unchanged for the same K, N, A, the plaintext recovery attack will be mounted easily. On the other hand, the internal state value still remains secret. Thus, the integrity may be ensured even for the repetition of the same nonce value. The CAESAR candidate PANDA aims to achieve this goal. PANDA-s, which is one of the members of the PANDA-family, is claimed to be nonce-misuse resistant with respect to the integrity.

Our Contributions. In this paper, we present a new cryptanalytic approach to recover the internal state value or to break the integrity of authenticated encryptions belonging to the class in Fig. 1 in the nonce-repeating model. The overall idea is inspired by the length extension attack for hash function based MACs specified in [12], thus we call it the *message extension attack*.

The message extension attack firstly aims to recover the internal state value between the message processing part and the tag generation part. Let s and n be the size of the internal state and the tag, respectively. The attacker first observes an n-bit tag T for any pair of (A, M). The attacker can obtain n bits out of s bits of the state after the tag generation function from T. Here, we have two observations: 1) input values to the tag generation function, i.e. $A_{len}, M_{len}, A^*, M^*$, are usually derived only from (A, M), and 2) functions to update the internal state are usually identical in the message processing part and in the tag generation part in order to optimize the implementation cost. Whenever these observations apply, the attacker can extend the message M so that the input to the tag generation function is appended to the end of M. For this new message under the same (K, N, A), the attacker can obtain n bits of the target state. Once the internal state is fully recovered, the tag generation function can be simulated offline and thus the existential forgery, which produces a valid pair of (N, A, M) and (C, T), can be performed only by accessing the encryption oracle.

Note that several cryptanalytic results have already been proposed for ALE [13,14], FIDES [15] and PAES [16,17,18,19] that belong to the same class. We stress that the message extension attack is different from those attacks that are differential based approach mainly accessing to the decryption oracle.

---

[2] In Section 4, we identify features of some of these designs that make the attack presented in this paper in applicable.

We then apply the message extension attack to PANDA-s, which belongs to the class in Fig. 1 and claims 128-bit security in the nonce-repeating model. The internal state size for PANDA-s is 448 bits. A unique design feature of PANDA-s is that 192 bits of the state are not simply affected from the message input, and thus cannot be recovered. This prevents the simple application of the message extension attack. We then analyze the details of the round function of PANDA-s. By exploiting the key stream information, we show that the existential forgery attack is mounted with 2^5 chosen plaintexts, 2^{64} computations, and a negligible memory. This is the first result that breaks the security claim of PANDA.

Current Status of PANDA. Between the preprint version (25 March 2014) [20] and the formal publication of this paper, Feng *et al.* uploaded unreviewed work of the cryptanalysis on PANDA-s which requires 2^{64} computational cost but can work in the nonce-respecting model under the known-plaintext scenario [21] (06 May 2014). In a few days later (10 May 2014), Feng *et al.* improved their attack complexity to 2^{41} and claimed a practical forgery attack against PANDA-s [22].

PANDA was withdrawn from the CAESAR competition on 13 May 2014.

Paper Outline. The organization of this paper is as follows. We describe message extension attack in a generic form in Section 2. We then apply it to mount a forgery attack on PANDA-s in Section 3. Possible countermeasures are discussed in Section 4. Finally, we conclude the paper in Section 5.

2 Generic Approach with Message Extension Attack

In this section we introduce our approach for recovering the internal state value and forging the tag value against the computation structure in Fig. 1. More precisely, our goal is finding a valid pair of (N, A, M) and (C, T) which has not been queried before, i.e. the existential forgery attack in the nonce-repeating model in the chosen-plaintext scenario. Note that the attacker only needs to interact with the encryption oracle. The decryption oracle is never accessed.

We denote the lengths of the associated data A and the message M as A_{len} and M_{len}, respectively. We also denote four parts of the class as follows.

F_{ini}: generates an s-bit state from the initial value IV, key K, and nonce N.

F_{AD}: updates the s-bit state depending on the associated data A.

F_{M}: updates the s-bit state depending on the message M, and generates the key stream of M_{len} bits. In practice, M_{len} bits of the key stream are not generated at once. A small function generating a certain bit size, say b bits, of the key stream is iteratively performed until M_{len} bits are generated.

F_{T}: computes an n-bit tag value depending on the s-bit state, A_{len}, and M_{len}. It can also take as input some values computed from A or M, e.g. the checksum of A or M. The class in Fig. 1 assumes that the input value to F_{T} can be determined easily when A and M are fixed. We denote its value by $\mathcal{I}(A, M)$.

With the message extension attack, we aim to recover n bits of internal state value which is input to the tag generation function F_T by exploiting the tag value obtained by queries of different messages. One natural approach is utilizing the last key stream value, which can be recovered by taking XOR of the last b bits of the message and the ciphertext. Because the key stream is generated from the state, it may derive at most b-bit information about the internal state value. The difficulty of this attempt is that the size of b is usually much smaller than the state size s and thus is not enough to recover the entire state. For instance, the sizes of b and s are 10 bits and 160 bits for FIDES respectively, and 64 bits and 448 bits for PANDA-s respectively. By using the key stream for multi-blocks, the amount of known bits increases. However, this also increases the amount of unknown bits. Thus, even with multi-blocks, the ratio of the number of known bits to the number of unknown bits does not increase.

Our observation is that when the computations to update the state are identical between F_M and F_T, we can utilize the n-bit tag value to recover the internal state, in which n is often larger than b, and thus the attacker can obtain more information. For instance, the tag size n of FIDES and PANDA-s are 80 bits and 128 bits, respectively.

Intuitively the attack works as follows. We first choose the associated data A and the message M, and then compute the corresponding input value to F_T, i.e. $\mathcal{I}(A, M)$. Then, the input value for updating the state in F_M and F_T is represented as $M \| \mathcal{I}(A, M)$. We then choose another message M' such that $M' \leftarrow M \| \mathcal{I}(A, M)$. That is, M is extended to M' by appending its input value to F_T. This is illustrated in Fig. 2. n bits of the state after the F_M function

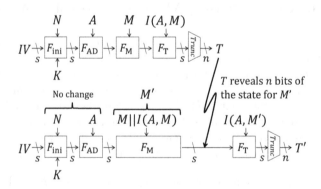

Fig. 2. Generic Approach with Message Extension Attack

for M' is already known to the attacker as the tag value T for M. This gives significant information to the attacker about the internal state value.

How many internal state bits are directly recovered from the obtained n-bit information is dependent on the specification. If the tag is generated by the truncation of the state, it immediately derives n bits of the state. If the tag is generated by some function of the state, it does not reveal the state bits directly. For example, PANDA generates the tag by taking the XOR of internal state bits. Thus, the attacker can know the result of the XOR, but cannot know the state bits directly. However, in any case, n-bit information is derived.

The security of the class shown in Figure 1 tends to be proved up to $\mathcal{O}(2^{s/2})$ queries. Hence, the parameter $s = 2n$ is very natural. With the recovered n bits, the remaining unknown bit size is n bits. To recover those n bits efficiently[3], we need more information. Let M'' be a message in which another message block is appended to M', i.e. $M'' = M'\|X$. Then, besides the obtained n-bit information, another b-bit key stream generated by the target state is obtained. How the b-bit key stream relates to the s-bit state depends on the specification. Here we suppose that the size of the exhaustive search is reduced from n bits to $n - b$ bits. For example, when b-bit key stream is unknown state bits of the state or the XOR of the several unknown state bits, the assumption can hold.

The correctness of the exhaustive guess on $n - b$ bits can be verified by computing F_T offline, and by checking the n-bit match of the result and T' (the tag value for M'). Moreover, by appending longer X, the key stream can also be used for the verification. Thus, false positives can be eliminated. Once the internal state value is recovered, the attacker can forge the tag value for any message starting from M', namely any message of the form $M'\|Y$, where Y can be an arbitrary string but for already queried X.

The attack also needs to obtain the ciphertext of the message to be forged. This is easily obtained by querying a message in which at least 1 random block is appended to the end. The ciphertext for the extended message contains the ciphertext for the message to be forged. The attacker can copy it.

The detailed attack procedure is described in Algorithm 1.

As shown in Algorithm 1, the attack requires to repeat the same nonce three times. Hence, the attack can work only in the nonce-repeating model. The attacker needs to specify the queried message. Therefore, the attack only works in the chosen-plaintext scenario. In the end, the attacker can find a valid pair of (N, A, M'') and (C'', T'') which have not been queried before. Thus, the attack breaks the notion of the existential forgery attack only by accessing the encryption oracle.

The data complexity is 2 chosen-plaintext queries. Note that the data complexity is usually measured by the number of queried message blocks, which cannot be determined without giving the detailed specification of F_T. Thus, we only count the number of queries here, and later will discuss the details in the application to a specific design. The time complexity is 2^{s-n} computations of F_T. The memory requirement is negligible.

---

[3] A forgery attack may be able to be performed without recovering all the internal state value. For generality, the attack goal is set to recovering the $2n$-bit state value.

Algorithm 1. Existential Forgery with Message Extension Attack

---

Output: a valid pair of (N, A, M) and (C, T)

1: Choose values of N, A, and M at random.
2: Query (N, A, M) to the encryption oracle to obtain the corresponding C and T.
3: Compute the corresponding $\mathcal{I}(A, M)$ offline and set $M' \leftarrow M \| \mathcal{I}(A, M)$.
4: Query (N, A, M') to the encryption oracle to obtain the corresponding C' and T'.
5: Compute the corresponding $\mathcal{I}(A, M')$ offline.
6: Query $M' \| X$ for a random message block X to obtain b-bit key stream.
7: **for** the remaining $s - n - b$ bits of the state after F_M for processing M' **do**
8:     With the knowledge of the state and $\mathcal{I}(A, M')$, compute F_T offline.
9:     **if** the result of F_T and received T' match **then**
10:         Choose the value of message $Y (\neq X)$ to be appended at random.
11:         Set $M'' \leftarrow M' \| Y$, and compute the corresponding $\mathcal{I}(A, M'')$ offline.
12:         With the knowledge of the state and $\mathcal{I}(A, M'')$, compute F_T offline. Let T''
             be the resulted output from F_T.
13:         Choose 1-block sting Z and query $M'' \| Z$ to obtain the ciphertext $C'' \| C_Z$.
14:         **return** (N, A, M'') and (C'', T'').
15:     **end if**
16: **end for**

---

3   Application: Existential Forgery Attack on PANDA-s

In this section, we apply the message extension attack for PANDA-s, which is claimed to be nonce-misuse resistant with respect to integrity. In Section 3.1, we briefly introduce the specification of PANDA-s. Its computation structure belongs to the class in Fig. 1, with the state size $s = 448$ and the tag size $n = 128$. Because n is not big enough, we cannot attack PANDA-s with the straight-forward application of the generic approach. In Section 3.2, we improve the attack by looking inside the round function of PANDA-s. By further exploiting the key stream value, we can successfully mount the existential forgery attack.

3.1   Specification of PANDA-s

PANDA-s is a member of the PANDA-family [8] designed by Ye *et al.* which was submitted to CAESAR. The PANDA-s encryption function takes a 128-bit key K, a 128-bit nonce N, variable length associated data A, and variable length plaintext M as input, and outputs the ciphertext C and a 128-bit tag T.

The encryption function consists of 4 parts: initialization, processing associated data, processing plaintext, and finalization, which are computed in this order. The computation structure is illustrated in Fig. 3, where the bit size of each arrow line is 64 bits. 64-bit values are called "blocks" in PANDA-s.

Initialization. A 128-bit key K and a 128-bit nonce N are mixed and expanded to 448-bit internal state. We omit the details due to the irrelevance to our attack.

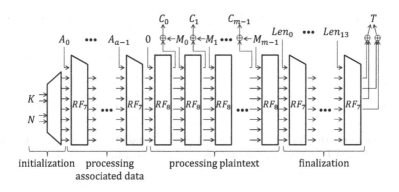

Fig. 3. Computation Structure of `PANDA-s`

Processing Associated Data. The associated data A is first padded to a multiple of 64 bits $(A_0, A_1, \ldots, A_{a-1})$, and then processed block by block with the round function RF. The round function RF of `PANDA-s` generally takes an 8-block (or 512-bit) value as input, of which 448 bits are for the previous internal state value and 64 bits are for mixing new input data to the state. The output of RF is either a 7-block value (updated internal state) or a 8-block value (updated internal state and 1-block key stream). We denote the round function by RF_7 when the output size is 7 blocks, and by RF_8 when the output size is 8 blocks.

In RF_7, a 7-block internal state value is split into seven 1-block variables $w, x, y, z, S^{(0)}, S^{(1)}, S^{(2)}$. Let m be another 1-block input value. Then, the updated state value $w', x', y', z', S'^{(0)}, S'^{(1)}, S'^{(2)}$ are computed as follows:

$$w' \leftarrow \texttt{SubNibbles}(w \oplus x \oplus m),$$
$$x' \leftarrow \texttt{SubNibbles}(x \oplus y),$$
$$y' \leftarrow \texttt{SubNibbles}(y \oplus z),$$
$$z' \leftarrow \texttt{SubNibbles}(S^{(0)}),$$
$$(S'^{(0)}, S'^{(1)}, S'^{(2)}) \leftarrow \texttt{LinearTrans}(S^{(0)} \oplus w, S^{(1)}, S^{(2)}),$$

where `SubNibbles` is a parallel application of a 4-bit S-box and `LinearTrans` applies a linear transformation. We omit their full specifications due to the irrelevance to our attack. RF_7 is illustrated in Fig. 4. Finally, by taking the 7-block state value after the initialization, $state$, as input, the associated data is processed by computing $state \leftarrow RF_7(state, A_i)$ for $i = 0, 1, \ldots, a - 1$.

Processing Plaintext. The plaintext M is first padded to a multiple of 64 bits $(M_0, M_1, \ldots, M_{m-1})$, and then processed block by block with the round function RF_8. RF_8 is almost the same as RF_7. The only difference is that it produces another 1-block output value r by $r \leftarrow x \oplus x'$ as illustrated in Fig. 5.

The additional 1-block output value r_i in round i is used as a key stream. Namely, the ciphertext block C_i for the plaintext block M_i is computed by

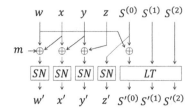 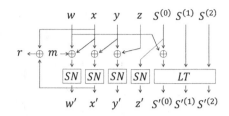

Fig. 4. Round Function for 7-block Output **Fig. 5.** Round Function for 8-block Output
SN and LT stand for SubNibbles and LinearTrans, respectively.

$C_i \leftarrow M_i \oplus r_i$. Finally, by taking the 7-block state value after the associated data processing, $state$, as input, the plaintext is processed as follows:

$$(state, r_0) \leftarrow RF_8(state, 0),$$
for $i = 0$ **to** $m - 1$ **do**
$\quad C_i \leftarrow M_i \oplus r_i,$
$\quad (state, r_{i+1}) \leftarrow RF_8(state, M_i).$
end for

The extra key stream r_m after the last message block M_{m-1} is discarded.

Finalization. In the finalization, the state is updated by using the bit length of the associated data A_{len} and the bit length of the plaintext M_{len}. Let Len_i be A_{len} when i is even and M_{len} when i is odd. The finalization consists of 14-round state update by using Len_i and the tag generation to produce a 128-bit tag T. In details, the finalization computes the following operations.

for $i = 0$ **to** 13 **do**
$\quad state \leftarrow RF_7(state, Len_i).$
end for
$T \leftarrow (w \oplus y)\|(x \oplus z).$

Claimed Security. The claimed security of PANDA-s is given in Table 1. In particular, 128-bit security is claimed for integrity in the nonce-repeating model.

3.2 Existential Forgery Attack against PANDA-s

We first observe that the following properties of PANDA-s enable the application of the message extension attack.

1. The computations for updating the state by RF_7 and RF_8 are exactly the same, i.e. $RF_7(state, m)$ and $RF_8(state, m)$ produce the same state value.
2. The 1-block input values in the finalization, A_{len} and M_{len}, can be computed by the attacker only from A and M.

Table 1. Bits of Security for PANDA-s in Two Models [8, Table 3.1]

Goal	Model	
	Nonce-respect	**Nonce-repeat**
confidentiality for the plaintext	128	/
integrity for the plaintext	128	**128**
integrity for the associated data	128	**128**
integrity for the public message number	128	**128**

Overall Strategy and Message Choices. We start by applying the message extension attack to PANDA-s. The attack requires only two encryption oracle calls under the same key and nonce. The associated data can be fixed to any value. Hereafter, we always set A to Null for simplicity. We set the first query $\mathcal{Q}_1$ as $\mathcal{Q}_1 \leftarrow \alpha$, where α can be any string. Let $\ell(\alpha)$ be the 14-block value that will be processed in the finalization part for α, i.e. $\ell(\alpha) = A_{len}\|M_{len}\| \dots \|A_{len}\|M_{len}$.

By following the generic approach in Section 2, we should set the second query $\mathcal{Q}_2$ as $\mathcal{Q}_2 \leftarrow \alpha\|\ell(\alpha)$. However, the 128-bit tag for $\mathcal{Q}_1$ only reveals 128 bits of the 448-bit state after the processing plaintext part for $\mathcal{Q}_2$. As later explained, we aim to recover 256 bits of the state. Hence, we need more information, at least additional 128 bits, of the state. Here, our strategy is appending 2 more message blocks after $\alpha\|\ell(\alpha)$, and obtaining 2-block (128-bit) key stream value, which allows us to recover 256 bits of the state. Hence, we set $\mathcal{Q}_2 \leftarrow \alpha\|\ell(\alpha)\|\beta$, where β can be any string as long as its length is at least 2 blocks. Then, only with 2 queries of $\mathcal{Q}_1$ and $\mathcal{Q}_2$, 256 bits of the state after $\alpha\|\ell(\alpha)$ is processed are recovered.

We then choose a target message $\mathcal{M}$ to be forged. By following the generic approach, we should append some string X to $\alpha\|\ell(\alpha)$. Namely, $\mathcal{M} \leftarrow \alpha\|\ell(\alpha)\|X$. Then $\ell(\alpha\|\ell(\alpha)\|X)$ is processed during the finalization. The generic approach in Section 2 computes the state while X and $\ell(\alpha\|\ell(\alpha)\|X)$ are processed. However, because we only partially recover the state (256 bits out of 448 bits), the generic approach cannot work for PANDA-s. As later explained, to recover the internal state, we need the corresponding key stream value. While $\ell(\alpha\|\ell(\alpha)\|X)$ is processed in the finalization, the key stream is never generated, and thus the internal state cannot be recovered. Here, our strategy is using a query $\mathcal{Q}_3$ in which $\alpha\|\ell(\alpha)\|X\|\ell(\alpha\|\ell(\alpha)\|X)$ is included inside. Then, the key stream is obtained while $\ell(\alpha\|\ell(\alpha)\|X)$ is processed, and thus the corresponding internal state can be recovered. Finally, by setting $\mathcal{M} \leftarrow \alpha\|\ell(\alpha)\|X$, the tag for $\mathcal{M}$ can be computed offline. Note that, precisely speaking, we need at least 1 block after $\alpha\|\ell(\alpha)\|X\|\ell(\alpha\|\ell(\alpha)\|X)$ in $\mathcal{Q}_3$ by a similar reason to append 2 blocks in $\mathcal{Q}_2$.

The purpose of $\mathcal{Q}_2$ and $\mathcal{Q}_3$ can be achieved by 1 query. Namely, we set $\mathcal{Q}_2 \leftarrow \alpha\|\ell(\alpha)\|\beta\|\ell(\alpha\|\ell(\alpha)\|\beta)\|\gamma$, where β is any string and γ is any string as long as its length is at least 1 block. Finally, the tag for $\mathcal{M} \leftarrow \alpha\|\ell(\alpha)\|\beta$ can be computed offline. In summary, we choose the queries of the following forms:

$$\mathcal{Q}_1 \leftarrow \alpha, \qquad \mathcal{Q}_2 \leftarrow \alpha\|\ell(\alpha)\|\beta\|\ell(\alpha\|\ell(\alpha)\|\beta)\|\gamma, \qquad \mathcal{M} \leftarrow \alpha\|\ell(\alpha)\|\beta.$$

Because $\mathcal{M}$ is included inside $\mathcal{Q}_2$, the ciphertext of $\mathcal{M}$ can be directly copied from a part of the ciphertext of $\mathcal{Q}_2$.

As you can see, except for 14 blocks (112 bytes) of $\ell(\alpha)$, any message can be the target of our forgery attack. Therefore, though this attack is the existential forgery attack, it can forge the tag for a huge variety of messages.

Recovering 256-bit Internal State After Processing $\alpha\|\ell(\alpha)$. The attacker first queries the message $\mathcal{Q}_1 = \alpha$ and obtains the corresponding tag T_1. This reveals some information about the internal state x, y, z, w after processing $\alpha\|\ell(\alpha)$. The attacker then appends the message block $\beta = \beta_0\|\beta_1\|\cdots$. Let the internal state value after processing $\alpha\|\ell(\alpha)$ be $(w_{\beta_0}, x_{\beta_0}, y_{\beta_0}, z_{\beta_0}, S_{\beta_0}^{(0)}, S_{\beta_0}^{(1)}, S_{\beta_0}^{(2)})$. Remember that the tag is computed by $T \leftarrow (w \oplus y)\|(x \oplus z)$. The obtained tag T_1 indicates that the internal state value satisfies the following equations.

$$w_{\beta_0} \oplus y_{\beta_0} = T_1^L, \tag{1}$$

$$x_{\beta_0} \oplus z_{\beta_0} = T_1^R, \tag{2}$$

where T_1^L and T_1^R are 64-bit values satisfying $T_1^L\|T_1^R = T_1$.

Then, the attacker queries $\mathcal{Q}_2 = \alpha\|\ell(\alpha)\|\beta\|\ell(\alpha\|\ell(\alpha)\|\beta)\|\gamma$, and obtains the corresponding ciphertext blocks and tag T_2. The computation to process β is shown in Fig. 6. As a result of $RF_8(w_{\beta_0}, x_{\beta_0}, y_{\beta_0}, z_{\beta_0}, S_{\beta_0}^{(0)}, S_{\beta_0}^{(1)}, S_{\beta_0}^{(2)}, \beta_0)$, the attacker obtains the ciphertext block C_{β_0}, which is computed by $r_{\beta_0} \oplus M_{\beta_0}$. Hence, the key stream value r_{β_0} can be computed as $M_{\beta_0} \oplus C_{\beta_0}$. From the computation structure of the key stream, the attacker obtains the equation

$$r_{\beta_0} = x_{\beta_0} \oplus \texttt{SubNibbles}(x_{\beta_0} \oplus y_{\beta_0}). \tag{3}$$

Here, the attacker guesses the 64-bit value of x_{β_0}. For each guess, the corresponding z_{β_0} is obtained from Eq. (2), the corresponding y_{β_0} is obtained from Eq. (3), and the corresponding w_{β_0} is obtained from Eq. (1). Hence, for each guess of x_{β_0}, 256-bit internal state value $(w_{\beta_0}, x_{\beta_0}, y_{\beta_0}, z_{\beta_0})$ is determined. Moreover, the knowledge of $(w_{\beta_0}, x_{\beta_0}, y_{\beta_0}, z_{\beta_0})$ leads to the knowledge of $w_{\beta_1}, x_{\beta_1}, y_{\beta_1}, w_{\beta_2}, x_{\beta_2}$, and r_{β_1}. These give another 64-bit relation

$$r_{\beta_1} = x_{\beta_1} \oplus \texttt{SubNibbles}(x_{\beta_1} \oplus y_{\beta_1}), \tag{4}$$

and 1 guess of x_{β_0} out of 2^{64} possibilities is expected to satisfy this equation. Therefore, the 256-bit internal state value $(w_{\beta_0}, x_{\beta_0}, y_{\beta_0}, z_{\beta_0})$ is almost uniquely determined. In Fig. 6, the focused variables up to here are stressed by bold circles. Note that with some probability, several candidates of $(w_{\beta_0}, x_{\beta_0}, y_{\beta_0}, z_{\beta_0})$ will remain. Those false positives only give negligible impact to the attack complexity. Moreover, if the key leak value is obtained for a few more message blocks, those false positives can be eliminated easily.

Recovering w, x, y, z in All Rounds. In the round function of PANDA-s, the input message affects the right most 3 blocks (=192 bits) of the state in a

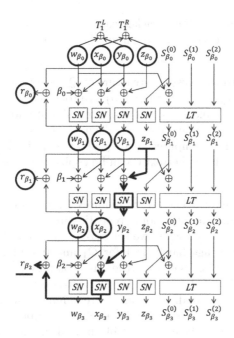

Fig. 6. Recovery of 256 Bits of the Internal State

complicated way through `LinearTrans`. Therefore, without the exhaustive guess for those 192 bits, recovering all 448-bit internal state seems impossible. However, 2^{192} is already more expensive than the cost of the brute force attack.

To solve this problem, our strategy is to keep revealing the 256-bit state values w, x, y, z for all rounds by using the knowledge of $(w_{\beta_0}, x_{\beta_0}, y_{\beta_0}, z_{\beta_0})$. This can be done with negligible cost for `PANDA-s`. Let us recall Fig. 6. Once the 256-bit state values w_i, x_i, y_i, z_i are recovered for some i, the attacker can easily obtain 192-bit state values for the next round, i.e. $w_{i+1}, x_{i+1}, y_{i+1}$. Therefore, if the 64-bit state value z_{i+1} can be recovered efficiently, the attacker can reveal the 256-bit state values w, x, y, z for any number of rounds. In Fig. 6, in order to recover the 64-bit value of z_{β_1}, the attacker uses the key stream value after 1 round, i.e. r_{β_2}. In details, the attacker focuses on the following 64-bit relation.

$$r_{\beta_2} = x_{\beta_2} \oplus \texttt{SubNibbles}(x_{\beta_2} \oplus y_{\beta_2}),$$
$$= x_{\beta_2} \oplus \texttt{SubNibbles}\big(x_{\beta_2} \oplus \texttt{SubNibbles}(y_{\beta_1} \oplus z_{\beta_1})\big).$$

The above equation is converted to

$$z_{\beta_1} = y_{\beta_1} \oplus \texttt{SubNibbles}^{-1}\big(\texttt{SubNibbles}^{-1}(r_{\beta_2} \oplus x_{\beta_2}) \oplus x_{\beta_2}\big). \qquad (5)$$

Then, z_{β_1} is recovered only with 1 computation. In Fig. 6, the focused variables to recover z_{β_1} are stressed by bold lines. By iterating the same procedure for all the subsequent blocks, the attacker can recover $(w_{\beta_i}, x_{\beta_i}, y_{\beta_i}, z_{\beta_i})$ for any block-length i as long as the key stream for the next block, $r_{\beta_{i+1}}$, is obtained.

Forging Tag. Due to the message structure of $\mathcal{Q}_2$, the attacker can recover the internal state after $\alpha \| \ell(\alpha) \| \beta \| \ell(\alpha \| \ell(\alpha) \| \beta)$ is processed. Note that the length of γ must be at least 1 block so that the internal state after the last block of $\alpha \| \ell(\alpha) \| \beta \| \ell(\alpha \| \ell(\alpha) \| \beta)$ can be recovered. Then, the tag value for a new message $\mathcal{M}(= \alpha \| \ell(\alpha) \| \beta)$ is easily computed by $(w \oplus y) \| (x \oplus z)$ of this state. Because $\mathcal{M}$ is included inside $\mathcal{Q}_2$, the ciphertext $\mathcal{C}$ can be copied from the ciphertext of $\mathcal{Q}_2$.

Complexity Evaluation. The attack requires 2 encryption oracle calls in the chosen-plaintext scenario and the nonce repeating model. The number of queried message blocks is minimized when we set $\alpha, \beta \leftarrow$ Null and $|\gamma| \leftarrow 1$. Then, the number of queried message blocks is 1 for $\mathcal{Q}_1$ and $0 + 14 + 0 + 14 + 1 = 29$ for $\mathcal{Q}_2$, in total 30 blocks. Therefore, the data complexity is about 2^5 chosen-plaintext message blocks. To recover the 256-bit state $(w_{\beta_0}, x_{\beta_0}, y_{\beta_0}, z_{\beta_0})$, 2^{64} computational cost is required. Then, all the remaining cost is 1. Thus, the time complexity of this attack is less than 2^{64} PANDA-s computations. The memory requirement is to store all the ciphertext blocks and the tag, which is negligible.

Attack Procedure. The attack procedure for the parameter $\alpha, \beta \leftarrow$ Null and $|\gamma| \leftarrow 1$ in the algorithmic form is given in Algorithm 2. For simplicity, the associated data is supposed to be Null.

Algorithm 2. Existential Forgery Attack on PANDA-s

Input: nonce N, $\mathcal{Q}_1 = $ Null, $\mathcal{Q}_2 = \ell(\text{Null}) \| \ell(\ell(\text{Null})) \| \gamma$
Output: ciphertext $\mathcal{C}$ and tag $\mathcal{T}$ in which $(N, \mathcal{C}, \mathcal{T})$ is valid
1: Query $\mathcal{Q}_1$ to the encryption oracle to obtain the tag $T_1 = T_1^L \| T_1^R$.
2: Query $\mathcal{Q}_2$ to obtain the key stream $r_{\beta_0}, r_{\beta_1}, \ldots, r_{\beta_{14}}$ and set $\mathcal{C}$ to the first 14 blocks of the ciphertext of $\mathcal{Q}_2$.
3: **for** 2^{64} guesses of x_{β_0} **do**
4:    Compute $w_{\beta_0}, y_{\beta_0}, z_{\beta_0}$ with equations (1),(2),(3).
5:    **if** Equation (4) is satisfied **then**
6:       Fix the values of $w_{\beta_0}, x_{\beta_0}, y_{\beta_0}, z_{\beta_0}$.
7:    **end if**
8: **end for**
9: **for** $i = 1, 2, \ldots, 14$ **do**
10:    With $r_{\beta_{i+1}}$ and equation (5), compute z_{β_i} to recover $(w_{\beta_i}, x_{\beta_i}, y_{\beta_i}, z_{\beta_i})$.
11: **end for**
12: Set $\mathcal{T} \leftarrow (w_{\beta_{14}} \oplus y_{\beta_{14}}) \| (x_{\beta_{14}} \oplus z_{\beta_{14}})$
13: **return** $(\mathcal{C}, \mathcal{T})$.

---

4   Countermeasures

The message extension attack seems to be possible to prevent with some extra cost. To apply the message extension attack, two conditions must be satisfied.

1. The functions to update the state in F_M and in F_T are identical.
2. $\mathcal{I}(A, M)$ can be derived only from A and M.

In order to break the first condition, giving a small tweak to the state, e.g. XORing a constant at the beginning of F_T, is a possible option. The XOR must be done to the state which is not directly updated by the message input. Otherwise, the impact of the tweak can be canceled by the attacker by modifying the message. For example, for PANDA-s, it is hard for the attacker to control the impact to $S^{(0)}, S^{(1)}, S^{(2)}$ from a message block. Therefore, if a constant is XORed to one of $S^{(0)}, S^{(1)}, S^{(2)}$ at the beginning of F_T, the attacker cannot cancel its impact and thus the message extension attack can be prevented. Indeed, AEGIS adopts such a mechanism, i.e. XORing some constant at the begging of F_T. This prevents the message extension attack on AEGIS though it does not claim the security in the nonce-repeating model to begin with.

In order to break the second condition, the simplest way is to use the key K in F_T. Actually, many of known secure block-cipher based MACs run the full-round encryption both in the beginning and the end, and many of hash function based MACs use the key both in the beginning and the end. Compared to those, using K in F_T may be a reasonable extra cost to increase the security. Actually, the message extension attack can be prevented by masking the final output with a key-dependent value.

5   Concluding Remarks

In this paper, we proposed the new approach called message extension attack for a class of authenticated encryptions, which includes many of currently discussed designs. The message extension attack aims to mount the internal state recovery attack or the existential forgery attack only with the encryption oracle in the nonce-repeating model. The attack exploits the similarity of the state updating function for processing the message and generating the tag.

We applied the message extension attack to PANDA-s, which is one of the designs submitted to the CAESAR competition. Due to the state size and the computation structure particular to PANDA-s, the simple application cannot work. With some detailed analysis, we found that the forgery attack can be performed with 2^5 chosen plaintexts, 2^{64} computational complexity, and negligible memory. The result clearly breaks the designers' security claim of PANDA-s.

To apply the message extension attack, several conditions must be satisfied. Thus it can be prevented with a small cost. Nevertheless, we believe that the message extension attack is an useful object to learn. Accumulating the knowledge of generic approaches at this stage is important to discuss the authenticated encryption security in future. We hope that future authenticated encryption designers understand the approach and make their designs resistant to it.

Acknowledgments. The authors would like to thank anonymous reviewers of CANS 2014 for their helpful comments. Lei Wang is supported by the Singapore National Research Foundation Fellowship 2012 (NRF-NRFF2012-06).

References

1. Bernstein, D.: CAESAR Competition (2013),
   http://competitions.cr.yp.to/caesar.html
2. AlFardan, N.J., Paterson, K.G.: Lucky Thirteen: Breaking the TLS and DTLS Record Protocols. In: IEEE Symposium on Security and Privacy, pp. 526–540. IEEE Computer Society (2013)
3. Bertoni, G., Daemen, J., Peeters, M., Van Assche, G.: Duplexing the Sponge: Single-Pass Authenticated Encryption and Other Applications. In: Miri, A., Vaudenay, S. (eds.) SAC 2011. LNCS, vol. 7118, pp. 320–337. Springer, Heidelberg (2012)
4. Wu, H., Preneel, B.: AEGIS: A Fast Authenticated Encryption Algorithm. In: Lange, T., Lauter, K., Lisonek, P. (eds.) SAC 2013. LNCS, vol. 8282, pp. 185–201. Springer, Heidelberg (2013)
5. Wu, H., Preneel, B.: AEGIS: A Fast Authenticated Encryption Algorithm (v1). Submitted to the CAESAR competition (2014)
6. Zhang, L., Wu, W., Wang, Y., Wu, S., Zhang, J.: LAC: A Lightweight Authenticated Encryption Cipher. Submitted to the CAESAR competition (2014)
7. Ye, D., Wang, P., Hu, L., Wang, L., Xie, Y., Sun, S., Wang, P.: PAES v1. Submitted to the CAESAR competition (2014)
8. Ye, D., Wang, P., Hu, L., Wang, L., Xie, Y., Sun, S., Wang, P.: PANDA v1. Submitted to the CAESAR competition (2014)
9. Jakimoski, G., Khajuria, S.: ASC-1: An Authenticated Encryption Stream Cipher. In: Miri, A., Vaudenay, S. (eds.) SAC 2011. LNCS, vol. 7118, pp. 356–372. Springer, Heidelberg (2012)
10. Bogdanov, A., Mendel, F., Regazzoni, F., Rijmen, V., Tischhauser, E.: ALE: AES-Based Lightweight Authenticated Encryption. In: Moriai, S. (ed.) FSE 2013. LNCS, vol. 8424, pp. 447–466. Springer, Heidelberg (2013)
11. Bilgin, B., Bogdanov, A., Knežević, M., Mendel, F., Wang, Q.: FIDES: Lightweight Authenticated Cipher with Side-Channel Resistance for Constrained Hardware. In: Bertoni, G., Coron, J.-S. (eds.) CHES 2013. LNCS, vol. 8086, pp. 142–158. Springer, Heidelberg (2013)
12. U.S. Department of Commerce, National Institute of Standards and Technology: Federal Register/Vol. 72, No. 212/Friday, November 2, 2007/Notices (2007),
    http://csrc.nist.gov/groups/ST/hash/documents/FR_Notice_Nov07.pdf.
13. Khovratovich, D., Rechberger, C.: The LOCAL Attack: Cryptanalysis of the Authenticated Encryption Scheme ALE. In: Lange, T., Lauter, K., Lisonek, P. (eds.) SAC 2013. LNCS, vol. 8282, pp. 174–184. Springer, Heidelberg (2013)
14. Wu, S., Wu, H., Huang, T., Wang, M., Wu, W.: Leaked-State-Forgery Attack against the Authenticated Encryption Algorithm ALE. In: Sako, K., Sarkar, P. (eds.) ASIACRYPT 2013, Part I. LNCS, vol. 8269, pp. 377–404. Springer, Heidelberg (2013)
15. Dinur, I., Jean, J.: Cryptanalysis of FIDES. In: Cid, C., Rechberger, C. (eds.) FSE. LNCS. Springer (to appear, 2014)

16. Sasaki, Y., Wang, L.: A Practical Universal Forgery Attack against PAES-8. Cryptology ePrint Archive, Report 2014/218 (2014),
    https://eprint.iacr.org/2014/218
17. Jean, J., Nikolić, I.: Using AES Round Symmetries to Distinguish PAES (2014),
    http://www1.spms.ntu.edu.sg/~syllab/m/images/6/6e/
    Using_AES_Round_Symmetries_to_Distinguish_PAES.pdf
18. Saarinen, M.J.O.: PAES and rotations (2014),
    https://groups.google.com/#forum/topic/crypto-competitions/vRmJdRQBzOo
19. Jean, J., Nikolić, I., Sasaki, Y., Wang, L.: Practical Cryptanalysis of PAES. In: Joux, A., Youssef, A. (eds.) SAC. LNCS. Springer (to appear, 2014)
20. Sasaki, Y., Wang, L.: A Forgery Attack against PANDA-s. Cryptology ePrint Archive, Report 2014/217 (2014), https://eprint.iacr.org/2014/217
21. Feng, X., Zhang, F., Wang, H.: A Forgery and State Recovery Attack on the Authenticated Cipher PANDA-s. Cryptology ePrint Archive, Report 2014/325 (2014)
22. Feng, X., Zhang, F., Wang, H.: A Practical Forgery and State Recovery Attack on the Authenticated Cipher PANDA-s (2014),
    http://www.amss.ac.cn/xwdt/kydt/201405/t20140506_4109871.html

New Second Preimage Attack Variants against the MD-Structure

Tuomas Kortelainen[1] and Juha Kortelainen[2]

[1] Mathematics Division, University of Oulu, Finland
[2] Department of Information Processing Science, University of Oulu, Finland

Abstract. We consider a situation where the adversary performs a second preimage attack and is able to influence slightly the preconditions under which the iterated hash function is used. In the first variant of the attack, the adversary is able to choose the initial value of the hash function after receiving the original message. In the second variant, the adversary is allowed to determine a prefix of the original message and has to create a second preimage with the same prefix. Both of these attacks use diamond structures and the expected number of compression function calls required to complete each of them successfully is in $O(\sqrt{n} \cdot 2^{\frac{2n}{3}})$ while on random oracle hash function it is in $O(2^n)$. We also show that it is possible to decrease the before mentioned expected value to $O(2^{\frac{2n-l}{3}})$ if the length of the original message is 2^l and l is sufficiently large. Furthermore, we generalize these attacks to work against concatenated hash functions as well.

1 Introduction

Hash functions are defined to be mappings which take an arbitrary length string over a fixed alphabet (usually assumed to be the binary alphabet $\{0,1\}$) and return a (binary) string of a fixed length. These functions are employed to put up various cryptographic structures that are in turn used to form cryptographic protocols for various purposes such as message authentication, digital signatures and electronic voting. Traditionally there are three security properties required from a cryptographic hash function, *preimage resistance, second preimage resistance* and *collision resistance.*

Most hash functions widely used in practice follow the design principles proposed by Merkle and Damgård [5, 21]. There have been several attacks against these functions, based on the flaws in the underlying compression function [7, 12, 13, 23–26]. In recent years, theoretical study has also found some weaknesses in the iterative structure itself [4, 8–11, 14–19, 22].

One of the most interesting results concerning the iterative structure in a theoretical sense was presented in [10]. The paper introduces the so called *herding attack* which relies on *diamond structures*, a tree construction where several hash values are herded towards one final hash value. Diamond structures proved to be very useful in attack construction. They were employed in [1] and [2] to create herding and second preimage attacks against several iterated hash

D. Gritzalis et al. (Eds.): CANS 2014, LNCS 8813, pp. 98–110, 2014.

function variants also beyond Merkle-Damgård. The results concerning diamond structures have been further studied and improved in [3] and [19].

This paper applies diamond structures to create two new variants of preimage attacks. In the Chosen Initial Value Attack (CIVA) the attacker, after receiving the message, is allowed to choose the initial value of the hash function. In the Chosen Prefix Attack (CPA) the state of affairs is as follows: The attacker A wants to create a second preimage for some message generated by the victim B and A can affect the message slightly by choosing a prefix to it. However, the second preimage the attacker creates has to contain the same prefix. A situation like this could occur for example when A and B wish to form a secret contract and A can choose the time when the contract will be signed, that is public information, but is not allowed to formalize its details freely.

We analyze the the effectiveness of both CIVA and CPA and generalize them to the case where we are either dealing with long messages or attacking against concatenated hash function.

This paper is organized in the following way. In the second section, we give some basic definitions and results that are needed later. In the third section, we introduce necessary earlier results concerning the topic. The fourth section presents the details of CIVA and CPA. In Section 5 we generalize our results to concatenated hash functions. The paper ends with a short conclusion.

2   Basic Concepts and Notation

Some basic definitions concerning hash functions follow.

2.1   Words, Hash Functions and Security Properties

Let $\mathbb{N}_+$ be the set of all positive integers and $\mathbb{N} = \mathbb{N}_+ \cup \{0\}$. An *alphabet* is any finite nonempty set of abstract symbols called *letters*. Given an alphabet A, a *word* (over A) is any finite sequence of symbols in A. Let w be a word over A. Then $w = a_1 a_2 \cdots a_r$ where $r \in \mathbb{N}$ and $a_i \in A$ for $i = 1, 2, \ldots, r$. Here r is the (*symbol*) *length* of w. If $r = 0$, then w is the *empty word*, denoted by ϵ. For each $s \in \mathbb{N}$, denote by A^s the set of all words of length s over A. Furthermore, let A^+ be the set of all nonempty words over A and $A^* = A^+ \cup \{\epsilon\}$. The *concatenation* of two words u and v in A^+ is the word $u||v$ obtained by writing u and v after one another. For any two sets U and V of words, let $U||V = \{u||v \mid u \in U, v \in V\}$.

A *hash function* (of length n, where $n \in \mathbb{N}_+$) is a mapping $H : \{0,1\}^+ \to \{0,1\}^n$. An ideal hash function $H : \{0,1\}^+ \to \{0,1\}^n$ is a (*variable input length*) *random oracle*: for each $x \in \{0,1\}^+$, the value $H(x) \in \{0,1\}^n$ is chosen uniformly at random.

There are three basic security properties of hash functions: *collision resistance*, *preimage resistance* and *second preimage resistance*. In this work our main interest is second preimage that has been historically defined as follows.

Second preimage resistance. Given any $x \in \{0,1\}^+$, it is computationally infeasible to find $x' \in \{0,1\}^+$, $x \neq x'$, such that $H(x) = H(x')$.

2.2 Iterated Hash Functions

The design principles of [21, 5] create a so called *iterated hash function*. A (finite) compression function forms the core of an iterated hash function.

Definition 1. *A compression function (of block size m and length n) is a mapping $f : \{0,1\}^n \times \{0,1\}^m \to \{0,1\}^n$ where $m, n \in \mathbb{N}_+$.*

Let $m, n \in \mathbb{N}_+$, $m > n$, and the compression function $f : \{0,1\}^n \times \{0,1\}^m \to \{0,1\}^n$ be given. The *iterative closure* f^+ of f is a function: $\{0,1\}^n \times (\{0,1\}^m)^+ \to \{0,1\}^n$ defined as follows: Given h in $\{0,1\}^n$ and $x = x_1||x_2||\cdots||x_l$, where $l \in \mathbb{N}_+$, and $x_1, x_2, \ldots, x_l \in \{0,1\}^m$, let $h_i = f(h_{i-1}, x_i)$ for $i = 1, 2, \ldots, l$. Then $f^+(h, x) = h_l$. Note that the assumption $m > n$ is made for the sake of notational simplicity, not because of necessity.

We wish to be able to compute the hash value of any word in $\{0,1\}^+$ and, moreover, make use of f^+ in our hashing process. Since all words in $\{0,1\}^+$ do not have length that is divisible by m, it is necessary to preprocess the word by adding extra bits (*padding*) at the end of the word to attain the suitable symbol (or bit) length. The padding usually includes also the bit length of the original message, so in fact all words are padded. This is known as *Merkle-Damgård strengthening*.

Let us define the *iterated hash function* $H : \{0,1\}^+ \to \{0,1\}^n$ (based on f and with initial value $h_0 \in \{0,1\}^n$) as follows. Let $x \in \{0,1\}^+$ and pad_x be the aforementioned padding of x: pad_x contains the bit length of x and the length of the concatenated word $x||pad_x$ is divisible by m. We then set $H(x) = f^+(h_0, x||pad_x)$.

Usually, the initial value h_0 (often denoted also by IV) is assumed to be a fixed constant, but we will consider a situation where the attacker can choose the initial value from some predetermined set.

From now on, we assume that all the words that are to be hashed have already been appropriately padded; the words are thus in $(\{0,1\}^m)^+$, i.e., their lengths are divisible by m. The elements of $(\{0,1\}^m)^+$ are called *messages*. Let $x = x_1||x_2\cdots||x_l$ where $l \in \mathbb{N}_+$ and $x_i \in \{0,1\}^m$ for $i = 1, 2, \ldots, l$. Then the *length* of the message x, denoted by $|x|$, is l.

2.3 Attack Complexity

In this work we define the (*message*) *complexity* of a given attack algorithm to be the expected number of queries on the compression function f required to complete the attack successfully. This means that the complexity of both a preimage attack and a second preimage attack should be $O(2^n)$ while the complexity of a collision attack should be $O(2^{\frac{n}{2}})$.

2.4 Concatenated Hash Functions

In practice, a natural way to build hash functions with large hash values, is to take hash functions with smaller hash values and concatenate their results (see for example [20]). This means that, given the iterative closures $f_1^+ : \{0,1\}^{n_1} \times (\{0,1\}^m)^+ \to \{0,1\}^{n_1}$ and $f_2^+ : \{0,1\}^{n_2} \times (\{0,1\}^m)^+ \to \{0,1\}^{n_2}$ of the compression functions f_1 and f_2, respectively, one can simply set $C(h_{0,1}, h_{0,2}, x) = f_1^+(h_{0,1}, x) \| f_2^+(h_{0,2}, x)$, where $h_{0,1} \in \{0,1\}^{n_1}$, $h_{0,2} \in \{0,1\}^{n_2}$ and x is a message.

Ideally $C : \{0,1\}^{n_1} \times \{0,1\}^{n_2} \times (\{0,1\}^m)^+ \to \{0,1\}^{n_1+n_2}$ should be random oracle. This, however, is not the case and such structure has severe weaknesses as has been shown before [9, 1]. From the perspective of this work it is important to notice that [9] presents a second preimage attack against concatenated hash function with the complexity $O(2^{\max\{n_1,n_2\}})$ while it should be in $O(2^{n_1+n_2})$.

We shall later create new ways to attack concatenated hash functions.

3 Earlier Work

We will now present earlier results that we will need to create our new attacks.

3.1 Joux's Multicollision Attack

In [9] Joux presents a clever way to find a 2^r-collision for any $r \in \mathbb{N}_+$. The attacker starts from the initial value h_0 and searches two distinct message block x_1, x_1' such that $f(h_0, x_1) = f(h_0, x_1')$ and denotes $h_1 = f(h_0, x_1)$ and $M_1 = \{x_1, x_1'\}$. By the birthday paradox, the expected number of queries is in $O(2^{\frac{n}{2}})$. Then, for each $i = 2, 3, \ldots, r$, the attacker continues by searching message blocks x_i and x_i' such that $x_i \neq x_i'$ and $f(h_{i-1}, x_i) = f(h_{i-1}, x_i')$ and stating $h_i = f(h_{i-1}, x_i)$ and $M_i = \{x_i, x_i'\}$.

After r steps the attacker has created a set $M = M_1 \| M_2 \cdots \| M_r$ such that:

(i) for each $i \in \{1, 2, ..., r\}$, the set M_i consists of two distinct message blocks; and

(ii) $f^+(h_0, x) = f^+(h_0, x')$ for all $x, x' \in M = M_1 M_2 \cdots M_r$.

Due to the birthday paradox, a two colliding message blocks can be found with complexity $O(2^{\frac{n}{2}})$. Thus the expected number of queries on f to create a 2^r-collision is clearly in $O(r \cdot 2^{\frac{n}{2}})$. In certain instances r may depend on n.

3.2 Creating a Diamond Structure

Collision trees or diamond structures were originally presented in [10]. The idea of the diamond structure is to take a large set of different hash values and force these to converge towards a single hash value along equal length paths. The definition of diamond structure that can be found for example in [19] follows.

A *diamond structure* that is based on 2^d hash values, or of breadth 2^d, where $d \in \mathbb{N}_+$, is a both node labeled and edge labeled complete binary tree D satisfying the following conditions.

1. The tree D has 2^d leaves, i.e., the height of the tree is d.
2. The nodes of the tree D are labeled by hash values (strings in the set $\{0,1\}^n$) so that the labels of nodes that are on the same distance from the root of D are pairwise disjoint.
3. The edges of the tree D are labeled by message blocks (strings in the set $\{0,1\}^m$).
4. Let v_1, v_2, and v with labels h_1, h_2, and h, respectively, be any nodes of the tree D such that v_1 and v_2 are children of v. Suppose furthermore that x_1 and x_2 are (message) labels of the edges connecting v_1 to v and v_2 to v, respectively. Then $f(h_1, x_1) = f(h_2, x_2) = h$.

The important thing to notice is that we have 2^d hash values (leaves) h_i and a single final hash value h'. For each leaf there exists a d message blocks long message x_i such that $f^+(h_i, x_i) = h'$. We will skip the details of creating a diamond structure in this work. They can be found for example in [19].

The complexity of creating a diamond structure has been under close examination. In their original article Kelsey and Kohno [10] propose that the complexity of creating a diamond structure would be in $O(2^{\frac{n+d}{2}})$. However a study by Blackburn et al [3] has shown, that creating diamond structure is not that simple and that the assertion concerning complexity in [10] is incorrect. It was proven that the complexity of creating a diamond structure with the same kind of approach used in [10] is $O(\sqrt{d} \cdot 2^{\frac{n+d}{2}})$.

The reasoning of [3] is sound. However later work [19] has shown that it is possible to use a different kind of an algorithm to create a diamond structure with complexity $O(2^{\frac{n+d}{2}})$.

Assume now that we have a Joux's type multicollision set M of size 2^{dn}. In [1] it is shown that it is possible to create a variant of a diamond structure based on M. The variant structure has 2^d hash values (leaves) h_i and for each of these a $n \cdot d$ message blocks long message $x_i \in M$ that satisfy $f^+(h_i, x_i) = h'$, where h' is the final hash value of the structure. In the following we call this variant *multicollision diamond structure*.

3.3   Expandable Messages

With *expandable message*, based on initial value h_0, we mean a set of messages X, such that for any two distinct messages $x, x' \in X$ we have $|x| \neq |x'|$ and $f^+(h_0, x) = f^+(h_0, x')$. Then $f^+(h_0, x)$ is called the *final value* of the expandable message.

The first use of expandable messages against the iterated compression function f^+ was carried out in [6]. The creation method presented in [6] requires a weak compression function in order to work. However, later Kelsey and Schneier showed [11], that one can with complexity $O(k \cdot 2^{\frac{n}{2}})$ create an expandable messages X, such that it is possible to choose any integer s between k and $k + 2^k - 1$ and find a message $x \in X$ that satisfies property $|x| = s$.

4 Second Preimage Attack Variants against MD Structure

4.1 Chosen Initial Value Attack (CIVA)

Consider the iterative closure $f^+ : \{0,1\}^n \times (\{0,1\}^m)^+ \to \{0,1\}^n$ of the compression function f where $m > n$. The attacker receives a message and has to provide a second preimage to it. After receiving the message, the attacker is allowed to choose the initial value of from a subset $I = \{h_1, h_2, \ldots, h_{2^d}\}$ of $\{0,1\}^n$ of cardinality 2^d where $d \in \mathbb{N}_+$ is smaller than n. For the sake of simplicity we will assume that the length of the message is at least $d + 1$, i.e., the message consists of at least $d + 1$ message blocks. This is not a necessary requirement by itself, but makes the notation easier to follow. The following is assumed.

- The attacker is provided with a message y, with the length of at least $d + 1$ message blocks.
- The attacker picks up an initial value $h_0 \in I$ and message $x \neq y$ such that $f^+(h_0, x) = f^+(h_0, y)$.

The question arises: How hard it should be for the attacker to complete such an attack?

Let $H : \{0,1\}^n \times (\{0,1\}^m)^+ \to \{0,1\}^n$ be a hash function, where, given $h \in \{0,1\}^n$ and $x \in (\{0,1\}^m)^+$, the value $H(h, x)$ in $\{0,1\}^n$ is chosen uniformly at random. Surely the expected number of hash function calls required to carry out the second step when f^+ is replaced with H successfully is $O(2^n)$. It seems unlikely that the attacker can gain any advantage whatsoever from the ability to choose the initial value of the hash function, so the only way to attack is through exhaustive search. The probability that $H(h_0, x) = H(h_0, y)$ for a random message x is 2^{-n}, so the expected number of messages the attacker has to try before finding the right one is $O(2^n)$.

Let us now return to the use of f^+ and assume that the attacker receives a message $y = y_1||y_2|| \cdots ||y_k$ where y_i is a message block for all $i \in \{1, 2, \cdots, k\}$ and $k > d$. Consider the following procedure. The attacker

1. creates a diamond structure based on the initial values $h_1, h_2, \ldots, h_{2^d}$ of I; let h' be the final hash value of the diamond structure. The attacker denotes the final hash value of the diamond structure with h';
2. searches a message block x' such that
$f(h', x') = f^+(h_i, y_1||y_2|| \cdots ||y_{d+1})$ where $i \in \{1, 2, \cdots, 2^d\}$; and
3. chooses h_i to be the initial value of the hash function and offers the string $x = z_1||x'||y_{d+2}||y_{d+3}|| \cdots ||y_k$, where z_1 is message that takes h_i to h', as the second preimage for y.

Clearly the lengths of x and y in message blocks are equal and

$$f^+(h_i, y) = f^+(h_i, y_1||y_2|| \cdots ||y_k) = f^+(h', x'||y_{d+2}||y_{d+3}|| \cdots ||y_k)$$

$$= f^+(h_i, z_1||x'||y_{d+2}||y_{d+3}|| \cdots ||y_k) = f^+(h_i, x)$$

so x really is a second preimage for y.

The complexity of the attack depends on d. The complexity of creating a diamond structure is in $O(2^{\frac{n+d}{2}})$ (see [19]). The attacker can optimize the complexity of finding suitable x' in step 2 to be in $O(\sqrt{d} \cdot 2^{n-d})$. It follows that the total complexity of the attack is in $O(2^{\frac{n+d}{2}} + \sqrt{d} \cdot 2^{n-d})$. If we can choose $d = \frac{n}{3}$ we can minimize this complexity to $O(\sqrt{n} \cdot 2^{\frac{2n}{3}})$.

Remark 1. The important property that allows the attacker to gain advantage from the Chosen Initial Value Attack is the adversary's ability to influence, on some level, the circumstances where the iterated hash function is applied. This influence does not necessarily have to include the initial value of the hash function and soon we will describe a variant of the Chosen Prefix Attack that is based on adversary's ability to impact the current situation in another way.

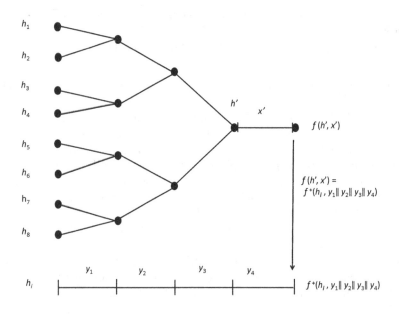

Fig. 1. Example of the Chosen Initial Value Attack when $d = 3$

4.2   CIVA against a Long Message

It is possible to combine second preimage attack against long messages presented in [11] and the Chosen Initial Value Attack presented above. Assume that $y = y_1||y_2||\cdots||y_{2^l}$, where y_i is a message block for all $i \in \{1, 2, \cdots, 2^l\}$ and l is fairly large, while still $l \leq \frac{n}{2}$. Instead of the standard version of the CIVA, the attacker

1. creates a diamond structure based on initial values
   $h_1, h_2, \cdots, h_{2^d}$ and denotes by h' the final value of the diamond structure;
2. creates an expandable message based on h', with maximum length 2^l and
   miminum length $l + 1$ and denotes by h'' the final hash value of the expandable message.
3. searches for a message block x'' such that
   $f(h'', x'') = f^+(h_i, y_1 || y_2 || \cdots || y_j)$ where $i \in \{1, 2, \cdots, 2^d\}$ and $j \in \{d + l + 2, d + l + 3, \cdots, 2^l\}$; and
4. chooses h_i to be the initial value of the hash function and offers $x = z_1 || z_2 || x'' || y_{j+1} || y_{j+2} || \cdots || y_{2^l}$, where z_1 is message that takes h_i to h' and z_2 is the expandable message chosen so that $|x| = 2^l$, as the second preimage for y.

Clearly x has the same length as y and $f^+(h_i, x) = f^+(h_i, y)$ so x is a second preimage for y.

The complexity of creating a diamond structure is in $O(2^{\frac{n+d}{2}})$ as before, while the complexity of creating an expandable message is in $O(l \cdot 2^{\frac{n}{2}})$. The attacker can optimize the complexity of finding suitable x'' and h_i in step 3 to be in $O(2^{d+l} + 2^{n-(d+l)})$.

Once again we can optimize this by setting $d = \frac{n-2l}{3}$. The total complexity of the attack is thus in $O(2^{\frac{2n-l}{3}})$, while it should be 2^n.

Remark 2. Thus far the lowest complexity for the second preimage attack on iterated hash function has been presented in [11]. The attack offers the complexity $O(2^{n-l})$ when the length of the original message in message blocks is 2^l and l is sufficiently large.

4.3   Chosen Prefix Attack   (CPA)

We can describe the situation in the Chosen Prefix Attack as the following game.

- The attacker is challenged with an initial value $h_0 \in \{0, 1\}^n$ and a suffix message y such that the length of y is at least $d + 1$. Here d is a positive integer fixed in advance.
- The attacker creates a prefix p and a suffix x such that $x \neq y$ and $f^+(h_0, p||x) = f^+(h_0, p||y)$.

Above we assumed that the length of the message is at least $d+1$ message blocks to simplify the notation. Again, this is not a necessary requirement and is simply a matter of convenience.

If in the construction above the mapping f^+ is replaced by a random oracle hash function H, then the only way to attack is to make random queries on H. This means that the best possible strategy for the attacker is simply to fix the prefix p, calculate $H(h_0, p||y)$ and then use a random search to find such $x \neq y$ that $H(h_0, p||x) = H(h_0, p||y)$. The complexity of this kind of an attack is certainly $O(2^n)$.

However, against the iterative structure f^+, the adversary can construct the attack almost in the same manner as in CIVA. Assume now that the attacker receives an initial value h_0 and a suffix $y = y_1||y_2||\cdots||y_k$ where y_i is a message block for all $i \in \{1, 2, \cdots, k\}$ and $k > d$. Denote $k_1 = d + 1$. Now the attacker

1. chooses 2^d random message blocks $p_1, p_2, \cdots, p_{2^d}$;
2. creates a diamond structure based on hash values $f^+(h_0, p_1), f^+(h_0, p_2), \ldots,$ $f^+(h_0, p_{2^d})$ and denotes the final value of diamond structure by h';
3. searches a message block x' such that $f(h', x') = f^+(h_0, p_i||y_1||y_2||\cdots||y_{k_1})$ where $i \in \{1, 2, \cdots, 2^d\}$; and
4. chooses p_i to be the prefix of the second preimage and offers $p_i||z||x'||y_{k_1+1}$ $||y_{k_2+2}||\cdots||y_k$, where z is message that takes $f^+(h_0, p_i)$ to h', as the second preimage for $p_i||y$ i.e. $x = z||x'||y_{k_1+1}||y_{k_2+2}||\cdots||y_k$.

Creating a diamond structure possesses the complexity $O(2^{\frac{n+d}{2}})$. The complexity of finding a suitable x' is $O(\sqrt{d}\cdot 2^{n-d})$. This means that the if the attacker chooses $d = \frac{n}{3}$ the total complexity of the attack is in $O(\sqrt{n}\cdot 2^{\frac{2n}{3}})$.

It is also easy to show that the attacker can make use of the length of the original message in the same manner as in the Chosen Initial Value Attack, i.e., by creating an expandable message after the diamond structure and then searching for a collision with any suitable chaining value in original message. If the original message has the length 2^l the attacker can reduce the complexity to $O(2^{\frac{2n-l}{3}})$, when we assume l to be large enough.

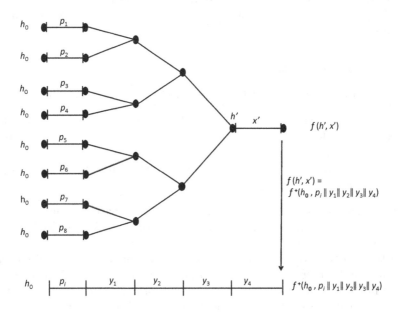

Fig. 2. Example of the Chosen Prefix Attack when $d = 3$

5   Second Preimage Attacks on Concatenated Hash Functions

We will now generalize our attacks to concern also concatenated hash functions.

Assume in the following that we are provided with the iterative closures f_1^+ : $\{0,1\}^{n_1} \times (\{0,1\}^m)^+ \to \{0,1\}^{n_1}$ and f_2^+ : $\{0,1\}^{n_2} \times (\{0,1\}^m)^+ \to \{0,1\}^{n_2}$ of the compression functions $f_1 : \{0,1\}^{n_1} \times \{0,1\}^m \to \{0,1\}^{n_1}$ and $f_2 : \{0,1\}^{n_2} \times \{0,1\}^m \to \{0,1\}^{n_1}$ where $n_1 \le n_2 < m$. Assume further that the concatenated hash function $C : \{0,1\}^{n_1} \times \{0,1\}^{n_2} \times (\{0,1\}^m)^+ \to \{0,1\}^{n_1+n_2}$ is defined by setting $C(h_{0,1}, h_{0,2}, x) = f_1^+(h_{0,1}, x) \| f_2^+(h_{0,2}, x)$.

5.1   CIVA on a Concatenated Hash Function

Assume that the attacker receives a message $y = y_1 \| y_2 \| \cdots \| y_k$, where y_i is a message block for all $i \in \{1, 2, \cdots, k\}$ and k at least $d + (d+1)n_2 + 1$. Denote $k_1 = d + (d+1)n_2 + 1$. The adversary now has to create a second preimage for y while she/he can choose the initial values for both f_1^+ and f_2^+. The attacker

1. chooses a set I_1 with 2^d possible initial values for f_1^+, creates a diamond structure based on these initial values, and denotes the final value of diamond structure by h_1;
2. creates a large Joux type multicollision of cardinality $2^{d\,n_2}$ on f_1^+ with initial value h_1, names the common hash value of the collision messages to h_2, and denotes the set of multicollision messages with M_1; the attacker creates a Joux type multicollision of cardinality 2^{n_2} on f_1^+ with initial value h_2, denotes this collision set with M_2, and the common hash value of M_2 with h_3;
3. creates a message block x' such that $f_1^+(h_3, x') = f_1^+(h_{0,1}', y_1 \| y_2 \| \cdots y_{k_1})$ for some $h_{0,1}' \in I_1$, and denotes the path from $h_{0,1}'$ to h_1 in the diamond structure by z_1;
4. chooses a set I_2 with 2^d possible initial values for f_2^+, creates a multicollision diamond structure based on hash values $\{f_2^+(h, z_1) | h \in I_2\}$ by using the multicollision set M_1, and denotes the final hash value of this diamond structure by h_4; and
5. searches for a message $z_3 \in M_2$ for which $f_2^+(h_4, z_3 \| x') = f_2^+(h_{0,2}', y_1 \| y_2 \| \cdots y_{k_1})$ where $h_{0,2}' \in I_2$, and denotes by z_2 the path from $f_2^+(h_{0,2}', z_1)$ to h_4 (note that $z_2 \in M_1$); and
6. chooses $h_{0,1}'$ and $h_{0,2}'$ to be the initial values of f_1^+ and f_2^+ and offers $z_1 \| z_2 \| z_3 \| x' \| y_{k_1+1} \| y_{k_1+2} \| \cdots \| y_k$ as the second preimage for y.

The complexity of creating diamond structures in steps 1 and 4 are $O(2^{\frac{n_1+d}{2}})$ and $O(2^{\frac{n_2+d}{2}})$, respectively. The complexity of creating multicollision sets in step 2 is in $O(dn_2 \cdot 2^{\frac{n_1}{2}})$ while the complexity of finding suitable x', z_3, $h_{0,1}'$ and $h_{0,2}'$ in steps 3 and 5 can be optimized to be in $O(\sqrt{d\,n_2} \cdot 2^{n_2-d})$. If the attacker is allowed to choose $d = \frac{n_2}{3}$, i.e., the length of the original message is about $\frac{(n_2)^2}{3}$, the total complexity of the attack is $O(n_2 \cdot 2^{\frac{2n_2}{3}})$. If the original message is shorter then the complexity will be greater.

5.2   CPA on a Concatenated Hash Function

Assume now that initial values for f_1^+ and f_2^+ are fixed to be $h_{0,1}$ and $h_{0,2}$, respectively. Assume furthermore that s and d are positive integers and $s, d < \frac{n_2}{2}$. The attacker receives a suffix y and now has to find a prefix p and another suffix $x \neq y$ such that $C(h_{0,1}, h_{0,2}, p||x) = C(h_{0,1}, h_{0,2}, p||y)$. Assume that $y = y_1||y_2|| \cdots ||y_k$, where $y_1, y_2, \ldots, y_k$ are message blocks and k at least $d + n_2(s + 1) + 1$. Denote $k_1 = d + n_2(s + 1) + 1$. The attacker

1. chooses 2^d random message blocks $x_1, x_2, \cdots, x_{2^d}$ and computes
   $h_{i,1} = f_1(h_{0,1}, x_i)$ for $i = 1, 2, \ldots, 2^d$;
2. creates 2^d Joux type multicollision sets $M_1, M_2, \ldots, M_{2^d}$ on f_1^+ each of cardinality 2^s such that the initial value for M_i is $h_{i,1}$, and denotes the common collision value of M_i by $h'_{i,1}$ $(i = 1, 2, \ldots, 2^d)$;
3. creates a diamond structure based on hash values $\{h'_{i,1} | i = 1, 2, \cdots, 2^d\}$ and denotes the final hash value of the diamond structure by h_1;
4. creates a Joux type multicollision set M'_1 of cardinality $2^{n_2 s}$ on f_1^+ based on the initial value h_1 and denotes the common collision hash value of the set M'_1 with h_2;
5. creates a Joux type multicollision set M'_2 of cardinality 2^{n_2} on f_1^+ based on initial value h_2 and denotes the common collision hash value of the set M'_2 with h_3;
6. searches a message block x' and an integer $j \in \{1, 2, \cdots, 2^d\}$ such that $f_1(h_3, x') = f_1^+(h'_{j,1}, y_1||y_2|| \cdots ||y_{k_1})$ and denotes the path in diamond structure from $h'_{j,1}$ to h_1 with z_1;
7. makes use of messages in the set M'_1 to createa a multicollision diamond structure on f_2^+ based on hash values $\{f_2^+(h_{0,2}, x_j||p'||z_1)|p' \in M_j\}$, and denotes the final hash value of the diamond structure by h_4;
8. searches a message $z_3 \in M'_2$ such that $f_2^+(h_4, z_3||x') = f_2^+(h_{0,2}, x_j||p_j||y_1||y_2|| \cdots ||y_{k_1})$ where $p_j \in M_j$ and denotes by z_2 the path from $f_2^+(h_{0,2}, x_j||p_j||z_1)$ to h_4;
9. offers the message $x_j||p_j$ as a common prefix and the message $x_j||p_j||z_1||z_2||z_3||x'||y_{k_1+1}||y_{k_1+2}|| \cdots ||y_k$ as a second preimage for $x_j||p_j||y$.

The complexity of the step 2 is $O(s \cdot 2^{d + \frac{n_1}{2}})$, while the complexity of the step 3 is in $O(2^{\frac{n_1 + d}{2}})$. The total complexity of steps 4 and 5 is in $O(n_2 \cdot s \cdot 2^{\frac{n_1}{2}})$ and the complexity of finding suitable x' and j in the step 6 can be optimized to be in $O(\sqrt{(s + k_1)} \cdot 2^{n_1 - d})$. The complexity of the step 7 is in $O(2^{\frac{n_2 + d}{2}})$ and finally the complexity of the step 8 is in $O(\sqrt{s + k_1} \cdot 2^{n_2 - s})$.

The attacker can choose for example $s = \frac{n_2}{3}, d = \frac{n_1}{4}$. This results to the total complexity $O(n_2 \cdot 2^{\frac{3n_1}{4}} + 2^{\frac{2n_2}{3}})$. The exact efficiency of this attack depends on the difference between n_1 and n_2. Certainly, however, in any case the complexity of the attack is $O(n_2 \cdot 2^{\frac{3n_2}{4}})$.

This is clearly significantly better than the complexity $O(2^{n_2})$ offered by Joux's attack against concatenated hash functions (see [9]). If the concatenated structure would work as a random oracle hash function the complexity should be in $O(2^{n_1 + n_2})$.

6   Conclusion

In this article, we have considered a case where the attacker is able to influence the situation where the second preimage attack takes place by either choosing the initial value of the iterated hash function used or by choosing a common prefix that the original message and the second preimage must include. We have shown that in these situations by using diamond structures the attacker is able to reduce the expected number of compression function calls required to $O(\sqrt{n} \cdot 2^{\frac{2n}{3}})$, while it should be $O(2^n)$. In addition we have shown that against long messages with 2^l message blocks these attacks work even better by reducing the complexity to $O(2^{\frac{2n-l}{3}})$.

We have also generalized these attacks to work against concatenated hash functions. The Chosen Initial Value Attack possesses the complexity $O(n_2 \cdot 2^{\frac{2n_2}{3}})$ while the complexity of the Chosen Prefix Attack is $O(n_2 \cdot 2^{\frac{3n_2}{4}})$. The best known second preimage attack up to now has been of the complexity $O(2^{n_2})$ [9].

The basic idea of the presented attacks lie in the adversary's ability to influence in some manner the circumstances where the iterated hash function is applied and, by making use of the diamond structure, to gain advantage in the game; this advantage would be impossible to achieve against a random oracle hash function. A robust research is needed to find the actual limits of these kind of attacks.

References

1. Andreeva, E., Bouillaguet, C., Dunkelman, O., Kelsey, J.: Herding, second preimage and Trojan message attacks beyond Merkle-Damgård. In: Jacobson Jr., M.J., Rijmen, V., Safavi-Naini, R. (eds.) SAC 2009. LNCS, vol. 5867, pp. 393–414. Springer, Heidelberg (2009)
2. Andreeva, E., Bouillaguet, C., Fouque, P.-A., Hoch, J.J., Kelsey, J., Shamir, A., Zimmer, S.: Second preimage attacks on dithered hash functions. In: Smart, N.P. (ed.) EUROCRYPT 2008. LNCS, vol. 4965, pp. 270–288. Springer, Heidelberg (2008)
3. Blackburn, S., Stinson, D., Upadhyay, J.: On the complexity of the herding attack and some related attacks on hash functions. Designs, Codes and Cryptography 64(1-2), 171–193 (2012)
4. Coron, J.-S., Dodis, Y., Malinaud, C., Puniya, P.: Merkle-Damgård revisited: How to construct a hash function. In: Shoup, V. (ed.) CRYPTO 2005. LNCS, vol. 3621, pp. 430–448. Springer, Heidelberg (2005)
5. Damgård, I.B.: A design principle for hash functions. In: Brassard, G. (ed.) CRYPTO 1989. LNCS, vol. 435, pp. 416–427. Springer, Heidelberg (1990)
6. Dean, R.: Formal aspects of mobile code security. PhD thesis, Princeton University (1999)
7. Dobbertin, H.: Cryptanalysis of MD4. Journal of Cryptology 11(4), 253–271 (1998)
8. Hoch, J.J., Shamir, A.: Breaking the ICE - finding multicollisions in iterated concatenated and expanded (ICE) hash functions. In: Robshaw, M. (ed.) FSE 2006. LNCS, vol. 4047, pp. 179–194. Springer, Heidelberg (2006)
9. Joux, A.: Multicollisions in iterated hash functions. Application to cascaded constructions. In: Franklin, M. (ed.) CRYPTO 2004. LNCS, vol. 3152, pp. 306–316. Springer, Heidelberg (2004)

10. Kelsey, J., Kohno, T.: Herding hash functions and Nostradamus attack. In: Vaudenay, S. (ed.) EUROCRYPT 2006. LNCS, vol. 4004, pp. 183–200. Springer, Heidelberg (2006)
11. Kelsey, J., Schneier, B.: Second preimage on n-bit hash functions for much less than 2^n work. In: Cramer, R. (ed.) EUROCRYPT 2005. LNCS, vol. 3494, pp. 474–490. Springer, Heidelberg (2005)
12. Klima, V.: Finding MD5 collisions on a notebook PC using multi-message modifications, Cryptology ePrint Archive, Report 2005/102 (2005), http://eprint.iacr.org/2005/102
13. Klima, V.: Huge multicollisions and multipreimages of hash functions BLENDER-n, Cryptology ePrint Archive, Report 2009/006 (2009), http://eprint.iacr.org/2009/006
14. Kortelainen, J., Halunen, K., Kortelainen, T.: Multicollision attacks and generalized iterated hash functions. J. Math. Cryptol. 4, 239–270 (2010)
15. Kortelainen, J., Kortelainen, T., Vesanen, A.: Unavoidable regularities in long words with bounded number of symbol occurrences. In: Fu, B., Du, D.-Z. (eds.) COCOON 2011. LNCS, vol. 6842, pp. 519–530. Springer, Heidelberg (2011)
16. Kortelainen, J., Kortelainen, T., Vesanen, A.: Unavoidable regularities in long words with bounded number of symbol occurrences. J. Comp. Optim. 26, 670–686 (2013)
17. Kortelainen, T., Kortelainen, J., Halunen, K.: Variants of multicollision attacks on iterated hash functions. In: Lai, X., Yung, M., Lin, D. (eds.) Inscrypt 2010. LNCS, vol. 6584, pp. 139–154. Springer, Heidelberg (2011)
18. Kortelainen, T., Vesanen, A., Kortelainen, J.: Generalized iterated hash functions revisited: New complexity bounds for multicollision attacks. In: Galbraith, S., Nandi, M. (eds.) INDOCRYPT 2012. LNCS, vol. 7668, pp. 172–190. Springer, Heidelberg (2012)
19. Kortelainen, T., Kortelainen, J.: On diamond structures and Trojan message attacks. In: Sako, K., Sarkar, P. (eds.) ASIACRYPT 2013, Part II. LNCS, vol. 8270, pp. 524–539. Springer, Heidelberg (2013)
20. Menezes, A., van Oorschot, P., Vanstone, S. (eds.): Handbook of Applied Cryptography, pp. 321–376. CRC Press (1996)
21. Merkle, R.C.: One way hash functions and DES. In: Brassard, G. (ed.) CRYPTO 1989. LNCS, vol. 435, pp. 428–446. Springer, Heidelberg (1990)
22. Nandi, M., Stinson, D.: Multicollision attacks on some generalized sequential hash functions. IEEE Trans. Inform. Theory 53, 759–767 (2007)
23. Stevens, M.: Fast collision attack on MD5, Cryptology ePrint Archive, Report 2006/104 (2006), http://eprint.iacr.org/2006/104
24. Wang, X., Yu, H.: How to break MD5 and other hash functions. In: Cramer, R. (ed.) EUROCRYPT 2005. LNCS, vol. 3494, pp. 19–35. Springer, Heidelberg (2005)
25. Wang, X., Yin, Y.L., Yu, H.: Finding collisions in the full SHA-1. In: Shoup, V. (ed.) CRYPTO 2005. LNCS, vol. 3621, pp. 17–36. Springer, Heidelberg (2005)
26. Yu, H., Wang, X.: Multi-collision attack on the compression functions of MD4 and 3-pass HAVAL. In: Nam, K.-H., Rhee, G. (eds.) ICISC 2007. LNCS, vol. 4817, pp. 206–226. Springer, Heidelberg (2007)

Negotiating DNSSEC Algorithms
over Legacy Proxies

Amir Herzberg[1,2] and Haya Shulman[2]

[1] Computer Science Department,
Bar Ilan University, Ramat Gan, Israel
[2] Fachbereich Informatik,
Technische Universität Darmstadt, Darmstadt, Germany
{amir.herzberg,haya.shulman}@gmail.com

Abstract. To ensure best security and efficiency, cryptographic protocols should allow parties to negotiate the use of the 'best' cryptographic algorithms supported by the different parties; this is usually referred to as *cipher-suite negotiation*, and considered an essential feature of such protocols, e.g., TLS and IPsec. However, such negotiation is absent from protocols designed for *distribution* of cryptographically-signed objects, such as DNSSEC. One reason may be the challenges of securing the choice of the 'best' algorithm, especially in the presence of intermediate 'proxies' (crucial for performance), and in particular, providing solutions, compatible with the existing legacy servers and proxies; another reason may be a lack of understanding of the security and performance damages due to lack of negotiation.

We show that most DNSSEC signed domains, support only RSA 1024-bit signatures, which are considered insecure, and are also larger than alternatives; the likely reason is lack of negotiation mechanisms. We present a *DNSSEC-negotiation mechanism*, allowing name-servers to send responses containing only the keys and signatures required by the requesting resolver. Our design is compatible with intermediary proxies, and even with legacy proxies, that do not support our negotiation mechanism. We show that our design enables incremental deployment and will have negligible performance impact on overhead of DNSSEC as currently deployed, and significant improved performance to DNSSEC if more domains support multiple algorithms; we also show significant security benefits from the use of our design, under realistic, rational adoption model. Ideas of our design apply to other systems requiring secure and efficient distribution of signed data, such as wireless sensor networks (WSNs).

1 Introduction

A *cipher-suite* is an ordered set of (one or more) cryptographic algorithms, each implementing a corresponding function among the functions used by a cryptographic protocol. For example, the RSA_WITH_RC4_128_MD5 cipher suite uses RSA for key exchange, RC4 with a 128-bit key for bulk encryption, and MD5 for message authentication. *Cipher-suite negotiation* refers to the process of selecting

D. Gritzalis et al. (Eds.): CANS 2014, LNCS 8813, pp. 111–126, 2014.

the cipher-suite to be used in a protocol between two (or more) parties, among multiple cipher-suites supported by each of the participants. Many standard cryptographic protocols, e.g., IKE, SSH, SSL and TLS, [RFC2409, RFC4253, RFC6101, RFC5246] use cipher-suite negotiation to ensure that the parties select the 'best' cipher-suite among those they jointly support, in order to avoid broken algorithms and to facilitate migration to better (more secure, more efficient) algorithms.

Currently, DNSSEC is an exception: it allows the use of multiple signature algorithms and hash functions, e.g., RSA and elliptic curves (see [7] for a complete list of cryptographic algorithms). However, no mechanism allows name servers to identify the best set of algorithms, keys and signatures to send in response to a particular request, i.e., for cipher-suite negotiation. As a result, during a DNS transaction between a resolver and a name server, *all* the keys and signatures, supported by the target zone, are sent to the resolver, even if some of those algorithms are unsupported or unvalidated by the resolver.

We collected responses' sizes from Top Level Domains (TLDs) and Alexa-top-million domains, [1]; our measurements are plotted in Figure 1. The measurements show that the overhead of signed DNS responses is significant in comparison to plain DNS responses. For instance, non-existent domain (NXD) is a very common response, which often occurs due to a typo in a DNS query: the size of NXD responses without DNSSEC is less than 400 bytes, while with DNSSEC, 70% of the responses exceed 1000 bytes and 10% are even larger than the link's Maximal Transmission Unit (MTU) (which also holds for more than 30% of DNSKEY responses). Signed responses for ANY query type can reach even 5000 bytes and more, while plain ANY type responses are less than 1000 bytes.

Large DNSSEC signed responses inflict significant overhead on the network and on the end points to the DNS transation, and often result in failures; we describe the problems in Section 3. We believe that the problems with large responses, and the lack of cipher-suite negotiation mechanism, motivate administrators to use only a limited number of cipher-suites. In particular, without cipher-suite negotiation mechanism administrators are likely to avoid algorithms with larger

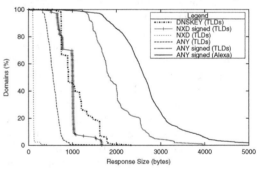

Fig. 1. Length of responses for signed and non-signed Alexa and TLDs, for ANY, DNSKEY and A resource records; A records were sent for random subdomains of tested domains, and resulted in NXD responses.

keys/signatures, e.g., 2048 or 4096 bit RSA; these may offer better security, but surely will increase response length significantly and as a result also exacerbate the interoperability problems and exposure to attacks.

Paradoxically, for a different motivation, administrators are also likely to avoid offering alternative algorithms which may provide good security even with shorter keys/signatures, e.g., elliptic curves. Without cipher-suite negotiation, there is no motivation to offer such shorter alternatives, since when sent in addition to the existing keys/signatures, e.g., 1024-bit RSA (which is mandatory to support), the resulting length of the response is even *larger*.

With the growing awareness of powerful, nation-state adversaries who may be able to crack such key length, we find it alarming that 1024-bit RSA implementations are still dominant. Furthermore, 1024-bit RSA is entrenched, by the lack of cipher-suite negotiation as well as by being mandated by NIST as well as by IETF standards [RFC4033-4035], as well as by being the default choice in key generation procedure of DNSSEC implementations.

Indeed, as our measurements on top-million Alexa, [1], and TLD domains, in Figure 3 show, current adoption of DNSSEC algorithms by signed domains seems to support our conclusions: the 1024-bit RSA algorithm, already considered not-sufficiently-secure, is, by far, the most popular (and mandatory), while the elliptic curve (EC) variant, in spite of its shorter keys and signatures and fast computation, and although it was standardised [RFC6605], is still not deployed. For example, to provide equivalent security to 1024-bit RSA, an ECC scheme only needs 160 bits on various parameters, such as 160-bit finite field operations and 160-bit key size. Other signature algorithms which may have advantages (esp. over RSA), do not even have the (negligible!) penetration of EC signatures.

This situation further demotivates resolvers to support elliptic curve, or other non-RSA algorithms; and, surely, zones cannot sign using *only* elliptic curve signatures, since that is likely to be incompatible with most resolvers. As we show in Section 4.6, this results in a 'vicious cycle' which essentially prevents adoption of new algorithms, and hence in significant security exposure - as well as in significant performance penalty, once security sufficiently deteriorates to force adoption of new algorithms.

Notice that similar need for cipher-suite negotiation exists in other systems, such as Wireless Sensor Networks (WSNs), where efficient authentication and short keys and signatures are critical for functionality and availability. In WSNs different public key ciphers are not widely adopted due to resource constraints on sensor platforms, and limited battery power (although some proposals for short signatures and keys using Elliptic Curves were proposed, e.g., [5,10,9]). In particular, to avoid overloading the network with multiple keys and signatures and to reduce signatures validation complexity, implementors often prefer to support weakest cipher(s) that most clients support, and not to send keys and signatures that corresponds to a number of cryptographic options.

We conclude that cipher-suite negotiation for DNSSEC is essential for security, interoperability and efficiency of DNS and DNSSEC. Furthermore, it may allow end-to-end cryptographic protection of DNS, in particular, in mobile devices.

We present a *cipher-suite negotiation mechanism for DNSSEC*, allowing nameservers to send responses containing only the keys and signatures required by the requesting resolver. Our design supports seamlessly intermediate resolvers (proxies), without even requiring adoption by the proxies. Proxies are widely used by DNS servers. Prior work showed that proxies are common among the recursive resolvers, [12,6]. We also find that proxies are common on the name servers side: (at least) 38% of top 50,000 Alexa domains and 3.73% of TLDs are configured in the following way: a recursive resolver is registered as an authoritative name server (in the parent domain and in the zone file of the child domain), and it receives DNS requests from the clients to the target domain (for which it is authoritative). The resolver then forwards the requests to the name server hosting the zone file for the target domain. Upon responses from the name server, the resolver caches them and subsequently returns them to the requesting client.

Proxies pose a well-known challenge to cipher-suite negotiation. Essentially, cipher-suite negotiation requires proxies to provide responses which depend on the preferences of each requesting client, contrary to the basic design of the proxies, which utilise caches. Our design overcomes these obstacles, without requiring any change or adoption by the proxies.

Although our work is focused on DNS and DNSSEC, the ideas can be benefit WSNs and other systems.

Cipher-suite negotiation for DNSSEC cannot use the design principles of existing standardised cipher-suite negotiation mechanisms, e.g., IKE and TLS. These mechanisms are *interactive*, i.e., operate in two rounds. However, such a two-round, interactive mechanism, would add too much overhead to a DNS transaction and is not suitable for DNS, which is a pure request-response protocol. In contrast, our proposed secure cipher-suite negotiation protocol is *non-interactive*; it only adds few, short fields, to the messages exchanged during a DNS transaction. This is important, since adding another round would cause significant extra delay, as well as make deployment much harder.

The cipher-suite negotiation mechanism for DNSSEC would alleviate deployment obstacles, and would speed up adoption of DNSSEC both by resolvers and zones. We also review obstacles to DNSSEC adoption and report on our measurements study of factors impeding DNSSEC adoption.

Organisation

In Section 2, we review background on DNS and DNSSEC and in Section 3 we discuss deployment status of DNSSEC and review obstacles towards wide adoption thereof. We provide a design of cipher-suite negotiation for DNSSEC in Section 4. In Section 4.6 we investigate the performance impact of our design, on current and projected adoption rates of different signing algorithms, and the resulting impact on security. Finally we conclude this work in Section 5.

2   Overview: DNS and DNSSEC

The domain name system (DNS), [RFC1034, RFC1035], is a distributed data base of Internet mappings (also called *resource records (RRs)*), from *domain names* to different values. The most popular and widely used mappings, [4], are for IP addresses, represented by A type RRs, that map a domain name to its IPv4 address, and name servers, represented by NS type RRs, that map a name server to domain name; see [RFC1035] for a list of standard DNS mappings.

The client side of the DNS infrastructure is composed of resolvers, which lookup records in zones by sending DNS requests to corresponding name servers. The resolvers communicate to the name servers using a simple request-response protocol (typically over UDP); for instance, (abstracting out subtleties) to translate www.foo.bar resolvers locate the name server ns.foo.bar, authoritative for foo.bar, and obtain the IP address of the machine hosting the web server of the website www.foo.bar, see Figure 2. Resolvers store DNS records, returned in responses, in their caches for the duration indicated in the Time To Live (TTL) field of each record set.

The resource records in DNS correspond to the different services run by the organisations and networks, e.g., hosts, servers, network blocks.

The zones are structured hierarchically, with the root zone at the first level, Top Level Domains (TLDs) at the second level, and millions of Second Level Domains (SLDs) at the third level. The IP addresses of the 13 root servers are provided via the *hints* file, or compiled into DNS resolvers software and when a resolver's cache is empty, every resolution process starts at the root. According to the query in the DNS request, the root name server redirects the resolver, via a

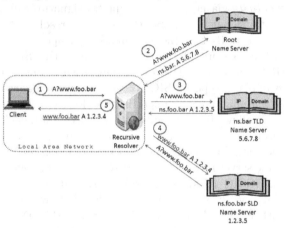

Fig. 2. DNS resolution process for www.foo.bar and the involved DNS servers.

referral response type, to a corresponding TLD, under which the requested resource is located. There are a number of TLDs types, most notably: *country code TLD* (ccTLD), which domains are (typically) assigned to countries, e.g., us, il, de, and *generic TLD* (gTLD), whose domains are used by organisations, e.g., com, org, and also US government and military, e.g., gov, mil. Domains in SLDs can also be used to further delegate subdomains to other entities, or can be directly managed by the organisations, e.g., as in the case of ibm.com, google.com.

A DNS *domain* is divided into zones, and includes all the nodes of the subtree rooted at the zone. A DNS *zone* constitutes a portion of a domain name space. A zone can be divided into subdomains, with its own DNS name servers. For instance, when querying the root zone for foo.bar., the resolver will be redirected to bar. domain, via a referral to the authoritative servers for bar. zone. When querying the name servers of bar., the resolver receives another referral for foo.bar. zone. Notice that bar. zone does not include subdomains, e.g., like foo.bar., but those are delegated from bar to their name servers.

Domains and their mappings are also administered hierarchically; the mappings of each domain foo.bar are provided by a *name server*, managed by the owner of the domain.

DNS Security (DNSSEC). When no protection is employed, DNS requests and responses can be inspected and altered by a MitM attacker. For example, a malicious wireless client can tap the communication of other clients and can respond to their DNS requests with maliciously crafted DNS responses, containing a spoofed IP address, e.g., redirecting the clients to a phishing site. Domain Name System Security Extensions (DNSSEC) standard [RFC4033-RFC4035] was designed to prevent cache poisoning, by providing *data integrity* and *origin authenticity* via cryptographic digital signatures over DNS resource records. The digital signatures enable the receiving resolver, that supports DNSSEC validation, to verify that the data in a DNS response is the same as the data published in the zone file of the target domain. DNSSEC defines new resource records (RRs) to store signatures and keys used to authenticate the DNS responses. For example, a type RRSIG record contains a signature authenticating an RR-set, i.e., all mappings of a specific type for a certain domain name.

To allow clients to authenticate DNS data, each zone generates a signing and verification key pair, (sk, vk). The signing key sk is used to sign the zone data, and should be secret and kept offline. Upon queries for records in a domain, the name server returns the requested RRs, along with the corresponding signatures (in RRSIG RRs). The resolvers should also obtain the zone's public verification key vk, stored in a DNSKEY RR, which is then used by the clients to authenticate the origin and integrity of the DNS data.

Keys for two different purposes can be stored in a DNSKEY RR: (1) Key Signing Key (KSK) and (2) Zone Signing Key (ZSK). ZSK signs the RRs for which a zone is authoritative, the ZSK is signed with the KSK and the KSK is stored in the DS RR at the parent. This separation mainly allows to reduce the overhead associated with updating the parent each time the ZSK is replaced.

Resolvers are configured with a set of verification keys for specific zones, called *trust anchors*; in particular, all resolvers have the verification key (trust anchor) for the root zone. The resolver obtains other verification keys, which are not trust anchors, by requesting a DNSKEY RR from the domain. To validate these verification keys obtained from the DNSKEY RR, the resolver obtains a corresponding DS RR from the parent zone, which contains a hash of the DNSKEY of the child; the resolver accepts the DNSKEY RR of the child as authentic if the hashed value in the DNSKEY RR is the same as the value in the DS record at the parent, and the DS record is properly signed (with a signature stored in a corresponding RRSIG record). Since the DS record is signed with the DNSKEY of the parent, authenticity is guaranteed. Hence, the resolver can establish a *chain of trust* from the trust anchor of the root, following the signed delegations all the way to the target domain, and authenticate the public verification key (stored in a DNSKEY RR) of the target zone.

3 DNSSEC Deployment Obstacles and Challenges

DNS responses, signed with DNSSEC, are much larger than traditional DNS responses, often exceeding the typical Maximal Transmission Unit (MTU) of the Internet. In particular, due to their increased size, signed responses are often exploited for attacks, e.g., cache poisoning and DDoS, [2,3], and incur interoperability problems with intermediate devices disrupting DNS functionality and availability. As a result, zone operators are often hesitant about signing their zones, and resolvers' operators typically do not enforce validation of DNSSEC records. The outcome is impeded deployment of DNSSEC. The fact that there is currently limited deployment of DNSSEC further reduces a motivation for early adopters, since protection of DNSSEC only 'kicks in' when all the entities, involved in a resolution of a domain name, support DNSSEC.

3.1 DNSSEC Deployment Status

DNSSEC Validation at Resolvers. A significant fraction of the resolvers currently signal DNSSEC support; however, *less than 3%* actually *enforce DNSSEC validation* [8]. Obviously, for such non-validating resolvers, DNSSEC does not provide added security.

DNSSEC Deployment at Zones. To make DNSSEC validation effective in resolvers the zones have to adopt DNSSEC. However, most do not. Recently, the root and some important top-level domains (TLDs), such as com, org, were signed; through experimental study we found that currently 62% of the TLDs are signed and less than one percent (0.46%) of top million Alexa domains are signed.

3.2 DNSSEC Overhead

DNS Infrastructure. Adopting DNSSEC requires a significant increase in the DNS infrastructure, both in resolvers and name servers platforms, [11]. In particular, most devices are needed, to support the increased number of requests, processing and storage overhead.

Communication. Large responses cause noticeable overhead: (1) on the name server that is required to transmit them,(2) on the recepient that needs to receive and process them (allocate buffers to store and reassemble) and (3) on the network, and intermediate devices, e.g., routers and proxies, causing load spikes and increasing processing. Not only much more data, than needed, is sent: the name server sends all the keys and signatures that correspond to the cryptographic options that the zone supports, but also such large responses often result in fragmentation or cause resolvers to use TCP for the DNS transaction.

Computation. Signatures generation increases the computational overhead on name servers and is significant for dynamic zones, e.g., the common content distribution networks. Signatures verification imposes overhead on busy resolvers and is prohibitive for mobile devices, making support of DNSSEC on end-hosts impractical.

3.3 Interoperability Problems with DNSSEC

DNSSEC signed DNS responses often exceed the 512B maximal DNS size specified in [RFC1035], requiring use of the EDNS [RFC6891] extension mechanism; EDNS is also used to signal support of DNSSEC. Some firewalls interpret such large DNS packets as malicious and drop them. Indeed, DNSSEC responses often exceed the maximal transmission unit (MTU) and thus may get dropped or fragmented. Fragments are also blocked by some firewalls, mainly for security concerns.

Due to concerns for the interoperability issues with large signed-DNS responses, many resolvers that support DNSSEC, accept and cache unvalidated responses, thereby exposing themselves to a *downgrade attack*, [RFC4035]; for instance, to avoid interoperability problems, **unbound** resolver supports a 'permissive' mode, accepting responses with missing or incorrect signatures.

In a downgrade attack an attacker sends fake responses that appear similar to responses passing through non-interoperable devices.

3.4 Common Ciphers

Most signed zones, among Alexa top million domains and TLDs, suppport different variations of RSA (with SHA1 or SHA256 hash functions) with weak keys, 1024 bits. The results are plotted in Figure 3. The categories are grouped according to key sizes[1] ranges and according to different variations of the RSA cipher; since all the domains were found to support different versions of RSA algorithm, we do not mention 'RSA' in the figure. The

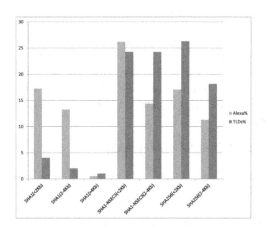

Fig. 3. Distribution of the ciphers and public key sizes supported by TLDs and Alexa top million domains.

measurements are consistent with the recommendations by NIST and IETF [RFC4641] for a mandatory support of RSA and also to avoid using large keys

---

[1] The transmitted keys and signatures are encoded in Base64 thus contain an extra byte of redundancy for every three bytes of actual data.

(specifying a range of 512-2048 bits for (ZSK) key size and recommending a default value of 1024 bits), in order to avoid fragmentation, communication and computation overhead and other problems with large keys and signatures. There is hardly any adoption of cryptographic algorithms that produce short signatures, such as ECC, since the motivation to add more overhead to the transmitted data is low. This supports our argument that cipher-suite negotiation mechanism is essential not only for deployment of stronger cryptography and adoption of new cryptographic ciphers, which currently the zone operators are hesitant to support, but also to mitigate the interoperability and overhead problems associated with DNSSEC.

4   Cipher-Suite Negotiation for DNSSEC

A cipher suite negotiation requires that one of the end points to the transaction signals to the other, the ciphers that it supports. The receiving end point would then apply its own priorities, over those signaled to it, and select an optimal cipher that reflects the priorities of both parties.

Recently, [RFC6975] standardised new options in the EDNS record, [RFC6891], enabling clients to signal the supported ciphers to the name servers. The signaling of deployed ciphers allows zone operators to determine whether they can adopt new cryptographic algorithms. However, the zones would still have to support the other algorithms, in order to serve the resolvers which have not adopted the new cipher. In addition, a mechanism that relies on the EDNS record would not be effective when resolvers or name servers communicate via the proxies (which is common). The problem is that EDNS is a hop-by-hop transport layer mechanism, and its records and options are not cached by the resolvers. Hence, it only allows to signal and coordinate options between two communicating hops, e.g., a proxy and a name server, or a resolver and a proxy, but not end-to-end, between a resolver and a name server. In particular, if a proxy has cached records according to the preferences supported and signaled in EDNS by other clients, it will serve those records to the subsequently requesting clients, and will be oblivious to the signaling of different options by the other clients. Enhancing the proxy with a cipher suite negotiation does not solve the problem. In particular, the proxy would serve the records to the clients according to its own preferences.

We present a design that does not require *any* changes to the proxies. Our design uses the DNS packets themselves for signaling of the supported cryptographic options. The signaling is performed by the name server. The resolver uses the options, signaled by the name server, to select the optimal cipher, according to its own priorities. Then, in the DNS requests that the resolver sends, it 'asks' the name server to return only the cryptographic DNSSEC algorithm that corresponds to that selection. This design is based on two mechanisms: (1) secure signaling from the name-server to the client, of the supported algorithms, encoded and cached as a record in a DNS response, and (2) retrieval of the preferred cryptographic (signature and hash) algorithms, encoded within the DNS query. We next elaborate on each of these mechanisms.

Signaling the algorithms supported by the zone. To facilitate signaling the (signature and hash) algorithms supported by the zone, we propose to dedicate a special algorithm number, say 99, whose meaning is a *'list of supported algorithms'*. The zones supporting cipher suite negotiation, should add a DS and a DNSKEY records, both with algorithm identifier 99 to every response containing DS or DNSKEY record set (RRSET); the DS RR would be served by the parent domain to the resolver during the establishment of a chain of trust, and the DNSKEY RR by the domain owner itself, upon DNSKEY requests from the resolver. The 'list of algorithms' record will contain the list of algorithms supported by that zone, in the order of preference, and an expiration date for that list. We expect the list of ciphers not to change frequently (as new algorithms are adopted rarely), hence we expect long validity periods (in the order of months and longer).

Once a resolver, enhanced with a cipher suite negotiation, receives that list, it learns that the name server is enhanced with the cipher suite negotiation mechanism and it learns the ciphers that the zone supports; the module, responsible for cipher suite negotiation stores that ciphers list (associated with the corresponding zone) for the duration specified in the expiration date field in the record. Next time that the resolver sends a request for a record within that domain, it will indicate the cryptographic options (the signature algorithm and the hash function) in its DNS request, as a subdomain concatenated to the original query (more details follow). Hence, our mechanism introduces only a negligible overhead, see Section 4.6. To minimise the chance of loss due to response truncation, the 'list of algorithms' record will be sent as the *first* record in the DNSKEY or DS RR-sets.

The validity of the 'list of algorithms' record, is established by the resolver as it validates the signature over the entire RR-set, namely, using the (already validated) key signing key (KSK) of the zone, stored in a DNSKEY record, or the parent's zone DNSKEY record. This ensures that the resolver establishes a chain of trust all the way from the root zone to the target domain.

The *indirect* signaling by the name servers to the resolvers implicitly supports interoperability with legacy resolvers and legacy name servers, which do not support the cipher suite negotiation mechanism – while not increasing the amount of DNS requests to the legacy DNS servers.

Encoding the preferred algorithms. We encode the preferred cryptographic (signature and hash) algorithm, as a subdomain in each DNS request sent by the cipher suite negotiation supporting resolver to the cipher suite negotiation supporting name server. As an example, to resolve the domain name `foo.bar` using `RSA/SHA1`, the client sends the query `_pAI_5.foo.bar`. Here, `_pAI_` is a fixed prefix identifying that this request contains a *preferred Algorithm Identifier*, and 5 is the algorithm number of `RSA/SHA1` as assigned by *IANA* [7]. These algorithm-numbers are already used in DNSSEC (DS, RRSIG and DNSKEY) records, to identify the cryptographic algorithm used to generate the hash and signature algorithms.

4.1 Query Processing

Suppose a resolver needs to make a query to a name server authoritative for foo.bar, and that the resolver prefers the use of algorithm number 7 (ECDSA Curve P-256 SHA-256). If the resolver does not have the 'list of algorithms' record for the zone foo.bar cached, then it sends a 'regular' query, e.g., query for a name server (NS) record of domain foo.bar. If the name server supports cipher suite negotiation, in response to its query for a DNSKEY record (or a DS record if the query is sent to the parent domain), the resolver receives the 'default/current' DNSKEY (resp. DS) record, that contains the 'list of algorithms'.

Note that all those records - the _pAI_5.foo.bar responses and the 'list of algorithms' - would automatically be cached by any intermediate 'legacy' DNS proxy, without requiring modifications to the existing proxies. Additional resolvers (or clients), requesting records recently requested by another client, e.g., to the domain _pAI_5.foo.bar, will receive the responses from the cache. Furthermore, clients which do not support cipher suite negotiation, will receive responses that contain all the cryptographic material supported by the target domain – as is done currently; the 'list of algorithms' in the DS and DNSKEY RR-sets will refer to an unknown algorithm and hence will be ignored by legacy resolvers, that do not support cipher suite negotiation.

4.2 Considering Limitations

The query size field in DNS is limited to 256 bytes. Thus, this encoding will fail if the original domain name is already at the limit or close to it. We measured the distribution of domains' lengths on Alexa top-50,000 and found that almost 72% are less than 10 characters, 88.45% are less than 20 characters, and the remaning are less than 100 characters. Namely, current query field does not pose a restriction for the prefix encoding.

4.3 Implementation

Our design does not require changes to the DNS software or protocol, and can be easily integrated into the existing DNS infrastructure. We implemented our cipher-suite negotiation mechanism as two separate user space modules, *cipher-suite client* and *cipher-suite server*.

Our mechanism requires a modification of the current signature procedure dnssec-keygen which currently signs each DNS record in a zone file with *all* the supported keys. We show how to extend it to enable cipher-suite negotiation, in Section 4.4.

To test our implementation, we extended the dig (domain information groper) DNS lookup utility[2], with the support for signaling of a list of ciphers.

To integrate support of cipher suite negotiation also into the process of signing the zone file we create separate copies of the zone file, such that each copy

---

[2] dig is a tool for performing DNS lookup by interrogating DNS name servers, and displaying the responses.

corresponds to a single cipher. This is instead of signing the same zone file with multiple ciphers as is currently performed.

4.4 Separate Zone File per Cipher

When supporting a number of cryptographic options, zone operators sign, typically using dnssec-keygen procedure, the same zone file with a number of algorithms. The signing process of DNSSEC creates a signature per each RR-set, i.e., set of resource records of the same type; for instance, all the name servers (NS) records (of a specific domain) are signed as a single unit, and for each supported cryptographic option a signature is attached to the NS RR-set. When a number of cryptographic options are supported (as is typically the case) a number of signatures are created and attached to each RR-set in the zone file. For instance, the entire DNSKEY RR-set is signed with each of the supported algorithmic options - and the responses, to DNS requests for a DNSKEY record, contain all those signatures. As a result, DNS responses typically contain multiple signatures (that correspond to all the supported cryptographic ciphers) for each RR-set that they return.

To encorporate support for a cipher-suite negotiation, we extended the dnssec-keygen procedure, to generate a separate zone file, per each cryptographic algorithm that the zone supports. Our ednssec-keygen (extended dnssec-keygen) performs the same number of signing operations as the number thereof that would have been performed by the dnssec-keygen procedure. However, instead of signing the same zone file with different keys (which results in a zone file where every RR-set is coupled with a set of signatures per each supported cipher), it creates a separate copy of the zone file for each supported cryptographic option. Each resulting RR-set in a signed zone file contains the signature that corresponds only to the algorithm that was used to sign that copy of the zone file.

4.5 Experimental Evaluation

We evaluated two key performance factors affected by our cipher-suite negotiation mechanism: the latency of a DNS request to a signed domain and the communication overhead. We configured an iptables firewall rule to capture all the packets to/from port 53 (DNS requests/responses) and to pass them to our user space modules on the resolver side and on the server side; cipher-suite client module running on the resolver side, and cipher-suite server module on name server side. In our implementation of the cipher-suite client and the cipher suite server we used the libipq module to retrieve the packets from the kernel queue for user space processing.

We measured the latency of a DNS request as the elapsed time between the transmission of the request by the resolver and the receipt of the response, with and without support of cipher-suite negotiation. We measured the communication overhead (Figure 4) by comparing the amount of bytes transmitted (Figure

5) with and without support of cipher-suite negotiation by the resolver and the name server.

For our evaluation we configured cipher-suite client and cipher-suite server as modules on separate hosts. The cipher-suite client was set up on the resolver's network, to capture all the DNS requests sent by the resolver; it adding the subdomain of the preferred cipher, in requests to zones supporting cipher suite negotiation, and stored DS and DNSKEY RRs containing the 'list of algorithms' record. Cipher suite client also validated that the DNS responses, from the zones supporting cipher suite negotiation, were signed with the correct algorithms, according to the option signaled in the DNS requests. The cipher-suite server was set up on name server's network, and was redirecting requests enhanced with cipher suite negotiation, to the correct zone file (according to the option signaled in the subdomain of the DNS query). We added firewall rules to redirect the DNS traffic via the cipher suite client and cipher suite server modules.

To test the impact of cipher suite negotiation mechanism on DNS requests to top-50,000 Alexa domains, we wrote a script that was stripping all the keys and signatures from the responses of the name servers and was adding keys and signatures according to a cipher that we selected - simulating the cipher-suite selection process. Due to its short keys and signatures size, we selected the EC algorithm, and the keys and signatures were computed with an EC secret signing key that we generated for this experiment; the resolver was configured with a corresponding trust anchor, i.e., public verification key, which enabled it to establish a chain of trust and to successfully validate the signatures over the RR-sets in the responses.

We performed two series of evaluations of requests' latency over a list of top-50,000 Alexa domains and TLDs: (1) we wrote a python script that receives in an input a list of TLDs and Alexa top domains, invokes the `dig` utility on each domain, and measures the time between the transmission of the request and the receipt of the response as well as the number of bytes received in the response; we used Bind-9.9.3 software to set up a recursive DNS resolver. (2) Then, to measure the impact of cipher-suite negotiation, we wrote a python script, which used the extended `dig` tool with our cipher-suite negotiation options for appending the algorithm as a subdomain to the query in the DNS requests. The measurements are plotted in Figures 4 and 5.

As can be seen, in Figure 4, cipher-suite negotiation reduces the latency for signed DNS responses both in TLDs and Alexa domains. The difference is more evident in signed TLDs, majority of which support more keys than signed Alexa domains. However, as can be seen in the figure, there is a significant latency difference in signed Alexa domains and in TLDs that do not support cipher-suite negotiation, after the point of 256 ms. This is due to transition to TCP for responses which exceed the path maximal transmission unit (MTU); some TLDs such as com, send large responses only over TCP.

We measured the impact of the cipher-suite negotiation on the amount of the transmitted bytes for queries to the domains within the signed TLDs, using the DNSKEY record type requests. The graph, plotted in Figure 5, with the

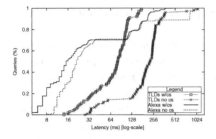
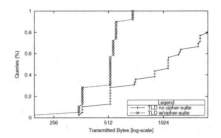

Fig. 4. Latency of DNS requests to TLDs and Alexa top 100,000 web sites, with and without support of cipher-suite negotiation.

Fig. 5. Amount of bytes transmitted in DNSKEY responses from TLDs, with and without support of cipher-suite negotiation.

cipher-suite negotiation shows three steps. Intuitively, one may expect to see an almost a straight line, however, the steps appear due to the fact that some domains are in a process of key rollover for ZSK and thus use two ZSK records (in addition to a KSK record). The improvement in traffic volume is the difference between the two lines: the upper (with cipher-suite negotiation) and the lower (without cipher-suite negotiation).

4.6 Impact on Performance and Security

In this section we discuss the impact of the proposed cipher suite negotiation mechanism on performance and security. We first discuss the impact on performance, which, we argue, is mixed, with reduced client to resolver communication, reduced latency to clients, and reasonable additional communication to resolvers, and storage kept by resolvers to accomodate for the additional records that reflect the priorities of the clients. We then argue that cipher suite negotiation can have significant positive impact on the adoption of new algorithms, and hence on security.

Impact on Performance. Our mechanism does not introduce a negative impact on performance, since it is invoked only when the resolver receives the new 'list of algorithms' record in a DNS response. Similarly, the performance impact on queries to zones enhanced with a cipher suite negotiation mechanism, by 'legacy' resolvers (that do not support cipher suite negotiation mechanism), is also negligible: just the addition of the few bytes required for the 'list of algorithms' record in DNSKEY or DS type responses; this addition constitutes less than 1% of the typical DNSSEC response length (see Introduction, Figure 1 for DNSSEC signed responses sizes. Therefore, the interesting comparison is between the case of full or partial adoption (by both resolvers and zones), vs. the case of no adoption.

The cipher suite negotiation mechanisms is expected to result in significant savings in bandwidth in the client to resolver connection, since the client will only receive the signatures and the keys that it uses. Cipher suite negotiation would reduce the latency significant for all DNSSEC responses that are fragmented due to excessive length, and those that are resent over TCP (e.g., responses from a com domain).

On the other hand, the algorithm-negotiation mechanism may cause a resolver to make multiple requests for the same domain name - one request for each of the algorithms supported by the zone (from different clients, each preferring a different algorithm). This results in overhead of additional request and response packets sent and received by resolver/proxy, and corresponding storage for these records. However, the largest part of the response are the signatures and keys, which are sent at most twice: in the 'legacy' response (containing all algorithms) and in the response to query specifying the required algorithm. Furthermore, since the responses are shorter, we avoid fragmentation and the use of TCP, which results in a significant reduction in resources in the resolver and the name servers (in particular, for buffering).

Impact on Adoption and Security. As can be seen in Figure 3, currently, essentially all domains support only RSA signatures. Indeed, without the proposed cipher suite negotiation mechanism, if a domain were to support an additional algorithm, e.g., one based on Elipitic Curves (EC), this would result in *larger* responses, hence in more truncation and fragmentation of responses, increasing communication overhead and latency and causing interoperability failures. Therefore, it is not surprising, that almost no domains have opted to use EC or other non-RSA signature schemes.

The proposed cipher suite negotiation mechanism removes this concern of fragmentation/truncation, for a domain offering a new, possibly better, cryptographic (signature, hashing) algorithm. Furthermore, there is no 'penalty' to the name server, unless and until the clients and the resolver begin requesting the new algorithm. Therefore, the domains have incentive to adopt such alternatives to RSA. This can have significant security value, by allowing the use of the secure alternatives.

5   Conclusions

It is well known that cryptographic protocols should allow parties to (securely) negotiate the 'best' cryptographic functions; such 'algorithm-agility' is often mentioned as a requirement from crypto-protocol standards. Indeed, appropriate, secure 'cipher-suite negotiation' mechanisms were designed for many crypto-protocol standards (TLS, IPsec, and others).

However, so far, such negotiation mechanisms were not proposed for protocols designed for secure distribution of signed information, such as DNSSEC, used for secure distribution of DNS records.

We show that currently, almost *all* (99.9% !) of domains use RSA with 1024 bit keys, for DNSSEC signatures, which is considered insecure (outdated). This choice results in larger signatures than the existing (more efficient) alternatives. The use of 2048-bit keys results in even larger DNS responses.

We present a simple, practical and efficient protocol allowing secure negotiation of signature algorithms. The protocol is secure and efficient since it supports caching by the intermediate devices (proxies), without requiring upgrade of the intermediaries.

Acknowledgements. We are grateful to the anonymous referees for their thoughtful comments on the earlier version of this work – in particular the proposal to emphasise the interoperability with legacy DNS servers and the insight of the impact of cipher suite negotiation on the caching of the proxy resolvers.

This research was supported by grant 1354/11 from the Israeli Science Foundation (ISF), and by the Ministry of Science and Technology, Israel and by projects EC SPRIDE (BMBF) and CASED (LOEWE).

References

1. Alexa: The web information company, `http://www.alexa.com/`
2. Ariyapperuma, S., Mitchell, C.J.: Security vulnerabilities in dns and dnssec. In: The Second International Conference on Availability, Reliability and Security, ARES 2007, pp. 335–342. IEEE (2007)
3. Bernstein, D.J.: Breaking DNSSEC. In: 3rd USENIX Workshop on Offensive Technologies (August 2009)
4. Gao, H., Yegneswaran, V., Chen, Y., Porras, P., Ghosh, S., Jiang, J., Duan, H.: An empirical reexamination of global dns behavior. In: Proceedings of the ACM SIGCOMM 2013 Conference on SIGCOMM, pp. 267–278. ACM (2013)
5. Gura, N., Patel, A., Wander, A., Eberle, H., Shantz, S.C.: Comparing elliptic curve cryptography and RSA on 8-bit CPUs. In: Joye, M., Quisquater, J.-J. (eds.) CHES 2004. LNCS, vol. 3156, pp. 119–132. Springer, Heidelberg (2004)
6. Herzberg, A., Shulman, H.: Vulnerable Delegation of DNS Resolution. In: Crampton, J., Jajodia, S., Mayes, K. (eds.) ESORICS 2013. LNCS, vol. 8134, pp. 219–236. Springer, Heidelberg (2013)
7. Internet Assigned Numbers Authority (IANA): Domain Name System Security (DNSSEC) Algorithm Numbers (March 2014),
   `http://www.iana.org/assignments/`
   `dns-sec-alg-numbers/dns-sec-alg-numbers.xhtml`
8. Lian, W., Rescorla, E., Shacham, H., Savage, S.: Measuring the Practical Impact of DNSSEC Deployment. In: Proceedings of USENIX Security (2013)
9. Liu, A., Ning, P.: Tinyecc: A configurable library for elliptic curve cryptography in wireless sensor networks. In: International Conference on Information Processing in Sensor Networks, IPSN 2008, pp. 245–256. IEEE (2008)
10. Malan, D.J., Welsh, M., Smith, M.D.: A public-key infrastructure for key distribution in tinyos based on elliptic curve cryptography. In: 2004 First Annual IEEE Communications Society Conference on Sensor and Ad Hoc Communications and Networks, IEEE SECON 2004, pp. 71–80. IEEE (2004)
11. Migault, D., Girard, C., Laurent, M.: A performance view on dnssec migration. In: 2010 International Conference on Network and Service Management (CNSM), pp. 469–474. IEEE (2010)
12. Schomp, K., Callahan, T., Rabinovich, M., Allman, M.: On measuring the client-side dns infrastructure. In: Proceedings of the 2013 Conference on Internet Measurement Conference, pp. 77–90. ACM (2013)

A Censorship-Resistant, Privacy-Enhancing and Fully Decentralized Name System

Matthias Wachs, Martin Schanzenbach, and Christian Grothoff

Network Architectures and Services
Fakultät für Informatik
Technische Universität München, Germany
{wachs,schanzen,grothoff}@in.tum.de

Abstract. The Domain Name System (DNS) is vital for access to information on the Internet. This makes it a target for attackers whose aim is to suppress free access to information. This paper introduces the design and implementation of the GNU Name System (GNS), a fully decentralized and censorship-resistant name system. GNS provides a privacy-enhancing alternative to DNS which preserves the desirable property of memorable names. Due to its design, it can also double as a partial replacement of public key infrastructures, such as X.509. The design of GNS incorporates the capability to integrate and coexist with DNS. GNS is based on the principle of a petname system and builds on ideas from the Simple Distributed Security Infrastructure (SDSI), addressing a central issue with the decentralized mapping of secure identifiers to memorable names: namely the impossibility of providing a global, secure and memorable mapping without a trusted authority. GNS uses the transitivity in the SDSI design to replace the trusted root with secure delegation of authority, thus making petnames useful to other users while operating under a very strong adversary model. In addition to describing the GNS design, we also discuss some of the mechanisms that are needed to smoothly integrate GNS with existing processes and procedures in Web browsers. Specifically, we show how GNS is able to transparently support many assumptions that the existing HTTP(S) infrastructure makes about globally unique names.

1   Introduction

The Domain Name System (DNS) is a unique distributed database and a vital service for most Internet applications. While DNS is distributed, it relies on centralized, trusted registrars to provide globally unique names. As the awareness of the central role DNS plays on the Internet rises, various institutions are using their power (including legal means) to engage in attacks on the DNS, thus threatening the global availability and integrity of information on the Web [1]. This danger has also been recognized by the European Parliament, which has emphasized the importance of maintaining free access to information on the Web in a resolution [2]. Tampering with the DNS can cause collateral damage, too: a recent study [3] showed that Chinese censorship of the DNS has had worldwide

D. Gritzalis et al. (Eds.): CANS 2014, LNCS 8813, pp. 127–142, 2014.

effects on name resolution. At the same time, we observe that the Internet's importance for free communication has dramatically risen: the events of the Green Revolution in Iran and the Arab Spring have demonstrated this. Dissidents need communication channels that provide the easy linking to information that is at the Web's core. This calls for a censorship-resistant name system which ensures that names of Internet servers can always be resolved correctly.

DNS was not designed with security as a goal. This makes it very vulnerable, especially to attackers that have the technical capabilities of an entire nation state at their disposal. The follow are some of the most severe weaknesses that the DNS exhibits even in the presence of the DNS Security Extensions (DNSSEC). DNSSEC [4] was designed to provide data integrity and origin authentication to DNS. DNSSEC maintains the hierarchical structure of DNS and thus places extensive trust in the root zone and TLD operators. More importantly, DNSSEC fails to provide any level of query privacy [5]: the content of DNS queries and replies can be read by any adversary with access to the communication channel and can subsequently be correlated with users. On a technical level, current DNSSEC deployment suffers from the use of the RSA crypto system, which leads to large key sizes. This can result in message sizes that exceed size restrictions on DNS packets, leading to additional vulnerabilities [6]. Finally, DNSSEC is not designed to withstand legal attacks. Depending on their reach, governments, corporations and their lobbies can legally compel operators of DNS authorities to manipulate entries and certify the changes, and Soghoian and Stamm have warned that similar actions might happen for X.509 server certificates [7]. There can also be collateral damage: DNSSEC cannot prevent problems such as the recent brief disappearance of thousands of legitimate domains during the execution of established censorship procedures, in which the Danish police accidentally requested the removal of 8,000 (legitimate) domain names from DNS and providers complied. The underlying attack vector in these cases is the same: names in the DNS have owners, and ownership can be taken away by different means.

This paper presents the GNU Name System (GNS), a censorship-resistant, privacy-preserving and decentralized name system designed to provide a secure alternative to DNS, especially when censorship or manipulation is encountered. As GNS can bind names to any kind of cryptographically secured token, it can double in some respects as an alternative to some of today's Public Key Infrastructures, in particular X.509 for the Web.

The foundation of the GNS system is a petname system [8], where each individual user may freely and securely map names to values. In a petname system, each user chooses a *nickname* as his preferred (but not necessarily globally unique) name. Upon introduction, users adopt the nickname by default as a *label* to refer to a new acquaintance; however, they are free to select and assign any *petname* of their choice in place of—or, in addition to—the nickname. Petnames thus reflect the personal choice of the individual using a name, while nicknames are the preferred name of the user that is being identified.

The second central idea is to provide users with the ability to securely delegate control over a subdomain to other users. This simple yet powerful mechanism is borrowed from the design of SDSI/SPKI. With the combination of petname system and delegation, GNS does not require nor depend on a centralized or trusted authority, making the system robust against censorship attempts. Decentralization and additional censorship resistance is achieved by using a distributed hash table (DHT) to enable the distribution and resolution of key-value mappings. In theory, any DHT can be used. However, depending on the properties of the DHT in question, varying degrees of censorship resistance will be the result. As such, the choice of the DHT is crucial to the system. Finally, GNS is privacy-preserving since both key-value mappings as well as queries and responses are encrypted such that an active and participating adversary can at best perform a confirmation attack, and can otherwise only learn the expiration time of a response.

While this combination yields a secure name system, it also violates a fundamental assumption prevailing on the Web, namely that names are globally unique. Thus, together with the working implementation of GNS[1], another key contribution of our work is the construction of system components to enable the use of GNS in the context of the Web. We provide ready-to-use components to enable existing Web applications to use GNS (and DNS in parallel, if desired) without any prior modifications and knowledge.

As a alternative public key infrastructure, GNS can also be combined with existing PKI approaches (such as X.509, DANE, Tor's ".onion" or the Web of Trust) to either provide memorable names or alternative means for verification with increased trust agility. In combination with TLSA records, GNS can replace existing X.509 certification authorities as described in Appendix A.3.

2   Background

In order to present GNS, we must first discuss technical background necessary to understand our design. We define the adversary model that GNS addresses and then provide some brief background on DNS, DNSSEC, SDSI/SPKI and distributed storage in P2P Networks.

2.1   Adversary Model

The adversary model used in this work is modeled after a state trying to limit access to information without causing excessive damage to its own economy. The goal of the adversary is to force name resolution to change in the respective name system, by either making the resolution fail or by changing the value to which an existing name (not originally under the control of the adversary) maps.

We allow the adversary to participate in any role in the name system. Note that this excludes the possibility of a global trusted third party. In addition, the adversary is allowed to assume multiple identities. We impose no bound on the fraction of collaborating malicious participants, and we assume that the

---

[1] Available under: https://gnunet.org/gns

adversary can take control of names using judicial and executive powers (for example by confiscating names or forcing third parties to misdirect users to adversary-controlled impostor sites). Computationally, the adversary is allowed to have more resources than all benign users combined.

The adversary may directly compromise the computers of individual users; for the security of the system as a whole, we only require that the impact of such attacks remains localized. The rationale for being able to make such an assumption is that the economic and political cost of such tailored methods is very high, even for a state actor. Similarly, the adversary cannot prevent the use of cryptography, free software, or encrypted network communication. The adversary is assumed to be unable to break cryptographic primitives. As far as network communication is concerned, we assume that communication between benign participants generally passes unhindered by the adversary.

Zooko's triangle [9], an insightful conjecture that is often used to define the possible design space of name systems, has important implications under this adversary model: it means that no name system can provide globally unique and memorable names and be secure [10]. It should be noted that in weaker adversary models, these implications do not hold [11].

2.2 DNS and DNSSEC

The Domain Name System is an essential part of the Internet as it provides mappings from host names to IP addresses, providing memorable names for users. DNS is hierarchical and stores name-value mappings in so-called *records* in a distributed database. A record consists of a name, type, value and expiration time. Names consist of *labels* delimited by dots. The root of the hierarchy is the empty label, and the right-most label in a name is known as the top-level domain (TLD). Names with a common suffix are said to be in the same *domain*. The *record type* specifies what kind of value is associated with a name, and a name can have many records with various types. The most common record types are "A" records that map names to IPv4 addresses.

The Domain Name System database is partitioned into *zones*. A *zone* is a portion of the namespace where the administrative responsibility belongs to one particular authority. A zone has unrestricted autonomy to manage the records in one or more domains. Very importantly, an authority can delegate responsibility for particular *subdomains* to other authorities. This is achieved with an "NS" record, whose value is the name of a DNS server of the authority for the subdomain. The *root zone* is the zone corresponding to the empty label. It is managed by the Internet Assigned Numbers Authority (IANA), which is currently operated by the Internet Corporation for Assigned Names and Numbers (ICANN). The National Telecommunications and Information Administration (NTIA), an agency of the United States Department of Commerce, assumes the (legal) authority over the root zone. The root zone contains "NS" records which specify names for the authoritative DNS servers for all TLDs.

The Domain Name System Security Extensions add integrity protection and data origin authentication for DNS records. DNSSEC does not add confidentiality nor denial-of-service protection. It adds record types for public keys ("DNSKEY") and for signatures on resource records ("RRSIG"). DNSSEC relies on a hierarchical public-key infrastructure in which all DNSSEC operators must participate. It establishes a trust chain from a zone's authoritative server to the trust anchor, which is associated with the root zone. This association is achieved by distributing the root zone's public key out-of-band with, for example, operating systems. The trust chains established by DNSSEC mirror the zone delegations of DNS. With TLD operators typically subjected to the same jurisdiction as the domain operators in their zone, these trust chains are at risk of attacks using legal means.

2.3 SDSI/SPKI

SDSI/SPKI is a merger of the Simple Distributed Security Infrastructure (SDSI) and the Simple Public Key Infrastructure (SPKI) [12]. It defines a public-key infrastructure that abandons the concept of memorable global names and does not require certification authorities. SDSI/SPKI has the central notion of *principals*, which are globally unique public keys. These serve as namespaces within which local names are defined. A name in SDSI/SPKI is a public key and a local identifier, e.g. $K - Alice$. This name defines the identifier *Alice*, which is only valid in the namespace of key K. Thus, $K_1 - Alice$ and $K_2 - Alice$ are different names. SDSI/SPKI allows namespaces to be linked, which results in compound names: $K_{Carol} - Bob - Alice$ is Carol's name for the entity which Bob refers to as $K_{Bob} - Alice$. Bob himself is identified by Carol as $K_{Carol} - Bob$. SDSI/SPKI allows assertions about names by issuing certificates[2]. A *name cert* is a tuple of *(issuer public key, identifier, subject, validity)*, together with a signature by the issuer's private key. The *subject* is usually the key to which a name maps. Compound names are expressed as certificate chains.

GNS applies these key ideas from SDSI/SPKI to a name resolution mechanism in order to provide an alternative to DNS. The transitivity at the core of SDSI/SPKI is found in GNS as *delegation of authority* over a name. In both systems, name resolution starts with a lookup in the local namespace.

2.4 Distributed Storage in P2P Overlay Networks

In peer-to-peer systems, it is common to use a DHT to exchange data with other participants in the overlay. A DHT creates a decentralized key/value store to make mappings available to other users and to resolve mappings not available locally. GNS uses a DHT to make local namespace and delegation information available to other users and to resolve mappings from other users. As mentioned previously, the choice of DHT strongly affects the availability of GNS data.

---

[2] Ultimately, SDSI/SPKI allows to create authorizations based on certificates and is a flexible infrastructure in general, but we will focus only on the names here.

3   Design of the GNU Name System

In the following, we describe the core concepts of GNS that are relevant to users. The cryptographic protocol used to ensure query privacy is explained in Section 4, and the protocol for key revocation in Section A.5.

3.1   Names, Zones and Delegations

GNS employs the same notion of names as SDSI/SPKI: principals are public keys, and names are only valid in the local namespace defined by that key. Namespaces constitute the *zones* in GNS: a zone is a public-private key pair and a set of records. GNS records consist of a label, type, value and expiration time. Labels have the same syntax as in DNS; they are equivalent to local identifiers in SDSI/SPKI. Names in GNS consists of a sequence of labels, which identifies a *delegation path*. Cryptography in GNS is based on elliptic curve cryptography and uses the ECDSA signature scheme with Curve25519 [13].

We realise a petname system by having each user manage his own zones, including, in particular, his own personal *master zone*.[3] Users can freely manage mappings for memorable names in their zones. Most importantly, they can delegate control over a subdomain to another user (which is locally known under the petname assigned to him). To this end, a special record type is used (see Section 3.5). This establishes the aforementioned delegation path. Each user uses his master zone as the starting point for lookups in lieu of the root zone from DNS. For interoperability with DNS, domain names in GNS use the pseudo-TLD ".gnu". ".gnu" refers to the GNS master zones (i. e. the starting point of the resolution). Note that names in the ".gnu" pseudo-TLD are always relative.

Publishing delegations in the DHT allows transitive resolution by simply following the delegation chains. Records can be private or public, and public records are made available to other users via a DHT. Record validity is established using signatures and controlled using expiration values. The records of a zone are stored in a *namestore* database on a machine under the control of the zone owner.

We illustrate the abstract description above with the example shown in Figure 1. The figure shows the paths Alice's GNS resolver would follow to resolve the names "www.dave.carol.gnu" and "www.buddy.bob.gnu", both of which refer to Dave's server at IP "192.0.2.1". For Carol, Dave's server would simply be "www.dave.gnu". It is known to Alice only because both Bob and Carol have published public records indicating Dave, and Alice can resolve the respective delegation chain via her known contacts. Recall that zones are identified using public keys and records must be cryptographically signed to ensure authenticity and integrity.

---

[3] Each user can create any number of zones, but must designate one as the master zone.

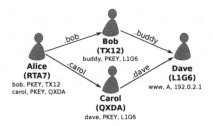

Fig. 1. Name resolution graph in GNS. Each user is shown with a fingerprint of his master zone and the public records from this zone in the format *name, type, value*.

3.2   Zone Management with Nicknames and Petnames

Suppose Alice runs a web server and wants to make it available with GNS. In the beginning she sets up her master zone using GNS. After the public-private key pair is generated, Alice can create a revocation notice to be able to immediately revoke their GNS zone in case she gets compromised. Suppose Alice wants to propose that her preferred nickname is "carol" to other users. She therefore uses the new "NICK" record that GNS provides. For her web server, she creates an appropriate public "A" record under the name "www". This "A" record is the same as in DNS. To make it resolvable by other users, this record is marked as public and published in the DHT.

Now suppose we have a second user, Bob. He performs the same setup on his system, except that his preferred nickname is just "bob". Bob gets to know Alice in real life and obtains her public key. To be able to contact Alice and access her web server, he then adds Alice to his zone by adding a new delegation using the new "PKEY" record. Bob can choose any name for Alice's zone in *his* zone. Nevertheless, Bob's software will default to Alice's preferences and suggest "carol", as long as "carol" has not already been assigned by Bob. This is important as it gives Alice an *incentive* to pick a nickname that is (sufficiently) unique to be available among the users that would delegate to her zone. By adding Alice's public key under "carol", Bob delegates queries to the "*.carol.gnu" subdomain to Alice. Thus, from Bob's point of view, Alice's web server is "www.carol.gnu". Note that there is no need for Alice's nickname "carol" to be globally unique, they should only not already be in use within Alice's social group.

3.3   Relative Names for Transitivity of Delegations

Users can delegate control over a subdomain to another user's zone by indicating this in a new record, "PKEY". Suppose Dave is Bob's friend. Dave has added a delegation to Bob with a "PKEY" record under the name "buddy"—ignoring Bob's preference to be called "bob". Now suppose Bob wants to put on his webpage a link to Alice's webpage. For Bob, Alice's website is "www.carol.gnu". For Dave, Bob website is "buddy.gnu". Due to delegation, Dave can access Alice's website under "www.carol.buddy.gnu". However, Bob's website cannot contain that link: Bob may not even know that he is "buddy" for Dave.

We solve this issue by having Bob use "www.carol.+" when linking to Alice's website. Here, the "+" stands for the originating zone. When Dave's client encounters "+" at the end of a domain name, it should replace "+" with the name of the GNS authority of the site of origin. This mechanism is equivalent to relative URLs, except that it works with hostnames.

3.4 Absolute Names

In GNS, the ".gnu" pseudo-TLD is used to provide secure and memorable names which are only defined relative to some master zone. However, introducing new zones into the system ultimately requires the ability to reference a zone by an absolute identifier, which must correspond to the public key of the zone. To facilitate dealing with public keys directly, GNS uses the pseudo-TLD ".zkey", which indicates that the specified domain name contains the public key of a GNS zone. As a result, the ".zkey" pseudo-TLD allows users to use secure and globally unique identifiers. Applications can use the ".zkey" pseudo-TLD to generate a domain name for a GNS zone for which the user does not (yet) have a memorable name. A label in the ".zkey" pseudo-TLD is the public key of the zone encoded within the 63 character limitations for labels imposed by DNS.

3.5 Records in GNS

As GNS is intended to coexist with DNS, most DNS resource records from [14,15] (e. .g., "A", "MX") are used with identical semantics and binary format in GNS. GNS defines various additional records to support GNS-specific operations. These records have record type numbers larger than 2^{16} to avoid conflicts with DNS record types that might be introduced in the future. Details on all record types supported by our current implementation can be found in our technical report [16].

4 Query Privacy

To enable other users to look up records of a zone, all public records for a given label are stored in a cryptographically signed block in the DHT. To maximize user privacy when using the DHT to look up records, both queries and replies are encrypted. Let $x \in \mathbb{Z}_n$ be the ECDSA private key for a given zone and $P = xG$ the respective public key where G is the generator of the elliptic curve. Let $n := |G|$ and $l \in \mathbb{Z}_n$ be a numeric representation of the label of a set of records $R_{l,P}$. Using

$$h := x \cdot l \mod n \tag{1}$$

$$Q_{l,P} := H(hG) \tag{2}$$

$$B_{l,P} := S_h(E_{\text{HKDF}(l,P)}R_{l,P}), hG \tag{3}$$

we can then publish $B_{l,P}$ under $Q_{l,P}$ in the DHT, where S_h represents signing with the private key h, HKDF is a hash-based key derivation function and E

represents symmetric encryption based on the derived key. Any peer can validate the signature (using the public key hG) but not decrypt $B_{l,P}$ without knowledge of both l and P. Peers knowing l and P can calculate the query

$$Q_{l,P} = H(lP) = H(lxG) = H(hG) \tag{4}$$

to retrieve $B_{l,P}$ and then decrypt $R_{l,P}$.

Given this scheme, an adversary can only perform a confirmation attack; if the adversary knows both the public key of the zone and the specific label, he can perform the same calculations as a peer performing a lookup and, in this specific case, gain full knowledge about the query and the response. As the DHT records are public, this attack cannot be prevented. However, users can use passwords for labels to restrict access to zone information to authorized parties. The presented scheme ensures that an adversary that is unable to guess both the zone's public key and the label cannot determine the label, zone or record data.

5   Security of GNS

One interesting metric for assessing the security of a system is to look at the size of the trusted computing base (TCB). In GNS, users explicitly see the trust chain and thus know if the resolution of a name requires trusting a friend, or also a friend-of-a-friend, or even friends-of-friends-of-friends—and can thus decide how much to trust the result. Naturally, the TCB for all names can theoretically become arbitrarily large—however, given the name length restrictions, for an individual name it is always less than about 125 entities. The DHT does not have to be trusted; the worst an adversary can do here is reduce performance and availability, but not impact integrity or authenticity of the data.

For DNS, the size of the TCB is first of all less obvious. The user may think that only the operators of the resolvers visible in the name and their local DNS provider need to be trusted. However, this is far from correct. Names can be expanded and redirected to other domains using "CNAME" and "DNAME" records, and resolving the address of the authority from "NS" records may require resolving again other names. Such "out-of-bailiwick" "NS" records were identified as one main reason for the collateral damage of DNS censorship by China [3]. requires correct information from "x.gtld-servers.net" (the authority for ".com"), which requires trusting "X2.gtld-servers.net" (the authority for ".net"). While the results to these queries are typically cached, the respective servers must be included in the TCB, as incorrect answers for any of these queries can change the ultimate result. Thus, in extreme cases, even seemingly simple DNS lookups may depend on correct answers from over a hundred DNS zones [17]; thus, with respect to the TCB, the main difference is that DNS is very good at obscuring the TCB from its users.

In the following, we discuss possible attacks on GNS within our adversary model. The first thing to note is that as long as the attacker cannot gain direct control over a user's computer, the integrity of master zones is preserved. Attacks on GNS can thus be classified in two categories: attacks on the network, and attacks on the delegation mechanism.

Attacks on the network can be staged as Eclipse attacks. The success depends directly on the DHT. Our choice, R^5N, shows a particularly good resistance against such attacks [18].

Concerning the delegation mechanism, the attacker has the option of tricking a user into accepting rogue mappings from his own zones. This requires social engineering. We assume that users of an anti-censorship system will be motivated to carefully check whose mappings they trust. Nevertheless, if the attacker succeeds, some damage will be done: all users that use this mapping will be affected. The effect thus depends on the "centrality" of the tricked user in the GNS graph. It is difficult to give estimates here, as the system is not deployed yet. In order to maximize the effects of his attack, the attacker would have to carry out his social engineering many times, which is naturally harder. Comparing this to DNSSEC, we note that even when a compromise has been detected, DNS users cannot choose whose delegations to follow. In GNS, they can attempt to find paths in the GNS graph via other contacts. The system that is most similar and in deployment is the OpenPGP Web of Trust. Ulrich et al. found that the Web of Trust has developed a strong mesh structure with many alternative paths [19]. If GNS develops a similar structure, users would greatly benefit.

Finally, censorship does not stop with the name system, and for a complete solution we thus need to consider censorship at lower layers. For example, an adversary might block the IP address of the server hosting the critical information. GNS is not intended as an answer to this kind of censorship. Instead, we advocate using tools like Tor [20] to circumvent the blockade.

6   Related Work

Timeline-based systems in the style of Bitcoin [21] have been proposed to create a global, secure and memorable name system [11]. Here, the idea is to create a single, globally accessible timeline of name registrations that is append-only. In the Namecoin system [22], a user needs to expend computational power on finding (partial) hash collisions in order to be able to append a new mapping. This is supposed to make it computationally infeasible to produce an alternative valid timeline. It also limits the rate of registrations. However, the Namecoin system is not strong enough in our adversary model, as the attacker has more computational power than all other participants, which allows him to create alternative valid timelines. Note that our adversary model is not a far-fetched assumption in this context: it is conceivable that a nation-state can muster more resources than the small number of other entities that participate in the system, especially for systems used as an alternative in places where censorship is encountered or during the bootstrapping of the network, when only a small number of users participate.

The first practical system that improves confidentiality with respect to DNS queries and responses was DNSCurve [5]. In DNSCurve, session keys are exchanged using Curve25519 [13] and then used to provide authentication and encryption between caches and servers. DNSCurve improves the existing Domain Name System with confidentiality and integrity, but the fundamental issues of DNS with respect to the adversary trying to modify DNS mapping is not within its focus.

GNS has much in common with the name system in the Unmanaged Internet Architecture (UIA) [23], as both systems are inspired by SDSI. In UIA, users can define personal names bound to self-certifying cryptographic identities and can access namespaces of other users. UIA's focus is on universal connectivity between a user's many devices. With respect to naming, UIA takes a clean-slate approach and simply assumes that UIA applications use the UIA client library to contact the UIA name daemon and thus understand the implications of relative names. In contrast, GNS was designed to interoperate with DNS as much as possible, and we have specifically considered what is needed to make it work as much as possible with the existing Internet. In terms of censorship resistance, both systems inherit basic security properties from SDSI with respect to correctness.

7   Summary and Conclusion

GNS is a censorship resistant, privacy-enhancing name system which avoids the use of trusted third parties. GNS provides names that are memorable, secure and transitive. Placing names in the context of each individual user eliminates ownership and effectively eliminates the possibility of executive or judicial control over these names.

GNS can be operated alongside DNS and begins to offer its advantages as soon as two parties using the system interact, enabling users to choose GNS or DNS based on their personal trade-off between censorship-resistance and convenience.

GNS and the related tools are available to the public as part of the GNUnet peer-to-peer framework and are free software under the GNU General Public License. The current implementation includes all of the features described in this paper. In the future, we will begin deployment to actual users and perform experiments to find out which usability problems arise with GNS.

Acknowledgments. This work was funded by the Deutsche Forschungsgemein-schaft (DFG) under ENP GR 3688/1-1. We thank Kenneth Almquist, Jacob Appelbaum, Daniel Bernstein, Ludovic Courtès, Tanja Lange, Luke Leighton, Simon Josefsson, Nikos Mavrogiannopoulos, Ondrej Mikle, Stefan Monnier, Niels Möller, Chris Palmer, Martin Pool, Richard Stallman, Neal Walfield and Zooko Wilcox-O'Hearn for insightful comments and discussions on an earlier draft of the paper. We thank Florian Dold for his implementation of Eppstein's efficient set reconciliation method. We thank Werner Koch for insightful discussions and for implementing ECDSA with RFC 6979 support in `libgcrypt`. We thank Krista Grothoff and Ralph Holz for editing the paper.

References

1. Essers, L.: German court finds domain registrar liable for torrent site's copyright infringement (February 2014), http://www.itworld.com/print/403869
2. European Parliament: Resolution on the EU-US Summit of 28 November 2011 (November 2011) P7-RC-2011-0577

3. Anonymous: The collateral damage of internet censorship by dns injection. ACM SIGCOMM Comp. Comm. Review 42(3), 22–27 (July 2012)

4. Arends, R., Austein, R., Larson, M., Massey, D., Rose, S.: DNS Security Introduction and Requirements. IETF RFC 4033 (March 2005)

5. Bernstein, D.J.: Dnscurve: Usable security for dns (August 2008), http://dnscurve.org/

6. Herzberg, A., Shulman, H.: Fragmentation Considered Poisonous: or one-domain-to-rule-them-all.org. In: The IEEE Conference on Communications and Network Secusrity, CNS 2013. IEEE (2013)

7. Soghoian, C., Stamm, S.: Certified lies: Detecting and defeating government interception attacks against SSL (Short paper). In: Danezis, G. (ed.) FC 2011. LNCS, vol. 7035, pp. 250–259. Springer, Heidelberg (2012)

8. Stiegler, M.: An introduction to petname systems. (February 2005), http://www.skyhunter.com/marcs/petnames/IntroPetNames.html

9. Wilcox-O'Hearn, Z.: Names: Decentralized, secure, human-meaningful: Choose two (January 2006), http://zooko.com/distnames.html

10. Wachs, M., Schanzenbach, M., Grothoff, C.: On the feasibility of a censorship resistant decentralized name system. In: Danger, J.-L., Debbabi, M., Marion, J.-Y., Garcia-Alfaro, J., Heywood, N.Z. (eds.) FPS 2013. LNCS, vol. 8352, pp. 19–30. Springer, Heidelberg (2014)

11. Swartz, A.: Squaring the triangle: Secure, decentralized, human-readable names (January 2011), http://www.aaronsw.com/weblog/squarezooko

12. Rivest, R.L., Lampson, B.: SDSI – a simple distributed security infrastructure (1996), http://groups.csail.mit.edu/cis/sdsi.html

13. Bernstein, D.J.: Curve25519: New diffie-hellman speed records. In: Yung, M., Dodis, Y., Kiayias, A., Malkin, T. (eds.) PKC 2006. LNCS, vol. 3958, pp. 207–228. Springer, Heidelberg (2006)

14. Mockapetris, P.: Domain names - implementation and specification. RFC 1035 (Standard) (November 1987)

15. Thomson, S., Huitema, C., Ksinant, V., Souissi, M.: DNS Extensions to Support IP Version 6. RFC 3596 (Draft Standard) (October 2003)

16. Wachs, M.: A Secure Communication Infrastructure for Decentralized Networking Applications. PhD thesis, Technische Universität München (under submission)

17. Deccio, C., Sedayao, J., Kant, K., Mohapatra, P.: Quantifying dns namespace influence. Comput. Netw. 56(2), 780–794 (2012)

18. Evans, N., Grothoff, C.: R^5N: Randomized Recursive Routing for Restricted-Route Networks. In: 5th Int. Conf. on Network and System Security, pp. 316–321 (2011)

19. Ulrich, A., Holz, R., Hauck, P., Carle, G.: Investigating the OpenPGP Web of Trust. In: Atluri, V., Diaz, C. (eds.) ESORICS 2011. LNCS, vol. 6879, pp. 489–507. Springer, Heidelberg (2011)

20. Dingledine, R., Mathewson, N., Syverson, P.: Tor: The second-generation onion router. In: Proc. 13th USENIX Security Symposium (August 2004)

21. Nakamoto, S.: Bitcoin: A peer-to-peer electronic cash system (2008), http://bitcoin.org/bitcoin.pdf

22. http://dot-bit.org/: The Dot-BIT project, A decentralized, open DNS system based on the bitcoin technology (April 2013), http://dot-bit.org/

23. Ford, B.A.: UIA: A Global Connectivity Architecture for Mobile Personal Devices. PhD thesis, Massechusetts Institute of Technology (2008)

A   Special Features

This appendix describes some additional special features in GNS that are used to deal with corner cases that a practical system needs to deal with, but that might only be relevant for a subset of the users.

A.1   Automatic Shortening

Once Dave's client translates "www.carol.+" to "www.carol.buddy.gnu", Dave can resolve "carol.buddy.gnu" to Alice's public key and then lookup the IP address for Alice's server under the respective key in the DHT. At this point, Dave's GNS system will also learn that Alice has set her "NICK" record to "carol". It will then check if the name "carol" is already taken in Dave's zone, and—if "carol" is free—offer Dave the opportunity to introduce a PKEY record into Dave's zone that would *shorten* "carol.buddy.gnu" to "carol.gnu".

Alternatively, the record could be automatically added to a special *shorten zone* that is, in addition to the master zone, under Dave's control. In this case, Alice would become available to Dave under "carol.shorten.gnu", thus highlighting that the name was created by automatic shortening within the domain name.

In either case, shortening eliminates Bob from the trust path for Dave's future interactions with Alice. Shortening is a variation of trust on first use (TOFU), as compromising Bob afterwards would no longer compromise Dave's path to Alice.

A.2   Relative Names in Record Values

GNS slightly modifies the rules for some existing record types in DNS. In particular, names in DNS values are always absolute; GNS allows the notation ".+" to indicate that a name is relative. For example, consider "CNAME" records in DNS, which map an alias (label) to a canonical name: as specified in RFC 1035 [14], the query can (and in GNS will) be restarted using the specified "canonical name". The difference between DNS and GNS is that in GNS, the canonical name can be a relative name (ending in ".+"), an absolute GNS name (ending in ".zkey") or a DNS name.

As with DNS, if there is a "CNAME" record for a label, no other records are allowed to exist for the same label in that zone. Relative names using the ".+" notation are not only legal in "CNAME" records, but in all records that can include names. This specifically includes "MX" and "SOA" records.

A.3   Dealing with Legacy Assumptions: Virtual Hosting and TLS

In order to integrate smoothly with DNS, GNS needs to accommodate some assumptions that current protocols make. We can address most of these with the "LEHO" resource record. In the following, we show how to do this for Web hosting. There are two common practices to address here; one is virtual hosting

(i. e. hosting multiple domains on the same IP address); the other is the practice of identifying TLS peers by their domain name when using X.509 certificates.

The problem we encounter is that GNS gives additional and varying names to an existing service. This breaks a fundamental assumption of these protocols, namely that they are only used with globally unique names. For example, a virtually hosted website may expect to see the HTTP header `Host: www.example.com`, and the HTTP server will fail to return the correct site if the browser sends `Host: www.example.gnu` instead. Similarly, the browser will expect the TLS certificate to contain the requested "www.example.gnu" domain name and reject a certificate for "www.example.com", as the domain name does not match the browser's expectations.

In GNS, each user is free to pick his own petname for the service. Hence, these problems cannot be solved by adding an additional alias to the HTTP server configuration or the TLS certificate. Our solution for this problem is to add the *legacy hostname* record type ("LEHO") for the name. This record type specifies that "www.example.gnu" is known in DNS as "www.example.com". A proxy between the browser and the web server (or a GNS-enabled browser) can then use the name from this record in the HTTP `Host:` header. Naturally, this is only a legacy issue, as a new HTTP header with a label and a zone key could also be introduced to address the virtual hosting problem. The LEHO records can also be used for TLS validation by relating GNS names to globally unique DNS names that are supported by the traditional X.509 PKI. Furthermore, GNS also supports TLSA records, and thus using TLSA records instead of CAs would be a better alternative once browsers support it.

A.4   Handling TLSA and SRV Records

TLSA records are of particular interested for GNS, as they allow TLS applications to use DNSSEC as an alternative to the X.509 CA PKI. With TLSA support in GNS, GNS provides an alternative to X.509 CAs and DNSSEC using this established standard. Furthermore, GNS does not suffer from the lack of end-to-end verification that currently plagues DNSSEC.

However, to support TLSA in GNS a peculiar hurdle needs to be resolved. In DNS, both TLSA and SRV records are special in that their domain names are used to encode the service and protocol to which the record applies. For example, a TLSA record for HTTPS (port 443) on `www.example.com` would be stored under the domain name `_443._tcp.www.example.com`.

In GNS, this would be a problem since dots in GNS domain names are supposed to always correspond to delegations to another zone. Furthermore, even if a special rule were applied for labels starting with underscores, this would mean that say the A record for `www.example.com` would be stored under a different key in the DHT than the corresponding TLSA record. As a result, an application would experience an unpredictable delay between receiving the A record and the TLSA record. As a TLSA record is not guaranteed to exist, this would make it difficult for the application to decide between delaying in hope of using a TLSA record (which may not exist) and using traditional X.509 CAs for authentication (which may not be desired and likely less secure).

GNS solves this problem by introducing another record type, the BOX record. A BOX record contains a 16-bit port, a 16-bit protocol identifier, a 32-bit embedded record type (so far always SRV or TLSA) and the embedded record value. This way, BOX records can be stored directly under `www.example.com` and the corresponding SRV or TLSA values are thus never delayed — not to mention the number of DHT lookups is reduced. When GNS is asked to return SRV or TLSA records via DNS, GNS recognizes the special domain name structure, resolves the BOX record and automatically unboxes the BOX record during the resolution process. Thus, in combination with the user interface (Figure 2) GNS effectively hides the existence of BOX records from DNS users.

We note that DNS avoids the problem of indefinite latency by being able to return NXDOMAIN in case a SRV or TLSA record does not exist. However, in GNS NXDOMAIN is not possible, largely due to GNS's provisions for query privacy. Furthermore, DNS can solve the efficiency problem of a second lookup by using its "additional records" feature in the reply. Here, a DNS server can return additional records that it believes may be useful but that were not explicitly requested. However, returning such additional records might not always work, as DNS implementations can encounter problems with the serious size restrictions (often just 512 bytes) on DNS packets. As GNS replies can contain up to 63 kB of payload data, we do not anticipate problems with the size limit in GNS even for a relatively large number of unusually big TLSA records.

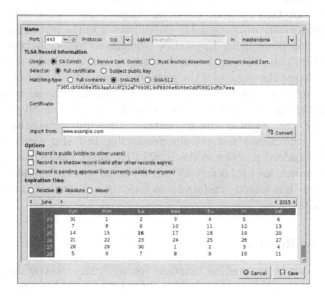

Fig. 2. The user can remain unaware of the behind-the-scenes boxing when creating TLSA records in the GNS zone management interface

A.5   Revocation

In case a zone's private key gets lost or compromised, it is important that the key can be revoked. Whenever a user decides to revoke a zone key, other users must be notified about the revocation. However, we cannot expect users to explicitly query to check if a key has been revoked, as this increases their latency (especially as reliably locating revocations may require a large timeout) and bandwidth consumption for every zone access just to guard against the relatively rare event of a revoked key. Furthermore, issuing a query for zone revocations would create the privacy issue of revealing that a user is interested in a particular zone. Existing methods for revocation checks using certificate revocation lists in X.509 have similar disadvantages in terms of bandwidth, latency increase and privacy.

Instead of these traditional methods, GNS takes advantage of the P2P overlay below the DHT to distribute revocation information by flooding the network. When a peer wants to publish a revocation notice, it simply forwards it to all neighbors; all peers do the same when the receive previously unknown valid revocation notices. However, this simple-yet-Byzantine fault-tolerant algorithm for flooding in the P2P overlay could be used for denial of service attacks. Thus, to ensure that peers cannot abuse this mechanism, GNS requires that revocations include a revocation-specific proof of work. As revocations are expected to be rare special events, it is acceptable to require an expensive computation by the initiator. After that, all peers in the network will remember the revocation forever (revocations are a few bytes, thus there should not be an issue with storage).

In the case of peers joining the network or a fragmented overlay reconnecting, revocations need to be exchanged between the previously separated parts of the network to ensure that all peers have the complete revocation list. This can be done using bandwidth proportional to the difference in the revocation sets known to the respective peers using Eppstein's efficient set reconciliation method. In effect, the bandwidth consumption for healing network partitions or joining peers will then be almost the same as if the peers had always been part of the network.

This revocation mechanism is rather hard to disrupt for an adversary. The adversary would have to be able to block the flood traffic on all paths between the victim and the origin of the revocation. Thus, our revocation mechanism is not only decentralized and privacy-preserving, but also much more robust compared to standard practice in the X.509 PKI today, where blocking of access to certificate revocation lists is an easy way for an adversary to render revocations ineffective. This has forced vendors to include lists of revoked certificates with software updates.

A.6   Shadow Records

GNS records can be marked as "shadow records"; the receiver only interprets shadow records if all other records of the respective type have expired. This is useful to ensure that upon the timeout of one set of records the next set of records is immediately available. This may be important, as propagation delays in the DHT are expected to be larger than those in the DNS hierarchy.

Universally Composable Oblivious Transfer Based on a Variant of LPN

Bernardo David[1,*], Rafael Dowsley[2], and Anderson C. A. Nascimento[3]

[1] Department of Computer Science,
Aarhus University, Denmark
bernardo@cs.au.dk
[2] Institute of Theoretical Informatics,
Karlsruhe Institute of Technology, Germany
rafael.dowsley@kit.edu
[3] Department of Electrical Engineering,
University of Brasilia, Brazil
andclay@ene.unb.br

Abstract. Oblivious transfer (OT) is a fundamental two-party cryptographic primitive that implies secure multiparty computation. In this paper, we introduce the first OT based on the Learning Parity with Noise (LPN) problem. More specifically, we use the LPN variant that was introduced by Alekhnovich (FOCS 2003). We prove that our protocol is secure against active static adversaries in the Universal Composability framework in the common reference string model. Our constructions are based solely on a LPN style assumption and thus represents a clear next step from current code-based OT protocols, which require an additional assumption related to the indistinguishability of public keys from random matrices. Our constructions are inspired by the techniques used to obtain OT based on the McEliece cryptosystem.

1   Introduction

Oblivious transfer (OT) [42,40,21] was introduced in the early days of public-key cryptography and has thereafter played an essential role in modern cryptography. They imply, among other things, the possibility of performing two-party secure computation [24,31] and multi-party computation [13]. Initially many variants of OT were considered, but they are equivalent [12] and therefore in this work we will focus on the most common one: one-out-of-two bit oblivious transfer. In this variant there is a sender who inputs two bits x_0 and x_1, and a receiver who chooses which bit x_c he wants to learn. On one hand, the receiver should learn

* Supported by European Research Council Starting Grant 279447. The author acknowledges support from the Danish National Research Foundation and The National Science Foundation of China (under the grant 61061130540) for the Sino-Danish Center for the Theory of Interactive Computation, and also from the CFEM research centre (supported by the Danish Strategic Research Council) within which part of this work was performed.

D. Gritzalis et al. (Eds.): CANS 2014, LNCS 8813, pp. 143–158, 2014.

x_c, but should have no information about $x_{\bar{c}}$. On the other hand, the sender should not learn the choice bit c.

Given the importance of OT protocols, constructions were extensively studied and nowadays solutions are known based on both generic computational assumptions such as enhanced trapdoor permutations [21], and also based on specific computational assumptions such as: the hardness of factoring [40,26], the Decisional Diffie-Hellman (DDH) assumption [4,35,1,43], the Quadratic Residuosity (QR) assumption [26], the N'th residuosity assumption [26], the hardness of the Subgroup Decision Problem [33], and the McEliece assumptions [19]. Since Shor's algorithm [41] would make factoring and computing discrete logarithms easy in the case that quantum computers become practical, an important question is determining which post-quantum assumptions are sufficient to implement OT protocols. LPN-based/code-based cryptography is one of the main alternatives for a post-quantum world and thus our result improves the understanding in this area.

As with most cryptographic primitives, the first OT protocols considered simple security models (in this case the stand alone model in which there is only one execution of the protocol isolated from the rest of the world). Afterwards, stronger models were considered, such as security in the Universal Composability (UC) framework by Canetti [5], which allows arbitrary composition of the protocols. This latter notion is the most desirable security goal for oblivious transfer protocols, since it allows these protocols to be used as building blocks of more complex primitives and protocols.

In this work we will present the first OT protocol based on a variant of the Learning Parity with Noise (LPN) problem that was introduced by Alekhnovich [2,3]. The protocol achieves UC security against active static adversaries following ideas similar to the ones that Dowsley et al. [19,20,15] used to build OT protocols based on the McEliece assumptions [34]. It is well-known that UC-secure oblivious transfer is impossible in the plain model [6,7], so our solution is in the common reference string (CRS) model.

1.1   Related Works

Cryptography Based on Codes and LPN: McEliece [34] proposed a cryptosystem based on the hardness of the syndrome decoding problem. Later on, Niederreiter [36] proposed a cryptosystem that is the dual of McEliece's cryptosystem. These cryptosystems can be modified to achieve stronger notions of security such as IND-CPA [37,38] and IND-CCA2 [18,22,16]. Based on these cryptosystems it is possible to implement both stand alone secure [19,20] and UC-secure [15] OT protocols. The main drawback of these code-based schemes is that, besides assuming the hardness of the decoding problem, they also assume that the adversary is not able to recover the hidden structure of the keys, which is formalized by assuming that the public-keys are indistinguishable from random matrices. But this later problem is far less studied than the decoding one.

Building public-key encryption schemes from the original LPN problem is a difficult task and so far the only schemes are based on a variant of the LPN problem introduced by Alekhnovich in [2,3], which yields semantically secure encryption [2,3,28] and IND-CCA2 secure encryption by Döttling et al. [17]. Moreover, other cryptographic primitives were built based solely on the Alekhnovich variant of the LPN problem, such as: pseudo random generators (PRG) [28], message authentication codes (MAC) [28], pseudo random functions (PRFs) [28], signature schemes with constant overhead [28], zero-knowledge [29], and commitments [29].

Furthermore, Ishai *et al.* present a protocol for secure two-party and multiparty computation with constant computational overhead in the semi-honest model and slightly superlinear computational overhead in the malicious model based on Alekhnovich's LPN [28]. However, their secure computation constructions assume the existence of bit oblivious transfer, which wasn't built from Alekhnovich's LPN until now (not even with stand-alone security).

Universally Composable OT: Peikert et al. developed a general framework for obtaining efficient, round optimal UC-secure OT in the CRS model [39] that provides instantiations based on the DDH, QR and Learning With Errors (LWE) [39]. Constructions of OT protocols that achieve UC security against different kinds of adversaries under various setup assumptions are also known to be possible under the Decisional Linear (DLIN) assumption [14,30], the DDH and the strong RSA assumptions [23] and the Decisional Composite Residuosity (DCR) assumption [30,11].

Another approach to obtain UC-secure oblivious transfer protocols is to take a stand alone secure OT protocol and use compilers [27,25,10] to achieve an UC-secure protocol. However these compilers require access to UC-secure string commitment schemes that were not yet built from the LPN assumption.

1.2 Our Contributions

In this work we address the open problem of constructing oblivious transfer based on the assumption that LPN is hard. We focus on the LPN variant introduced by Alekhnovich in [2,3]. Our main result is the first Oblivious Transfer protocol based on LPN. Our protocol is Universally Composable and offers security against active static adversaries, *i.e.* adversaries that may deviate in any arbitrary way from the protocol but are forced to corrupt their desired parties before protocol execution starts. It is well-known that UC realizing any interesting multiparty functionality (among them OT) is impossible in the plain model (*i.e.* without a setup assumption) [6,7]. Hence, we build our protocol in the Common Reference String (CRS) model, where the parties are assumed to have access to a fixed string generated before protocol execution starts.

The protocol is based on the cut-and-choose approach of [15], although with a different proof strategy. This approach basically requires a stand-alone passively secure OT protocol and an extractable commitment scheme as building blocks. We show that a stand alone OT protocol (with passive or active security) can be obtained in a similar way as in [19,20]. We also observe that we can obtain an extractable commitment scheme from an IND-CPA secure public key encryption scheme based on Alekhnovich's LPN assumption introduced in [17].

Besides proving that it is possible to construct oblivious transfer from variants of the LPN assumption, our results greatly improve on previous code-based OT protocols by relying on a weaker assumption. Moreover, together with the CCA2 secure Alekhnovich cryptosystem [17] and the LPN based proofs of knowledge and commitments [29], our results contribute towards obtaining more complex cryptographic protocols based on coding based assumptions weaker than McEliece. Unfortunately, the UC secure protocol we introduce is meant to demonstrate the feasibility of obtaining OT based on LPN and lacks on efficiency, having high round communication complexity. Addressing efficiency issues, as well as obtaining security against adaptive adversaries, is left as a future work.

1.3   Outline

In Section 2 we introduce the notation, assumptions and definitions used throughout the paper. In Section 3, we present the active secure universally composable OT protocol based on cut-and-choose techniques.

2   Preliminaries

In this section we introduce our notation and also recall the relevant definitions.

2.1   Notation

If x is a string, then $|x|$ denotes its length, while $|\mathcal{X}|$ represents the cardinality of a set $\mathcal{X}$. If $n \in \mathbb{N}$ then 1^n denotes the string of n ones. $s \leftarrow S$ denotes the operation of choosing an element s of a set S uniformly at random. $w \leftarrow \mathcal{A}^{\mathcal{O}}(x, y, \ldots)$ represents the act of running the algorithm $\mathcal{A}$ with inputs $x, y, \ldots$, oracle access to $\mathcal{O}$ and producing output w. $\mathcal{A}^{\mathcal{O}}(x; r)$ denotes the execution with coins r. We denote by $\Pr(E)$ the probability that the event E occurs. If a and b are two strings of bits or two matrices, we denote by $a|b$ their concatenation. The transpose of a matrix M is M^T. If a and b are two strings of bits, we denote by $\langle a, b \rangle$ their dot product modulo 2 and by $a \oplus b$ their bitwise XOR. $\mathcal{U}_n$ is an oracle that returns an uniformly random element of $\{0, 1\}^n$. If b is a bit, then $\bar{b}$ denotes its inverse (*i.e.* $1 - b$). Let $\mathbb{F}_2$ denote the finite field with 2 elements. For a parameter ρ, χ_ρ denotes the Bernoulli distribution that outputs 1 with probability ρ.

2.2   Encryption Scheme

In this section we describe the LPN-based public-key encryption scheme that was introduced by Döttling et al. [17] and that will be used in this paper. Note that we use the simplest version of their cryptosystem, the one which only achieves

IND-CPA security (which is already enough for our purposes) and does not allow witness recovery.

Let n be the security parameter, $\rho \in O(n^{-(1+2\epsilon)/(1-2\epsilon)})$, and $n_1, \ell_1, \ell_2 \in O(n^{2/(1-2\epsilon)})$. Let $G \in \mathbb{F}_2^{\ell_2 \times n_1}$ be the generator-matrix of a binary linear error-correcting code $\mathcal{C}$ and $\mathsf{Decode}_{\mathcal{C}}$ an efficient decoding procedure for $\mathcal{C}$ that corrects up to $\alpha \ell_2$ errors for a constant α.

Key Generation: Sample a uniformly random matrix $A \in \mathbb{F}_2^{\ell_1 \times n_1}$, a matrix T from $\chi_\rho^{\ell_2 \times \ell_1}$ and a matrix X from $\chi_\rho^{\ell_2 \times n_1}$. Set $B = TA + X$. Set $\mathsf{pk} = (A, B, G)$ and $\mathsf{sk} = T$. Output $(\mathsf{pk}, \mathsf{sk})$.

Encryption $\mathsf{Enc}(\mathsf{pk}, \mathsf{m})$: Given a message $\mathsf{m} \in \mathbb{F}_2^{n_1}$ and the public key $\mathsf{pk} = (A, B, G)$ as input, sample s from $\chi_\rho^{n_1}$, e_1 from $\chi_\rho^{\ell_1}$ and e_2 from $\chi_\rho^{\ell_2}$. Then set $\mathsf{ct}_1 = As + e_1$ and $\mathsf{ct}_2 = Bs + e_2 + G\mathsf{m}$. Output $\mathsf{ct} = (\mathsf{ct}_1, \mathsf{ct}_2)$.

Decryption $\mathsf{Dec}(\mathsf{sk}, \mathsf{ct})$: Given a ciphertext $\mathsf{ct} = (\mathsf{ct}_1, \mathsf{ct}_2)$ and a secret key $\mathsf{sk} = T$ as input, compute $y = \mathsf{ct}_2 - T\mathsf{ct}_1$ and $\mathsf{m} = \mathsf{Decode}_{\mathcal{C}}(y)$. Output m.

The IND-CPA security of this scheme was proved under the following assumption which is equivalent to Alekhnovich's hardness assumption [17].

Assumption 1 *Let $n_1 \in \mathbb{N}$ be the problem parameter, $m = O(n_1)$, $\epsilon > 0$ and $\rho = \rho(n_1) = O(n_1^{-1/2-\epsilon})$. Choose uniformly at random $A \in \mathbb{F}_2^{m \times n_1}$ and $x \in \mathbb{F}_2^{n_1}$. Sample e according to χ_ρ^m. The problem is, given A and $y \in \mathbb{F}_2^m$, to decide whether y is distributed according to $Ax + e$ or uniformly at random.*

The current best algorithms to attack this problem require time of the order $2^{n^{1/2-\epsilon}}$ and for this reason by setting $n_1 = O(n^{2/(1-2\epsilon)})$ where n is the security parameter of the encryption scheme the hardness is normalized to $2^{\Theta(n)}$.

2.3 Extractable Commitment Schemes

A string commitment scheme is said to be *extractable* if there exists a polynomial-time simulator that is able to obtain the committed value m before the *Open* phase. In the CRS model, we will build an extractable commitment scheme based on the encryption scheme from the previous section in the following way. The CRS contains a public key pk of the cryptosystem and the scheme works as follows:

- $\mathsf{Com}_{\mathsf{crs}}(\mathsf{m})$ The sender encrypts m under the public key pk with randomness (s, e_1, e_2) and sends the corresponding ciphertext ct to the receiver as a commitment.
- $\mathsf{Open}_{\mathsf{crs}}(\mathsf{m})$ The sender sends the message m and the randomness (s, e_1, e_2) used in the commitment phase. The receiver checks if the encryption of m with the randomness (s, e_1, e_2) results in the ciphertext ct that he received before. Additionally, for a fixed constant $\gamma > 1$ such that $\gamma \rho < \alpha/3$, he checks if the Hamming weights of s, e_1 and e_2 are respectively smaller than $\gamma \rho n_1$, $\gamma \rho \ell_1$ and $\gamma \rho \ell_2$. If all tests are passed, the receiver accepts the opening as correct.

Note that in the case that both parties are honest, the Hamming weight tests will be passed with overwhelming probability, as it was shown in the proof of the cryptosystem [17] that larger Hamming weights only occur with negligible probability, so the correctness of the commitment scheme follows. The hiding property follows trivially from the IND-CPA security of the encryption scheme. For the binding property, first notice that the Hamming weight tests performed during the opening phase ensure that the error term $Xs + e_2 - Te_1$ that would appear in a decryption operation of $\mathsf{Enc}(\mathsf{pk}, \mathsf{m}; s, e_1, e_2)$ would be within the decoding limit of $\mathcal{C}$ and so the decryption would have been successfully performed and m recovered (see the proof of correctness of [17] for details). I.e., for any opening information $(\mathsf{m}, s, e_1, e_2)$ that passes the tests, we have $\mathsf{Dec}(\mathsf{sk}, \mathsf{Enc}(\mathsf{pk}, \mathsf{m}; s, e_1, e_2)) = \mathsf{m}$ and $\mathsf{Enc}(\mathsf{pk}, \mathsf{m}; s, e_1, e_2) = \mathsf{ct}$. Thus, due to the uniqueness of the decryption, there is only one m that can pass all the tests performed in the opening phase.

In order to extract the committed values, the simulator generates a key pair $(\mathsf{pk}, \mathsf{sk})$ for the cryptosystem and sets the CRS to pk. With the knowledge of the secret key sk, he can extract from any ct the only value m that can be successfully opened in a later stage.

2.4 Universal Composability

The Universal Composability framework was introduced by Canetti in [5] to analyze the security of cryptographic protocols and primitives under arbitrary composition. In this framework, protocol security is analyzed by comparing an ideal world execution and a real world execution. The comparison is performed by an *environment* $\mathcal{Z}$, which is represented by a *PPT* machine and has direct access to all inputs and outputs of the individual parties and to the adversary $\mathcal{A}$. In the ideal world execution, dummy parties (possibly controlled by a *PPT simulator* $\mathcal{S}$) interact directly with the ideal functionality $\mathcal{F}$, which works as trusted third party that computes the desired function or primitive. In the real world execution, several *PPT* parties (possibly corrupted by a real world adversary $\mathcal{A}$) interact with each other by means of a protocol π that realizes the ideal functionality. The real world execution is represented by the ensemble $EXEC_{\pi,\mathcal{A},\mathcal{Z}}$, while the ideal execution is represented by the $IDEAL_{\mathcal{F},\mathcal{S},\mathcal{Z}}$. The rationale behind this framework lies in showing that the environment $\mathcal{Z}$ (that represents all the things that happen outside of the protocol execution) is not able to efficiently distinguish between $EXEC_{\pi,\mathcal{A},\mathcal{Z}}$ and $IDEAL_{\mathcal{F},\mathcal{S},\mathcal{Z}}$, thus implying that the real world protocol is as secure as the ideal functionality.[1]

Adversarial Model. In this work we consider security against static adversaries, *i.e.* the adversary corrupts parties before the protocol execution and corrupted parties remain so during the whole execution. Moreover, we consider active adversaries, which may arbitrarily deviate from the protocol in order to perform an attack.

---

[1] For the sake of brevity, we refer the reader to Canetti's work [5] for further details and definitions regarding the UC framework.

Setup Assumptions. The security of our protocol is proved in the Common Reference String (CRS) model (referred to as the $\mathcal{F}_{CRS} - hybrid$ model in [5]), where protocol parties are assumed to have access to a fixed string generated according to a specific distribution before protocol execution starts, in a so called setup phase. The CRS ideal functionality $\mathcal{F}_{CRS}$ is formally presented below.

Common Reference String Ideal Functionality. The formal definition of the CRS ideal functionality $\mathcal{F}_{CRS}^{\mathcal{D}}$ is taken from [9].

Functionality $\mathcal{F}_{CRS}^{\mathcal{D}}$
$\mathcal{F}_{CRS}^{\mathcal{D}}$ runs with parties $(P_1, ..., P_n)$ and is parametrized by an algorithm $\mathcal{D}$.   • When receiving a message (sid, P_i, P_j) from P_i, let $crs \leftarrow \mathcal{D}(1^n)$, send (sid, crs) to P_i and send (crs, P_i, P_j) to the adversary. Next, when receiving (sid, P_i, P_j) from P_j (and only P_j), send (sid, crs) to P_j and to the adversary, and halt.

Oblivious Transfer Ideal Functionality. The basic 1-out-of-2 oblivious transfer functionality $\mathcal{F}_{OT}$ as defined in [8] is presented bellow.

Functionality $\mathcal{F}_{OT}$
$\mathcal{F}_{OT}$ interacts with a sender **S** and a receiver **R**.   • Upon receiving a message $(\mathsf{sid}, \mathsf{sender}, x_0, x_1)$ from **S**, where each $x_i \in \{0,1\}^\ell$, store (x_0, x_1) (the length of the strings is fixed and known to all parties).   • Upon receiving a message $(\mathsf{sid}, \mathsf{receiver}, c)$ from **R**, check if a $(\mathsf{sid}, \mathsf{sender}, \cdots)$ message was previously sent. If yes, send (sid, x_c) to **R**, sid to the adversary $\mathcal{S}$ and halt. If not, send nothing to **R** (but continue running).

Similarly to the framework of [39], our protocols reuse the same CRS for multiple oblivious transfer invocations. In order to achieve this, we employ the same techniques of UC with joint state (JUC) [9].

3   Universally Composable Active Secure OT

In this section, we construct an universally composable OT protocol secure against active static adversaries in the Common Reference String model. Using cut-and-choose techniques similar to [15] we depart from a stand alone OT protocol. The stand alone protocol can be constructed from a IND-CPA secure cryptosystem following the paradigm of [4], previously employed in [19] to obtain OT based on the McEliece assumptions. Basically, the receiver **R** generates a valid public key, scrambles it with random matrices of the same size and sends both valid and scrambled keys to the sender **S**. **S** encrypts each of its messages under one of the public keys provided by **R** and sends the ciphertexts back. **R** is able to decrypt only the ciphertext created with the valid public key, obtaining only one of the messages. On the other hand, **S** cannot distinguish between the valid and scrambled public keys generated by **R**, thus not knowing which message **R** obtains.

In the universally composable protocol, **R** generates a number of valid public keys K_{i,d_i} for random d_i's and commits to them. Next, both players run a coin tossing protocol to generate the random paddings R_i that are used by **R** to scramble each valid public key as $K_{i,\bar{d}_i} = K_{i,d_i} + R_i$. **R** sends all $K_{i,1}$ keys to **S**, who retrieves keys $K_{i,0} = K_{i,1} + R_i$. Next, another coin tossing protocol is run between **S** and **R** to obtain a random string Ω. For each bit equal to 1 in Ω, **R** opens the corresponding commitments to valid public keys for verification. For each bit equal to 0 in Ω, **R** sends to **S** information that derandomizes the corresponding public key pairs such that the valid public key corresponds to his choice bit. **S** uses the corresponding public key pairs to encrypt an additive share of its messages such that **R** can only retrieve a message if it's able to decrypt all ciphertexts. An extractable commitment scheme is employed, allowing the simulator to cheat and obtain the information necessary to carry out the simulation.

We use the LPN-based IND-CPA secure public key cryptosystem from [17] (described in Section 2.2) as a building block for encryption and extractable commitments (described in Section 2.3). In the following protocol, parameter ω controls the number of parallel executions of randomized OTs. The protocol's security parameter is composed of ω and the underlying cryptosystem's security parameter n. The protocol has 10 rounds and communication complexity in the order of $O(\omega n)$. The exact communication complexity depends on the relation between ω and n, which in turn depends on the desired security level and the hardness of solving Alekhnovich's LPN problem with the currently best attack.

Protocol 1
Inputs: The sender **S** takes as input two bits x_0 and x_1, while the receiver **R** takes as input a choice bit c.
Common reference string: A random public key ck used for the commitment scheme.

1. Upon being activated with their inputs, the parties query $\mathcal{F}_{CRS}$ with (sid, **S**, **R**) and receive (sid, crs) as answer.
2. **R** initiates the first round by performing the following actions:
   (a) **R** initially samples a random bit string $d \leftarrow \{0,1\}^\omega$, where, d_i denotes each bit in d for $i = 1, \ldots, \omega$.
   (b) For $i = 1, \ldots, \omega$, **R** generates a public-key pk_i and a secret-key sk_i, and sets $K_{i,d_i} = \mathsf{pk}_i = (A_i, B_i, G_i)$.

(c) $\mathbf{R}$ commits to all public keys K_{i,d_i} by sending to $\mathbf{S}$ the message $(\mathtt{sid}, \mathsf{Com}_{\mathsf{ck}}(K_{1,d_1}), \ldots, \mathsf{Com}_{\mathsf{ck}}(K_{\omega,d_\omega}))$.

3. Both parties run a coin tossing protocol in order to obtain random matrices:

   (a) $\mathbf{S}$ samples uniformly random matrices of the same size as the public key matrices $A_i' \in \mathbb{F}_2^{\ell_1 \times n_1}$, $B_i' \in \mathbb{F}_2^{\ell_2 \times n_1}$, $G_i' \in \mathbb{F}_2^{\ell_2 \times n_1}$, assigns $R_i' = (A_i', B_i', G_i')$ and sends a commitment $(\mathtt{sid}, \mathsf{Com}_{\mathsf{ck}}(R_1'), \ldots, \mathsf{Com}_{\mathsf{ck}}(R_\omega'))$ to $\mathbf{R}$.

   (b) For $i = 1, \ldots, \omega$, $\mathbf{R}$ samples uniformly random $A_i'' \in \mathbb{F}_2^{\ell_1 \times n_1}$, $B_i'' \in \mathbb{F}_2^{\ell_2 \times n_1}$, $G_i'' \in \mathbb{F}_2^{\ell_2 \times n_1}$, assigns $R_i'' = (A_i'', B_i'', G_i'')$ and sends $(\mathtt{sid}, R_1'', \ldots, R_\omega'')$ to $\mathbf{S}$.

   (c) $\mathbf{S}$ opens its commitments and both parties compute $R_i = (\bar{A}_i = A_i' + A_i'', \bar{B}_i = B_i' + B_i'', \bar{C}_i = C_i' + C_i'')$ for $i = 1, \ldots, \omega$.

4. $\mathbf{R}$ computes the remaining keys as follows:

   (a) For $i = 1, \ldots, \omega$, $\mathbf{R}$ sets $K_{i,\overline{d_i}} = K_{i,d_i} + R_i = (A_i + \bar{A}_i, B_i + \bar{B}_i, G_i + \bar{G}_i)$, scrambling the valid keys related to the random choice bit using the random matrices obtained in the coin tossing.

   (b) $\mathbf{R}$ sends all the resulting keys $K_{i,1} = (\tilde{A}_i, \tilde{B}_i, \tilde{G}_i)$ to $\mathbf{S}$ as $(\mathtt{sid}, K_{1,1}, \ldots, K_{\omega,1})$.

5. $\mathbf{S}$ computes $K_{i,0} = K_{i,1} + R_i = (\tilde{A}_i + \bar{A}_i, \tilde{B}_i + \bar{B}_i, \tilde{G}_i + \bar{G}_i)$ obtaining the public key pairs $K_{i,0}, K_{i,1}$, for $i = 1, \ldots, \omega$.

6. Both parties run a coin tossing protocol in order to obtain a random bit string Ω:

   (a) $\mathbf{S}$ samples a random bit string $v \leftarrow \{0,1\}^\omega$ and sends a commitment $(\mathtt{sid}, \mathsf{Com}_{\mathsf{ck}}(v))$ to $\mathbf{R}$.

   (b) $\mathbf{R}$ chooses a random bit string v' and sends $(\mathtt{sid}, v')$ to $\mathbf{S}$.

   (c) $\mathbf{S}$ opens its commitment and both parties compute $\Omega = v \oplus v'$.

7. Let I be the set of indexes $i \in \{1, \ldots, \omega\}$ such that $\Omega_i = 1$ and let J be the set of indexes $j \in \{1, \ldots, \omega\}$ such that $\Omega_j = 0$. $\mathbf{R}$ performs the following actions:

   - **Verification:** For each $i \in I$, $\mathbf{R}$ opens the commitments to K_{i,d_i} by sending $(\mathtt{sid}, \mathsf{Open}_{\mathsf{ck}}(K_{i,d_i}))$.
   - **Derandomization:** For each $j \in J$, let ρ_j be a reordering bit such that if $\rho_j = 1$ the keys $K_{j,0}, K_{j,1}$ are swapped and if $\rho_j = 0$ they are left as they are. For each $j \in J$, $\mathbf{R}$ sends $(\mathtt{sid}, \rho_j)$ to $\mathbf{S}$ in such a way that, after the reordering, all the keys $K_{j,c}$ are valid.[2]

8. For each opening $(\mathtt{sid}, \mathsf{Open}_{\mathsf{ck}}(K_{i,d_i}))$ that it receives, $\mathbf{S}$ checks that the public key pair $K_{i,0}, K_{i,1}$ is honestly generated (*i.e.* that there exists $b \in \{0,1\}$ s.t. $K_{i,b} = K_{i,d_i}$ and $K_{i,\bar{b}} = K_{i,d_i} \oplus R_i$). If this check fails for at least one public key pair $\mathbf{S}$ aborts, otherwise it continues as follows:

---

[2] If the operation performed with ρ is seen as computing $(\hat{K}_{j,0}, \hat{K}_{j,1}) = K_{j,0\oplus\rho}, K_{j,1\oplus\rho}$, the choice of ρ can be seen as $\rho = d_j \oplus c$. Here $\mathbf{R}$ makes sure that the public keys in the unopened commitments that will be used to encrypt the bit x_c (related to its choice bit) are valid public keys.

- For each reordering bit ρ_j received by **S**, it derandomizes the corresponding public key pair by computing $(\hat{K}_{j,0}, \hat{K}_{j,1}) = K_{j,0 \oplus \rho}, K_{j,1 \oplus \rho}$.
- Let μ be the number of indexes in J, and let $j_1, ..., j_\mu$ denote each of these indexes. For $j = j_1, ..., j_\mu$, **S** generates μ bits $x_{j,0}$ such that $x_{j_1,0} \oplus \cdots \oplus x_{j_\mu,0} = x_0$ and μ bits $x_{j,1}$ such that $x_{j_1,1} \oplus \cdots \oplus x_{j_\mu,1} = x_1$.
- For $j = j_1, ..., j_\mu$, **S** encrypts $x_{j,0}$ under public key $\hat{K}_{j,0}$ and encrypts $x_{j,1}$ under public key $\hat{K}_{j,1}$ by computing $\mathsf{ct}_{j,0} = \mathsf{Enc}(\hat{K}_{j,0}, x_{j,0})$ and $\mathsf{ct}_{j,1} = \mathsf{Enc}(\hat{K}_{j,1}, x_{j,1})$.
- **S** sends all ciphertexts to **R** as $(\mathsf{sid}, (\mathsf{ct}_{j_1,0}, \mathsf{ct}_{j_1,1}), ..., (\mathsf{ct}_{j_\mu,0}, \mathsf{ct}_{j_\mu,1}))$.

9. For $j = j_1, ..., j_\mu$, **R** decrypts the ciphertexts related to x_c by computing $x_{j,c} = \mathsf{Dec}(\mathsf{sk}_j, \mathsf{ct}_{j,c})$. If any of the decryption attempts fail, **R** outputs a random $x_c \leftarrow \{0,1\}$. Otherwise, **R** outputs $x_c = x_{j_1,c} \oplus \cdots \oplus x_{j_\mu,c}$.

Correctness. It is clear that the protocol runs in polynomial time. The classical coin tossing protocol ensures that the string Ω and matrices R_i are uniformly distributed and the commitment hiding property ensures that **S** cannot obtain any information about the keys in the unopened commitments.

Notice that, after the reordering, all the public key pairs $(\hat{K}_{j,0}, \hat{K}_{j,1})$ are such that $\hat{K}_{j,c}$ is a valid public key and $\hat{K}_{j,\bar{c}}$ is a scrambled public key (*i.e.* summed with the random matrices in R_j). Thus, **R** is able to decrypt all of the ciphertexts $\mathsf{ct}_{j,c}$ for $j = j_1, ..., j_\mu$, obtaining all bits $x_{j,c}$ that are necessary to compute the bit $x_c = x_{j_1,c} \oplus \cdots \oplus x_{j_\mu,c}$. On the other hand, **R** cannot obtain $x_{\bar{c}}$ through decrypting the ciphertexts $\mathsf{ct}_{i,\bar{c}}$, since they were generated under the scrambled keys. **S** cannot obtain the choice bit c by distinguishing the valid public keys from randomized keys, since the public-key of the cryptosystem is pseudorandom [29,17].

Theorem 1. *Protocol 1 securely realizes the functionality $\mathcal{F}_{OT}$ in the $\mathcal{F}_{CRS}$-hybrid model under Assumption 1. Let π denote Protocol 1. For every PPT static malicious adversary $\mathcal{A}$ there is a PPT simulator $\mathcal{S}$ such that for all PPT environment $\mathcal{Z}$, the following holds:*

$$EXEC_{\pi,\mathcal{A},\mathcal{Z}} \stackrel{c}{\approx} IDEAL_{\mathcal{F}_{OT},\mathcal{S},\mathcal{Z}}$$

3.1   Security Proof

In this section we analyse the security of Protocol 1 by constructing a simulator $\mathcal{S}$ that interacts with $\mathcal{F}_{OT}$ such that no environment $\mathcal{Z}$ can distinguish between interactions with a static adversary $\mathcal{A}$ in the real world and interactions with $\mathcal{S}$ in the ideal world. The formal description of the simulator and the full proof of Theorem 1 showing that execution with $\mathcal{S}$ is indeed indistinguishable from execution with $\mathcal{A}$ are left for the full version of this paper. We first present trivial simulation cases (where both parties are honest or corrupted) and then consider the cases where only **S** or only **R** is corrupted separately. The simulators are based on techniques introduced in [32] and [15]. For each corruption scenario, $\mathcal{S}$ works as follows:

Simulating Communication with $\mathcal{Z}$. $\mathcal{S}$ writes all the messages received from $\mathcal{Z}$ in $\mathcal{A}$'s input tape, simulating $\mathcal{A}$'s environment. Also, $\mathcal{S}$ writes all messages from $\mathcal{A}$'s output tape to its own output tape, forwarding them to $\mathcal{Z}$.

Simulating Trivial Cases. If both **S** and **R** are corrupted, $\mathcal{S}$ simply runs $\mathcal{A}$ internally. Notice that $\mathcal{A}$ will generate the messages from both corrupted **S** and **R**. If neither **S** and **R** are corrupted, $\mathcal{S}$ runs the protocol between honest **S** and **R** internally on the inputs provided by $\mathcal{Z}$. All messages are delivered to $\mathcal{A}$.

Simulator for a Corrupted S. If only **S** is corrupted, the simulator $\mathcal{S}$ has to extract the bits x_0 and x_1 (the adversary's input) by interacting with adversary $\mathcal{A}$ through Protocol 1. The main trick for doing this lies in cheating the coin tossing phase by means of the underlying commitment scheme's extractability. The simulator will use this ability to construct public key pairs where both keys are valid (allowing it to obtain both bits) and pass the corrupted **S**'s verification without getting caught. $\mathcal{S}$ sends the x_0 and x_1 obtained after decryption to $\mathcal{F}_{OT}$ and terminates. The simulator $\mathcal{S}$ is formally described in Appendix A.

Simulator for a Corrupted R. In this case where only **R** is corrupted, the simulator has to extract the choice bit c (the adversary's input) by interacting with the adversary $\mathcal{A}$ through Protocol 1. First, simulator $\mathcal{S}$ sets the CRS in such a way that it can extract the commitments sent by $\mathcal{A}$ in the first step. $\mathcal{S}$ runs the protocol as an honest **S**, only deviating to extract the commitments containing the valid public key sent by $\mathcal{A}$. After the public key pairs are reordered, $\mathcal{S}$ verifies which key $\hat{K}_{j,0}$ or $\hat{K}_{j,1}$ corresponds to the valid public key $\hat{K}_{j,d_j}$ in the extracted (but unopened) commitment. The choice bit is determined as the bit c such that $\hat{K}_{j,c} = \hat{K}_{j,d_j}$. $\mathcal{S}$ sends c to $\mathcal{F}_{OT}$, obtaining x_c in return. $\mathcal{S}$ then encrypts x_c and a dummy x_{1-c} using the procedure of a honest sender, sends the corresponding message to $\mathcal{A}$ and terminates. The simulator $\mathcal{S}$ is formally described in Appendix B.

References

1. Aiello, W., Ishai, Y., Reingold, O.: Priced Oblivious Transfer: How to Sell Digital Goods. In: Pfitzmann, B. (ed.) EUROCRYPT 2001. LNCS, vol. 2045, pp. 119–135. Springer, Heidelberg (2001)
2. Alekhnovich, M.: More on average case vs approximation complexity. In: 44th FOCS, Cambridge, Massachusetts, USA, October 11-14, pp. 298–307. IEEE Computer Society Press (2003)
3. Alekhnovich, M.: More on average case vs approximation complexity. Computational Complexity 20, 755–786 (2011)

4. Bellare, M., Micali, S.: Non-interactive oblivious transfer and spplications. In: Brassard, G. (ed.) CRYPTO 1989. LNCS, vol. 435, pp. 547–557. Springer, Heidelberg (1990)
5. Canetti, R.: Universally composable security: A new paradigm for cryptographic protocols. In: 42nd FOCS, Las Vegas, Nevada, USA, October 14-17, pp. 136–145. IEEE Computer Society Press (2001)
6. Canetti, R., Fischlin, M.: Universally composable commitments. In: Kilian, J. (ed.) CRYPTO 2001. LNCS, vol. 2139, pp. 19–40. Springer, Heidelberg (2001)
7. Canetti, R., Kushilevitz, E., Lindell, Y.: On the limitations of universally composable two-party computation without set-up assumptions. Journal of Cryptology 19(2), 135–167 (2006)
8. Canetti, R., Lindell, Y., Ostrovsky, R., Sahai, A.: Universally composable two-party and multi-party secure computation. In: 34th ACM STOC, Montréal, Québec, Canada, May 19-21, pp. 494–503. ACM Press (2002)
9. Canetti, R., Rabin, T.: Universal composition with joint state. In: Boneh, D. (ed.) CRYPTO 2003. LNCS, vol. 2729, pp. 265–281. Springer, Heidelberg (2003)
10. Choi, S.G., Dachman-Soled, D., Malkin, T., Wee, H.: Simple, black-box constructions of adaptively secure protocols. In: Reingold, O. (ed.) TCC 2009. LNCS, vol. 5444, pp. 387–402. Springer, Heidelberg (2009)
11. Choi, S.G., Katz, J., Wee, H., Zhou, H.-S.: Efficient, adaptively secure, and composable oblivious transfer with a single, global CRS. In: Kurosawa, K., Hanaoka, G. (eds.) PKC 2013. LNCS, vol. 7778, pp. 73–88. Springer, Heidelberg (2013)
12. Crépeau, C.: Equivalence between two flavours of oblivious transfers. In: Pomerance, C. (ed.) CRYPTO 1987. LNCS, vol. 293, pp. 350–354. Springer, Heidelberg (1988)
13. Crépeau, C., van de Graaf, J., Tapp, A.: Committed oblivious transfer and private multi-party computation. In: Coppersmith, D. (ed.) CRYPTO 1995. LNCS, vol. 963, pp. 110–123. Springer, Heidelberg (1995)
14. Damgård, I., Nielsen, J.B., Orlandi, C.: Essentially optimal universally composable oblivious transfer. In: Lee, P.J., Cheon, J.H. (eds.) ICISC 2008. LNCS, vol. 5461, pp. 318–335. Springer, Heidelberg (2009)
15. David, B.M., Nascimento, A.C.A., Müller-Quade, J.: Universally composable oblivious transfer from lossy encryption and the mceliece assumptions. In: Smith, A. (ed.) ICITS 2012. LNCS, vol. 7412, pp. 80–99. Springer, Heidelberg (2012)
16. Döttling, N., Dowsley, R., Müller-Quade, J., Nascimento, A.C.A.: A cca2 secure variant of the mceliece cryptossystem. IEEE Transactions on Information Theory (to appear)
17. Döttling, N., Müller-Quade, J., Nascimento, A.C.A.: IND-CCA secure cryptography based on a variant of the LPN problem. In: Wang, X., Sako, K. (eds.) ASIACRYPT 2012. LNCS, vol. 7658, pp. 485–503. Springer, Heidelberg (2012)
18. Dowsley, R., Müller-Quade, J., Nascimento, A.C.A.: A CCA2 secure public key encryption scheme based on the McEliece assumptions in the standard model. In: Fischlin, M. (ed.) CT-RSA 2009. LNCS, vol. 5473, pp. 240–251. Springer, Heidelberg (2009)
19. Dowsley, R., van de Graaf, J., Müller-Quade, J., Nascimento, A.C.A.: Oblivious transfer based on the mceliece assumptions. In: Safavi-Naini, R. (ed.) ICITS 2008. LNCS, vol. 5155, pp. 107–117. Springer, Heidelberg (2008)

20. Dowsley, R., van de Graaf, J., Müller-Quade, J., Nascimento, A.C.A.: Oblivious transfer based on the mceliece assumptions. IEICE Transactions on Fundamentals of Electronics, Communications and Computer Sciences E95-A(2), 567–575 (2012)

21. Even, S., Goldreich, O., Lempel, A.: A randomized protocol for signing contracts. In: Chaum, D., Rivest, R.L., Sherman, A.T. (eds.) CRYPTO 1982, pp. 205–210. Plenum Press, New York (1982)

22. Freeman, D.M., Goldreich, O., Kiltz, E., Rosen, A., Segev, G.: More constructions of lossy and correlation-secure trapdoor functions. In: Nguyen, P.Q., Pointcheval, D. (eds.) PKC 2010. LNCS, vol. 6056, pp. 279–295. Springer, Heidelberg (2010)

23. Garay, J.A.: Efficient and universally composable committed oblivious transfer and applications. In: Naor, M. (ed.) TCC 2004. LNCS, vol. 2951, pp. 297–316. Springer, Heidelberg (2004)

24. Goldreich, O., Micali, S., Wigderson, A.: How to play any mental game or A completeness theorem for protocols with honest majority. In: Aho, A. (ed.) 19th ACM STOC, May 25-27, pp. 218–229. ACM Press, New York (1987)

25. Haitner, I.: Semi-honest to malicious oblivious transfer—the black-box way. In: Canetti, R. (ed.) TCC 2008. LNCS, vol. 4948, pp. 412–426. Springer, Heidelberg (2008)

26. Halevi, S., Kalai, Y.T.: Smooth projective hashing and two-message oblivious transfer. Journal of Cryptology 25(1), 158–193 (2012)

27. Ishai, Y., Kushilevitz, E., Lindell, Y., Petrank, E.: Black-box constructions for secure computation. In: Kleinberg, J.M. (ed.) 38th ACM STOC, Seattle, Washington, USA, May 21-23, pp. 99–108. ACM (2006)

28. Ishai, Y., Kushilevitz, E., Ostrovsky, R., Sahai, A.: Cryptography with constant computational overhead. In: Ladner, R.E., Dwork, C. (eds.) 40th ACM STOC, Victoria, British Columbia, Canada, May 17-20, pp. 433–442. ACM Press (2008)

29. Jain, A., Krenn, S., Pietrzak, K., Tentes, A.: Commitments and efficient zero-knowledge proofs from learning parity with noise. In: Wang, X., Sako, K. (eds.) ASIACRYPT 2012. LNCS, vol. 7658, pp. 663–680. Springer, Heidelberg (2012)

30. Jarecki, S., Shmatikov, V.: Efficient two-party secure computation on committed inputs. In: Naor, M. (ed.) EUROCRYPT 2007. LNCS, vol. 4515, pp. 97–114. Springer, Heidelberg (2007)

31. Kilian, J.: Founding cryptography on oblivious transfer. In: 20th ACM STOC, Chicago, Illinois, USA, May 2-4, pp. 20–31. ACM Press (1988)

32. Lindell, A.Y.: Efficient fully-simulatable oblivious transfer. In: Malkin, T. (ed.) CT-RSA 2008. LNCS, vol. 4964, pp. 52–70. Springer, Heidelberg (2008)

33. Lipmaa, H.: New communication-efficient oblivious transfer protocols based on pairings. In: Wu, T.-C., Lei, C.-L., Rijmen, V., Lee, D.-T. (eds.) ISC 2008. LNCS, vol. 5222, pp. 441–454. Springer, Heidelberg (2008)

34. McEliece, R.J.: A public-key cryptosystem based on algebraic coding theory. Technical Report DSN Progress Report 4244, Jet Propulsion Laboratory (1978)

35. Naor, M., Pinkas, B.: Efficient oblivious transfer protocols. In: Kosaraju, S.R. (ed.) 12th SODA, Washington, DC, USA, January 7-9, pp. 448–457. ACM-SIAM (2001)

36. Niederreiter, H.: Knapsack-type cryptosystems and algebraic coding theory. Problems of Control and Information Theory 15, 159–166 (1986)

37. Nojima, R., Imai, H., Kobara, K., Morozov, K.: Semantic security for the mceliece cryptosystem without random oracles. In: International Workshop on Coding and Cryptography (WCC), pp. 257–268 (2007)

38. Nojima, R., Imai, H., Kobara, K., Morozov, K.: Semantic security for the mceliece cryptosystem without random oracles. Des. Codes Cryptography 49(1-3), 289–305 (2008)
39. Peikert, C., Vaikuntanathan, V., Waters, B.: A framework for efficient and composable oblivious transfer. In: Wagner, D. (ed.) CRYPTO 2008. LNCS, vol. 5157, pp. 554–571. Springer, Heidelberg (2008)
40. Rabin, M.O.: How to exchange secrets by oblivious transfer. Technical Report Technical Memo TR-81, Aiken Computation Laboratory, Harvard University (1981)
41. Shor, P.W.: Algorithms for quantum computation: Discrete logarithms and factoring. In: 35th FOCS, Santa Fe, New Mexico, November 20-22, pp. 124–134. IEEE Computer Society Press (1994)
42. Wiesner, S.: Conjugate coding. SIGACT News 15(1), 78–88 (1983)
43. Zhang, B., Lipmaa, H., Wang, C., Ren, K.: Practical fully simulatable oblivious transfer with sublinear communication. In: Sadeghi, A.-R. (ed.) FC 2013. LNCS, vol. 7859, pp. 78–95. Springer, Heidelberg (2013)

A   Simulator for a Corrupted S

Simulating $\mathcal{F}_{CRS}$: $\mathcal{S}$ generates a commitment key $\mathsf{ck} \leftarrow \mathsf{Gen}(1^n)$ for which he knows the secret key tk and sets $\mathsf{crs} = (\mathsf{ck})$. Later on, the secret key will be used as a trapdoor to extract unopened commitments. When the parties query $\mathcal{F}_{CRS}$, $\mathcal{S}$ hands them (sid, crs).

When the dummy **S** is activated, $\mathcal{S}$ proceeds as follows:

1. $\mathcal{S}$ initiates the first round by performing the following actions:
   (a) $\mathcal{S}$ initially samples a random bit string $d \leftarrow \{0,1\}^\omega$, where d_i denotes each bit in d for $i = 1, \ldots, \omega$.
   (b) For $i = 1, \ldots, \omega$, $\mathcal{S}$ generates a public-key pk_i and a secret-key sk_i, and sets $K_{i,d_i} = \mathsf{pk}_i = (A_i, B_i, G_i)$.
   (c) $\mathcal{S}$ commits to all public keys K_{i,d_i} by sending to $\mathcal{A}$ the message $(\mathtt{sid}, \mathsf{Com}_{\mathsf{ck}}(K_{1,d_i}), \ldots, \mathsf{Com}_{\mathsf{ck}}(K_{\omega,d_i}))$.
2. $\mathcal{S}$ performs the coin tossing to generate the random matrices as follows:
   (a) Upon receiving $(\mathtt{sid}, \mathsf{Com}_{\mathsf{ck}}(R'_1), \ldots, \mathsf{Com}_{\mathsf{ck}}(R'_\omega))$ from $\mathcal{A}$, $\mathcal{S}$ extracts the $R'_i = (A'_i, B'_i, G'_i)$.
   (b) $\mathcal{S}$ chooses public-keys $\mathsf{pk}_{i,\overline{d_i}} = (\overline{A}_i, \overline{B}_i, \overline{G}_i)$ with the respective secret-key, sets $K_{i,\overline{d_i}} = \mathsf{pk}_{i,\overline{d_i}}$ and computes $R''_i = R'_i \oplus \mathsf{pk}_{i,\overline{d_i}} = (\overline{A}_i + A'_i, \overline{B}_i + B'_i, \overline{G}_i + G'_i)$ for $i = 1, \ldots, \omega$. $\mathcal{S}$ sends $(\mathtt{sid}, R''_1, \ldots, R''_\omega)$ to $\mathcal{A}$.
3. Upon receiving the openings from $\mathcal{A}$, $\mathcal{S}$ sends $\mathsf{pk}_{1,1}, \ldots, \mathsf{pk}_{\omega,1}$ to $\mathcal{A}$.
4. $\mathcal{S}$ simulates the coin tossing:
   – Upon receiving $(\mathtt{sid}, \mathsf{Com}_{\mathsf{ck}}(v))$ from $\mathcal{A}$, $\mathcal{S}$ chooses a random bit string $v' \leftarrow \{0,1\}^\omega$ and sends to $\mathcal{A}$.
   – Upon receiving an opening $(\mathtt{sid}, \mathsf{Open}_{\mathsf{ck}}(v))$ from $\mathcal{A}$, $\mathcal{S}$ computes $\Omega = v \oplus v'$ and stores $(\mathtt{sid}, \Omega)$. However, If $\mathcal{A}$ does not correctly open its commitment $(\mathtt{sid}, \mathsf{Com}_{\mathsf{ck}}(v))$, then $\mathcal{S}$ sends $\bot$ to $\mathcal{F}_{OT}$, simulating an invalid opening and halts.

5. After the coin tossing, S opens the commitments needed for verification and simulates reordering. Recall that i represents the indexes for which $\Omega_i = 1$ and j represents the indexes for which $\Omega_j = 0$.
   - **Verification:** For each i, S opens the commitments to K_{i,d_i} by sending $(\mathsf{sid}, \mathsf{Open}_{\mathsf{ck}}(K_{i,d_i}))$.
   - **Derandomization:** For every j, S samples a random reordering bit $\rho_j \leftarrow \{0,1\}$. For each j, S sends (sid, ρ_j) to $\mathcal{A}$. [3]
6. Upon receiving $(\mathsf{sid}, (\mathsf{ct}_{j_1,0}, \mathsf{ct}_{j_1,1}), \ldots, (\mathsf{ct}_{j_\mu,0}, \mathsf{ct}_{j_\mu,1}))$, S uses the instructions of an honest receiver to decrypt and reconstruct both bits x_0 and x_1. For $j = j_1, \ldots, j_\mu$, S decrypts the ciphertexts related to x_{d_i} by computing $x_{j,d_i} = \mathsf{Dec}(sk_{j,d_i}, \mathsf{ct}_{j,d_i})$ and the ciphertexts related to $x_{\overline{d}_i}$ by computing $x_{j,\overline{d}_i} = \mathsf{Dec}(sk_{j,\overline{d}_i}, \mathsf{ct}_{j,\overline{d}_i})$ (notice that S knows all secret keys $sk_{j,d_i}, sk_{j,\overline{d}_i}$ since it cheated in the random padding generation). S obtains $x_{d_i} = x_{j_1,d_i} \oplus \ldots \oplus x_{j_\mu,d_i}$ and $x_{\overline{d}_i} = x_{j_1,\overline{d}_i} \oplus \ldots \oplus x_{j_\mu,\overline{d}_i}$. However, if $\mathcal{A}$ does not reply with a valid message or any of the decryption attempts fail, then S samples two random bits $x_0, x_1 \leftarrow \{0,1\}$.
7. S completes the simulation by sending $(\mathsf{sid}, \mathsf{sender}, x_0, x_1)$ to $\mathcal{F}_{OT}$ as $\mathbf{S}$'s input and halts.

B   Simulator for a Corrupted R

Simulating $\mathcal{F}_{CRS}$: S generates a commitment key $\mathsf{ck} \leftarrow \mathsf{Gen}(1^n)$ for which he knows the secret key tk and sets $\mathsf{crs} = (\mathsf{ck})$. Later on, the secret key will be used as a trapdoor to extract unopened commitments. When the parties query $\mathcal{F}_{CRS}$, S hands them (sid, crs).

When the dummy $\mathbf{R}$ is activated, S proceeds as follows:

1. Upon receiving $(\mathsf{sid}, \mathsf{Com}_{\mathsf{ck}}(K_{1,d_i}), \ldots, \mathsf{Com}_{\mathsf{ck}}(K_{\omega,d_i}))$ from $\mathcal{A}$, S extract the commitments and stores $(\mathsf{sid}, K_{1,d_i}, \ldots, K_{\omega,d_i})$.
2. S simulates the coin tossing to obtain random matrices as follows:
   (a) S samples uniformly random matrices of the same size as the public key matrices $A'_i \in \mathbb{F}_2^{\ell_1 \times n_1}$, $B'_i \in \mathbb{F}_2^{\ell_2 \times n_1}$, $G'_i \in \mathbb{F}_2^{\ell_2 \times n_1}$, assigns $R'_i = (A'_i, B'_i, G'_i)$ and sends a commitment $(\mathsf{sid}, \mathsf{Com}_{\mathsf{ck}}(R'_1), \ldots, \mathsf{Com}_{\mathsf{ck}}(R'_\omega))$ to to $\mathcal{A}$.
   (b) Upon receiving $(\mathsf{sid}, R''_1, \ldots, R''_\omega)$ from $\mathcal{A}$, S opens its commitments and both parties compute $R_i = (\bar{A}_i = A'_i + A''_i, \bar{B}_i = B'_i + B''_i, \bar{C}_i = C'_i + C''_i)$ for $i = 1, \ldots, \omega$.
   (c) Upon receiving $(\mathsf{sid}, K_{1,1}, \ldots, K_{\omega,1})$ from $\mathcal{A}$ where $K_{i,1} = (\tilde{A}_i, \tilde{B}_i, \tilde{G}_i)$, S computes $K_{i,0} = K_{i,1} + R_i = (\tilde{A}_i + \bar{A}_i, \tilde{B}_i + \bar{B}_i, \tilde{G}_i + \bar{G}_i)$ obtaining the public key pairs $K_{i,0}, K_{i,1}$, for $i = 1, \ldots, \omega$. .
3. Simulating the coin tossing phase:

---

[3] The reordering bit performs the same function described in the protocol for a honest receiver.

- $\mathcal{S}$ samples a random bit string $v \leftarrow \{0,1\}^\omega$ and sends a commitment $(\text{sid}, \text{Com}_{\text{ck}}(v))$ to $\mathcal{A}$.
- Upon receiving $\mathcal{A}$'s string (sid, v'), $\mathcal{S}$ opens its commitment sending $(\text{sid}, \text{Open}_{\text{ck}}(v))$ to $\mathcal{A}$ and receives.
- $\mathcal{S}$ computes $\Omega = v \oplus v'$.

4. Let i represent the indexes for which $\Omega_i = 1$ and j represent the indexes for which $\Omega_j = 0$. Upon receiving the openings $(\text{sid}, \text{Open}_{\text{ck}}(pk_i|sk_i))$ and reordering bits (sid, ρ_j) from $\mathcal{A}$, $\mathcal{S}$ performs the following actions. However, if $\mathcal{A}$ send invalid openings, then $\mathcal{S}$ sends $\perp$ to $\hat{\mathcal{F}}_{OT}$, simulating an abortion and halts.

   - For each opening $(\text{sid}, \text{Open}_{\text{ck}}(K_{i,d_i}))$, s uses the key K_{i,d_i} and the instructions of an honest sender to check whether the public key pairs are valid (*i.e.* one of the keys is equal to K_{i,d_i} and the other is equal to $K_{i,d_i} \oplus R_i$). If this check fails, $\mathcal{S}$ sends $\perp$ to $\hat{\mathcal{F}}_{OT}$, simulating an abortion and halts. Otherwise it continues to the next step.
   - For each reordering bit ρ_j received by $\mathcal{S}$, it derandomizes the corresponding public key pair by computing $(\hat{K}_{j,0}, \hat{K}_{j,1}) = K_{j,0\oplus\rho}, K_{j,1\oplus\rho}$.
   - $\mathcal{S}$ uses the keys K_{j,d_j} obtained from the extracted commitments to find at least one valid reordered pair $(\hat{K}_{j,0}, \hat{K}_{j,1})$. If no such pair is found, $\mathcal{S}$ aborts, sending $\perp$ to $\hat{\mathcal{F}}_{OT}$ and halting. Otherwise, $\mathcal{S}$ obtains c by checking which key in the pair is equal to K_{j,d_j}, *i.e.* if $K_{j,0} = K_{j,d_j}$ then $c = 0$ and if $K_{j,1} = K_{j,d_j}$ then $c = 1$.
   - $\mathcal{S}$ sends $(\text{sid}, \text{receiver}, c)$ to $\hat{\mathcal{F}}_{OT}$, receiving (sid, x_c) in response.

5. $\mathcal{S}$ samples a random bit $x_{\bar{c}} \leftarrow \{0,1\}$, obtaining a pair (x_0, x_1) since it already learned x_c from $\hat{\mathcal{F}}_{OT}$. $\mathcal{S}$ completes the protocol by performing the following actions:

   - Let μ be the number of indexes j, and let $j_1, ..., j_\mu$ denote each of these indexes. For $j = j_1, ..., j_\mu$, $\mathcal{S}$ generates μ bits $x_{j,0}$ such that $x_{j_1,0} \oplus \cdots \oplus x_{j_\mu,0} = x_0$ and μ bits $x_{j,1}$ such that $x_{j_1,1} \oplus \cdots \oplus x_{j_\mu,1} = x_1$.
   - For $j = j_1, ..., j_\mu$, $\mathcal{S}$ encrypts $x_{j,0}$ under public key $\hat{K}_{j,0}$ and encrypts $x_{j,1}$ under public key $\hat{K}_{j,1}$ by computing $\text{ct}_{j,0} = \text{Enc}(\hat{K}_{j,0}, x_{j,0}; r_{j,0})$ and $\text{ct}_{j,1} = \text{Enc}(\hat{K}_{j,1}, x_{j,1}; r_{j,1})$, respectively.
   - $\mathcal{S}$ sends all ciphertexts to $\mathcal{A}$ as $(\text{sid}, (\text{ct}_{j_1,0}, \text{ct}_{j_1,1}), \ldots, (\text{ct}_{j_\mu,0}, \text{ct}_{j_\mu,1}))$.

Converting PKI-Based Authenticated Key Exchange to Identity-Based

Koutarou Suzuki and Kazuki Yoneyama

NTT Secure Platform Laboratories,
3-9-11 Midori-cho Musashino-shi Tokyo 180-8585, Japan
yoneyama.kazuki@lab.ntt.co.jp

Abstract. Fiore and Gennaro proposed an identity-based authenticated key exchange (ID-AKE) scheme without pairing. Though their scheme is very efficient both in communication and computation, the scheme is not secure against some advanced exposure attacks. In this paper, we achieve exposure-resilient ID-AKE schemes without pairings. Specifically, we introduce two *security preserving* generic conversions from ordinary PKI-based AKE (PKI-AKE) to ID-AKE (i.e., exposure resilience of PKI-AKE is preserved in converted ID-AKE). Our first conversion is for the post-specified peer model (i.e., the peer can be unknown at the beginning of the protocol), and our second conversion is for the pre-specified peer model (i.e., the peer must be fixed at the beginning of the protocol). The merit of the first conversion is *round-preserving* (i.e., converted ID-AKE has same round complexity as PKI-AKE). The merit of the second conversion is *rich instantiability* (i.e., it can be instantiated from various kinds of number-theoretic assumptions such as RSA and lattices as well as Diffie-Hellman variants) thanks to rich instantiability of known PKI-AKE schemes in the pre-specified peer model.

Keywords: ID-based authenticated key exchange, pre/post-specified peer model, exposure resilience.

1 Introduction

Authenticated Key Exchange (AKE) is a cryptographic primitive to share a common *session key* among multiple parties through unauthenticated networks such as the Internet. In the ordinary PKI-based setting, each party locally keeps his own *static secret key* and publish a *static public key* corresponding to the static secret key. Validity of static public keys is guaranteed by a certificate authority (CA). In a key exchange session, each party generates an *ephemeral secret key* and sends messages corresponding to the ephemeral secret key. A session key is derived from these keys with a *key derivation procedure*. Parties can establish a secure channel with the session key.

PKI-based AKE (PKI-AKE) assumes that each static public key is strictly bound with each party's ID through PKI and is known to all parties in advance. This setting allows us to easily design secure AKE protocols. However, in a practical viewpoint, it is problematic that each party must manage lots of static public keys. Thus, it is natural to consider the ID-based setting in order to avoid the burden of key managements. In

D. Gritzalis et al. (Eds.): CANS 2014, LNCS 8813, pp. 159–174, 2014.

ID-based cryptography, it is assumed that a *key generate center* (KGC) exists. The KGC manages a *master public key* and a *master secret key*, and generates static secret key of each party with the master secret key. Parties can use their IDs instead of static public keys. Especially, ID-based AKE (ID-AKE) is more suitable for mobile environment than PKI-AKE. For example, let's consider some P2P service for smart-phones. When a user wants to securely connect to a peer with a secure channel in such a service but he/she only knows the e-mail address or the phone number of the peer, PKI-AKE is not available because each party must know the public-key of the peer. On the other hand, ID-AKE can easily handle this situation by dealing with the e-mail address or the phone number as the ID of the peer.

Security models for ID-AKE are studied by following security models for PKI-AKE. For example, in the context of PKI-AKE, the Bellare-Rogaway (BR) model [1,2,3], the Canetti-Krawczyk (CK) model [4], the extended CK (eCK) model [5], and the CK^+ model [6] are introduced. The id-BR model [7,8], the id-CK model [9], the id-eCK model [10], and the id-CK^+ model [11] are ID-based setting versions of such security models. The distinguished point of models for ID-AKE is that we must consider security against the KGC. Even if the KGC is honest-but-curious, any information of session keys must be protected. Thus, models for ID-AKE allow an adversary to expose the master secret key in order to capture this situation. Also, it is desirable to capture security against various advanced attacks. For example, key-compromise impersonation (KCI) [3] can be a practical threat. Suppose a party A's static secret key is disclosed. Though, clearly, an adversary that knows the static secret key can now impersonate A, it may be desirable that this loss does not enable an adversary to impersonate other entities to A. Also, ephemeral secret key-exposure attacks [5] are another concern. If an adversary can guess the ephemeral secret key of one or both parties (e.g., due to a poor implementation of pseudo-random number generator), the secrecy of session keys should not be affected. Therefore, most of advanced attacks use *exposure of secret information*; thus, the security model must capture such exposure. Some security models for ID-AKE can guarantee *exposure-resilience*. The id-CK model allows to an adversary to expose static secret keys and session state (i.e., some intermediate computation result). However, the id-CK model only guarantees partial exposure-resilience because resistances to KCI and ephemeral secret key-exposure attacks are not guaranteed. The id-eCK model allows to an adversary to expose both static secret keys and ephemeral secret keys. Thus, the id-eCK model captures resistances to KCI and ephemeral secret key-exposure attacks. However, it is clarified that the id-eCK model is not stronger than the id-CK model because of the difference on session state reveal property [12,13]. Fujioka et al. [6,11] revisit security attributes of HMQV [14] as the CK^+ model and id-CK^+ model formulating exposure of static secret keys, ephemeral secret keys and session state. The id-CK^+ model captures all known advanced attacks, and is stronger than the id-CK model.

Most of known ID-AKE schemes rely on bilinear pairings. The ID-AKE scheme by Fiore and Gennaro [15] (FG scheme) is the only known scheme without pairings.[1] The FG scheme uses the Schnorr signature [16] in order to generate static secret keys for parties by the KGC. It is proved to be id-CK secure under the strong DH assumption in

---

[1] Though there are generic ID-AKE constructions based on ID-based KEM such as [9,11], ID-based KEM has not been achieved under Diffie-Hellman (DH) assumptions without pairings.

the random oracle (RO) model. Since the FG scheme is designed in the dedicated manner, there are some mysterious point why they can achieve ID-AKE without pairings. Indeed, as far as we know, there is no other exposure-resilient ID-AKE scheme without pairings. Also, it is not clear if we can remove ROs or can achieve stronger security like the id-CK^+ model.

Our Contribution. In this paper, we give generic conversions from PKI-AKE to ID-AKE. The main idea of our conversions comes from the FG scheme. The essential technique used in the FG scheme is to bind the static public key with the ID of the owner by the Schnorr signature. We revisit this paradigm, and generalize to a more generic case of any unforgeable signature scheme. Also, though the FG scheme is based on the DH key exchange, our conversions can be based on any PKI-AKE. Our conversions are security preserving; that is, the converted ID-AKE is secure in the model the underlying PKI-AKE satisfies. In this paper, we prove the case of the CK^+ model and the id-CK^+ model.

This methodology is very similar to the construction of ID-based signature from the normal signature [17]. However, since AKE protocols are interactive, the design of conversions has some subtle point. We must consider what timing the peer of a key exchange session is decided. There are two models: the *pre-specified peer model* and the *post-specified peer model* [18]. In the pre-specified peer model, the protocol must start after deciding the peer. Conversely, in the post-specified peer model, the protocol can start before deciding the peer. If the underlying PKI-AKE can work in the post-specified peer model, we can convert it with the same round complexity (i.e., When the underlying PKI-AKE scheme is a n-pass protocol, then the converted ID-AKE scheme is also a n-pass protocol). However, if the underlying PKI-AKE works in the pre-specified peer model, the conversion needs an additional round for sending the static public key and the signature. Since, in the ID-based setting, the peer's static public key is not known before starting the protocol, the session initiator must receive the peer's static public key before generating the 1st message.

Our conversions have various instantiations. The conversion in the post-specified peer model can be instantiated from some DH-variant assumptions without pairings like the FG scheme. The advantage against the FG scheme is to be able to satisfy stronger security (e.g., the id-CK^+ model). Also, some theoretical instantiation with neither pairing nor ROs is possible. The conversion in the pre-specified peer model can be instantiated from RSA or lattices. The instantiation from RSA is the first ID-AKE scheme based on such an assumption. Since we can use KEM-based PKI-AKE [9,6,19] in the pre-specified peer model, we enjoy rich instantiability of KEM-based PKI-AKE. We also have some theoretical instantiation from other hardness assumptions such as the factoring problem, code-based problems, subset-sum problems and multi-variate quadratic systems.

2 Preliminaries

In this section, we formally define syntaxes of PKI-AKE and ID-AKE in order to describe our conversions. Due to space limitation, we omit definitions of the CK^+ model, the id-CK^+ model and eUF-CMA. Please refer to [6,11,17].

2.1 Notations

Throughout this paper we use the following notations. If Set is a set, then by $m \in_R$ Set we denote that m is sampled uniformly from Set. If **ALG** is an algorithm, then by $y \leftarrow$ **ALG**$(x; r)$ we denote that y is output by **ALG** on input x and randomness r (if **ALG** is deterministic, r is empty).

2.2 Syntax of PKI-AKE

Here, we give a syntax of n-pass PKI-AKE. The syntax is applicable both to sequential protocols (i.e., a party sends the 1st message and the peer sends the 2nd message after receiving the 1st message) and to simultaneous protocols (i.e., a party can send the 2nd message without waiting the 1st message from the peer).[2] We denote a party by a party ID U_P, and party U_P and other parties are modeled as probabilistic polynomial-time Turing (PPT) machines w.r.t. security parameter κ.

In this paper, we classify PKI-AKE into two models: the *pre-specified peer model* and the *post-specified peer model* [18]. In the pre-specified peer model, the 1st message in the protocol must be generated with information of the peer (i.e., the 1st message must depend on the peer's static public key). In the post-specified peer model, the 1st message in the protocol can be generated without information of the peer (i.e., the 1st message is independent from the peer's static public key). We give the formal classification on the syntax, later.

A PKI-AKE scheme consists of the following algorithms.

Setup. The setup algorithm **Setup** takes a security parameter κ as input, and outputs a public parameter PP^{PKI}, i.e.,

$$PP^{PKI} \leftarrow \mathbf{Setup}(1^\kappa).$$

In the initialization of the system, PP^{PKI} is published.

Key Registration. The static key generation algorithm **StaticGen** for party U_P takes a public parameter PP^{PKI} as input, and outputs a static secret key SSK_P^{PKI} and a static public key SPK_P^{PKI}, i.e.,

$$(SPK_P^{PKI}, SSK_P^{PKI}) \leftarrow \mathbf{StaticGen}(PP^{PKI}).$$

Each party U_P registers his/her static public key SPK_P^{PKI} to the CA. After that, the party ID U_P is associated with the static public key SPK_P^{PKI}. It can be supposed that the CA securely distributes all pairs of party ID and static public key to all parties.

Key Exchange. An invocation of a protocol is called a *session*. The party U_A and the party U_B share a session key by performing the following n-pass protocol. The

---

[2] A typical example of sequential protocols is KEM-based schemes [9,6,19], and a typical example of simultaneous protocols is DH-variant schemes like HMQV [14].

ephemeral key generation algorithm **EpheGen** for party U_P takes a public parameter PP^{PKI} as input, and outputs a ephemeral secret key $ES K_P^{PKI}$, i.e.,

$$ES K_P^{PKI} \leftarrow \textbf{EpheGen}(PP^{PKI}).$$

In the pre-specified peer model, a session is activated with an incoming message of the forms $(\Pi, \mathcal{I}, U_A, U_B)$ or $(\Pi, \mathcal{R}, U_B, U_A, [Mes_1^{PKI}])$, where Π is a protocol identifier, and $\mathcal{I}$ and $\mathcal{R}$ are role identifiers. In the post-specified peer model, a session is activated with an incoming message of the forms $(\Pi, \mathcal{I}, U_A)$ or $(\Pi, \mathcal{R}, U_B, [U_A], [Mes_1^{PKI}])$. $\mathcal{I}$ stands for the initiator, and $\mathcal{R}$ stands for the responder. If U_A was activated with $\mathcal{I}$, then U_A is called the session *initiator*. If U_B was activated with $\mathcal{R}$, then U_B is called the session *responder*. $[U_A]$ and $[Mes_1^{PKI}]$ in $(\Pi, \mathcal{R}, U_B, U_A, [Mes_1^{PKI}])$ and $(\Pi, \mathcal{R}, U_B, [U_A], [Mes_1^{PKI}])$ means that, if Π is a simultaneous protocol, U_A and Mes_1^{PKI} are not contained.

A party U_P starts the protocol by generating ephemeral secret keys $ES K_P^{PKI}$. In the pre-specified peer model, if U_P generates the 1st message Mes_1^{PKI} in the protocol, U_P computes Mes_1^{PKI} by the algorithm **Message**^{pre} that takes the public parameter PP^{PKI}, U_P and the peer $U_{\bar{P}}$, the static secret key $S S K_P^{PKI}$, the ephemeral secret key $ES K_P^{PKI}$, the peer $U_{\bar{P}}$'s static public key $S PK_{\bar{P}}^{PKI}$, and outputs the 1st message Mes_1^{PKI}, i.e.,

$$Mes_1^{PKI} \leftarrow \textbf{Message}^{\text{pre}}(PP^{PKI}, U_P, U_{\bar{P}}, S S K_P^{PKI}, ES K_P^{PKI}, S PK_{\bar{P}}^{PKI}).$$

In the post-specified peer model, if U_P generates the 1st message Mes_1^{PKI} in the protocol, U_P computes Mes_1^{PKI} by the algorithm **Message**^{post} that takes the public parameter PP^{PKI}, U_P, the static secret key $S S K_P^{PKI}$, the ephemeral secret key $ES K_P^{PKI}$, and outputs the 1st message Mes_1^{PKI}, i.e.,

$$Mes_1^{PKI} \leftarrow \textbf{Message}^{\text{post}}(PP^{PKI}, U_P, S S K_P^{PKI}, ES K_P^{PKI}).$$

U_P sends Mes_1^{PKI} to the peer $U_{\bar{P}}$. In simultaneous protocols, Mes_2^{PKI} is generated without knowing Mes_1^{PKI}, i.e.,

$$Mes_2^{PKI} \leftarrow$$

$\textbf{Message}^{\text{pre}}(PP^{PKI}, U_{\bar{P}}, U_P, S S K_{\bar{P}}^{PKI}, ES K_{\bar{P}}^{PKI}, S PK_P^{PKI})$ (pre-specified peer model),

$Mes_2^{PKI} \leftarrow \textbf{Message}^{\text{post}}(PP^{PKI}, U_{\bar{P}}, S S K_{\bar{P}}^{PKI}, ES K_{\bar{P}}^{PKI})$ (post-specified peer model).

For $i = 2, ..., n$ in sequential protocols and $i = 3, ..., n$ in simultaneous protocols, upon receiving the $(i-1)$-th message Mes_{i-1}^{PKI}, the party U_P ($P = A$ or B) computes the i-th message by algorithm **Message**, that takes the public parameter PP^{PKI}, U_P and the peer $U_{\bar{P}}$, the static secret key $S S K_P^{PKI}$, the ephemeral secret key $ES K_P^{PKI}$, the peer $U_{\bar{P}}$'s static public key $S PK_{\bar{P}}^{PKI}$ and the sent and received messages $Mes_1^{PKI}, ..., Mes_{i-1}^{PKI}$, and outputs the i-th message Mes_i^{PKI}, i.e.,

$$Mes_i^{PKI} \leftarrow \textbf{Message}(PP^{PKI}, U_P, U_{\bar{P}}, S S K_P^{PKI}, ES K_P^{PKI}, S PK_{\bar{P}}^{PKI}, Mes_1^{PKI}, ..., Mes_{i-1}^{PKI}).$$

The party P sends Mes_i^{PKI} to the peer $U_{\bar{P}}$ ($\bar{P} = B$ or A). Formally, after activated with an incoming message of the forms $(\Pi, \mathcal{I}, U_A, U_B, Mes_1^{PKI}, ..., Mes_{k-1}^{PKI})$ from the responder U_B, the initiator U_A outputs Mes_k^{PKI}, then may be activated next by an incoming message of the forms $(\Pi, I, U_A, U_B, Mes_1^{PKI}, \ldots, Mes_{k+1}^{PKI})$ from the responder U_B. Similarly, after activated by an incoming message of the forms $(\Pi, \mathcal{R}, U_B, U_A, Mes_1^{PKI}, \ldots, Mes_k^{PKI})$ from the initiator U_A, the responder U_B outputs Mes_{k+1}^{PKI}, then may be activated next by an incoming message of the forms $(\Pi, \mathcal{R}, U_B, U_A, Mes_1^{PKI}, \ldots, Mes_{k+2}^{PKI})$ from the initiator U_A.

Upon receiving or after sending the final n-th message Mes_n^{PKI}, U_P computes a session key by algorithm **SesKey**, that takes the public parameter PP^{PKI}, U_P and the peer $U_{\bar{P}}$, the static secret key SSK_P^{PKI}, the ephemeral secret key ESK_P^{PKI}, the peer $U_{\bar{P}}$'s static public key $SPK_{\bar{P}}^{PKI}$ and the sent and received messages $Mes_1^{PKI}, \ldots, Mes_n^{PKI}$, and outputs an session key K^{PKI}, i.e.,

$$K^{PKI} \leftarrow \textbf{SesKey}(PP^{PKI}, U_P, U_{\bar{P}}, SSK_P^{PKI}, ESK_P^{PKI}, SPK_{\bar{P}}^{PKI}, Mes_1^{PKI}, \ldots, Mes_n^{PKI}).$$

A session is identified by a session ID. If U_A is the initiator of a session, the session ID sid is updated as $(\Pi, I, U_A, [U_B], Mes_1^{PKI})$, $(\Pi, I, U_A, U_B, Mes_1^{PKI}, Mes_2^{PKI}, Mes_3^{PKI})$, $\ldots$, $(\Pi, I, U_A, U_B, Mes_1^{PKI}, \ldots, Mes_n^{PKI})$ according to progress of the session. Similarly, if U_B is the responder of a session, the session ID sid is updated as $(\Pi, \mathcal{R}, U_B, [U_A], Mes_1^{PKI}, [Mes_2^{PKI}])$, $(\Pi, \mathcal{R}, U_B, U_A, Mes_1^{PKI}, Mes_2^{PKI}, Mes_3^{PKI}, [Mes_4^{PKI}])$, $\ldots$, $(\Pi, \mathcal{R}, U_B, U_A, Mes_1^{PKI}, \ldots, Mes_n^{PKI})$ according to progress of the session. We say that a session is *completed* if a session key is computed in the session. The *matching session* of a completed session $(\Pi, I, U_A, U_B, Mes_1^{PKI}, \ldots, Mes_n^{PKI})$ is a completed session with identifier $(\Pi, \mathcal{R}, U_B, U_A, Mes_1^{PKI}, \ldots, Mes_n^{PKI})$ and vice versa.

2.3 Syntax of ID-AKE

Here, we give a syntax of n-pass ID-AKE. As for PKI-AKE, the syntax is applicable both to sequential protocols and to simultaneous protocols. Also, we can consider the pre-specified peer model and the post-specified peer model in a similar manner.

We denote a party by U_P, and party U_P and other parties are modeled as PPT machines w.r.t. security parameter κ. Each party U_P has identity $ID_P \in \{0, 1\}^*$.

An ID-AKE scheme consists of the following algorithms.

Setup. The setup algorithm **IDSetup** takes a security parameter κ as input, and outputs a master secret key MSK^{ID} and a master public key MPK^{ID}, i.e.,

$$(MSK^{ID}, MPK^{ID}) \leftarrow \textbf{IDSetup}(1^\kappa).$$

In the initialization of the system, MSK^{ID} is given to the KGC, and MPK^{ID} is published.

Key Derivation. The key derivation algorithm **IDKeyDer** takes the master secret key MSK^{ID}, the master public key MPK^{ID}, and an ID ID_P given by a party U_P, and outputs a static secret key SSK_P^{ID} corresponding to ID_P, i.e.,

$$SSK_P^{ID} \leftarrow \textbf{IDKeyDer}(MSK^{ID}, MPK^{ID}, ID_P).$$

Each party U_P sends his/her ID ID_P to the KGC through a secure channel, and the KGC generates and sends SSK_P^{ID} to U_P.

Key Exchange. The party U_A and the party U_B share a session key by performing the following n-pass protocol. The ephemeral key generation algorithm **IDEpheGen** for party U_P takes a master public key MPK^{ID} as input, and outputs a ephemeral secret key ESK_P^{ID}, i.e.,

$$ESK_P^{ID} \leftarrow \textbf{IDEpheGen}(MPK^{ID}).$$

In the pre-specified peer model, a session is activated with an incoming message of the forms $(\varPi, \mathcal{I}, ID_A, ID_B)$ or $(\varPi, \mathcal{R}, ID_B, ID_A, [Mes_1^{ID}])$, where $\varPi$ is a protocol identifier, and $\mathcal{I}$ and $\mathcal{R}$ are role identifiers. In the post-specified peer model, a session is activated with an incoming message of the forms $(\varPi, \mathcal{I}, ID_A)$ or $(\varPi, \mathcal{R}, ID_B, [ID_A], [Mes_1^{ID}])$. $\mathcal{I}$ stands for the initiator, and $\mathcal{R}$ stands for the responder. $[ID_A]$ and $[Mes_1^{ID}]$ in $(\varPi, \mathcal{R}, ID_B, ID_A, [Mes_1^{ID}])$ and $(\varPi, \mathcal{R}, ID_B, [ID_A], [Mes_1^{ID}])$ means that, if $\varPi$ is a simultaneous protocol, ID_A and Mes_1^{ID} are not contained.

A party U_P starts the protocol by generating ephemeral secret keys ESK_P^{ID}. In the pre-specified peer model, if U_P generates the 1st message Mes_1^{ID} in the protocol, U_P computes Mes_1^{ID} by the algorithm **IDMessage**^{pre} that takes the master public key MPK^{ID}, ID_P and the peer $ID_{\bar{P}}$, the static secret key SSK_P^{ID}, the ephemeral secret key ESK_P^{ID}, and outputs the 1st message Mes_1^{ID}, i.e.,

$$Mes_1^{ID} \leftarrow \textbf{IDMessage}^{\text{pre}}(MPK^{ID}, ID_P, ID_{\bar{P}}, SSK_P^{ID}, ESK_P^{ID}).$$

In the post-specified peer model, if U_P generates the 1st message Mes_1^{ID} in the protocol, U_P computes Mes_1^{ID} by the algorithm **IDMessage**^{post} that takes the master public key MPK^{ID}, ID_P, the static secret key SSK_P^{ID}, the ephemeral secret key ESK_P^{ID}, and outputs the 1st message Mes_1^{ID}, i.e.,

$$Mes_1^{ID} \leftarrow \textbf{IDMessage}^{\text{post}}(MPK^{ID}, ID_P, SSK_P^{ID}, ESK_P^{ID}).$$

U_P sends Mes_1^{ID} to the peer $U_{\bar{P}}$. In simultaneous protocols, Mes_2^{ID} is generated without knowing Mes_1^{ID}, i.e.,

$$Mes_2^{ID} \leftarrow$$

$$\textbf{IDMessage}^{\text{pre}}(MPK^{ID}, ID_{\bar{P}}, ID_P, SSK_{\bar{P}}^{ID}, ESK_{\bar{P}}^{ID}) \quad \text{(pre-specified peer model)},$$

$$Mes_2^{ID} \leftarrow \textbf{IDMessage}^{\text{post}}(MPK^{ID}, ID_{\bar{P}}, SSK_{\bar{P}}^{ID}, ESK_{\bar{P}}^{ID}) \quad \text{(post-specified peer model)}.$$

For $i = 2, ..., n$ in sequential protocols and $i = 3, ..., n$ in simultaneous protocols, upon receiving the $(i-1)$-th message Mes_{i-1}^{ID}, the party U_P ($P = A$ or B) computes the i-th message by algorithm **IDMessage**, that takes the master public key MPK^{ID}, ID_P and $ID_{\bar{P}}$, the static secret key SSK_P^{ID}, the ephemeral secret key ESK_P^{ID}, and the sent and received messages $Mes_1^{ID}, ..., Mes_{i-1}^{ID}$, and outputs the ith message Mes_i^{ID}, i.e.,

$$Mes_i^{ID} \leftarrow \textbf{IDMessage}(MPK^{ID}, ID_P, ID_{\bar{P}}, SSK_P^{ID}, ESK_P^{ID}, Mes_1^{ID}, ..., Mes_{i-1}^{ID}).$$

The party P sends Mes_i^{ID} to the peer $U_{\bar{P}}$ ($\bar{P} = B$ or A). Formally, after activated with an incoming message of the forms $(\varPi, \mathcal{I}, ID_A, ID_B, Mes_1^{ID}, ..., Mes_{k-1}^{ID})$ from the responder U_B, the initiator U_A outputs Mes_k^{ID}, then may be activated next by an incoming message of the forms $(\Pi, \mathcal{I}, ID_A, ID_B, Mes_1^{ID}, \ldots, Mes_{k+1}^{ID})$ from the responder U_B. Similarly, after activated by an incoming message of the forms $(\Pi, \mathcal{R}, ID_B, ID_A, Mes_1^{ID}, \ldots, Mes_k^{ID})$ from the initiator U_A, the responder U_B outputs Mes_{k+1}^{ID}, then may be activated next by an incoming message of the forms $(\Pi, \mathcal{R}, ID_B, ID_A, Mes_1^{ID}, \ldots, Mes_{k+2}^{ID})$ from the initiator U_A.

Upon receiving or after sending the final n-th message Mes_n^{ID}, U_P computes a session key by algorithm **IDSesKey**, that takes the master public key MPK^{ID}, ID_A and $ID_{\bar{P}}$, the static secret key SSK_P^{ID}, the ephemeral secret key ESK_P^{ID}, and the sent and received messages $Mes_1^{ID}, \ldots, Mes_n^{ID}$, and outputs an session key K^{ID}, i.e.,

$$K^{ID} \leftarrow \textbf{IDSesKey}(MPK^{ID}, ID_P, ID_{\bar{P}}, SSK_P^{ID}, ESK_P^{ID}, Mes_1^{ID}, \ldots, Mes_n^{ID}).$$

A session is identified by a session ID. If U_A is the initiator of a session, the session ID sid is updated as $(\Pi, \mathcal{I}, ID_A, [ID_B], Mes_1^{ID})$, $(\Pi, \mathcal{I}, ID_A, ID_B, Mes_1^{ID}, Mes_2^{ID}, Mes_3^{ID})$, $\ldots, (\Pi, \mathcal{I}, ID_A, ID_B, Mes_1^{ID}, \ldots, Mes_n^{ID})$ according to progress of the session. Similarly, if U_B is the responder of a session, the session ID sid is updated as $(\Pi, \mathcal{R}, ID_B, [ID_A], Mes_1^{ID}, [Mes_2^{ID}])$, $(\Pi, \mathcal{R}, ID_B, ID_A, Mes_1^{ID}, Mes_2^{ID}, Mes_3^{ID}, [Mes_4^{ID}])$, $\ldots, (\Pi, \mathcal{R}, ID_B, ID_A, Mes_1^{ID}, \ldots, Mes_n^{ID})$ according to progress of the session. We say that a session is *completed* if a session key is computed in the session. The *matching session* of a completed session $(\Pi, \mathcal{I}, ID_A, ID_B, Mes_1^{ID}, \ldots, Mes_n^{ID})$ is a completed session with identifier $(\Pi, \mathcal{R}, ID_B, ID_A, Mes_1^{ID}, \ldots, Mes_n^{ID})$ and vice versa.

3 Fiore-Gennaro ID-AKE, Revisited

The Fiore-Gennaro (FG) ID-AKE [15] is the first scheme secure in the id-CK model without pairings. The protocol of the FG scheme is shown in Fig. 1.

The FG scheme is a simultaneous protocol in the post-specified peer model. ID of each party is certified by using the Schnorr signature [16]. Specifically, the master secret key is the signing key of the Schnorr signature, and ID is signed as a message. The exchanged message in ID-AKE contains a part of the signature (i.e., r_P), and it implicitly guarantees that the message is sent by the owner of the signature. The session key is the hash value of two group elements: one is the same as the Diffie-Hellman (DH) key exchange, and the other is using the other part of the signature (i.e., s_P). Since the Schnorr signature does not need any pairing operation, the resultant ID-AKE is also achievable without pairings.

The FG scheme provides us an interesting perspective about the design of ID-AKE. First, g^{s_P} plays the role of the static public key in PKI-AKE; that is, the generation of z_1 is the same way as many PKI-AKE scheme such as HMQV [14] when we regard g^{s_P} as the static public key. Also, s_P is generated by the KGC, and g^{s_P} is bound with ID as $s_P = k_P + xH_1(ID_P, r_P))$. Though the FG scheme depends on the structure of the Schnorr signature and the DH key exchange, it seems that this technique can be captured generically.

Thus, we try to generalize their idea by any signature scheme and PKI-AKE scheme. The essential point is that the static public key of PKI-AKE must be bound with ID. Hence, if the static public key and ID is signed by the KGC, this condition is satisfied. In this case, the signature scheme does not have to be the Schnorr signature, and we

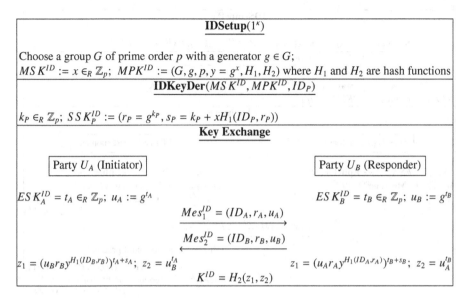

Fig. 1. Fiore-Gennaro ID-AKE

can use any unforgeable signature. If the static public key is certified by the KGC, a party can use the peer's static public key as in PKI-AKE by sending the certified static public key as a part of the 1st message. Thus, we can execute the session key generation procedure by the same way as PKI-AKE, and eUF-CMA is enough to prove. It means that we can use any PKI-AKE as well as the DH key exchange. Therefore, the above can be viewed as a generalization of the idea of the FG scheme.

However, we must consider the difference between the post-specified peer model and the pre-specified peer model. As the FG scheme, protocols in the post-specified peer model can be captured by the above generalization. On the other hand, in the pre-specified peer model, there is a problem. In order to generate the 1st message, the initiator needs the responder's static public key. But, in the generalization, since the responder sends the static public key with his/her 1st message, the initiator cannot know it. Hence, in the pre-specified peer model, the responder must sends the static public key in advance. It means that we need an additional round than the underlying PKI-AKE scheme. Therefore, we need to consider two constructions according to the difference between peer models.

4   Conversion in Post-specified Peer Model

In this section, we introduce a generic conversion of ID-AKE from PKI-AKE in the post-specified peer model, named GC_{post}. The GC_{post} preserves the number of round and security in the PKI-based setting. Specifically, if the underlying PKI-AKE scheme is CK^+ secure, then the converted ID-AKE scheme is id-CK^+ secure. Similarly, the cases of other known security models (the BR model, the CK model, and the eCK

$$\mathbf{IDSetup}(1^\kappa)$$

$PP^{PKI} \leftarrow \mathbf{Setup}(1^\kappa); \; (vk, sk) \leftarrow \mathbf{SigGen}(1^\kappa); \; MSK^{ID} = sk; \; MPK^{ID} = (vk, PP^{PKI})$

$$\mathbf{IDKeyDer}(MSK^{ID}, MPK^{ID}, ID_P)$$

$(SPK_P^{PKI}, SSK_P^{PKI}) \leftarrow \mathbf{StaticGen}(PP^{PKI}); \; cert_P \leftarrow \mathbf{Sign}(sk, (ID_P, SPK_P^{PKI}));$
$SSK_P^{ID} = (SSK_P^{PKI}, SPK_P^{PKI}, cert_P)$

Key Exchange

| Party U_A (Initiator) | Party U_B (Responder) |

$ESK_A^{ID} = ESK_A^{PKI} \leftarrow \mathbf{EpheGen}(PP^{PKI})$ $ESK_B^{ID} = ESK_B^{PKI} \leftarrow \mathbf{EpheGen}(PP^{PKI})$
$Mes_1^{PKI} \leftarrow \mathbf{Message}^{\mathrm{post}}(PP^{PKI},$ If Π_{PKI} is a simultaneous protocol,
$\qquad\qquad U_A, SSK_A^{PKI}, ESK_A^{PKI})$ $Mes_2^{PKI} \leftarrow \mathbf{Message}^{\mathrm{post}}(PP^{PKI}, U_B, SSK_B^{PKI},$
$\qquad\qquad\qquad\qquad\qquad\qquad ESK_B^{PKI})$

$$\xrightarrow{\quad Mes_1^{ID} = (Mes_1^{PKI}, SPK_A^{PKI}, cert_A) \quad}$$

If Π_{PKI} is a sequential protocol,
$\qquad\qquad 1 \stackrel{?}{\leftarrow} \mathbf{Ver}(vk, (ID_A, SPK_A^{PKI}), cert_A)$
$\qquad Mes_2^{PKI} \leftarrow \mathbf{Message}(PP^{PKI}, U_B, U_A, SSK_B^{PKI},$
$\qquad\qquad\qquad\qquad ESK_B^{PKI}, SPK_A^{PKI}, Mes_1^{PKI})$

$$\xleftarrow{\quad Mes_2^{ID} = (Mes_2^{PKI}, SPK_B^{PKI}, cert_B) \quad}$$

$1 \stackrel{?}{\leftarrow} \mathbf{Ver}(vk, (ID_B, SPK_B^{PKI}), cert_B)$ If Π_{PKI} is a simultaneous protocol,
$\qquad\qquad 1 \stackrel{?}{\leftarrow} \mathbf{Ver}(vk, (ID_A, SPK_A^{PKI}), cert_A)$

(For $i = 3, ..., n$)
$Mes_i^{PKI} \leftarrow \mathbf{Message}(PP^{PKI}, U_P, U_{\bar{P}}, SSK_P^{PKI}, ESK_P^{PKI}, SPK_P^{PKI}, Mes_1^{PKI}, ..., Mes_{i-1}^{PKI})$
$$\xleftarrow{\quad Mes_i^{ID} = Mes_i^{PKI} \quad}$$
$K^{ID} = K^{PKI} \leftarrow \mathbf{SesKey}(PP^{PKI}, U_P, U_{\bar{P}}, SSK_P^{PKI}, ESK_P^{PKI}, SPK_P^{PKI}, Mes_1^{PKI}, ..., Mes_n^{PKI})$

Fig. 2. Conversion in the post-specified peer model, $\mathsf{GC}_{\mathrm{post}}$

model) also hold. Due to space limitation, in this paper, we prove the case of CK^+ security.

4.1 Description of $\mathsf{GC}_{\mathrm{post}}$

$\mathsf{GC}_{\mathrm{post}}$ converts a PKI-AKE $\Pi_{PKI} = (\mathbf{Setup}, \mathbf{StaticGen}, \mathbf{EpheGen}, \mathbf{Message}^{\mathrm{post}},$ $\mathbf{Message}, \mathbf{SesKey})$ in the post-specified peer model to an ID-AKE $\Pi_{ID} = (\mathbf{IDSetup}, \mathbf{IDKeyDer}, \mathbf{IDEpheGen}, \mathbf{IDMessage}^{\mathrm{post}}, \mathbf{IDMessage}, \mathbf{IDSesKey})$. Π_{ID} becomes a simultaneous protocol if Π_{PKI} is also a simultaneous protocol. Fig. 2 shows the protocol of the generic conversion $\mathsf{GC}_{\mathrm{post}}$.

Π_{ID} is constructed as follows:

- $(MSK^{ID}, MPK^{ID}) \leftarrow \mathbf{IDSetup}(1^\kappa)$:
  $PP^{PKI} \leftarrow \mathbf{Setup}(1^\kappa); \; (vk, sk) \leftarrow \mathbf{SigGen}(1^\kappa); \; MSK^{ID} = sk; \; MPK^{ID} = (vk, PP^{PKI})$
- $SSK_P^{ID} \leftarrow \mathbf{IDKeyDer}(MSK^{ID}, MPK^{ID}, ID_P)$:
  $(SPK_P^{PKI}, SSK_P^{PKI}) \leftarrow \mathbf{StaticGen}(PP^{PKI}); \; cert_P \leftarrow \mathbf{Sign}(sk, (ID_P, SPK_P^{PKI}));$
  $SSK_P^{ID} = (SSK_P^{PKI}, SPK_P^{PKI}, cert_P)$

- $ESK_P^{ID} \leftarrow \textbf{IDEpheGen}(MPK^{ID})$:
  $ESK_P^{PKI} \leftarrow \textbf{EpheGen}(PP^{PKI}); ESK_P^{ID} = ESK_P^{PKI}$
- $Mes_1^{ID} \leftarrow \textbf{IDMessage}^{\text{post}}(MPK^{ID}, ID_P, SSK_P^{ID}, ESK_P^{ID})$:
  $Mes_1^{PKI} \leftarrow \textbf{Message}^{\text{post}}(PP^{PKI}, U_P, SSK_P^{PKI}, ESK_P^{PKI}); Mes_1^{ID} = (Mes_1^{PKI}, SPK_A^{PKI},$
  $cert_A)$
- $Mes_2^{ID} \leftarrow \textbf{IDMessage}^{\text{post}}(MPK^{ID}, ID_{\bar{P}}, SSK_{\bar{P}}^{ID}, ESK_{\bar{P}}^{ID})$ (simultaneous):
  $Mes_2^{PKI} \leftarrow \textbf{Message}^{\text{post}}(PP^{PKI}, U_{\bar{P}}, SSK_{\bar{P}}^{PKI}, ESK_{\bar{P}}^{PKI}); Mes_2^{ID} = (Mes_2^{PKI}, SPK_{\bar{P}}^{PKI},$
  $cert_{\bar{P}})$
- $Mes_2^{ID} \leftarrow \textbf{IDMessage}^{\text{post}}(MPK^{ID}, ID_{\bar{P}}, SSK_{\bar{P}}^{ID}, ESK_{\bar{P}}^{ID}, Mes_1^{ID})$ (sequential):
  Verify $1 \overset{?}{\leftarrow} \textbf{Ver}(vk, (ID_P, SPK_P^{PKI}), cert_P); Mes_2^{PKI} \leftarrow \textbf{Message}(PP^{PKI}, U_{\bar{P}}, U_P,$
  $SSK_{\bar{P}}^{PKI}, ESK_{\bar{P}}^{PKI}, SPK_P^{PKI}, Mes_1^{PKI}); Mes_2^{ID} = (Mes_2^{PKI}, SPK_{\bar{P}}^{PKI}, cert_{\bar{P}})$
- $Mes_i^{ID} \leftarrow \textbf{IDMessage}(MPK^{ID}, ID_P, ID_{\bar{P}}, SSK_P^{ID}, ESK_P^{ID}, Mes_1^{ID}, \ldots, Mes_{i-1}^{ID})$:
  Verify $1 \overset{?}{\leftarrow} \textbf{Ver}(vk, (ID_{\bar{P}}, SPK_{\bar{P}}^{PKI}), cert_{\bar{P}})$ (for $i = 3$, and $i = 4$ (simultaneous));
  $Mes_i^{PKI} \leftarrow \textbf{Message}(PP^{PKI}, U_P, U_{\bar{P}}, SSK_P^{PKI}, ESK_P^{PKI}, SPK_{\bar{P}}^{PKI}, Mes_1^{PKI}, \ldots,$
  $Mes_{i-1}^{PKI}); Mes_i^{ID} = Mes_i^{PKI}$
- $K^{ID} \leftarrow \textbf{IDSesKey}(MPK^{ID}, ID_P, ID_{\bar{P}}, SSK_P^{ID}, ESK_P^{ID}, Mes_1^{ID}, \ldots, Mes_n^{ID})$:
  $K^{PKI} \leftarrow \textbf{SesKey}(PP^{PKI}, U_P, U_{\bar{P}}, SSK_P^{PKI}, ESK_P^{PKI}, SPK_{\bar{P}}^{PKI}, Mes_1^{PKI}, \ldots, Mes_n^{PKI})$;
  $K^{ID} = K^{PKI}$

4.2 Security

We show the following theorem.

Theorem 1. *If signature scheme* (**SigGen, Sign, Ver**) *is eUF-CMA and* $\Pi_{PKI} = ($**Setup, StaticGen, EpheGen, Message**^{post}, **Message, SesKey**$)$ *is* CK$^+$ *secure, then protocol* $\Pi_{ID} = ($**IDSetup, IDKeyDer, IDEpheGen, IDMessage**^{post}, **IDMessage, IDSesKey**$)$ *converted by* GC$_{\text{post}}$ *is id-CK$^+$-secure.*

Here, we show a proof sketch of Theorem 1.

In GC$_{\text{post}}$, messages and the session key generation procedure are same as the underlying PKI-AKE. Thus, if an adversary cannot obtain any advantage by using the additional message (i.e., spk_P and $cert_P$), the same level of security is preserved.

We transform the id-CK$^+$ security game such that the game halts if an adversary does not pose MasterRev and poses Send query containing spk_P and $cert_P$ which is valid for some ID not registered to the KGC. If the event occurs, it means that the adversary can bind a static public key with a non-registered ID. We can prove that the difference of advantages between two games is negligible due to eUF-CMA of the underlying signature scheme. In the transformed game, all static public keys are strictly bound with registered IDs unless the master secret key is not exposed. Thus, the situation is same as PKI-AKE, and we easily obtain security for ID-AKE from security for PKI-AKE.

We show the proof of Theorem 1 in the full paper.

4.3 Instantiations

We can instantiate GC$_{\text{post}}$ with CK$^+$ secure PKI-AKE in the post-specified peer model and an eUF-CMA signature scheme. For example, an instantiation based on the gap

DH assumption and the discrete logarithm (DLog) assumption in the RO model is with HMQV [14] as CK^+ secure PKI-AKE, and with the Schnorr sigature as eUF-CMA signature. This instantiation achieves ID-AKE without pairings like the FG scheme, and is secure in the stronger security model (i.e., the id-CK^+ model) than the model of the FG scheme (i.e., the CK model).

Theoretically, we can also achieve ID-AKE without either of pairings and ROs in the post-specified peer model. We can construct eUF-CMA signature from any one-way function by combining the Lamport-Diffie one-time signature [20] and the Merkle signature [21]. Thus, we can obtain eUF-CMA signature based on the DLog assumption. Also, Okamoto [22] proposed exposure-resilient 2-pass PKI-AKE under a DH-variant assumption without ROs in the post-specified peer model. Therefore, with these building blocks, we have exposure-resilient 2-pass ID-AKE without either of pairings and ROs in the post-specified peer model.

5   Conversion in Pre-specified Peer Model

In this section, we introduce a generic conversion of ID-AKE from PKI-AKE in the pre-specified peer model, named GC_{pre}. Compared with GC_{post}, GC_{pre} needs an additional round to send the static public key. As GC_{post}, we can prove that the converted ID-AKE scheme preserves security of the underlying PKI-AKE.

5.1   Description of GC_{pre}

GC_{pre} converts a PKI-AKE Π_{PKI} = (**Setup, StaticGen, EpheGen, Message**^{post}, **Message, SesKey**) in the pre-specified peer model to an ID-AKE Π_{ID} = (**IDSetup, IDKeyDer, IDEpheGen, IDMessage**^{post}, **IDMessage, IDSesKey**). We note that Π_{ID} becomes a sequential protocol regardless of Π_{PKI} because the responder must wait the initiator's message in order to derive Mes_2^{ID}. Fig. 3 shows the protocol of the generic conversion GC_{pre}.

Π_{ID} is constructed as follows:

- $(MSK^{ID}, MPK^{ID}) \leftarrow$ **IDSetup**$(1^\kappa), SSK_P^{ID} \leftarrow$ **IDKeyDer**$(MSK^{ID}, MPK^{ID}, ID_P)$, and $ESK_P^{ID} \leftarrow$ **IDEpheGen**(MPK^{ID}):
  The same as GC_{post} in Section 4.1
- $Mes_1^{ID} \leftarrow$ **IDMessage**$^{pre}(MPK^{ID}, ID_P, ID_{\bar{P}}, SSK_P^{ID}, ESK_P^{ID})$:
  $Mes_1^{ID} = (SPK_P^{PKI}, cert_P)$
- $Mes_2^{ID} \leftarrow$ **IDMessage**$(MPK^{ID}, ID_{\bar{P}}, ID_P, SSK_{\bar{P}}^{ID}, ESK_{\bar{P}}^{ID}, Mes_1^{ID})$:
  Verify $1 \overset{?}{\leftarrow}$ **Ver**$(vk, (ID_P, SPK_P^{PKI}), cert_P)$; $Mes_1^{PKI} \leftarrow$ **Message**$^{pre}(PP^{PKI}, U_{\bar{P}}, U_P,$ $SSK_{\bar{P}}^{PKI}, ESK_{\bar{P}}^{PKI}, SPK_P^{PKI})$; $Mes_2^{ID} = (Mes_1^{PKI}, SPK_{\bar{P}}^{PKI}, cert_{\bar{P}})$
- $Mes_3^{ID} \leftarrow$ **IDMessage**$(MPK^{ID}, ID_P, ID_{\bar{P}}, SSK_P^{ID}, ESK_P^{ID}, Mes_1^{ID}, Mes_2^{ID})$ (simultaneous) :
  Verify $1 \overset{?}{\leftarrow}$ **Ver**$(vk, (ID_{\bar{P}}, SPK_{\bar{P}}^{PKI}), cert_{\bar{P}})$; $Mes_2^{PKI} \leftarrow$ **Message**$^{pre}(PP^{PKI}, U_P, U_{\bar{P}},$ $SSK_P^{PKI}, ESK_P^{PKI}, SPK_{\bar{P}}^{PKI})$; $Mes_3^{ID} = Mes_2^{PKI}$

$$\textbf{IDSetup}(1^\kappa)$$

$PP^{PKI} \leftarrow \textbf{Setup}(1^\kappa);\ (vk, sk) \leftarrow \textbf{SigGen}(1^\kappa);\ MSK^{ID} = sk;\ MPK^{ID} = (vk, PP^{PKI})$

$$\textbf{IDKeyDer}(MSK^{ID}, MPK^{ID}, ID_P)$$

$(SPK_P^{PKI}, SSK_P^{PKI}) \leftarrow \textbf{StaticGen}(PP^{PKI});\ cert_P \leftarrow \textbf{Sign}(sk, (ID_P, SPK_P^{PKI}));$
$SSK_P^{ID} = (SSK_P^{PKI}, SPK_P^{PKI}, cert_P)$

$$\textbf{Key Exchange}$$

Party U_A (Initiator)			Party U_B (Responder)

$ESK_A^{ID} = ESK_A^{PKI} \leftarrow \textbf{EpheGen}(PP^{PKI})$ $\qquad\qquad ESK_B^{ID} = ESK_B^{PKI} \leftarrow \textbf{EpheGen}(PP^{PKI})$

$$\xrightarrow{\quad Mes_1^{ID} = (SPK_A^{PKI}, cert_A) \quad}$$

$$1 \overset{?}{\leftarrow} \textbf{Ver}(vk, (ID_A, SPK_A^{PKI}), cert_A)$$
$$Mes_1^{PKI} \leftarrow \textbf{Message}^{\text{pre}}(PP^{PKI}, U_B, U_A,$$
$$SSK_B^{PKI}, ESK_B^{PKI}, SPK_A^{PKI})$$

$$\xleftarrow{\quad Mes_2^{ID} = (Mes_1^{PKI}, SPK_B^{PKI}, cert_B) \quad}$$

$1 \overset{?}{\leftarrow} \textbf{Ver}(vk, (ID_B, SPK_B^{PKI}), cert_B)$
If Π_{PKI} is a simultaneous protocol,
$Mes_2^{PKI} \leftarrow \textbf{Message}^{\text{pre}}(PP^{PKI}, U_A, U_B, SSK_A^{PKI},$
$\qquad\qquad ESK_A^{PKI}, SPK_B^{PKI})$
Otherwise,
$\quad Mes_2^{PKI} \leftarrow \textbf{Message}(PP^{PKI}, U_A, U_B, SSK_A^{PKI},$
$\qquad\qquad ESK_A^{PKI}, SPK_B^{PKI}, Mes_1^{PKI})$

$$\xrightarrow{\quad Mes_3^{ID} = Mes_2^{PKI} \quad}$$

$$\text{(For } i = 3, ..., n)$$
$Mes_i^{PKI} \leftarrow \textbf{Message}(PP^{PKI}, U_P, U_{\bar{P}}, SSK_P^{PKI}, ESK_P^{PKI}, SPK_{\bar{P}}^{PKI}, Mes_1^{PKI}, ..., Mes_{i-1}^{PKI})$
$$Mes_{i+1}^{ID} = Mes_i^{PKI}$$

$$\xleftrightarrow{\quad \quad}$$

$K^{ID} = K^{PKI} \leftarrow \textbf{SesKey}(PP^{PKI}, U_P, U_{\bar{P}}, SSK_P^{PKI}, ESK_P^{PKI}, SPK_{\bar{P}}^{PKI}, Mes_1^{PKI}, ..., Mes_n^{PKI})$

Fig. 3. Conversion in the pre-specified peer model, GC_{pre}

- $Mes_3^{ID} \leftarrow \textbf{IDMessage}(MPK^{ID}, ID_P, ID_{\bar{P}}, SSK_P^{ID}, ESK_P^{ID}, Mes_1^{ID}, Mes_2^{ID})$ (sequential):
  Verify $1 \overset{?}{\leftarrow} \textbf{Ver}(vk, (ID_{\bar{P}}, SPK_{\bar{P}}^{PKI}), cert_{\bar{P}});\ Mes_2^{PKI} \leftarrow \textbf{Message}(PP^{PKI}, U_P, U_{\bar{P}},$
  $SSK_P^{PKI}, ESK_P^{PKI}, SPK_{\bar{P}}^{PKI}, Mes_1^{PKI});\ Mes_3^{ID} = Mes_2^{PKI}$
- $Mes_{i+1}^{ID} \leftarrow \textbf{IDMessage}(MPK^{ID}, ID_P, ID_{\bar{P}}, SSK_P^{ID}, ESK_P^{ID}, Mes_1^{ID}, ..., Mes_i^{ID})$:
  $Mes_i^{PKI} \leftarrow \textbf{Message}(PP^{PKI}, U_P, U_{\bar{P}}, SSK_P^{PKI}, ESK_P^{PKI}, SPK_{\bar{P}}^{PKI}, Mes_1^{PKI}, ...,$
  $Mes_{i-1}^{PKI});\ Mes_{i+1}^{ID} = Mes_i^{PKI}$
- $K^{ID} \leftarrow \textbf{IDSesKey}(MPK^{ID}, ID_P, ID_{\bar{P}}, SSK_P^{ID}, ESK_P^{ID}, Mes_1^{ID}, ..., Mes_{n+1}^{ID})$:
  $K^{PKI} \leftarrow \textbf{SesKey}(PP^{PKI}, U_P, U_{\bar{P}}, SSK_P^{PKI}, ESK_P^{PKI}, SPK_{\bar{P}}^{PKI}, Mes_1^{PKI}, ...,$
  $Mes_n^{PKI});\ K^{ID} = K^{PKI}$

5.2 Security

We show the following theorem.

Theorem 2. *If signature scheme* (**SigGen, Sign, Ver**) *is eUF-CMA and* Π_{PKI} = (**Setup, StaticGen, EpheGen, Message**^{post}, **Message, SesKey**) *is* CK^{+} *secure, then protocol* Π_{ID} = (**IDSetup, IDKeyDer, IDEpheGen, IDMessage**^{post}, **IDMessage, IDSesKey**) *converted by* GC$_{pre}$ *is* id-CK^{+}-*secure*.

The proof sketch is almost same as the case of GC$_{post}$. Please see Section 4.2. We show the proof of Theorem 2 in the full paper.

5.3 Instantiations

We can instantiate GC$_{pre}$ with CK^{+} secure PKI-AKE in the pre-specified peer model and an eUF-CMA signature scheme. We have a wider class of instantiations in the pre-specified peer model than in the post-specified peer model thanks to KEM-based PKI-AKE such as [9,6,19]. Though KEM-based PKI-AKE can not be used to instantiate ID-AKE in the post-specified peer model because the initiator must know the peer's static public key for KEM, it is no problem in the pre-specified peer model. For example, an instantiation based on lattices (without ROs) is with KEM-based PKI-AKE [6] from the Peikert PKE [23], and with the Gentry-Peikert-Vaikuntanathan signature [24]. Moreover, we have an instantiation based on the standard RSA problem (without ROs), which is with KEM-based PKI-AKE from the Hofheinz-Kiltz PKE [25], and with the Hohenberger-Waters signature [26]. This instantiation is the first ID-AKE scheme from the RSA assumption.

We can also construct ID-AKE schemes from other hardness assumptions in a theoretical sense. Fujioka et al. [6] proposed KEM-based PKI-AKE from the factoring problem and code-based problem, and Yoneyama [19] proposed KEM-based PKI-AKE from subset-sum problems and multi-variate quadratic systems. With one-way function-based signature (see Section 4.3), we can have ID-AKE schemes from such assumptions.

In [11], Fujioka et al. introduce a 2-pass generic construction of ID-AKE in the pre-specified peer model from ID-based KEM. Their construction is instantiated from pairings or lattices. Compared with GC$_{pre}$, though their construction has an advantage in round efficiency, possible instantiations are limited.

References

1. Bellare, M., Rogaway, P.: Entity Authentication and Key Distribution. In: Stinson, D.R. (ed.) CRYPTO 1993. LNCS, vol. 773, pp. 232–249. Springer, Heidelberg (1994)
2. Bellare, M., Rogaway, P.: Provably secure session key distribution: the three party case. In: STOC 1995, pp. 57–66 (1995)
3. Blake-Wilson, S., Johnson, D., Menezes, A.: Key Agreement Protocols and Their Security Analysis. In: Darnell, M.J. (ed.) Cryptography and Coding 1997. LNCS, vol. 1355, pp. 30–45. Springer, Heidelberg (1997)

4. Canetti, R., Krawczyk, H.: Analysis of Key-Exchange Protocols and Their Use for Building Secure Channels. In: Pfitzmann, B. (ed.) EUROCRYPT 2001. LNCS, vol. 2045, pp. 453–474. Springer, Heidelberg (2001)
5. LaMacchia, B.A., Lauter, K., Mityagin, A.: Stronger Security of Authenticated Key Exchange. In: Susilo, W., Liu, J.K., Mu, Y. (eds.) ProvSec 2007. LNCS, vol. 4784, pp. 1–16. Springer, Heidelberg (2007)
6. Fujioka, A., Suzuki, K., Xagawa, K., Yoneyama, K.: Strongly Secure Authenticated Key Exchange from Factoring, Codes, and Lattices. In: Fischlin, M., Buchmann, J., Manulis, M. (eds.) PKC 2012. LNCS, vol. 7293, pp. 467–484. Springer, Heidelberg (2012)
7. Boyd, C., Choo, K.-K.R.: Security of Two-Party Identity-Based Key Agreement. In: Dawson, E., Vaudenay, S. (eds.) Mycrypt 2005. LNCS, vol. 3715, pp. 229–243. Springer, Heidelberg (2005)
8. Chen, L., Cheng, Z., Smart, N.P.: Identity-based Key Agreement Protocols From Pairings. Int. J. Inf. Sec. 6(4), 213–241 (2007)
9. Boyd, C., Cliff, Y., Gonzalez Nieto, J.M., Paterson, K.G.: Efficient One-Round Key Exchange in the Standard Model. In: Mu, Y., Susilo, W., Seberry, J. (eds.) ACISP 2008. LNCS, vol. 5107, pp. 69–83. Springer, Heidelberg (2008)
10. Huang, H., Cao, Z.: An ID-based Authenticated Key Exchange Protocol Based on Bilinear Diffie-Hellman Problem. In: ASIACCS 2009, pp. 333–342 (2009)
11. Fujioka, A., Suzuki, K., Xagawa, K., Yoneyama, K.: Strongly Secure Authenticated Key Exchange from Factoring, Codes, and Lattices. In: Designs, Codes and Cryptography (2014)
12. Cremers, C.J.F.: Session-state Reveal Is Stronger Than Ephemeral Key Reveal: Attacking the NAXOS Authenticated Key Exchange Protocol. In: Abdalla, M., Pointcheval, D., Fouque, P.-A., Vergnaud, D. (eds.) ACNS 2009. LNCS, vol. 5536, pp. 20–33. Springer, Heidelberg (2009)
13. Cremers, C.J.F.: Examining Indistinguishability-Based Security Models for Key Exchange Protocols: The case of CK, CK-HMQV, and eCK. In: ASIACCS 2011, pp. 80–91 (2011)
14. Krawczyk, H.: HMQV: A High-Performance Secure Diffie-Hellman Protocol. In: Shoup, V. (ed.) CRYPTO 2005. LNCS, vol. 3621, pp. 546–566. Springer, Heidelberg (2005)
15. Fiore, D., Gennaro, R.: Making the Diffie-Hellman Protocol Identity-Based. In: Pieprzyk, J. (ed.) CT-RSA 2010. LNCS, vol. 5985, pp. 165–178. Springer, Heidelberg (2010)
16. Schnorr, C.P.: Efficient Identification and Signatures for Smart Cards. J. Cryptology 4(3), 161–174 (1991)
17. Bellare, M., Namprempre, C., Neven, G.: Security Proofs for Identity-Based Identification and Signature Schemes. In: Cachin, C., Camenisch, J.L. (eds.) EUROCRYPT 2004. LNCS, vol. 3027, pp. 268–286. Springer, Heidelberg (2004)
18. Menezes, A., Ustaoglu, B.: Comparing the Pre- and Post-specified Peer Models for Key Agreement. In: Mu, Y., Susilo, W., Seberry, J. (eds.) ACISP 2008. LNCS, vol. 5107, pp. 53–68. Springer, Heidelberg (2008)
19. Yoneyama, K.: Compact Authenticated Key Exchange from Bounded CCA-Secure KEM. In: Paul, G., Vaudenay, S. (eds.) INDOCRYPT 2013. LNCS, vol. 8250, pp. 161–178. Springer, Heidelberg (2013)
20. Lamport, L.: Constructing digital signatures from a one-way function. Technical Report SRI-CSL-98, SRI International Computer Science Laboratory (1979)
21. Merkle, R.C.: A Certified Digital Signature. In: Brassard, G. (ed.) CRYPTO 1989. LNCS, vol. 435, pp. 218–238. Springer, Heidelberg (1990)
22. Okamoto, T.: Authenticated Key Exchange and Key Encapsulation in the Standard Model. In: Kurosawa, K. (ed.) ASIACRYPT 2007. LNCS, vol. 4833, pp. 474–484. Springer, Heidelberg (2007)
23. Peikert, C.: Public-key cryptosystems from the worst-case shortest vector problem: extended abstract. In: STOC 2009, pp. 333–342 (2009)

24. Gentry, C., Peikert, C., Vaikuntanathan, V.: Trapdoors for hard lattices and new cryptographic constructions. In: STOC 2008, pp. 197–206 (2008)
25. Hofheinz, D., Kiltz, E.: Practical Chosen Ciphertext Secure Encryption from Factoring. In: Joux, A. (ed.) EUROCRYPT 2009. LNCS, vol. 5479, pp. 313–332. Springer, Heidelberg (2009)
26. Hohenberger, S., Waters, B.: Short and Stateless Signatures from the RSA Assumption. In: Halevi, S. (ed.) CRYPTO 2009. LNCS, vol. 5677, pp. 654–670. Springer, Heidelberg (2009)

Proving Correctness and Security of Two-Party Computation Implemented in Java in Presence of a Semi-honest Sender*

Florian Böhl[1], Simon Greiner[1], and Patrik Scheidecker[2]

[1] Karlsruhe Institute of Technology,
Institute of Theoretical Informatics, Germany
firstname.lastname@kit.edu
[2] FZI Research Center for Information Technology, Germany
lastname@fzi.de

Abstract. We provide a proof of correctness and security of a two-party-computation protocol based on garbled circuits and oblivious transfer in the presence of a semi-honest sender. To achieve this we are the first to combine a machine-assisted proof of correctness with advanced cryptographic primitives to prove security properties of Java code. The machine-assisted part of the proof is conducted with KeY, an interactive theorem prover.

The proof includes a correctness result for the construction and evaluation of garbled circuits. This is particularly interesting since checking such an implementation by hand would be very tedious and error-prone. Although we stick to the secure two-party-computation of an n-bit AND in this paper, our approach is modular, and we explain how our techniques can be applied to other functions.

To prove the security of the protocol for an honest-but-curious sender and an honest receiver, we use the framework presented by Küsters et al. for the cryptographic verification of Java programs. As part of our work, we add oblivious transfer to the set of cryptographic primitives supported by the framework. This is a general contribution beyond our results for concrete Java code.

1 Introduction

Motivation and overview Protocols for secure two-party computation allow two parties to evaluate a function f such that both parties provide a part of the input. Neither of the parties must learn more about the input of the other than can be inferred by its own input, the function f and the computed output. Since first solutions for two-party computation protocols have been presented by Yao [35, 36], the problem has received a lot of attention (e.g., [14, 8, 25, 26, 29]).

* This work was partially funded by the KASTEL project by the Federal Ministry of Education and Research, BMBF 01BY1172. Florian Böhl was supported by MWK grant "MoSeS".

D. Gritzalis et al. (Eds.): CANS 2014, LNCS 8813, pp. 175–190, 2014.

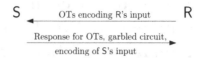

Fig. 1. Yao's protocol for two-party computations

Yao's approach Following the initial ideas of Yao, one can construct a two-party computation protocol from garbled circuits [35, 36] and oblivious transfer [32] (see Figure 1). The basic idea is to first encode the function f as a circuit consisting of gates and wires. Such a circuit can then be transformed into a garbled circuit by one of the parties, say the sender S. Instead of a bitstring, the garbled circuit takes an encoding for each bit as input. These encodings are initially only known to the creator of the garbled circuit (S here). When the receiver R wants to evaluate the garbled circuit on a given input $x \in \{0,1\}^n$, it needs to know the corresponding encoding for each input bit.

The encodings for the input bits of R are transmitted via oblivious transfer from S to R. The oblivious transfer protocol guarantees that R learns exactly one encoding for each of its own input bits and that S remains oblivious to which encodings R learned. Subsequently, S transmits the garbled circuit and the encodings of its own input bits to R. These encodings don't tell R anything about S's input bits. Finally, R can evaluate the garbled circuit. Note that R only knows the corresponding encoding for one bitstring $x \in \{0,1\}^n$ and hence can only use the garbled circuit to compute $f(x)$.

From theory to practice While they have always been of theoretical interest, two-party computation protocols seemed far away from being applicable to practical problems for a long time. Beginning with Fairplay [28], methods to construct (garbled) circuits for generic functions have drastically improved (e.g., [20, 16]). This inspired various protocols for practical problems [19, 12, 30, 17]. As performance of garbled circuits is going to increase, we are going to see more practical applications of garbled circuits in the future.

Mind the gap Although all of those protocols come equipped with security proofs of abstractions of the protocol, there remains a gap between the security of the specification in a theoretical model and a real world implementation, e.g., in Java. There are aspects of actual implementations, which have no counterpart in the abstract world. For example, even if a protocol itself is secure, minor mistakes in its realization can completely break security as the recent Heartbleed bug in the OpenSSL library shows. Under this point of view it is important not only to prove the security and correctness of a protocol in the abstract world but also to verify its actual implementation. This can be achieved by using machine-based verification techniques, and in this work we present a first step to close this gap. We chose Java for being a widely used programming language in the real world, unlike e.g. EasyCrypt [2], which offers verification in its own specific language.

Our contributions We use the KeY tool[3], a deductive verification tool for Java programs, to show the correctness of a two-party computation protocol implemented in Java. KeY was previously used for verification of functional properties[33], non-interference properties[15], and security properties of programs making use of public key encryption[22]. Our first contribution is to extend this body of work by using KeY to prove correctness of an implementation that uses symmetric encryption for garbled circuits. The machine-assisted proof is done for a concrete function f, namely an n-bit AND. While this might seem limited at first glance, the proof is modular, i.e., it uses the correctness of the implementation of garbled gates in a black-box way. Additionally, we explain how correctness proofs for other functions can be conducted in the same fashion. As a proof of concept, we also prove the correctness of a XOR gate. The correctness of our implementation of an n-bit AND can be used in a black-box way to show the correctness of more complicated circuits. This is the first paper that presents a security and correctness proof of an implementation in a real-world programming language. Alternative tools for languages like Java, C, and C#, are, for example, Spec# [1], Krakatoa [13] or VCC [34]. Another tool using symbolic execution for Java and C programs is the VeriFast system [18].

Our second contribution is to show the security of the implementation in presence of a passive adversary for corrupted sender S and honest receiver R; independently of the function f. To achieve this, we add oblivious transfer as a cryptographic building block to the framework for Cryptographic Verification of Java-like programs by Küsters et al. [23, 21]. That is, we provide an ideal interface in Java for oblivious transfer following the ideal OT functionality of [8] for Canetti's UC-framework [7]. We show that this ideal interface can be implemented by any UC-secure oblivious transfer protocol (e.g., [31, 11, 10]).

On our restrictions. We would like to point out that – although we only consider honest-but-curious security in this paper – our work is a necessary step towards proving security of implementations of adaptively secure protocols based on garbled circuits (like [27] for example). Every security argument for these protocols assumes that the actual implementation is correct; this is where our result is needed. Furthermore, we would like to point out that it is sufficient that the output is only learned by R as explained in [26].

Outline The structure of this paper is as follows. In the next section we introduce some preliminaries. We briefly introduce the cryptographic building blocks used in this paper, the specification language *Java Modelling Language* and the interactive theorem prover *KeY*. Subsequently, in Section 3, we describe the protocol we analyze in this work. In Section 4 we present details on an abstraction for the secret key encryption scheme, followed by a description of the modular implementation for the cryptographic building blocks introduced earlier. We then show two lemmas stating the correctness of the implementation. In Section 5 we prove the security of our protocol for a semi-honest sender S using the results from Section 4. In Section 6 we present potential directions for future work. A full version of this paper is available online[6].

2   Preliminaries

2.1   The CVJ Framework

Due to the limited space we cannot present the framework for Cryptographic Verification of Java Programs here. We therefore would like to refer readers interested in a summary of the framework to the full version of this paper [6] and readers who are interested in the full details to the original paper [23].

2.2   Cryptographic Building Blocks

SKE A *secret key encryption scheme* (SKE scheme) with keyspace $\mathcal{K}$ and message space $\mathcal{M}$ features three probabilistic-polynomial-time algorithms:
- Gen takes the security parameter λ and generates a key $k \in \mathcal{K}$,
- E takes a key $k \in \mathcal{K}$ and a message $M \in \mathcal{M}$ and outputs a ciphertext, and
- D takes a key $k \in \mathcal{K}$ and a ciphertext C and outputs the plaintext if decryption works and $\perp$ otherwise.

We say that an SKE scheme is *correct* if for all $k \in \mathcal{K}$ and all $M \in \mathcal{M}$ we have $D(k, E(k, M)) = M$. Furthermore, we stipulate for SKE schemes throughout the paper that $\mathbf{Pr}\left[D(k', E(k, M)) \neq \perp : k, k' \leftarrow \text{Gen}(\lambda)\right]$ is negligible in λ. Note that this already implies that two honestly generated keys are equal only with negligible probability independent of the security of the SKE scheme.

The algorithms Gen, E and D can be provided in many ways; in our implementation they are provided by the interface $\mathcal{I}_{\mathsf{SKE}}$ (see [6] for details). The methods `GenKey`, `Encrypt` and `Decrypt` provide the respective functionality. The classes `Key` and `Cipher` provide a constructor, which we do not further specify and the identifier `ident` which represents the numerical representation of a byte array. An implementation can use the `ident` field to store an arbitrary representation of the object. We use this concept throughout the paper for all abstract objects we have. Although identifiers are defined here as of data type *int*, these fields can hold arbitrary natural numbers during verification. Hence, they are merely a placeholder and an actual representation would not be bounded by a 32 or 64 bit integer size. The method `GenKey` creates a key which is not distinguishable from a random number. $\mathcal{I}_{\mathsf{SKE}}$ contains methods `Encrypt` and `Decrypt` that provide the expected functionality for symmetric encryption.

Circuits A *circuit* consists of input pins, output pins, gates and wires. Each gate has two input pins and one output pin. Each wire connects exactly two pins and each pin is connected to exactly one wire. Furthermore, each wire connects an input pin of the circuit to an input pin of a gate. An output pin of a gate is connected to an input pin of a gate or an output pin of the circuit. If the gates, the input pins, and the output pins of the circuits are viewed as nodes of a graph and the wires are viewed as the edges, a circuit must be a directed acyclic graph. Each wire can take a value from $\{0, 1\}$ and each gate resembles an arbitrary binary function $g : \{0, 1\}^2 \to \{0, 1\}$. [1] To *evaluate* a circuit having n

---

[1] Although there are more general definitions of circuits, this one is simple and doesn't restrict our results.

input wires for an input $x \in \{0,1\}^n$, we assign x_i to the wire connected to the ith input pin and then evaluate gate after gate in a straightforward way. Obviously, for every function $f : \{0,1\}^n \to \{0,1\}^m$ we can find a circuit encoding f, i.e., evaluating the circuit for $x \in \{0,1\}^n$ yields $f(x)$.

Garbled Circuits [2] Given a circuit, the idea behind garbling is basically to obfuscate the function encoded by it to some extend. Using an SKE scheme, we can *garble* a circuit as follows: First, we generate two keys k_0, k_1 for each wire. These keys represent the two possible values the wire can take. The input of each gate are now two keys $l \in \{l_0, l_1\}$ and $r \in \{r_0, r_1\}$. The output must be a key $out \in \{out_0, out_1\}$. For l_b and $r_{b'}$ we compute $\mathsf{E}(l_b, \mathsf{E}(r_{b'}, out_{g(b,b')}))$ which yields a list of four ciphertexts (as above, $g\{0,1\}^2 \to \{0,1\}$ is the binary function describing the functionality of the gate). A random permutation of that list, also referenced as *evaluation table* later, is the description of the gate. To evaluate a garbled gate, one can, given the input keys l and r, try all ciphers and see which one decrypts correctly to retrieve the output key. In this manner, the garbled circuit can be evaluated gate by gate.

Oblivious Transfer The protocol we describe uses a cryptographic primitive called *oblivious transfer* (OT), introduced by [32]. More concretely, we use a 2-1 oblivious transfer for two parties. One party (S) has two secrets of which another party (R), may learn exactly one. S must not learn the choice of R while R must learn only one of the secrets.

In our Java code, we use an interface called $\mathcal{I}_{OT}$ resembling an abstraction of a two message OT protocol (see [6] for details): The receiver R starts by generating some secret information OTKey. This is used to prepare the request OTReq which is then sent to S. From the request S can generate a response by providing inputs in0 and in1. If R receives the response, it can extract in0 or in1 depending on the value of choice used for generating the request.

2.3 The Verification Setup

We use *JML**, an extension of the Java Modelling Language (JML) for specification of Java programs and the *KeY-tool* as a prover. A full account of JML can be found in [24]. Specifications are given as annotations in the source code of a program. The main concept follows a design-by-contract approach, whose central specification artefacts are *method contracts* and *class invariants*.

A method contract consists of a precondition and a postcondition. A method satisfies its contract if for all states satisfying the method's precondition it terminates in a state that satisfies the postcondition. A class invariant describes a global state which has to be preserved by all methods (except special "'helper"' methods).

Pre-, postconditions and invariants are boolean valued JML expressions. A JML expression can be almost any side-effect free Java expression. Besides the

---

[2] A thorough and comprehensive state-of-the-art description can be found in [4].

built-in operators in Java, some additional ones can be used; we explain the ones relevant for our work in [6]. We make use of *ghost variables*, which are variables that can be used for specifications. They do not influence the actual behaviour of a program, but allow us to perform bookkeeping of information during execution of a program within proofs. Ghost variables cannot be referred to by Java code.

We use the KeY-tool [3] to prove our correctness result. This interactive theorem prover is based on a generalization of Hoare logic. During a KeY proof, a program is *symbolically executed*, i.e., transformed into a set of logical constraints representing the behaviour of the program. Using first-order reasoning, the KeY tool evaluates the postcondition, given the constraints.

3 The Protocol

We model a two-party computation of an n-bit AND between a sender S and a receiver R following Yao's initial construction (see Figure 1). During a normal run of a protocol, both parties send exactly one message (we omit distributing the output computed by the receiver).

Intuitively, the protocol works as follows: R starts by preparing oblivious transfers (OTs) according to its own input. E.g., if R's ith input bit is 1, it will prepare the OT such that it will learn the second input of S to this OT later. R then sends the OTs to S. S generates a garbled circuit. S generates for each input and each output wire of the circuit a pair of keys that corresponds to the possible bit-value of the wire (0 or 1). For the input wires that belong to R's input, S fills the OTs received from R with the corresponding key pairs. R will receive only the corresponding key (and, by the security of the OT, R's choice remains hidden from S). S then sends the garbled circuit, the keys corresponding to its own input, the filled OTs and the key pairs for the output wires to R. R extracts the keys corresponding to its inputs from the OTs, evaluates the garbled circuit and can – using the key pairs for the output wires – interpret the resulting keys as a bitstring. This bitstring is the result of the two-party computation.

The interfaces of sender and receiver are given in Figure 2 in the appendix.

4 Correctness of Our Protocol

In this section we describe the proof of correctness for our implementation. We will present only the idea behind the proof here. A more thorough description can be found in the full version of this paper [6]. Additionally, the complete implementation and machine-assisted proofs are available online[5].

A word on modularity and re-usability One of the most tedious tasks during the verification of a program is finding a correct and sufficient specification. This is especially true in the case of garbled gates and circuits, because a lot of information is given implicitly by the code and the interworking of methods following after another. In order to prove correctness, we have to make this information explicit in the form of class invariants.

Our implementation is modular in the way that only the contracts of other objects are used for verification, not their actual implementation. In order to implement binary gates with different algorithms the same functionality the specification provided can be re-used. Also, when binary gates realizing a different function are implemented, our specification can be reused, by only changing the specification of the truth table and fixing two lines in the postcondition of one method. As a proof of concept, we implemented and verified an additional garbled gate with XOR-functionality, which can be found in the online sources [5]. The proof process is essentially the same for both gates.

A circuit is built by wiring gates (which are used in a black-box fashion but may again be circuits themselves) in a certain way. The way gates are wired is called the *topology* of the circuit. In our work we use something one could call a *linear topology* for the circuit that then forms the n-bit AND. Our specification can easily be re-used for other circuits with a linear topology. For example, realizing an n-bit OR would only require straightforward changes in two lines of the postcondition of the evaluate method. Realizations of n-bit AND and n-bit OR are particularly interesting to us because they are the basis for disjunctive and conjunctive normal forms.

4.1 Encryption Abstraction

Instead of using a real implementation for the interfaces $\mathcal{I}_{\mathsf{SKE}}$ we provide an abstract specification of this cryptographic primitive.

A `Cipher` has two ghost fields we use for specifying the encryption information. The ghost field `key` holds the key, which was used for encryption of a message. We call two objects of type `Key` corresponding, if they have the same `ident` value. The ghost field `msg` holds the message that is encrypted in the cipher by a key corresponding to the value of `key`.

Instead of directly using constructors or methods provided by `Key` or `Cipher`, we encapsulate this functionality in a secret key encryption scheme, providing the interface $\mathcal{I}_{\mathsf{SKE}}$.

The `SKE` class has two static ghost fields. The field `randoms` holds a collection of numbers, which represent random byte arrays. The content of `randoms` can be seen as a stream of random numbers from which elements can be drawn. This makes the methods provided by `SKE` deterministic and we can treat randomisation independent from execution of our actual code.

A field `counter` is a pointer to the element in `randoms` which is drawn the next time a random number is needed. The management of this pointer is ensured by the methods provided by `SKE`. To create a new key, we use the method `GenKey`. It returns a new `Key` object, where the identifier has the same value as the next element in `randoms`.

The method `SKE.Encrypt` encapsulates the encryption functionality in our program. The `Cipher` object returned by the method has a fresh random number as identifier. The ghost field `key` remembers the key which was used for encryption, while the ghost field `msg` remembers the clear text information.

The method SKE.Decrypt provides decryption functionality, which ensures that a null object is returned, if the key passed as parameter does not correspond to the key originally used for encryption of the message. If the encrypted message is of type Key, the Decrypt method has to return a key corresponding to the originally encrypted key object. So the object structure is preserved by decryption. For other cases, we leave the behaviour of Decrypt underspecified.

4.2 Implementation Details

Our realization of a garbled circuit consists of two classes. The class GarbledANDGate implements a garbled gate with binary AND functionality. The class GCnBitAND makes use of GarbledANDGate to realize the interface $\mathcal{I}_{GC}$.

GarbledANDGate The class GarbledANDGate (see Figure 3 in the appendix) defines the field Cipher[] eT, representing the evaluation table as explained in Section 2.2. Additionally, we introduce several ghost variables for bookkeeping of the state of a GarbledANDGate to explicitly store information given by the structure of the evaluation table.

The variables kl0 and kl1 store an object of type Key which represents the key expected as 0- or 1-valued input on the left pin. The variables kr0 and kr1 do the same for the right pin. The variables out0 and out1 hold the objects representing the keys used as 0- and 1-valued output.

The evaluation table holds on each position an encryption either of out0 or out1, first encrypted by one of the input keys for the right pin and then encrypted by one of the input keys for the left pin. As explained in Section 2.2, the evaluation table contains a random permutation of the ciphers and we use the ghost variables ci0, ci1, ci2, ci3 to store the indices of the ciphers after permutation. For example, the encryption of out0 with the keys kr0 and kl0 is stored at position eT[ci0]. For a full account of the definition of the specification, we refer the reader to the implementation.

Further, we provide a method contract for the constructor and the method evaluate provided by the gate. These contracts ensure that the gate does realize a garbled AND functionality, assuming some preconditions. The correctness of the implementation according to the contract is used as a lemma during the proof of correctness of the garbled circuit.

Garbled n-bit AND circuit The class GCnBitAND (see Figure 4 in the appendix), realizing $\mathcal{I}_{GC}$, defines an array gates. The gates stored in this array are responsible for the functionality implemented by the circuit. The correct wiring of the circuit is indirectly ensured by the constructor and the evaluate method.

We define four ghost variables to store the expected in- and output of the circuit. The keys expected by the circuit as 0-valued input are stored in the array in0, those representing a 1-valued input are stored in the array in1. The ghost variables out0 and out1 store the keys representing the 0- and 1-valued outputs.

The invariant of GCnBitAND ensures a well-definedness property. First, it is ensured that the expected input of a gate on the left pin corresponds to the output of the previous gate, i.e., the circuit implements a linear structure. Second, it is ensured that the keys expected as an input on the right pin by the gates correspond to the keys expected as input by the circuit. A special case here is the first gate, for which both inputs come from the user. Finally, the invariant ensures that the output of the last gate corresponds to the output the circuit is supposed to provide.

4.3 Correctness of the Implementation

We prove the correctness of our implementation of the methods provided by GCnBitAND against their contracts.

The contract of the constructor of class GCnBitAND (see Figure 5 in the appendix) requires that as many keys provided as 0-valued input are also provided as 1-valued input. The amount of keys provided determines the number of pins provided by the circuit. At least two keys have to be provided for each value, which expresses the circuit to be built provides at least two pins.

Further, the precondition of the contract states that the keys used as possible input for each pin do not correspond, neither do the keys used as possible input on two subsequent gates. Both of these conditions are necessary for the correctness of the gates, which are built during execution of the constructor. Finally the possible output keys must not correspond, i.e., it can be distinguished between a 0- and a 1-valued output.

The postcondition of the contract states that the identifier representing expected input keys in the ghost fields in0 and in1 are the same as the identifiers of the keys used as input to the constructor. Additionally, the invariant of class GCnBitAND is required to hold after termination of the constructor, which is an implicit postcondition for the constructor.

Theorem 1 states the correctness of the constructor of $\mathcal{I}_{GC}$, since its implementation is correct with respect to its specification.

Theorem 1. *Let GCnBitAND be the realization of $\mathcal{I}_{GC}$; let in0 and in1 be arrays of keys, such that the length of in0 equals the length of in1, all elements in in0 and in1 are not null and in0 contains at least two elements; let out0 and out1 be keys that are not null and let all keys in in0, in1 and the keys out0 and out1 have pairwise different identifier.*

Then a call $\mathcal{I}_{GC}$.GCnBitAND(in0, in1, out0, out1) returns an object gc realizing $\mathcal{I}_{GC}$ such that the invariant of gc holds and; for all $i \in \{0 .. length\ of\ in0 - 1\}$ the keys expected by gc as input on pin n representing a 0-valued input corresponds to the key in0[n] and the key expected by gc as input on pin n representing a 1-valued input corresponds to the key in1[n] and the key provided by gc as output representing a 0-valued output corresponds to out0 and the key provided by gc as output representing a 1-valued output corresponds to out1.

Proof. The conditions stated as preconditions in Theorem 1 imply the preconditions of the constructor of class GCnBitAND. The postconditions stated in

Theorem 1 are equivalent to the postcondition of class GCnBitAND. The realization of $\mathcal{I}_{GC}$ is given by the class GCnBitAND.

We proved with the KeY-tool that GCnBitAND.GCnBitAND satisfies its contract. Therefore Theorem 1 holds.

The contract of evaluate of GCnBitAND (see Figure 6 in the appendix) requires R to provide exactly one key for each pin of the circuit, while each key either has to correspond to the key expected by the circuit on the respective pin as 0- or 1-valued input. Implicitly it is also required that the invariant of the circuit holds right before a call to evaluate. The postcondition of evaluate of GCnBitAND states that a correct implementation of evaluate returns a key corresponding to the 1-valued output key, if all input keys correspond to 1-valued input. If at least one input key does not correspond to a 1-valued input, the circuit returns a 0-valued output. It is easy to see that the postcondition expresses a n-bit AND functionality.

Theorem 2 states the correctness of method evaluate of $\mathcal{I}_{GC}$, since the implementation of the constructor is correct due to its specification.

Theorem 2. *Let GCnBitAND be the realization of $\mathcal{I}_{GC}$; let gc be the object giving access to $\mathcal{I}_{GC}$; let the invariant of gc hold; let in be an array of keys with the same length as the amount of expected input keys by gc and let in[i] correspond to the 0-valued or 1-valued input key expected by gc.*

Then a call $\mathcal{I}_{GC}.evaluate(in)$ returns a key o such that o represents a 1-valued output if all keys in in represent 1-valued inputs and o represents a 0-valued output if not all keys in in represent 1-valued inputs.

Proof. The proof can be found in the full version of this paper [6].

5   Security of Our Protocol

In this section we prove that our protocol (see Section 3) is secure against an honest-but curious adversary if the sender S is corrupted. Security in this setting means, that the inputs of the receiver R remain secret. This follows from the correctness of the protocol and the UC-security of oblivious transfer.

$\mathcal{I}_{(\hat{S},R)}$ (see [6] for details) describes the interface of the two-party computation in presence of a corrupted sender to the environment. In addition to what a passive adversary can usually observe during a run of the protocol (using methods getReceiverMessage, getSenderMessage, and getOutput), $\mathcal{I}_{(\hat{S},R)}$ now provides it with methods getSenderInput and getSenderKeys which leak S's secrets. In particular, getSenderKeys returns the list of all encryption keys generated by S to construct the garbled circuit. Note that the adversary cannot change the behavior of S.

We now introduce two implementations of the interface $\mathcal{I}_{(\hat{S},R)}$.

– The real implementation $2PC_{real}^{(\hat{S},R)}$ runs the two-party protocol in the constructor on the given inputs and saves the exchanged messages, generated encryption keys, etc. for later retrieval by the adversary through the corresponding getters.

- The ideal implementation $2\mathsf{PC}_{\mathsf{ideal}}^{(\hat{\mathsf{S}},\mathsf{R})}$ doesn't run the protocol but uses a simulator implementing the interface $\mathcal{I}_{\mathsf{Sim}}$ which provides all getters except getOutput. It resembles a wrapper for the ideal functionality (for corrupted S and honest R) running in parallel with a simulator. Note that the simulator is only given the input of the sender and the length of the receiver's input.

$\mathsf{OT}_{\mathsf{ideal}}$ is an ideal implementation of the interface for oblivious transfer $\mathcal{I}_{\mathsf{OT}}$ (see [6] for details) resembling the ideal functionality $\mathcal{F}_{\mathsf{OT}}$. Internally, $\mathsf{OT}_{\mathsf{ideal}}$ maintains a list of tuples (OTKey k, boolean choice, OTResp r, Object in0, Object in1) each representing one OT instance. Constructing an OT request creates a new entry in that list with r, in0 and in1 set to null. Upon genResponse for an OTKey the corresponding r, in0 and in1 are set according to the given values (which must not be null and the length of their serialization must not exceed a fixed maximum). On getOutput for OTResp r and OTKey k, depending on the value of choice, in0 or in1 is returned. The ident attributes of keys, responses and requests are set to uniformly random values on object creation.[3] As usual throughout the paper, these idents are placeholders that can be used for data by a real implementation.

Theorem 3. *Let* $2\mathsf{PC}_{\mathsf{real}}^{(\hat{\mathsf{S}},\mathsf{R})}$, $2\mathsf{PC}_{\mathsf{ideal}}^{(\hat{\mathsf{S}},\mathsf{R})}$ *and* $\mathsf{OT}_{\mathsf{ideal}}$ *be the programs introduced above and* $\mathsf{SKE}_{\mathsf{real}}$ *be a correct implementation of* $\mathcal{I}_{\mathsf{SKE}}$, *then we have*

$$\mathsf{SKE}_{\mathsf{real}} \cdot \mathsf{OT}_{\mathsf{ideal}} \cdot 2\mathsf{PC}_{\mathsf{real}}^{(\hat{\mathsf{S}},\mathsf{R})} \leq^{(\mathcal{I}_{\mathsf{out}}, \emptyset, \emptyset, \mathcal{I}_{\mathsf{Sim}})} \mathsf{SKE}_{\mathsf{real}} \cdot \mathsf{OT}_{\mathsf{ideal}} \cdot 2\mathsf{PC}_{\mathsf{ideal}}^{(\hat{\mathsf{S}},\mathsf{R})}$$

where $\mathcal{I}_{\mathsf{out}} := \mathcal{I}_{(\hat{\mathsf{S}},\mathsf{R})} \cup \mathcal{I}_{\mathsf{OT}} \cup \mathcal{I}_{\mathsf{SKE}}$ *and* $\mathcal{I}_{\mathsf{Sim}}$ *the interface described above.*

Proof. The simulator can successfully fake getReceiverMessage because the OT keys are random handles independent of choice in $\mathsf{OT}_{\mathsf{ideal}}$. It creates inR_length OTs and returns the corresponding OT requests on a call of getReceiverMessage. To simulate the sender, it generates a garbled circuit as an honest S would do and prepares the OT responses accordingly to assemble the sender response. The correctness of the garbled circuit (see Theorem 1, Theorem 2) guarantees that the output in the real world actually matches that in the ideal world.

What remains to do is to show that we can replace the ideal implementation for oblivious transfer by a real one.

Security of Oblivious Transfer We first describe the simplified functionality for oblivious transfer [8]. $\mathcal{F}_{\mathsf{OT}}$ interacts with a sender S and a receiver R.
- Upon receiving a message (in_0, in_1) from S, store (in_0, in_1).
- Upon receiving a message b from R, check if a (in_0, in_1) message was previously sent by S. If yes, send in_b to R. If not, send nothing to R (but continue running).

Let $\mathsf{OT}_{\mathsf{real}}$ be a system that implements the OT $\mathcal{I}_{\mathsf{OT}}$ interface (see [6] for details). We show that the system $\mathsf{OT}_{\mathsf{ideal}}$ can safely be replaced by $\mathsf{OT}_{\mathsf{real}}$ if $\mathsf{OT}_{\mathsf{real}}$ suitably implements a two-party-two-message realization of $\mathcal{F}_{\mathsf{OT}}$. Such

---

[3] Theoretically, other distributions are also possible. For Theorem 3 we just need that the idents of OT requests are independent of the choice bit.

realizations exists under standard cryptographic assumptions, e.g., decisional Diffie-Hellman, quadratic residuosity, or learning with errors [31].[4]

Theorem 4. *If* OT_{real} *implements a realization* $\mathcal{R}$ *of* $\mathcal{F}_{OT}$, *then* $OT_{real} \leq^{(\mathcal{I}_{OT}, \emptyset, \emptyset, \emptyset)} OT_{ideal}$

Proof. The basic idea is that, since $\mathcal{R}$ realizes $\mathcal{F}_{OT}$, there is a simulator $\mathcal{S}$ such that $\mathcal{R}$ and $\mathcal{S} \cdot \mathcal{F}_{OT}$ are indistinguishable for every environment in the computational UC model (for a suitable composition $\cdot$ in that model). The output of $\mathcal{S}$ is independent from the original inputs of the parties S and R (it doesn't get those values from $\mathcal{F}_{OT}$). As output distribution for OT_{ideal} we can hence pick that of $\mathcal{S}$. Since we can simulate Turing machines with Jinja+ programs, strong simulatability in the CVJ framework follows.

6   Future Work

This work provides the proof of security of a two-party computation implemented in Java against a semi-honest sender. In particular, we prove correctness of the implementation of a garbled circuit using cryptographic primitives via a formally specified interface.

One obvious direction for future work is to prove security for the two remaining scenarios, i.e., security against a corrupted receiver and security if both parties are honest (all in presence of a passive adversary).

One interesting challenge towards this goal is to prove at code level that the evaluation of a garbled circuit does not leak more than the encoded function f and the output $f(x)$.[5] For this, implementation details of the garbled circuit (e.g., that the evaluation table is randomized) will become important.

Since the security against a corrupted receiver will also depend on the security of the used encryption scheme, a suitable functionality for secret key encryption will be necessary. This functionality should be realizable in the sense of strong simulatability and sufficient for the construction of garbled circuits.

Finally, it would be interesting to build a compiler from functions to (garbled) circuits that automatically outputs Java code that is verifiably correct. E.g., if we have the description of a function in conjunctive normal form (one multi-bit AND, a number of multi-bit ORs and NOTs) we can use the modularity of our correctness proof as explained in Section 4. However, more work would be needed to get from the proof for a conjunctive normal form to a high-level description of the function like "addition of two integers given as bitstrings".

---

[4] These realizations need a common reference string functionality [9] which can be part of OT_{real}.

[5] Actually, a garbled circuit should leak f only to some extent. However, since f is public in our setting, even a complete leakage of f would not be problematic which relaxes the difficulty of the proof.

References

1. Barnett, M., Rustan M. Leino, K., Schulte, W.: The spec# programming system: An overview. In: Barthe, G., Burdy, L., Huisman, M., Lanet, J.-L., Muntean, T. (eds.) CASSIS 2004. LNCS, vol. 3362, pp. 49–69. Springer, Heidelberg (2005)
2. Barthe, G., Grégoire, B., Heraud, S., Béguelin, S.Z.: Computer-aided security proofs for the working cryptographer. In: Rogaway, P. (ed.) CRYPTO 2011. LNCS, vol. 6841, pp. 71–90. Springer, Heidelberg (2011)
3. Beckert, B., Hähnle, R., Schmitt, P.H. (eds.): Verification of Object-Oriented Software. LNCS (LNAI), vol. 4334. Springer, Heidelberg (2007)
4. Bellare, M., Hoang, V.T., Rogaway, P.: Foundations of garbled circuits. In: Yu, T., Danezis, G., Gligor, V.D. (eds.) ACM CCS 2012, pp. 784–796. ACM Press (October 2012)
5. Böhl, F., Greiner, S., Scheidecker, P.: Java sources and proofs for the implementation in this paper, http://formal.iti.kit.edu/~greiner/cans2014/CodeAndProofCANS2014.zip
6. Böhl, F., Greiner, S., Scheidecker, P.: Proving correctness and security of two-party computation implemented in Java in presence of a semi-honest sender. IACR Cryptology ePrint Archive, 2014: 618 (2014), https://eprint.iacr.org/2014/618
7. Canetti, R.: Universally composable security: A new paradigm for cryptographic protocols. In: 42nd FOCS, pp. 136–145. IEEE Computer Society Press (October 2001)
8. Canetti, R., Lindell, Y., Ostrovsky, R., Sahai, A.: Universally composable two-party and multi-party secure computation. In: 34th ACM STOC, pp. 494–503. ACM Press (May 2002)
9. Canetti, R., Rabin, T.: Universal composition with joint state. In: Boneh, D. (ed.) CRYPTO 2003. LNCS, vol. 2729, pp. 265–281. Springer, Heidelberg (2003)
10. Choi, S.G., Katz, J., Wee, H., Zhou, H.-S.: Efficient, adaptively secure, and composable oblivious transfer with a single, global CRS. In: Kurosawa, K., Hanaoka, G. (eds.) PKC 2013. LNCS, vol. 7778, pp. 73–88. Springer, Heidelberg (2013)
11. Damgård, I., Nielsen, J.B., Orlandi, C.: Essentially optimal universally composable oblivious transfer. In: Lee, P.J., Cheon, J.H. (eds.) ICISC 2008. LNCS, vol. 5461, pp. 318–335. Springer, Heidelberg (2009)
12. Erkin, Z., Franz, M., Guajardo, J., Katzenbeisser, S., Lagendijk, I., Toft, T.: Privacy-preserving face recognition. In: Goldberg, I., Atallah, M.J. (eds.) PETS 2009. LNCS, vol. 5672, pp. 235–253. Springer, Heidelberg (2009)
13. Filliâtre, J.-C., Marché, C.: The why/krakatoa/caduceus platform for deductive program verification. In: Damm, W., Hermanns, H. (eds.) CAV 2007. LNCS, vol. 4590, pp. 173–177. Springer, Heidelberg (2007)
14. Goldreich, O., Micali, S., Wigderson, A.: How to play any mental game or A completeness theorem for protocols with honest majority. In: Aho, A. (ed.) 19th ACM STOC, pp. 218–229. ACM Press (May 1987)
15. Greiner, S., Birnstill, P., Krempel, E., Beckert, B., Beyerer, J.: Privacy preserving surveillance and the tracking-paradox. In: Lauster, M. (ed.) Proceedings of the 8th Future Security. Security Research Conference, pp. 296–302. Fraunhofer Verlag, Berlin (2013)

16. Huang, Y., Evans, D., Katz, J., Malka, L.: Faster secure two-party computation using garbled circuits. In: USENIX Security Symposium (2011a)
17. Huang, Y., Malka, L., Evans, D., Katz, J.: Efficient privacy-preserving biometric identification. In: NDSS (2011b)
18. Jacobs, B., Smans, J., Philippaerts, P., Vogels, F., Penninckx, W., Piessens, F.: Verifast: A powerful, sound, predictable, fast verifier for c and java. In: Bobaru, M., Havelund, K., Holzmann, G.J., Joshi, R. (eds.) NFM 2011. LNCS, vol. 6617, pp. 41–55. Springer, Heidelberg (2011)
19. Jha, S., Kruger, L., Shmatikov, V.: Towards practical privacy for genomic computation. In: 2008 IEEE Symposium on Security and Privacy, pp. 216–230. IEEE Computer Society Press (May 2008)
20. Kolesnikov, V., Schneider, T.: Improved garbled circuit: Free XOR gates and applications. In: Aceto, L., Damgård, I., Goldberg, L.A., Halldórsson, M.M., Ingólfsdóttir, A., Walukiewicz, I. (eds.) ICALP 2008, Part II. LNCS, vol. 5126, pp. 486–498. Springer, Heidelberg (2008)
21. Küsters, R., Scapin, E., Truderung, T., Graf, J.: Extending and applying a framework for the cryptographic verification of java programs. IACR Cryptology ePrint Archive, 2014:38 (2014)
22. Küsters, R., Truderung, T., Beckert, B., Bruns, D., Graf, J., Scheben, C.: A hybrid approach for proving noninterference and applications to the cryptographic verification of Java programs. In: Hammer, C., Mauw, S. (eds.) Grande Region Security and Reliability Day 2013, Luxembourg (2013)
23. Küsters, R., Truderung, T., Graf, J.: A framework for the cryptographic verification of java-like programs. In: CSF 2012, pp. 198–212. IEEE (2012)
24. Gary, T., Leavens, A.L.: Baker, and Clyde Ruby. Preliminary design of jml: A behavioral interface specification language for java. SIGSOFT Softw. Eng. Notes 31(3), 1–38 (2006) ISSN 0163-5948
25. Lindell, Y., Pinkas, B.: A proof of yao's protocol for secure two-party computation. Electronic Colloquium on Computational Complexity (ECCC) (063) (2004)
26. Lindell, Y., Pinkas, B.: An efficient protocol for secure two-party computation in the presence of malicious adversaries. In: Naor, M. (ed.) EUROCRYPT 2007. LNCS, vol. 4515, pp. 52–78. Springer, Heidelberg (2007)
27. Lindell, Y., Pinkas, B., Smart, N.P.: Implementing two-party computation efficiently with security against malicious adversaries. In: Ostrovsky, R., De Prisco, R., Visconti, I. (eds.) SCN 2008. LNCS, vol. 5229, pp. 2–20. Springer, Heidelberg (2008)
28. Malkhi, D., Nisan, N., Pinkas, B., Sella, Y.: Fairplay - secure two-party computation system. In: USENIX Security Symposium, pp. 287–302 (2004)
29. Nielsen, J.B., Orlandi, C.: LEGO for two-party secure computation. In: Reingold, O. (ed.) TCC 2009. LNCS, vol. 5444, pp. 368–386. Springer, Heidelberg (2009)
30. Osadchy, M., Pinkas, B., Jarrous, A., Moskovich, B.: SCiFI - a system for secure face identification. In: 2010 IEEE Symposium on Security and Privacy, pp. 239–254. IEEE Computer Society Press (May 2010)
31. Peikert, C., Vaikuntanathan, V., Waters, B.: A framework for efficient and composable oblivious transfer. In: Wagner, D. (ed.) CRYPTO 2008. LNCS, vol. 5157, pp. 554–571. Springer, Heidelberg (2008)
32. Rabin, M.O.: How to exchange secrets with oblivious transfer. In: Technical Report TR-81. Harvard University (1981)

33. Schmitt, P.H., Tonin, I.: Verifying the mondex case study. In: SEFM, pp. 47–58. IEEE Computer Society (2007) ISBN 978-0-7695-2884-7
34. Schulte, W., Songtao, X., Smans, J., Piessens, F.: A glimpse of a verifying c compiler. In: C/C++ Verification Workshop 2007 (2007)
35. Yao, A.C.-C.: Protocols for secure computations (extended abstract). In: 23rd FOCS, pp. 160–164. IEEE Computer Society Press (November 1982)
36. Yao, A.C.-C.: How to generate and exchange secrets (extended abstract). In: 27th FOCS, pp. 162–167. IEEE Computer Society Press (October 1986)

Appendix

```
 1 public final class SenderMessage {
   GarbledCircuit gc;
 3 Key[] sender_keys;
   OTResp[] ots;
 5 Key out0, out1;
   }
 7 public final class Sender {
   public Sender(boolean[] input);
 9 public SenderMessage
   getMessage(Receiver r,
11    ReceiverMessage m);
   }
13
   public final class ReceiverMessage {
15 OTReqt[] ots;
   }
17 public final class Receiver {
   public Receiver(boolean[] input);
19 public ReceiverMessage getMessage();
   public boolean
21    getOutput(Sender s,
        SenderMessage m);
23 }
```

Fig. 2. Interface for sender and receiver in our protocol.

```
 1 public final class GarbledANDGate {
   Cipher[] eT;
 3 /*@ ghost Key kl0, kl1, kr0, kr1,
      @ out0, out1;
 5    @ ghost int ci0, ci1, ci2, ci3;*/
   public GarbledANDGate(
 7    Key kl0, kl1, kr0, k1,
        out0, out1){...}
 9 public Key evaluate(Key inl, inr){...}
   }
```

Fig. 3. Definition of `GarbledANDGate` including Ghost variables.

```
 public final class GCnBitAND {
 2 GarbledANDGate[] gates;
   /*@ ghost Key[] in0, in1;
 4    @ ghost Key out0, out1;*/
   }
```

Fig. 4. Definition of `GCnBitAND` including ghost variables.

```
 1 /*@ requires
   @ inkeys0.length==inkeys1.length &&
 3 @ inkeys0.length >= 2 &&
   @ (\forall int i;
 5 @    1 <= i < inkeys0.length;
   @ \distct (inkeys0[i−1],
 7 @    inkeys1[i−1], inkeys0[i],
   @    inkeys1[i].ident)) &&
 9 @ \distct (outkey0, outkey1); */
   @ ensures
11 @ (\forall int i;
   @    0 <= i < in0.length;
13 @ inkeys0[i].ident==in0[i].ident &&
   @ inkeys1[i].ident==in1[i].ident) &&
15 @ outkey0.ident==out0.ident &&
   @ outkey1.ident==out1.ident;
17 public GarbledNBitANDCircuit(
   Key[] inkeys0, inkeys1;
19    Key outkey0, outkey1) {...}
```

Fig. 5. Contract of constructor of `GCnBitAND`.

```
 1 /*@ requires
   @ in.length == in0.length &&
 3 @ (\forall int i;
   @    0 <= i < in.length;
 5 @  in[i].ident == in0[i].ident ||
   @  in[i].ident == in1[i].ident);
 7 @ ensures
   @ \if (\forall int i;
 9 @    0 <= i < in.length;
   @  in[i].ident==in1[i].ident)
11 @ \then (\result.ident==out1.ident)
   @ \else (\result.ident==out0.ident); */
13 public Key evaluate(Key[] in) {...}
```

Fig. 6. Contract of `evaluate` for `GCnBitAND`.

Mining API Calls and Permissions for Android Malware Detection

Akanksha Sharma and Subrat Kumar Dash

Department of Computer Science and Engineering,
The LNM Institute of Information Technology, Jaipur, India
{akshasharma.sharma,subrat.dash}@gmail.com

Abstract. The popularity of Android platform is increasing very sharply due to the large market share of Android and openness in nature. The increased popularity is making Android an enticing target for malwares. A worrying trend that is alarming is the increasing sophistication of Android malware to evade detection by traditional signature based scanners. Several approaches have been proposed in literature for Android malware detection. However, most of them are less effective in terms of true positive rate and involves computational overheads. In this paper, we propose an effective approach to attenuate the problem of Android malware detection using static code analysis based models. The proposed models, in this paper, are built to capture features relevant to malware behaviour based on API calls as well as permissions present in various Android applications. Thereafter, models are evaluated using Naive Bayesian as well as K-Nearest Neighbour classifiers. Proposed models are able to detect real malwares in the wild and achieve an accuracy of 95.1% and true positive rate with highest value one.

Keywords: Android malware detection, API calls, Permissions, Feature Selection, Classification.

1 Introduction

Smartphones are becoming popular these days as they serve the user with same utilities as desktop computers like web browsing, on-line shopping, social networking, on-line banking etc. Smartphones have additional features of SMS messaging, location services, constantly updated data and global access. This rich functionality and popularity is making them an enticing target for malicious activities. In fact, malware developers can take advantage of these features by stealing users credentials, accessing private data and charging users with premium rate SMSes and calls. It is estimated that there are around 657,000 applications available on Google's official Android market. According to a report from Fortinet (issued in November 2011) [1], there exists 2000 malwares from 80 different families [2]. As stated in a report by Symantec (issued in October 2013) [3], the number of Android malware families increased by 69% between June 2012 and June 2013. The reason for Android being the most popular platform is that Android is open source and freely available to manufacturers for

D. Gritzalis et al. (Eds.): CANS 2014, LNCS 8813, pp. 191–205, 2014.

customization. As new families are evolving, it is becoming more difficult to detect malwares using traditional signature based techniques. Oberheide et al. [4] revealed some security challenges including resource constraints, lack of visibility in mobile platforms, network obscurity, use of customized applications that utilizes the native capabilities etc. for mobile malware detection. Several permission based malware detection approaches have been proposed earlier [5,6]. But the presence of certain permissions does not solely ensure the malicious behaviour of an application. It is not necessary that the permissions declared in *Android-Manifest.xml* are utilized by the application code. On the other hand, there are existing approaches [8] that take into account only API level information to extract features on the basis of frequency analysis over a large data set. But these techniques utilizes large feature sets for detection of malwares. Clearly, there is a need for an effective approach that can detect malwares from unknown families and at the same time uses a minimal feature set to avoid high computational overheads.

In this paper, we propose a proactive approach towards Android malware detection using static code analysis. In this approach, features based on API calls as well as permissions present in applications are considered. Correlation based feature selection and information gain feature selection techniques are employed to select most relevant features. The profile build from this selected feature set is validated using Naive Bayesian and K-Nearest Neighbor (kNN) classifiers. The main contributions of this paper are:

- Extraction of a minimal set of features which is able to detect malwares with an accuracy and true positive rate (TPR) of 94% and 97.5% respectively.
- Comparison of Naive Bayesian and kNN classifier in terms of performance with same feature set shows that TPR is better in case of Naive Bayesian classifier but higher accuracy is attained by kNN classifier.
- A TPR of value 1 is achieved using a feature set of 25 features indicating that all the malwares present in the data set are detected.
- When tested using real world malwares, our approach is able to detect various unknown malwares.

The rest of the paper is organised as follows. Section 2 gives description about related work. Section 3 and 4 describes feature extraction process and feature selection techniques used in our proposed approach. Section 5 provides detailed discussion of data set used and the classification techniques employed. Section 6 includes experimental results and their discussion. Section 7 concludes the paper giving some future work.

2 Related Work

Several studies have been done in the field of Android malware detection. Felt et al. [5] developed a tool called *Stowaway*, which identifies the API calls used in an Android application and maps those API calls to permissions. Based on this, the tool can further detect over-privileged Android applications. As reported by the authors [5], when tested with 900 applications, it categorized 323 applications having unnecessary permissions. Another approach towards permission based malware detection proposed by Aung et al. [6] used K-means clustering cascaded with Random Forest decision tree and CART (Classification And Regression Tree) algorithm. This method reports highest accuracy of 91.75% with Random Forest decision tree and highest true positive rate of 97.8% with CART.

Dini et al. [7] introduced MADAM (Multi-Level Anomaly Detector for Android Malware), first real time anomaly based detector developed for real devices, which is able to detect real malware of different categories. This technique uses a detector that monitors Android both at kernel level as well as user level. A data set of 1000 samples (900 standard and 100 malicious) with 13 features is used including system calls and the state of system, whether it is idle or sending unwanted outgoing SMSes, is used to test the technique. It shows overall 93% detection rate and in particular 100% detection rate with rootkits. Aafer et al. [8] used generic data mining approach to build a classifier for Android applications (apps). They compared performance of four classifiers in terms of both the methods of feature extraction i.e. permission based and API calls based feature set with package level and parameter information. Their data set consists of 3987 malware samples from Android Malware Genome Project and 500 applications from each category in Google Play. Asfer et al. reported that kNN is best performing model with an accuracy of 99.9% and false positive rate as low as 2.2% with a feature set of 189 features. Yerima et al. [9] proposed an effective approach of malware detection based on Naive Bayesian classification using static code analysis. A data set of 2000 samples containing 1000 benign and 1000 malware samples from 49 different families are analysed to obtain feature vectors containing 48 features based on API calls and system commands. Information gain feature selection technique is used to reduce feature set. With top 20 features when applied to Naive Bayesian classifier model it reported an accuracy of 92.1% and TPR value of 0.906.

3   Feature Extraction

In this section, we describe extraction of a feature set that is utilized for building a profile of an Android application. Each Android application contain a corresponding .apk file which describes the functionalities present in the application.To obtain feature set for samples present in data set, we used a Java-based Android package profiling tool for automated reverse engineering of the .apk files named as ApkAnalyser [12]. This tool unpacks and decompiles the input .apk files to corresponding .dex and AndroidManifest.xml files. After doing reverse engineering, a set of detectors are applied to the reverse engineered .apk files to detect properties used to build the profile for APK file. The feature vector obtained after property detection contains values for selected features as binary numbers (0 and 1), which is a sequence of comma separated values. Let an application characteristic f_i obtained from the *ApkAnalyser* detector be defined by a random variable:

$$F = \begin{cases} 1, & \text{if discovered by the detectors} \\ 0, & \text{otherwise} \end{cases}. \tag{1}$$

Property detectors applied to the reverse engineered applications belong to either of the following two categories:

- **API call detectors**: These are used to record API calls invoked by applications. Since API calls provide means to apps to interact with the device, static inspection of API calls gives information about their runtime activities.
- **Permission detectors**: These are used to gather information about permissions requested in the manifest file of an application.

3.1 API Call Based Features

API calls basically refer to built-in code libraries. Our strategy is to reliably identify the major APIs that malwares invoke by statically analysing our samples. We analyse a large number of malware samples and benign apps to identify a set of API calls that describes the profile of malicious applications. We categorize these APIs according to type of resources requested and their functionalities as follows [8], [13]:

Android Framework Related APIs

- **Broadcast Receiver**: This class enables the application to respond to the intents sent by other applications using *sendBroadcast()* method. The breakdown of APIs chosen from this class is shown in Table 1.

Table 1. Broadcast Receiver APIs and their utilities

API call	Utility
AutoSmsReceiver	Receives incoming messages automatically
BootReceiver	Start up process that runs other processes at boot
PhoneCallReceiver	Call back which fires off when phone changes state
abortBroadcast	Abort the current broadcast

- **PackageManager:** This class has information about the packages that get installed on the device. Malware apps call the *getInstalledPackages()* to scan the system against a list of known anti-virus and take suitable actions (eg. remain dormant, kill the anti-virus process etc.)
- **Telephony/SmsManager** and **telephony/gsm/SmsManager**: This class manages all the SMS operations for sending data, text and PDU SMS

messages. *sendTextMessage()* is used by malwares to send messages to premium rate numbers without user's consent and thus incur financial losses. *getServiceCenterAddress()* is used by malwares to obtain the address of SMS service center that relayed the message.

– **TelephonyManager:** This class provides access to telephony services present on the device. Malwares collect private data such as subscriber information etc. and send it to remote servers to build user profile and track them. The methods of this class which are frequently used by malware samples in our data set are listed in Table 2.

Table 2. Telephony Manager APIs and their utilities

API call	Utility
getCallState()	returns call state
getDataActivity()	returns a constant indicating the type of activity
getDeviceId()	returns IMEI number
getLine1number()	returns number string for line 1 e.g. MSISDN
getNetworkType()	returns network type for current data connection
getSimOperator()	returns MCC+MNC(mobile country code + mobile network) code of the provider of the sim
getSimSerialNumber()	returns serial number of sim card
getSimState()	returns information about sim state
getSubscriberId()	returns IMSI number of the device

DVM Related Resource APIs

– **DexClassLoader**: This class allows to load classes from external *.jar* and *.apk* files containing classes *.dex* entry. *loadClass()* is a commonly invoked API by malwares and is used to execute the code which is not installed as part of the application.

System Resources API

– **ConnectivityManager**: This class gives information about the state of network connectivity. It notifies the application about the change in network state. The method used by malware samples often use *getActiveNetworkInfo()*, which gives information about currently active default data network.
– **WifiManager**: This class is used to establish network connection and interact with malicious remote servers. The method *getConnectionInfo()* is used by malwares to get dynamic information about the Wi-Fi connection.
– **SupplicantState**: This class gives information about the current WPA (wifi protected access) supplicant state. The API call invoked by malwares of this call is *getSupplicantState()*.

3.2 Permissions Based Features

Permissions are declared by Android developer in *AndroidManifest.xml* file to provide the application access to some protected APIs of Android. But some applications request permissions that are not needed for their normal execution. We identify a set of permissions that can be needed by malware applications to steal private information and communicate to remote servers for charging revenue from customers. The permissions along with their serviceabilities are shown in Table 3 [13].

Table 3. Permissions and their services

Permission	Functionality
ACCESS_NETWORK_STATE	Allows to access information about networks
ACCESS_WI-FI_STATE	Allows to access information about wi-fi networks
CALL_PHONE	Allows to call any number without going through Dailer
CHANGE_NETWORK_STATE	Allows to change network connectivity state
GET_ACCOUNTS	Allows access to the list of accounts in the account service
INTERNET	Allows to open network sockets
INSTALL_PACKAGES	Allows to install packages
READ_CONTACTS	To read user's contacts data
READ_LOGS	Allows to read low-level system log files
READ_PHONE_STATE	Allows read only access to phone state
READ_SMS	Allows to read SMS messages
RECEIVE_BOOT_COMPLETED	Allows to receive signals after system finishes booting
RESTART_PACKAGES	Deprecated in API level 8. This API is no longer supported
RECEIVE_SMS	Record incoming SMS messages and perform processing on them
SEND_SMS	To send SMS messages

4 Feature Selection

Feature selection is the process of removing as much irrelevant and redundant information as possible. Presence of irrelevant information may lead to several problems such as difficulty in learning phase, over-fitting of data, increased complexity and runtime of classifier, effecting accuracy of model [11]. We used a Java based suite of data mining algorithms named as *WEKA* [10] for implementing correlation based feature selection technique.

4.1 Correlation Based Feature Selection (CFS)

CFS is basically a filter algorithm. The aim is to remove irrelevant features that have low correlation with the class and also eliminate redundant features that are highly correlated with one or more of the remaining features. CFS feature subset evaluation function is given by Equation 2 [11] :

$$F_s = \frac{n\overline{r_{cf}}}{\sqrt{n + n(n-1)\overline{r_{ff}}}} \tag{2}$$

where F_s is the heuristic "merit" of a feature subset S containing n features, $\overline{r_{cf}}$ is the mean feature-class correlation ($f \in S$), and $\overline{r_{ff}}$ is the average feature-feature inter-correlation. The numerator of Equation 2 shows how predictive of the class a set of features are; the denominator shows how much redundancy is there among the features [11].

The ranking of features obtained for our data set in decreasing order of significance is listed in Table 4.

Table 4. Feature ranking using CFS method

Feature	Ranking	Feature	Ranking
getSubscriberId	1	Access_Wifi_State	18
Read_Phone_State	2	Call_Phone	19
Read_SMS	3	Change_Network_State	20
getSimSerialNumber	4	getSupplicantState	21
Send_SMS	5	getNetworkType	22
getInstalledPackages	6	BootReceiver	23
getServiceCenterAddress	7	Receive_Boot_Completed	24
getLine1Number	8	Internet	25
SendTextMsg	9	getSimOperator	26
Install_Packages	10	getCallState	27
getDeviceId	11	Read_Logs	28
PhoneCallReceiver	12	getConnectionInfo	29
get_accounts	13	DexClassLoader	30
Restart_Packages	14	Receive_SMS	31
getDataActivity	15	AutoSmsReceiver	32
getActivityNetworkInfo	16	getSimState	33
Read_Contacts	17	Access_Network_State	34
		abortBroadcast	35

4.2   Information Gain Method

Information gain method measures the amount of information about class prediction, if the only information available is the presence of a feature and the corresponding class distribution. This method is also known as mutual information method. Let D be the training set containing samples from two calsses (malware and benign), then the entropy of D is defined as

$$H(D) = -\sum_i (P(f_i)log_2P(f_i)), \tag{3}$$

where p_i is the probability that an arbitrary tuple in D belongs to class C_i. Suppose the samples in D are partitioned into two classes based on some feature f_i (which can take only two possible values, i.e. 0 and 1, as explained in Section 3), then the entropy of D given f_i is as follows:

$$H(D|f_i) = - \sum_{v \in f_i} P(v) \sum_i P(f_i|c_i) log_2 P(f_i|c_i). \qquad (4)$$

The amount by which the entropy of D is reduced reflects the additional information provided by f_i about D and is called information gain, which is defined as

$$Gain(D|f_i) = H(D) - H(D|f_i). \qquad (5)$$

The ranking of features based on decreasing order of information gain is shown in Table 5.

Table 5. Feature ranking using Information Gain method

Feature	Ranking	Feature	Ranking
getSubscriberId	1	getCallState	18
Read_Phone_State	2	Access_Wifi_State	19
Read_SMS	3	Change_Network_State	20
getSimSerialNumber	4	getSimOperator	21
Send_SMS	5	Receive_Boot_Completed	22
getLine1Number	6	Internet	23
SendTextMsg	7	getActivityNetworkInfo	24
getDeviceId	8	get_accounts	25
getInstalledPackages	9	AutoSmsReceiver	26
Receive_SMS	10	abortBroadcast	27
Call_Phone	11	getSupplicantState	28
BootReceiver	12	Read_Logs	29
Read_Contacts	13	getNetworkType	30
Install_Packages	14	getSimState	31
getServiceCenterAddress	15	Access_Network_State	32
PhoneCallReceiver	16	getDataActivity	33
Restart_Packages	17	DexClassLoader	34
		getConnectionInfo	35

5   Classification

In this section, we first describe the data set that we have used for experimentation purpose followed by the classification models used and the evaluation metrics.

5.1   Data Set

For the purpose of feature mining and further evaluation of classification models we collect a data set of total 1600 applications. The 1600 *apk* files includes 800 samples of Android malwares and 800 samples of benign Android applications downloaded from official and third party Android markets. The malware samples are obtained from The Android Malware Genome Project [14]. Our malware samples have occurrences from the following 49 different families.

```
ADRD, AnserverBot, Asroot, BaseBridge, BeanBot, Bgserve,
CoinPirate, CruseWins, Dogwars, DroidCoupon, DroidDeluxe,
DroidDream, DroidDreamLight, DroidKungFu1, DroidKungFu2,
DroidKungFu3, DroidKungFu4, DroidKungFuSapp, DroidKungFuUpdate,
EndOfDay, FakeNetFlix, FakePlayer, GamblerSMS, Geinimi, GGTracker,
GingerMaster, GoldDream, Gone60, GPSMSSpy, HippoSMS, JiFake,
jSMSHider, KMin, LoveTrap, NickyBot, NickySpy, PjApps, Plankton,
RogueLemon, RogueSPPush, SMSReplicator, SndApps, Spitmo, Tapsnake,
WalkinWat, YZHC, zHash, Zitmo, Zsone.
```

5.2   Classification Models

We evaluate the feature ranking obtained during feature selection procedure using different classification models. For this purpose, we use two classifiers: Naive Bayesian and kNN. In our experiments, we use five fold stratified cross validation. Thus, 1280 samples (640 each from benign and malware classes) are used as the training set, while the remaining 320 samples (160 from each class) for testing purpose in each fold.

5.3   Evaluation Metrics

There are several measures that have been proposed in the literature for evaluating the accuracy of classifiers. The applicable measures utilized in our experiments are discussed below. Let $k_{ben \to ben}$ be the number of benign applications correctly classified as benign, $k_{ben \to mal}$ the number of misclassified benign applications, $k_{mal \to mal}$ the number of malwares applications correctly classified as malwares, $k_{mal \to ben}$ the number of misclassified malicious applications. Accuracy (Acc) and error rate (Err) are given by Equation 6 and Equation 7 respectively.

$$Acc = \frac{k_{ben \to ben} + k_{mal \to mal}}{k_{ben \to ben} + k_{mal \to mal} + k_{ben \to mal} + k_{mal \to ben}}. \tag{6}$$

$$Err = \frac{k_{ben \to mal} + k_{mal \to ben}}{k_{ben \to ben} + k_{mal \to mal} + k_{ben \to mal} + k_{mal \to ben}}. \tag{7}$$

We also define *true positive rate* (TPR), *true negative rate* (TNR), *false positive rate* (FPR), *false negative rate* (FNR) and *precision* (p) as follows:

$$TPR = \frac{k_{mal \to mal}}{k_{mal \to ben} + k_{mal \to mal}}. \tag{8}$$

$$TNR = \frac{k_{ben \to ben}}{k_{ben \to ben} + k_{ben \to mal}}. \tag{9}$$

$$FPR = \frac{k_{ben \to mal}}{k_{ben \to ben} + k_{ben \to mal}}. \tag{10}$$

$$FNR = \frac{k_{mal \to ben}}{k_{mal \to ben} + k_{mal \to mal}}. \tag{11}$$

$$p = \frac{k_{mal \to mal}}{k_{ben \to mal} + k_{mal \to mal}}. \tag{12}$$

6   Results and Discussion

In our experiments, we evaluated different feature sets obtained from ranking generated by both the feature selection techniques with both the classifiers. The purpose is to find minimal feature set that best describes the profile of malicious applications.

Table 6, Fig. 1 and Fig. 2 show the results for Naive Bayesian classification using five different feature sets containing 5, 10, 15, 20 and 25 features respectively. In Column 1 of Table 6, 5f, 10f, 15f, 20f, 25f refer to the top 5, 10, 15, 20 and 25 ranked features respectively. From the results, we observe that the TPR and FNR values for 5f, 10f, 15f, 20f and 25f sets are similar i.e 0.975 and 0.025 respectively. But the value of FPR for 10f set is relatively low than for all other feature sets. FPR is not considered as critical as FNR since the latter directly affects the malware that left undetected. On the other hand, a low value of FPR means that less benign applications will need to be subjected to further scrutiny; it then becomes more cost effective and less time consuming to do so. The accuracy value is highest for 10f set.

Table 6. Experimental results from Naive Bayesian classification model for different feature sets using CFS method

	ERR(%)	ACC(%)	TNR	FPR	TPR	FNR	PREC	AUC
5f	6.5	93.4	0.894	0.106	0.975	0.025	0.902	0.979
10f	5.9	94.0	0.906	0.094	0.975	0.025	0.912	0.985
15f	6.5	93.4	0.894	0.106	0.975	0.025	0.902	0.985
20f	8.1	91.8	0.862	0.138	0.975	0.025	0.876	0.984
25f	9.6	90.3	0.831	0.169	0.975	0.025	0.852	0.983
35f	8.7	91.25	0.825	0.175	1.00	0.00	0.851	0.985

This approach shows the capability of detecting unknown malwares as both the training and testing sets have malware samples from various different malware families, as described in Section 5.1. Table 6 also includes precision (PREC)

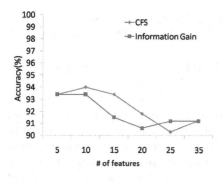 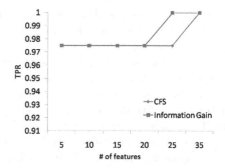

Fig. 1. Accuracy of Naive Bayesian classifier for different number of features

Fig. 2. TPR of Naive Bayesian Classifier for different number of features

and area under the curve (AUC) measures for each of the feature sets. Precision shows the precision of the model in terms of suspicious samples and AUC represents the total area under the Receiver Operation Characteristic (ROC) curve, which is a plot between TPR and FPR for every possible detection cutoff. An AUC of 1 implies perfect classification. So, if the value of AUC is closer to 1 that indicates better classifier predictive power. Also, the error parameter (ERR) shows a subsequent decrease while moving from 25f to 10f. For 10f set, the value of ERR is minimum. We observe that results for 10f feature set are better than all other feature sets.

Table 7 shows the results for Naive Bayesian classification using five different feature sets retrieved using information gain method of feature selection. We observe that the values of TPR and FNR remains same for 5, 10, 15 and 20 feature sets i.e. 0.975 and 0.025 respectively. From Fig. 2, we see that the value of TPR for 25 feature is 1 and also FNR is 0 which means all the malwares present in the data set are detected using this feature set. The values for accuracy for 5f and 10f are highest. Both 5f and 10f sets have same values for all the evaluation metrics but 10f set has higher AUC area than 5f set.

Table 7. Experimental results from Naive Bayesian classification model for different feature sets using Information Gain method

	ERR(%)	ACC(%)	TNR	FPR	TPR	FNR	PREC	AUC
5f	6.5	93.4	0.894	0.106	0.975	0.025	0.902	0.979
10f	6.5	93.4	0.894	0.106	0.975	0.025	0.902	0.985
15f	8.4	91.5	0.856	0.144	0.975	0.025	0.975	0.978
20f	9.3	90.6	0.838	0.162	0.975	0.025	0.857	0.984
25f	8.7	91.2	0.825	0.175	1.00	0.00	0.851	0.984
35f	8.7	91.2	0.825	0.175	1.00	0.00	0.851	0.985

Thus, we deduce from the results that 25f feature set gives the highest TPR but slightly less accuracy than 10f set. So it can be chosen when the undetected malware can lead to serious problems. But in situations requiring cost effective and less time consuming detection methods, we choose 10f feature set (which has high accuracy of 93.4%).

For kNN classifier, we test the data set for different k values and observe that k=1 gives better results in comparison to other k values.

Table 8 shows the results of using kNN classifier for calculating evaluation metrics using five different feature sets. From Fig. 3 and Fig. 4 we observe that, the TPR value shows improvement while increasing the feature set from 5f to 20f but decreases for 25f set, while the TNR value do not show much variation. Also accuracy improves with increasing feature set until we reach 20f set but, remains unchanged for 25f set. As 20f set has better TPR as well as TNR and high AUC value, it is chosen as better performing feature set.

Table 8. Experimental results from kNN classification model for different feature sets using CFS method

	ERR(%)	ACC(%)	TNR	FPR	TPR	FNR	PREC	AUC
5f	10.8	89.1	0.929	0.071	0.854	0.146	0.923	0.952
10f	6.2	93.8	0.960	0.040	0.915	0.085	0.958	0.966
15f	5.5	94.5	0.955	0.045	0.934	0.066	0.954	0.973
20f	4.8	95.2	0.940	0.060	0.962	0.038	0.941	0.977
25f	4.6	95.4	0.951	0.049	0.956	0.044	0.951	0.980
35f	4.4	95.6	0.952	0.048	0.960	0.040	0.953	0.981

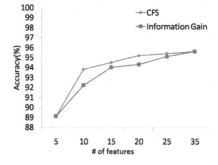

Fig. 3. Accuracy of kNN classifier for different number of features

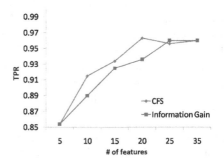

Fig. 4. TPR of kNN classifier for different number of features

Table 9 shows the results for evaluation metrics using five different feature sets. A high TPR depicts greater malware detection rate, so feature set with high TPR is considered as a better feature set to profile a class. It can be observed from the results that the AUC value for 35f set is closest to 1 among all other values. From this, it can also be inferred that the performance of 35f is better than the other feature set when considered in relation to accuracy and TPR.

Table 9. Experimental results from kNN classification model for different feature sets using Information Gain method

	ERR(%)	ACC(%)	TNR	FPR	TPR	FNR	PREC	AUC
5f	10.8	89.1	0.929	0.071	0.854	0.146	0.923	0.952
10f	7.8	92.2	0.954	0.046	0.890	0.110	0.951	0.961
15f	5.9	94.0	0.956	0.044	0.925	0.075	0.955	0.966
20f	5.6	94.3	0.950	0.050	0.936	0.064	0.949	0.968
25f	4.8	95.1	0.942	0.058	0.960	0.040	0.943	0.977
35f	4.4	95.6	0.952	0.048	0.960	0.040	0.953	0.981

6.1 Comparative Analysis between Naive Bayesian and kNN Classifiers

Table 10 shows the performance metrics of both Naive Bayesian and kNN classifiers for feature sets selected using CFS method. As we can see that we get better accuracy with kNN classifier but it utilizes feature set of Top 20 features and has relatively low TPR. In case of Naive Bayesian classifier, the accuracy is marginally low (1.1%), but it achieves higher TPR with a feature set of top 10 features. So, Naive Bayesian classifier achieves high TPR and comparable accuracy with a feature set of 10 features which is just half the feature set deployed for kNN. So we conclude that Naive Bayesian classifier performs better with CFS method.

Table 10. Comparative analysis between Naive Bayesian and kNN classifiers using CFS method

Feature Set	Classifier	TPR	Accuracy(%)
10f	Naive Bayesian	0.975	94.0
20f	K-Nearest Neighbour	0.963	95.1

Table 11. Comparative analysis between Naive Bayesian and kNN classifiers using Information Gain method

Feature Set	Classifier	TPR	Accuracy(%)
25f	Naive Bayesian	1.00	91.2
35f	K-Nearest Neighbour	0.960	95.1

Similarly, Table 11 shows the evaluation metrics for both Naive Bayesian and kNN classifiers using Information Gain feature selection method. We can clearly see that TPR value for Naive Bayes classifier is much better than that for kNN classifier but accuracy improves for kNN in comparison to Naive Bayes classification. As TPR has more significance in comparison to accuracy, and considering the number of features, we conclude that Naive Bayesian classifier performs better with Information Gain method.

7   Conclusions and Future Work

In this paper, we have proposed an effective approach of detecting malwares using static code analysis. It takes into account various features based on API calls and permissions declared in *AndroidManifest.xml* file. We have extracted 35 features for all 1600 samples in the data set and implemented two feature selection methods, namely CFS and Information Gain. It is observed that a subset of 10 features gives better performance metrics than the whole feature set. Small feature set will help in reducing computational overheads that is beneficial in mobile devices having resource constraints regarding memory and power consumption. Information Gain feature selection when applied to features yields a TPR of value 1 indicating the superior detection power of proposed approach in comparison to existing approaches of Android malware detection. CFS is more effective approach towards feature selection to remove irrelevant and redundant features as it attains higher evaluation metrics with smaller feature set than Information Gain using naive Bayesian classifier. kNN classifier achieved high accuracy (95%) than Naive Bayesian but TPR is elevated with Naive Bayesian classifier in comparison to kNN classification. For future work classification models can be tested with larger number of malwares as more malwares are discovered in the wild. Ensemble of classifiers can be used to improve the performance of build models.

References

1. Google celebrates as Android hits 25 billion downloads,
   http://www.theregister.co.uk/2012/09/26/google_play_25bn_downloads/
2. Apvrille, A., Strazzere, T.: Reducing the Window of Opportunity for Android Malware Gotta catchem all. Journal in Computer Virology 8(1-2), 61–71 (2012)
3. Secuirty Response: Moblie Adware and Malware Analysis,
   http://www.symantec.com/content/en/us/enterprise/media/
   security_response/whitepapers/madware_and_malware_analysis.pdf
4. Oberheide, J., Jahanian, F.: When mobile is harder than fixed (and vice versa): demystifying security challenges in mobile environments. In: Proceedings of the Eleventh Workshop on Mobile Computing Systems & Applications, pp. 43–48. ACM (2010)
5. Felt, A.P., Chin, E., Hanna, S., Song, D., Wagner, D.: Android permissions demystified. In: Proceedings of the 18th ACM Conference on Computer and Communications Security, pp. 627–638. ACM (2011)
6. Aung, Z., Zaw, W.: Permission-Based Android Malware Detection. International Journal of Scientific and Technology Research vol 2(3), 228–234 (2013)
7. Dini, G., Martinelli, F., Saracino, A., Sgandurra, D.: MADAM: A Multi-level Anomaly Detector for Android Malware. In: Kotenko, I., Skormin, V. (eds.) MMM-ACNS 2012. LNCS, vol. 7531, pp. 240–253. Springer, Heidelberg (2012)
8. Aafer, Y., Du, W., Yin, H.: DroidAPIMiner: Mining API-level features for robust malware detection in android. In: Zia, T., Zomaya, A., Varadharajan, V., Mao, M. (eds.) SecureComm 2013. LNICST, vol. 127, pp. 86–103. Springer, Heidelberg (2013)

9. Yerima, S.Y., Sezer, S., McWilliams, G., Muttik, I.: A New Android Malware Detection Approach Using Bayesian Classification. In: 27th International Conference on Advanced Information Networking and Applications (AINA), pp. 121–128. IEEE (2013)
10. WEKA 3.7, http://www.cs.waikato.ac.nz/ml/weka/downloading.html
11. Hall, M.A.: Correlation-based feature selection for machine learning. The University of Waikato (1999)
12. ApkAnalyser 5.2,
    http://developer.sonymobile.com/knowledge-base/
    tools/analyse-your-apks-with-apkanalyser/
13. Android Developer, http://developer.android.com/guide/index.html
14. Zhou, Y., Jiang, X.: Dissecting android malware: Characterization and evolution. In: IEEE Symposium on Security and Privacy (SP), pp. 95–109. IEEE (2012)

Direct Anonymous Attestations
with Dependent Basename Opening

Nicolas Desmoulins[1], Roch Lescuyer[2*], Olivier Sanders[1,3], and Jacques Traoré[1]

[1] Orange Labs, Applied Crypto Group, Caen, France
[2] Morpho, Issy-Les-Moulineaux, France
[3] École Normale Supérieure, Paris, France

Abstract. We introduce a new privacy-friendly cryptographic primitive we call Direct Anonymous Attestations with Dependent Basename Opening (DAA-DBO). Such a primitive is a Direct Anonymous Attestation in which the anonymity can be revoked only if a specific authority, called the admitter, allowed to revoke the DAA signatures that include a specific basename. We also present an efficient scheme that achieves this functionality, secure in the random oracle model. Furthermore, we provide a prototype implementation of an anonymous transit pass system, based on this new primitive. Compared to previous privacy-friendly cryptographic primitives with partial linkability, we provide a way to share the power to open signatures between two entities which is more practical than the use of conventional techniques from threshold cryptography.

Keywords. Privacy-enhancing cryptography, Direct anonymous attestations, Dependent anonymity revocation.

1 Introduction

Preserving privacy of users even during access control to services is a major concern. As an evidence, the German BSI agency has recently introduced a mechanism allowing owners of ID documents to authenticate to different service providers while being unlinkable across these services (a property called, *cross-domain anonymity*) [1]. Another example is the Big Brother award received in 2012 by the Belgium transport operator STIB for its contactless transport card. Ensuring both authentication and anonymity is necessary to reconcile the users' and the service providers' interests. One solution could be the use of a group signature, a primitive introduced by Chaum and Van Heyst [14] in 1991. Indeed, it enables members of a group to anonymously sign on behalf of the group. To prevent abuse, a specific entity has the ability to open (*i.e.* to identify the issuer of) any signature. However the strong anonymity provided by this primitive may also be a drawback for some applications such as public transports or authentication of ID documents. Regarding the former, the use of group signatures makes clone detection impossible since signatures produced

---

* This work was done while the author was at ENSICAEN/GREYC/UCBN, Caen, France.

D. Gritzalis et al. (Eds.): CANS 2014, LNCS 8813, pp. 206–221, 2014.

with the same key are unlinkable. Regarding the latter, the recommendations of the BSI specifies that the service provider should be able to link users inside its service which is not possible using group signatures. There is thus a need for controlled-anonymity as in Direct Anonymous Attestation (DAA) [10,6]. This primitive, close to group signatures, adds an element, called the basename, which enables anyone to link signatures produced by the same user with the same basename. Therefore, if each service provider uses a specific basename for its domain it will be able to link users in its service but not across them, achieving then the cross-domain anonymity property. For public transports, if a user in some time slot uses the same basename, clones could be detected. Of course, this slot has to be long enough to catch clones but not too much to avoid the traceability of the user. Since corrupting the transport card in which the keys are embedded requires a large amount of resource we may assume that the adversary will have to produce many clones to be profitable which ensures a significant probability of detection even within a short time slot.

REVOCATION IN DAA. However DAA schemes do not consider an opening authority but only a *RogueList* constructed using the secret keys we want to revoke. This means, in some sense, that a user is the only person able to revoke his keys. Most of the time however, the revocation will be performed without the help of the user. The authors of [5,12,11] use Domain-Specific Pseudonym Signatures (DSPS) for authentication of ID documents. This primitive can be seen as a kind of DAA extended to allow the issuer to revoke users. As noticed in [9], revocation offers a way to open signatures. The issuer in the DSPS is then also the opener. To the contrary, we would like here to split the managing abilities into different entities. One way to achieve this could be to share the opening information among several entities in such a way that none of them can open signatures alone. Unfortunately, running such a distributed protocol may be a practical concern, especially if there are many signatures to open. This can be the case, for example, if we want to find witnesses of a crime in transport system because every signatures issued during a specific time slot (and so with the same basename) will have to be opened.

DEPENDENT BASENAME OPENING. This problem has already been considered for group signatures, leading the authors of [22] to propose a new primitive called group signature with dependent message opening (GS-DMO). In a GS-DMO scheme, the power of the opener is divided between an entity, called the admitter, which issues a token τ_m corresponding to a message m, and another one, called the opener, which can open any signature on m using τ_m. Their security model ensures that the admitter is unable to open a signature without the help of the opener and that the opener is unable to open a signature on a message m without the corresponding token. Unfortunately, identity-based encryption was proved necessary to build such schemes, leading to signatures with significant sizes [22,19].

In this paper, we provide a similar extension of DAA, that we call DAA with Dependent Basename Opening (DAA-DBO), where tokens issued by the admitter now correspond to basenames. We substitute the message by the basename because in our use cases the latter has a specific meaning (the time slot for public transport or the domain name for authentication of ID documents). Unlike GS-DMO, we do not need identity based encryption for our primitive which permits more efficient constructions. The reason is that signatures issued by the same user with the same basename must be linkable whereas we want the opposite for signatures on the same message in a GS-DMO scheme. A benefit of splitting the opening power in such a way is that we can now consider authorities of different computational power. Indeed, the complexity for the admitter does not depend on the number of signatures to open, which implies that this role can be played by an entity with a low computing power.

OUR CONTRIBUTION. In this work, we introduce a new cryptographic primitive, a variant of Direct Anonymous Attestation, that we call DAA with Dependent Basename Opening tailored to the context of access control such as transit pass systems or authentication of ID documents. We provide a formal security model for this primitive along with an instantiation that we prove secure, under conventional assumptions, in the random oracle model. Furthermore, we provide a prototype implementation of an anonymous transit pass system, based on this primitive, which complies with the functional requirements [2] of existing standards.

2   A Security Model for DAA-DBO Schemes

DEFINITION. A *DAA scheme with dependent-basename opening* is defined by the following algorithms:

Setup(λ): This probabilistic algorithm outputs *param*, a description of the system parameters, such as the underlying groups.

Keygen(*param*): This probabilistic algorithm outputs the description of two registers, **Reg** and **Sreg**, and the two following public/secret key pairs: (tsk, tpk) for the admitter and (isk, ipk) for the group manager. The group public key *gpk* is eventually set as ($param$, **Reg**, ipk, tpk).

UKeygen(*gpk*): This probabilistic algorithm outputs a key pair (sk_i, pk_i) for a digital signature scheme. The value pk_i is public, and we assume that anyone can get an authentic copy of it for any user.

(Join, Issue): This is an interactive protocol between a new group user i, whose inputs are (sk_i, gpk), the group manager, whose inputs are (isk, gpk, **Reg**) and the opening authority, whose input is **Sreg**. As a result of this protocol the user obtains his group signing key gsk_i and some data that are stored in **Reg** (the public part) and **Sreg** (the secret part).

Sign(gpk, gsk_i, m, bsn): This probabilistic algorithm takes as input the user's signing key, a message m and a basename bsn and outputs a signature σ.

Verify(gpk, σ, m, bsn): This deterministic algorithm outputs 1 if σ is a valid signature on m with basename bsn and 0 otherwise.

Link($gpk, \sigma, m, \sigma', m', bsn$): This deterministic algorithm outputs 1 if σ and σ' are two valid signatures with the same basename bsn and were issued by the same user.

Token(gpk, tsk, bsn): This deterministic algorithm outputs a token τ enabling the opening authority to open any signature with basename bsn.

Open($gpk, \sigma, m, bsn, \tau, \mathbf{Reg}, \mathbf{Sreg}$): This algorithm first checks that σ is a valid signature on m with basename bsn and then outputs an index i and a proof π that user i produced the signature σ or $\perp$ if it did not succeed.

Judge($gpk, i, \sigma, m, bsn, \mathbf{Reg}, \pi$): This deterministic algorithm outputs 1 if π is a valid proof that user i issued σ and 0 otherwise.

SECURITY PROPERTIES. The sets of honest and dishonest users will be denoted $\mathcal{HU}$ and $\mathcal{DU}$. Note that the adversaries of anonymity experiments have to select targeted users from $\mathcal{HU}$. This restriction, called *selfless anonymity* for group signatures [9], is unavoidable for DAA schemes. Indeed, anyone knowing the secret keys will be able to open the challenge signature by computing a new signature with the same basename and running the Link algorithm. The security notions make use of the following oracles ($\mathcal{O}\text{Alg}\neg(x)$ means that an oracle query on x is not allowed).

$\mathcal{O}\text{Join}_{UD}(gpk, isk)$ is an oracle that executes the user's side of the join protocol for the input user $i \in \mathcal{HU}$. This oracle will be used by an adversary playing the role of the corrupted group manager.

$\mathcal{O}\text{Join}_{DM}(gpk)$ is an oracle that executes the join protocol with the honest group manager. This oracle will be used by an adversary to register a corrupted user.

$\mathcal{O}\text{Sign}(gpk, i, m, bsn)$ is an oracle that takes as input an identity i, a message m and a basename bsn and returns a signature σ if the user i is honest and registered.

$\mathcal{O}\text{Token}(gpk, bsn)$ is an oracle that takes as input a basename bsn and outputs a token τ.

$\mathcal{O}\text{Open}(gpk, \sigma, m, bsn, \tau)$ inputs a signature σ on m with basename bsn and a token τ and returns the result of a call to Open($gpk, \sigma, m, bsn, \tau, \mathbf{Reg}, \mathbf{Sreg}$).

$\mathcal{O}\text{ReadSreg}(i)$ inputs an identity i and outputs the content of the secret registration table $\mathbf{Sreg}[i]$.

Correctness. Defining correctness is not a matter of concern. Due to space limitations, a formal definition is given in Appendix A.1. Informally, a DAA-DBO scheme is correct if *(i)* honestly computed signatures are accepted, *(ii)* valid signatures that share the same basename are linkable, *(iii)* honestly computed tokens enable to open signature and, *(iv)* valid opening proofs are accepted by the judge.

Admitter Anonymity. Informally, admitter anonymity requires that signatures do not reveal the signer's identity even if the admitter is dishonest. The adversary cannot obviously request a signature from users selected in the challenge phase with the challenge basename since the adversary could use the Link algorithm to retrieve the identity. We define the admitter-anonymity experiment $\mathbf{Exp}_{\mathcal{A}}^{ad\text{-}anon\text{-}b}(\lambda)$ as follows:

1. $\mathcal{DU} \leftarrow \mathcal{A}(1^\lambda)$.
2. $\mathcal{HU} \leftarrow \{1..n\} \setminus \mathcal{DU}$.
3. $(gpk, isk, tsk) \leftarrow \texttt{Keygen}(1^\lambda)$.
4. For $i \in \mathcal{HU}$:
   (a) $(usk_i, upk_i) \leftarrow \texttt{UKeygen}(gpk)$
   (b) $(gsk_i, \mathbf{Reg}[i], \mathbf{SReg}[i]) \leftarrow \langle \texttt{Join}(gpk, usk_i), \texttt{Issue}(gpk, isk) \rangle$
5. $(i_0, i_1, m, bsn) \leftarrow \mathcal{A}^{\mathcal{O}\texttt{Sign}, \mathcal{O}\texttt{Open}, \mathcal{O}\texttt{Join}_{UD}}(gpk, isk, tsk)$ with $(i_0, i_1 \in \mathcal{HU})$.
6. If $\mathcal{O}\texttt{Sign}(gpk, i_b, \cdot, bsn)$ was requested for $b \in \{0,1\}$ then abort.
7. Else $\sigma \leftarrow \texttt{Sign}(gpk, gsk_{i_{b'}}, m, bsn)$ for $b' \xleftarrow{\$} \{0,1\}$.
8. $b^* \leftarrow \mathcal{A}^{\mathcal{O}\texttt{Sign}\neg(gpk, i_b, \cdot, bsn), \mathcal{O}\texttt{Open}\neg(gpk, \sigma, m, bsn, \cdot), \mathcal{O}\texttt{Join}_{DM}}(gpk, isk, tsk)$.
9. Return b^*.

We define $\mathbf{Adv}_{\mathcal{A}}^{ad\text{-}anon\text{-}b}(\lambda) = |\Pr[b' = b^*] - \frac{1}{2}|$. The scheme is *admitter-anonymous* if for any probabilistic polynomial time $\mathcal{A}$, this advantage is negligible.

Opener Anonymity. Informally, opener-anonymity requires that the opening authority is unable to identify the issuers of signatures with basename bsn without the help of the admitter. We define the opener-anonymity experiment $\mathbf{Exp}_{\mathcal{A}}^{op\text{-}anon\text{-}b}(\lambda)$ as follows:

1. $\mathcal{DU} \leftarrow \mathcal{A}(1^\lambda)$.
2. $\mathcal{HU} \leftarrow \{1..n\} \setminus \mathcal{DU}$.
3. $(gpk, isk, tsk) \leftarrow \texttt{Keygen}(1^\lambda)$.
4. For $i \in \mathcal{HU}$:
   (a) $(usk_i, upk_i) \leftarrow \texttt{UKeygen}(gpk)$
   (b) $(gsk_i, \mathbf{Reg}[i], \mathbf{SReg}[i]) \leftarrow \langle \texttt{Join}(gpk, usk_i), \texttt{Issue}(gpk, isk) \rangle$
5. $(i_0, i_1, m, bsn) \leftarrow \mathcal{A}^{\mathcal{O}\texttt{Sign}, \mathcal{O}\texttt{Token}, \mathcal{O}\texttt{Join}_{UD}}(gpk, isk, \mathbf{SReg})$ with $(i_0, i_1 \in \mathcal{HU})$.
6. If $\mathcal{O}\texttt{Sign}(gpk, i_b, \cdot, bsn)$ or $\mathcal{O}\texttt{Token}(gpk, bsn)$ was requested for $b \in \{0,1\}$ then abort.
7. Else $\sigma \leftarrow \texttt{Sign}(gpk, gsk_{i_{b'}}, m, bsn)$ for $b' \xleftarrow{\$} \{0,1\}$.
8. $b^* \leftarrow \mathcal{A}^{\mathcal{O}\texttt{Sign}\neg(gpk, i_b, \cdot, bsn), \mathcal{O}\texttt{Token}\neg(gpk, bsn), \mathcal{O}\texttt{Join}_{DM}}(gpk, isk, \mathbf{SReg})$.
9. Return b^*.

We define $\mathbf{Adv}_{\mathcal{A}}^{op\text{-}anon\text{-}b}(\lambda) = |\Pr[b' = b^*] - \frac{1}{2}|$. The scheme is *opener-anonymous* if for any probabilistic polynomial time $\mathcal{A}$, this advantage is negligible.

Traceability. Traceability requires that no adversary is able to create a valid signature that cannot be traced to some user already registered. We define the traceability experiment as follows:

1. $\mathcal{DU} \leftarrow \{1..n\}$.
2. $(gpk, isk, tsk) \leftarrow \texttt{Keygen}(1^\lambda)$.
3. $(\sigma, m, bsn) \leftarrow \mathcal{A}^{\mathcal{O}\texttt{ReadSreg}, \mathcal{O}\texttt{Join}_{DM}}(gpk, tsk)$.
4. $\tau \leftarrow \texttt{Token}(gpk, tsk, bsn)$
5. If $\texttt{Verify}(gpk, \sigma, m, bsn) = 1$ and $\texttt{Open}(gpk, \sigma, m, bsn, \tau, \mathbf{Reg}, \mathbf{Sreg}) = \perp$ then return 1.
6. Return 0.

We define $\mathbf{Adv}_{\mathcal{A}}^{trace}(\lambda) = \Pr[\mathbf{Exp}_{\mathcal{A}}^{trace}(\lambda) = 1]$. The scheme is *traceable* if for any probabilistic polynomial time adversary, this advantage is negligible.

Non-frameability. Informally, non-frameability requires that no one can falsely accuse an honest user of having signed a given message m with basename bsn. We define the non-frameability experiment as follows:

1. $\mathcal{DU} \leftarrow \mathcal{A}(1^\lambda)$.
2. $\mathcal{HU} \leftarrow \{1..n\} \setminus \mathcal{DU}$.
3. $(gpk, isk, tsk) \leftarrow \text{Keygen}(1^\lambda)$.
4. For $i \in \mathcal{HU}$:
   (a) $(usk_i, upk_i) \leftarrow \text{UKeygen}(gpk)$
5. $(i, \sigma, m, bsn, \tau, \pi) \leftarrow \mathcal{A}^{\mathcal{O}\text{Sign}, \mathcal{O}\text{Join}_{UD}}(gpk, isk, tsk, \mathbf{Sreg})$.
6. If $i \notin \mathcal{HU}$ or $\text{Verify}(gpk, \sigma, m, bsn) = 0$ then return 0.
7. If σ was returned by $\mathcal{O}\text{Sign}(gpk, i, m, bsn)$ then return 0.
8. If $\text{Judge}(gpk, i, \sigma, m, bsn, \tau, \mathbf{Reg}, \pi) = 0$ then return 0.
9. Return 1.

We define $\mathbf{Adv}_\mathcal{A}^{nf}(\lambda) = \Pr[\mathbf{Exp}_\mathcal{A}^{nf}(\lambda) = 1]$. The scheme is *non-frameable* if for any probabilistic polynomial time adversary, this advantage is negligible.

3 Our DAA-DBO Scheme

We now introduce our DDA-DBO scheme, fulfilling the requirements of Section 2.

BILINEAR GROUPS. A *bilinear environment* is given by a set of three groups $\mathbb{G}_1, \mathbb{G}_2, \mathbb{G}_T$ of prime order p along with a bilinear map $e : \mathbb{G}_1 \times \mathbb{G}_2 \to \mathbb{G}_T$ with the following properties:

1. For all $X_1 \in \mathbb{G}_p, X_2 \in \mathbb{G}_2$ and $a, b \in \mathbb{Z}_p$, $e([a]X_1, [b]X_2) = e(X_1, X_2)^{ab}$.
2. For $X_1 \neq 1_{\mathbb{G}_1}$ and $X_2 \neq 1_{\mathbb{G}_2}$, $e(X_1, X_2) \neq 1_{\mathbb{G}_T}$.
3. e is efficiently computable.

In the following, we will write $\mathbb{G}_1$ and $\mathbb{G}_2$ additively and $\mathbb{G}_T$ multiplicatively.

ALGORITHMS AND PROTOCOLS OF OUR DAA-DBO SCHEME. Given bilinear environments, our scheme is described as follows.

$\text{Setup}(1^\lambda)$: outputs $param \leftarrow (p, \mathbb{G}_1, \mathbb{G}_2, \mathbb{G}_T, e, \mathcal{H}, \mathcal{H}_1, G_1, H, G_2)$ where $\mathbb{G}_1, \mathbb{G}_2$ and $\mathbb{G}_T$ are groups of prime order p, $\mathcal{H} : \{0,1\}^* \to \mathbb{Z}_p$ and $\mathcal{H}_1 : \{0,1\}^* \to \mathbb{G}_1$ are hash functions (modelled as random oracles in the proofs of security), and $G_1, H \overset{\$}{\leftarrow} \mathbb{G}_1$ and $G_2 \overset{\$}{\leftarrow} \mathbb{G}_2$ are random generators. Finally, this algorithm outputs the description of a digital signature scheme $\mathcal{S}$ whose message space is $\mathcal{M}$ and of a hash function $\mathcal{H}_0 : \mathbb{G}_1 \to \mathcal{M}$.

$\text{Keygen}(param)$: The group manager picks $\gamma \overset{\$}{\leftarrow} \mathbb{Z}_p$ and sets $(sk_M, pk_M) \leftarrow (\gamma, W)$ where $W \leftarrow [\gamma]G_2$. The admitter picks $\delta \overset{\$}{\leftarrow} \mathbb{Z}_p$ and sets $(sk_T, pk_T) \leftarrow (\delta, T)$ where $T \leftarrow [\delta]G_2$. The group public key gpk is $(param, W, T)$.

$\text{UKeygen}(gpk)$: Each user i generates a key pair (sk_i, pk_i) for the scheme $\mathcal{S}$.

$(\text{Join}, \text{Issue})$: The user first chooses $y' \in \mathbb{Z}_p$ and computes $(C_1', C_2') \leftarrow ([y']H, [y']G_2)$. Then, he sends (C_1', C_2') to the opening authority who tests whether $e(C_1', G_2) = e(H, C_2')$. If the equality holds, this last entity stores (C_1', C_2') in his secret register $\mathbf{Sreg}$. To register with the group manager, the user begins the Join protocol given Figure 1[1]. At the end of the interaction, the user sets

---

[1] The first moves are a proof of knowledge of a discrete logarithm. To prove full traceability, we must add an extractable commitment of y' together with a proof of equality with the discrete logarithm of C_1' (see [15], Section 4.1.)

$$\underline{User(y', sk_i, gpk) \hspace{6cm} GM(\gamma, gpk)}$$

$User(y', sk_i, gpk)$		$GM(\gamma, gpk)$
$r \overset{\$}{\leftarrow} \mathbb{Z}_p; \ R \leftarrow [r]H$	$\xrightarrow{\quad i, C_1', R \quad}$	
	$\xleftarrow{\quad c \quad}$	$c \overset{\$}{\leftarrow} \mathbb{Z}_p$
$z \leftarrow r + y' \cdot c$	$\xrightarrow{\quad z \quad}$	If $[s]H = R + [c]C_1'$ then $y'', x \overset{\$}{\leftarrow} \mathbb{Z}_p$
$C_1 \leftarrow C_1' + [y'']H$	$\xleftarrow{\quad y'' \quad}$	$A \leftarrow [\frac{1}{\gamma+x}](G_1 + C_1' + [y'']H)$
$v \leftarrow \mathcal{S}.\mathtt{Sign}(sk_i, \mathcal{H}_0(C_1))$	$\xrightarrow{\quad v \quad}$	If $\mathcal{S}.\mathtt{Verify}(pk_i, v, \mathcal{H}_0(C_1)) = 1$
$y \leftarrow y' + y''$	$\xleftarrow{\quad A, x \quad}$	then send A, x

Fig. 1. The DAA-DBO (`Join`, `Issue`) protocol

$gsk_i \leftarrow (A, x, y)$ while the group manager stores (i, C_1, v) in **Reg**. We assume that the group manager ensured that the interaction between the user and the opening authority was complete before issuing the user's certificate. Users can, for example, receive a signature from the opening authority whose validity will be checked by the group manager at the beginning of the interaction. After the interaction, the later sends $([y'']H, [y'']G_2)$ to the opener, who updates **Sreg** by recording $(C_1' + [y'']H, C_2' + [y'']G_2)$ instead of (C_1', C_2').

`Sign`: The protocol to sign a message m with basename bsn is described in Figure 2. As in DAA schemes, the signer is divided into two entities, the TPM and the Host.

`Verify`(gpk, σ, m, bsn): To check the validity of the signature σ, the verifier parses σ as $(C, K, c, s_x, s_y, s_d, s_z)$, computes $R_1 \leftarrow e([s_x]C - [s_z]H - [s_d]G_1, G_2) \cdot e(C, W)^c$, $R_2 \leftarrow e([s_y]\mathcal{H}_1(bsn), T) \cdot K^{-c}$, $R_3 \leftarrow e([s_z]\mathcal{H}_1(bsn), T) \cdot K^{-s_d}$, and checks whether $c = \mathcal{H}(m, bsn, C, K, R_1, R_2, R_3)$. If the equality holds then the signature is valid.

`Link`$(gpk, \sigma, m, \sigma', m', bsn)$: To test if σ and σ' were produced by the same user, the algorithm first checks that σ is a valid signature on m with basename bsn and that σ' is a valid signature on m' with the same basename. If this is true then it parses σ as $(C, K, c, s_x, s_y, s_d, s_z)$ and σ' as $(C', K', c', s_x', s_y', s_d', s_z')$. If $K = K'$ then it returns *true*, else it returns *false*.

`Token`(gpk, tsk, bsn): To issue a token τ on a basename bsn the admitter outputs $\tau \leftarrow [\delta]\mathcal{H}_1(bsn)$.

`Open`$(gpk, \sigma, m, bsn, \tau, \mathbf{Reg}, \mathbf{Sreg})$: If τ is a valid token on the basename bsn (*i.e.* if $e(\tau, G_2) = e(\mathcal{H}_1(bsn), T)$) and σ is a valid signature on m and bsn then the opening authority will parse σ as $(C, K, c, s_x, s_y, s_d, s_z)$ and test, for each $(i, [y_i]G_2)$ in **Sreg**, if $K = e(\tau, [y_i]G_2)$ until he gets a match. Then, he outputs i and π, a non-interactive zero-knowledge proof of knowledge (using, for example, the proof systems of [17]) of τ and C_2 such that $K = e(\tau, C_2)$, $e(C_1, G_2) = e(H, C_2)$ and $1 \leftarrow \mathcal{S}.\mathtt{Verify}(pk_i, v, \mathcal{H}_0(C_1))$ (C_1, v and i are stored in a public register **Reg**).

$TPM(gpk, x, y, bsn, m)$		$Host(gpk, A, x)$
$k_y, k_z \xleftarrow{\$} \mathbb{Z}_p$		$k_x, k_d, d \xleftarrow{\$} \mathbb{Z}_p$
$J \leftarrow \mathcal{H}_1(bsn)$	$\xleftarrow{\quad k_x, k_d, d, C \quad}$	$C \leftarrow [d]A$
$(T_1, T_2) \leftarrow ([k_z]H, [k_z]J)$		
$(T_3, T_4) \leftarrow ([y]J, [k_y]H)$	$\xrightarrow{\quad T_1, T_2, T_3, T_4 \quad}$	
		$(K, R_2) \leftarrow (e(T_3, T), e(T_4, T))$
		$R_1 \leftarrow e([k_x]C - T_1 - [k_d]G_1, G_2)$
	$\xleftarrow{\quad K, R_1, R_2, R_3 \quad}$	$R_3 \leftarrow e(T_2, T) \cdot K^{-k_d}$
$c \leftarrow \mathcal{H}(m, bsn, C, K, R_1, R_2, R_3)$		
$s_x \leftarrow k_x + c \cdot x \; [p]; s_y \leftarrow k_y + c \cdot y \; [p]$		
$s_d \leftarrow k_d + c \cdot d \; [p]; s_z \leftarrow k_z + c \cdot d \cdot y \; [p]$		
$\sigma = (C, K, c, s_x, s_y, s_d, s_z)$		
$\xrightarrow{\hspace{5cm}}$		

Fig. 2. The DAA-DBO Sign protocol

Judge($gpk, i, \sigma, m, bsn, \mathbf{Reg}, \pi$): To check the validity of the opening, the algorithm first recovers the data (i, C_1, v) in $\mathbf{Reg}$. If π is a valid proof of knowledge of two elements τ and C_2 such that $K = e(\tau, C_2)$, $e(C_1, G_2) = e(H, C_2)$ and $1 \leftarrow \mathcal{S}.\mathsf{Verify}(pk_i, v, \mathcal{H}_0(C_1))$ then it outputs 1. Else, it returns 0.

4   Security Analysis of Our Scheme

We now present our results concerning the security of our scheme. Verifying its correctness is not hard from its description. The security of our protocols rely on the difficulty of the following problems.

Symmetric Discrete Logarithm (SDLP). This assumption, formalized in [7], underlies many asymmetric pairing protocols or assumptions.
Given a tuple $(G_1, [x]G_1, G_2, [x]G_2) \in \mathbb{G}_1^2 \times \mathbb{G}_2^2$ *computing* x *is a hard problem.*

Strong Diffie-Hellman (SDH). This well-know assumption [8] enables to compute short signatures in bilinear environments.
Given $(G_1, [\theta]G_1, [\theta^2]G_1, \ldots, [\theta^q]G_1, G_2, [\theta]G_2) \in \mathbb{G}_1^{q+1} \times \mathbb{G}_2^2$, *computing a pair* $(c, [\frac{1}{\theta+c}]G_1)$, *for some* $c \in \mathbb{Z}_p \setminus \{-\theta\}$, *is a hard problem.*

External Diffie-Hellman (XDH). This assumption, formalized in the full version of [13] is the Decisional Diffie-Hellman one extended to the bilinear setting.
Given $(G_1, [a]G_1, [b]G_1, [z]G_1) \in \mathbb{G}_1^4$, *deciding whether* $z = a \cdot b$ *is a hard problem.*

Decisional Bilinear Diffie-Hellman (DBDH). This assumption is the asymmetric version of the one originally stated in [18] for symmetric pairings.
Given $(G_1, [a]G_1, [b]G_1, [c]G_1, G_2, [a]G_2, [c]G_2, e(G_1, G_2)^z) \in \mathbb{G}_1^4 \times \mathbb{G}_2^3 \times \mathbb{G}_T$, *deciding whether* $z = a \cdot b \cdot c$ *is a hard problem.*

Given these assumptions, our security result is stated by the following theorem.

Theorem 1. *In the random oracle model, the DAA-DBO scheme is admitter anonymous under the XDH assumption in $\mathbb{G}_1$, opener anonymous under the DBDH assumption, traceable under the SDH assumption and non-frameable under the SDLP assumption and the EUF-CMA security of $\mathcal{S}$.*

Due to space limitations, here we only provide the proofs of admitter and opener anonymities. The other proofs, including the proof that the `Sign` algorithm is a zero-knowledge proof of knowledge of a valid certificate on x and y such that $K = e(\mathcal{H}_1(bsn), T)^y$, are more classical and are given in Appendix A.2.

Proof of Admitter Anonymity. Let $\mathcal{A}$ be an ϵ-adversary against the admitter anonymity, we construct a reduction $\mathcal{R}$ using $\mathcal{A}$ against XDH challenges in $\mathbb{G}_1$. Let $(H, [a]H, [b]H, [z]H)$ be such a challenge, $\mathcal{R}$ has to decide whether $z = a \cdot b$. After the adversary has chosen the set $\mathcal{DU}$, $\mathcal{R}$ randomly selects i^* from $\mathcal{HU}$ and j^* in $[1; q_H]$, where q_H is the number of hash queries.

[Keygen] $\mathcal{R}$ proceeds as usual and sends δ and γ to $\mathcal{A}$.

[Join queries] $\mathcal{R}$ proceeds as usual for dishonest users. For honest users, $\mathcal{R}$ will act as follows: (i) If $i \neq i^*$, then it selects $y_i \xleftarrow{\$} \mathbb{Z}_p$ and gets a certificate on x_i and y_i for a random x_i. (ii) If $i = i^*$, then it acts as if $y_i = a$ and uses $[a]H$ to get a valid certificate A^* on a and some random x_i.

[Hash queries] Upon receiving the jth hash request on bsn, $\mathcal{R}$ proceeds as follows: (i) If no previous request was made on bsn then we distinguish two cases. If $j \neq j^*$, then $\mathcal{R}$ selects $u_j \xleftarrow{\$} \mathbb{Z}_p$, stores $(j, bsn, u_j, [u_j]H)$ and outputs $[u_j]H$. Else, it selects $v \xleftarrow{\$} \mathbb{Z}_p$, stores $(j^*, bsn, -, [b \cdot v]H)$ and returns $[b \cdot v]H$. (ii) If bsn has already been queried, then $\mathcal{R}$ returns the output of the first time.

[Sign queries] Upon receiving a signature query on m, with basename bsn, for $i \in \mathcal{HU}$, $\mathcal{R}$ proceeds as usual if $i \neq i^*$, else, we distinguish the two following cases. If bsn was the one requested in the j^*th hash request, then $\mathcal{R}$ aborts. Else, it selects $d \xleftarrow{\$} \mathbb{Z}_p$, computes $C \leftarrow [d]A$, $K \leftarrow ([a]H, T)^{u_j}$, simulates the proof of knowledge, stores the resulting signature (σ, m, bsn) in **SignReg** and outputs σ.

[Open queries] Upon receiving an opening query on (σ, m, bsn), R checks if $(\sigma, m, bsn) \in$ **SignReg**. If so, then it returns i^*, else it proceeds as usual.

Challenge phase. $\mathcal{A}$ outputs two honest identities i_0 and i_1, a message m and a basename bsn. If a hash request on this basename was already submitted during the jth query then $\mathcal{R}$ aborts if $j \neq j^*$. Now, $\mathcal{R}$ randomly selects a bit b and aborts if $i_b \neq i^*$. Else, it has to issue a valid signature on m and bsn on behalf of i^*. It proceeds as follows: (i) If no hash request was submitted on bsn, then $\mathcal{R}$ programs the random oracle to return $[b]H$. (ii) It randomly selects $d \in \mathbb{Z}_p$, computes $C \leftarrow [d]H$ and $K \leftarrow e([z]H, T)^v$ (with $v = 1$ if no hash request on bsn was made before the challenge phase), simulates the proof of knowledge and outputs the resulting signature.

After the Challenge phase, $\mathcal{R}$ proceeds as in the first phase. The probability that $\mathcal{R}$ aborts is then smaller than $(1 - \frac{1}{q_H \cdot |\mathcal{HU}|})$. If it did not aborted, its behaviour is the same as the challenger in the original anonymity experiment. So if $c = a \cdot b$, the signature issued by $\mathcal{R}$ in the challenge phase is indistinguishable from an original one, else it is a random element from the signature space. Then, the probability of success of $\mathcal{R}$ in breaking the XDH problem in $\mathbb{G}_1$ is greater than $\frac{1}{q_H \cdot |\mathcal{HU}|} \cdot \frac{\epsilon}{2}$. □

Proof of Opener Anonymity. Let $\mathcal{A}$ be an ϵ-adversary against the opener anonymity, we construct a reduction $\mathcal{R}$ using $\mathcal{A}$ against DBDH challenges. Let $(H, [a]H, [b]H, [c]H, G_2, [a]G_2, [c]G_2, e(G_1, G_2)^z)$ be such a challenge, $\mathcal{R}$ has to decide whether $z = a \cdot b \cdot c$. After $\mathcal{A}$ chose the set $\mathcal{DU}$, $\mathcal{R}$ randomly selects i^* from $\mathcal{HU}$ and j^* in $[1; q_H]$, where q_H is the number of hash queries.

[Keygen] $\mathcal{R}$ proceeds as usual except that it sets $T \leftarrow [a]G_2$.

[Join queries] $\mathcal{R}$ proceeds as usual for dishonest users. For honest users, $\mathcal{R}$ will act as follows. (i) If $i \neq i^*$, then it selects $y_i \xleftarrow{\$} \mathbb{Z}_p$ and gets a certificate on x_i and y_i for a random x_i. (ii) If $i = i^*$, then it acts as if $y_i = c$ and uses $[c]H$ to get a valid certificate A^* on c and some random x_i and sends $[c]G_2$ to $\mathcal{A}$.

[Hash queries] Upon receiving the jth hash request on bsn, $\mathcal{R}$ proceeds as follows: (i) If no previous request was made on bsn then we distinguish two cases. If $j \neq j^*$, then $\mathcal{R}$ selects $u_j \xleftarrow{\$} \mathbb{Z}_p$, stores $(j, bsn, u_j, [u_j]H)$ and outputs $[u_j]H$. Else, it selects $v \xleftarrow{\$} \mathbb{Z}_p$, stores $(j^*, bsn, -, [b \cdot v]H)$ and returns $[b \cdot v]H$. (ii) If bsn has already been queried, then $\mathcal{R}$ returns the output of the first time.

[Sign queries] Upon receiving a signature query on m, with basename bsn, for $i \in \mathcal{HU}$, $\mathcal{R}$ proceeds as usual if $i \neq i^*$, else, we distinguish the two following cases. If bsn was the one requested in the j^*th hash request, then $\mathcal{R}$ aborts. Else, it selects $d \xleftarrow{\$} \mathbb{Z}_p$, computes $C \leftarrow [d]A$, $K \leftarrow ([c]H, T)^{u_j}$, simulates the proof of knowledge and outputs σ.

[Token queries] Upon receiving a token query on bsn, $\mathcal{R}$ aborts if bsn was the basename used in the j^*th hash request and returns $[u_j \cdot a]H$ otherwise.

Challenge phase. $\mathcal{A}$ outputs two honest identities i_0 and i_1, a message m and a basename bsn. If a hash request on this basename was already submitted during the jth query then $\mathcal{R}$ aborts if $j \neq j^*$. Now, $\mathcal{R}$ randomly selects a bit b and aborts if $i_b \neq i^*$. Else, it has to issue a valid signature on m and bsn on behalf of i^*. It proceeds as follows: (i) If no hash request was submitted on bsn, then $\mathcal{R}$ programs the random oracle to return $[b]H$. (ii) It randomly selects $d \in \mathbb{Z}_p$, computes $C \leftarrow [d]H$ and $K \leftarrow [e(H, G_2)^z]^v$ (with $v = 1$ if no hash request on bsn was made before the challenge phase), simulates the proof of knowledge and outputs the resulting signature. After the Challenge phase, $\mathcal{R}$ proceeds as in the first phase. The probability that $\mathcal{R}$ aborts is then smaller than $(1 - \frac{1}{q_H \cdot |\mathcal{HU}|})$. If it did not aborted, its behaviour is the same as the challenger in the original anonymity experiment. So if $z = a \cdot b \cdot c$, the signature issued by $\mathcal{R}$ in the challenge phase is indistinguishable from an original one, else it is a random element from the signature space. Then, the probability of success of $\mathcal{R}$ in breaking the DBDH problem is $\frac{1}{q_H \cdot |\mathcal{HU}|} \cdot \frac{\epsilon}{2}$. □

5   Implementation

UNTRACEABLE TRANSIT PASSES ON NFC-ENABLED MOBILE PHONE. We designed and implemented an anonymous public transit pass system based on our new primitive. A transit pass refers to a transport subscription card that allows a passenger of the transport service to take unlimited trips within a fixed period of time (a week or a month). Our DAA-DBO scheme enables strong authentication and anonymity properties for the mobile phone, while being very effective. To enter the public transport system the users will sign a random message m received from the turnstile with the basename corresponding to the current time slot. The architecture is that of a secure element embedded in the phone. This fits DAA schemes were the signer is divided into the TPM, a low-power but trusted entity, here the SIM card, and the host, a powerful but untrusted entity, here the mobile phone.

CURVE AND PAIRING PARAMETERS. We use a 256 bits Barreto-Naehrig curve [4] over $\mathbb{F}_q$ since this family of curves provides an optimal size for $\mathbb{G}_1$ and $\mathbb{G}_2$ while preventing the MOV attack [20] due to their embedding degree, equal to 12. The curve is thus defined by the equation $E : y^2 = x^3 + b$, $\mathbb{G}_1$ is the group of $\mathbb{F}_q$-rational points (of order p) and $\mathbb{G}_2$ is the subgroup of trace zero points in $E(\mathbb{F}_{q^{12}})[p]$ (our pairing is thus of type-3 [16]). We use the following parameters:

$q = 8243401665430090752057404098378368203946728292799613002465591229288 9294264593$

$p = 8243401665430090752057404098378368203918016968090658713689664525546 5309139857$

$b = 5$

EQUIPMENT. Our scheme was tested on a smartcard provided by a smartcard manufacturer enabling the use of low level APIs to access smartcard functions handling elliptic curves operations and a Samsung galaxy S3 NFC phone (ARM ARMv7 @ 1.40 GHz 1 processor, 4 cores). The verification was performed by a PC (Intel(R) Celeron(R) CPU E3300 @ 2.50GHz, 2-core CPU) under Linux (64-bit architecture). The NFC reader is an Omnikey 5321.

PRECOMPUTATIONS. Our Sign protocol (Figure 2) can be divided into two phases: the offline phase where the TPM interacts with the host to precompute a part of the signature, and the online phase, where the former issues a signature more quickly using these precomputations. In our scheme, only operations involving the message m cannot be performed in the offline phase since m is only known when accessing the service. Therefore, every elements of the signature can be precomputed, except c, s_x, s_y, s_d, s_z. With this methodology, the Sign procedure can be performed very quickly. Indeed, given a message m and the precomputations, it only remains to compute a hash value and some operations in $\mathbb{Z}_p$.

PERFORMANCE. Figure 3 describes the timings of the precomputations. The slowness of the communication protocol between a SIM card and a smartphone affects the efficiency of these precomputations. The total size of the elements that the card has to store for one signature is 1665 bytes.

Figure 4 describes the timings of the online part of the signature. Since the card only has to compute one hash value and cheap operations in $\mathbb{Z}_p$, all the

Card Computations	Smartphone Computations	Data sending and storage	Total
360-390 ms	138-150 ms	990-1000 ms	1488-1540 ms

Fig. 3. Precomputations

Card Signature	Verif. by PC	Total
90-92 ms	38-46 ms	128-138 ms

Fig. 4. Signature and verification performance

validation process (*online* signature and verification) can be performed quickly. It is worthy to note that our system fulfils the challenging functional requirements of public transport [2] specifying that access control should be performed in less than 300ms. The size of the signature is 577 bytes.

6   Conclusion

We introduced the notion of Direct Anonymous Attestations with Dependent Basename Opening (DAA-DBO), where the anonymity of a Direct Anonymous Attestation can be revoked only if a specific authority, called the admitter, allowed to revoke the DAA signatures that includes a specific basename. We gave an efficient scheme that achieves this notion. We implemented our scheme on mobile phone, showing that this primitive is well-suited for practical uses such as, for example, the design of a public transportation card embedded in a mobile phone.

Acknowledgments. This work has been supported by the French ANR-11-INS-0013 LYRICS Project. The opinions expressed in this document only represent the authors' view. They does not reflect the view of their employers.

References

1. Advanced security mechanism for machine readable travel documents extended access control (eac). technical report (bsi-tr-03110) version 2.05 release candidate, bsi (2010)
2. White paper: Mobile nfc in transport, gsma (2012),
   http://www.uitp.org/public-transport/
   technology/Mobile-NFC-in-Transport.pdf
3. Atluri, V., Pfitzmann, B., McDaniel, P.D. (eds.): Proceedings of the 11th ACM Conference on Computer and Communications Security, CCS 2004, October 25-29. ACM, Washington, DC (2004)
4. Barreto, P.S.L.M., Naehrig, M.: Pairing-friendly elliptic curves of prime order. In: Preneel, B., Tavares, S. (eds.) SAC 2005. LNCS, vol. 3897, pp. 319–331. Springer, Heidelberg (2006)

5. Bender, J., Dagdelen, Ö., Fischlin, M., Kügler, D.: Domain-specific pseudonymous signatures for the german identity card. In: Gollmann, D., Freiling, F.C. (eds.) ISC 2012. LNCS, vol. 7483, pp. 104–119. Springer, Heidelberg (2012)
6. Bernhard, D., Fuchsbauer, G., Ghadafi, E., Smart, N.P., Warinschi, B.: Anonymous attestation with user-controlled linkability. Int. J. Inf. Sec. 12(3), 219–249 (2013)
7. Bichsel, P., Camenisch, J., Neven, G., Smart, N.P., Warinschi, B.: Get shorty via group signatures without encryption. In: Garay, J.A., De Prisco, R. (eds.) SCN 2010. LNCS, vol. 6280, pp. 381–398. Springer, Heidelberg (2010)
8. Boneh, D., Boyen, X.: Short signatures without random oracles and the sdh assumption in bilinear groups. J. Cryptology 21(2), 149–177 (2008)
9. Boneh, D., Shacham, H.: Group signatures with verifier-local revocation. In: Atluri et al [3], pp. 168–177
10. Brickell, E.F., Camenisch, J., Chen, L.: Direct anonymous attestation. In: Atluri et al [3], pp. 132–145
11. Bringer, J., Chabanne, H., Lescuyer, R., Patey, A.: Efficient and strongly secure dynamic domain-specific pseudonymous signatures for id documents. IACR Cryptology ePrint Archive, 2014:67 (2014)
12. Bringer, J., Chabanne, H., Patey, A.: Collusion-resistant domain-specific pseudonymous signatures. In: Lopez, J., Huang, X., Sandhu, R. (eds.) NSS 2013. LNCS, vol. 7873, pp. 649–655. Springer, Heidelberg (2013)
13. Camenisch, J., Hohenberger, S., Lysyanskaya, A.: Compact e-cash. In: Cramer, R. (ed.) EUROCRYPT 2005. LNCS, vol. 3494, pp. 302–321. Springer, Heidelberg (2005)
14. Chaum, D., van Heyst, E.: Group signatures. In: Davies, D.W. (ed.) EUROCRYPT 1991. LNCS, vol. 547, pp. 257–265. Springer, Heidelberg (1991)
15. Delerablée, C., Pointcheval, D.: Dynamic fully anonymous short group signatures. In: Nguyên, P.Q. (ed.) VIETCRYPT 2006. LNCS, vol. 4341, pp. 193–210. Springer, Heidelberg (2006)
16. Galbraith, S.D., Paterson, K.G., Smart, N.P.: Pairings for cryptographers. Discrete Applied Mathematics 156(16), 3113–3121 (2008)
17. Groth, J., Sahai, A.: Efficient non-interactive proof systems for bilinear groups. In: Smart, N.P. (ed.) EUROCRYPT 2008. LNCS, vol. 4965, pp. 415–432. Springer, Heidelberg (2008)
18. Joux, A.: A one round protocol for tripartite diffie-hellman. J. Cryptology 17(4), 263–276 (2004)
19. Libert, B., Joye, M.: Group signatures with message-dependent opening in the standard model. In: Benaloh, J. (ed.) CT-RSA 2014. LNCS, vol. 8366, pp. 286–306. Springer, Heidelberg (2014)
20. Menezes, A., Vanstone, S.A., Okamoto, T.: Reducing elliptic curve logarithms to logarithms in a finite field. In: Koutsougeras, C., Vitter, J.S. (eds.) STOC, pp. 80–89. ACM (1991)
21. Pointcheval, D., Stern, J.: Security arguments for digital signatures and blind signatures. J. Cryptology 13(3), 361–396 (2000)
22. Sakai, Y., Emura, K., Hanaoka, G., Kawai, Y., Matsuda, T., Omote, K.: Group signatures with message-dependent opening. In: Abdalla, M., Lange, T. (eds.) Pairing 2012. LNCS, vol. 7708, pp. 270–294. Springer, Heidelberg (2013)

A Appendix

A.1 Formal Definition of Correctness

We define the correctness of a DAA scheme with dependent-basename opening through a game in which an adversary is allowed to request a signature on two messages with the same basename by any of the honest group members. The adversary wins if the resulting signatures are not linkable, do not pass the verification test or are opened as if they were produced by a different user. The scheme is correct if for any adversary $\mathcal{A}$ and any security parameter λ (we keep this notation in the following experiments), $\Pr[\mathbf{Exp}_{\mathcal{A}}^{corr}(\lambda) = 1]$ is negligible in λ, where $\mathbf{Exp}_{\mathcal{A}}^{corr}(\lambda)$ is defined as follows:

1. $\mathcal{HU} \leftarrow \{1..n\}$.
2. $(gpk, isk, tsk) \leftarrow \mathsf{Keygen}(\lambda)$.
3. For $i \in \mathcal{HU}$:
   (a) $(usk_i, upk_i) \leftarrow \mathsf{UKeygen}(gpk)$
   (b) $(gsk_i, \mathbf{Reg}[i], \mathbf{SReg}[i]) \leftarrow \langle \mathsf{Join}(gpk, usk_i), \mathsf{Issue}(gpk, isk) \rangle$
4. $(i, m_0, m_1, bsn) \leftarrow \mathcal{A}(gpk)$.
5. If $i \notin \mathcal{HU}$ then return 0.
6. $\sigma_0 \leftarrow \mathsf{Sign}(gpk, gsk_i, m_0, bsn)$.
7. $\sigma_1 \leftarrow \mathsf{Sign}(gpk, gsk_i, m_1, bsn)$.
8. If $\mathsf{Verify}(gpk, \sigma_0, m_0, bsn) = 0$ or $\mathsf{Verify}(gpk, \sigma_1, m_1, bsn) = 0$, return 1.
9. If $\mathsf{Link}(gpk, \sigma_0, m_0, \sigma_1, m_1, bsn) = 0$, return 1.
10. $\tau \leftarrow \mathsf{Token}(gpk, tsk, bsn)$
11. If $\mathsf{Open}(gpk, \sigma_b, m_b, bsn, \tau, \mathbf{Reg}, \mathbf{Sreg}) = (j, \pi_b)$ with $j \neq i_b$ for $b \in \{0, 1\}$, return 1.
12. If $\mathsf{Judge}(gpk, i_b, \sigma_b, m_b, bsn, \tau, \mathbf{Reg}, \pi_b) = 0$, return 1.

A.2 Additional Proofs

Proof of Knowledge of a Valid Certificate. The Sign procedure of our scheme is a proof of knowledge transformed into a signature by applying the Fiat-Shamir heuristic, in a classical way [21]. More precisely, the Sign procedure proves knowledge of a valid certificate on x and y where y is such that $K := e(\mathcal{H}_1(bsn), T)^y$.

The proof is complete. We have

$$
\begin{aligned}
e([s_x]C &- [s_z]H - [s_d]G_1, G_2) \cdot e(C, W)^c \\
&= R_1 \cdot e([x]C - [z]H - [d]G_1, G_2)^c \cdot e(C, W)^c \\
&= R_1 \cdot e([x]A - [y]H - G_1, G_2)^{d \cdot c} \cdot e(A, W)^{d \cdot c} = R_1.
\end{aligned}
$$

Moreover, $e([s_y]\mathcal{H}_1(bsn), T) \cdot K^{-c} = R_2 \cdot e([y]\mathcal{H}_1(bsn), T)^c \cdot K^{-c} = R_2$.
Finally, we have $e([s_z]\mathcal{H}_1(bsn), T) \cdot K^{-s_d} = R_3 \cdot e([z]\mathcal{H}_1(bsn), T)^c \cdot K^{-d \cdot c} = R_3$.

The proof is sound. Assume that the prover is able to answer (s_x, s_y, s_z, s_d) and (s'_x, s'_y, s'_z, s'_d) for two different challenges c and c' (with the same commitments). Let $\tilde{x} = \frac{s_x - s'_x}{c - c'}$, $\tilde{y} = \frac{s_y - s'_y}{c - c'}$ and $\tilde{d} = \frac{s_d - s'_d}{c - c'}$. From:

$$e(\mathcal{H}_1(bsn), T)^{s_y} \cdot K^{-c} = e(\mathcal{H}_1(bsn), T)^{s'_y} \cdot K^{-c'}$$

$$e(\mathcal{H}_1(bsn), T)^{s_z} \cdot K^{-s_d} = e(\mathcal{H}_1(bsn), T)^{s'_z} \cdot K^{-s'_d},$$

we get $e(\mathcal{H}_1(bsn), T)^{\tilde{y}} = K$, $e(\mathcal{H}_1(bsn), T)^{s_z - s'_z} = K^{s_d - s'_d}$ and thus $s_z - s'_z = \tilde{y}(s_d - s'_d)$. Then, since

$$e([s_x]C - [s_z]H - [s_d]G_1, G_2) \cdot e(C, W)^c = e([s'_x]C - [s'_z]H - [s'_d]G_1, G_2) \cdot e(C, W)^{c'}$$

so we have:

$$e(C, G_2)^{s_x - s'_x} \cdot e(C, W)^{c - c'} = e(H, G_2)^{s'_z - s_z} \cdot e(G_1, G_2)^{s_d - s'_d},$$

$$e(C, G_2)^{s_x - s'_x} \cdot e(C, W)^{c - c'} = e(H, G_2)^{\tilde{y}(s_d - s'_d)} \cdot e(G_1, G_2)^{s_d - s'_d},$$

$$e(C, G_2)^{\tilde{x}} \cdot e(C, W) = e(H, G_2)^{\tilde{y} \cdot \tilde{d}} \cdot e(G_1, G_2)^{\tilde{d}}.$$

(i) If $\tilde{d} = 0$ then $\tilde{x} = -\gamma$, the prover thus knows the secret key of the group manager and so a valid certificate on $\tilde{x}$ and $\tilde{y}$ (since he is able to issue it). (ii) Now, if $\tilde{d} \neq 0$ then $e([\tilde{d}^{-1}]C, G_2)^{\tilde{x}} \cdot e([\tilde{d}^{-1}]C, W) = e(H, G_2)^{\tilde{y}} \cdot e(G_1, G_2)$, proving that $[\tilde{d}^{-1}]C$ is a valid certificate on $\tilde{x}$ and $\tilde{y}$.

The proof is zero-knowledge. The simulator first selects $C \overset{\$}{\leftarrow} \mathbb{G}_1$, $c \overset{\$}{\leftarrow} \{0,1\}^l$ and $s_x, s_y, s_d, s_z \overset{\$}{\leftarrow} \mathbb{Z}_p$. Then it computes $R_1 \leftarrow e([s_x]C - [s_z]H - [s_d]G_1, G_2) \cdot e(C, W)^c$, $R_2 \leftarrow e([s_y]\mathcal{H}_1(bsn), T) \cdot K^{-c}$ and $R_3 \leftarrow e([s_z]\mathcal{H}_1(bsn), T) \cdot K^{-s_d}$. Since C is a random element from $\mathbb{G}_1$, then the transcript $C, R_1, R_2, R_3, c, s_x, s_y, s_d, s_z$ is indistinguishable from those a real prover may generate.

Proof of Non-frameability. Let $\mathcal{A}$ be an adversary against the non-frameability. A corruption of the public register **Reg** implies that $\mathcal{A}$ has successfully produced a forgery for $\mathcal{S}$. Due to the EUF-CMA security of this scheme we can consider that such an event will not occur so we only describe a reduction $\mathcal{R}$ using $\mathcal{A}$ against SDLP challenges. Let $(H, [a]H, G_2, [a]G_2)$ be such a challenge, $\mathcal{R}$ must then output a.

[Keygen] $\mathcal{R}$ proceeds as usual.

[Join queries] Given a honest user $i \in \mathcal{HU}$, $\mathcal{R}$ randomly selects $r_i \in \mathbb{Z}_p$, sends $([r_i]([a]H), [r_i]([a]G_2))$ to $\mathcal{A}$ (as corrupted opening authority) and uses $[r_i]([a]H)$ to register with $\mathcal{A}$ (as corrupted group manager).

[Sign queries] Upon receiving a signature query on m, with basename bsn, for $i \in \mathcal{HU}$, $\mathcal{R}$ proceeds as follows: it computes $C \leftarrow [d]A_i$ for a random d and computes $K \leftarrow e(\mathcal{H}_1(bsn), [a]G_2)^{(r_i \cdot \delta)}$. Then, $\mathcal{R}$ simulates the proof of knowledge of a and sends the resulting group signature to $\mathcal{A}$.

If $\mathcal{A}$ is successful then it outputs (i, σ, m, bsn, π) such that $i \in \mathcal{HU}$ and (gpk, i, m, bsn) was never queried to the Sign oracle. Assuming that π was produced using a sound proof system, σ is thus a valid signature opening to i, $\mathcal{R}$ can thus extract the witness $r_i \cdot a$ and output a.

Proof of Traceability. Let $\mathcal{A}$ be an adversary against the traceability. We construct a reduction $\mathcal{R}$ using $\mathcal{A}$ against q-SDH challenges, where q is the number of the dishonest users. Let $(G_1, [\theta]G_1, [\theta^2]G_1, \ldots, [\theta^q], G_2, [\theta]G_2)$ be a SDH challenge. $\mathcal{R}$ must output $(c, [\frac{1}{\theta+c}]G_1)$, for some $c \in \mathbb{Z}_p \setminus \{-\theta\}$.

Simulating parameters. $\mathcal{R}$ picks $k \xleftarrow{\$} [1, q]$ and $x_n, s_n \xleftarrow{\$} \mathbb{Z}_p^*$ for $n \in [1, q]$ (with distinct x_n). Let P, P_m and P_{m-} be the polynomials $P := \prod_{n=1}^{q}(X + x_n - x_k)$, $P_m := \prod_{\substack{n=1 \\ n \neq m}}^{q}(X + x_n - x_k)$, $P_{m-} := \prod_{\substack{n=1 \\ n \neq m, n \neq k}}^{q}(X + x_n - x_k)$. Thanks to the q-SDH challenge, $\mathcal{R}$ is able to compute $[P(\theta)]G_1$. $\mathcal{R}$ sets $W \leftarrow ([\theta]G_2) + [-x_k]G_2$, picks $\beta, \delta, \rho \xleftarrow{\$} \mathbb{Z}_p^*$ and computes $T \leftarrow [\delta]G_2$, $G_1' \leftarrow [\beta(\rho P(\theta) - s_k P_k(\theta))]G_1$ and $H \leftarrow [\beta P_k(\theta)]G_1$. $\mathcal{R}$ gives $\mathcal{A}$ $(p, \mathbb{G}_1, \mathbb{G}_2, \mathbb{G}_T, e, G_1', H, G_2)$ as parameters and W, T as keys.

Simulating Join *queries.* $\mathcal{R}$ maintains a counter n for the queries. $\mathcal{R}$ obtains y' from the extractable commitment and sets $A_n \leftarrow [\beta(\rho P_n(\theta) + P_{n-}(\theta)(y' + s_n - s_k))]G_1$. $(y' + s_n, A_n, x_n)$ is a valid certificate under W.

Probability to win. If $\mathcal{A}$ is successful then, through the forking Lemma ([21]), we extract a certificate (A_*, x_*, y_*) where y_* does not correspond to any existing user. We have: $A_* = [\frac{1}{\gamma+x_*}](G_1' + [s_*]H) = [\frac{1}{\theta - x_k + x_*}]([\beta(\rho P(\theta) - s_k P_k(\theta))]G_1 + [\beta y_* P_k(\theta)]G_1) = [\beta P_k(\theta)(\rho\theta + y_* - s_k)\frac{1}{\theta + x_* - x_k}]G_1$. Two cases (I) and (II) arise.

(I) $x_* \notin \{x_1, \ldots, x_q\}$. Let us see $\beta P_k(\theta)(\rho\theta + y_* - s_k)$ as a polynomial A in θ. The Euclidean division of A by $(\theta + x_* - x_k)$ gives Q and R such that $A(\theta) = (\theta + x_* - x_k) \cdot Q(\theta) + R(\theta)$. Since $(\theta + x_* - x_k)$ is of the form $X - (x_k - x_*)$, then $R(\theta) = A(x_k - x_*)$. $\mathcal{R}$ computes $C \leftarrow R(\theta) = A(x_k - x_*) = \left[\prod_{n=1, n \neq k}^{q}(x_n - x_*)\right](\rho(x_k - x_*) + y_* - s_k)$. Since $A_* = [\frac{C}{\theta + x_* - x_k} + Q(\theta)]G_1$, $\mathcal{R}$ can compute $[Q(\theta)]G_1$ from the SDH challenge. We have two cases. (i) If $(y_* - s_k) \neq \rho(x_* - x_k)$, then $C \neq 0$. $\mathcal{R}$ computes $g^{\frac{1}{\theta + x_* - x_k}} = (A_* \cdot g^{-Q(\theta)})^{\frac{1}{C}}$, sets $c \leftarrow x_* - x_k$, and returns $(c, g^{1/(\theta+c)})$ as SDH solution. (ii) If $(y_* - s_k) = \rho(x_* - x_k)$, then $\mathcal{R}$ aborts.

(II) $x_* \in \{x_1, \ldots, x_q\}$. We have two cases. (i) If $x_* \neq x_k$, then $\mathcal{R}$ aborts. (ii) If $x_* = x_k$, then : $[\frac{1}{s_k - y_*}]([s_k]A_* + [-y_*]A_k) = [\beta(P(\theta)(\rho(s_k - y_*))\frac{1}{s_k - y_*} - P_k(\theta)s_k)\frac{1}{\theta}]G_1$. The point is that P vanishes in 0, but not P_k. Then the division of $\beta(P(\theta)(\rho(s_k - y_*))\frac{1}{s_k - y_*} - P_k(\theta)s_k)$ by θ gives R and Q such that $C \leftarrow R(0) = -\beta s_k \prod_{\substack{n=1 \\ n \neq k}}^{q}(x_n - x_*)$ and $[\frac{1}{s_k - y_*}]([s_k]A_* + [-y_*]A_k) = [\frac{C}{\theta} + Q(\theta)]G_1$ where $C \neq 0$. $\mathcal{R}$ computes $[\frac{1}{\theta}]G_1 \leftarrow [\frac{1}{s_k - y_*}]([s_k]A_* + [-y_*]A_k) + [\frac{1}{C}][-Q(\theta)]G_1$, sets $c \leftarrow 0$ and returns $(0, [\frac{1}{\theta}]G_1)$ as SDH solution.

k is hidden from the adversary's view. So if $x_* \in \{x_1, \ldots, x_q\}$, then $x_* = x_k$ with probability $1/q$, and if $x_* \notin \{x_1, \ldots, x_q\}$, then $(y_* - s_k) = \rho(x_* - x_k)$ with probability at most $1/q$. Hence if $\mathcal{A}$ as advantage ϵ, $\mathcal{R}$ has advantage ϵ/q.

A Storage-Efficient and Robust Private Information Retrieval Scheme Allowing Few Servers

Daniel Augot[1,2], Françoise Levy-dit-Vehel[1,2,3], and Abdullatif Shikfa[4]

[1] INRIA, France
[2] Laboratoire d'informatique de l'École polytechnique, France
[3] ENSTA ParisTech/U2IS, France
[4] Alcatel-Lucent, France

Abstract. Since the concept of locally decodable codes was introduced by Katz and Trevisan in 2000 [11], it is well-known that information theoretically secure private information retrieval schemes can be built using locally decodable codes [15]. In this paper, we construct a Byzantine robust PIR scheme using the multiplicity codes introduced by Kopparty *et al.* [12]. Our main contributions are on the one hand to avoid full replication of the database on each server; this significantly reduces the global redundancy. On the other hand, to have a much lower locality in the PIR context than in the LDC context. This shows that there exists two different notions: LDC-locality and PIR-locality. This is made possible by exploiting geometric properties of multiplicity codes.

1 Introduction

Private information retrieval allows a user to privately retrieve a record of a database, in the sense that the database server does not know which record the user is asking for. The applications of this functionality are numerous. Imagine for instance doctors having to query a company-wide database storing medical for patients, or a police officer wanting to request financial data from the fiscal administration. In both cases, to respect privacy of the patient, or secrecy of the inquiry, it is desirable that the central administration does not know about the queries sent by these users (the doctor or the police officer). A private information retrieval protocol will allow these users to send their queries to the databases, without revealing what they are asking for (either the name of patient, or the name of the suspect under inquiry). Another example is an Internet user who wants to use cloud-based remote storage services, like DropBox, GoogleDrive, CloudMe, hubiC, etc, to store data, and retrieve portion of its data without revealing to these remote services anything about what he is after.

Related work. The problem of Private Information retrieval (PIR) was introduced in 1995 by Chor, Goldreich, Kushilevitz and Sudan [4]. A PIR protocol is a cryptographic protocol the purpose of which is to protect the privacy of

D. Gritzalis et al. (Eds.): CANS 2014, LNCS 8813, pp. 222–239, 2014.

a user accessing a public database via a server, in the sense that it makes it possible for a user to query a particular record of the database without revealing to the server which record he wants to retrieve. We here deal with *information theoretic* PIR, as opposed to *computationally secure* PIR [13]. In an *information theoretic* PIR setting, a server gets no information about the identity of the record of user interest even if it has unlimited computing power: the queries sent to the server must not be correlated to the actual record the user is looking for. In [4] it is shown that when accessing a database located on a single server, to completely guarantee the privacy of the user in an information theoretic sense, one needs to download the entire database, which results in a communication complexity of $O(N)$, N being the bit-size of the database. Thus scenarios have been introduced where the database is replicated across several, say ℓ, servers, and the proposed schemes have communication complexity $O(N^{1/\ell})$, for $\ell \geq 3$. Such multiple-server settings have been investigated since then, and the best communication complexity to date is $N^{O(1/(\log_2 \log_2 N))}$ for 3-server PIR protocols (from matching vector codes construction [14,6]) and $N^{O((\log_2 \log_2 \ell)/\ell \log_2 \ell)}$ for $\ell \geq 3$ [1] .

Beimel and Stahl [2,3] have proposed several robust information theoretic PIR protocols, based on polynomial interpolation, as well as on Shamir's secret sharing scheme. They have built a generic transformation from regular to robust PIR protocols that relies on perfect hash families. They also addressed the Byzantine setting. Recently, Devet, Goldberg and Heninger [5] proposed an Information-Theoretic PIR tolerating the maximum possible number of Byzantine servers. In all these previous proposals, the (encoded or not) database is fully replicated among the servers.

Our contribution. Our main concern is to reduce the global storage overhead. We achieve this by avoiding full replication of the database among the servers. We use multiplicity codes and exploit the geometry of $\mathbb{F}_q^m$ to partition the encoded database (codeword) of bit-size N into q shares of equal size, and distribute them among the servers (one share for one server). This way, we reduce the storage on each server from N bits down to N/q bits, q being the number of servers, while totally preserving the information theoretic security of the PIR protocol. Here $N = \log_2(q^{\sigma q^m}) = \sigma q^m \log_2 q$, with $\sigma = \binom{m+s-1}{m}$, and s is an auxiliary small integer (say $s \leq 6$) used in the construction of multiplicity codes. Given that the code has rate R, the storage overhead of our scheme is thus $\frac{1}{R}$ instead of $\frac{1}{R}\ell$ for schemes with full replication of the encoded database (as in the standard LDC to PIR reduction), ℓ being the number of servers ($\ell = q$ in our scheme). The number of servers is also drastically reduced, from $\sigma(q-1)$ to q, see Fig 3.

The communication complexity in bits (total number of bits sent by the user to all the servers as queries of our protocol) is $(m-1)q\sigma \log_2 q$, and the total number of bits answered by the servers is $q\sigma^2 \log_2 q$. Thus the communication complexity is $(m-1+\sigma)q\sigma \log_2 q$ bits. Putting $\ell = q$ the number of servers, and in contexts where s is small, say $s \leq 6$, this gives a communication complexity of $O(\ell(\log_2 N)^s)$.

Our protocol tolerates $\nu = \lfloor t \rfloor$ byzantine servers, $t = 1/2(q - 1 - d/s)$, d being the degree of the multiplicity code, in the sense that even if ν out of q servers always answer wrongly, then the database item can still be correctly recovered by the user. Thus our protocol is a ν-Byzantine robust PIR protocol. The property of being robust is a built-in feature of the decoding algorithms that are involved in the process of retrieving the database item.

Organization of the paper. In section 2 we recall the basics of locally decodable and self-correctable codes, private information retrieval schemes, and the link between the two notions; we also set the necessary material and notation to define multiplicity codes, namely Hasse derivatives. Section 3 describes the multiplicity codes [12] as a generalization of Reed Muller codes, and explains their local decoding. Section 4 contains our main ideas: we explain how we use multiplicity codes in a PIR scenario in such a way as to avoid full replication of the encoded database. We also explain how we achieve the Byzantine robustness property of our protocol. We end the paper by numerical tables showing the main features of the codes (rate, locality) for various parameter sizes.

2   Preliminaries

2.1   Locally Decodable and Locally Self-correctable Codes

A code in the ambient space is seen as an encoding map, which encodes a message of k symbols on an alphabet Δ into code-vectors, or *codewords* of n symbols on some alphabet Σ (possibly different from Δ). That is, it is a one-to-one map $C : \Delta^k \to \Sigma^n$. The decoding problem is to find codewords close enough to any element y in the ambient space (the "received word" in coding theory language). Formally, given a distance $d()$, code $C \subset \Sigma^n$, for a given $y = (y_1, \ldots, y_n) \in \Sigma^n$, one has to find one, some, or all codewords $c \in C$ such that $d(c, y)$ is small. In our setting, the distance $d(x, y)$ is the Hamming distance which is the number of indices i where $x_i \neq y_i$. A major concern is to build codes with small redundancy, or equivalently, large *rate*, where the rate is $(k \log |\Delta|)/(n \log |\Sigma|)$. In classical settings, $\Delta = \Sigma$, and the rate is simply k/n.

Locally decodable codes, in short LDCs, allow efficient sublinear time decoding. More precisely, an ℓ-query LDC allows to probabilistically recover any symbol of a message by looking at only $\ell \leq k$ randomly chosen coordinates of its - possibly corrupted - encoding. The major objective is to have $\ell \ll k$. Although LDCs appeared in the PCP literature in early 90's [15], their first formal definition is due to Katz and Trevisan in 2000 [11]. The number ℓ of queried symbols is the *query complexity*, that we also call here *locality*. Formally:

Definition 1. *A code* $C : \Delta^k \to \Sigma^n$ *is* (ℓ, δ)-*locally decodable if there exists a randomized decoding algorithm* $\mathcal{A}$ *such that*

1. *for any* message $x \in \Delta^k$ *and any* $y \in \Sigma^n$ *with* $d(C(x), y) < \delta n$, *we have, for all* $i \in [k]$, $\Pr[\mathcal{A}^y(i) = x_i] \geq \frac{2}{3}$,

2. $\mathcal{A}$ makes at most ℓ queries to y.

Here, and in the following, $\mathcal{A}^y$ means that $\mathcal{A}$ is given query access to y, and the probability is taken over all internal random coin tosses of $\mathcal{A}$. In the case when one wants to probabilistically recover *any* codeword symbol and not only information symbols, one has the following definition.

Definition 2. *A code* $C : \Delta^k \to \Sigma^n$ *is* (ℓ, δ)-*locally self-correctable* (LCC) *if there exists a randomized decoding algorithm* $\mathcal{A}$ *such that*

1. *for any codeword* $c \in \Sigma^n$ *and* $y \in \Sigma^n$ *with* $d(c, y) < \delta n$, *we have, for all* $i \in [k]$, $\Pr[\mathcal{A}^y(i) = c_i] \geq \frac{2}{3}$,
2. $\mathcal{A}$ *makes at most* ℓ *queries to* y.

When $\Delta = \Sigma = \mathbb{F}_q$, the finite field with q elements, and when the code is $\mathbb{F}_q$-linear, one can easily construct an LDC from a LCC [16]. No known constructions of LDCs or LCCs minimize both ℓ and the length n simultaneously. The oldest class of LDCs are the Reed-Muller codes over $\mathbb{F}_q$, whose codewords are the evaluations of m-variate polynomials of total degree at most d over $\mathbb{F}_q$ on all the points of $\mathbb{F}_q^m$. The main issues are thus to minimize one parameter given that the other one is fixed. With this respect, constructions of subexponential length codes with constant query complexity $\ell \geq 3$ exist [15]. On the other side, constant rate LDCs feature an ℓ which is known to lie between $\Omega(\log_2 k)$ and $\Theta(k^\epsilon)$, with explicit constructions for the latter bound. A major result is the construction of high-rate (i.e. $> 1/2$) locally self-correctable codes with sublinear query complexity, in the presence of a constant (as a function of the distance of the code) fraction of errors. Those codes are known as *Multiplicity Codes* and were introduced by Kopparty, Saraf and Yekhanin in 2011 [12]. They generalize the Reed-Muller codes by evaluating high degree multivariate polynomials as well as their partial derivatives up to some order s. Using high-degree polynomials improves on the rate, while evaluating their partial derivatives compensates for the loss in distance. Other LDC constructions achieving rate $> 1/2$ and query complexity n^ϵ are the one of Guo *et al.* [8] based on lifting affine-invariant codes (namely, Reed-Solomon codes), and the Expander codes of Hemenway *et al.* [10].

In this work, we use Multiplicity codes, but recall Reed-Muller codes and their local decoding for the sake of comprehension. These codes provide the simplest geometric setting for partitioning a codeword and laying it out on servers. We think such a partition can be done for other families of LDC codes, e.g. matching-vector codes, affine invariant codes and possibly Expander codes.

2.2 Private Information Retrieval Schemes

We model the database as a string x of length k over Δ. An ℓ-server PIR scheme involves ℓ servers $S_1, \ldots, S_\ell$, each holding the same database x, and a user who knows k and wants to retrieve some value x_i, $i \in [k]$, without revealing any information about i to the servers.

Definition 3 (Private Information Retrieval (PIR)). *An* ℓ-*server p-PIR protocol is a triple* $(\mathcal{Q}, \mathcal{A}, \mathcal{R})$ *of algorithms running as follows:*

1. *User obtains a random string s; then he invokes $\mathcal{Q}$ to generate an ℓ-tuple of queries $(q_1, \ldots, q_\ell) = \mathcal{Q}(i, s)$.*
2. *For $1 \leq j \leq \ell$, User sends q_j to server S_j;*
3. *Each S_j answers $a_j = \mathcal{A}(j, x, q_j)$ to User;*
4. *User recovers x_i by applying the reconstruction algorithm $\mathcal{R}(a_1, \ldots, a_\ell, i, s)$.*

Furthermore the protocol has the Correctness *property: for any $x \in \Delta^k$, $i \in [k]$, User recovers x_i with probability at least p; and the* Privacy *property: each server individually can obtain no information about i.*

The Privacy property can be obtained by requiring that for all $j \in [\ell]$, the distribution of the random variables $\mathcal{Q}(i, \cdot)_j$ are identical for all $i \in [k]$. Katz and Trevisan [11], introduced a notion very relevant in the context of locally decodable codes: that of *smooth codes*. The notion of smooth codes captures the idea that a decoder cannot read the same index too often, and implies that the distributions $\mathcal{Q}(i, \cdot)_j$ are close to uniform. All known examples are such that the distribution $\mathcal{Q}(i, \cdot)_j$ are actually uniform. Uniform distribution of the queries among codeword (or received word) coordinates is what is needed in the PIR setting in order to achieve information theoretic privacy of the queries. The locality as a core feature of LDCs, together with the fact that in all known constructions of LDCs the queries made by the local decoding algorithm $\mathcal{A}$ are uniformly distributed, make the application of LDCs to PIR schemes quite natural. Note also that conversely PIR schemes can be used to build LDCs with best asymptotic code-lengths [1,14,6]. The lemma below describes how it formally works.

Lemma 1 (Application of LDCs to PIR schemes). *Suppose there exists an ℓ-query locally decodable code $C : \Delta^k \to \Sigma^n$, in which each decoder's query is uniformly distributed over the set of codeword coordinates. Then there exists an ℓ-server 1-PIR protocol with $O(\ell(\log_2 n + \log_2 |\Sigma|))$ communication to access a database $x \in \Delta^k$.*

Proof. Given an LDC $C : \Delta^k \to \Sigma^n$ as in the lemma, one constructs the following PIR protocol. First, in a preprocessing step, for $1 \leq j \leq \ell$, server S_j encodes x with C. Then, to actually run the protocol, User tosses random coins and invokes the local decoding algorithm to determine the queries $(q_1, \ldots, q_\ell) \in [n]^\ell$ such that x_i can be computed from $\{C(x)_{q_j}\}_{1 \leq j \leq \ell}$. For $1 \leq j \leq \ell$, User sends $q_j \in [n]$ to server S_j, and each server S_j answers $C(x)_{q_j} \in \Sigma$. Finally, User applies the local decoding algorithm of C to recover x_i.

This protocol has the communication complexity claimed in the lemma. Furthermore, as the user applies the local decoding algorithm with non corrupted inputs $\{C(x)_{q_j}\}_{1 \leq j \leq \ell}$, he retrieves x_i with probability 1. Uniformity of the distribution of the decoder's queries over $[n]$ ensures the information-theoretic privacy of the protocol.

2.3 Hasse Derivative for Multivariate Polynomials

Notation Considering m indeterminates $X_1, \ldots, X_m$, and m positive integers $i_1, \ldots, i_m$, we use the short-hand notation

$$X = (X_1, \ldots, X_m) \qquad X^i = X_1^{i_1} \cdots X_m^{i_m}, \quad \mathbb{F}_q[X] = \mathbb{F}_q[X_1, \ldots, X_m]$$
$$i = (i_1, \ldots, i_m) \in \mathbb{N}^m \qquad |i| = i_1 + \cdots + i_m \qquad P = (p_1, \ldots, p_m) \in \mathbb{F}_q^m$$

i.e. we use bold symbols for vectors, points, etc, and standard symbols for uni-dimensional scalars, variables, etc. In general, we write polynomials $Q \in \mathbb{F}_q[X] = \mathbb{F}_q[X_1, \ldots, X_m]$ without parenthesis and without variables, and $Q(X)$ (resp. $Q(P)$) when the evaluation on indeterminates (resp. points) has to be specified. For $i, j \in \mathbb{N}^m$, $i \gg j$ means $i_t \geq j_t \forall 1 \leq t \leq m$.

Hasse derivative Given a multi-index i, and $F \in \mathbb{F}_q[X]$, the i-th Hasse derivative of F, denoted by $H(F, i)$, is the coefficient of Z^i in the polynomial $F(X + Z) \in \mathbb{F}_q[X, Z]$, where $Z = (Z_1, \ldots, Z_m)$. More specifically, let $F(X) = \sum_{j \gg 0} f_j X^j$, then

$$F(X + Z) = \sum_j f_j (X + Z)^j = \sum_i H(F, i)(X) Z^i,$$

where Z^i stands for $Z_1^{i_1} \cdots Z_m^{i_m}$, and

$$H(F, i)(X) = \sum_{j \gg i} f_j \binom{j}{i} X^{j-i} \quad \text{with} \quad \binom{j}{i} = \binom{j_1}{i_1} \cdots \binom{j_m}{i_m}.$$

Considering a vector $V \in \mathbb{F}_q^m \setminus \{0\}$, and a base point P, we consider the restriction of F to the line $D = \{P + tV : t \in \mathbb{F}_q\}$, which is a univariate polynomial that we denote by $F_{P,V}(T) = F(P + TV) \in \mathbb{F}_q[T]$. We have the following relations:

$$F_{P,V}(T) = \sum_j H(F, j)(P) V^j T^{|j|}, \tag{1}$$

$$\operatorname{coeff}(F_{P,V}, i) = \sum_{|j|=i} H(F, j)(P) V^j, \tag{2}$$

$$H(F_{P,V}, i)(\alpha) = \sum_{|j|=i} H(F, j)(P + \alpha V) V^j, \quad \text{for all } \alpha \in \mathbb{F}_q \tag{3}$$

3 Multiplicity Codes

3.1 Local Decoding of Reed-Muller Codes

We enumarte the finite field $\mathbb{F}_q$ with q elements as $\mathbb{F}_q = \{\alpha_0 = 0, \alpha_1, \ldots, \alpha_{q-1}\}$. We denote by $\mathbb{F}_q[X]_d$ the set of polynomials of degree less than or equal to d, which has dimension $k = \binom{m+d}{d}$. We enumerate all the points in $\mathbb{F}_q^m$:

$$\mathbb{F}_q^m = \{P_1, \ldots, P_n\} \tag{4}$$

where $P_i = (P_{i,1}, \ldots, P_{i,m}) \in \mathbb{F}_q^m$, is an m-tuple of $\mathbb{F}_q$-symbols, and $n = q^m$. We encode a polynomial F of degree $\leq d$ into a codeword c of length n using the evaluation map

$$
\begin{aligned}
\mathrm{ev} : \mathbb{F}_q[\boldsymbol{X}]_d &\to \mathbb{F}_q^n \\
F &\mapsto (F(\boldsymbol{P}_1), \ldots, F(\boldsymbol{P}_n))
\end{aligned}
$$

and the d-th order Reed-Muller code is $\mathrm{RM}_d = \{\mathrm{ev}(F) \mid F \in \mathbb{F}_q[\boldsymbol{X}]_d\}$. The evaluation map ev encodes k symbols into n symbols, and the rate is $R = k/n \in [0,1]$. A codeword $c \in RM_d$ can be indexed by integers as $c = (c_1, \ldots, c_n)$ or by points as $c = (c_{\boldsymbol{P}_1}, \ldots, c_{\boldsymbol{P}_n})$, where $c_i = c_{\boldsymbol{P}_i}$.

Assuming $d < q$, we now recall how RM_d achieves a locality of $\ell = q - 1$ as follows. Suppose that $c = \mathrm{ev}(F) \in \mathrm{RM}_d$ is a codeword, and that $c_j = c_{\boldsymbol{P}_j}$ is looked for. Then, the local decoding algorithm randomly picks a non-zero vector $\boldsymbol{V} \subset \mathbb{F}_q^m \setminus \{0\}$ and considers the line D of direction $\boldsymbol{V}$ passing through $\boldsymbol{P}_j$:

$$
\begin{aligned}
D &= \{\boldsymbol{P}_j + t \cdot \boldsymbol{V} \mid t \in \mathbb{F}_q\} = \{\boldsymbol{P}_j + 0 \cdot \boldsymbol{V}, \boldsymbol{P}_j + \alpha_1 \cdot \boldsymbol{V}, \ldots, \boldsymbol{P}_j + \alpha_{q-1} \cdot \boldsymbol{V}\} \\
&= \{\boldsymbol{R}_0 = \boldsymbol{P}_j, \ldots, \boldsymbol{R}_{q-1}\} \subset \mathbb{F}_q^m.
\end{aligned}
$$

Then, the points $\boldsymbol{R}_1, \ldots, \boldsymbol{R}_{q-1}$ are sent as queries, and the decoding algorithm receives the answer:

$$
(y_{\boldsymbol{R}_1}, \ldots, y_{\boldsymbol{R}_{q-1}}) \in \mathbb{F}_q^{q-1}.
$$

In case of no errors, $(y_{\boldsymbol{R}_1}, \ldots, y_{\boldsymbol{R}_{q-1}}) = (c_{\boldsymbol{R}_1}, \ldots, c_{\boldsymbol{R}_{q-1}})$. Now

$$
c_{\boldsymbol{R}_u} = F(\boldsymbol{P}_j + \alpha_u \cdot \boldsymbol{V}) = F_{\boldsymbol{P}, \boldsymbol{V}}(\alpha_u), \ u = 1, \ldots, q - 1,
$$

where

$$
F_{\boldsymbol{P}, \boldsymbol{V}} = F(\boldsymbol{P} + T \cdot \boldsymbol{V}) \in \mathbb{F}_q[T] \tag{5}
$$

is the restriction of F to the line D, which is a univariate polynomial of degree less than or equal to d. That is, $(c_{\boldsymbol{R}_1}, \ldots, c_{\boldsymbol{R}_{q-1}})$ belongs to a Reed-Solomon code RS_d of length $q-1$ and dimension $d+1$. In case of errors, $(y_{\boldsymbol{R}_1}, \ldots, y_{\boldsymbol{R}_{q-1}})$ is a noisy version of it. Using a decoding algorithm of RS_d, one can recover $F_{\boldsymbol{P}, \boldsymbol{V}}$, and then $c_{\boldsymbol{P}_j}$ is found as $c_{\boldsymbol{P}_j} = F_{\boldsymbol{P}, \boldsymbol{V}}(0)$.

The main drawback of these codes is the condition $d < q$, which imposes a dimension $k = \binom{d+m}{m} < \binom{q+m}{m} \sim q^m/m!$. For a fixed alphabet $\mathbb{F}_q$, the rate $R = k/q^m < 1/m!$ goes to zero very fast when the codes get longer.

3.2 Multiplicity Codes and Their Local Decoding

To obtain codes with higher rates, we need a derivation order $s > 0$ and an extended notion of evaluation. There are $\sigma = \binom{m+s-1}{m}$ Hasse derivatives $H(F, \boldsymbol{i})$ of a polynomial F for multi-indices $\boldsymbol{i}$ such that $|\boldsymbol{i}| < s$. Letting $\Sigma = \mathbb{F}_q^\sigma$, we generalize the evaluation map at a point $\boldsymbol{P}$:

$$
\begin{aligned}
\mathrm{ev}_{\boldsymbol{P}}^s : \mathbb{F}_q[\boldsymbol{X}] &\to \mathbb{F}_q^\sigma \\
F &\mapsto (H(F, \boldsymbol{v})(\boldsymbol{P}))|_{|\boldsymbol{v}|<s}
\end{aligned}
$$

and, given an enumeration of the points as in Eq. 4, the total evaluation rule is

$$\mathrm{ev}^s : \mathbb{F}_q[\boldsymbol{X}] \to \Sigma^n$$
$$F \mapsto \left(\mathrm{ev}^s_{\boldsymbol{P}_1}(F), \dots, \mathrm{ev}^s_{\boldsymbol{P}_n}(F)\right).$$

Given $y = \mathrm{ev}^s_{\boldsymbol{P}}(F) \in \Sigma$, we denote by y_v the coordinate of y corresponding to the v-th derivative of F. As in the case of classical Reed-Muller codes, we denote by $(c_1, \dots, c_n) = (c_{\boldsymbol{P}_1}, \dots, c_{\boldsymbol{P}_n}) = \mathrm{ev}^s(F)$, i.e. $c_i = c_{\boldsymbol{P}_i} = \mathrm{ev}^s_{\boldsymbol{P}_i}(F)$. We can consider $\mathbb{F}_q[\boldsymbol{X}]_d$, with $d < s(q-1)$ [12], and the corresponding code is

$$\mathrm{Mult}^s_d = \{\mathrm{ev}^s(F) \mid F \in \mathbb{F}_q[\boldsymbol{X}]_d\}.$$

Using the language of locally decodable codes, we have a code $\mathrm{Mult}^s_d : \Delta^k \to \Sigma^n$, with $\Delta = \mathbb{F}_q$, and $\Sigma = \mathbb{F}_q^\sigma$. The code Mult^s_d, is a $\mathbb{F}_q$-linear space, whose dimension over $\mathbb{F}_q$ is $k = \binom{m+d}{d}$. Its rate is $R = (\log_q |\mathbb{F}_q[\boldsymbol{X}]_d|)/(\log_q |\Sigma^n|) = k/(\sigma n) = \binom{m+d}{m}/\left(\binom{m+s-1}{m} \cdot q^m\right)$. Its minimum distance is (from Generalized Schwartz-Zippel Lemma) $q^m - \frac{d}{s}q^{m-1}$.

This family of codes has a locality of $(q-1)\sigma = (q-1)\binom{m+s-1}{m}$ queries. Here is how the local decoding algorithm works. Let j be the index of the point where we want to local decode, i.e. $c_j = c_{\boldsymbol{P}_j}$ is looked for. The algorithm randomly picks σ vectors $\boldsymbol{U}_i \in \mathbb{F}_q^m \setminus \{0\}$, $i = 1, \dots, \sigma$. For each $\boldsymbol{U}_i$, $i = 1, \dots, \sigma$, consider the line of direction $\boldsymbol{U}_i$ passing through $\boldsymbol{P}_j$:

$$D_i = \{\boldsymbol{P}_j + 0 \cdot \boldsymbol{U}_i, \boldsymbol{P}_j + \alpha_1 \cdot \boldsymbol{U}_i, \dots, \boldsymbol{P}_j + \alpha_{q-1} \cdot \boldsymbol{U}_i\}$$
$$= \{\boldsymbol{R}_{i,0} = \boldsymbol{P}_j, \boldsymbol{R}_{i,1}, \dots, \boldsymbol{R}_{i,q-1}\} \subset \mathbb{F}_q^m$$

For each i, $1 \le i \le \sigma$, the algorithm queries the received word at points $\boldsymbol{R}_{i,1}, \dots, \boldsymbol{R}_{i,q-1}$, and gets the answers

$$\left(y_{\boldsymbol{R}_{i,1}}, \dots, y_{\boldsymbol{R}_{i,q-1}}\right) \in \Sigma^{q-1},$$

thus a total of $(q-1)\sigma$ queries in $\mathbb{F}_q^m$, and $\sigma(q-1)$ answers from Σ. In case of no errors, we have

$$(y_{\boldsymbol{R}_{i,b}})_v = H(F, v)(\boldsymbol{R}_{i,b}), \quad b = 1, \dots, q-1,$$

where $(y_{\boldsymbol{R}_{i,b}})_v$ is the v-th coordinate of $y_{\boldsymbol{R}_{i,b}}$, and, using Eq. 3, we can compute

$$H(F_{\boldsymbol{P}_j, \boldsymbol{U}_i}, e)(\alpha_b) = \sum_{|v|=e} H(F, v)(\boldsymbol{R}_{i,b})\boldsymbol{U}_i^v \quad \begin{cases} 1 \le b \le q-1, \\ 0 \le e < s \end{cases} \tag{6}$$

Having the values $H(F_{\boldsymbol{P}_j, \boldsymbol{U}_i}, e)(\alpha_b)$, for $1 \le b \le q-1$ and $|v| < s$, we can then recover $F_{\boldsymbol{P}_j, \boldsymbol{U}_i}$ by Hermite interpolation. Next we solve, for the indeterminates $H(F, v)(\boldsymbol{P}_j)$, $|v| < s$, the linear system derived from Eq. 2:

$$\mathrm{coeff}(F_{\boldsymbol{P}_j, \boldsymbol{U}_i}, e) = \sum_{|v|=e} H(F, v)(\boldsymbol{P}_j)\boldsymbol{U}_i^v \quad \begin{cases} e = 0, \dots, s-1, \\ i = 1, \dots, \sigma, \end{cases}$$

and we output $\{H(F, v)(\boldsymbol{P}_j), |v| < s\} = \mathrm{ev}^s_{\boldsymbol{P}_j}(F)$.

In case of errors, for each direction U_i, we define a function $h_i : \mathbb{F}_q^* \to \mathbb{F}_q^{\{0,\dots,s-1\}}$, $\alpha_b \mapsto h_i(\alpha_b)$, such that

$$(h_i(\alpha_b))(e) = \sum_{|v|=e} (y_{R_{i,b}})_v U_i^v, \quad \begin{cases} 1 \le b \le q-1 \\ 0 \le e < s \end{cases} \tag{7}$$

By virtue of Eq. 6, note that $h_i(\alpha_b)(e)$ is the (erroneous) e-th Hasse derivative of F_{P_j,U_i} at α_b.

Having $h_i(\alpha_b)(e)$ for all $e \in \{0,\dots,s-1\}$ and all $b \in \{1,\dots,q-1\}$, F_{P_j,U_i} is recovered using a decoding algorithm of univariate multiplicity codes (see [12]), provided $d(\text{ev}^s(F_{P_j,U_i}), h_i) \le \frac{(q-1)-d/s}{2}$. Once we have recovered F_{P_j,U_i}, we solve for the indeterminates $H(F,v)(P_j)$, $|v| < s$, the linear system derived from Eq. 2:

$$\text{coeff}(F_{P_j,U_i}, e) = \sum_{|v|=e} H(F,v)(P_j)U_i^v \quad \begin{cases} t = 0,\dots,s-1, \\ i = 1,\dots\sigma \end{cases} \tag{8}$$

and we output $\{H(F,v)(P_j), |v| < s\} = \text{ev}_{P_j}^s(F)$. This local decoding algorithm is sketched in Alg 1. In case of more than $\frac{(q-1)-d/s}{2}$ errors in some directions, the linear system 8 may have erroneous equations. In this case, due to lack of space, we refer the reader to [12].

Algorithm 1. Local decoding algorithm for Multiplicity Codes

Require: Oracle Access to $y = (y_1,\dots,y_n)$, a noisy version of $c = \text{ev}^s(F) \in \text{Mult}_d$.
Input: $j \in [n]$, the index of the symbol c_j looked for in c
Output: $c_j = c_{P_j} = \text{ev}_{P_j}^s(F)$
1: Pick distinct σ non zero random vectors $U_1,\dots,U_\sigma$ giving σ different lines
2: **for** i=1 to σ **do**
3:     Consider the line

$$D_i = \{P_j + 0 \cdot U_i, P_j + \alpha_1 \cdot U_i, \dots, P_j + \alpha_{q-1} \cdot U_i\} = \{R_{i,0}, \dots, R_{i,q-1}\}$$

4:     Send $R_{i,1},\dots,R_{i,q-1}$, as queries,
5:     Receive the answers: $y_{R_{i,1}},\dots,y_{R_{i,q-1}}, y_{R_{i,b}} \in \mathbb{F}_q^\sigma$.
6:     Recover F_{P_j,U_i} from $(y_{R_{i,1}},\dots,y_{R_{i,q-1}})$ using a univariate decoding algorithm on the values $(h_i(\alpha_b))(e)$ defined in Eq. 7.
7: **end for**
8: Solve for the indeterminates $H(F,v)(P_j)$, $|v| < s$, the linear system 8.
9: **return** $\{H(F,v)(P_j), |v| < s\} = \text{ev}_{P_j}^s(F)$.

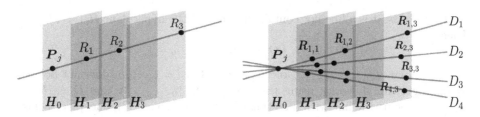

Fig. 1. Transversal lines for simple Reed-Muller codes (a), for Multiplicity Codes (b), assuming that the point P_j corresponding to query j lies on the H_0 hyperplane. Parameters are $q = 4$, $m = 3$, $s = 2$, $\sigma = 4$. Not all point names are displayed for readability.

4 Hyperplane Partitions and Their Use in PIRs

4.1 Affine Hyperplanes and Servers

Considering Mult_d^s, we show how to equally share a codeword

$$c = \text{ev}^s(f) = \left(\text{ev}_{P_1}^s(f), \ldots, \text{ev}_{P_n}^s(f) \right)$$

on $\ell = q$ servers, using the geometry of $\mathbb{F}_q^m$. This is done as follows: consider H a $\mathbb{F}_q$-linear subspace of $\mathbb{F}_q^m$ of dimension $m - 1$. It can be seen as the kernel of a linear map

$$f_H : \qquad \mathbb{F}_q^m \to \mathbb{F}_q$$
$$(x_1, \ldots, x_m) \mapsto h_1 x_1 + \cdots h_m x_m$$

for some $(h_1, \ldots, h_m) \in \mathbb{F}_q^m \setminus \{0\}$. Now $\mathbb{F}_q^m$ can be split as the disjoint union of affine hyperplanes $\mathbb{F}_q^m = H_0 \cup H_1 \cup \cdots \cup H_{q-1}$, where

$$H_i = \left\{ P \in \mathbb{F}_q^m \mid f_H(P) = \alpha_i \right\}, \quad i = 0, \ldots, q - 1.$$

As a simple example, consider the $\mathbb{F}_q$-linear hyperplane H of $\mathbb{F}_q^m$:

$$H = \{ P = (x_1, \ldots, x_m) \mid x_m = 0 \}.$$

Then we have $\mathbb{F}_q^m = H_0 \cup H_1 \cup \ldots H_{q-1}$ where

$$H_i = \left\{ P = (x_1, \ldots, x_m) \in \mathbb{F}_q^m \mid x_m = \alpha_i \right\}, \quad i = 0, \ldots, q - 1.$$

Up to a permutation of the indices, we can write any codeword $c = \left(c_{H_0} | \cdots | c_{H_{q-1}} \right)$, where

$$c_{H_i} = (\text{ev}_P^s(f))_{P \in H_i}, \quad i = 0 \ldots, q - 1.$$

Now consider an affine line, which is *transversal* to all the hyperplanes. It is a line which can be given by any direction $U \in \mathbb{F}_q^m \setminus \{0\}$ such that $f_H(U) \neq 0$, and which contains a point P:

$$D = \{ P + t \cdot U \mid t \in \mathbb{F}_q \}.$$

In other words, it is a line not contained in any of the hyperplane $H_0, \ldots, H_{q-1}$. Then,

$$D \cap H_j = \{Q_j\}, \quad j = 0, \ldots, q-1,$$

for some points $Q_0, \ldots, Q_{q-1}$. Now, as long as U_i, $i = 1, \ldots, \sigma$, does not belong to H, Algorithm 1 works, using the points $\{Q_{i,j}\}_{0 \le j \le q-1}$, where $D_i \cap H_j = \{Q_{i,j}\}$, D_i being the line with direction U_i passing through P_j, one query being a fake one (see section 4.2 below).

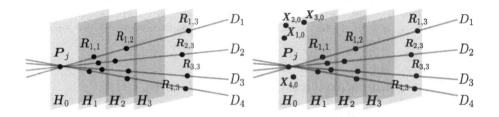

Fig. 2. Parameters are $q = 4$, $m = 3$, $s = 2$, $\sigma = 4$. Queries for a Multiplicity code used as an LDC codes (a), used in PIR scheme (b), assuming that the point P_j corresponding to query j lies on the H_0 hyperplane. In the PIR scheme, random points $X_{1,0}, \ldots, X_{4,0}$ are sent to the server S_0 to hide him the fact that he hosts the index of the request. Not all point names are displayed for readability.

4.2   Use in PIR Schemes

Given $\mathbb{F}_q^m = H_0 \cup H_1 \cup \ldots H_{q-1}$, the PIR scheme can be built by requiring that, for $i = 1, \ldots, q$, Server S_i is given c_{H_i} to store. Local decoding must be done using transversal lines. The user will first select σ transversal lines D_i, $i = 1, \ldots, \sigma$, which passes through the point P_j which corresponds to the requested symbol, and query each server S_i at the point $D \cap H_i$. In algorithms 1, 2, the main and only change is to make sure that all lines under consideration are indeed transversal to the chosen hyperplanes. We here explain how this works: the code requires $(q-1)$ queries along each line. In our context, when P_j is requested, all σ lines have to pass through P_j. For a direction U_i, the queries sent to the servers correspond to $q-1$ points on the line D_i defined by U_i, those points being all different from P_j. Assume for instance that $P_j = (x_1, \ldots, x_m)$ with $x_m = \alpha_u$, for some u. Query P_j must not be sent to server S_u who stores the c_{H_u} part of the encoded word: S_u would then know that it has the index of the requested coordinate among its possibly queried indices. A solution to this problem is to send σ fake (i.e. random) queries $X_{i,u}$, $i = 1, \ldots, \sigma$, to server S_u, see Fig 2. This is enough to obfuscate server S_u. See Algorithm 2.

Algorithm 2. PIR Protocol from transversal lines on hyperplanes

Preprocessing Phase: The user:

1: chooses q, m, d, s so that the original data x of bit-size k can be encoded using $\text{Mult}_d^s(q)$, i.e. parameters such that $\binom{m+d}{d} \log_2 q \geq k$;

2: encodes the data x into the codeword $c = \text{ev}^s(F)$, where the coefficients of F represent the original data x;

3: sends each server S_ℓ the c_{H_ℓ} part of the codeword.

Online Protocol: To recover $c_j = \text{ev}_{\boldsymbol{P}_j}^s(F)$ for an index $j \in [n]$, the user:

4: User selects σ distinct lines $D_i, 1 \leq i \leq \sigma$, transversal to the hyperplanes, and passing through $\boldsymbol{P}_j$;

5: Let ℓ_j be such that $D_i \cap H_{\ell_j} = \boldsymbol{P}_j$, $i = 1, \dots, \sigma$

6: For $1 \leq \ell \leq q, \ell \neq \ell_j$, user sends the queries $\{D_i \cap H_\ell = R_{i,\ell}\}_{1 \leq i \leq \sigma}$ to server ℓ.

7: User sends σ random queries $X_{i,\ell_j}, i = 1, \dots, \sigma$ to server S_{ℓ_j};

8: For $1 \leq \ell \leq q$, server sends the answers $\{y_{R_{i,\ell}}\}_{1 \leq i \leq \sigma}$. Answers $\{y_{R_{i,u}}\}_{1 \leq i \leq \sigma}$ are discarded by the user.

9: User then proceeds as in steps 5 to 8 of algorithm 1 to retrieve $\text{ev}_{\boldsymbol{P}_j}^s(F)$.

5   Analysis of the Protocol Given in Algorithm 2

5.1   Overall Storage Overhead

The natural reduction from locally decodable codes to information theoretically secure private information retrieval schemes leads to two overheads: the first one is $1/R$ where R is the rate of the code used for encoding the data, the second one is ℓ, where ℓ is the number of servers. The total overhead is thus $\ell \cdot 1/R$. Our scheme has an overhead of only $1/R$, which is the natural overhead of the code. With respect to the amount of storage required in each server for encoding k symbols, only k/Rq symbols are required per server. In particular, when $R \geq 1/q$, each server stores less than k symbols, which is the amount of information without redundancy.

5.2   Communication Complexity

We count the communication complexity in terms of the number of exchanged bits during the online protocol, discounting the preprocessing phase. The user has to send σ points to each server S_j, $j = 1, \dots, q$. A point consists in m coordinates in $\mathbb{F}_q$, but since it belongs to an hyperplane, it can be specified with $(m-1)$ coordinates, i.e. $(m-1) \log_2 q$ bits. Thus $\sigma(m-1) \log_2 q$ bits are sent to each server S_j, $1 \leq j \leq q$, for a total of $q\sigma(m-1) \log_2 q$. For his response, each server sends σ field elements for each of the σ points it receives in the query: σ^2 field elements, i.e. $\sigma^2 \log_2 q$ bits, and thus a total of $q\sigma^2 \log_2 q$ bits for all the servers. The overall communication complexity for the queries and the answers is $q\sigma(m-1) \log_2 q + q\sigma^2 \log_2 q = (m - 1 + \sigma)q\sigma \log_2 q = O(q\sigma^2 \log_2 q)$, since $m \leq \sigma$ as soon as $s > 1$.

Parameters					Locality		Storage overhead		Comm. complexity	
q	m	s	d	k	♯ queries	♯ servers	std	ours	std	ours
16	2	1	14	120	15	16	32	2.1	180	128
16	2	2	29	465	45	16	25	1.7	900	768
16	2	3	44	1035	90	16	22	1.5	2880	2688
16	2	4	59	1830	150	16	21	1.4	7200	7040
16	2	5	74	2850	225	16	20	1.3	15300	15360
16	2	6	89	4095	315	16	20	1.3	28980	29568
16	3	1	14	680	15	16	90	6.0	240	192
16	3	2	29	4960	60	16	50	3.3	1680	1536
16	3	3	44	16215	150	16	38	2.5	7800	7680
16	3	4	59	37820	300	16	32	2.2	27600	28160
16	3	5	74	73150	525	16	29	2.0	79800	82880
16	3	6	89	125580	840	16	27	1.8	198240	207872
16	4	1	14	3060	15	16	320	21	300	256
16	4	2	29	40920	75	16	120	8.0	2700	2560
16	4	3	44	194580	225	16	76	5.1	17100	17280
16	4	4	59	595665	525	16	58	3.9	81900	85120
16	4	5	74	1426425	1050	16	48	3.2	310800	327040
16	4	6	89	2919735	1890	16	42	2.8	982800	1040256
256	2	1	254	32640	255	256	510	2.0	6120	4096
256	2	2	509	130305	765	256	380	1.5	30600	24576
256	2	3	764	292995	1530	256	340	1.3	97920	86016
256	2	4	1019	520710	2550	256	320	1.3	244800	225280
256	2	5	1274	813450	3825	256	310	1.2	520200	491520
256	2	6	1529	1171215	5355	256	300	1.2	985320	946176
256	3	1	254	2796160	255	256	1500	6.0	8160	6144
256	3	2	509	22238720	1020	256	770	3.0	57120	49152
256	3	3	764	74909055	2550	256	570	2.2	265200	245760
256	3	4	1019	177388540	5100	256	480	1.9	938400	901120
256	3	5	1274	346258550	8925	256	430	1.7	2713200	2652160
256	3	6	1529	598100460	14280	256	400	1.6	6740160	6651904
256	4	1	254	180352320	255	256	6100	24	10200	8192
256	4	2	509	2852115840	1275	256	1900	7.5	91800	81920
256	4	3	764	14382538560	3825	256	1100	4.5	581400	552960
256	4	4	1019	45367119105	8925	256	840	3.3	2784600	2723840
256	4	5	1274	110629606725	17850	256	690	2.7	10567200	10465280
256	4	6	1529	229222001295	32130	256	600	2.4	33415200	33288192

Fig. 3. Properties of our scheme for $q = 16$ and $q = 256$. We have to distinguish LDC-locality (i.e. ♯ queries) and PIR-locality (i.e. ♯ servers), since they are not the same using our construction. The storage overhead is the global overhead among all the servers: in the standard case, using the standard LDC to PIR reduction as in Lemma 1, it is $(q-1)/R$; in our case, using partitioning on the servers, it is $1/R$, R being the rate of the code. Similarly the communication complexities (in bits) are shown. The degree d has been chosen to be $d = s(q-1) - 1$, the maximum possible value, with no correction capability.

5.3 PIR-Locality

Our construction leads to introduce the notion of "PIR-locality": when an LDC code admits a nice layout as multiplicity codes do, the number of servers can be smaller than the locality of the code. We call this the *PIR-locality*. Here the (LDC-)locality, i.e. the number of queries, is $(q-1)\sigma$, while the PIR-locality, i.e. the number of servers, is q. The tables show the obtained parameters for $q = 256$ and $q = 16$ in Fig. 3. We can see that the rate and LDC-locality of the code grow with s, while the PIR-locality is constant for a fixed q. The global storage overhead is much smaller, and the communication complexities are very similar.

5.4 Robustness of the Protocol

Algorithm 1 involves σ applications of decoding of univariate multiplicity codes of length $q - 1$. From [12], we can decode if the word $y_i = (y_{R_{i,1}}, \dots, y_{R_{i,q-1}})$ is t-far from a codeword $ev^s(F)$, for a polynomial $F \in \mathbb{F}_q[X_1]_d$, where $t = 1/2(q - 1 - d/s)$. The received word y_i corresponds to the answers of the $q - 1$ servers (all q servers except server u) for direction $\boldsymbol{U}_i$. Tolerating $\nu = \lfloor t \rfloor$ errors here means that ν servers can answer wrongly. Thus, following the terminology of Beimel and Stahl [3], our protocol is a ν-Byzantine robust protocol.

We sum up features of the protocol presented in Algorithm 2 in the following

Theorem 1. *Let q be a power of a prime, $m, s \in \mathbb{N}^*$, and d be an integer with $d < s(q-1)$. Set $\sigma = \binom{m+s-1}{m}$, with the constraint $\sigma \le (q^m - 1)/(q-1)$. Protocol from Algorithm 2 has:*

- *LDC-locality (i.e. number of queries) $\sigma(q-1)$;*
- *PIR-locality (i.e. number of servers) $\ell = q$;*
- *Communication complexity $(m - 1 + \sigma)q\sigma \log_2 q$ bits;*
- *Storage overhead $1/R$, where $R = \binom{m+d}{m}/(q^m \sigma)$ is the rate of the underlying multiplicity code;*
- *ν-Byzantine robustness, where $\nu = \lfloor 1/2(q - 1 - d/s) \rfloor$, in the sense that it can tolerate up to ν servers answering wrongly.*

6 Discussing Parameters

6.1 Impact of the Byzantine Robustness on the Storage Overhead

Expressing d in terms of t for a given s gives $d = (q - 1)s - 2st$, which then gives a rate, say R_t, to be compared with the rate R found for $d = s(q - 1) - 1$, when no error can be tolerated. For small m and $s(q - 1)$ large enough, we have a relative loss:

$$R_t/R = \frac{\binom{s(q-1)-2st+m}{m}/\sigma q^m}{\binom{s(q-1)+m-1}{m}/\sigma q^m} \approx \left(\frac{(q - 1 - 2t + m/s)}{(q - 1 + (m - 1)/s)} \right)^m$$

For $m = s = 1$, we find $(q - 2t)/(q - 1)$, which is almost the rate of the t-error correcting classical Reed-Solomon code. Otherwise, we get, for small t

$$R_t/R \approx \left(1 - \frac{2t - 1/s}{q - 1 + (m - 1)/s}\right)^m$$

For $t = 1$ or 2 and m small, the relative loss is not drastic. But, if t is large, say $(q - 1)/2$

$$R_t/R \approx (1/(sq))^m$$

and the loss is bigger.

6.2   Choice of q

We discuss how the size of q may be chosen independently of the size of entries on the database. Consider a simple database, which is a table, with E entries, each entry having S records, all of the same bit-size b. I.e. the total bit-size of the database is thus $N = E \cdot S \cdot b$. A multiplicity code of $\mathbb{F}_q$-dimension k enables to encode $k \log_2 q$ bits. Thus, to encode the whole database, we need $k \log_2 q \geq N = E \cdot S \cdot b$. If furthermore $a = b/\log_2 q$ is an integer, then, to recover a record of size b, the user needs to apply the PIR protocol a times. By definition of information theoretic PIR schemes, Protocol. 2 can be run any number of times, with no information leakage. This implies that q does not need to have a special relationship with the original data.

For instance, imagine a database of 90 000 IPV6 adresses. An IPV6 address consists in 128 bits addresses, i.e. 16 bytes. The database has $E = 90\,000$, $S = 1$, $b = 128$, and requires $90\,000 \cdot 16 = 144\,0000$ bytes of storage. We first design a PIR scheme using $q = 256 = 2^8$. Mapping a byte to an $\mathbb{F}_q$-symbol, we need a code of $\mathbb{F}_q$-dimension at least 144 000. From Table 3, using $m = 3$, $s = 1$, we find a code of $\mathbb{F}_q$-dimension 2796160 $\sim 2, 7 \cdot 10^6$, and expansion 6. The LDC-locality is 255, and its PIR-locality is 256. The communication cost is 6144 bits.

But we could also use $q_0 = 2^4 = 16$. Then 144 0000 bytes require $2 \cdot 144\,0000 = 2, 88 \cdot 10^6$ $\mathbb{F}_{q_0}$-symbols. From Table 3, with $m = 4$ and $s = 6$, we find a code of $\mathbb{F}_{q_0}$-dimension 2919735 $\sim 2.9 \cdot 10^6$, and expansion 2.8. Its LDC-locality is $(q_0 - 1)\binom{4+6-1}{4} = 15 \cdot 126 = 1890$ while its PIR-locality is 16. This is better in many aspects since less servers are needed, and a better rate is achieved. But the communication cost is now 1040256 bits.

7   Conclusion

Starting from multiplicity codes, we have designed a layout of the encoded data which leads to a new PIR scheme. It features a very small PIR-locality and much smaller global redundancy compared to PIR schemes naturally arising from LDCs, as well as Byzantine robustness. This layout is quite natural in the context of multiplicity codes. A straightforward question, to be investigated in a future work, is to construct layouts for other locally decodable codes, like affine-invariant codes [8] and matching vector codes [14,6]. This seems feasible due to the very multidimensional and geometric nature of these constructions.

References

1. Beimel, A., Ishai, Y., Kushilevitz, E., Raymond, J.-F.: Breaking the $n^{1/(2k-1)}$ barrier for information-theoretic private information retrieval. In: Chazelle, B. (ed.) The 43rd Annual IEEE Symposium on Foundations of Computer Science, 2002. Proceedings, vol. 59, pp. 261–270 (2002)
2. Beimel, A., Stahl, Y.: Robust Information-Theoretic Private Information Retrieval. In: Cimato, S., Galdi, C., Persiano, G. (eds.) SCN 2002. LNCS, vol. 2576, pp. 326–341. Springer, Heidelberg (2003)
3. Beimel, A., Stahl, Y.: Robust information-theoretic private information retrieval. J. Cryptology 20(3), 295–321 (2007)
4. Chor, B., Goldreich, O., Kushilevitz, E., Sudan, M.: Private information retrieval. Journal of the ACM 45(6), 965–981 (1998); Earlier version in FOCS 1995
5. Devet, C., Goldberg, I., Heninger, N.: Optimally robust private information retrieval. In: 21st USENIX Security Symposium, Security 2012, pp. 269–283. USENIX Association, Berkeley (2012)
6. Efremenko, K.: 3-query locally decodable codes of subexponential length. In: STOC 2009. Proceedings of the Forty-first Annual ACM Symposium on Theory of Computing, pp. 39–44. ACM (2009)
7. Gemmell, P., Sudan, M.: Highly resilient correctors for polynomials. Information Processing Letters 43(4), 169–174 (1992)
8. Guo, A., Kopparty, S., Sudan, M.: New affine-invariant codes from lifting. In: Proceedings of the 4th Conference on Innovations in Theoretical Computer Science, ITCS 2013, pp. 529–540. ACM, New York (2013)
9. Guruswami, V., Wang, C.: Linear-algebraic list decoding for variants of Reed–Solomon codes. IEEE Transactions on Information Theory 59(6), 3257–3268 (2013)
10. Hemenway, B., Ostrovsky, R., Wootters, M.: Local correctability of expander codes. CoRR, abs/1304.8129 (2013)
11. Katz, J., Trevisan, L.: On the efficiency of local decoding procedures for error-correcting codes. In: Yao, F., Luks, E. (eds.) Proceedings of the Thirty-Second Annual ACM Symposium on Theory of Computing, STOC 2000, pp. 80–86. ACM (2000)
12. Kopparty, S., Saraf, S., Yekhanin, S.: High-rate codes with sublinear-time decoding. In: Proceedings of the Forty-Third Annual ACM Symposium on Theory of Computing, STOC 2011, pp. 167–176. ACM, New York (2011)
13. Kushilevitz, E., Ostrovsky, R.: Replication is not needed: single database, computationally-private information retrieval. In: Proceedings of the 38th Annual Symposium on Foundations of Computer Science 1997, pp. 364–373 (October 1997)
14. Yekhanin, S.: Towards 3-query locally decodable codes of subexponential length. J. ACM 1, 1:1–1:16 (2008)
15. Yekhanin, S.: Locally Decodable Codes and Private Information Retrieval Schemes. In: Information Security and Cryptography. Springer (2010)
16. Yekhanin, S.: Locally Decodable Codes. Foundations and Trends in Theoretical Computer Science, vol. 6. NOW Publisher (2012)

A   Possible Ranges for d

In order the encoding function ev^s to be injective, it is sufficient to choose $d < sq$. Indeed:

$$\mathrm{ev}^s(f) = \mathrm{ev}^s(g) \Leftrightarrow \mathrm{ev}^s(f - g) = (0, \ldots, 0),$$

which means that $f - g$ admits sq^m zeroes, counting multiplicities. By Schwartz-Zippel lemma, we have:

$$\sum_{P \in \mathbb{F}_q^m} \mathrm{mult}(f - g, P) \le dq^{m-1}$$

that is here

$$sq^m \le dq^{m-1}$$

Thus, if we want $f - g$ to be identically zero, it suffices that $d < sq$.

Now during the decoding phase, in the case of errors, one has to perform Reed-Solomon with multiplicities decoding (indeed, σ Reed-Solomon applications of decoding). In this case, the length of the Reed-Solomon code is always $q - 1$ as we have $q - 1$ noisy evaluations of the original polynomial F on each line. In order such a Reed-Solomon code to realize proper (i.e. injective) encoding, we need $d < s(q - 1)$, as shown below.

$$\mathrm{ev}^s(f) = \mathrm{ev}^s(g) \Leftrightarrow \mathrm{ev}^s(f - g) = (0, \ldots, 0),$$

i.e. $f - g$ admits $s(q-1)$ zeroes, where here $\mathrm{ev}^s(f)$ is the encoding of a univariate degree $\le d$ polynomial $f \in \mathbb{F}_q[X]$ with a Reed-Solomon code of length $q - 1$ and multiplicity s. But a univariate polynomial cannot have more zeroes, counted with multiplicities, than its degree:

$$\sum_{P \in \mathbb{F}_q^*} \mathrm{mult}(f - g, P) \le d,$$

thus if we want $f - g$ to be identically zero, it suffices that $d < s(q - 1)$.

B   Decoding Univariate Multiplicity Codes

When the number m of variables is 1, then the codes lead to Reed-Solomon codes, also called derivative codes in [9]. We briefly recall how to decode these codes, using the so-called Berlekamp-Welch framework [7]. We consider univariate polynomials in $\mathbb{F}_q[X]$. For $s > 0$, we have $\Sigma = \mathbb{F}_q^s$, and the code is the set of codewords of length $n = q - 1$:

$$\{c = \mathrm{ev}^s(F) \mid F \in \mathbb{F}_q[X]_d\}.$$

Decoding up to distance t is, for a given vector $y \in \Sigma^n$, find all polynomials $F \in \mathbb{F}_q[X]_d$ such that

$$d_\Sigma(\mathrm{ev}^s(F), y) \le t$$

where d_Σ is the Hamming distance in Σ^n. We first look for two polynomials $N, E \in \mathbb{F}_q[X]$ of degree $(sn + d)/2$ and $(sn - d)/2$ respectively, as follows. Write the linear system of equations:

$$\begin{cases} N(\alpha_i) = E(\alpha_i) \cdot y_{i,0} \\ H(N, 1)(\alpha_i) = E(\alpha_i) y_{i,1} + H(E, 1)(\alpha_i) \cdot y_{i,0} \\ \quad\vdots \\ H(N, s-1)(\alpha_i) = \sum_{j=0}^{s-1} H(E, j)(\alpha_i) \cdot y_{i,s-1-j} \end{cases}$$

for $i = 1, \ldots, n$, where the indeterminates are the coefficients of N and E. This is a system of sn homogeneous linear equations in $(sn - d)/2 + 1 + (sn + d)/2 + 1 = sn + 2$ unknowns. Thus a non-zero solution (N, E) always exists. Given any solution, F can then be recovered as N/E.

Assuming that $t = (n - d/s)/2$, we can show the correctness of this algorithm: any univariate polynomial F of degree $\leq d$, such that $d_\Sigma(\mathrm{ev}^s(F), y) \leq t$ will satisfy $N - EF = 0$ where (N, E) is a solution of the above system. Indeed, for any α_u such that $\mathrm{ev}^s_{\alpha_u}(F) = y_u$, the system is satisfied at α_u, and hence the polynomial $N - EF$ has a zero of multiplicity s at α_u. Thus

$$\sum_{i=1,\ldots,n} \mathrm{mult}(N - EF, \alpha_i) > (n - t)s = (sn + d)/2.$$

But $\deg(N - EF) \leq \max\{(sn + d)/2, d + (sn - d)/2\} = (sn + d)/2$. Thus $N - EF$, having more zeroes than its degree, is identically zero.

Should Silence be Heard? Fair Rational Secret Sharing with Silent and Non-silent Players

Sourya Joyee De[1], Sushmita Ruj[2], and Asim K. Pal[1]

[1] Management Information Systems Group,
Indian Institute of Management Calcutta, India
[2] R.C. Bose Center for Cryptology and Security,
Indian Statistical Institute, Kolkata, India

Abstract. Parties in a rational secret sharing protocol may use mobile devices which are severely resource-constrained. Therefore, it may be in the interest of such parties to try to obtain the secret while spending as little as possible on communication and computation. This preference is different from a traditional rational player and is similar to *freeriding*. We call such players *'silent'*. The traditional rational player is represented as a *'non-silent'* player and we modify its preference to incorporate the fact that 1) it is indifferent between incurring a cost and not incurring a cost when everybody is able to reconstruct the secret and 2) it prefers that nobody obtains the secret over some players obtaining the secret free-of-cost while others incur a cost in reconstructing the secret. We thus introduce a *mixed-utility model* consisting of the utility of obtaining the secret and the cost of computation in order to obtain the secret. We propose new rational secret reconstruction protocols in the simultaneous channel model for both online and offline dealer scenario, that satisfy a new notion of fairness which we call *cost-aware complete fairness*, in the presence of both silent and non-silent players. Our protocol with the offline dealer makes use of a simplified version of the Boneh-Gentry-Waters [21] broadcast encryption scheme. Both types of parties find it to be in (Bayesian) computational Nash Equilibrium to follow our protocols and the protocols are ($\lceil \frac{t}{2} \rceil - 1$) resilient for non-silent players.

1 Introduction

Threshold secret sharing comprises the distribution of shares of a secret s among n players $P_1, \ldots, P_n$ such that at least t of these players must cooperate in order to reconstruct the secret from the shares they possess. By cooperation, we mean that at least t players must communicate their shares so that in the end, each player has at least t shares with them. An example of such a threshold secret sharing scheme is Shamir's scheme [10] that uses the concept of polynomial interpolation for generation and distribution of shares from the secret by a dealer and subsequent reconstruction of the secret by players. It is often considered that players that are 'good' or 'honest' cooperate to reconstruct the secret, while players that are 'bad' or malicious do not cooperate [6]. So, for successful reconstruction of the secret, at most, $n - t$ players may be 'bad'. However, since

D. Gritzalis et al. (Eds.): CANS 2014, LNCS 8813, pp. 240–255, 2014.

each 'good' party communicates its share, the 'bad' parties too receive these shares and are able to reconstruct the secret, even without actively participating in the reconstruction mechanism. Halpern and Teague [6] introduced the concept of rational players in threshold secret sharing. This area which came to be known as *rational secret sharing (RSS)* and its application in secure multi-party computation (known as *rational multi-party computation or RMPC*) has attracted a lot of fruitful research [1,2,4,8,11,12,13,17]. Rational players are neither 'good' nor 'bad' but simply utility maximizing. Each rational party wishes to learn the secret itself while allowing as few others as possible to learn the secret. So, rational parties are inherently selfish. In the presence of such players, Shamir's scheme fails because, during secret reconstruction, it is in Nash Equilibrium for each player to remain silent (instead of broadcasting its share). Since the behavior of rational players favor an unfair outcome, achieving 'fairness' is one of the central problems that rational secret reconstruction protocols need to address. RSS protocols suggest a strategy for accomplishing a fair outcome (where everybody gets the secret or nobody gets it) such that each player finds it to be in its best interest to follow this suggested strategy.

In existing rational secret sharing protocols, what happens if a player is silent but is still listening to the communication channel? If there are less than t players that communicate, then the secret cannot be reconstructed. Otherwise, since, in each round, the protocol requires the players to communicate their shares with all the other players, irrespective of whether they are silent or not, the player who remains silent is able to obtain the shares in each round. Along with the parties that communicated all the while, this player who remained silent throughout also comes to know the secret. The following example describes a practical scenario where a rational party may prefer to remain silent. In a standard rational secret sharing scenario, the costs incurred by each party include the cost of message transfer and the cost of computation in each round. Now, parties in a rational secret reconstruction mechanism may be using different types of devices such as PCs and mobile devices. A party using a mobile device is energy constrained. Apart from obtaining the secret, minimizing energy consumptions is also of interest to the party. It wants to perform as little computation and data transfer as possible. However it also wants to know the value of a secret that other parties may be reconstructing. For this to be possible, its strategy is to remain silent all the while and listen to all messages communicated by other parties. In this way, it minimizes its costs by not actively communicating or computing anything till all the shares of the actual secret are obtained. It only incurs the cost of downloading messages and cost for the final reconstruction of the secret. Prior protocols addressed only deviations that referred to remaining silent to obtain the secret alone. Our main focus is to eliminate silence resulting from the desire to obtain no cost.

Our Contributions. In this paper, we introduce a *mixed-utility model* consisting of the utility of obtaining the secret and cost of computation in order to obtain the secret. We propose new rational secret reconstruction protocols in the simultaneous channel model for both online and offline dealer scenario, that satisfies a new notion of fairness which we call *cost-aware complete fairness*, in the presence of both silent and non-silent players. The solution approach that we adopt is inspired by the approach of Asharov and Lindell [2] for achieving utility independence. Our protocol with the offline dealer makes use of a simplified version of the Boneh-Gentry-Waters [21] broadcast encryption scheme. Finally, we show that both types of parties find it to be in Bayesian Nash Equilibrium to follow our protocols and the protocols are ($\lceil \frac{t}{2} \rceil - 1$) resilient for both types of players.

Why should we bother at all about 'silent' rational parties? In rational secret reconstruction protocols, the reconstructed secret reaches all parties irrespective of their participation. So even though a player is active, it still prefers to remain silent and gets the secret. This is unfair because parties who have communicated during the protocol have incurred some cost. The others get the secret for free. The silence of an active party may even prevent the secret from being reconstructed which is again to the disadvantage of parties who communicate. This requires us to introduce the new notion of 'cost-aware complete fairness' in order to redefine the concept of 'fairness' for this new situation, with respect to cost of communicating as opposed to remaining silent. To ensure that such a party communicates, we must ensure that only parties that communicate during the reconstruction protocol get the secret. A protocol that takes care of the situation described above would inevitably cause the total cost of computation (i.e., the cost of computation of all parties taken together) to increase by making silent players incur some cost in order to obtain the secret. Although this may seem to be a disadvantage at first, we must remember that players in a rational setting are not concerned about the benefits of the whole group of players. Rather, each of them is selfish and maximizes its own utility. We would like to observe here that this situation is very similar to the classic example of the freerider problem, *"Tragedy of the Commons"* [5], where selfish behavior by individuals cause them to be worse off than if they had considered the interest of the group or community as a whole [3,9]. So even though the solution approach may lead to the overall increase in the cost, it should not be a concern to any of the non-silent players as long as each of them is able to reconstruct the secret while incurring an acceptable cost for preventing silent players from freeriding.

To successfully threaten silent parties that they would be thrown away from the protocol once they start remaining silent is a major challenge in our solution. Keeping track of parties remaining silent is another hurdle. In the online dealer case, we have achieved this by employing the dealer itself to keep track of the silent players and not to send them further shares once they start remaining silent. For offline dealer case, we achieve the same by using broadcast encryption.

1.1   Related Work

Halpern and Teague (2004) [6] first demonstrated how Shamir's secret sharing failed in the presence of rational parties and showed that a fair rational secret sharing protocol cannot be achieved if the secret revelation round is known to the parties beforehand. They proposed a (t, n) RSS protocol (with $n \geq 3$) that survives iterated deletion of weakly dominated strategies in the presence of an online dealer and with simultaneous broadcast channel. Improving on their work, Gordon and Katz (2006) [4], under similar assumptions about dealer and channel, proposed a protocol that works even for $n = 2$. In 2008, Kol and Naor [8], for the first time, discussed rational secret sharing in the non-simultaneous channel model and in the presence of an offline dealer. Henceforth, almost all works on rational secret sharing assume the dealer to be offline. As pointed out later by Asharov and Lindell (2010) [2], Kol and Naor's protocol is fair but not correct, since they assume that players prefer obtaining a fair outcome where all players prefer obtaining the correct secret rather than causing the other players to obtain an incorrect secret. Ong et al (2009) [13] proposed a two-round protocol for rational secret sharing in the presence of a minority of honest parties, in non-simultaneous channel and with offline dealer. In 2010, the work of Asharov and Lindell [2], introduced the concept of utility independence. One of the most significant results they arrived at was a fair (t, n) (where $n \geq 3$) RSS protocol, independent of any utility value in the simultaneous channel model. They were also the first to achieve both correctness and fairness in the non-simultaneous channel even when players may mislead others into believing in an incorrect value of the secret. They also proved the impossibility of achieving independence of the utility of misleading in the $(2, 2)$ case in non-simultaneous channel model and the impossibility of obtaining a fair reconstruction protocol in the presence of side information. However, future works such as [18] and [17] achieve these respectively. Fuchsbauer et al (2010) [12] demonstrated an interesting use of Verifiable Random Function (VRF) in non-simultaneous as well as point-to-point channel. They were also the first to propose an exact t-out-of-n RSS protocol in the point-to-point network. In 2010, Lysysanksaya and Segal [17] showed that it is possible to achieve fairness even in the presence of arbitrary auxiliary information using the Time Delayed Encryption scheme. De and Pal [18] (2013), use the result of [17] to show that it is possible to achieve both correctness and fairness with U^{NF}-independence in the non-simultaneous channel model. The earliest reference to 'different' rational behavior than expected by the mechanism designer in the literature appears in the work of Abraham et al [1]. They refer to agents who are 'altruists' and prefer more agents learning the secret contrary to the normal assumption of selfishness of rational agents. Specifically, they cite the example of peer-to-peer file sharing networks like Kazaa or Gnutella which work on the basis of cooperative behavior of participants rather than selfishness. Lysyanskaya and Triandopoulos [11] consider the presence of irrational adversaries and rational players for their general secure rational multi-party computation protocol. Groce et al. [20] consider rational adversaries while revisiting the Byzantine Agreement problem in the rational setting. They argue that it may be sometimes beneficial to consider that even adversaries, like other players, try to maximize their utility by moving towards their desired goal instead of just behaving arbitrarily, a worst-case scenario that is typically assumed in cryptography. Similarly, De and Pal [19], introduce the concept of rational adversary in the context of first and second price sealed bid auctions. Kol and Naor [8] briefly describe a strategy of a rational player who wants to obtain the secret alone, in which it communicates its share in the first round but remains silent in all the subsequent rounds. They argue that such strategies are not ruled out by the iterated admissibility solution concept used by Halpern and Teague [6].

In our work, the preferences of the silent and non-silent players are influenced by their utility of obtaining the secret and the cost of computation to obtain the secret. Some other works in the literature also consider this mixed utility model. In their work on privacy enhanced auctions with rational players, Miltersen et al. [15] discuss about privacy consciousness of rational players and propose a hybrid utility model which is a linear combination of monetary utility, i.e., the monetary gain related to participating in the auction and information utility, i.e., the utility related to maintaining privacy. On a similar note, De and Pal [19] also discuss about a hybrid utility consisting of auction utility and information utility in the context of the role of a rational adversary in auctions. Halpern and Pass [7] provide an interesting case where the utility of a player not only depends on the actions and types of players but also on the complexity of the chosen strategy. The complexity may be represented by cost in terms of running time or space etc.

Organization of the paper. In section 2, we introduce preliminary concepts of our work. In sections 3 and 4, we discuss the problem and various possible solution approaches respectively. We propose our protocols in section 5 and conclude in section 6.

2   Preliminaries

2.1   Preference of 'Silent' and 'Non-silent' Players

In this paper, we associate a cost incurred by each party to the mechanism and this cost can be denoted by $\overrightarrow{c((\Gamma, \overrightarrow{\sigma})_{t,n})} = (c_1, \ldots, c_n)$, where c_i is the cost incurred by party P_i and $c_i \geq 0$. We then define the utility function u_i of each party P_i defined over the set of possible outcomes of the game and the cost incurred by the players and are polynomial in the security parameter k. Thus, in this work, $U_i^{TN} = u_i(1^k, (o_i = s, o_{-i} = \bot), (c_i > 0, c_{-i} > 0)), U_i^{T_cT} = u_i(1^k, (o_i = s, o_{-i} = s), (c_i = 0, c_{-i} > 0))$ (where o_{-i} and c_{-i} refer to the outputs and costs respectively corresponding to the players P_{-i} other than P_i). T refers to obtaining the correct secret, N refers to not obtaining the secret and F refers to obtaining an incorrect value of the secret.

Table 1 represents different outcomes, costs incurred and utility of the parties corresponding to outcomes and incurred costs. There are other possible outcomes and utilities which we have not considered in this work. Players have their preferences based on the different possible outcomes of the secret reconstruction game. We shall refer to the following preferences of a party P_i throughout our work:

1. $\mathcal{R}'_1 : U^{TN} > U^{T_cT} = U^{TT} > U^{NN} > U^{TT_c} > U^{NT}$
2. $\mathcal{R}'_2 : U^{TN} > U^{T_cT} > U^{NN} > U^{TT} > U^{TT_c} > U^{NT}$

Table 1. Outcomes and Utilities for (t, n) rational secret reconstruction

Outcome P_i, (o_i)	of Outcome P_{-i}	of Cost incurred by P_i, (c_i)	Cost incurred by P_{-i}, (c_{-i})	Utility of P_i, $(U_i(o_i, o_{-i}))$	Utility of P_{-i}, $(U_{-i}(o_i, o_{-i}))$
$o_i = s$	$o_{-i} = s$	$c_i > 0$	$c_{-i} > 0$	U_i^{TT}	U_{-i}^{TT}
$o_i = \perp$	$o_{-i} = \perp$	$c_i > 0$	$c_{-i} > 0$	U_i^{NN}	U_{-i}^{NN}
$o_i = s$	$o_{-i} = \perp$	$c_i > 0$	$c_{-i} > 0$	U_i^{TN}	U_{-i}^{NT}
$o_i = \perp$	$o_{-i} = s$	$c_i > 0$	$c_{-i} > 0$	U_i^{NT}	U_{-i}^{TN}
$o_i = s$	$o_{-i} = s$	$c_i = 0$	$c_{-i} > 0$	$U_i^{T_cT}$	$U_{-i}^{TT_c}$
$o_i = s$	$o_{-i} = s$	$c_i > 0$	$c_{-i} = 0$	$U_i^{TT_c}$	$U_{-i}^{T_cT}$

We call a party having the preference $\mathcal{R}'_2$ a silent party and that having $\mathcal{R}'_1$ a non-silent party. We assume that silent and non-silent parties may be present in a secret reconstruction game simultaneously. Incurring any cost for obtaining the secret is a strict no-no for the silent player, unless incurring such cost will enable it to get the secret alone. However, existing rational secret reconstruction mechanisms already prevent one from obtaining the secret alone. Therefore, any behavior that allows the silent party to freeride (i.e., obtain the secret but not incur any cost, U^{T_cT}) is highly preferable. For non-silent players, on the other hand, the priority is to obtain the secret and for that they do not mind incurring a cost, given that others also incur a cost (i.e., not freeriding). Therefore, to such players, $U^{T_cT} = U^{TT}$. Neither silent nor non-silent players like others to freeride (i.e., the situation where $U^{NN} > U^{TT_c}$). When others freeride, the chances of obtaining the secret without incurring a cost reduces for a silent player. For a non-silent player, tolerating a freeriding player is synonymous to reducing the chance of reconstructing the secret because the number of communicating players may fall below t. We note here that we do not intend to model envy. Instead, we model the situations where 1) players who are willing to incur some costs in order to reconstruct the secret (or in other words to cooperate) do not tolerate players who freeride (i.e., silent players) and 2) players who freeride do not want others (i.e., other silent players) to freeride so as to keep intact the chances of being able to reconstruct the secret without incurring any cost. Both these situations reinforce the fact that both silent and non-silent players are inherently selfish.

2.2 Cost-Aware Complete Fairness in the Presence of Silent Players

Let $(\Gamma, \overrightarrow{\sigma})_{t,n}$ be a (t, n) rational secret reconstruction mechanism. Following previous convention [2], we define cost-aware complete fairness as follows:

Definition 1. *(Cost-aware Complete Fairness) A rational secret reconstruction mechanism $(\Gamma, \overrightarrow{\sigma})$ is said to be completely fair in the presence of silent and non-silent players if for every arbitrary alternative strategy σ'_i followed by party P_i, $i \in \{1, \ldots, n\}$ there exists a negligible function μ in the security parameter k such that the following hold:*

1. $Pr[o_i(\Gamma, (\sigma_i', \sigma_{-i})) = s] \leq Pr[o_{-i}(\Gamma, (\sigma_i', \sigma_{-i})) = s] + \mu(k)$ *and*

2. $Pr[o_i(\Gamma, (\sigma_i', \sigma_{-i})) = s | (o_{-i}(\Gamma, (\sigma_i', \sigma_{-i})) = s) \wedge (c_i(\Gamma, (\sigma_i', \sigma_{-i}))) < c_{-i}(\Gamma, (\sigma_i', \sigma_{-i}))] < \mu(k)$

The first condition implies that if a party with a deviating strategy obtains the secret, then a non-deviating party should also obtain the secret, except with negligible probability. On the other hand, the second condition implies that, the situation where a deviating player obtains the secret given that a non-deviating player has also obtained the secret and the deviating player incurs a cost less than the non-deviating player, occurs with negligible probability. Existing rational secret sharing protocols do not satisfy the notion of cost-aware complete fairness in the presence of silent and non-silent players. The preference of rational players as defined in existing works deals only with their utility of obtaining the secret, with respect to others. For example, a rational player in such works prefers to obtain the secret alone and that everybody obtains the secret over nobody obtaining it. In this work we introduce an additional component, the cost of computation. In Shamir's secret sharing scheme, a player would remain silent in order to obtain the secret alone. However, existing works in rational secret sharing, prevent such a deviation and enforce that either everybody gets the secret (when there are at least t communicating players) or nobody gets the secret (when there are less than t communicating players). However, the silent players that we define has an additional reason to remain silent: cost of computation. A silent player, by not communicating its share, either obtains the secret free of cost (when there are at least t communicating players) or denies everybody the secret (when there are less than t communicating players). In all existing protocols (assuming simultaneous or non-simultaneous broadcast or point-to-point channel) in rational secret sharing, players are supposed to stop sending out their shares as soon the number of shares received in the previous round falls below t. The effect of this is that, if there are less than t players who communicate, the secret is not reconstructed at all. However, this does not in any way stop a silent player (as we define) from being silent i.e. from deviating, because it prefers nobody obtaining the secret to everybody obtaining the secret after it incurs some cost. As an example, let us consider the t-out-of-n protocol using non-simultaneous broadcast channel proposed in [8]. In the presence of both silent and non-silent players, all silent players would get the secret in a round as long as the total number of communicating players is at least t. In the n-out-of-n point-to-point channel protocol proposed in [17], none of the players obtain the secret even if there is one silent player. In this case, all the players obtain a utility U^{NN}, but the silent player is strictly better off in comparison to the non-silent player because the main motive of the silent player, i.e., not incurring any cost is successful while the main motive of the non-silent player, i.e., obtaining the secret is not achieved.

2.3 Rational Secret Reconstruction with Silent Players as a Bayesian Game

Our problem of rational secret reconstruction in the presence of silent players can be represented as a Bayesian game or a game of incomplete information.

Definition 2. *(Bayesian Game [16]) A Bayesian game or a game with incomplete information $G = (\theta, S, \phi, u)$ consists of:*

1. *A set $\Theta = \Theta_1 \times \Theta_2 \ldots \times \Theta_n$, where Θ_i is the finite set of possible types for player P_i;*
2. *A set $S = S_1 \times S_2 \times \ldots \times S_n$, where S_i is the set of possible strategies for player P_i;*
3. *A joint probability distribution $\phi(\theta_1, \ldots, \theta_n)$ over types where $\phi(\theta_i) > 0$ for all $\theta_i \in \Theta_i$ for finite type space;*
4. *Utility functions $u_i : S \times \Theta \to \mathbb{R}$.*

In our rational secret reconstruction game, a player may have either preference $\mathcal{R}_1$ or preference $\mathcal{R}_2$. Each player knows its own preference but is not aware of the preference of the other players. Therefore, we refer to these preferences as types of the players such that $\Theta_i = \{\mathcal{R}_1, \mathcal{R}_2\}$. We can assume that each player has a prior belief that the other players' preferences are drawn uniformly from $\{\mathcal{R}_1, \mathcal{R}_2\}$. These prior beliefs are assumed to be common knowledge.

Definition 3. *(Bayesian Nash Equilibrium [16]) The suggested strategy $\overrightarrow{\sigma}$ in the mechanism $(\Gamma, \overrightarrow{\sigma})$ is a Bayesian Nash Equilibrium if for every player P_i, type θ_i and every strategy σ_i',*

$$\sum_{\theta_{-i} \in \Theta_{-i}} u_i(\sigma_i(\theta_i), \sigma_{-i}(\theta_{-i}), \theta_i, \theta_{-i})\phi(\theta_{-i}|\theta_i) \geq \sum_{\theta_{-i} \in \Theta_{-i}} u_i(\sigma_i'(\theta_i), \sigma_{-i}(\theta_{-i}), \theta_i, \theta_{-i})\phi(\theta_{-i}|\theta_i)$$

2.4 Collusion Resilience

In general (t, n) rational secret reconstruction protocols are $t - 1$ resilient, with a few exceptions. The completely utility-independent (t, n) rational secret reconstruction protocol suggested by Asharov and Lindell [2] is $\lceil \frac{t}{2} \rceil - 1$ resilient. The (t, n) rational secret sharing protocol proposed by Kol and Naor[8] is also susceptible to collusions between a long player and a short player. For the problem scenario that we address, there may be three types of collusion: 1) collusion among silent players; 2) collusion among non-silent players and 3) collusion between silent and non-silent players. Formally, a k-resilient equilibrium has been defined as follows:

Definition 4. *(k-resilient Equilibrium [1]) Given a non-empty set $C \subseteq N$, $\sigma_C \in S_C$ is a group best response for C to $\sigma_{-C} \in S_{-C}$ if, for all $\tau_C \in S_C$ and all $i \in C$, we have, $u_i(\sigma_C, \sigma_{-C}) \geq u_i(\tau_C, \sigma_{-C})$. A joint strategy $\overrightarrow{\sigma} \in S$ is a k-resilient equilibrium if for all $C \subseteq N$ with $|C| \leq k$, σ_C is a group best response for C to σ_{-C}. A strategy is strongly resilient if it is k resilient for all $k \leq n - 1$.*

3 Fair Rational Secret Sharing with Silent and Non-silent Players

3.1 Our Assumptions

In this work, we assume that silent players remain silent at all points of time, i.e., a silent player never becomes non-silent, or more specifically, does not change its preference to $\mathcal{R}_1'$. Moreover, which players are silent and which are not is not known beforehand. We also assume that parties do not know the number of players that may communicate in a secret reconstruction protocol. The channel between the dealer and each player is considered secure. Our protocols use simultaneous broadcast channel. By nature, a silent player does not want to incur any cost by communicating its shares. Even when it colludes with players like itself, it has to communicate in order to reconstruct the secret among those that collude. Thus, collusion among silent players for reconstructing the secret is not practical. However, the aim of colluding silent players may be to prevent communicating players from reconstructing the secret. In this work, we consider that the number of silent players is at most $\lceil \frac{t}{2} \rceil - 1$. Hence, in our protocols where the least secret reconstruction threshold that we use is $\lceil \frac{t}{2} \rceil$ whereas the required threshold is t (since it is a (t, n) secret reconstruction scheme where $n \geq 3$ and $2 < t \leq n$), no collusion of silent players can prevent communicating players from reconstructing the secret. In addition, we assume that silent and non-silent players do not collude with each other and that collusion takes place only among non-silent players.

3.2 Solution Concept

We assume that the exact number and identities of communicating parties is not known to any of the parties or to the dealer before the protocol execution begins. In the first round, shares of a secret are distributed to all parties supposed to take part in the secret sharing. In subsequent rounds, shares are only distributed to or exchanged among those that communicated in the previous round. If the dealer is online, then in each round with probability β, the dealer distributes the shares of the correct secret and with probability $1 - \beta$ it distributes the shares of a fake secret. If, on the other hand, the dealer is offline it simply sends a list of shares to all the players where the position of the shares of the actual secret in the list is chosen according to a geometric distribution $\mathcal{G}(\beta)$ with parameter β. In the online case, the dealer keeps track of the communicating parties in each round and sends shares only to those that communicated in the previous one. It also facilitates players to exchange their shares with only those that communicated in the previous round. In the offline case, the dealer does not have the opportunity to give out shares selectively, unlike the online case. So, each communicating player has the responsibility of exchanging its share only with those that communicated in the previous round. In both the cases, the first round requires at least t players to communicate, while in subsequent rounds it is sufficient if only $\lceil \frac{t}{2} \rceil$ players communicate. As usual [1,2,4,8,11,12,13,6,17], the dealer is assumed to be honest and signs all shares sent to the players.

In the first round, messages are sent to each party (since it is not known whether a party is active or not) while in the subsequent rounds communication occurs only among those parties which communicated in the previous round. If less than t messages are received by a party in the first round then the protocol is aborted. So, in the first round, silent parties get the chance to know how many communicating parties t^* are there. Due to the nature of their preferences, any silent party may wish to quit after this round 1) if it finds that $t^* \leq t - 1$ thus ensuring a utility of U^{NN} or 2) if it finds that $t^* \geq t$ ensuring a utility of U^{T_cT}. However, the tricks in our protocol are that 1) after the first round it is sufficient if $\lceil \frac{t}{2} \rceil$ parties communicate and 2) in any round (except the first), shares are distributed only to those parties that communicated in the previous round. The first clause ensures that the secret can be reconstructed even without any communication from the silent player beyond the first round. The second clause ensures that a silent player that does not communicate does not obtain the secret without any cost incurred. So in each round after the first one, if a player gets less than $\lceil \frac{t}{2} \rceil$ messages then it quits. Since the first round requires at least t players to communicate, it is a (t, n) secret reconstruction mechanism. In our solution approach, the following cases arise:

Case I: $t^* < t - 1$. In this case, secret reconstruction is anyway not possible, irrespective of whether the silent player communicates or not.

Case II: $t^* = t - 1$. Here, the utility of the silent player due to non-communication is U^{NN}. Although the silent player is able to reconstruct the secret in the first round, it is not the actual secret. Moreover, the other parties abort the protocol because each of them receive less than t shares. If the silent player communicated it would have obtained the secret and hence its utility would have been U^{TT}.

Case III: $t^* \geq t$. In this case, if the silent party does not communicate then it puts an end to all future scope of reconstructing the secret, because only parties that communicate in a particular round get the shares corresponding to the next round. Non-silent players have the incentive to communicate and reconstruct the secret whereas the silent player does not get it. So the utility of the silent player in this case becomes U^{NT}. On the other hand, if the silent player did communicate, then it would have received the reconstructed secret giving it the utility of U^{TT}.

Even in our approach, we observe that communication in the first round does not dominate non-communication. However, we have assumed that none of the players know the number of communicating parties in the protocol until the end of the first round. Now, suppose a silent player decides not to participate in the protocol. Let us also assume that with probability β' the number of communicating players $t^* = t - 1$, while with probability $(1 - \beta')$, the number of communicating players is $t^* \geq t$. Here, we do not consider $t^* < t - 1$ because in this case none of the parties can reconstruct the secret irrespective of whether silent players communicate or not. Then for communication in the first round to be beneficial for a silent player, the expected utility of communication must be greater than that of non-communication for each silent player P_i: $U_i^{TT} > \beta' U_i^{NN} + (1 - \beta') U_i^{NT}$ So the overall condition on β' is: $\beta' < \min_i \left(\frac{U_i^{TT} - U_i^{NT}}{U_i^{NN} - U_i^{NT}} \right)$ However, β' cannot be controlled by the protocol designer and hence is not a parameter of the protocol. We assume that the value of β' follows the above defined condition or in other words, our protocol works only if β' satisfies the above condition.

Choice of β. Since the protocol must be fair, so we must make an appropriate choice of β like previous rational secret sharing protocols. Reconstructions in rounds after the first round require only $\lceil \frac{t}{2} \rceil$ players. Suppose a non-silent party

P_j does not communicate in one of the rounds after the first. If this round is the revelation round, P_j only obtains a utility of U_j^{TT} instead of U_j^{TN} because there are extra players who communicate in this round. If this round is not the revelation round, then it obtains a utility of U_j^{NT} because the dealer will not distribute shares to it in any subsequent rounds and hence even when others obtain the secret, P_j will never be able to reconstruct the secret again. So, for non-silent players, β must satisfy the condition: $\beta U_j^{TT} + (1 - \beta)U_j^{NT} < U_j^{TT}$ Since for non-silent players $U_j^{TT} > U_j^{NT}$, the above condition is true for any value of β. Now, suppose a silent party P_i does not communicate in one of the rounds after the first. If this round is the revelation round, P_i only obtains a utility of $U_i^{T_cT}$ instead of U_i^{TN} because there are extra players who communicate in this round. If this round is not the revelation round, then it obtains a utility of U_i^{NT} because neither the dealer will distribute shares to it nor other players will send their shares to it in any subsequent rounds and hence even when others obtain the secret, P_i will never be able to reconstruct the secret again. So, for silent players, β must satisfy the condition: $\beta U_i^{T_cT} + (1 - \beta)U_i^{NT} < U_i^{TT}$ So we have, $\beta < \frac{U_i^{TT} - U_i^{NT}}{U_i^{T_cT} - U_i^{NT}}$. Therefore, the overall choice of β satisfies the condition: $\beta < \min_i \left(\frac{U_i^{TT} - U_i^{NT}}{U_i^{T_cT} - U_i^{NT}} \right)$. For the remaining rounds, we require the active parties to multicast their messages only to those parties that communicated in the first round. This can be achieved with the help of broadcast encryption technique when broadcast channel is being used.

4   Fair Rational Secret Sharing Protocols with Silent and Non-silent Players

4.1   Protocol with Online Dealer

Our approach is inspired by Asharov and Lindell's [2] completely utility independent protocol. The only difference is that, in our protocol, the online dealer has to keep track of the number and identities of parties that are participating in each round and should send shares of the secret to these parties only.

Protocol π_{s-RSS}^{online}

The Dealer's Protocol:

Input. The secret s to be shared using (t, n) threshold secret sharing.

Computation and Communication: In the ith round, the dealer does the following:

1. If this is the first round ($i = 1$), then the dealer chooses a random value r and generates (t, n) shares of $r \oplus s$ and distributes this share to all the n parties.

2. Else if the dealer had received an abort signal from the players at the end of the $(i - 1)$th round, then it aborts.

3. Otherwise, the dealer does the following:
   - It identifies the players who communicated in the $(i - 1)$th round from broadcast messages received from players. If the number of players that

communicated in the last round $n_{i-1} < \lceil \frac{t}{2} \rceil$, then abort. For each of these n_{i-1} identified players, the dealer does the following:

- It communicates a secret key sk_i.
- It then communicates a $(\lceil \frac{t}{2} \rceil, n)$ share $s_{i,j}$ of the actual value r with probability β or that of a fake value r^f with probability $(1 - \beta)$.

Output. The output for round i is a share $s_{i,j}$ and a secret key sk_i for a player P_j.

The Players' Protocol:

In the ith round, each player does the following:

1. Each player P_j computes $c_{i,j} \leftarrow Enc_{sk_i}(s_{i,j})$ and broadcasts this encrypted share simultaneously with other players.
2. If this is the first round ($i = 1$), then the player aborts if it has received less than t shares at the end of this round. Else, if $i > 1$, then the player aborts if it has received less than $\lceil \frac{t}{2} \rceil$ shares at the end of this round. Else the player continues to the next step.
3. On receiving sufficient encrypted shares from other players at the end of a round, each player first decrypts each of the encrypted share to obtain the share in plain-text as follows: $s_{i,j} \leftarrow Dec_{sk_i}(c_{i,j})$. It then reconstructs a value s_i from the shares obtained in this round.
   - If $i > 1$, the player computes $s' \leftarrow s_1 \oplus s_i$. If $i = 1$ then simply store s_1.
   - If $s' \in S$ (where S is the set of possible secrets), then the player aborts the protocol, informs the dealer and outputs s' as the correct secret. Otherwise continue with the next iteration.

Output. Each party outputs the secret s if it has been reconstructed. If the protocol aborts before the secret is obtained then, it outputs a default value.

Theorem 1. *Let $n \geq 3$ and $2 < t \leq n$ be integers. Then the proposed protocol π_{s-RSS}^{online} which is a prescribed strategy $\overrightarrow{\sigma}$ of the game $(\Gamma, \overrightarrow{\sigma})$ is a (Bayesian) computational Nash Equilibrium for both silent as well as non-silent parties for suitable value of β' and an appropriate choice of β. The protocol is also $(\lceil \frac{t}{2} \rceil - 1)$ resilient with respect to non-silent players.*

Proof. Since shares are signed by the honest dealer, players cannot send false shares undetected.

Case I: Silent Players. Let us trace the actions of a silent player P_i throughout the protocol. P_i **is not silent in the first round.** We have assumed that players do not know the number of communicating players beforehand. Suppose, P_i decides not to participate in the first round of the protocol. With probability β' we have $t^* = t - 1$ and with probability $(1 - \beta')$, we have $t^* \geq t$. Then the expected utility of the silent player in not participating is $\beta' U^{NN} + (1 - \beta') U^{NT}$ whereas that of participation is U^{TT}. Since, β' has been assumed to satisfy the condition $\beta' < \frac{U^{TT} - U^{NT}}{U^{NN} - U^{NT}}$, the expected utility of communicating is strictly greater than that of remaining silent. Therefore, P_i communicates in the first round of the protocol.

P_i **is not silent in the remaining rounds.** Since P_i has participated in the first round, it receives its share from the dealer and hence is capable of communicating this share in the next round. After the first round, the cooperation of only at least $\lceil \frac{t}{2} \rceil$ parties are required. Suppose P_i decides to remain silent. Now, if this is not the revelation round, then P_i does not learn the secret in this round and also forgoes all possibilities of learning the secret in future rounds. If this is the revelation round, then P_i learns the secret. But since the number of shares available is more than the threshold value of $\lceil \frac{t}{2} \rceil$, everybody who communicated in the previous round learns the secret. So the expected utility of P_i for remaining silent is $\beta U^{T_c T} + (1 - \beta) U^{NT}$. Now, suppose, P_i decides to communicate. Then it will be able to reconstruct the secret and hence gain a utility of U^{TT}. For our choice of β, for P_i, the utility of communicating is strictly greater than the expected utility of remaining silent. So P_i will also communicate in the rounds after the first round.

Case II: Non-silent Players. As we saw in case of previous RSS protocols, a non-silent player P_j is most interested in getting the secret alone. Since for P_j, $U^{TT} > U^{NN}$, it communicates in the first round irrespective of the number of communicating players. After the first round, the cooperation of only at least $\lceil \frac{t}{2} \rceil$ parties are required. Suppose P_j decides to remain silent. Now, if this is not the revelation round, then P_j does not learn the secret in this round and also forgoes all possibilities of learning the secret in future rounds. If this is the revelation round, then P_j learns the secret. But since the number of shares available is more than the threshold value of $\lceil \frac{t}{2} \rceil$, everybody who communicated in the previous round learns the secret. So the expected utility of P_j for remaining silent is $\beta U^{TT} + (1 - \beta) U^{NT}$. Now, suppose, P_j decides to communicate. Then it will be able to reconstruct the secret and gain a utility of U^{TT}. We observe that irrespective of the value of β, for P_j, the expected utility of communicating is strictly better than that of remaining silent because $U^{NT} < U^{TT}$.

For both types of players $U^{TT} > U^{TT_c}$. By sending shares to everybody, each of these players will enable other silent players to reconstruct the secret free of cost. On the other hand, communicating shares to only those that communicated in the previous rounds helps to eliminate players that take advantage by remaining silent. Moreover, even if a player communicates its shares to only a subset of players that communicated in the previous round, since the number of shares available is more than the threshold value of $\lceil \frac{t}{2} \rceil$, the remaining players still have enough shares and hence are not eliminated from the protocol. Hence it is in (Bayesian) computational Nash Equilibrium for both P_i and P_j to communicate shares to only those that communicated in the last round.

$(\lceil \frac{t}{2} \rceil - 1)$ **resilience.** Since in our protocol $r \oplus s$ is shared using $(\lceil \frac{t}{2} \rceil, n)$ Shamir's secret sharing scheme, it is impossible for any group of $(\lceil \frac{t}{2} \rceil - 1)$ players to reconstruct $r \oplus s$ and hence the secret s. So, our protocol is $(\lceil \frac{t}{2} \rceil - 1)$ resilient for non-silent players. ∎

4.2 Protocol with Offline Dealer

The offline dealer cannot keep track of the players who are participating in each round. It is not possible for it to distribute encryption/decryption keys selectively.

Protocol $\pi_{s-RSS}^{offline}$

The Dealer's Protocol: Let s be the secret to be shared using (t, n) threshold secret sharing.

Input. The secret s, number of players n and the threshold value t.

The dealer then proceeds through the following phases:

Key Set-up and Distribution Phase. In this phase, the dealer does the following:

1. Choose randomly the following:
   - $\alpha \in \mathbb{Z}_p$;
   - $r_1, r_2, \ldots, r_n \in \mathbb{Z}_p$;
   - $u_1, u_2, \ldots, u_n \in \mathbb{G}$

   (where p is a prime power and $\mathbb{G}$ is a bilinear group with generator g).
2. Define public parameters $PP = (e(g, g)^\alpha, u_1, u_2, \ldots, u_n)$.
3. Define the secret key for player P_i as follows:
   $K_i = (K_{i,1}, K_{i,2}, u_1^{r_i}, \ldots, u_{i-1}^{r_i}, u_{i+1}^{r_i}, \ldots, u_n^{r_i})$ with $K_{i,1} = g^\alpha u_i^{r_i}$, $K_{i,2} = g^{r_i}$.
4. Broadcast PP to all players.
5. Send secret key K_i to player P_i.

Share Generation and Distribution Phase. In this phase, the dealer does the following:

1. Choose randomly a value $r \in \{0, 1\}^{|s|}$.
2. Generate n shares r_i, $(i = 1, \ldots, n)$, of r using (t, n) Shamir's secret sharing scheme.
3. Generate $j^* \sim \mathcal{G}(\beta)$.
4. Generate n shares s_{i,j^*}, $(i = 1, \ldots, n)$, of $s_j = r \oplus s$ using $(\lceil \frac{t}{2} \rceil, n)$ Shamir's secret sharing scheme.
5. Generate d sets of fake values $s_{i,j}$, $(j = 1, \ldots, d; i = 1, \ldots, n)$.
6. Generate indicator bits b_j for each round $(j = 1, \ldots, d)$. Each indicator bit is supposed to indicate whether the last round was the revelation round.
   - If $j = j^*$, the dealer sets $b_{j+1} = 1$, else, $b_j = 0$.
   - Generate (t, n) shares $b_{i,j}$, $(i = 1, \ldots, n)$ of b_j.
7. Create n lists $list_i$, $(i = 1, \ldots, n)$ each containing the following:
   $(r_i, b_{i,1}), (s_{i,1}, b_{i,2}), \ldots, (s_{i,j^*}, b_{i,j^*}), \ldots, (s_{i,d+1}, b_{i,d+1})$.

Output. The dealer distributes the list $list_i$ and secret key K_i to player P_i and broadcasts public parameter PP to all players.

The Players' Protocol:

Input. The list $list_i$ for party P_i.

Communication Phase. Each player P_i does the following in round j:

1. Check the number of shares obtained in the last round, i.e., in round $j - 1$. Denote this by n_{j-1}. Also, note the identities of the players who communicated in the last round. Denote this by the set $\mathcal{S}_{j-1}$. Skip this round if $j = 1$.
   - If $j = 2$ and $n_{j-1} \geq t$, proceed, else abort.
   - Else, if $j > 2$ and $n_{j-1} \geq \lceil \frac{t}{2} \rceil$, proceed, else abort.
2. If $j = 1$, simply broadcast the first share in list $list_i$. Else, if $j > 1$, do the following:
   - Compute function $F(\mathcal{S}_{j-1}) = \prod_{i \in \mathcal{S}_{j-1}} u_i$.

- Choose a random number $s_{ran} \in \mathbb{Z}_p$.
- Then compute $C_{j,1} = Me(g,g)^{\alpha s_{ran}}$ (where $M = s_{i,j}||b_{i,j}$, the current share of the secret in the list $list_i$), $C_{j,2} = g^{s_{ran}}$ and $C_{j,3} = F(\mathcal{S}_{j-1})^{s_{ran}}$.
- Broadcast the ciphertext $C_j = (C_{j,1}, C_{j,2}, C_{j,3})$ to all players.

Reconstruction Phase. Each player P_i does the following in round j:

1. If $j = 1$, reconstruct the value r from t shares obtained in this round.
2. If $j > 1$, do the following for the encrypted share received from each player P_{-i}:
   - Decrypt the share as follows:
     - Divide $e(K_{i,2}, C_{j,3}) = e(g, \prod_{l \in S_{j-1}} u_l)^{r_i s_{ran}}$ by
       $e(\prod_{l \in S_{j-1}} u_l^{r_i}, C_2) = e(g, \prod_{l \in S_{j-1}} u_l)^{r_i s_{ran}}$ This can be used to divide $e(K_{i,1}, C_{j,2}) = e(g,g)^{\alpha s_{ran}} e(g, u_i)^{r_i s_{ran}}$ to get the blinding factor $e(g,g)^{\alpha s_{ran}}$.
     - Remove the blinding factor $e(g,g)^{\alpha s_{ran}}$ from $C_{j,1}$ to get $M = s_{-i,j}||b_{-i,j}$.
   - Reconstruct the current share as follows:
     - Reconstruct the secret s_j and the indicator bit b_j from all the decrypted shares.
3. If $b_j = 0$, then continue. Else if $b_j = 1$, then compute $s = s_{j-1} \oplus r$ and output s as the secret.

Output. Output the secret s.

Theorem 2. *Let $n \geq 3$ and $2 < t \leq n$ be integers. Then the proposed protocol $\pi_{s-RSS}^{offline}$ which is a prescribed strategy $\overrightarrow{\sigma}$ of the game $(\Gamma, \overrightarrow{\sigma})$ is a (Bayesian) computational Nash Equilibrium for both silent as well as non-silent parties for suitable value of β' and an appropriate choice of β. The protocol is also $(\lceil \frac{t}{2} \rceil - 1)$ resilient with respect to non-silent players.*

Proof. The only difference between protocol $\pi_{s-RSS}^{offline}$ and π_{s-RSS}^{online} is that in the first case the dealer is offline and cannot keep track of which players are communicating in each round. In both cases however, players may try to choose a deviating strategy where they give out the shares to only to a particular set of players or none at all. We already proved for π_{s-RSS}^{online} that even though such deviating strategies exist, players will have no incentive to follow them. Players do not get any extra advantage due to the offline dealer. Hence, it is in (Bayesian) computational Nash Equilibrium for players to follow $\pi_{s-RSS}^{offline}$ and that this protocol is $(\lceil \frac{t}{2} \rceil - 1)$ resilient with respect to non-silent players. ∎

Acknowledgements. We thank the anonymous reviewers for their insightful comments and suggestions. This work is partially supported by DRDO sponsored project Centre of Excellence in Cryptology (CoEC), under MOC ERIP/ER/1009002/M/01/1319/788/D (R&D) of ER&IPR, DRDO.

References

1. Abraham, I., Dolev, D., Gonen, R., Halpern, J.: Distributed computing meets game theory: robust mechanisms for rational secret sharing and multiparty computation. In: Proceedings of the 25th Annual ACM Symposium on Principles of Distributed Computing, pp. 53–62. ACM (2006)

2. Asharov, G., Lindell, Y.: Utility Dependence in Correct and Fair Rational Secret Sharing. Journal of Cryptology 24(1), 157–202 (2010)
3. Albanese, R., Van Fleet, D.D.: Rational behavior in groups: The free-riding tendency. Academy of Management Review 10(2), 244–255 (1985)
4. Gordon, S.D., Katz, J.: Rational Secret Sharing, Revisited. In: De Prisco, R., Yung, M. (eds.) SCN 2006. LNCS, vol. 4116, pp. 229–241. Springer, Heidelberg (2006)
5. Harding, G.: The tragedy of the commons. Science 162(3859), 1243–1248 (1968)
6. Halpern, J., Teague, V.: Rational secret sharing and multiparty computation: extended abstract. In: Proceedings of the 36th Annual ACM Symposium on Theory of Computing, pp. 623–632. ACM (2004)
7. Halpern, J.Y., Pass, R.: Algorithmic rationality: Game theory with costly computation. Journal of Economic Theory (2014)
8. Kol, G., Naor, M.: Games for exchanging information. In: Proceedings of the 40th Annual ACM Symposium on Theory of Computing, pp. 423–432. ACM (2008)
9. Stroebe, W., Frey, B.S.: Self-interest and collective action:The economics and psychology of public goods. British Journal of Social Psychology 21(2), 121–137 (1982)
10. Shamir, A.: How to share a secret. Communications of the ACM 22(11), 612–613 (1979)
11. Lysyanskaya, A., Triandopoulos, N.: Rationality and Adversarial Behavior in Multi-party Computation. In: Dwork, C. (ed.) CRYPTO 2006. LNCS, vol. 4117, pp. 180–197. Springer, Heidelberg (2006)
12. Fuchsbauer, G., Katz, J., Naccache, D.: Efficient Rational Secret Sharing in Standard Communication Networks. In: Micciancio, D. (ed.) TCC 2010. LNCS, vol. 5978, pp. 419–436. Springer, Heidelberg (2010)
13. Ong, S.J., Parkes, D.C., Rosen, A., Vadhan, S.: Fairness with an Honest Minority and a Rational Majority. In: Reingold, O. (ed.) TCC 2009. LNCS, vol. 5444, pp. 36–53. Springer, Heidelberg (2009)
14. Kol, G., Naor, M.: Cryptography and Game Theory: Designing Protocols for Exchanging Information. In: Canetti, R. (ed.) TCC 2008. LNCS, vol. 4948, pp. 320–339. Springer, Heidelberg (2008)
15. Miltersen, P.B., Nielsen, J.B., Triandopoulos, N.: Privacy-enhancing auctions using rational cryptography. In: Halevi, S. (ed.) CRYPTO 2009. LNCS, vol. 5677, pp. 541–558. Springer, Heidelberg (2009)
16. Osborne, M., Rubinstein, A.: A Course in Game Theory. MIT, Cambridge (2004)
17. Lysyanskaya, A., Segal, A.: Rational Secret Sharing with Side Information in Point-to-Point Networks via Time Delayed Encryption.IACR Cryptology ePrint Archive:Report2010/540 (2010)
18. De, S.J., Pal, A.K.: Achieving Correctness in Fair Rational Secret Sharing. In: Abdalla, M., Nita-Rotaru, C., Dahab, R. (eds.) CANS 2013. LNCS, vol. 8257, pp. 139–161. Springer, Heidelberg (2013)
19. De, S.J., Pal, A.K.: Auctions with Rational Adversary. In: Bagchi, A., Ray, I. (eds.) ICISS 2013. LNCS, vol. 8303, pp. 91–105. Springer, Heidelberg (2013)
20. Groce, A., Katz, J., Thiruvengadam, A., Zikas, V.: Byzantine agreement with a rational adversary. In: Czumaj, A., Mehlhorn, K., Pitts, A., Wattenhofer, R. (eds.) ICALP 2012, Part II. LNCS, vol. 7392, pp. 561–572. Springer, Heidelberg (2012)
21. Boneh, D., Gentry, C., Waters, B.: Collusion resistant broadcast encryption with short ciphertexts and private keys. In: Shoup, V. (ed.) CRYPTO 2005. LNCS, vol. 3621, pp. 258–275. Springer, Heidelberg (2005)

Attribute-Based Signatures
with User-Controlled Linkability

Ali El Kaafarani[1,*], Liqun Chen[2], Essam Ghadafi[3], and James Davenport[1]

[1] University of Bath, UK
[2] HP Laboratories, Bristol, UK
[3] University of Bristol, UK

Abstract. In this paper, we introduce Attribute-Based Signatures with User-Controlled Linkability (ABS-UCL). Attribute-based signatures allow a signer who has enough credentials/attributes to anonymously sign a message w.r.t. some public policy revealing neither the attributes used nor his identity. User-controlled linkability is a new feature which allows a user to make some of his signatures directed at the same recipient linkable while still retaining anonymity. Such a feature is useful for many real-life applications. We give a general framework for constructing ABS-UCL and present an efficient instantiation of the construction that supports multiple attribute authorities.

Keywords. Attribute-based signatures, security definitions, user-controlled linkability.

1 Introduction

Attribute-based cryptography can play a tremendous role in providing security to cloud computing, whether for privacy/access control (encryption) or for authentication (signatures). Attribute-based encryption [21,35] is a *natural* generalization of Identity-Based Encryption (IBE) [34,9,13] and its subsequent fuzzy variant [35] in the sense that it enables fine-grained control of access to encrypted data.

Attribute-Based Signatures (ABS) [27] allow a signer owning a set of attributes to sign messages w.r.t. any public access policy satisfied by his attributes revealing neither his identity nor the set of attributes used in the signing. Attribute-based signatures proved to be a powerful primitive and many existing signature-related notions such as ring signatures [33] and group signatures [10] could be viewed as special cases of attribute-based signatures. For a comparison with other primitives, we refer to [30]. The authors in [30] also showed many application of ABS including attribute-based messaging [8], trust negotiation [17] and leaking secrets.

Some constructions of ABS consider multiple authorities while others only support a single attribute authority. Okamoto et al. [32] and El Kaafarani et al.

---

* This work was done while at HP Labs, Bristol, UK.

D. Gritzalis et al. (Eds.): CANS 2014, LNCS 8813, pp. 256–269, 2014.

[14] provide the first schemes working in a decentralized fashion, where multiple attribute authorities are involved in the scheme, with no reliance on a central authority. To add accountability to attribute-based signatures, [25,15,14,20] grant a designated tracing authority the power to revoke anonymity and reveal the identity of the signer in the case of a dispute. [20] strengthen the security notions of [14] but at the expense of having a public key infrastructure. Direct Anonymous Attestation (DAA) [5,3] adds a new interesting feature, namely, the *user-controlled linkability* (UCL). This is a lightweight solution that avoids having a designated tracing authority, which had previously represented a bottleneck to users' privacy. In addition, it allows the user to opt to make some of his signatures directed at the same verifier linkable without sacrificing anonymity. Unlike the reliance on tracing authorities, which are generally thought of as "for trouble-shooting", UCL is intended to be built into normal use. For example, in the world of attributes, assume that a signer wants to establish a session (in a analogous way to the idea of cookies) with a recipient and maintain this session in a convincing way that he is indeed the same person whom the recipient is communicating with, not someone else who also has enough credentials to satisfy the same policy in question; the tracing authority cannot help here, whereas user-controlled linkability is an ideal functionality for such a scenario.

Existing ABS schemes differ from each other by the expressiveness of the policies they support. For instance, we have constructions supporting non-monotonic policies, e.g. [31,15], and those supporting monotonic policies, e.g. [30], both with signatures' size linear in the length of the policy. There are also constructions supporting threshold policies, e.g. [36,26,23,18], where some of them yield constant-size signatures.

Contribution. We provide security definitions and a general framework for constructing attribute-based signatures with user-controlled linkability. Instantiations of the tools used in our generic construction exist in both the random oracle [1] and the standard models. For efficiency reasons, we provide an instantiation in the random oracle model.

Paper Organization. In Section 2, we define the notion of ABS-UCL, giving its syntax along with the security definitions. In Section 3, we give the cryptographic building blocks needed for ABS-UCL. We present our general framework in Section 4, whereas in Section 5, we give a concrete construction of ABS-UCL along with the security analysis. We conclude the paper by comparing our notion to other notions in Section 6.

2 Definition and Security of ABS-UCL

In this section, we define the notion of Attribute-Based Signatures with User-Controlled Linkability (ABS-UCL), and present its security requirements. Our notion supports multiple attribute authorities, each responsible for a subset of attributes.

2.1 Syntax of ABS-UCL

In an ABS-UCL scheme, we have a set $\mathbb{AA} = \{AA_i\}_{i=1}^n$ of attribute authorities, where $\mathbb{A}_i$ is the space of attributes managed by attribute authority AA_i. The universe of attributes is defined as $\mathbb{A} = \bigcup_{i=1}^n \mathbb{A}_i$. Assume that $\mathcal{A} \subset \mathbb{A}$ is a set of attributes for which a certain predicate Ω is satisfied, i.e. $\Omega(\mathcal{A}) = 1$. We have, $a \in \mathcal{A} \Rightarrow \exists \mathbb{A}_i$, s.t. $a \in \mathbb{A}_i$, so attribute a is managed by attribute authority AA_i. Below are the definitions of the algorithms used in an ABS-UCL scheme, where all algorithms (bar the first three) take as implicit input pp produced by Setup.

- Setup(1^λ): On input a security parameter, it returns public parameters pp.
- AASetup(aid, pp): Is run locally by attribute authority AA_{aid} to generate its public/secret key pair (vk_{AA}, sk_{AA}). The authority publishes vk_{AA} and keeps sk_{AA} secret.
- UKeyGen(id, pp): Is run by user id to generate his personal secret key sk_{id}.
- AttKeyGen(id, $f(sk_{id})$, a, sk_{AA}): Is run by attribute authority AA that is responsible for the attribute a, where f is an injective one-way function, it gives the user id the secret key $sk_{id,a}$, bound to his identity id and $f(sk_{id})$.
- Sign(m, Ω, sk_{id}, $sk_{id,\mathcal{A}}$, recip): If a user has enough attributes to satisfy the predicate Ω, i.e. $\Omega(\mathcal{A}) = 1$, then he uses the corresponding secrets keys $sk_{id,\mathcal{A}} = \{sk_{id,a_i}\}_{a_i \in \mathcal{A}}$ to produce a valid signature $\sigma = \{\sigma_{ABS}, \sigma_{UCL}\}$ on the message m and the recipient tag recip w.r.t. the predicate Ω; if recip $= \perp$ then $\sigma_{UCL} = \perp$.
- Verify(σ, $\{vk_{AA_i}\}_i$, Ω, m, recip): Takes a signature σ on the message m and the possibly empty recipient tag recip w.r.t. a predicate Ω, the verification keys $\{vk_{AA_i}\}_i$ of the attribute authorities managing attributes involved in Ω, and returns 1 if the signature is valid, and 0 otherwise.
- Link(σ_0, m_0, $\{vk_{AA_i}\}_i$, Ω_0, σ_1, m_1, $\{vk_{AA_j}\}_j$, Ω_1, recip): On input two signatures, two messages, two signing policies and the verification keys of the attribute authorities managing the attributes involved in the policies, and a recipient tag, it returns 1 if the signatures are valid on their respective messages and the same non-empty recipient tag recip (w.r.t. the respective policy), i.e. if recip $\neq \perp$ and ($\sigma_{UCL0} = \sigma_{UCL1} \neq \perp$), and 0 otherwise.
- Identify(σ, m, recip, $\{vk_{AA_i}\}_i$, Ω, sk): Is only used in the security model for capturing linkability. It checks whether the valid signature σ (w.r.t. the signing policy Ω) on the message m and the non-empty recipient tag recip was produced by the secret key sk, outputting 0/1 accordingly.

2.2 Security Definitions

We define here the security requirements of an ABS-UCL scheme.

Correctness. This requires that signatures produced by honest users verify correctly and that signatures produced by the same user to the same valid recipient (i.e. on the same non-empty recipient tag) link.

Linkability. As specified in [37], there are two methods to support user-controlled linkability in anonymous digital signatures: In the first, a designated linking authority can determine whether or not two signatures are linked; whereas in the second method, there exists a public linking algorithm which can be run by any party. Our model supports the latter. We require that only valid signatures directed at the same recipient and which were produced by the same user link. In the game the adversary can choose all the secret keys of the users and attribute authorities. The adversary outputs $(\sigma_1, \mathsf{recip}_1, m_1, \{\mathsf{vk}_{\mathsf{AA}_i}\}_i, \Omega_1, \mathsf{sk}_1)$ and $(\sigma_2, \mathsf{recip}_2, m_2, \{\mathsf{vk}_{\mathsf{AA}_j}\}_j, \Omega_2, \mathsf{sk}_2)$. It wins if σ_i is valid (w.r.t. Ω_i) on m_i and recip_i, for $i = 1, 2$ and either of the following holds:

- σ_1 was produced by sk_1 and σ_2 was produced by sk_2 where $\mathsf{sk}_1 = \mathsf{sk}_2$ and $\mathsf{recip} = \mathsf{recip}_1 = \mathsf{recip}_2 \neq\perp$ but $\mathsf{Link}(\sigma_1, m_1, \{\mathsf{vk}_{\mathsf{AA}_i}\}_i, \Omega_1, \sigma_2, m_2, \{\mathsf{vk}_{\mathsf{AA}_j}\}_j, \Omega_2, \mathsf{recip}) = 0$.
- σ_1 was produced by sk_1 and σ_2 was produced by sk_2 where $\mathsf{sk}_1 = \mathsf{sk}_2$ and $\mathsf{Link}(\sigma_1, m_1, \{\mathsf{vk}_{\mathsf{AA}_i}\}_i, \Omega_1, \sigma_2, m_2, \{\mathsf{vk}_{\mathsf{AA}_j}\}_j, \Omega_2, \mathsf{recip}_k) = 1$ for $k \in \{1, 2\}$ and either $\mathsf{recip}_k =\perp$ or $\mathsf{recip}_1 \neq \mathsf{recip}_2$.
- σ_1 was produced by sk_1 and σ_2 was produced by sk_2 where $\mathsf{sk}_1 \neq \mathsf{sk}_2$ and $\mathsf{recip} = \mathsf{recip}_1 = \mathsf{recip}_2 \neq\perp$ and $\mathsf{Link}(\sigma_1, m_1, \{\mathsf{vk}_{\mathsf{AA}_i}\}_i, \Omega_1, \sigma_2, m_2, \{\mathsf{vk}_{\mathsf{AA}_j}\}_j, \Omega_2, \mathsf{recip}) = 1$.

In summary, this requires that signatures by the same user on the same non-empty recipient tag link. Also, signatures by different users but on the same recipient tag or those by the same user but on different recipient tags do not link.

Anonymity. This requires that a signature reveals neither the identity of the signer nor the attributes used in the signing. In the anonymity game, we have the following:

- Adversary's Capabilities: Full control over *all* attribute authorities. It can also ask for the secret keys of signers of its choice; those signers will be referred to as corrupt users. In addition, the adversary can ask for the secret key of any attribute and has a signing oracle that it can query on messages and recipient tags on behalf of honest users.
- Adversary's Challenge: The adversary outputs $(m, \mathsf{id}_0, \mathcal{A}_0, \mathsf{id}_1, \mathcal{A}_1, \Omega, \mathsf{recip})$ where $\Omega(\mathcal{A}_i) = 1$ for $i = 0, 1$. If $\mathsf{recip} \neq\perp$ then we require that throughout the game (i.e. even after the challenge phase) id_0 and id_1 must be honest (i.e. their personal secret keys are not revealed to the adversary), and that neither of $(\mathsf{id}_0, \mathsf{recip})$, $(\mathsf{id}_1, \mathsf{recip})$ is queried to the signing oracle. This ensures that the adversary cannot trivially win by exploiting the linkability feature. The adversary gets back a signature σ_b produced using $(\mathsf{id}_b, \mathcal{A}_b)$ for $b \leftarrow \{0, 1\}$. After this, the adversary can continue accessing its oracles as long as it does not violate the above two conditions.
- Adversary's Output: The adversary outputs its guess b^* and wins if $b^* = b$.

Unforgeability. This requires that users cannot output signatures on (message, recipient tag) pairs w.r.t. to a signing policy not satisfied by their set of attributes, even if they pool their attributes together, which ensures collusion-resistance. In addition, since our notion supports user-controlled linkability, we additionally require that an adversary cannot produce signatures which link to other signatures by an honest user, i.e. one whose personal secret key has not been revealed to the adversary, even if all other users and attribute authorities in the system are corrupt. Note that, unlike in DAA, e.g. [2,3], in our notion even if a user's personal secret key is revealed, only signatures on non-empty recipient tags by the user can be traced, i.e. it is impossible to trace signatures on empty recipient tags.

In the unforgeability game, we have the following:

- Adversary's Capabilities: Access to a signing oracle. Moreover, it can corrupt any attribute authority. We refer to the non-corrupted attribute authorities as honest ones. It can also ask for the personal secret key of any user. We refer to the non-corrupted users as honest ones. It can also ask for the secret key for any attribute.
- Winning Conditions: The adversary wins if either:
  - Adversary outputs a valid signature σ on m and recip w.r.t. Ω, where $(m, \mathsf{recip}, \Omega)$ was not queried to the signing oracle, and there exists no subset of attributes $\mathcal{A}^*$ whose keys have been revealed to the adversary or managed by corrupt attribute authorities s.t. $\Omega(\mathcal{A}^*) = 1$. In other words, $\forall \mathcal{A}^*$ s.t. $\Omega(\mathcal{A}^*) = 1$, $\exists a^* \in \mathcal{A}^*$ s.t. $\Omega(\mathcal{A}^* \setminus \{a^*\}) = 0$ and a^*'s key has never been revealed to the adversary and it is managed by an honest attribute authority.
  - Adversary outputs a tuple $(m_0, \sigma_0, \{\mathsf{vk}_{\mathsf{AA}_i}\}_i, \Omega_0, m_1, \sigma_1, \{\mathsf{vk}_{\mathsf{AA}_j}\}_j, \Omega_1, \mathsf{recip} \neq \bot, \mathsf{id})$, where σ_0 is valid on m_0 and recip w.r.t. Ω_0, σ_1 is valid on m_1 and recip w.r.t. Ω_1, user id is honest, $\mathsf{Link}(\sigma_0, m_0, \{\mathsf{vk}_{\mathsf{AA}_i}\}_i, \Omega_0, \sigma_1, m_1, \{\mathsf{vk}_{\mathsf{AA}_j}\}_j, \Omega_1, \mathsf{recip}) = 1$ and either $(\mathsf{id}, m_0, \mathsf{recip}, \Omega_0)$ or $(\mathsf{id}, m_1, \mathsf{recip}, \Omega_1)$ was not queried to the signing oracle.

  Note here the adversary has more freedom than it has in the anonymity game because it is allowed to ask for signatures by the honest user it intends to frame on any recipient tag.

3 Building Blocks

Bilinear Groups. A bilinear group is a tuple $\mathcal{P} = (\mathbb{G}_1, \mathbb{G}_2, \mathbb{G}_T, p, g_1, g_2, e)$ where $\mathbb{G}_1$, $\mathbb{G}_2$ and $\mathbb{G}_T$ are groups of a prime order p and g_1 and g_2 generate $\mathbb{G}_1$ and $\mathbb{G}_2$, respectively. The function e is a non-degenerate bilinear map $\mathbb{G}_1 \times \mathbb{G}_2 \longrightarrow \mathbb{G}_T$. According to [19], prime-order bilinear groups can be categorized into three main types. We will use Type-3 where $\mathbb{G}_1 \neq \mathbb{G}_2$ and no efficiently computable isomorphisms between $\mathbb{G}_1$ and $\mathbb{G}_2$ are known. This type is considered to be more efficient than Type-2, and definitely more efficient than Type-1, when the latter is implemented over fields of large prime characteristic.[1]

---

[1] One can implement Type-1 using supersingular curves over fields of small characteristics (2 or 3), however recent records on solving DLog in these fields [22], with the help of the MOV attack [28], *ring a warning bell* to avoid using Type-1 pairings in new cryptographic applications.

Digital Signatures. We require a Digital Signature (DS) scheme that is correct and existentially unforgeable. In our construction realised in the ROM, we will use different variants of the full Boneh-Boyen signature scheme [6]. We refer to original full Boneh-Boyen scheme as the BB scheme, whereas we refer to its modified variant originally defined in [6], and used in, e.g. [12], as the BB† scheme. Both schemes are secure under the q-SDH assumption.

Let $\mathcal{P} = (\mathbb{G}_1, \mathbb{G}_2, \mathbb{G}_T, p, g_1, g_2, e)$ be the description of a bilinear group and $h_1 \in \mathbb{G}_1$ is a random element. The schemes are described below:

- KeyGen($\mathcal{P}$): Choose $x, y \leftarrow \mathbb{Z}_p$, set $(X, Y) = (g_2^x, g_2^y)$. The secret key is (x, y) and the verification key is (X, Y).
- BB.Sign(sk, m): To sign $m \in \mathbb{Z}_p$, choose $r \leftarrow \mathbb{Z}_p$ such that $x + ry + m \neq 0$ and compute the signature $\sigma = g_1^{1/(x+ry+m)}$. In the BB† scheme, the signature is $\sigma = (g_1 \cdot h_1^z)^{1/(x+ry+m)}$, where the BB† signer need not know the value z.
- Verify(vk, m, σ): if $e(\sigma, X \cdot Y^r \cdot g_2^m) = e(g_1, g_2)$ output 1, otherwise 0.
  In the BB† scheme, the verification equation is $e(\sigma, X \cdot Y^r \cdot g_2^m) = e(g_1 \cdot h_1^z, g_2)$

Linkable Indistinguishable Tags. A Linkable Indistinguishable Tag (LIT) scheme [3] is similar to a Message Authentication Code (MAC) but requires different security properties. It consists of a couple of algorithms KeyGen and Tag. The former, on input a security parameter, produces a secret key sk, whereas the latter, on input a message m and the secret key, outputs a tag.

Besides correctness, the security of LIT [3] requires Linkability and f-Indistinguishability. Linkability requires that an adversary who is allowed to control both the secret key and the message cannot produce equal tags unless they are tags on the same message/key pair. Indistinguishability, which is defined w.r.t. a one-way function f of the secret key, requires that an adversary who gets $f(\mathsf{sk})$ and access to a tag oracle, cannot determine whether or not a new tag on a message of its choice was produced using the same key used by the tag oracle.

As in [3], we instantiate the LIT in the ROM with the Boneh-Lynn-Shacham (BLS) signature scheme [7]. The LIT instantiation is secure under the DDH and the discrete logarithm problems [3].

Non-interactive Zero-Knowledge Proofs. Let R be an NP relation on pairs (x, y) with a corresponding language $\mathcal{L}_\mathsf{R} = \{y \mid \exists x \; s.t. (x, y) \in \mathsf{R}\}$. A NIZK proof system Π for a relation R is a tuple of algorithms (Setup, Prove, Verify, Extract, SimSetup, SimProve) defined as follows: Setup outputs a reference string crs and an extraction key xk which allows for witness extraction. On input (crs, x, y), Prove outputs a proof π if R(x, y) = 1. On input (crs, y, π), Verify outputs 1 if π is a valid proof that $y \in \mathcal{L}_\mathsf{R}$, and 0 otherwise. Extract outputs the witness x from a valid proof π. Finally, SimSetup outputs a simulated reference string crs$_{\mathsf{sim}}$ and a trapdoor tr, which is used by SimProve to simulate proofs without a witness.

We require: completeness, soundness and zero-knowledge. Completeness requires that honestly generated proofs are accepted; Soundness requires that it is infeasible to produce a convincing proof for a false statement; Zero-knowledge requires that a proof reveals no information about the witness used. For formal definitions refer to [4].

In our construction in the random oracle model, we use the Fiat–Shamir transformation [16] applied to interactive Σ-protocols.

Span Programs. A span program [24] is defined as follows:

Definition 1. *Given a monotone boolean function $\Phi : \{0,1\}^n \rightarrow \{0,1\}$, a $l \times t$ matrix M with entries in a field $\mathbb{F}$, and a labelling function $a : [l] \rightarrow [n]$ that associates M's rows to Φ's input variables. We say that M is a monotone span program for ϕ over a field $\mathbb{F}$ if for every $(x_1, \ldots, x_n) \in \{0,1\}^n$, we have the following:*

$$[\Phi(x_1, \ldots, x_n) = 1] \Leftrightarrow [\exists v \in \mathbb{F}^{1 \times t} : v \cdot M = [1, 0, 0, \cdots, 0]$$
$$\wedge (\forall i : x_{a(i)} = 0 \Rightarrow v_i = 0)]$$

4 Framework for ABS with User-Controlled Linkability

Overview of the Framework. The tools we use in our generic construction are: a NIZK system Π that is sound and zero-knowledge, two existentially unforgeable signature schemes DS_1 and DS_2, a collision-resistant hash function $\mathcal{H}$ and a f-indistinguishable linkable indistinguishable tag scheme LIT. The Setup algorithm of ABS-UCL generates the common reference string crs for the NIZK system Π. It also generates a key pair $(\mathsf{vk}_{\mathsf{psdo}}, \mathsf{sk}_{\mathsf{psdo}})$ for the digital signature schemes DS_2. The public parameters of the system is set to $\mathsf{pp} = (\mathsf{crs}, \mathsf{vk}_{\mathsf{psdo}}, \mathbb{A}, \mathcal{H})$, where $\mathbb{A}$ is the universe of attributes. For a new attribute authority to join the system, it creates a secret/verification key pair $(\mathsf{sk}_{\mathsf{aid}}, \mathsf{vk}_{\mathsf{aid}})$ for signature scheme DS_1. To generate a signing key for attribute $a \in \mathbb{A}$ for signer id, the managing attribute authority signs the signer identity along with the attribute and the image of the one-way function on his secret key, i.e. $(\mathsf{id}, a, f(\mathsf{sk}_{\mathsf{id}}))$, using $\mathsf{sk}_{\mathsf{aid}}$. The resulting signature is used as the secret key for that attribute by signer id.

To sign a message m w.r.t. a signing policy Ω, there are two cases; if the signature is linkable (i.e. on a non-empty recipient tag recip $\neq \bot$), the signer first uses LIT and his secret key to compute a tag σ_{UCL} on the recipient name recip and a NIZK proof π that such a tag verifies w.r.t. his personal secret key $\mathsf{sk}_{\mathsf{id}}$, and that he either has a digital signature on a pseudo-attribute (following [30,14]), i.e. the hash of the combination of the signing predicate, the message and the recipient name recip, i.e. $a_{\mathsf{psdo}} = \mathcal{H}(\Omega, m, \mathsf{recip})$, that verifies w.r.t. the verification key $\mathsf{vk}_{\mathsf{psdo}}$ or that she has enough credentials (DS_1 signatures on $(\mathsf{id}, f(\mathsf{sk}_{\mathsf{id}}), a_i)$) to satisfy the original signing predicate Ω. For non-linkable signatures (i.e. when recip $= \bot$), it suffices to produce a NIZK proof that the signer has enough attributes to satisfy the modified predicate, i.e $\hat{\Omega} = \Omega \vee a_{\mathsf{psdo}}$, and therefore, no need for the linking part that uses LIT. Note that in this case $a_{\mathsf{psdo}} = \mathcal{H}(\Omega, m)$.

Before we define the languages for the NIZK proofs $\mathcal{L}_1$ for linkable and $\mathcal{L}_2$ for non-linkable signatures, we will generically define the format of these languages, where the secret values, aka witnesses for proofs, are underlined:

$$\mathcal{L} : \left\{ (\text{public values} \quad \mathsf{pv}), (\text{witness} \quad \underline{\mathsf{w}}) : \mathsf{R}_i(\mathsf{pv}, \underline{\mathsf{w}}) \right\}$$

- **Linkable signatures** (recip $\neq \bot$):

$$\mathcal{L}_1 : \Big\{ ((\mathbf{vk} = \{\mathsf{vk}_i\}_{i=1}^{|\hat{\Omega}|}, \boldsymbol{a} = \{a_i\}_{i=1}^{|\hat{\Omega}|}), (\underline{\mathsf{sk}_{\mathsf{id}}}, \underline{\mathsf{id}}, \underline{\boldsymbol{v}}, \underline{\boldsymbol{\sigma}} = \{\sigma_{a_i}\}_{i=1}^{|\hat{\Omega}|})) :$$

$$\Big(\underline{\boldsymbol{v}}\mathbf{M} = [1,0,\ldots,0] \Big) \bigwedge_{i=1}^{|\hat{\Omega}|-1} \Big(\underline{v_i} = 0 \vee \mathsf{DS}_1.\mathsf{Verify}(\mathsf{vk}_i, \underline{\mathsf{id}}, \underline{\mathsf{sk}_{\mathsf{id}}}, a_i, \underline{\sigma_{a_i}}) = 1 \Big)$$

$$\bigwedge \Big(v_{|\hat{\Psi}|} = 0 \vee \mathsf{DS}_2.\mathsf{Verify}(\mathsf{vk}_{\mathsf{psdo}}, a_{\mathsf{psdo}}, \underline{\sigma_{a_{\mathsf{psdo}}}}) = 1 \Big)$$

$$\bigwedge \Big(\mathsf{LIT}.\mathsf{Tag}(\underline{\mathsf{sk}_{\mathsf{id}}}, \mathsf{recip}) = \sigma_{\mathsf{UCL}} \Big\}.$$

- **Non-Linkable signatures** (recip $= \bot$):

$$\mathcal{L}_2 : \Big\{ ((\mathbf{vk} = \{\mathsf{vk}_i\}_{i=1}^{|\hat{\Omega}|}, \boldsymbol{a} = \{a_i\}_{i=1}^{|\hat{\Omega}|}), (\underline{\mathsf{sk}_{\mathsf{id}}}, \underline{\mathsf{id}}, \underline{\boldsymbol{v}}, \underline{\boldsymbol{\sigma}} = \{\sigma_{a_i}\}_{i=1}^{|\hat{\Omega}|})) :$$

$$\Big(\underline{\boldsymbol{v}}\mathbf{M} = [1,0,\ldots,0] \Big) \bigwedge_{i=1}^{|\hat{\Omega}|-1} \Big(\underline{v_i} = 0 \vee \mathsf{DS}_1.\mathsf{Verify}(\mathsf{vk}_i, \underline{\mathsf{id}}, \underline{\mathsf{sk}_{\mathsf{id}}}, a_i, \underline{\sigma_{a_i}}) = 1 \Big)$$

$$\bigwedge \Big(v_{|\hat{\Psi}|} = 0 \vee \mathsf{DS}_2.\mathsf{Verify}(\mathsf{vk}_{\mathsf{psdo}}, a_{\mathsf{psdo}}, \underline{\sigma_{a_{\mathsf{psdo}}}}) = 1 \Big)$$

We use a span program (Section 3) to prove the satisfiability of the extended predicate $\hat{\Omega}$. Using a public matrix $\mathbf{M}$, the signer needs to prove the ownership of a *secret* vector $\boldsymbol{v} \in \mathbb{Z}_p^{|\hat{\Omega}|}$ for which $\boldsymbol{v}\mathbf{M} = [1,0,\ldots,0]$. The zero elements in this vector $\boldsymbol{v}$ corresponds to attributes that the signer does not actually need in order to satisfy the predicate. For these values, the signer can safely choose random signatures. For the non-zero elements in $\boldsymbol{v}$, the signer needs to prove ownership of their corresponding attributes/pseudo-attribute.

The hiding property of the Π system ensures that the proof π does not reveal how the modified predicate $\hat{\Omega}$ was satisfied.

The pseudo-attribute is used for two reasons; firstly, it binds the signature to the message, the signing predicate, and the recipient name recip if the the signature is linkable. Secondly, the secret signing key $\mathsf{sk}_{\mathsf{psdo}}$ for the digital signature scheme DS will be used as a trapdoor in the security proofs to allow its holder to simulate signatures and sign on behalf of any signer without knowing their secret keys. That could be done by producing a signature on the pseudo-attribute associated with the message and the signing predicate.

The full proof for the following Theorem is in the full version.

Theorem 1. *The generic construction of the attribute-based signature with user-controlled linkability* ABS-UCL *given above is secure if the underlying building blocks are secure.*

5   A Concrete Construction of **ABS-UCL**

Description of the Construction. The signer's task is to provide a zero-knowledge proof of knowledge π w.r.t. the languages defined earlier, i.e. $\mathcal{L}_1$ and

$\mathcal{L}_2$, depending on whether or not the signature is linkable. We instantiate DS_1 using the BB† scheme and DS_2 using the BB scheme. The proof will be made of 3 parts (or 2 if non-linkable). The first deals with the Span program to show how to hide which subset of attributes the signer has used to satisfy the modified predicate $\hat{\Omega}$. For this, the signer proves that he has used a secret vector v to span the public matrix $\mathbf{M} \in \mathbb{Z}_p^{\alpha \times \theta}$ of the span program, where $\alpha = |\hat{\Omega}|$. The second part is to show that the signatures verify correctly w.r.t. their corresponding verification keys, where the span program can safely let the signer choose random signatures for the attributes which he does not own/want to use. The third part is to show that, when the signature is supposed to be linkable, the linking part indeed uses the same user secret key used in the rest of the proof. Not that the group elements used later in the commitments, i.e. k_1, k_2 and k_3 are parts of the public parameters pp whereas sk is the signer's secret key.

Part 1: Span program

Prove that $\underline{v}\mathbf{M} = [1, 0, \ldots, 0]$, this can be done by proving the following:

$$\sum_{i=1}^{|\hat{\Omega}|} v_i \mathbf{M}_{ij} = \begin{cases} 1 & j = 1 \\ 0 & 2 \leq j \leq \theta \end{cases} \tag{1}$$

- Commitments of vector v
  - $\beta_{v_i}, \beta_{t_i}, t_i \leftarrow \mathbb{Z}_p, i = 1 \ldots \alpha$.
  - $\mathcal{V}_i = g_1^{\beta_{v_i}} \cdot k_3^{\beta_{t_i}}; \quad \hat{v}_i = g_1^{v_i} \cdot k_3^{t_i}$
- Proof of Statement
  - $\forall j \in [1, \theta]$ compute: $\Lambda_j = \prod_{i=1}^{\alpha} k_3^{t_i \cdot M_{ij}}; \quad \lambda_j = \prod_{i=1}^{\alpha} (k_3^{M_{ij}})^{\beta_{t_i}}$

Part 2: DS_1 and DS_2

Now each verification equation is as follows:

$$e(\sigma_{a_i}{}^{v_i}, X \cdot Y^r \cdot g_2^{a_i || \mathsf{id}}) = e(g_1, g_2) \cdot e(h_1^{\mathsf{sk}}, g_2)$$

DS_1 is instantiated using the BB† scheme whereas DS_2 is instantiated using the BB scheme. The signatures are as follows:

$$\sigma_{a_i} = \begin{cases} (g_1 \cdot h_1^{\mathsf{sk}})^{1/(x_i + y_i r_i + a_i || \mathsf{id})} & \text{regular attributes} \\ g_1^{1/(x_i + y_i r_i + a_{\mathsf{psdo}})} & \text{pseudo-attributes} \end{cases}$$

Where the public keys of an attribute a_i is the couple of group elements $X_i = g_2^{x_i}$ and $Y_i = g_2^{y_i}$. The identity of the signer is id and his secret key is sk. In order to use the secret vector v to hide the subset of attributes used to satisfy the predicate Ω, we can simply raise each σ_{a_i} to its corresponding vector value v_i, when v_i is zero, the signer does not want to this attribute, and therefore he can replace the signature by a random value.

- Commitments of $(\sigma_{a_i}, r_i), i \in [1, \alpha]$ and the signer identity id:
  Pick $\rho_{v_i}, \rho_{id}, \rho_{r_i}, \rho_{sk}, \beta_{\rho_{sk}}, \beta_{id\rho_{v_i}}, \beta_{r_i}, \beta_{\rho_i}, \beta_{id}, \beta_{\rho_{r_i}}, \beta_{\rho_{id}}, \beta_{cs}, \leftarrow \mathbb{Z}_p$, and compute:

$$T_i = \sigma_{a_i}{}^{v_i} \cdot k_1^{\rho_{v_i}}, \quad K_i = Y^{r_i} \cdot k_2^{\rho_{r_i}}, \quad Z = h_1^{sk} \cdot k_1^{\rho_{sk}} \quad U = g_2{}^{id} \cdot k_2^{\rho_{id}}$$

$$\hat{K}_i = Y_i^{\beta_{r_i}} \cdot k_2^{\beta_{\rho_{r_i}}}, \quad \hat{Z} = h_1^{\beta_{sk}} \cdot k_1^{\beta_{\rho_{sk}}}, \quad \hat{U} = g_2^{\beta_{id}} \cdot k_2^{\beta_{\rho_{id}}}$$

Let, $\forall i \in [1, \alpha - 1] : \rho_i = \rho_{r_i} + \rho_{id}$ whereas $\rho_\alpha = \rho_{r_\alpha}$.
- Simplification: (can be done by both prover and verifier)

$$X'_i = e(k_1, X_i \cdot g_2^{a_i \cdot 2^{|id|}}) \quad Y'_i = e(k_1, Y_i) \quad R = e(k_1, g_2)$$

$$T'_i = e(T_i, k_2) \quad D' = e(k_1, G_2^{\alpha_{psdo}})$$

- Knowledge of Exponents
  $\forall i \in [1, \alpha]$ and $\forall j \in [1, \theta]$, compute:

$$\mathcal{X}'_{ij} = (X_i'^{M_{ij}})^{\beta_{\rho_{v_i}}} \quad \mathcal{Y}'_{ij} = (Y_i'^{M_{ij}})^{\beta_{r_i}\rho_{v_i}} \quad \mathcal{T}'_{ij} = (T_i'^{M_{ij}})^{\beta_{\rho_i}}$$

$\forall i \in [1, \alpha - 1], \forall j \in [1, \theta]$, compute:

$$\mathcal{R}_{ij} = (R^{M_{ij}})^{\beta_{id\rho_{v_i}}}$$

$\forall j \in [1, \theta]$:

  ○ $\mathcal{D}'_{\alpha j} = (M'^{z_{\alpha j}})^{\beta_{\rho_{v_i}}}$
  ○ $\mathcal{P}_j = \mathcal{X}'_{\alpha j} \cdot \mathcal{Y}'_{\alpha j} \cdot \mathcal{T}'_{\alpha j} \cdot \mathcal{D}'_{\alpha j}$
  ○ $\mathcal{B}_j = \mathcal{P}_j \cdot \prod_{i=1}^{\alpha-1} \mathcal{X}'_{ij} \cdot \mathcal{Y}'_{ij} \cdot \mathcal{R}_{ij} \cdot \mathcal{T}'_{ij}$

Part 3:Linkability- LIT
The signer needs to prove the following equation:

$$\mathsf{BLS.Sign}(\underline{sk}, recip) = \sigma_{\mathsf{UCL}}$$

If the signature is linkable, then compute:

$$\mathcal{N} = \mathcal{H}(recip)^{\beta_{sk}}, \quad \mathcal{L} = \left(\frac{h_1}{H(recip)}\right)^{\beta_{sk}} \cdot k_1^{\beta_{\rho_{sk}}} \quad \sigma_{\mathsf{UCL}} = \mathcal{H}(recip)^{sk},$$

otherwise; $\sigma_{\mathsf{UCL}} = \perp$.
Finally, compute the challenge c:

$$c = \mathcal{H}_{\mathsf{FS}}(\underbrace{\mathcal{N}||\mathcal{L}}_{\text{if linkable}} ||\lambda_j||\mathcal{S}_i||T_i||K_i||U||\hat{K}_i||\hat{U}||\mathcal{B}_j||Z), \forall i \in [1, \alpha], \forall j \in [1, \theta].$$

- Responses

$\circ\ s_{v_i} = \beta_{v_i} + cv_i,\ s_{t_i} = \beta_{t_i} + ct_i,\ s_{id} = \beta_{id} + cid,\quad s_{sk} = \beta_{sk} + csk,\quad s_{\rho_{sk}} = \beta_{\rho_{sk}} + c\rho_{sk},\quad s_{\rho_{id}} = \beta_{\rho_{id}} + c\rho_{id}$

$\circ\ \forall i \in [1, \alpha]:$
$s_{\rho_{v_i}} = \beta_{\rho_{v_i}} + c\rho_{v_i},\ s_{r_i\rho_{v_i}} = \beta_{r_i\rho_{v_i}} + c(r_i\rho_{v_i}),\ s_{\rho_i} = \beta_{\rho_i} + c\rho_i,\ s_{r_i} = \beta_{r_i} + cr_i,$
$s_{\rho_{r_i}} = \beta_{\rho_{r_i}} + c\rho_{r_i};$

$\circ\ \forall i \in [1, \alpha - 1],$ compute:
$s_{id\rho_{v_i}} = \beta_{id\rho_{v_i}} + c(id\rho_{v_i})$

Let $\Sigma = \{s_{\rho_{v_i}}, s_{r_i\rho_{v_i}}, s_{id_i}, s_{\rho_i}, s_{r_i}, s_{\rho_{r_i}}, s_{id}, s_{\rho_{id}}, s_{v_i}, s_{t_i}, s_{sk}, s_{\rho_{sk}}\}$, the signature is:

$$\sigma_{\mathsf{ABS-UCL}} = (\Sigma, c, \{\Lambda_j\}_1^\theta, \{\hat{v}_i, T_i, K_i\}_1^\alpha, U, Z, \sigma_{\mathsf{UCL}})$$

Verification

Compute:

$$\Delta_j = e(T_\alpha, (X_\alpha \cdot K_{1\alpha} \cdot G_2^{\alpha_{psdo}})^{M_{\alpha j}})$$

$$E_j = \begin{cases} \Delta_1 \cdot \displaystyle\prod_{i=1}^{\alpha-1} e(T_i, (X_i \cdot K_i \cdot U)^{M_{ij}})/e(g_1, g_2) \cdot e(Z, g_2) & j = 1 \\ \Delta_j \cdot \displaystyle\prod_{i=1}^{\alpha-1} e(T_i, (X_i \cdot K_i \cdot U)^{M_{ij}}) & 2 \leq j \leq \theta \end{cases}$$

- $\hat{U} = g_2^{s_{id}} \cdot k_2^{s_{\rho_{id}}} \cdot U^{-c}, \quad \hat{Z} = h_1^{s_{sk}} \cdot k_1^{s_{\rho_{sk}}} \cdot Z^{-c}$
- $\forall i \in [1, \alpha]:$
  $\mathcal{S}_i = g_1^{s_{v_i}} \cdot k_3^{s_{t_i}} \cdot \hat{v}_i^{-c} \quad \hat{K}_i = Y_i^{s_{r_i}} \cdot k_2^{s_{\rho_{r_i}}} \cdot K_i^{-c}$
- $\forall j \in [1, \theta]:$
  $\circ\ \lambda_j = \Lambda_j^{-c} \cdot \prod_{i=1}^\alpha (k_3^{M_{ij}})^{s_{t_i}}$
  $\circ\ \mathcal{P}_j = (X'^{M_{\alpha j}}_\alpha)^{s_{\kappa_\alpha}} \cdot (Y'^{M_{\alpha j}}_\alpha)^{s_{r_\alpha\kappa_\alpha}} \cdot (T'^{M_{\alpha j}}_\alpha)^{s_{\rho_\alpha}} \cdot (D'^{M_{\alpha j}})^{s_{\kappa_\alpha}}$
  $\circ\ \mathcal{B}_j = E_j^{-c} \cdot \mathcal{P}_j \cdot \displaystyle\prod_{i=1}^{\alpha-1} (X'^{M_{ij}}_i)^{s_{\rho_{v_i}}} \cdot (Y'^{M_{ij}}_i)^{s_{r_i\rho_{v_i}}} \cdot (R^{M_{ij}})^{s_{id_i}} \cdot (T'^{M_{ij}}_i)^{s_{\rho_i}}$

- For the linkablility:
  $\circ$ If $\sigma_{\mathsf{UCL}} \neq \perp$, then compute:

$$\mathcal{N} = \mathcal{H}(\mathsf{recip})^{s_{sk}} \cdot (\sigma_{\mathsf{UCL}})^{-c}, \quad \mathcal{L} = \left(\frac{h_1}{\mathcal{H}(\mathsf{recip})}\right)^{s_{sk}} \cdot k_1^{s_{\rho_{sk}}} \cdot \left(\frac{Z}{\sigma_{\mathsf{UCL}}}\right)^{-c}$$

- Let $\hat{c} = \mathcal{H}_{\mathsf{FS}}(\ \underbrace{\mathcal{N}||\mathcal{L}}_{\text{if linkable}}\ ||\lambda_j||\mathcal{S}_i||T_i||K_i||U||\hat{K}_i||\hat{U}||\mathcal{B}_j||Z),$

- Verify that $\hat{c} = c$ and that the following statement holds:

$$\prod_{i=1}^\alpha \hat{v}_i^{M_{ij}} = \begin{cases} g_1 \cdot \Lambda_1 & j = 1 \\ \Lambda_j & 2 \leq j \leq \theta \end{cases}$$

The full proof for the following Theorem is in the full version.

Theorem 2. *The construction is secure in the random oracle model if the q-SDH, DDH and Dlog assumptions hold, and the hash function $\mathcal{H}$ is collision resistant.*

Table 1. Existing ABS schemes and their features

Scheme	Anonymity	Traceability	Decentralisation	UCL
[14,20]	✓	✓	✓	✗
[32]	✓	✗	✓	✗
[29]	✓	✗	✗	✗
Ours	✓	✗	✓	✓

6 Comparison

In Table 1, we compare the properties offered by our notion with those offered by related attribute-based signature notions. We note that the size of the signature of our concrete construction, which uses Type-3 bilinear groups is $\mathbb{G}_1^{2\cdot|\hat{\Omega}|+\theta+2}$ + $\mathbb{G}_2^{|\hat{\Omega}|+1} + \mathbb{Z}_p^{8\cdot|\hat{\Omega}|+4}$, where θ is the number of columns in the span program matrix **M**.

Our main concern in this paper was efficiency, hence the use of random oracles. There are alternative building blocks in the literature to instantiate ABS-UCL in the standard model.

Acknowledgments. We would like to thank Russell Bradford. The third author was supported by ERC Advanced Grant ERC-2010-AdG-267188-CRIPTO and EPSRC via grant EP/H043454/1.

References

1. Bellare, M., Rogaway, P.: Random oracles are practical: A Paradigm for Designing Efficient Protocols. In: ACM-CCS 1993, pp. 62–73. ACM (1993)
2. Bernhard, D., Fuchsbauer, G., Ghadafi, E.: Efficient signatures of knowledge and DAA in the standard model. In: Jacobson, M., Locasto, M., Mohassel, P., Safavi-Naini, R. (eds.) ACNS 2013. LNCS, vol. 7954, pp. 518–533. Springer, Heidelberg (2013)
3. Bernhard, D., Fuchsbauer, G., Ghadafi, E., Smart, N.P., Warinschi, B.: Anonymous attestation with user-controlled linkability. International Journal of Information Security 12(3), 219–249 (2013)
4. Blum, M., Feldman, P., Micali, S.: Non-interactive zero-knowledge and its applications. In: STOC 1988, pp. 103–112 (1988)
5. Brickell, E., Chen, L., Li, J.: Simplified Security Notions of Direct Anonymous Attestation and a Concrete Scheme from Pairings. International Journal of Information Security 8(5), 315–330 (2009)
6. Boneh, D., Boyen, X.: Short signatures without random oracles. In: Cachin, C., Camenisch, J.L. (eds.) EUROCRYPT 2004. LNCS, vol. 3027, pp. 56–73. Springer, Heidelberg (2004)
7. Boneh, D., Lynn, B., Shacham, H.: Short Signatures from the Weil Pairing. Journal of Cryptology, 297–319 (2004)
8. Bobba, R., Fatemieh, O., Khan, F., Gunter, C.A., Khurana, H.: Using Attribute-Based Access Control to Enable Attribute-Based Messaging. In: ACSAC 2006, vol. 3027, pp. 403–413. IEEE Computer Society (2006)

9. Boneh, D., Franklin, M.: Identity-based encryption from the weil pairing. In: Kilian, J. (ed.) CRYPTO 2001. LNCS, vol. 2139, p. 213. Springer, Heidelberg (2001)

10. Chaum, D., van Heyst, E.: Group signatures. In: Davies, D.W. (ed.) EUROCRYPT 1991. LNCS, vol. 547, pp. 257–265. Springer, Heidelberg (1991)

11. Chen, L., Morrissey, P., Smart, N.P.: Pairings in trusted computing. In: Galbraith, S.D., Paterson, K.G. (eds.) Pairing 2008. LNCS, vol. 5209, pp. 1–17. Springer, Heidelberg (2008)

12. Chen, L.: A DAA scheme requiring less TPM resources. In: Bao, F., Yung, M., Lin, D., Jing, J. (eds.) Inscrypt 2009. LNCS, vol. 6151, pp. 350–365. Springer, Heidelberg (2010)

13. Cocks, C.: An identity based encryption scheme based on quadratic residues. In: IMA Int., pp. 360–363 (2001)

14. El Kaafarani, A., Ghadafi, E., Khader, D.: Decentralized traceable attribute-based signatures. In: Benaloh, J. (ed.) CT-RSA 2014. LNCS, vol. 8366, pp. 327–348. Springer, Heidelberg (2014)

15. Escala, A., Herranz, J., Morillo, P.: Revocable attribute-based signatures with adaptive security in the standard model. In: Nitaj, A., Pointcheval, D. (eds.) AFRICACRYPT 2011. LNCS, vol. 6737, pp. 224–241. Springer, Heidelberg (2011)

16. Fiat, A., Shamir, A.: How to prove yourself: Practical solutions to identification and signature problems. In: Odlyzko, A.M. (ed.) CRYPTO 1986. LNCS, vol. 263, pp. 186–194. Springer, Heidelberg (1987)

17. Frikken, K.B., Li, J., Atallah, M.J.: Trust negotiation with hidden credentials, hidden policies, and policy cycles. In: NDSS 2006, pp. 157–172. The Internet Society (2006)

18. Gagné, M., Narayan, S., Safavi-Naini, R.: Short pairing-efficient threshold-attribute-based signature. In: Abdalla, M., Lange, T. (eds.) Pairing 2012. LNCS, vol. 7708, pp. 295–313. Springer, Heidelberg (2013)

19. Galbraith, S., Paterson, K., Smart, N.P.: Pairings for cryptographers. Discrete Applied Mathematics 156, 3113–3121 (2008)

20. Ghadafi, E.: Stronger Security Notions for Decentralized Traceable Attribute-Based Signatures and More Efficient Constructions. In: Cryptology ePrint Archive, Report 2014/278 (2014)

21. Goyal, V., Pandey, O., Sahai, A., Waters, B.: Attribute-Based Encryption for Fine-Grained Access Control of Encrypted Data. In: CCS 2006, pp. 89–98. ACM (2006)

22. Granger, R., Kleinjung, T., Zumbragel, J.: Breaking '128-bit Secure' Supersingular Binary Curves (or how to solve discrete logarithms in $\mathbb{F}_{2^{4 \cdot 1223}}$ and $\mathbb{F}_{2^{12 \cdot 367}}$). In: CoRR 2014 (2014)

23. Herranz, J., Laguillaumie, F., Libert, B., Ràfols, C.: Short attribute-based signatures for threshold predicates. In: Dunkelman, O. (ed.) CT-RSA 2012. LNCS, vol. 7178, pp. 51–67. Springer, Heidelberg (2012)

24. Karchmer, M., Wigderson, A.: On span programs. In: 8th IEEE Structure in Complexity Theory, pp. 102–111 (1993)

25. Khader, D., Chen, L., Davenport, J.H.: Certificate-free attribute authentication. In: Parker, M.G. (ed.) Cryptography and Coding 2009. LNCS, vol. 5921, pp. 301–325. Springer, Heidelberg (2009)

26. Li, J., Au, M.H., Susilo, W., Xie, D., Ren, K.: Attribute-based signature and its applications. In: ASIACCS 2010, pp. 60–69. ACM (2010)

27. Maji, H.K., Prabhakaran, M., Rosulek, M.: Attribute-Based Signatures: Achieving Attribute-Privacy and Collusion-Resistance. In: Cryptology ePrint Archive, Report 2008/328, http://eprint.iacr.org/2008/328.pdf

28. Menezes, A., Vanstone, S.A., Okamoto, T.: Reducing Elliptic Curve Logarithms to Logarithms in a Finite Field. Transactions on Information Theory, 80–89 (1993)
29. Maji, H.K., Prabhakaran, M., Rosulek, M.: Attribute-Based Signatures. In: Cryptology ePrint Archive, Report 2010/595, http://eprint.iacr.org/2010/595.pdf
30. Maji, H.K., Prabhakaran, M., Rosulek, M.: Attribute-based signatures. In: Kiayias, A. (ed.) CT-RSA 2011. LNCS, vol. 6558, pp. 376–392. Springer, Heidelberg (2011)
31. Okamoto, T., Takashima, K.: Efficient attribute-based signatures for non-monotone predicates in the standard model. In: Catalano, D., Fazio, N., Gennaro, R., Nicolosi, A. (eds.) PKC 2011. LNCS, vol. 6571, pp. 35–52. Springer, Heidelberg (2011)
32. Okamoto, T., Takashima, K.: Decentralized attribute-based signatures. In: Kurosawa, K., Hanaoka, G. (eds.) PKC 2013. LNCS, vol. 7778, pp. 125–142. Springer, Heidelberg (2013)
33. Rivest, R.L., Shamir, A., Tauman, Y.: How to leak a secret. In: Boyd, C. (ed.) ASIACRYPT 2001. LNCS, vol. 2248, p. 552. Springer, Heidelberg (2001)
34. Shamir, A.: Identity-based cryptosystems and signature schemes. In: Blakely, G.R., Chaum, D. (eds.) CRYPTO 1984. LNCS, vol. 196, pp. 47–53. Springer, Heidelberg (1985)
35. Sahai, A., Waters, B.: Fuzzy identity-based encryption. In: Cramer, R. (ed.) EUROCRYPT 2005. LNCS, vol. 3494, pp. 457–473. Springer, Heidelberg (2005)
36. Shahandashti, S.F., Safavi-Naini, R.: Threshold attribute-based signatures and their application to anonymous credential systems. In: Preneel, B. (ed.) AFRICACRYPT 2009. LNCS, vol. 5580, pp. 198–216. Springer, Heidelberg (2009)
37. ISO/IEC 20008 (all parts) Information technology – Security techniques – Anonymous digital signatures (2013)

Towards a Full-Featured Implementation of Attribute Based Credentials on Smart Cards⋆

Antonio de la Piedra, Jaap-Henk Hoepman, and Pim Vullers

Radboud University Nijmegen, ICIS DS, Nijmegen, The Netherlands
{a.delapiedra,jhh,pim}@cs.ru.nl

Abstract. Attribute-based Credentials (ABCs) allow citizens to prove certain properties about themselves without necessarily revealing their full identity. Smart cards are an attractive container for such credentials, for security and privacy reasons. But their limited processing power and random access storage capacity pose a severe challenge. Recently, we, the IRMA team, managed to fully implement a limited subset of the Idemix ABC system on a smart card, with acceptable running times. In this paper we extend this functionality by overcoming the main hurdle: limited RAM. We implement an efficient extended Pseudo-Random Number Generator (PRNG) for recomputing pseudorandomness and reconstructing variables. Using this we implement Idemix standard and domain pseudonyms, AND proofs based on prime-encoded attributes, and equality proofs of representation modulo a composite, together with terminal verification and secure messaging. In contrast to prior work that only addressed the verification of one credential with only one attribute (particularly, the master secret), we can now perform multi-credential proofs on credentials of 5 attributes and complex proofs in reasonable time. We provide a detailed performance analysis and compare our results to other approaches.

1 Introduction

In Europe several eID systems supporting electronic transactions (particularly in Austria, Belgium, Estonia, Finland, Germany, Netherlands, Portugal, Spain and Sweden) exist. These systems vary a lot in terms of functionality, security levels, and the amount of privacy protection and user control they offer [28, 32], and are extensively studied in projects such as Future ID and STORK [1, 2]. Using eIDs, the massive utilization of username/password pairs on the Internet could be replaced by a Single-Sign-On (SSO) approach. For this reason a wide range of identity federation systems have been proposed in the last decade, such

⋆ The work described in this paper has been supported under the ICT theme of the Cooperation Programme of the 7th Framework Programme of the European Commission, GA number 318424 (Future ID). This research is conducted within the Privacy and Identity Lab (PI.lab) and funded by SIDN.nl (http://www.sidn.nl). The authors would like to thank the anonymous reviewers for their valuable comments and suggestions to improve the quality of the paper.

D. Gritzalis et al. (Eds.): CANS 2014, LNCS 8813, pp. 270–289, 2014.

as SAML [20] and OpenID [33]. These systems rely on a three-party scheme, distinguishing a user, a Service Provider (SP), and an Identity Provider (IdP). To access the service, the user logs in to the IdP, who provides an authentication token to the SP containing all the necessary information. Several security and privacy risks associated with this approach have been identified [30]. For example, the IdP knows every transaction its user performs [5].

Attribute Based Credentials (ABC) solve these problems, as follows. Credentials are secure containers of attributes, that can be selectively disclosed to the SP by the user. Moreover, the underlying cryptographic protocols are unlinkable, ensuring that repeated use of the same credential cannot be linked to one another. Despite the growing number of ABC systems (e.g. [6, 10, 14]), there are very few applications of such systems in practice. ABC systems rely on the secrecy of a master secret that binds all credentials to a single user. For security and privacy reasons it is therefore preferable to store this master secret and the associated credentials on a smart card, and run all cryptographic protocols (e.g. for issuing credentials and selectively disclosing attributes) on the smart card itself. This way the master secret never leaves the card. However, the limited processing power and random access storage capacity of the smart card pose a severe challenge for implementing the complex cryptographic protocols. Only recently, the IRMA[1] team, managed to fully implement a limited subset of the Idemix ABC system on a smart card, with acceptable running times [36]. In this paper we extend this functionality by overcoming the main hurdle: limited RAM.

Our Contributions. We first describe, in Section 2, different architectures and implementations of attribute based credentials presented in the literature. Then, in Section 3 we introduce the actual capabilities of the IRMA card, its execution model and its current limitations. In Section 4, we present the design of a PRNG for reducing the RAM requirements of the execution of proofs of knowledge in smart cards. This enables us to extend the number of attributes per credential, beyond the current IRMA limit of 5 attributes per credential. Our construction for recomputing randomness incurs an overhead of only 39.81 ms (3.66 %). Next, we broaden that approach to implement standard and domain pseudonyms in Section 5. Standard pseudonyms add 401.60 ms overhead, while domain pseudonyms in combination with standard pseudonyms add 658.63 ms overhead. Moreover, we can now perform equality proofs of representation across different credentials by combining this technique with variable reconstruction in RAM (e.g. 2,261.19 ms in the best case across 2 credentials, while the rest of proposed works in the literature only addressed the case of verifying one credential with one attribute (namely, the master secret) and obtained performance figures beyond 4 and 7 seconds [9,35]). This is discussed in Section 6. We implement the terminal verification and a secure channel for ABCs from [4] in Section 7. For each of these constructions we provide a detailed performance analysis, providing performance figures of our own constructions as well as giving those

---

[1] https://www.irmacard.org (accessed August 11, 2014)

of alternative approaches (tested on the same hardware), and comparing the results. Finally, we provide a performance analysis of all these operations using prime-encoded attributes [13] in Appendix A. In this respect, Bichsel et al. estimated an extra computation time of 1,684 ms over their verification operation with one attribute (i.e. the master secret) using a modulus of 1,536 bits in the prime-encoded AND proof [9]. That is 1.684 + 10.550 = 12.234 seconds. In our case (Appendix A) we can perform AND proofs with credentials of 5 attributes in 1,214.24 ms (hiding all the attributes) and we only require 1,547.83 ms for proving the ownership of the 5 attributes revealing them all using a modulus of 1,024 bits. In this case, we required 1,579.53 ms when proving the ownership of a pseudonym. Moreover, we show that the computation of equality proofs of representation involving several credentials on the smart card is also feasible relying on prime-encoding attributes.

2   Related Work

Generally, private ABCs rely on the idea of a blind and randomizable signature over a set of attributes [21]. A user that owns this type of signature can perform authentication operations by selectively disclosing a subset of attributes that describes her digital identity. Moreover, it is not possible to link transactions to signatures. Modern anonymous credential systems such as Idemix [14] and U-Prove [10] rely on that building block in combination with proofs of knowledge [22]. In the last few years, a myriad of credential systems has been implemented in smart cards [8,9,31,35,36]. Due to their availability in the market and their functionalities, the Java Card and MULTOS platforms are generally the preferred targets. Bichsel et al. presented the first implementation of Idemix on the Java Card platform in 2009. Proving the possession of one credential with one attribute (i.e. the master secret), required 7.4 seconds (1,280-bit modulus) and 10.55 seconds with a modulus of 1,536 bits [9]. Sterckx et al. followed a similar approach for implementing the signing protocol of Direct Anonymous Attestation (DAA) in Java Cards [35]. In their design, one transaction requires 4.2 seconds using a modulus of 1,024 bits. Nonetheless, the Java Cards 2 that Bichsel et al. and Sterckx et al. relied on do not provide direct access to modular arithmetic operations. Consequently, these authors had to rely on different strategies for performing modular multiplications and exponentiations, thus undermining the overall performance of the implementation. The IRMA card is based on the MULTOS platform embedded on the Infineon SLE78 chip. In contrast, this chip supports a variety of modular arithmetic operations that are crucial in the implementation of anonymous credentials together with asymmetric encryption primitives (RSA), signature schemes (RSA, ECDSA), symmetric encryption techniques (AES, 3DES) and hashing algorithms (SHA-1, SHA-2). Vullers et al. implemented in this platform the issuing and selective disclosure operations of Idemix. Using credentials of 5 attributes, the disclosure of all the attributes requires 0.947 seconds whereas the worst case (hiding the 5 attributes) is performed in 1.454 seconds [36].

3   The IRMA Card

IRMA relies on the specification of the Identity Mixer Anonymous Credential System [14] and is the first full card (i.e. no off-card or precomputation based) implementation of Idemix on smart cards suitable for real life transactions i.e the performance of a typical operation is reduced to 1–1.5 seconds [36] in comparison to the first attempts for implementing anonymous credentials in the literature (Section 2). Idemix provides different functionalities for proving the possession of attribute-based credentials and their properties e.g. [12, 18].

Idemix relies on different cryptographic blocks such as the Camenisch-Lysyanskaya (CL) signature, secure under the Strong RSA assumption [16]. Each credential can be categorized as an attribute container, protected by a CL signature generated by an issuer. This signature guarantees the integrity of the credentials i.e. modification, deletion or adding new attributes to a credential by the user can be easily detected by a verifier. Moreover, each credential is linked to the cardholder by her master secret, securely stored on the card in IRMA.

After the issuing process, the users owns a CL signature over one credential, represented by the triple (A, e, v) over $(m_0, m_1, ..., m_5)$. This information is stored in the card for each credential. The CL signature is created by an issuer according to its public key $(S, Z, R_0, R_1, ..., R_5 \in QR_n, n)$ using its secret key (p, q). For instance, a CL signature over a set of attributes $(m_0, ..., m_5)$ is computed by selecting A, e and v s.t. $A^e = Z R_0^{-m_0} R_1^{-m_1} R_2^{-m_2} R_3^{-m_3} R_4^{-m_4} R_5^{-m_5} S^{-v}$ mod n. Then, a third party can check the validity of the signature by using the issuer's public key and the tuple (A, e, v) as $Z \equiv A^e R_0^{m_0} R_1^{m_1} R_2^{m_2} R_3^{m_3} R_4^{m_4} R_5^{m_5} S^v$ mod n. In IRMA, for performance reasons, the size of the modulus n is restricted to $l_n = 1,024$ bits whereas the attributes are represented as $l_m = 256$ bits. The rest of parameters are set as $l_e' = 120$, $l_\emptyset = 80$, $l_H = 256$, $l_e = 504$, and $l_v = 1,604$ bits[2].

The key property of the CL signature in Idemix is to prove its possession without revealing additional information and performing the selective disclosure of the cardholder's attributes (Protocol 1) via discrete logarithm representation modulo a composite proofs of knowledge [25].

The typical 3-movement protocol (commitment, challenge and response) depicted in Protocol 1 is transformed into a Non-Interactive Proof of Knowledge (NIZK) via the Fiat-Shamir heuristic [24]. Therefore, the challenge c is computed by the card via a collision-resistant hash-function over the commitments and common values. Accordingly, an empty proof of possession over a set of attributes $(m_0, ..., m_5)$ is represented using the Camenisch-Staedler notation [19] as: NIZK: $\{(\varepsilon', \nu', \alpha_0, ..., \alpha_5) : Z \equiv \pm R_0^{\alpha_0} R_1^{\alpha_1} R_2^{\alpha_2} R_3^{\alpha_3} R_4^{\alpha_4} R_5^{\alpha_5} A^{\varepsilon'} S^{\nu'} \mod n\}$ being the Greek letters (ε', ν') and $(\alpha_0, ..., \alpha_5)$ the values of the signature and the

---

[2] The term l_e' represents the size of the interval where the e values are selected, $l_\emptyset$ is the security parameter of the statistical ZKP, and l_H is the domain of the hash function used in the Fiat-Shamir heuristic (we use SHA-256). Finally l_e and l_v are related to the size of e and v parameters of the CL signature.

Protocol 1. Message flow for proving the ownership of a CL signature over a set of attributes

Prover $Z \prod_{i \in A_r} R_i^{-m_i} = A'^e S^{v'} \prod_{i \in A_{\bar{r}}} R_i^{m_i}$	Public $S, Z, R_0, R_1, ..., R_5 \in QR_n, n$	Verifier $A', v', m_{i \in A_r}$
Signature randomization $r_A \in_R \{0,1\}^{l_n + l_\emptyset}$ $A' = A S^{r_A} \bmod n$ $v' = v - e r_A$ $e' = e - 2^{l_e - 1}$ **Generation of t_values** $\tilde{e} \in_R \pm\{0,1\}^{l'_e + l_\emptyset + l_H}$ $\tilde{v}' \in_R \pm\{0,1\}^{l_v + l_\emptyset + l_H}$ $\tilde{m}_i \in_R \pm\{0,1\}^{l_m + l_\emptyset + l_H} (i \in A_{\bar{r}})$ $\tilde{Z} = A'^{\tilde{e}} (\prod_{i \in A_{\bar{r}}} R_i^{\tilde{m}_i}) S^{\tilde{v}'}$ **Generation of s_values** $\hat{e} = \tilde{e} + ce'$ $\hat{v}' = \tilde{v}' + cv'$ $\hat{m}_i = \tilde{m}_i + cm_i (i \in A_{\bar{r}})$	$\xrightarrow{\quad \tilde{Z} \quad}$ $\xleftarrow{\quad c \quad}$ $\xrightarrow{\hat{e}, \hat{v}', \{\hat{m}_i\}_{i \in A_{\bar{r}}}}$	 $c \in_R \{0,1\}^{l_H}$ $A'^{\hat{e}} S^{\hat{v}'} \prod_{i \in A_{\bar{r}}} R_i^{\hat{m}_i} \stackrel{?}{=}$ $\tilde{Z} (Z \prod_{i \in A_r} R_i^{-m_i})^c$

set of attributes proved in zero knowledge and not revealed i.e. $\in A_{\bar{r}}$. The set of revealed attributes is represented by A_r. Similarly, one can prove the CL signature over a set of attributes revealing some of them. For instance, revealing m_1 and hiding $(m_0, m_2, m_3, m_4, m_5)$ would be represented in zero knowledge as NIZK: $\{(\varepsilon', \nu', \alpha_0, \alpha_2, \alpha_3, \alpha_4, \alpha_5) : Z R_1^{-m_1} \equiv \pm R_0^{\alpha_0} R_2^{\alpha_2} R_3^{\alpha_3} R_4^{\alpha_4} R_5^{\alpha_5} A^{\varepsilon'} S^{\nu'} \bmod n\}$.

In IRMA, the prover part of Idemix is implemented in the card as a set of states (PROVE_CREDENTIAL, PROVE_COMMITMENT, PROVE_SIGNATURE and PROVE_ATTRIBUTE) that mimics the Prover-Verifier interaction between a terminal and the smart card[3]. In each transaction, both entities exchange ISO 7816 APDUs that retrieve and write data in the smart card volatile (RAM) and non-volatile (EEPROM) memories [27]. When the card receives a verification request, it changes its initial state to PROVE_CREDENTIAL. Then, it acquires a presentation policy with the description of the attributes that must be revealed (i.e. those $\{m_i\}_{i \in A_r}$) and hidden (i.e. $\{m_i\}_{i \in A_{\bar{r}}}$). Then, the card performs the operations depicted in Protocol 1 (PROVE_COMMITMENT). Afterwards, the card changes its working state to PROVE_SIGNATURE. In this state, the verifier can request the

---

[3] We refer the reader to [36] for a description about how a (A, e, v) triple is obtained by the card.

randomized tuple $(A', \hat{e}, \hat{v}')$. Finally, the card switches to PROVE_ATTRIBUTE, where the verifier is allowed to request the set of revealed and hidden attributes related to the proof.

3.1   Execution Model

The latency of the verification operation can be modeled first according to the number of attributes per credential ($n = 5$ in the case of IRMA) together with the number of attributes that are revealed (r) or hidden. If we consider the worst case (all the attributes are hidden), $n - r + 1$ extra computations will be required for generating each $\hat{m}_i$ value (one extra operation is considered since the master secret is always hidden). Otherwise, the m_i attributes are sent in clear to the verifier. Eq. 1 represents the overall latency of the four states described above according to the (n, r) parameters.

$$T_{verify}(n,r) = T_{sel\_cred} + T_{gen\_commit}(n,r) + \sum_{i=A,e,v} T_{get\_sig}(i) + \sum_{i=1}^{n} T_{get\_attr}(i) \quad (1)$$

The time that T_{sel_cred} comprises is related to the PROVE_CREDENTIAL state whereas
$T_{gen\_commit}(n,r)$ represents PROVE_COMMITMENT and $T_{get\_sig}(i)\backslash T_{get\_attr}(i)$ are related to the PROVE_SIGNATURE and PROVE_ATTRIBUTE states respectively. Furthermore, the latency of the
PROVE_COMMITMENT state can be expanded to the following expression:

$$T_{gen\_commit}(n,r) = \sum_{i=A,v} T_{rand\_sig}(i) + T_{gen\_t\_values}(n-r+1) + T_{hash} + T_{gen\_s\_values}(n-r+1)$$

$$(2)$$

Eq. 2 represents the randomization of the CL signature and the generation of the t_values, s_values and the challenge c. Further, $T_{gen\_t\_values}$ represents the latency due to the computation of the commitment according to the number of non-disclosed values i.e. $\Sigma_{i=1}^{n-r+1} T_{mul\_exp}(R_i^{\tilde{m}_i})$. This value is then multiplied by $A'^{\tilde{e}} \cdot S^{\tilde{v}'}$ as described in Section 3. In addition, $n - r$ random $\tilde{m}_i$ values must be generated. Finally, the s_values are generated according to the number of hidden attributes:

$$T_{gen\_s\_values}(n-r+1) = T_{gen\_\hat{e}} + T_{gen\_\hat{v}'} + \sum_{i=0}^{r} T_{gen\_\hat{m}_i} \quad (3)$$

From the Equations 1-3 we notice the following. First, that the pseudorandomness used to derive the ($\tilde{e}$, $\tilde{v}'$) tuple and the $\tilde{m}_i$ values are used in both $T_{gen\_t\_values}$ and $T_{gen\_s\_values}$. Second, that the overall verification time is dominated by the number of non-revealed attributes ($n - r$) that requires: (1) the modular exponentiations computed during the generation of the t_values and (2), the random generation of the $\tilde{m}_i$ values and the computation of the correspondent $\hat{m}_i$ value as $\hat{m}_i = \tilde{m}_i + cm_i$. All in all, any possible optimization in the implementation must be driven by: (1) recomputing the pseudorandomness utilized in the $\tilde{m}$ values and (2) reducing the overhead of the required computation for hiding the selected attributes.

3.2   Memory Model

In the current IRMA implementation, the CL signatures and the credential attributes are stored in EEPROM. Besides, the intermediate values $\hat{m}_i$ and the randomized signature are computed in RAM in order to speed-up the overall performance of the verification operation. Since the RAM only comprises 960 bytes (together with 1,160 bytes of transient memory), we must consider how to scale the operations with credentials of a large number of attributes in order to deal with those intermediate values. In this respect, independently storing each $\hat{m}_i$ value for large credentials is impossible due to the RAM restrictions. In the current implementation, based on $5 + 1$ $\hat{m}_i$ values (taking into account the master secret, which is always hidden), one verification session requires $74 \cdot 6 = 444$ bytes of RAM, 74 bytes is the required space for storing one $\hat{m}_i$ value. Finally, given the current memory utilization, any optimization should be based on rearranging the storage of the random $\tilde{m}_i$ values.

4   Preliminary Optimizations

Our goal is to generate as many $\hat{m}_i$ values as needed without being limited by the current RAM size . This would make it possible to operate with larger credentials in the card. As noted before, these values are used in two parts of the generation of the NIZK: (1) during the computation of the commitment and (2) for hiding the desired attributes in the generation of the s_values. In the seminal paper of Bichsel et al. they suggested the utilization of a PRNG to regenerate the random exponent of the Idemix verification operation in the case of one credential with one attribute (i.e. the master secret) [9]. Consequently, we can extend this approach to regenerate all the involved pseudorandomness, not only the random exponents, for supporting credentials with a large number of attributes and implementing: pseudonyms, domain pseudonyms and AND proofs. Moreover, we coupled this technique with variable reconstruction in RAM for making possible to compute multi-credential proofs in the case of the equality proofs of representation.

Using cryptographic primitives such as block ciphers and Message Authentication Codes (MACs), conjectured as pseudorandom generators under the assumption that one-way functions exist (cf. [26,29]), a wide range of PRNGs has been proposed in the literature e.g. [7,23]. Therefore, it is expected that the output of these constructions would be indistinguishable from random by any probabilistic polynomial time algorithm or distinguisher. Among the schemes described in [7,23] (e.g. Fortuna, HMAC_DBRG and HASH_DBRG), all share the same behaviour: (1) acquire new entropy, (2) process the entropy into a seed and, if needed, add a personalizing string, and (3) generate pseudorandom bits using a cryptographic primitive (e.g. a block cipher) categorized as Generator Function (GF). The HASH_DBRG PRNG utilizes SHA-1/-2 for generating pseudorandomness whereas the HMAC_DBRG PRNG can optionally rely on one of those primitives following the HMAC construction, where a key k is also part of the initial state. Finally, a PRNG can be constructed using a block cipher such as Fortuna [23], which only enciphers a counter using a key derived from an entropy input and processed via SHA-256.

In Table 1, we present the performance results in our target device for computing one $\hat{m}_i$ value (74 bytes) using six different PRNGs. We also present the number of calls to the GF in each case to generate $|\hat{m}_i|$ bytes. Notice that the PRNGs based on HMACs are considerably slower due to the fact that they require performing two hash operations per call together with two updating functions [7]. Moreover, the performance of using Fortuna and the PRNG based on SHA-1 is similar, given that the number of calls to the SHA-1 hash algorithm is almost equal in both cases (26.33 ms and 29.32 ms respectively). However, when a considerable amount of pseudorandomness per session is generated (particularly, during the execution of a proof that involves more than one credential), a difference of 3 ms can be significant[4]. In this respect, we have lowered the security level to AES-128 (24.76 ms per $\hat{m}_i$).

Table 1. Performance of PRNG candidates in the IRMA card for generating an $\hat{m}_i$ value of 74 bytes

Work	PRNG	GF	Block size (bytes)	No. calls (GF)	Delay (ms)
[7]	HMAC_DBRG	SHA-1	20	12	48.64
[7]	HASH_DBRG	SHA-1	20	5	26.33
[7]	HMAC_DBRG	SHA-256	32	10	106.78
[7]	HASH_DBRG	SHA-256	32	4	47.47
[23]	Fortuna	AES-256	16	5	29.32
This work	IRMA	AES-128	16	5	24.76

In our case, during each verification session, a seed k is generated as the last 128 bits of the SHA-1 hash operation of the concatenation of the MULTOS PRNG output together with the string "IRMA". Then, this seed is fed into the GF (AES-128) as the key. At the beginning of each verification session a counter c is initialized to 0 and incremented in the generation of each pseudorandom block of 128 bits. When the verification process is finished the seed stored in RAM is erased by the discharge of the capacitors of the smart card and in the next verification session, a new seed is generated. Thus, this design provides backtracking resistance between verification sessions. Moreover, prediction resistance

---

[4] See, for instance, the number of required calls in our approach for performing equality proofs of representation (Section 6, Table 4). In that case, only generating the pseudorandomness associated to a $(A', \hat{e}, \hat{v}')$ triple for one credential of 5 attributes needs $9 + 16 + 4 + 5 \cdot 6 = 59$ calls to the PRNG if all the attributes are hidden.

is ensured if we rely on the security of the AES block cipher. The PRNG runs the following sequence in this case: $init_{PRNG}() \Rightarrow \tilde{m}_i \Rightarrow reset_{PRNG}() \Rightarrow \tilde{m}_i$.

4.1   Results for Verifying a Full Credential

In our implementation we proceed as follows. We replace the former $74 \cdot 6$ bytes for storing all the $\tilde{m}_i$ values by three values maintained in RAM during the verification session: the seed/AES key ($128/8 = 16$ bytes), the counter c (16 bytes) and 74 bytes for the $\tilde{m}_i$ values that are generated when required. Thus, when an $\tilde{m}$ value needs to be generated, we get as many blocks as needed for filling the 74 random bytes space and the counter c is incremented after each block is computed. This process is repeated two times. First, during the computation of the t_value and second, during the s_values generation. In the second part, the PRNG is reset to its initial state (by choosing $c = 0$ again) in order to obtain the same output as the first time without storing all the reconstructed $\tilde{m}$ values. This requires $74 + 16 + 16 = 106$ bytes of RAM instead of $74 \cdot 6 = 444$ bytes. Nonetheless, an extra latency for computing all the $\tilde{m}$ values at run time is expected. This is depicted in Table 2[5]. We have considered both worst cases (WC, where all the attributes are hidden) and best cases (BC, where only the master secret (m_0) is hidden).

Table 2. Performance overhead while verifying five attributes using a custom PRNG for generating the $\tilde{m}$ values (ms)

Work	Encoding	Case	T_{sel_cred}	T_{gen_commit}	$T_{get\_sig}(A, e, v)$	$T_{get\_attr}(m_0, ..., m_5)$	Total
This work	normal	BC	103.10	840.73	14.12, 11.52, 19.54	38.32, 11.51*5	1,084.91
This work	normal	WC	104.95	1,307.35	15.11, 11.48, 19.49	38.30*6	1,688.20
[36]	normal	BC	104.12	826.25	14.16, 11.48, 19.50	12.10, 11.49*5	1,045.10
[36]	normal	WC	105.20	1,259.24	16.10, 11.49, 19.48	12.13*6	1,484.32

According to Eq. 1–3, the calculation of the $\tilde{m}$ values as $\tilde{m}_i + cm_i$ was performed in $T_{gen\_commit}(n, r)$. Now, that generation operation is performed on demand in $T_{get\_attr}(i)$ i.e. when the verifier asks for those values. Therefore, $T_{gen\_s\_values}$ is represented as $T_{gen\_s\_values} = T_{gen\_\hat{e}} + T_{gen\_\hat{v}'}$ and $\sum_{i=1}^{n} T_{get\_attr}(i)$ includes the generation of $\tilde{m}_i$ as $T_{gen\_\tilde{m}_i}$ for r $\tilde{m}_i$ values. This means, that we reduce the

---

[5] The notation and abbreviations in Tables 2–3 and 5–9 are utilized as follows. First, for those latencies that are related to the same operation e.g. $T_{get\_attr}(i)$, only one element appears multiplied by the number of elements of its type that are involved e.g. 11.51*5. Then, for each element that is optional according to the different proofs represented in the same table, a vertical bar (|) appears in the header of the table (e.g. Table 3). For those values that do not belong to the proof an horizontal bar (−) is utilized. Finally, we represent the best performance figures in **bold**.

overall time in $T_{gen\_commit}(n, r)$ but add an extra delay according to the random generation of the $\tilde{m}_i$ values. We also obtained an extra delay in $T_{get\_attr}(i)$, consisting of (1) recomputing the pseudorandomness for each $\tilde{m}_i$ value and (2) computing $\hat{m}_i = \tilde{m}_i + cm_i$. All in all, we obtained a reduction of RAM of 338 bytes with an added overall latency of 203.88 ms in the worst case whereas the extra latency in the best case is only restricted to the generation of the $\hat{m}_i$ value for hiding the master secret, where only 39.81 ms are required[6].

5   Implementation of Standard and Domain Pseudonyms

Given the optimizations described in the past section, now it is possible to implement additional proofs in combination to proving the ownership of a CL signature over a set of attributes. In this section, we relate our implementation of Idemix pseudonyms [15]. They provide extended operations to basic protocols such as issuing a credential associated to a pseudonym or connect the cardholder's verification process to a given pseudonym. The latter, would guarantee being recognized the next time an user visited the same SP. Besides standard pseudonyms (described as randomized commitments to the cardholder's master secret i.e. $\mathsf{Nym} = g^{m_0} h^r \mod \Gamma$ where both generators (g, h) and modulo Γ are public and part of the system group parameters) it is possible to create pseudonyms associated to a certain domain such as an organization. They are derived as $\mathsf{dNym} = g_{dom}^{m_0}$ where $g_{dom} = \mathcal{H}(\mathsf{dom})^{(\Gamma-1)/\rho}$ and the group Z_Γ^* has order $\Gamma - 1 = \rho \cdot b$ for a prime ρ [15]. For instance, proving the ownership of both a standard and domain pseudonyms can be performed in zero knowledge as NIZK: $\{(\varepsilon', \nu', \alpha_0, ..., \alpha_5, \psi) : Z \equiv \pm R_0^{\alpha_0} R_1^{\alpha_1} R_2^{\alpha_2} R_3^{\alpha_3} R_4^{\alpha_4} R_5^{\alpha_5} A^{\varepsilon'} S^{\nu'} \mod n \wedge \mathsf{nym} \equiv g^{\alpha_0} h^{\psi} \mod \Gamma \wedge \mathsf{dNym} \equiv g_{dom}^{\alpha_0} \mod \Gamma\}$ without revealing any attribute. However, performing a certain degree of selective disclosure would provide the SP with more identification details linked to the pseudonym. In order to design a RAM-efficient implementation of standard/domain pseudonyms, the associated pseudorandomness to r and m_0 must be recomputed by the PRNG that we presented in Section 4. Therefore, the PRNG would follow the $init_{PRNG}() \Rightarrow \tilde{m}_i \Rightarrow \tilde{r} \Rightarrow \tilde{m}_0 \Rightarrow r \Rightarrow reset_{PRNG}() \Rightarrow \tilde{m}_i \Rightarrow \tilde{r} \Rightarrow \tilde{m}_0$ sequence in order to recompute the required pseudorandom values during the generation of both t- and s_values in the case of proving the ownership of a standard pseudonym and a domain pseudonym.

5.1   Results for Verifying a Full Credential with an Associated Pseudonym

The user must store in EEPROM the two generators (g, h), together with r and the modulus Γ. Given that our target device is comprised of 80KB of EEPROM and the current implementation is 31,897 bytes we have plenty of space for

---

[6] Extending the number of attributes of the credential also involves modifying the issuing protocol implementation. Given the space limits, we opted for showing how to compute complex proofs.

Table 3. Performance analysis of proving the ownership of standard and domain pseudonyms (normal encoding, ms)

Implementation	Case	T_{sel_cred}	T_{gen_commit}	$T_{get\_sig}(A,e,v)$	$T_{get\_attr}(m_0,...,m_5,nym,\hat{r}|dNym)$	Total
Nym	BC	103.10	1,176.02	15.30, 11.41, 19.57	38.42, 11.55*5, 13.95, 50.99	**1,486.51**
Nym	WC	103.15	1,647.33	15.35, 11.54, 19.57	38.11*6, 13.99, 50.86	2,065.42
Nym ∧ dNym	BC	103.01	1,373.37	15.28, 11.41, 19.35	38.39, 11.83*5, 14.02, 58.37 | 51.12	**1,743.54**
Nym ∧ dNym	WC	104.23	1,836.00	15.19, 11.59, 19.24	38.02*6, 13.84, 58.32 | 51.42	2,338.01

storing different pseudonyms. In this respect, encoding pseudonyms as strings of 32 bytes would allow to store up to $80K-(31,897/32) = 1,503$ pseudonyms in the card. Finally, in addition to the revealed or hidden attributes that the cardholder sends to the verifier, the commitments nym and dNym together with the s_value $\hat{r}$ are recomputed and their respective delay is added to $T_{get\_attr}(i)$. As in Table 2, we have represented the best case/worst case scenarios for each type of pseudonym in Table 3. In comparison to Table 2, performing the extra number of modular exponentiations related to the pseudonyms commitments (e.g. nym) required $1,176.02 - 840.73 = 335.29$ ms in the best case. However, due to the optimizations described in Section 4, is also possible to store extra commitments in RAM in order to avoid recomputing them during T_{get_attr}.

6   Tailored Execution of Equality Proofs of Representation

Sometimes, it is useful to prove that two or more credentials share some values [17]. This type of proof would enable verifiers to evaluate different properties in the credentials of the cardholder, for instance, proving that two or more credentials belong to the same cardholder via the master secret that is included in all the credentials with independence of the issuer. This is essential to prevent credential pooling attacks.

In this section, we restrict ourselves to equality proofs of two credentials, where the ownership of the cardholder is proved through the equality of the master secret, and where independent selective disclosures can be performed in each credential. Given two credentials issued by different issuers over the same master secret (m_0) and two different CL signatures (A_1, e_1, v_1) and (A_2, e_2, v_2), we describe an empty (i.e. where all the attributes of the first and second credentials are hidden) equality proof of this type as: NIZK: $\{(\varepsilon_1', \nu_1', \varepsilon_2', \nu_2', \mu, (\alpha_1, ..., \alpha_5), (\beta_1, ..., \beta_5))$: $Z^{(1)} \equiv \pm R_0^{(1)\mu} R_1^{(1)\alpha_1} R_2^{(1)\alpha_2} R_3^{(1)\alpha_3} R_4^{(1)\alpha_4} R_5^{(1)\alpha_5} A^{(1)\varepsilon_1'} S^{(1)\nu_1'} \mod n_1 \wedge Z^{(2)} \equiv \pm R_0^{(2)\mu} R_1^{(2)\beta_1} R_2^{(2)\beta_2} R_3^{(2)\beta_3} R_4^{(2)\beta_4} R_5^{(2)\beta_5} A^{(2)\varepsilon_2'} S^{(2)\nu_2'} \mod n_2\}$. Where μ represents the non-disclosed master secret[7] and the two public keys of the issuers consists of $(S^{(1)}, Z^{(1)}, R_0^{(1)}, R_1^{(1)}, ..., R_5^{(1)} \in QR_{n_1}, n_1)$ and

---

[7] In this case $\alpha_0 = \beta_0$ if both credentials belong to the same cardholder. We represent the non-disclosed master secret as μ following the Camenisch-Staedler notation [19].

$(S^{(2)}, Z^{(2)}, R_0^{(2)}, R_1^{(2)}, ..., R_5^{(2)} \in QR_{n_2}, n_2)$. Moreover, the following s_values for the groups of attributes of each credential and the master secret need to be computed: $\hat{m}_0 = \tilde{m}_0 + cm_0, \hat{m}_1^{(1)} = \tilde{m}_1^{(1)} + cm_1^{(1)}, \hat{m}_2^{(1)} = \tilde{m}_2^{(1)} + cm_2^{(1)}, \hat{m}_3^{(1)} = \tilde{m}_3^{(1)} + cm_3^{(1)}, \hat{m}_4^{(1)} = \tilde{m}_4^{(1)} + cm_4^{(1)}, \hat{m}_5^{(1)} = \tilde{m}_5^{(1)} + cm_5^{(1)}, \hat{m}_1^{(2)} = \tilde{m}_1^{(2)} + cm_1^{(2)}, \hat{m}_2^{(2)} = \tilde{m}_2^{(2)} + cm_2^{(2)}, \hat{m}_3^{(2)} = \tilde{m}_3^{(2)} + cm_3^{(2)}, \hat{m}_4^{(2)} = \tilde{m}_4^{(2)} + cm_4^{(2)}, \hat{m}_5^{(2)} = \tilde{m}_5^{(2)} + cm_5^{(2)}$.

Finally, $\hat{v}_1 = \tilde{v}_1' + cv_1'$, $\hat{v}_2 = \tilde{v}_2' + cv_2'$, $\hat{e}_1' = \tilde{e}_1 + ce_1$ and $\hat{e}_2' = \tilde{e}_2 + ce_2$ are computed for each CL signature in $T_{get\_sig}(i)$.

6.1   Design

In order to implement these proofs, we must address three types of requirements in terms of: (1) space, (2) performance and (3) cryptographic capabilities of the card. First, we need space to store and/or maintain in RAM two or more (A, e, v) tuples in order to generate each t_value of the proof. Moreover, we also require space for storing the $(\hat{e}, \hat{v}')$ tuples for each credential during the computation of each s_value. Furthermore, we need to perform all these computations in a reasonable time. In this respect, performing the operations in RAM would be a top priority. Finally, we need a hash primitive for computing multiple and subsequent blocks of data (t_values) in order to generate the challenge c. In this case, we need to include the set of the $t\_$ and common values for each credential in the proof. Since the MULTOS hash function for obtaining a SHA-256 digest requires the full input in memory, and that resource is limited in our target device, we must find an alternative function that can compute hashes with partial inputs in a subsequent manner.

In order to implement the equality proof on the card and be able to cope with multiple signatures of different issuers we extend the PRNG described in Section 4 and couple it with variable reconstruction in RAM. We notice that the $(\hat{e}, \hat{v}')$ values only depend on the $(\tilde{e}, \tilde{v})$ pseudorandom variables. Since they do not depend on $\tilde{m}$, the same space reserved in RAM for such value (74 bytes as described in Section 4) can be reused for $(\hat{e}, \hat{v}')$ if their size is adapted to the largest value (i.e. 255 bytes in the case of $\tilde{v}$). This approach, makes it possible to sequentially reconstruct via the deterministic PRNG $\hat{e}$ and $\hat{v}'$ (i.e. as $\hat{e} = \tilde{e} + ce'$ and $\hat{v}' = \tilde{v} + cv'$) for each credential during the generation of the $t\-$ and s_values. Furthermore, the randomized computation of the signature component A' requires r_A, another random value that can be derived from the PRNG. Moreover, since the randomization of this value is independent form the rest of the signature (e, v) and the $\hat{m}_i$ values, we can compute all these variables in a sequentially way. After each pseudorandom value has been recomputed, the reconstructed variable is temporary stored in the transaction memory of the card till it is requested by the verifier.

Therefore, the generation and recomputing of these values for an equality proof of two credentials would be orchestrated by the PRNG as $init_{PRNG}() \Rightarrow r_A^{(1)} \Rightarrow \tilde{v}^{(1)} \Rightarrow \tilde{e}^{(1)} \Rightarrow \tilde{m}_i^{(1)} \Rightarrow r_A^{(2)} \Rightarrow \tilde{v}^{(2)} \Rightarrow \tilde{e}^{(2)} \Rightarrow \tilde{m}_i^{(2)} \Rightarrow reset_{PRNG}() \Rightarrow r_A^{(1)} \Rightarrow \tilde{v}^{(1)} \Rightarrow \tilde{e}^{(1)} \Rightarrow \tilde{m}_i^{(1)} \Rightarrow r_A^{(2)} \Rightarrow \tilde{v}^{(2)} \Rightarrow \tilde{e}^{(2)} \Rightarrow \tilde{m}_i^{(2)}$. We describe two[8]

---

[8] We provide a third alternative via prime encoding in Appendix A.

Table 4. Time required for reconstructing A_i', $\hat{v}_i'$, $\hat{e}_i$, and $\hat{m}_i$ in RAM

Variable	Operation	Size (bytes)	No. of calls to PRNG	Delay (ms)
A_i'	AS^{r_A}	138	9	235.191
$\hat{v}_i'$	$v' = v - e \cdot r_A$	255	16	104.365
	$\hat{v} = \tilde{v}' + c \cdot v'$			
$\hat{e}_i$	$\tilde{e} + c \cdot e'$	57	4	30.710
$\hat{m}_i$	$\tilde{m}_i + c \cdot m_i$	74	5	36.708

different alternatives for performing this proof according to different scenarios and speed requirements.

Alternative A: Equality Proofs Across n Credentials. We have depicted in Table 4 the performance of recomputing the randomness for the $(A', \hat{v}', \hat{e}, \hat{m}_i)$ values and reconstructing their values in RAM. Despite the required number of calls to the PRNG is higher in $\hat{v}'$, the overall execution time is dominated by the reconstruction of A' that requires recomputing the S^{r_A} modular exponentiation (235.191 ms). In contrast to the execution model described in Section 3.2, we have rearranged the computation of $(A', \hat{e}, \hat{v}')$ to $(A', \hat{v}', \hat{e})$ since the computation of $\hat{v}'$ requires r_A. On the contrary, $\hat{e}$ does not depend on other values.

Finally, in relation to the third requirement, we rely on the PRIM_SECURE_HASH_IV primitive of the MULTOS card in order to subsequently hash each t_value. This primitive makes possible to avoid maintaining a long string of bytes in RAM with all the required inputs for generating the challenge. Therefore, each A' and t_value is generated in an iterative way and sequentially added to the temporary digest. After the last t_value, the transaction nonce is hashed and the final digest is derived. In contrast to Eq. 2, the s_values for each credential signature $(\hat{e}, \hat{v}')$ are now recomputed on demand when the verifier request them. Consequently, that latency is added to $T_{get\_sig}(i)$.

Alternative B: Equality Proofs Across 2 Credentials. In this alternative, we work under the assumption that each card stores only two credentials i.e. one root credential with different information about an issuing organization, an expiration date or a revocation state together with a second credential that includes the cardholders attributes. In both credentials the master secret is shared and an equality proof can be performed across the two in order to proof the validity of the card or the attributes. In this case, it can be possible to store both $A'^{(1)}$ and $A'^{(2)}$ and avoid recomputing them two times as described in the first alternative (Table 4). Moreover, the randomization factors $r_A^{(1)}$ and $r_A^{(2)}$ can be stored too in order to avoid regenerate them via the PRNG during the computing of $\hat{v}_i'$. In this case, we use the transient memory of the card for storing these four values. Given that its size is 1,016 bytes and the APDU buffer is limited to 256 bytes according to the ISO 7816 standard we can use up to 1,016 - 256 = 760 bytes for storing these values. In this respect, we need 2·128 bytes for $A'^{(1)}$, $A'^{(2)}$ and 2·138 bytes for $r_A^{(1)}$ and $r_A^{(2)}$ in our case. Finally, the PRNG sequence for this approach is represented by $init_{PRNG}() \Rightarrow r_A^{(1)} \Rightarrow \tilde{v}^{(1)} \Rightarrow \tilde{e}^{(1)} \Rightarrow \tilde{m}_i^{(1)} \Rightarrow r_A^{(2)} \Rightarrow \tilde{v}^{(2)} \Rightarrow \tilde{e}^{(2)} \Rightarrow \tilde{m}_i^{(2)} \Rightarrow reset_{PRNG}() \Rightarrow \tilde{v}^{(1)} \Rightarrow \tilde{e}^{(1)} \Rightarrow \tilde{m}_i^{(1)} \Rightarrow \tilde{v}^{(2)} \Rightarrow \tilde{e}^{(2)} \Rightarrow \tilde{m}_i^{(2)}$ skipping the regenerated values $r_A^{(1)}, r_A^{(2)}$ (stored).

6.2 Results for Performing an Equality Proof of Representation with Two Full Credentials

We have depicted in Table 5[9] the performance of equality proofs using the two described alternatives (a, b) for proving that the credentials (2 in this example) of the cardholder share their master secret and therefore, are linked to her.

Table 5. Performance overhead while verifying two credentials with 5 attributes using the equality proof (normal encoding, ms)

Alternative	Case	T_{sel_cred} (ms)	T_{gen_commit}	$T_{get\_sig}(A,e,v)$	$T_{get\_attr}(m_0,...,m_5)$	Total
a	BC	104.12	1,805.24	$(231.95, 91.63, 27.47)^{(1,2)}$	$(32.02, 10.11*5)^{(1)}, (10.10*5)^{(2)}$	2,744.51
a	WC	105.23	2,738.78	$(228.38, 91.64, 27.55)^{(1,2)}$	$(31.50*6)^{(1)}, (31.13*5)^{(2)}$	3,883.83
b	BC	103.99	1,743.37	$(17.82, 91.58, 27.40)^{(1,2)}$	$(32.05, 10.49*5)^{(1)}, (10.53*5)^{(2)}$	**2,261.19**
b	WC	103.47	2,673.60	$(14.78, 91.25, 27.37)^{(1,2)}$	$(31.86*6)^{(1)}, (31.19*5)^{(2)}$	3,390.60

Using the second alternative (b), it can be possible to perform an equality proof of representation in 2,261.19 ms revealing all the attributes, whereas hiding all the attributes would require 1,129.40 extra ms. Finally, the first alternative (a), due to the fact that we recompute $(\hat{e}, \hat{v}')$ for each credential in the generation of each t_value, increases the execution time of $T_{gen\_commit}(n, r)$ from 840.73 ms (verification of one credential, best case, Table 2) to 1,805.24 ms (best case, all the attributes are revealed) and from 1,307.35 ms (verification of one credential, all the attributes hidden, Table 2) to 2,738.78 ms (worst case, all the attributes remain hidden). However, given the case that the user is requested to perform an equality proof of her credentials, it would be rare to hide all the attributes in the case that one of the credentials (e.g. a root credential) would contain information about the issuing operation required to be revealed e.g. a date, the name of an organization, etc.

7 Authenticated Secure Channel

We have depicted in Table 6 the results for performing all the operations described in Sections 4-6 through terminal verification and secure channel. We rely

---

[9] We use the superscripts 1 and 2 for referring to the operations related to the credentials 1 and 2 of the equality proof. During the randomization of the CL signatures the operations for each credential are the same. We have put together the operations related to each credential in the worst case. Therefore, two pairs of 5 attributes are hidden together with the master secret i.e. $6 + 5$ operations if the master secret is hidden during the computation of the s_values of the first credential.

Table 6. Performance analysis of a full operation using terminal verification and secure channel (normal encoding, ms)

Operation	Case	T_{set_sc}	T_{sel_cred}	T_{gen_commit}	$T_{get\_sig}(A, e, v_1, v_2)$	$T_{get\_attr}(m_0, ..., m_5|nym, \hat{r}|dNym)$	Total
verify 1 cred	BC	203.31	183.50	889.53	82.49, 49.40, 81.25, 68.82	76.04, 49.40*5	**1,881.30**
verify 1 cred	WC	203.29	183.53	1,360.42	82.47, 49.38, 81.24, 68.80	76.14*6	2,484.10
Nym	BC	203.32	185.26	1,226.26	81.99, 49.21, 80.88, 68.54	75.75, 49.28*5 | 81.01, 93.62	**2,392.21**
Nym	WC	203.28	182.27	1,690.50	82.18, 49.35, 81.01, 68.57	75.70*6 | 81.32, 93.67	2,986.42
Nym ∧ dNym	BC	203.29	182.41	1,419.52	82.19, 49.43, 81.02, 68.63	75.97, 49.41*5 | 81.38, 93.63 | 124.23	**2,708.82**
Nym ∧ dNym	WC	203.31	182.56	1,893.67	82.02, 49.45, 81.02, 68.50	75.08*6 | 81.21, 93.75 | 124.26	3,310.23
eq. proof b	BC	203.31	182.56	1,809.39	$(82.10, 49.41, 81.05, 68.54)^{1,2}$	$83.37, (49.99*5)^{1,2}$	**3,340.71**
eq. proof b	WC	203.33	182.56	2,743.20	$(82.12, 49.43, 81.02, 68.50)^{1,2}$	$84.10, (84.33*5)^{1,2}$	4,618.62

on the secure channel for ABCs proposed by Alpár et al. in [4] and we perform terminal verification via ECDSA signatures using the light secp160r1 (160 bits) curve [34]. Besides, we rely on the normative for secure messaging of the German ID [11] for providing authentication and confidentiality (CBC-MAC and 3DES-CBC are used [11]). If we compare our results depicted in Table 6 with the works described in Section 2, Bichsel et al. required 7.4 seconds for verifying a credential of one attribute (i.e. master secret, modulo 1,280 bits) whereas we can perform an equality proof of 5 credentials in the same time (Appendix A, Figure 1). Besides, one transaction in the implementation of Sterckx et al. required 4.25 s using a modulus of 1,024 bits whereas we can perform all the operations described in Sections 4–6 (best cases) within the same time [10].

We have made available our prototypes[11] for public verifiability under the General Public License (GPL) together with a terminal code based on the CHARM cryptographic framework [3].

8   Conclusions

We have presented the performance evaluation and our design options for implementing Idemix on a smart card together with a variety of operations for executing complex proofs. We relied on recomputing all the involved pseudorandommness using a PRNG. Moreover, we have described our results in combination with a secure channel coupled with terminal verification based on ECC. All our operations required between 1–3.3 seconds (best cases) and between 1–4.6 (all cases) while the prior art only addressed the case of one credential with one attribute (i.e. the master secret). In contrast, our performance figures can be acceptable in on-line settings and could be adapted to off-line scenarios.

References

1. EU FP7 Future ID (2014), http://www.futureid.eu/ (accessed August 11, 2014)

---

[10] We also note that these results can be probably reproduced in other devices relying on the Infineon SLE78 chip.

[11] https://github.com/adelapie/irma_phase_2 (accessed August 11, 2014)

2. EU FP7 Secure idenTity acrOss boRders linKed (STORK) 2.0 (2014), https://www.eid-stork2.eu/ (accessed August 11, 2014)
3. Akinyele, J.A., Garman, C., Miers, I., Pagano, M.W., Rushanan, M., Green, M., Rubin, A.D.: Charm: a framework for rapidly prototyping cryptosystems. J. Cryptographic Engineering 3(2), 111–128 (2013)
4. Alpár, G., Hoepman, J.-H.: A secure channel for attribute-based credentials: [short paper]. In: Digital Identity Management, pp. 13–18 (2013)
5. Alpár, G., Hoepman, J.-H., Siljee, J.: The identity crisis. security, privacy and usability issues in identity management. CoRR, abs/1101.0427 (2011)
6. Baldimtsi, F., Lysyanskaya, A.: Anonymous credentials light. In: ACM Conference on Computer and Communications Security, pp. 1087–1098 (2013)
7. Barker, E., Kelsey, J.: NIST Special Publication 800-90A: Recommendation for Random Number Generation Using Deterministic Random Bit Generators (2012)
8. Batina, L., Hoepman, J.-H., Jacobs, B., Mostowski, W., Vullers, P.: Developing efficient blinded attribute certificates on smart cards via pairings. In: Gollmann, D., Lanet, J.-L., Iguchi-Cartigny, J. (eds.) CARDIS 2010. LNCS, vol. 6035, pp. 209–222. Springer, Heidelberg (2010)
9. Bichsel, P., Camenisch, J., Groß, T., Shoup, V.: Anonymous credentials on a standard Java Card. In: ACM Conference on Computer and Communications Security, pp. 600–610 (2009)
10. Brands, S.A.: Rethinking Public Key Infrastructures and Digital Certificates: Building in Privacy. MIT Press, Cambridge (2000)
11. BSI. TR-03110: Advanced Security Mechanisms for Machine Readable Travel Documents
12. Camenisch, J., Chaabouni, R., Shelat, A.: Efficient protocols for set membership and range proofs. In: Pieprzyk, J. (ed.) ASIACRYPT 2008. LNCS, vol. 5350, pp. 234–252. Springer, Heidelberg (2008)
13. Camenisch, J., Groß, T.: Efficient attributes for anonymous credentials (extended version). IACR Cryptology ePrint Archive, 2010:496 (2010)
14. Camenisch, J., Van Herreweghen, E.: Design and implementation of the *idemix* anonymous credential system. In: ACM Conference on Computer and Communications Security, pp. 21–30 (2002)
15. Camenisch, J., Lysyanskaya, A.: An efficient system for non-transferable anonymous credentials with optional anonymity revocation. In: Pfitzmann, B. (ed.) EUROCRYPT 2001. LNCS, vol. 2045, pp. 93–118. Springer, Heidelberg (2001)
16. Camenisch, J., Lysyanskaya, A.: A signature scheme with efficient protocols. In: Cimato, S., Galdi, C., Persiano, G. (eds.) SCN 2002. LNCS, vol. 2576, pp. 268–289. Springer, Heidelberg (2003)
17. Camenisch, J., Michels, M.: Separability and efficiency for generic group signature schemes (Extended abstract). In: Wiener, M. (ed.) CRYPTO 1999. LNCS, vol. 1666, pp. 413–430. Springer, Heidelberg (1999)
18. Camenisch, J., Shoup, V.: Practical verifiable encryption and decryption of discrete logarithms. In: Boneh, D. (ed.) CRYPTO 2003. LNCS, vol. 2729, pp. 126–144. Springer, Heidelberg (2003)
19. Camenisch, J., Stadler, M.: Efficient group signature schemes for large groups. In: Kaliski Jr., B.S. (ed.) CRYPTO 1997. LNCS, vol. 1294, pp. 410–424. Springer, Heidelberg (1997)
20. Cantor, S., Kemp, J., Philpott, R., Maler, E.: Assertions and Protocols for the OASIS Security Assertion Markup Language (SAML) V2.0. Technical report (March 2005)

21. Chaum, D.: Blind signatures for untraceable payments. In: CRYPTO, pp. 199–203 (1982)
22. Damgård, I.: Commitment schemes and zero-knowledge protocols. In: Damgård, I. (ed.) EEF School 1998. LNCS, vol. 1561, pp. 63–86. Springer, Heidelberg (1999)
23. Ferguson, N., Schneier, B., Kohno, T.: Cryptography Engineering: Design Principles and Practical Applications. Wiley Publishing (2010)
24. Fiat, A., Shamir, A.: How to prove yourself: Practical solutions to identification and signature problems. In: Odlyzko, A.M. (ed.) CRYPTO 1986. LNCS, vol. 263, pp. 186–194. Springer, Heidelberg (1987)
25. Fujisaki, E., Okamoto, T.: Statistical zero knowledge protocols to prove modular polynomial relations. In: Kaliski Jr., B.S. (ed.) CRYPTO 1997. LNCS, vol. 1294, pp. 16–30. Springer, Heidelberg (1997)
26. Impagliazzo, R., Luby, M.: One-way functions are essential for complexity based cryptography. In: Proceedings of the 30th Annual Symposium on Foundations of Computer Science, SFCS 1989, pp. 230–235. IEEE Computer Society, Washington, DC (1989)
27. ISO/IEC. International standard 7816-4
28. Lehmann, A., Bichsel, P., Bruegger, B., Camenisch, J., Garcia, A.C., Gross, T., Gutwirth, A., Horsch, M., Houdeau, D., Hühnlein, D., Kamm, F.-M., Krenn, S., Neven, G., Rodriguez, C.B., Schmölz, J., Bolliger, C.: Survey and analysis of existing eid and credential systems. Technical Report Deliverable D32.1, FutureID (2013)
29. Luby, M., Rackoff, C.: Pseudo-random permutation generators and cryptographic composition. In: Proceedings of the Eighteenth Annual ACM Symposium on Theory of Computing, STOC 1986, pp. 356–363. ACM, New York (1986)
30. Maler, E., Reed, D.: The Venn of Identity: Options and Issues in Federated Identity Management. IEEE Security and Privacy 6(2), 16–23 (2008)
31. Mostowski, W., Vullers, P.: Efficient U-Prove implementation for anonymous credentials on smart cards. In: Rajarajan, M., Piper, F., Wang, H., Kesidis, G. (eds.) SecureComm 2011. LNICST, vol. 96, pp. 243–260. Springer, Heidelberg (2012)
32. Naumann, I., Hogben, G.: Privacy features of European eID card specifications. Network Security 2008(8), 9–13 (2008)
33. Recordon, D., Reed, D.: OpenID 2.0: A Platform for User-centric Identity Management. In: Proceedings of the Second ACM Workshop on Digital Identity Management, DIM 2006, pp. 11–16. ACM, New York (2006)
34. Standards for Efficient Cryptography Group. Sec 2: Recommended elliptic curve domain parameters. SECG2 (2000)
35. Sterckx, M., Gierlichs, B., Preneel, B., Verbauwhede, I.: Efficient implementation of anonymous credentials on java card smart cards. In: 1st IEEE International Workshop on Information Forensics and Security (WIFS 2009), pp. 106–110. IEEE, London (2009)
36. Vullers, P., Alpár, G.: Efficient selective disclosure on smart cards using idemix. In: Fischer-Hübner, S., de Leeuw, E., Mitchell, C. (eds.) IDMAN 2013. IFIP AICT, vol. 396, pp. 53–67. Springer, Heidelberg (2013)

Appendix A: Equality Proofs of Representation via Prime-Encoded Attributes

The main operation of Idemix is the modular exponentiation where the number of these operations is related to the amount of the cardholder's attributes that are hidden i.e. $\mathcal{O}(l)$ for l attributes. Recently, Camenisch et al, proposed an alternative method for encoding attributes that reduces the overall number of modular exponentiations to 2 [13]. They utilize a base R_1 for encoding all the attributes, which are represented as prime numbers. Therefore, the attribute corresponding to R_1 consists of the product $m_t = \prod_{i=1}^{l} m_i$ for l attributes. Proving the presence of an attribute m_i in m_t is performed via the coprime property: one shows that a certain attribute m_i can divide the product m_t. For instance, proving that the attribute m_1 belongs to m_t is represented in zero knowledge as NIZK: $\{(\varepsilon', \nu', \alpha_0, \alpha_1) : Z \equiv \pm R_0^{\alpha_0}(R_1^{m_1})^{\alpha_1} A^{\varepsilon'} S^{\nu'} \mod n\}$. In addition, the commitment $C = Z^{m_t} S^r \mod n$ and the t_values $\tilde{C} = (Z^{m_1})^{\tilde{m}_h} S^r \mod n$ and $\tilde{C}_0 = Z^{\tilde{m}_t} S^{\tilde{r}} \mod n$ must be computed, where $m_h = m_t/m_r$ and m_r consists on the product of attributes m_i that are revealed (in this case $m_r = m_1$). Moreover, $Z, S \in QR_n$ are both part of the issuer public key as described in Section 3. Finally, the verifier checks C and C_0 as $\tilde{C} \stackrel{?}{=} C^{-c}(Z^{m_r})^{\tilde{m}_h} S^{\hat{r}} \mod n$ and $\tilde{C}_0 \stackrel{?}{=} C^{-c} Z^{\hat{m}} S^{\hat{r}} \mod n$ together with the verification of the ownership of the CL signature as described in Protocol 1. This is performed using the following s_values computed and sent by the card: $\hat{m}_0 = \tilde{m}_0 + cm_0$, $\hat{m} = \tilde{m} + cm$, $\hat{m}_h = \tilde{m}_h + cm_h$ and $\hat{r} = \tilde{r} + cr$. In this case, the PRNG would compute the following sequence: $init_{PRNG}() \Rightarrow \tilde{m}_i \Rightarrow \tilde{m}_h \Rightarrow \tilde{r} \Rightarrow r \Rightarrow \tilde{m}_t \Rightarrow reset_{PRNG}() \Rightarrow \tilde{m}_i \Rightarrow \tilde{m}_h \Rightarrow \tilde{r}$. Otherwise, not revealing any attribute, that is, only proving the ownership of the signature would be represented as NIZK: $\{(\varepsilon', \nu', \alpha_0, \alpha_1) : Z \equiv \pm R_0^{\alpha_0} R_1^{\alpha_1} A^{\varepsilon'} S^{\nu'} \mod n\}$. This requires two exponentiations with independence of the number of attributes hidden. In this case, the PRNG would follow the same sequence depicted in Section 4.

Table 7. Performance overhead while verifying five attributes using a custom PRNG for generating the $\hat{m}$ values (ms)

Work	Encoding	Case	T_{sel_cred}	T_{gen_commit}	$T_{get\_sig}(A,e,v)$	$T_{get\_attr}(m_0,...,m_5|C,\hat{r},\hat{m}_h)$	Total
This work	prime	BC	103.13	1,250.10	15.40, 11.61, 19.67	38.31, 11.53 | 13.94, 32.97, 51.14	1,547.83
This work	prime	WC	103.71	987.10	15.54, 11.44, 19.62	38.30*2	**1,214.24**

As depicted in Table 7 we notice that what we considered the worst case for normal encoding is the opposite here. We reuse the notation utilized in Sections 4–7 i.e. WC for hiding all the attributes and BC for revealing the content of a credential with the exception of m_0. Hence, only proving the ownership of a CL signature over a set of attributes without revealing any only requires 1,214.24 ms. In contrast, revealing all the attributes requires the computation of C, $\tilde{C}$ and $\tilde{C}_0$. Thanks to the optimizations carried out in Section 4 we can store C in

RAM to avoid its recomputing when the verifiers requests its value. However, revealing all the attributes requires 492.20 ms more in comparison to the utilization of traditional encoding due to the additional modular exponentiations and multiplications required by the generation of C, $\tilde{C}$ and $\tilde{C}_o$.

We have recomputed the performance of standard and domain pseudonyms from Table 3 in Table 8 relying on prime-encoded attributes. In this respect, all the performance figures concerning the worst cases were improved i.e. 485.89 ms (standard pseudonyms) and 499.76 ms (domain pseudonyms in combination with standard pseudonyms, Section 5). However, revealing all the attributes requires the computation of three commitments that need a larger number of modular arithmetic operations in comparison to normal encoding (Table 3).

Table 8. Performance analysis of proving the ownership of standard and domain pseudonyms (prime encoding, ms)

Implementation	Case	T_{sel_cred}	T_{gen_commit}	$T_{get\_sig}(A, e, v)$	$T_{get\_attr}(m_0, ..., m_5 \mid C, \hat{r}, \hat{m}_h \mid nym, \hat{r}\mid dNym)$	Total
Nym	BC	103.13	1,720.73	15.41, 11.23, 19.46	38.42, 11.55 | 14.13, 32.48, 52.17 | 13.98, 50.33	2,083.01
Nym	WC	104.11	1,288.88	15.54, 11.64, 19.22	38.11*2 | − | 13.99, 50.86	1,579.53
Nym ∧ dNym	BC	103.17	2,255.31	15.29, 11.51, 19.12	38.39, 11.83 | 14.17, 32.44, 52.05 | 14.16, 58.34 | 51.12	2,676.92
Nym ∧ dNym	WC	104.33	1,487.86	15.22, 11.49, 19.48	38.02*2 | − | 13.58, 58.11 | 52.12	1,838.25

It can be possible to rely on prime encoding attributes for performing equality proofs with a better performance in comparison to the first two alternatives. In this respect, while the performance of the best case would be slightly worst due to the computation of the extra commitments, it can be possible to improve the performance of the worst one by reducing the number of exponentiations to $\mathcal{O}(1+1)$ per credential instead of $\mathcal{O}(5)$ per credential as in the alternatives a and b (Table 5). Proving that 2 credentials share m_0 without revealing any attributes would be represented in zero knowledge as NIZK: $\{(\varepsilon'_1, \nu'_1, \varepsilon'_2, \nu'_2, \mu, \alpha_1, \alpha_2) : Z^{(1)} \equiv \pm R_0^{(1)\mu} R_1^{(1)\alpha_1} A^{(1)\varepsilon'_1} S^{(1)\nu'_1} \mod n_1 \wedge Z^{(2)} \equiv \pm R_0^{(2)\mu} R_1^{(2)\beta_1} A^{(2)\varepsilon'_2} S^{(2)\nu'_2} \mod n_2\}$. We note that there is an improvement of 496.59 ms and 989.82 ms in comparison to the alternatives b and a respectively (Table 9)

However, the computation of C, $\tilde{C}_o$ and $\tilde{C}$ together with the two extra s_values undermines any possibility of improving the figures related to the best cases from b and a.

Table 9. Performance overhead while verifying two credentials with 5 attributes using the equality proof (ms)

Alternative	Case	T_{sel_cred} (ms)	T_{gen_commit}	$T_{get\_sig}(A, e, v)$	$T_{get\_attr}(m_0, ..., m_5 \mid C, \hat{r}, \hat{m}_h)$	Total
c	BC	103.23	3,145.11	$(232.69, 91.37, 27.72)^{(1,2)}$	$(32.11, 11.01)^{(1)}, (11.14)^{(2)} \mid (13.90, 32.95, 51.14)^{(1,2)}$	4,202.74
c	WC	104.17	2,023.94	$(232.61, 91.52, 27.62)^{(1,2)}$	$(31.19*2)^{(1,2)}$	2,894.01

We have also estimated the time that requires computing equality proofs up to 8 credentials using the alternatives a and c (Figure 1). We consider 4–5 seconds the acceptable time for an on-line setting. Hence, performing equality proofs with 3 and 4 credentials revealing all the attributes would be possible whereas execution times beyond 6 seconds (worst cases with 3 credentials and beyond and best cases with 5 credentials and beyond) are unrealistic in practical scenarios.

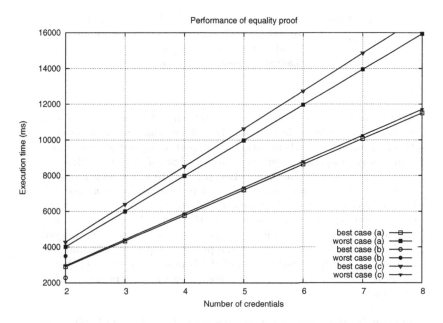

Fig. 1. Performance of the equality proof (credentials of five attributes)

We notice that it is possible to improve the performance results of an equality proof of 2 credentials hiding all the attributes by using this type of encoding. This approach would be only useful in systems where an user should prove the ownership of n credentials without revealing her attributes.

Security of a Privacy-Preserving
Biometric Authentication Protocol Revisited

Aysajan Abidin[1], Kanta Matsuura[2], and Aikaterini Mitrokotsa[1]

[1] Chalmers University of Technology, Gothenburg, Sweden
{aysajan.abidin,aikaterini.mitrokotsa}@chalmers.se
[2] University of Tokyo, Japan
kanta@iis.u-tokyo.ac.jp

Abstract. Biometric authentication establishes the identity of an individual based on biometric templates (*e.g.* fingerprints, retina scans etc.). Although biometric authentication has important advantages and many applications, it also raises serious security and privacy concerns. Here, we investigate a biometric authentication protocol that has been proposed by Bringer *et al.* and adopts a distributed architecture (*i.e.* multiple entities are involved in the authentication process). This protocol was proven to be secure and *privacy-preserving* in the *honest-but-curious* (or *passive*) attack model. We present an attack algorithm that can be employed to mount a number of attacks on the protocol under investigation. We then propose an improved version of the Bringer *et al.* protocol that is secure in the *malicious* (or *active*) insider attack model and has *forward security*.

Keywords: Biometrics, privacy-preserving biometric authentication, homomorphic encryption, active attack, forward security.

1 Introduction

Biometric authentication offers important advantages mainly due to the uniqueness of biometric identifiers and other favorable properties since biometrics cannot be lost or forgotten. A biometric authentication system consists of two phases, namely, the *enrollment phase* and the *authentication phase*; and it typically involves two entities: a client and a server. During the enrollment phase, the client provides the server with his biometric data for storage in a database. Then, during the authentication phase, the server authenticates the client if his fresh biometric template matches the one that is stored in the database.

Since the server often has to perform many tasks (*e.g.* retrieving from the database the client's reference biometric template, checking if it matches the fresh template) its role can be divided into several parts. Thus, the execution of the protocol involves different entities where each entity performs a specific task. For instance, a biometric authentication protocol could involve the following entities: a user $\mathcal{U}$, a biometric sensor $\mathcal{S}$, an authentication server $\mathcal{AS}$, a database $\mathcal{DB}$ and a matcher $\mathcal{M}$. This architecture of a biometric authentication system

D. Gritzalis et al. (Eds.): CANS 2014, LNCS 8813, pp. 290–304, 2014.
© Springer International Publishing Switzerland 2014

has been proposed by Bringer *et al.* [1]. In this new setup, a biometric authentication system works as follows. Let N be the number of users registered in the authentication system. We denote by $\mathcal{U}_i$ the i-th user where $1 \leq i \leq N$. In the *enrolment phase* the user $\mathcal{U}_i$ registers his biometric data b_i which is then stored in the database $\mathcal{DB}$. In the *authentication phase* a user $\mathcal{U}_i$ first provides a fresh biometric trait b_i' and his identity ID_i to the sensor $\mathcal{S}$, which in turn forwards these data to the authentication server $\mathcal{AS}$. $\mathcal{AS}$ then asks $\mathcal{DB}$ for $\mathcal{U}_i$'s biometric data b_i that is already stored in $\mathcal{DB}$. After getting b_i from $\mathcal{DB}$, $\mathcal{AS}$ sends b_i and b_i' to the matcher $\mathcal{M}$, which checks whether b_i and b_i' match and sends back the result of the comparison to $\mathcal{AS}$, which then makes the decision of whether to grant authentication to the user depending on the matcher's response.

Note that it is assumed that the output of the authentication process denoted as $\mathsf{Out}_{\mathcal{AS}}$ (*i.e.* knowing whether the authentication has been granted or not) is publicly available; something that is quite common in the literature [2,3,4,5,6]. For instance, in case the biometric authentication system is used to restrict access to a building then the event that the door opens corresponds to a successful authentication.

However, biometric authentication has also many serious security and privacy implications. Compromised biometric templates may lead to serious threats to identity, while the inherent irrevocability of biometrics renders this risk even more serious. Furthermore, biometric information may reveal very sensitive and private information such as genetic [7] and medical information [8]. Additional issues of linkability, profiling and tracking of individuals are raised by cross-matching biometric traits. Therefore, privacy-preserving biometric authentication protocols are of utmost importance. Many existing protocols rely on the use of secure multi-party computation techniques including homomorphic encryption [9] and oblivious transfer [10,11].

Contributions and Related Work. In this paper, we review a privacy-preserving biometric authentication protocol that has been proposed by Bringer *et al.* [1]. This protocol relies on the Goldwasser-Micali (GM) cryptosystem [12] which is a homomorphic encryption. Bringer *et al.* [1] have shown that their protocol is secure under the assumption that the system entities do not collude and are *honest-but-curious*. Here, we improve upon the original protocol to safeguard it against *malicious* insider attacks.

We first present a generic algorithm that can be employed by an adversary to mount a number of attacks to the protocol under investigation. One of the enablers of the attacks is the bit-by-bit encryption of the biometric data using the GM encryption scheme. Then, we propose an improved protocol that is secure and privacy-preserving in the *malicious* adversarial model. In particular, the improved protocol is secure against *malicious, but non-colluding* insider attacks and has *forward security*. We also compare our protocol with the original protocol.

Some attacks on the protocol under study were presented by Barbosa *et al.* [13] and Simoens *et al.* [14]. Barbosa *et al.* [13] present a simple attack that allows the authentication server $\mathcal{AS}$ to learn some bits of the reference biometric templates due to non-randomisation of the response by the database $\mathcal{DB}$ to the authentication server $\mathcal{AS}$. Simoens et al. [14] present possible insider attack ideas and attacks by a single or multiple, colluding malicious entities. In this paper, we extend some of their attack ideas and present a simple yet powerful attack algorithm.

Bringer and Chabanne [15] presented an improvement of the protocol under study, where they replaced the matching algorithm by an error correction procedure using secure sketches and discussed how it can be integrated into the *Private Information Retrieval (PIR)* scheme due to Lipmaa [16]. In their scheme, the database stores encryptions of the biometric templates. However, this scheme is computationally expensive. There are also several biometric authentication protocols proposed by Stoianov [17] that employ the Blum-Goldwasser (BG) [18,19] encryption scheme. But in these protocols, there are three entities, namely a client, a computation server (or database), and an authentication server. There are many other works related to privacy-preserving biometrics. However, to the best of our knowledge, Barbosa et al. [13] and Simoens et al. [14] are the only ones that study the security of the protocol under investigation.

Outline. After giving some definitions and our threat model in Section 2, we present the protocol under study in Section 3. Then, in Section 4, we describe the attack algorithm. Section 5 presents an improvement of the Bringer et al. protocol while Section 6 presents its security analysis and compares it with the original protocol. Finally, Section 7 concludes the paper and highlights some future work.

2   Preliminaries

We give notations and definitions of some of the key concepts used throughout the paper. Also, we present a threat model in which we analyse the security and privacy of the biometric authentication protocol under study.

Communication Model. In our modifications to the protocol under investigation, we assume that there is a secure and authentic channel between the system entities. In particular, we assume that there are shared secret keys between $\mathcal{S}$ and $\mathcal{M}$, $\mathcal{AS}$ and $\mathcal{M}$, $\mathcal{DB}$ and $\mathcal{M}$, that are used to encrypt and authenticate messages sent to $\mathcal{M}$. In addition, $\mathcal{M}$ has a public encryption key to which all other system entities have access, and $\mathcal{S}$ and $\mathcal{DB}$ have a shared secret key that they use to derive a permutation to permute the biometric templates before encrypting them. Since we omit the underlying infrastructure for the public-key primitive (*i.e.* the protocol does not explicitly use certificates), we also assume the authenticity of the matcher's public key. In this paper, we focus on the case where there is only a single $\mathcal{S}$, a single $\mathcal{AS}$, and a single $\mathcal{DB}$ in the system. Therefore, security in the case of multiple entities communicating with each other in parallel is outside the scope of this paper.

Definitions. We use the following as a definition of privacy-preserving biometric authentication.

Definition 1 (Privacy-preserving biometric authentication). *We say a biometric authentication protocol is* privacy-preserving *if no probabilistic polynomial-time (PPT) adversary can recover any of the following information, if they are not already known: a fresh biometric b'_i, a stored biometric b_i or the correspondence between the identity ID_i and b_i.*

We also use provably secure message authentication codes (MACs) in our modification to the protocol under study. A MAC scheme MAC consists of a key generation algorithm KeyGen, a tag generation algorithm TAG, and a verification algorithm VRFY. When we say a MAC scheme is ϵ-secure, we refer to the following definition.

Definition 2. *A MAC scheme is called ϵ-secure if no PPT adversary $\mathcal{A}$ can generate a valid message-tag pair, even after making polynomially many tag generation and verification queries, except with probability ϵ.*

Furthermore, when we say secure pseudorandom number generator (PNG) we mean a PNG that satisfies the following definition.

Definition 3. *A PNG is called an ϵ-secure if no PPT distinguisher D can distinguish its output from a randomly chosen bitstring of equal length except for a negligible probability ϵ.*

Lastly, we use symmetric key encryption, denoted by SKE, in our modification. We require SKE to have indistinguishability against ciphertext-only attacks (IND-COA) (cf. Appendix A). Note that we use Enc (and Dec) to denote the GM encryption (and decryption), and Enc_K (and Dec_K) to denote symmetric key encryption (and decryption) with a key K.

Threat Model. In our threat model, we go beyond the *honest-but-curious* (or *passive*) model that is adopted in the original protocol by Bringer *et al.* [1] and extend the adversary model investigated by Simoens *et al.* [14]. Hence, we consider as an adversary $\mathcal{A}$ any passive (or active) internal entity that can violate the protocol specifications and that attempts to recover any of the following information, if they are *not* yet known: the fresh biometric b'_i, the stored template b_i, and/or the correspondence of a user identity ID_i to the stored template b_i. Thus, each of the entities – the user ID_i, the sensor $\mathcal{S}$, the authentication server $\mathcal{AS}$, the database $\mathcal{DB}$, and the matcher $\mathcal{M}$ – may pose threats to privacy of biometric reference, biometric sample and user identity [14].

Assumptions. When security and privacy of a biometric authentication system are analysed, there are always certain assumptions that must hold. In our case, we make the following assumptions.

Assumption 1. *We assume that the sensor $\mathcal{S}$ is honest, has not been compromised and captures the biometric templates from alive human users.*

This assumption is important because if the sensor $\mathcal{S}$ is compromised, then the adversary can wait until a legitimate user comes and authenticates himself to the system, and hence easily learns the identity and fresh biometric template of a legitimate user. This is possible because as we mentioned earlier the output of the authentication server to the user is assumed to be publicly known.

A malicious user may attempt to get himself authenticated to the system by a fake identity and a fake biometric template. Also, a series of successful consecutive authentication attempts by the same user identity may also be an indication of a malicious behaviour if there is a specific pattern in the biometric templates used. Therefore, we assume that the system has appropriate measures to limit the number of such trials. This brings us to our next assumption.

Assumption 2. *We assume that the biometric authentication system has a limit on the maximum allowed consecutive failed trials to grant access. This limit does not allow an adversary to create a fake fresh biometric b_i' that is accepted by the matcher $\mathcal{M}$. Also, we assume that the system has a limit on the maximum allowed consecutive successful trials to grant access. This limit helps the system to detect hill climbing attacks; see Simoens et al. [14] for details on this attack.*

Finally, we assume that the system entities are not colluding. We note that this assumption is valid when an adversary has compromised *only* one of the entities. And we believe that this is an important first step towards achieving a protocol secure against *malicious and colluding* insider attacks.

Assumption 3. *We assume that the entities $\mathcal{AS}$, $\mathcal{DB}$, $\mathcal{M}$ may not collude with each other.*

3   The Bringer *et al.* Protocol

Bringer *et al.* [1] have proposed a protocol for privacy-preserving biometric authentication that follows the above described model and involves four entities in the biometric authentication process. According to this protocol the sensor $\mathcal{S}$, the authentication server $\mathcal{AS}$ and the database $\mathcal{DB}$ store the public key pk while the matcher $\mathcal{M}$ stores the secret key sk. $\mathcal{AS}$ also stores the mapping (ID_i, i), for $i = 1, \ldots, N$, where i corresponds to user $\mathcal{U}_i$ and N is the total number of users of the biometric authentication system. Furthermore, $\mathcal{DB}$ stores the reference biometric template b_i. The protocol is based on the GM cryptosystem. We denote by $\mathsf{Enc}(b_i)$ the *bit-by-bit* encryption of the template b_i, i.e. $\mathsf{Enc}(b_{i,1} \ldots b_{i,M}) = \big(\mathsf{Enc}(b_{i,1}), \ldots, \mathsf{Enc}(b_{i,M})\big)$, where M is the bit length of the template.

In the enrolment phase, user $\mathcal{U}_i$ registers (b_i, i) at $\mathcal{DB}$, and (ID_i, i) at the $\mathcal{AS}$. The authentication phase comprises the following phases.

PHASE 1 - COMMUNICATION $\mathcal{U}_i \to \mathcal{S} \to \mathcal{AS}$:

- $\mathcal{U}_i$ provides a fresh biometric trait b_i' and his identity ID_i to $\mathcal{S}$.
- Then, $\mathcal{S}$ sends the fresh biometric b_i' encrypted under the public key pk (*i.e.* $\mathsf{Enc}(b_i')$) as well as the claimed identity ID_i to $\mathcal{AS}$.

PHASE 2 - COMMUNICATION $\mathcal{AS} \leftrightarrow \mathcal{DB}$:

- $\mathcal{AS}$ performs the mapping from ID_i to i and then using a PIR mechanism sends i and requests the corresponding stored biometric template b_i. More precisely, $\mathcal{AS}$ sends to $\mathcal{DB}$ the encrypted value $\mathsf{Enc}(t_j)$, where $1 \leq j \leq N$ and $t_j = 1$, if $j = i$, 0 otherwise.
- $\mathcal{DB}$ computes: $\mathsf{Enc}(b_{i,k}) = \prod_{j=1}^{N} \mathsf{Enc}(t_j)^{b_{j,k}}$ where $1 \leq k \leq M$ and then sends the computed values $\mathsf{Enc}(b_{i,k})$ to $\mathcal{AS}$.

PHASE 3 - COMMUNICATION $\mathcal{AS} \leftrightarrow \mathcal{M}$:

- $\mathcal{AS}$ computes $v_k = \mathsf{Enc}(b'_{i,k})\mathsf{Enc}(b_{i,k}) = \mathsf{Enc}(b'_{i,k} \oplus b_{i,k})$, where $1 \leq k \leq M$. Then, $\mathcal{AS}$ permutes v_k and sends $\lambda_k = v_{\pi(k)}$ $(1 \leq k \leq M)$ to $\mathcal{M}$.
- $\mathcal{M}$ decrypts the permuted vector λ_k and checks whether the Hamming weight (HW) of the decrypted vector is less than a predefined threshold τ. The result of this control is sent to $\mathcal{AS}$.

PHASE 4 - COMMUNICATION $\mathcal{AS} \rightarrow \mathcal{U}_i$: Finally, $\mathcal{AS}$ accepts or rejects the authentication request ($\mathsf{Out}_{\mathcal{AS}} = 1$ or $\mathsf{Out}_{\mathcal{AS}} = 0$ respectively) depending on the value returned by $\mathcal{M}$.

4   Description of the Attacks

Barbosa et al. [13] and Simoens et al. [14] presented several attacks on the above protocol when the adversary is a single entity or a combination of multiple entities. In addition, Simoens et al. [14] presented a framework for analysing security and privacy of biometric data in biometric authentication systems. In this section, we present a simple yet powerful algorithm (*Algorithm 1*) that can be used as a basis for a number of attacks. The attack algorithm takes a ciphertext as input and returns the corresponding plaintext by querying the matcher. The main enabler of this attack algorithm is the *bit-by-bit encryption* of the communication between the involved parties and the use of Hamming distance as the measure of whether the fresh biometric template matches the stored biometric profile. The algorithm uses as a subroutine the algorithm for the *center search attack*, but it is called only if the condition $\mathsf{HW}(b_i) \leq \tau$ holds; we urge the interested reader to consult Simoens et al. [14] for details on the attack

The Attack Idea. Upon receiving from $\mathcal{AS}$ a vector λ of ciphertexts, the matcher $\mathcal{M}$ first decrypts λ component-by-component and then compares the Hamming weight of the resulting bitstring with a predefined threshold τ. $\mathcal{M}$ responds YES to $\mathcal{AS}$ if the Hamming weight is less than τ; otherwise, responds NO. Therefore, in order to find b_i from $\lambda := \mathsf{Enc}(b_i) = (\mathsf{Enc}(b_{i1}), \mathsf{Enc}(b_{i2}), \cdots, \mathsf{Enc}(b_{iM}))$, an adversary (say, $\mathcal{AS}$) first finds a bitstring whose Hamming weight is equal to the threshold $\tau + 1$ by repeatedly replacing the components of $(\mathsf{Enc}(0), \cdots, \mathsf{Enc}(0))$ with the corresponding components of λ until it gets rejected by $\mathcal{M}$. By using this bitstring with Hamming weight $\tau + 1$, the adversary is able to recover all bits of b_i one by one, as shown in Algorithm 1.

In the following attacks, we only consider the case when the authentication server $\mathcal{AS}$ (attacks 1 and 2) or the database $\mathcal{DB}$ (attack 3) is compromised, respectively.

Attack 1 - *Compromised $\mathcal{AS}$*. $\mathcal{AS}$ receives from $\mathcal{DB}$ the biometric reference template in encrypted form i.e. $\mathsf{Enc}(b_i) = c_1, \ldots, c_M$. Then, $\mathcal{AS}$ follows Algorithm 1. After executing the Algorithm 1, $\mathcal{AS}$ can successfully deduce all bits of b_i. The worst case complexity of this algorithm is $\max\big(2(\tau + M), 4\tau + M\big)$, where τ is the threshold. We may note here that the complexity of the center search attack is $\max\big(2\tau + M, 4\tau\big)$ [14]. After executing this algorithm $\mathcal{AS}$ has successfully deduced k out of the M bits of b_i, where $M - k = \tau$ are the maximum allowed errors. By following a similar algorithm for the remaining τ bits, it can recover all bits of b_i.

Attack 2 - *Compromised $\mathcal{AS}$*. A variation of the previous attack can be performed if $\mathcal{AS}$ has also at his disposal a valid value $\mathsf{Enc}(b_i' \oplus b_i)$. In this case Algorithm 1 can be executed twice: once for $\lambda = \mathsf{Enc}(b_i')$ and once for $\lambda = \mathsf{Enc}(b_i' \oplus b_i)$. Thus, $\mathcal{AS}$ will be able to recover b_i and $b_i' \oplus b_i$ and subsequently b_i'.

Attack 3 - *Compromised $\mathcal{DB}$*. A variation of attack 1 can also be performed if $\mathcal{DB}$ is compromised. $\mathcal{DB}$ sets $\lambda = \mathsf{Enc}(t_1), \ldots, \mathsf{Enc}(t_M)$ if $M < N$; otherwise, $\lambda = \mathsf{Enc}(t_1), \ldots, \mathsf{Enc}(t_N), \mathsf{Enc}(0), \cdots, \mathsf{Enc}(0)$. This way, $\mathcal{DB}$ is able to recover t_j's by sending multiple queries to $\mathcal{M}$. Note that in the case of $M \leq N$, if it turns out that $t_j = 0$, for all $j = 1, \ldots, M$, then λ can be chosen to be the encryption of the remaining t_j's. Here we remark that $\mathcal{DB}$ on its own cannot send queries to $\mathcal{M}$ directly. But since $\mathcal{M}$ does not check the integrity of received queries, the adversary can replace $\mathcal{AS}$'s query to $\mathcal{M}$ with his own. In other words, here $\mathcal{DB}$ impersonates $\mathcal{AS}$ to $\mathcal{M}$.

Algorithm 1.

```
Input: Enc(b_i) = c_1, ···, c_M
Output: b_i
Initialise: b_i = 00 ··· 0
For k = 1 to M:
        Set λ = c_1, ..., c_k, Enc(0), ..., Enc(0)
        If λ is rejected Then
                break
        If k == M Then
                Return centerSearch(b_i)
Set k* = k and b_{i,k*} = 1
If k* ≥ 2 Then
        For k = 1 to k* − 1:
                Set λ = c_1, ..., c_{k−1}, Enc(0), c_{k+1} ··· c_{k*}, Enc(0), ..., Enc(0)
                If λ is accepted Then
                        b_{i,k} = 1
For k = k* + 1 to M:
        Set λ = c_1, ..., c_{k*−1}, Enc(0), ..., Enc(0), c_k, Enc(0), ..., Enc(0)
        If λ is rejected Then
                b_{i,k} = 1
Return b_i
```

Thus, the Bringer *et al.* protocol is not secure or privacy-preserving in the *malicious insider* attack model. Because of the *bit-by-bit* encryption of the communication between the entities, the above presented attacks are straightforward and easy to mount. Plus, the complexity of the attacks is low. To mitigate the attacks, we next propose some modifications to the original protocol to improve its security and privacy preservation.

5   Countermeasure

Now, we propose modifications to the protocol under study to restore its security against the Attacks 1-3 presented in the previous section. Let us first discuss how we can protect the system against the Attack 1. We note that in this case the attacker has $\mathsf{Enc}(b_i)$ and wants to find out what b_i is. If the matcher $\mathcal{M}$ does *not* directly compute the Hamming weight (HW) of the resulting bit-string from the decryption of the received ciphertext, we may be able to protect the system against the Attack 1. So, in our modification, $\mathcal{M}$ shares two secret keys K_1 and K_2 with $\mathcal{S}$, a secret key K_3 with $\mathcal{AS}$, and two more secret keys K_4 and K_5 with $\mathcal{DB}$. These keys are used for symmetric key schemes, therefore the length of these keys are *not* as long as the length of the key for the GM encryption. As before, pk and sk are $\mathcal{M}$'s public and secret keys for GM encryption. $\mathcal{S}$ and $\mathcal{DB}$ also share a key $K_{\mathcal{S}\leftrightarrow\mathcal{DB}}$ that is used to derive a permutation π. In addition, $\mathcal{S}$ has a key K that it uses to encrypt the user identity ID_i.

During the *enrollment phase*, $\mathcal{S}$ stores (b_i, i) at $\mathcal{DB}$ and (id_i, i), where $\mathsf{id}_i = \mathsf{Enc}_K(\mathsf{ID}_i)$ (a symmetric key encryption of ID_i with key K), at $\mathcal{AS}$.

The main changes take place in the *authentication phase*.

PHASE 1 - COMMUNICATION $\mathcal{U}_i \rightarrow \mathcal{S} \rightarrow \mathcal{AS}$:

- $\mathcal{U}_i \rightarrow \mathcal{S}$: $\mathcal{U}_i$ provides a fresh biometric trait b'_i and ID_i to $\mathcal{S}$.
- $\mathcal{S} \rightarrow \mathcal{AS}$: $\mathcal{S}$ derives a permutation π using the key $K_{\mathcal{S}\leftrightarrow\mathcal{DB}}$ (shared with $\mathcal{DB}$) and permutes b'_i. Then, it generates two random bitstrings S and K'_1 of length M and encrypts $(b'_i)_\pi \oplus S$ with the public key pk (i.e. $a = \mathsf{Enc}((b'_i)_\pi \oplus S)$). In order to achieve *forward security*, K'_1 is generated to replace K_1. $\mathcal{S}$ proceeds to compute $\omega = \mathsf{Enc}_{K_1}(S, K'_1)$, an encryption of S and K'_1 with K_1, and computes $\sigma = \mathsf{TAG}(\omega, K_2)$. Also, $\mathcal{S}$ replaces K_1 with K'_1, which will be used in the next run of the protocol and deletes K_1 permanently. Finally, $\mathcal{S}$ sends a and (ω, σ) along with the encryption of the claimed identity $\mathsf{id}_i = \mathsf{Enc}_K(\mathsf{ID}_i)$ to $\mathcal{AS}$. Note that this encryption of ID_i is done to protect it from an adversary observing the communication from $\mathcal{S}$ to $\mathcal{AS}$.

PHASE 2 - COMMUNICATION $\mathcal{AS} \leftrightarrow \mathcal{DB}$:

- $\mathcal{AS} \rightarrow \mathcal{DB}$: $\mathcal{AS}$ extracts the index i from id_i and sends $d_j = \mathsf{Enc}(t_j)$ to $\mathcal{DB}$, for $j = 1, \cdots, N$, where t_j is the same as before.
- $\mathcal{DB} \rightarrow \mathcal{AS}$: $\mathcal{DB}$ derives π from $K_{\mathcal{S}\leftrightarrow\mathcal{DB}}$, generates two random bit-strings S' and K'_4 of length M, and computes $c_k = \mathsf{Enc}((b_{i,k})_\pi \oplus S'_k) = \prod_{j=1}^N \mathsf{Enc}(t_j)^{(b_{j,k})_\pi \oplus S'_k}$, where $1 \leq k \leq M$. $\mathcal{DB}$ then encrypts S' and K'_4 using K_4 to get $\omega' = \mathsf{Enc}_{K_4}(S', K'_4)$, and computes $\sigma' = \mathsf{TAG}(\omega', K_5)$. After that, $\mathcal{DB}$ replaces K_4 with K'_4 (to guarantee *forward security*) and deletes K_4. Finally, $\mathcal{DB}$ sends c, (ω', σ') to $\mathcal{AS}$.

PHASE 3 - COMMUNICATION $\mathcal{AS} \leftrightarrow \mathcal{M}$:

- $\mathcal{AS} \rightarrow \mathcal{M}$: $\mathcal{AS}$ computes $\lambda_k = a_k c_k = \mathsf{Enc}((b'_{i,k})_\pi \oplus S)\mathsf{Enc}((b_{i,k})_\pi \oplus S') = \mathsf{Enc}((b'_{i,k} \oplus b_{i,k})_\pi \oplus S \oplus S')$, for $1 \leq k \leq M$, computes $\sigma'' = \mathsf{TAG}(\lambda, K_3)$, and sends (ω, σ), (ω', σ'), and (λ, σ'') to $\mathcal{M}$.
- $\mathcal{M} \rightarrow \mathcal{AS}$: $\mathcal{M}$ first checks the authenticity of ω, ω' and λ by respectively running $\mathsf{VRFY}(\omega, \sigma, K_2)$, $\mathsf{VRFY}(\omega', \sigma', K_5)$, and $\mathsf{VRFY}(\lambda, \sigma'', K_3)$. If any one of them is not authentic, it outputs $\bot$ (*i.e.* aborts the protocol). Otherwise, it proceeds to obtain $S, K'_1 \leftarrow \mathsf{Dec}_{K_1}(\omega)$, $S', K'_4 \leftarrow \mathsf{Dec}_{K_4}(\omega')$, and $(b'_i \oplus b_i)_\pi \leftarrow \mathsf{Dec}(\lambda) \oplus S \oplus S'$; and replaces K_1 and K_4 with K'_1 and K'_4, respectively. Lastly, $\mathcal{M}$ checks whether the $\mathsf{HW}((b'_i \oplus b_i)_\pi) \leq \tau$ and sends the result of this control to $\mathcal{AS}$.

PHASE 4 - COMMUNICATION $\mathcal{AS} \to \mathcal{U}_i$: Finally, $\mathcal{AS}$ accepts or rejects the authentication request ($\mathsf{Out}_{\mathcal{AS}} = 1$ or $\mathsf{Out}_{\mathcal{AS}} = 0$ respectively) depending on the value returned by $\mathcal{M}$.

We should note here that the reason for replacing K_1 and K_4 with new independently generated K_1' and K_4', respectively, was to ensure *forward security* and thus to limit the damage in case the keys are compromised. The main question we want to answer now is: *How secure is the improved protocol against the presented attacks?* We address this question in the following section.

6   Security Analysis

Let us assess the security of the modified protocol. Before we proceed, we recall that we aim for security in the *malicious, but non-colluding* model, meaning that any entity can deviate from the protocol specifications but none of the entities may collude with each other. Therefore, we focus on security against *malicious insider* attacks. Since our primary goal is to assure security and privacy of biometric templates and user identity, we do not consider denial of service type of attacks in our analysis.

To begin with, let us analyse case-by-case what may happen when the entities, except for the sensor S which we assume to be honest and cannot be compromised, are malicious.

- *Attacker* = $\mathcal{AS}$: $\mathcal{AS}$ has knowledge of K_3, so it can send arbitrary queries to $\mathcal{M}$. In addition, it has at its disposal the encrypted user identity $\mathsf{id}_i = \mathsf{Enc}_K(\mathsf{ID}_i)$, encrypted biometric templates $\mathsf{Enc}((b_i')_\pi \oplus S)$ and $\mathsf{Enc}((b_i)_\pi \oplus S')$, $\omega = \mathsf{Enc}_{K_1}(S, K_1')$, $\omega' = \mathsf{Enc}_{K_4}(S', K_4')$, their authentication tags $\sigma = h_{K_2}(\omega)$, $\sigma' = h_{K_5}(\omega')$. He wants to use all this information to gain knowledge of b_i', b_i, and the linkage between ID_i and a biometric template b_i. It may arbitrarily deviate from the protocol specifications, except that it is not allowed to compromise or collude with another protocol entity. Note that $\mathcal{AS}$ can always cause denial of service to legitimate users by providing wrong input to $\mathcal{M}$.
- *Attacker* = $\mathcal{DB}$: $\mathcal{DB}$ has knowledge of all stored biometric templates and of K_4, K_5, S' and π. However, it does not know which b_i is related to which user identity $\mathcal{U}_i$. It also does not know which user is attempting to authenticate himself to the server $\mathcal{AS}$. Therefore, its goal is to learn which user is trying to authenticate himself and to which user a biometric template belongs. It may also deviate from the protocol specifications, but it cannot collude with other entities.
- *Attacker* = $\mathcal{M}$: $\mathcal{M}$ has the secret keys sk, K_1, K_2, K_3, K_4, and K_5. Its goal is to distinguish whether two authentication attempts are from the same user. Since we assume that communications between the entities cannot be eavesdropped, it cannot use the secret keys to learn b_i and b_i', unless it colludes with $\mathcal{AS}$.

The modified protocol is secure and preserves the privacy of biometric templates and user identity. In particular, none of the entities $\mathcal{AS}$, $\mathcal{DB}$, and $\mathcal{M}$, all *malicious but non-colluding* and PPT, can link a biometric template to a user identity and a malicious $\mathcal{DB}$ cannot distinguish whether two authentication attempts are from the same user. More precisely, Theorem 1 and Theorem 2 stated in Bringer *et al.* [1] also hold in the proposed modified protocol. We provide their proofs for the modified protocol in Appendix B. Finally, the modified proposed protocol is secure against malicious authentications servers $\mathcal{AS}$ as stated in the following theorem (we provide its proof in Appendix C).

Theorem 1. *If the Assumptions 1-3 hold and if (a) S and S' are generated using ϵ-secure PNGs (cf. Definition 3), (b) the symmetric encryption schemes SKE used between the sensor $\mathcal{S}$ and the matcher $\mathcal{M}$, and between the database $\mathcal{DB}$ and the matcher $\mathcal{M}$, is IND-COA-secure, and (c) the GM scheme is IND-CPA-secure. Then, our modified protocol is secure against any malicious authentication server $\mathcal{AS}$.*

Forward Security. Informally, *forward security* means that the disclosure of a secret key material does not compromise the secrecy of the exchanged communications from previous rounds. As we briefly mentioned in the previous section, our modified protocol has *forward security*. In particular, the biometric templates exchanged will not be affected by a future disclosure of the secret key used to encrypt them. The original protocol, on the other hand, does not provide forward security. This is because if the matcher $\mathcal{M}$'s secret key is compromised, then all biometric templates exchanged in the past can be learned. But in the modified protocol, the adversary learns the biometric templates in the present round (and onwards) only.

Comparison. In comparison with the original protocol, in our modification each protocol entity performs additional cryptographic computations such as, symmetric key encryption/decryption, MAC generation/verification, and generation of pseudo-random numbers. In particular, in the case of $\mathcal{S}$, in the original protocol, $\mathcal{S}$ only computes the encryption of the fresh biometric samples using the GM encryption. But in the modified protocol, in addition to that, $\mathcal{S}$ first generates S, K_1' and then computes $\omega = \mathsf{Enc}_{K_1}(S, K_1')$ and $\mathsf{Enc}_K(\mathsf{ID}_i)$ using a symmetric encryption and computes an authentication tag for ω using a suitable MAC. In the case of $\mathcal{AS}$, the only additional computation done in the modified protocol is the authentication tag generation for λ, *i.e.* $\sigma'' = h_{K_3}(\lambda)$. In the case of $\mathcal{DB}$, in the modified protocol, $\mathcal{DB}$ first generates S', K_4' and then $\omega' = \mathsf{Enc}_{K_4}(S', K_4')$, $\sigma' = \mathsf{TAG}_{K_5}(\omega')$. In the case of $\mathcal{M}$, in the modified protocol, the additional computations done by $\mathcal{M}$ are: $\mathsf{VRFY}(\omega, \sigma, K_2)$, $\mathsf{VRFY}(\omega', \sigma', K_5)$, $\mathsf{VRFY}(\lambda, \sigma'', K_3)$, $\mathsf{Dec}_{K_1}(\omega)$ and $\mathsf{Dec}_{K_4}(\omega')$. Also, it XORs S and S' with $\mathsf{Dec}(\lambda)$. It is evident that in the modified protocol, each system entity performs some additional computations than required in the original protocol. However, as they are symmetric cryptographic operations, these computations are *not* as heavy as those done in the GM encryption.

7   Conclusions

We investigated the security of a *privacy-preserving biometric authentication* protocol proposed by Bringer *et al.* that uses the Goldwasser-Micali cryptosystem in the *malicious* attack model. We presented a simple attack algorithm that can be employed to mount a number of attacks on the system to either obtain the reference biometric template (b_i) or the identity (ID_i) of a user associated with a biometric template (b_i). Furthermore, we proposed an improved version of the Bringer *et al.* [1] protocol and proved its security against *malicious, but non-colluding* insider attacks. As future work, we would like to investigate how to achieve security and privacy against colluding internal adversaries.

Acknowledgements. We would like to thank Serge Vaudenay for suggesting the attack algorithm and Julien Bringer for the helpful discussions. This work was partially supported by the FP7-STREP project "BEAT: Biometric Evaluation and Testing", grant number: 284989.

References

1. Bringer, J., Chabanne, H., Izabachène, M., Pointcheval, D., Tang, Q., Zimmer, S.: An application of the Goldwasser-Micali cryptosystem to biometric authentication. In: Pieprzyk, J., Ghodosi, H., Dawson, E. (eds.) ACISP 2007. LNCS, vol. 4586, pp. 96–106. Springer, Heidelberg (2007)
2. Ouafi, K., Vaudenay, S.: Strong Privacy for RFID Systems from Plaintext-Aware Encryption. In: Pieprzyk, J., Sadeghi, A.-R., Manulis, M. (eds.) CANS 2012. LNCS, vol. 7712, pp. 247–262. Springer, Heidelberg (2012)
3. Vaudenay, S.: On Privacy Models for RFID. In: Kurosawa, K. (ed.) ASIACRYPT 2007. LNCS, vol. 4833, pp. 68–87. Springer, Heidelberg (2007)
4. Hermans, J., Pashalidis, A., Vercauteren, F., Preneel, B.: A new RFID privacy model. In: Atluri, V., Diaz, C. (eds.) ESORICS 2011. LNCS, vol. 6879, pp. 568–587. Springer, Heidelberg (2011)
5. Juels, A., Weis, S.A.: Authenticating pervasive devices with human protocols. In: Shoup, V. (ed.) CRYPTO 2005. LNCS, vol. 3621, pp. 293–308. Springer, Heidelberg (2005)
6. Gilbert, H., Robshaw, M.J.B., Sibert, H.: Active attack against HB+: a provably secure lightweight authentication protocol. Electronic Letters 41, 1169–1170 (2005)
7. Penrose, L.: Dermatoglyphic topology. Nature 205, 544–546 (1965)
8. Bolling, J.: A window to your health. Jacksonville Medicine, Special Issue: Retinal Diseases 51 (2000)
9. Rivest, R.L., Adleman, L., Dertouzos, M.L.: On data banks and privacy homomorphisms. In: Foundations of Secure Computation, pp. 165–179. Academic Press (1978)
10. Rabin, M.O.: How to exchange secrets with oblivious transfer. Technical Report TR-81, Aiken Computation Lab, Harvard University (1981)
11. Even, S., Goldreich, O., Lempel, A.: A randomized protocol for signing contracts. Commun. ACM 28(6), 637–647 (1985)
12. Goldwasser, S., Micali, S.: Probabilistic encryption & how to play mental poker keeping secret all partial information. In: Proceedings of ACM Symposium on Theory of Computing, STOC 1982, pp. 365–377 (1982)
13. Barbosa, M., Brouard, T., Cauchie, S., de Sousa, S.M.: Secure Biometric Authentication with Improved Accuracy. In: Mu, Y., Susilo, W., Seberry, J. (eds.) ACISP 2008. LNCS, vol. 5107, pp. 21–36. Springer, Heidelberg (2008)

14. Simoens, K., Bringer, J., Chabanne, H., Seys, S.: A framework for analyzing template security and privacy in biometric authentication systems. IEEE Transactions on Information Forensics and Security 7(2), 833–841 (2012)

15. Bringer, J., Chabanne, H.: An authentication protocol with encrypted biometric data. In: Vaudenay, S. (ed.) AFRICACRYPT 2008. LNCS, vol. 5023, pp. 109–124. Springer, Heidelberg (2008)

16. Lipmaa, H.: An oblivious transfer protocol with log-squared communication. In: Zhou, J., López, J., Deng, R.H., Bao, F. (eds.) ISC 2005. LNCS, vol. 3650, pp. 314–328. Springer, Heidelberg (2005)

17. Stoianov, A.: Cryptographically secure biometrics. In: SPIE 7667, Biometric Technology for Human Identification VII 76670C, pp. 76670C–76670C–12 (2010)

18. Blum, M., Goldwasser, S.: An probabilistic public key encryption scheme which hides all partial information. In: Blakely, G.R., Chaum, D. (eds.) CRYPTO 1984. LNCS, vol. 196, pp. 289–299. Springer, Heidelberg (1985)

19. Menezes, A., van Oorschot, P.C., Vanstone, S.A.: Handbook of Applied Cryptography. CRC Press (1996)

A Appendix

$\mathsf{Exp}_{\mathsf{SKE},\mathcal{A}}^{\mathsf{IND\text{-}COA}}$ is the IND-COA game against an SKE scheme defined as follows.

$$
\begin{array}{ll}
\mathsf{Exp}_{\mathsf{SKE},\mathcal{A}}^{\mathsf{IND\text{-}COA}}: K & \leftarrow \mathsf{KeyGen}(1^\ell) \\
\qquad\qquad m_0, m_1 & \leftarrow A_1(1^\ell) \\
\qquad\qquad c & \leftarrow \mathsf{Enc}(m_\beta, K),\ \beta \xleftarrow{R} \{0,1\} \\
\qquad\qquad \beta' & \leftarrow A_2(m_0, m_1, c) \\
\text{Return 1 if } \beta' = \beta,\ 0 \text{ otherwise}
\end{array}
$$

The adversary's advantage in this game is defined as $\mathsf{Adv}_{\mathsf{SKE},\mathcal{A}}^{\mathsf{IND\text{-}COA}} = \left| 2\Pr\left(\mathsf{Exp}_{\mathsf{SKE},\mathcal{A}}^{\mathsf{IND\text{-}COA}} = 1\right) - 1 \right|$. A SKE scheme is said to be IND-COA-secure, if $\forall$ PPT adversary $\mathcal{A}$, $\mathsf{Adv}_{\mathsf{SKE},\mathcal{A}}^{\mathsf{IND\text{-}COA}} \leq \mathsf{negl}(\ell)$, where (and below) $\mathsf{negl}(\ell): \mathbf{N} \mapsto [0,1]$ is a negligible function meaning that for all positive polynomials P and all sufficiently large $\ell \in \mathbf{N}$, we have $\mathsf{negl}(\ell) < 1/P(\ell)$.

$\mathsf{Exp}_{\mathsf{GM},\mathcal{A}}^{\mathsf{IND\text{-}CPA}}$ is the IND-CPA game against the GM encryption and is defined as in the previous game, but now the adversary has access to the public key. This scheme is said to be IND-CPA secure if $\forall$ PPT adversary $\mathcal{A}$, $\mathsf{Adv}_{\mathsf{GM},\mathcal{A}}^{\mathsf{IND\text{-}CPA}} = \left| 2\Pr\left(\mathsf{Exp}_{\mathsf{GM},\mathcal{A}}^{\mathsf{IND\text{-}CPA}} = 1\right) - 1 \right| \leq \mathsf{negl}(\ell)$.

B Appendix

Here we prove the Theorem 1 and 2 in Bringer et al. [1] in the case of our improved protocol.

Theorem 2. *For any ID_{i_0} and two biometric templates b'_{i_0}, b'_{i_1}, where $i_0, i_1 \geq 1$ and b'_{i_0} is the biometric template related to ID_{i_0}, any of the malicious, but not colluding $\mathcal{AS}$, $\mathcal{DB}$, and $\mathcal{M}$ can only distinguish between $(\mathsf{ID}_{i_0}, b'_{i_0})$ and $(\mathsf{ID}_{i_0}, b'_{i_1})$ with a negligible advantage.*

Proof. Since $\mathcal{DB}$ and $\mathcal{M}$ have no access to user identities, their advantage is 0 in distinguishing between $(\mathsf{ID}_{i_0}, b'_{i_0})$ and $(\mathsf{ID}_{i_0}, b'_{i_1})$.

In the case of $\mathcal{AS}$, it has access to $\mathsf{id}_{i_0} = \mathsf{Enc}_K(\mathsf{ID}_{i_0})$, where $\mathsf{Enc}_K(\cdot)$ is a symmetric encryption with the sensor $\mathcal{S}$'s key K. However, even if $\mathcal{AS}$ knows ID_{i_0}, it cannot distinguish between $(\mathsf{ID}_{i_0}, b'_{i_0})$ and $(\mathsf{ID}_{i_0}, b'_{i_1})$, except with a negligible probability, as we see below.

Suppose that $\mathcal{AS}$ has a non-negligible advantage in distinguishing between $(\mathsf{ID}_{i_0}, b'_{i_0})$ and $(\mathsf{ID}_{i_0}, b'_{i_1})$. Then, we can construct an adversary $\mathcal{A}$, consisting of algorithms A_1 and A_2, such that $\mathcal{A}$'s advantage in the following game is non-negligible, contradicting the IND-CPA-security of GM cryptosystem:

$$
\begin{aligned}
&\mathsf{Exp}^{\mathsf{IND\text{-}CPA}}_{\mathsf{GM},\mathcal{A}}: \; \mathsf{pk} = (n,x), \mathsf{sk} = (p,q) && \leftarrow \mathsf{KeyGen}(1^\ell) \\
&\quad m_{i_0} = m'_{i_0} \oplus S, m_{i_1} = m'_{i_1} \oplus S, \; m'_{i_0} \neq m'_{i_1} && \leftarrow A_1(1^\ell, \mathsf{pk}) \\
&\quad c && \leftarrow \mathsf{Enc}(m_{i_\alpha}), \; \alpha \xleftarrow{R} \{0,1\} \\
&\quad \alpha' = \mathsf{guess}_{\mathcal{AS}} && \leftarrow A_2(\mathcal{AS}(m_{i_0}, m_{i_1}), c, \mathsf{pk}) \\
&\mathsf{Return}\ 1\ \mathsf{if}\ \beta' = \beta,\ 0\ \mathsf{otherwise}
\end{aligned}
$$

In the experiment, A_2 simulates the biometric authentication protocol by letting pk be $\mathcal{M}$'s public key and storing m'_{i_0} and m'_{i_1} in $\mathcal{DB}$. A_2 then asks $\mathcal{AS}$ to guess β from $c = \mathsf{Enc}(m_{i_\beta}) = \mathsf{Enc}(m'_{i_\beta} \oplus S)$ and returns β as the guess for α. So, $\mathcal{A}$ wins if $\mathcal{AS}$ wins in his guess. Thus, $\mathcal{AS}$ can only distinguish between $(\mathsf{ID}_{i_0}, b'_{i_0})$ and $(\mathsf{ID}_{i_0}, b'_{i_1})$ with negligible probability. □

The next theorem shows that a malicious database $\mathcal{DB}$ cannot distinguish whether two authentication attempts are from the same user.

Theorem 3. *For any two users $\mathcal{U}_{i_0}$ and $\mathcal{U}_{i_1}$, where $i_0, i_1 \geq 1$, if $\mathcal{U}_{i_\beta}$ where $\beta \in \{0,1\}$ makes an authentication attempt, then the malicious $\mathcal{DB}$ can only guess β with a negligible advantage. Here, the adversary's advantage is defined as $\big| \Pr\{\beta = \beta'\} - 1/2 \big|$, where β' is $\mathcal{DB}$'s guess.*

Proof (of Theorem 3). $\mathcal{DB}$ guesses β from $\mathsf{Enc}(t_j)$, for $j = 1, \cdots, N$, where $t_j = 1$ when $j = i_\beta$ ($\beta \in \{0,1\}$), otherwise $t_j = 0$. The proof is similar to that of Theorem 2 in Bringer *et al.* [1].

Suppose that $\mathcal{DB}$ can guess β with non-negligible advantage. Then, we can construct a PPT adversary $\mathcal{A}$, consisting of A_1 and A_2, that uses $\mathcal{DB}$ as a black-box to win in the following game with non-negligible advantage; contradicting the IND-CPA-security of GM cryptosystem:

$$
\begin{aligned}
&\mathsf{Exp}^{\mathsf{IND\text{-}CPA}}_{\mathsf{GM},\mathcal{A}}: \; \mathsf{pk} = (n,x), \mathsf{sk} = (p,q) && \leftarrow \mathsf{KeyGen}(1^\ell) \\
&\quad m_0 = 0, m_1 = 1 && \leftarrow A_1(1^\ell, \mathsf{pk}) \\
&\quad c && \leftarrow \mathsf{Enc}(m_\alpha), \; \alpha \xleftarrow{R} \{0,1\} \\
&\quad \alpha' = \mathsf{guess}_{\mathcal{DB}} && \leftarrow A_2(\mathcal{DB}(\mathsf{Enc}(t_j)), \mathsf{pk}), \; j = 1, \cdots, N \\
&\mathsf{Return}\ 1\ \mathsf{if}\ \beta' = \beta,\ 0\ \mathsf{otherwise}
\end{aligned}
$$

where $\mathsf{Enc}(t_{i_1}) = c$, $\mathsf{Enc}(t_{i_0}) = y^2 xc, y \xleftarrow{R} \mathbb{Z}_n^\star$, $t_j = 0$, $\forall j \neq i_0, i_1$. Note that if $c = \mathsf{Enc}(m_0)$, then $y^2 xc$ is not a quadratic residue mod n, so $\mathcal{DB}$'s guess, which is 0, and α coincide. Similarly, if $c = \mathsf{Enc}(m_1)$, then $y^2 xc$ is a quadratic residue mod n, so $\mathcal{DB}$'s guess, which is 1, and α coincide. Hence, $\mathcal{DB}$'s advantage of guessing β correctly should be negligible. □

C Appendix

Here, we present the proof of Theorem 1. Let $\mathcal{A}$ be any PPT adversary, consisting of two algorithms A_1 and A_2. Let us consider the following game against the modified biometric authentication protocol Π. Let KeyGen be an algorithm that generates both symmetric and asymmetric keys needed in the protocol, upon 1^ℓ (a string of 1s of length ℓ) as an input. As usual, ℓ is a security parameter.

$$
\begin{aligned}
\mathsf{Exp}_{\Pi,\mathcal{A}}^{\text{biometric-privacy}}: (\text{pk, sk}), K, K_{\mathcal{S}\leftrightarrow\mathcal{DB}}, K_1, \cdots, K_5 &\leftarrow \mathsf{KeyGen}(1^\ell) \\
S, S' &\leftarrow \mathsf{PNG}(s),\ s \xleftarrow{R} \{0,1\}^{r>0} \\
a, (\omega,\sigma),\ c,\ (\omega',\sigma') &\leftarrow \Pi(\text{pk}, K, K_{\mathcal{S}} \leftrightarrow \mathcal{DB}, K_1, K_2, K_4, K_5) \\
\gamma_0 = (\lambda^{(0)}, \sigma_0''),\ \gamma_1 = (\lambda^{(1)}, \sigma_1'') &\leftarrow A_1(a, c, K_3, (\omega,\sigma), (\omega',\sigma')) \\
\beta &\xleftarrow{R} \{0,1\} \\
\mathsf{Out}_{\mathcal{M}} &\leftarrow \mathcal{M}(\gamma_\beta, (\omega,\sigma), (\omega',\sigma'), \text{sk}, K_1, \cdots, K_5) \\
\beta' &\leftarrow A_2(\gamma_0, \gamma_1, \mathsf{Out}_{\mathcal{M}}) \\
\text{Return } (\beta' = \beta, \mathsf{Out}_{\mathcal{M}})
\end{aligned}
$$

The adversary's advantage $\mathsf{Adv}_{\Pi,\mathcal{A}}^{\text{biometric-privacy}}$ at the end of this game is defined as $\mathsf{Adv}_{\Pi,\mathcal{A}}^{\text{biometric-privacy}} = |\Pr\{\beta' = \beta\} - 1/2|$, where $\beta \in \{0,1\}$ is $\mathcal{M}$'s choice and β' is the adversary's guess for β. We say that the biometric authentication protocol is secure against malicious $\mathcal{AS}$, if $\mathsf{Adv}_{\Pi,\mathcal{A}}^{\text{biometric-privacy}} \leq \mathsf{negl}(\ell)$.

Note that as stated in Assumption 2, we assume that the adversary does not have access to an acceptable biometric template, because otherwise the adversary can easily produce two challenges so that it wins the above experiment with non-negligible advantage.

Proof (of Theorem 1). Case 1. $\mathsf{HW}\big(\mathsf{Dec}(\lambda^{(\beta)}) \oplus S \oplus S'\big) \leq \tau$, for $\forall \beta \in \{0,1\}$. In this case, $\mathcal{M}$'s output always be the same (i.e., $\mathsf{Out}_{\mathcal{M}} = \mathsf{YES}$.) Hence, the adversary's advantage in this case is 0.
Case 2. $\mathsf{HW}\big(\mathsf{Dec}(\lambda^{(\beta)}) \oplus S \oplus S'\big) > \tau$, for $\forall \beta \in \{0,1\}$. Also in this case, $\mathcal{M}$'s output always be the same (i.e., $\mathsf{Out}_{\mathcal{M}} = \mathsf{NO}$). Hence, the adversary's advantage in this case is 0.
Case 3. $\mathsf{HW}\big(\mathsf{Dec}(\lambda^{(\beta)}) \oplus S \oplus S'\big) \leq \tau$ and $\mathsf{HW}\big(\mathsf{Dec}(\lambda^{(1-\beta)}) \oplus S \oplus S'\big) > \tau$. Suppose that a PPT adversary $\mathcal{A}$ has a non-negligible advantage δ of winning the game $\mathsf{Exp}_{\Pi,\mathcal{A}}^{\text{biometric-privacy}}$. Then we can construct a PPT adversary $\bar{\mathcal{A}}$ that wins in $\mathsf{Exp}_{\mathsf{SKE},\bar{\mathcal{A}}}^{\text{IND-COA}}$ and/or $\mathsf{Exp}_{\mathsf{GM},\bar{\mathcal{A}}}^{\text{IND-CPA}}$ with advantage δ. The construction of such an adversary $\bar{\mathcal{A}}$, for example in the case of $\mathsf{Exp}_{\mathsf{SKE},\bar{\mathcal{A}}}^{\text{IND-COA}}$, may proceed as follows:

$$
\begin{aligned}
\mathsf{Exp}_{\mathsf{SKE},\bar{\mathcal{A}}}^{\text{IND-COA}}: K' &\leftarrow \mathsf{KeyGen}(1^\ell) \\
\begin{cases} m_0 = (m_{00}, m_{01}),\ \mathsf{HW}(m_{00}) \leq \tau\ \&\ \mathsf{HW}(\neg m_{00}) > \tau \\ m_1 = (m_{10}, m_{11}),\ \mathsf{HW}(m_{10}) > \tau\ \&\ \mathsf{HW}(\neg m_{10}) \leq \tau \end{cases} &\leftarrow \bar{\mathcal{A}}(1^\ell) \\
c &\leftarrow \mathsf{Enc}_{K'}(m_\alpha),\ \alpha \xleftarrow{R} \{0,1\} \\
\alpha' = \begin{cases} \mathsf{guess}_{\mathcal{A}}, & \text{if } \mathsf{Out}_{\mathcal{M}} = \mathsf{YES}, \\ 1 - \mathsf{guess}_{\mathcal{A}}, & \text{if } \mathsf{Out}_{\mathcal{M}} = \mathsf{NO}. \end{cases} &\leftarrow \bar{\mathcal{A}}(\mathcal{A}(m_0, m_1, c)) \\
\text{Return } 1 \text{ if } \alpha' = \alpha,\ 0 \text{ otherwise}
\end{aligned}
$$

where $|m_{00}| = |m_{10}| = |S|$ and $|m_{01}| = |m_{11}| = |K_1|$. $\bar{\mathcal{A}}$ then simulates the biometric authentication protocol and replaces, without loss of generality, the symmetric key encryption scheme between the sensor $\mathcal{S}$ and the matcher $\mathcal{M}$. More precisely, $\bar{\mathcal{A}}$ replaces ω with the challenge ciphertext c and ω' with an encryption of a bitstring of all zeros. $\bar{\mathcal{A}}$ then runs A_1 to obtain $\gamma_0 = (\mathsf{Enc}_{\mathsf{GM}}(0), \sigma_0'')$

and $\gamma_1 = (\mathsf{Enc}_{\mathsf{GM}}(1), \sigma_1'')$, where 0 and 1 respectively stand for bitstrings of all zeros and ones. If $\mathsf{Out}_\mathcal{M} = \mathsf{YES}$, $\bar{\mathcal{A}}$ outputs $\mathcal{A}$'s guess β' as α'; if $\mathsf{Out}_\mathcal{M} = \mathsf{NO}$, $\bar{\mathcal{A}}$ outputs $1 - \beta'$ as α'. This is because, when $\mathsf{Out}_\mathcal{M} = \mathsf{YES}$, $\beta' = 0$ would indicate that $\mathsf{HW}(m_{\alpha 0}) \leq \tau$, and $\beta' = 1$ would indicate that $\mathsf{HW}(1 \oplus m_{\alpha 0}) > \tau$. And similarly, when $\mathsf{Out}_\mathcal{M} = \mathsf{NO}$, $\beta' = 0$ would indicate that $\mathsf{HW}(m_{\alpha 0}) > \tau$, and $\beta' = 1$ would indicate that $\mathsf{HW}(1 \oplus m_{\alpha 0}) \leq \tau$. Hence, if $\mathcal{A}$ wins, so does $\bar{\mathcal{A}}$.   □

Private and Dynamic Time-Series Data Aggregation with Trust Relaxation

Iraklis Leontiadis, Kaoutar Elkhiyaoui, and Refik Molva

EURECOM, Sophia Antipolis, France
{firstname.lastname}@eurecom.fr

Abstract. With the advent of networking applications collecting user data on a massive scale, the privacy of individual users appears to be a major concern. The main challenge is the design of a solution that allows the data analyzer to compute global statistics over the set of individual inputs that are protected by some confidentiality mechanism. Joye *et al.* [7] recently suggested a solution that allows a centralized party to compute the sum of encrypted inputs collected through a smart metering network. The main shortcomings of this solution are its reliance on a trusted dealer for key distribution and the need for frequent key updates. In this paper we introduce a secure protocol for aggregation of time-series data that is based on the Joye *et al.* [7] scheme and in which the main shortcomings of the latter, namely, the requirement for key updates and for the trusted dealer are eliminated. Moreover our scheme supports a dynamic group management, whereby as opposed to Joye *et al.* [7] leave and join operations do not trigger a key update at the users.

Keywords: data aggregation, privacy, time-series data.

1 Introduction

Progress in statistical data processing enables data analyzers to infer extremely useful information from the massive amount of data collected through networks and distributed applications. Such data analysis has tremendous benefits in a wide range of applications. In an e-health scenario, statistics derived from the collected data sets would greatly help field studies about diseases and the effect of a specific medicine. Another scenario entails a different environment whereby data is produced by a set of users that hold smart meters. Smart meters can report accurately at specific time intervals energy, gas or water consumption. Considering electricity consumption for instance, a data analyzer with cooperation of an energy provider can compute useful statistics such as average electricity consumption over large population of users along a specific time period. These statistics can then help the energy provider perform various operations such as load balancing and forecasting for potential acquirement.

Despite its merits, statistical data processing is challenged with privacy issues such as the confidentiality of private data. Frequent smart-readings with inappropriate analysis by companies may leak private information such as the number of people that live in a place, the time period in which the house is empty and personal habits that can be a valuable asset to marketing retailers [10]. Serious privacy breaches are possible without

D. Gritzalis et al. (Eds.): CANS 2014, LNCS 8813, pp. 305–320, 2014.

any doubt in the medical scenario as well, in which the disclosure of personal data to untrusted data analyzers jeopardizes user personal information in various ways: It affects insurance coverage since records are exposed to insurance companies. Moreover, a social discrimination is possible owing to the exposure of medical treatments.

While encryption of data would protect data privacy, data analysis by an untrusted aggregator would become challenging. The most prominent privacy preserving solutions for data analysis benefit from cryptographic algorithms [13] that either introduce a high computation cost at the aggregator or restrict the possible range of values that users can submit due to the need of discrete logarithm computation. To mitigate this drawback, Joye et al. [7] proposed a nifty construction which as the solution in [13] calls for a fully trusted dealer. The reliance on trusted key dealer however can be deemed unrealistic for real world applications. In addition, this solution builds upon a static key management scheme where user joins and leaves induce a significant overhead in terms of communication.

In this paper, we improve the design of the privacy preserving aggregation protocol suggested by Joye et al. [7] by eliminating the need for key redistribution following a user join or leave and the need for fully trusted key dealer. The features of the enhanced protocol can be summarized as follows:

- *No key dealer.* Contrary to most previous privacy preserving aggregation protocols, there is no trusted key dealer in our scheme. In contrast, we introduce a *semi-trusted* party called *collector* which gathers partial key information from users through a *secure* channel.
- *Support for dynamic user populations.* No coordination is required to manage changes in the population of users. This is possible due to a self-generated key mechanism by which no key agreement between users is required.
- *Privacy.* With respect to privacy, the scheme assures *aggregator obliviousness* as introduced by Elaine Shi et al. [13]. That is, the untrusted aggregator only learns the sum and the average over users' private data at the end of the protocol execution. Moreover, we show that the collector does not derive any information about the users' private data.
- *Efficiency.* Like Joye et al. [7] our scheme enables the computation of the sum and the average over a large number of users without restrictions on the range of users' values. It is also scalable in the sense that decryptions performed by the aggregator do not depend on the number of users.

2   Problem Statement

We consider a scenario where an aggregator $\mathcal{A}$ would like to compute the aggregate sum of the private data of some users $\mathcal{U}_i$. Similarly to the work of [7] and [13], we restrict ourselves to time-series data which is a series of data point observations measured at equally spaced time intervals. A straightforward approach to compute the aggregate sum would be encrypting $\mathcal{U}_i$'s individual data using the public key of $\mathcal{A}$. This solution however relies on a *trusted* aggregator which first decrypts the users' individual data using its secret key then computes the sum. To tackle this issue, [7] and [13] employ a combination of secret sharing techniques and additively homomorphic encryption to enable aggregator $\mathcal{A}$ to compute the sum of users' data without compromising users' privacy. The idea is to have a *trusted third party* called *key dealer* that provides each user $\mathcal{U}_i$ with a secret share sk_i while supplying the aggregator $\mathcal{A}$ with the secret key sk_A defined as $-\sum sk_i$. Each user $\mathcal{U}_i$ encrypts its private data using its secret share sk_i and forwards the resulting ciphertext to the aggregator, which in turn combines the received ciphertexts so as to obtain an encryption of the sum of the users' data that can be decrypted using the aggregator's secret key sk_A.

Although such solutions prevent the aggregator from learning users' confidential data, they suffer from two main limitations which we aim to address in this paper. The first limitation is that they build upon the assumption that the key dealer is *trusted* and does not have any interest in undermining user privacy. Whereas the second shortcoming –which is generally overlooked– is that these solutions only support static groups of users and as a result they are fault intolerant. Namely, in the case of user failures, aggregator $\mathcal{A}$ cannot compute the aggregate sum. Along these lines, we propose a solution for privacy preserving data aggregation of time-series data that draws upon the work of [7] and which in addition to supporting *dynamic group management* and arbitrary *user failures* does not depend on trusted key dealers. The idea is to introduce an *intermediary untrusted party* that we call *collector*, who helps the aggregator $\mathcal{A}$ with the computation of the sum of users' individual data, without any prior distribution of secret keys by a trusted dealer.

2.1 Entities

A scheme for dynamic and privacy preserving data aggregation for time-series involves the following entities:

- Users $\mathcal{U}_i$: At each specific time interval t, each user $\mathcal{U}_i$ produces a data point $x_{i,t}$ that it wants to send to an aggregator. Each data point contains private sensitive information pertaining to user $\mathcal{U}_i$. To protect the confidentiality of the value of $x_{i,t}$ against the aggregator and eavesdroppers, user $\mathcal{U}_i$ encrypts $x_{i,t}$ using some secret input sk_i and forwards the resulting ciphertext $c_{i,t}$ to the aggregator. It also sends to the collector some auxiliary information $aux_{i,t}$ that will be used later to compute the aggregate sum of individual data. Without loss of generality, we denote $\mathbb{U}$ the set of users $\mathcal{U}_i$ in the system.
- Collector $\mathcal{C}$: It is an *untrusted party* which upon receiving the auxiliary information $aux_{i,t}$ sent by users $\mathcal{U}_i \in \mathbb{U}$ at time interval t computes a function g of $aux_{i,t}$. Hereafter, we denote aux_t the output of function g at time interval t.
- Aggregator $\mathcal{A}$: It is an *untrusted entity* which upon receipt of ciphertexts $c_{i,t}$ and the auxiliary information aux_t at time interval t computes the sum $\sum_{\mathcal{U}_i \in \mathbb{U}} x_{i,t}$ over the data points $x_{i,t}$ underlying ciphertexts $c_{i,t}$.

2.2 Privacy Preserving and Dynamic Time-Series Data Aggregation

A privacy preserving and dynamic time-series data aggregation protocol consists of the following algorithms:

- Setup$(1^\tau) \to (\mathcal{P}, \mathsf{sk}_A, \mathsf{sk}_C, \{\mathsf{sk}_i\}_{\mathcal{U}_i \in \mathbb{U}})$: It is a randomized algorithm which on input of a security parameter τ, outputs the public parameters $\mathcal{P}$ that will be used by subsequent algorithms, the secret key sk_A of aggregator $\mathcal{A}$, the secret key sk_C of collector $\mathcal{C}$ and the secret keys $\{\mathsf{sk}_i\}_{\mathcal{U}_i \in \mathbb{U}}$ of users $\mathcal{U}_i$.
- Encrypt$(t, \mathsf{sk}_i, x_{i,t}) \to c_{i,t}$: It is a deterministic algorithm which on input of time interval t, secret key sk_i of user $\mathcal{U}_i$ and data point $x_{i,t}$, encrypts $x_{i,t}$ and outputs the resulting ciphertext $c_{i,t}$.
- Collect$((\mathsf{aux}_{i,t})_{\mathcal{U}_i \in \mathbb{U}}, \mathsf{sk}_C) \to \mathsf{aux}_t$: It is a deterministic algorithm executed by collector $\mathcal{C}$ which on input of the auxiliary information $(\mathsf{aux}_{i,t})_{\mathcal{U}_i \in \mathbb{U}}$ provided by individual users $\mathcal{U}_i$ and collector $\mathcal{C}$'s secret key sk_C computes a function g over $\mathsf{aux}_{i,t}$ and outputs the result aux_t.
- Aggregate$(\{c_{i,t}\}_{\mathcal{U}_i \in \mathbb{U}}, \mathsf{aux}_t, \mathsf{sk}_A) \to \sum x_{i,t}$: It is a deterministic algorithm run by aggregator $\mathcal{A}$. It takes as inputs ciphertexts $\{c_{i,t}\}_{\mathcal{U}_i \in \mathbb{U}}$, auxiliary information aux_t supplied by collector $\mathcal{C}$ and aggregator $\mathcal{A}$'s secret key sk_A, and outputs the sum $\sum x_{i,t}$, where $x_{i,t}$ is the plaintext underlying ciphertext $c_{i,t}$.

2.3   Privacy Definitions

In accordance with the work of [7,13], we assume in this paper an honest-but-curious model. This means that while the participants in the protocol are interested in learning the individual data of users, they still comply with the aggregation protocol. Namely, users are always presumed to submit a correct input to the aggregation protocol. Actually, data pollution attacks where users submit bogus values to the aggregator is orthogonal to the problem of privacy preserving data aggregation. We also assume that while users $\mathcal{U}_i$ may collude with either aggregator $\mathcal{A}$ or collector $\mathcal{C}$ by disclosing their private inputs, aggregator $\mathcal{A}$ and collector $\mathcal{C}$ never collude.

In this section, we present two formalizations: The first one defines privacy against aggregator $\mathcal{A}$ which we call in compliance with previous work *aggregator obliviousness*, whereas the second formalization defines privacy against collector $\mathcal{C}$ which we refer to as *collector obliviousness*.

Aggregator Obliviousness. Aggregator Obliviousness (AO) ensures that for each time interval t, the aggregator learns nothing other than the value of $\sum_{\mathcal{U}_i \in \mathbb{U}} x_{i,t}$ from ciphertexts $c_{i,t}$ and the auxiliary information aux_t that it receives from users $\mathcal{U}_i \in \mathbb{U}$ and collector $\mathcal{C}$ respectively. It ensures also that even if aggregator $\mathcal{A}$ colludes with an arbitrary set of users $\mathbb{K} \subset \mathbb{U}$, it will only be able to learn the value of the aggregate sum of honest users (i.e. $\displaystyle\sum_{\mathcal{U}_i \in \mathbb{U} \setminus \mathbb{K}} x_{i,t}$) and nothing else.

To formally capture the capabilities of an aggregator $\mathcal{A}$ against the privacy of aggregation protocols, we assume that $\mathcal{A}$ is given access to the following oracles:

- $\mathcal{O}_{\mathsf{setup}, \mathcal{A}}$: When called, this oracle provides aggregator $\mathcal{A}$ with the public parameters denoted $\mathcal{P}$ of the aggregation protocol and any secret information sk_A that may be needed by aggregator $\mathcal{A}$ to perform the aggregation.

- $\mathcal{O}_{\text{encrypt}}$: When queried with time t, identifier uid$_i$ of some user $\mathcal{U}_i$ and a data point $x_{i,t}$, oracle $\mathcal{O}_{\text{encrypt}}$ outputs the encryption $c_{i,t}$ of $x_{i,t}$ in time interval t using $\mathcal{U}_i$'s secret key sk$_i$.
- $\mathcal{O}_{\text{corrupt}}$: When queried with the identifier uid$_i$ of some user $\mathcal{U}_i$, the oracle $\mathcal{O}_{\text{corrupt}}$ returns the secret key sk$_i$ of user $\mathcal{U}_i$.
- $\mathcal{O}_{\text{collect},\mathcal{A}}$: When called with time t, this oracle returns the auxiliary information aux$_t$ that collector $\mathcal{C}$ computed during time interval t. We note that in schemes such as [13,7] where a collector is not needed, the aggregator will not call this oracle.
- $\mathcal{O}_{\text{AO}}$: When called with a subset of users $\mathbb{S} \subset \mathbb{U}$ and with two time-series $(\mathcal{U}_i, t, x_{i,t}^0)_{\mathcal{U}_i \in \mathbb{S}}$ and $(\mathcal{U}_i, t, x_{i,t}^1)_{\mathcal{U}_i \in \mathbb{S}}$ such that $\sum x_{i,t}^0 = \sum x_{i,t}^1$, this oracle flips a random coin $b \in \{0, 1\}$ and returns an encryption of the time-serie $(\mathcal{U}_i, t, x_{i,t}^b)_{\mathcal{U}_i \in \mathbb{S}}$ (that is the tuple of ciphertexts $(c_{i,t}^b)_{\mathcal{U}_i \in \mathbb{S}}$) and the corresponding auxiliary information aux$_t^b$ that aggregator $\mathcal{A}$ should receive from the collector in time interval t.

Aggregator $\mathcal{A}$ has access to the above oracles in two phases:

Learning Phase. The learning phase is executed in two steps:

1. *Setup*: Aggregator $\mathcal{A}$ calls $\mathcal{O}_{\text{setup},\mathcal{A}}$ which provides $\mathcal{A}$ with the set of public parameters $\mathcal{P}$ associated with the aggregation protocol together with any secret information sk$_A$ that aggregator $\mathcal{A}$ may need to execute the aggregation correctly.
2. *Queries*: After calling $\mathcal{O}_{\text{setup},\mathcal{A}}$, aggregator $\mathcal{A}$ issues three types of queries:
   - **Corruption queries**: Aggregator $\mathcal{A}$ calls $\mathcal{O}_{\text{corrupt}}$ with a user identifier uid$_i$ and gets in return the secret key sk$_i$ matching the identifier uid$_i$.
   - **Encryption queries**: Aggregator $\mathcal{A}$ queries $\mathcal{O}_{\text{encrypt}}$ with time interval t, a user identifier uid$_i$ and a data point $x_{i,t}$. The oracle $\mathcal{O}_{\text{encrypt}}$ outputs accordingly the cipherext $c_{i,t}$ corresponding to the query $(t, \text{uid}_i, x_{i,t})$.
   - **Auxiliary information queries**: Aggregator $\mathcal{A}$ invokes the oracle $\mathcal{O}_{\text{collect}}$ with time interval t to receive the auxiliary information aux$_t$ that collector $\mathcal{C}$ computed at time t.

Challenge Phase. The challenge phase involves the following three operations:

1. *Challenge selection*: Aggregator $\mathcal{A}$ chooses a subset $\mathbb{S}^*$ of users that were not compromised and a challenge time interval t^* for which it did not make an encryption query during the learning phase. $\mathcal{A}$ then selects two time-series $\mathcal{X}_{t^*}^0 = (\mathcal{U}_i, t^*, x_{i,t^*}^0)_{\mathcal{U}_i \in \mathbb{S}^*}$ and $\mathcal{X}_{t^*}^1 = (\mathcal{U}_i, t^*, x_{i,t^*}^1)_{\mathcal{U}_i \in \mathbb{S}^*}$, such that $\sum x_{i,t}^0 = \sum x_{i,t}^1$.
2. *Query*: Aggregator $\mathcal{A}$ submits the time-series $\mathcal{X}_{t^*}^0$ and $\mathcal{X}_{t^*}^1$ to the oracle $\mathcal{O}_{\text{AO}}$. Oracle $\mathcal{O}_{\text{AO}}$ accordingly flips a coin $b \in \{0, 1\}$ and returns the encryption $(c_{i,t^*}^b)_{\mathcal{U}_i \in \mathbb{S}^*}$ of the time-serie $\mathcal{X}_{t^*}^b$ and the auxiliary information aux$_{t^*}^b$ computed by collector $\mathcal{C}$ for time interval t^*.
3. *Guess*: Aggregator $\mathcal{A}$ outputs a guess b^* for the bit b.

We say that aggregator $\mathcal{A}$ succeeds in the aggregator obliviousness game, if $b^* = b$.

Definition 1 (Aggregator Obliviousness). *An aggregation protocol is said to ensure aggregator obliviousness if for any aggregator $\mathcal{A}$, the probability $\Pr(b = b^*) \leqslant \frac{1}{2} + \epsilon$, where ϵ is a negligible function.*

Collector Obliviousness. Collector Obliviousness (CO) guarantees that collector $\mathcal{C}$ cannot infer any information about the private input of individual users $\mathcal{U}_i$ either from the messages it receives directly from the users or the protocol exchange between the users and the aggregator. It also entails that even in the case where collector $\mathcal{C}$ colludes with a set of users $\mathbb{K}$, it does not gain any additional information about the individual values of honest users $\mathcal{U}_i$ in $\mathbb{U} \setminus \mathbb{K}$.

To formally reflect the adversarial capabilities of collector $\mathcal{C}$ against aggregation protocols, we assume that in addition to the oracles $\mathcal{O}_{\text{encrypt}}$ and $\mathcal{O}_{\text{corrupt}}$, collector $\mathcal{C}$ is given access to the following oracles:

- $\mathcal{O}_{\text{setup},\mathcal{C}}$: When queried, this oracle supplies collector $\mathcal{C}$ with the public parameters denoted $\mathcal{P}$ of the aggregation protocol and any secret information $\text{sk}_\mathcal{C}$ that collector $\mathcal{C}$ may need during the aggregation protocol.
- $\mathcal{O}_{\text{collect},\mathcal{C}}$: When invoked with time t, identifier uid_i of some user $\mathcal{U}_i$ and ciphertext $c_{i,t}$, this oracle returns the auxiliary information $\text{aux}_{i,t}$ that corresponds to ciphertext $c_{i,t}$ that user $\mathcal{U}_i$ computed during time interval t.
- $\mathcal{O}_{\text{CO}}$: When called with a subset of users $\mathbb{S} \subset \mathbb{U}$ and with two time-series $(\mathcal{U}_i, t, x_{i,t}^0)_{\mathcal{U}_i \in \mathbb{S}}$ and $(\mathcal{U}_i, t, x_{i,t}^1)_{\mathcal{U}_i \in \mathbb{S}}$, this oracle flips a random coin $b \in \{0,1\}$ and returns to collector $\mathcal{C}$ an encryption of the time-serie $(\mathcal{U}_i, t, x_{i,t}^b)_{\mathcal{U}_i \in \mathbb{S}}$ (i.e. the ciphertexts $(c_{i,t}^b)_{\mathcal{U}_i \in \mathbb{S}}$) and the corresponding auxiliary information computed by users $\mathcal{U}_i \in \mathbb{S}$ (i.e. $(\text{aux}_{i,t}^b)_{\mathcal{U}_i \in \mathbb{S}}$).

Collector $\mathcal{C}$ accesses the aforementioned oracles in two phases:

Learning Phase. In the learning phase, collector $\mathcal{C}$ proceeds as follows:

1. *Setup*: Collector $\mathcal{C}$ queries $\mathcal{O}_{\text{setup},\mathcal{C}}$ which supplies $\mathcal{C}$ with the set of public parameters $\mathcal{P}$ of the aggregation protocol and the secret information $\text{sk}_\mathcal{C}$ that collector $\mathcal{C}$ should have to execute the aggregation properly.
2. *Queries*: After querying $\mathcal{O}_{\text{setup},\mathcal{C}}$, collector $\mathcal{C}$ issues three types of queries.
   - **Corruption queries**: Collector $\mathcal{C}$ calls $\mathcal{O}_{\text{corrupt}}$ with user identifiers uid_i to compromise users in the system.
   - **Encryption queries**: Collector $\mathcal{C}$ selects a time interval t, a user identifier uid_i and a data point $x_{i,t}$ and submits the query $(t, \text{uid}_i, x_{i,t})$ to $\mathcal{O}_{\text{encrypt}}$ which outputs the corresponding ciphertext $c_{i,t}$.
   - **Auxiliary information queries**: Collector $\mathcal{C}$ picks a time interval t, a user identifier uid_i and a ciphertext $c_{i,t}$ and queries $\mathcal{O}_{\text{collect},\mathcal{C}}$ to get the auxiliary information $\text{aux}_{i,t}$ generated by user $\mathcal{U}_i$ for time interval t and ciphertext $c_{i,t}$.

Challenge Phase. The challenge phase is performed in three steps:

1. *Challenge selection*: Collector $\mathcal{C}$ selects a subset $\mathbb{S}^*$ of honest users and a challenge time interval t^* for which it did not make an encryption query in the learning phase. Then, collector $\mathcal{C}$ chooses two time-series $\mathcal{X}_{t^*}^0 = (\mathcal{U}_i, t^*, x_{i,t^*}^0)_{\mathcal{U}_i \in \mathbb{S}^*}$ and $\mathcal{X}_{t^*}^1 = (\mathcal{U}_i, t^*, x_{i,t^*}^1)_{\mathcal{U}_i \in \mathbb{S}^*}$.
2. *Query*: Collector $\mathcal{C}$ queries the oracle $\mathcal{O}_{\text{CO}}$ with $\mathcal{X}_{t^*}^0$ and $\mathcal{X}_{t^*}^1$ which in turn selects randomly a bit $b \in \{0,1\}$ and returns the tuple $((\langle c_{i,t^*}^b, \text{aux}_{i,t^*}^b \rangle))_{\mathcal{U}_i \in \mathbb{S}^*}$.

3. *Guess*: Collector $\mathcal{C}$ outputs a guess b^* for the bit b.

We say that collector $\mathcal{C}$ succeeds in the collector obliviousness game, if $b^* = b$.

Definition 2 (Collector Obliviousness). *An aggregation protocol is said to ensure collector obliviousness if for any collector $\mathcal{C}$, the probability $\Pr(b = b^*) \leqslant \frac{1}{2} + \epsilon$, where ϵ is a negligible function.*

3   Idea of Solution

The homomorphic scheme suggested by Joye and Libert [7] allows an untrusted aggregator to evaluate the sum or the average without any access to individual data. However to support this functionality, a fully trusted dealer has to distribute secret keys to each user $\mathcal{U}_i$ and as a result, it will be able to decrypt. Our scheme extends Joye and Libert scheme [7] through two major enhancements :

- **No key dealer:** Our scheme does not require a trusted key dealer that might get individual private data samples.
- **Dynamic group management:** In the Joye and Libert scheme [7], each join or leave operation triggers a new key redistribution for all the users in the aggregation system, whereas in our protocol, join and leave operations are possible without any key update at the users. Hence, dynamic group management is assured with significantly lower communication and computation overhead. The proposed protocol is also resilient to user failures that may occur due to communication errors or hardware failures.

In order to eliminate the need for a fully trusted dealer and to support *dynamic group management*, we employ two techniques:

- *Responsibility splitting mechanism*: Each user $\mathcal{U}_i$ sends an encryption of its private data sample to aggregator $\mathcal{A}$ and an obfuscated version of its secret key sk_i to the semi trusted collector $\mathcal{C}$, in such a way that neither the aggregator nor the collector can violate the privacy of individual data points provided by users.
- *Self-generation of secret keys:* The secret keys used to encrypt individual data points are generated independently by users *without a trusted key dealer*.

Actually, each user $\mathcal{U}_i$ chooses independently its secret key sk_i whereas the untrusted aggregator generates a random key sk_A. For each time interval t, aggregator $\mathcal{A}$ publishes an obfuscated version $\mathsf{pk}_{A,t}$ of the secret key sk_A. Users $\mathcal{U}_i$ on the other hand encrypt their private data samples $x_{i,t}$ with their secret keys sk_i using the Joye-Libert cryptosystem, and send the corresponding ciphertexts $c_{i,t}$ to aggregator $\mathcal{A}$. They also obfuscate their secret keys sk_i using $\mathsf{pk}_{A,t}$ and sends the resulting auxiliary information $\mathsf{aux}_{i,t}$ to collector $\mathcal{C}$ through a secure channel. Collector $\mathcal{C}$ computes a function $g(t)$ of the auxiliary information $\mathsf{aux}_{i,t}$ it has received and forwards the output aux_t to aggregator $\mathcal{A}$. Upon receiving the ciphertexts $c_{i,t}$ and the auxiliary information aux_t, $\mathcal{A}$ uses its secret key sk_A and learns the sum $\sum x_{i,t}$ for the time interval t.

4   Protocol Description

Without loss of generality, we assume in the remainder of this section that the aggregation system comprises n users denoted $\mathbb{U} = \{\mathcal{U}_1, ..., \mathcal{U}_n\}$.

Now before providing the description of our solution, we first give a brief overview of the Joye-Libert (JL) scheme [7].

4.1   Joye-Libert Scheme

- $\mathsf{Setup}_{\mathsf{JL}}$: A trusted dealer $\mathcal{D}$ selects randomly two safe prime numbers p and q and sets $N = pq$. Then, it defines a cryptographic hash function $H : \mathbb{Z} \rightarrow \mathbb{Z}_{N^2}^*$ and outputs the public parameters $\mathcal{P}_{\mathsf{JL}} = (N, H)$. Finally, the dealer $\mathcal{D}$ distributes to each user $\mathcal{U}_i \in \mathbb{U}$ a secret key $\mathsf{sk}_i \in [0, N^2]$ and sends $\mathsf{sk}_A = -\sum_{i=1}^n \mathsf{sk}_i$ to the untrusted aggregator $\mathcal{A}$.
  We note that hereafter all computations are performed "$\mathrm{mod} N^2$" unless mentioned otherwise.
- $\mathsf{Encrypt}_{\mathsf{JL}}$: For each time interval t, each user $\mathcal{U}_i$ encrypts its private data $x_{i,t}$ using the secret key sk_i and outputs the ciphertext $c_{i,t} = (1 + x_{i,t}N)H(t)^{\mathsf{sk}_i} \mod N^2$. We point out that ciphertexts $c_{i,t}$ fulfills the following property:

$$\prod_{i=1}^n c_{i,t} = \prod_{i=1}^n (1 + x_{i,t}N)H(t)^{\mathsf{sk}_i} = (1 + \sum_{i=1}^n x_{i,t}N)H(t)^{\sum_{i=1}^n \mathsf{sk}_i}$$

$$= (1 + \sum_{i=1}^n x_{i,t}N)H(t)^{-\mathsf{sk}_A}$$

- $\mathsf{Aggregate}_{\mathsf{JL}}$: Upon receiving $c_{i,t}$ the untrusted aggregator computes

$$P_t = \prod_{i=1}^n c_{i,t} H(t)^{\mathsf{sk}_A} = 1 + \sum_{i=1}^n x_{i,t}N \mod N^2$$

and recovers $\sum_{i=1}^n x_{i,t}$ by computing $\frac{P_t - 1}{N}$ in $\mathbb{Z}$. The value $\frac{P_t - 1}{N}$ is meaningful as long as $\sum_{i=1}^n x_{i,t} < N$.

We recall that the JL scheme is aggregator oblivious in the random oracle model under the decisional composite residuosity (DCR) assumption (cf. [7]).

4.2   Description

Our protocol runs in four phases:

- Setup: A trusted third party $\mathcal{TP}$ selects two safe primes p and q, sets $N = pq$, and picks a cryptographic hash function $H : \{0,1\}^* \rightarrow \mathbb{Z}_{N^2}^*$. $\mathcal{TP}$ then publishes the public parameters $\mathcal{P} = (N, H)$ and goes offline. Next, aggregator $\mathcal{A}$ generates a random secret key $\mathsf{sk}_A \in \mathbb{Z}_{N^2}^*$, and each user $\mathcal{U}_i \in \mathbb{U}$ independently chooses its random secret key $\mathsf{sk}_i \in [0, N^2]$ *without any coordination by a trusted key dealer.*
  It is important to note here that contrary to the JL scheme, the trusted third party $\mathcal{TP}$ does not know the individual secret keys of users $\mathcal{U}_i$, and once the public parameters $\mathcal{P}$ are published it can go offline.

- Encrypt: For each time interval t, each user $\mathcal{U}_i$ encrypts its private data $x_{i,t}$ using its secret key sk_i and the algorithm $\mathsf{Encrypt}_{\mathsf{JL}}$ as shown in subsection 4.1, and sends the resulting ciphertext $c_{i,t} = (1 + x_{i,t}N)H(t)^{\mathsf{sk}_i} \mod N^2$ to aggregator $\mathcal{A}$.
- Collect: For each time interval t, aggregator $\mathcal{A}$ publishes $\mathsf{pk}_{A,t} = H(t)^{\mathsf{sk}_A}$. Each user $\mathcal{U}_i$ then computes the auxiliary information $\mathsf{aux}_{i,t} = \mathsf{pk}_{A,t}^{\mathsf{sk}_i} = H(t)^{\mathsf{sk}_A\mathsf{sk}_i}$ using its secret key sk_i and sends $\mathsf{aux}_{i,t}$ to collector $\mathcal{C}$ through a *secure channel*.
  Upon receiving $\mathsf{aux}_{i,t}$ $(1 \leqslant i \leqslant n)$ from users $\mathcal{U}_i \in \mathbb{U}$, collector $\mathcal{C}$ computes

$$\mathsf{aux}_t = \prod_{i=1}^{n} \mathsf{aux}_{i,t} = \prod_{i=1}^{n} H(t)^{\mathsf{sk}_A\mathsf{sk}_i} = H(t)^{\mathsf{sk}_A \sum_{i=1}^{n} \mathsf{sk}_i}$$

and sends the result to aggregator $\mathcal{A}$.
Notice here that $\mathcal{C}$ does not obtain the secret value $H(t)^{\mathsf{sk}_i}$ employed by users $\mathcal{U}_i$ during the encryption, rather it only learns an obfuscated encoding of it which is $\mathsf{aux}_{i,t} = H(t)^{\mathsf{sk}_A\mathsf{sk}_i}$.
- Aggregate: Upon receiving the ciphertexts $c_{i,t}$ $(1 \leqslant i \leqslant n)$ and the auxiliary information aux_t, aggregator $\mathcal{A}$ calculates:

$$P_t = (\prod_{i=1}^{n} c_{i,t})^{\mathsf{sk}_A} = ((1 + \sum_{i=1}^{n} x_{i,t}N)H(t)^{\sum_{i=1}^{n} \mathsf{sk}_i})^{\mathsf{sk}_A}$$

$$= (1 + \sum_{i=1}^{n} x_{i,t}N)^{\mathsf{sk}_A} H(t)^{\mathsf{sk}_A \sum_{i=1}^{n} \mathsf{sk}_i}$$

Since the order of $(1 + \sum_{i=1}^{n} x_{i,t}N)$ in $\mathbb{Z}_{N^2}^*$ is either N or divisor of N, we have:

$$P_t = (1 + \sum_{i=1}^{n} x_{i,t}N)^{\mathsf{sk}'_A} H(t)^{\mathsf{sk}_A \sum_{i=1}^{n} \mathsf{sk}_i} = (1 + \mathsf{sk}'_A \sum_{i=1}^{n} x_{i,t}N) H(t)^{\mathsf{sk}_A \sum_{i=1}^{\mathsf{sk}_i}}$$

where $\mathsf{sk}'_A = \mathsf{sk}_A \mod N$.
Finally, aggregator $\mathcal{A}$ computes $I_t = \frac{\frac{P_t}{\mathsf{aux}_t} - 1}{N} = \mathsf{sk}'_A \sum_{i=1}^{n} x_{i,t}$ in $\mathbb{Z}$ and evaluates $R_t = \mathsf{sk}'_A{}^{-1} I_t \mod N = \sum_{i=1}^{n} x_{i,t} \mod N$ to obtain the sum of $x_{i,t}$. Notice that since $\mathsf{sk}_A \in \mathbb{Z}_{N^2}^*$, sk'_A is in $\mathbb{Z}_N^*$. Now to obtain the average of the data points $x_{i,t}$, aggregator $\mathcal{A}$ computes $\frac{R_t}{n}$ in $\mathbb{Z}$.
As in [7], the result of the aggregation is meaningful as long as $\sum_{i=1}^{n} x_{i,t} < N$.

Now the privacy of the above scheme can be stated as follows:

Theorem 1. *The solution described above ensures aggregator obliviousness under the decisional composite residuosity (DCR) assumption in $\mathbb{Z}_{N^2}^*$.*

Theorem 2. *The solution described above assures collector obliviousness in the random oracle model under the decisional composite residuosity (DCR) assumption in $\mathbb{Z}_{N^2}^*$, the quadratic residuosity (QR) assumption in $\mathbb{Z}_N^*$ and the decisional Diffie-Hellman (DDH) assumption in the subgroup of quadratic residues in $\mathbb{Z}_N^*$.*

Due to space limitations, the proofs of Theorem 1 and Theorem 2 are deferred to Appendix A and Appendix B respectively.

4.3 Dynamic Group Management

Suppose at time interval t a set of users $\mathbb{F}$ fail to participate in the protocol execution. This event does not affect the computation of the aggregate sum by the aggregator $\mathcal{A}$. Indeed, each user $\mathcal{U}_i \notin \mathbb{F}$ computes: $\mathsf{aux}_{i,t} = \mathsf{pk}_{A,t}^{\mathsf{sk}_i}$ and encrypts its data by computing $c_{i,t} = (1 + x_{i,t}N)H(t)^{\mathsf{sk}_i}$. Upon receiving the auxiliary information $\mathsf{aux}_{i,t}$ from users $\mathcal{U}_i \notin \mathbb{F}$, collector $\mathcal{C}$ computes $\mathsf{aux}_t = \prod_{\mathcal{U}_i \notin \mathbb{F}} \mathsf{aux}_{i,t} = \prod_{\mathcal{U}_i \notin \mathbb{F}} H(t)^{\mathsf{sk}_A \mathsf{sk}_i}$. When aggregator $\mathcal{A}$ receives the ciphertexts $c_{i,t}$ from users $\mathcal{U}_i \notin \mathbb{F}$ and aux_t from collector $\mathcal{C}$, it first computes the product $\prod_{\mathcal{U}_i \notin \mathbb{F}} c_{i,t}$ and computes as depicted above the value of $\sum_{\mathcal{U}_i \notin \mathbb{F}} x_{i,t}$. Thus, our solution will still function correctly even when an arbitrary number of users fail to submit their contributions to the protocol as long as collector $\mathcal{C}$ operates properly.

Similarly, if a set of k new users $\mathbb{J} = \{\mathcal{U}_1^*, ..., \mathcal{U}_k^*\}$ join the protocol at time t, nothing changes from the point of view of aggregator $\mathcal{A}$ and collector $\mathcal{C}$. Notably, the new users $\mathcal{U}_i^*$ compute the auxiliary information $\mathsf{aux}_{i,t}^* = \mathsf{pk}_{A,t}^{\mathsf{sk}_i^*}$ corresponding to their ciphertexts $c_{i,t}^*$. The collector $\mathcal{C}$ in turn evaluates the product $\mathsf{aux}_t = \prod_{\mathcal{U}_i \in \mathbb{U}} \mathsf{aux}_{i,t} \times \prod_{\mathcal{U}_i^* \in \mathbb{J}} \mathsf{aux}_{i,t}^*$, whereas the aggregator $\mathcal{A}$ calculates the product $\prod_{\mathcal{U}_i \in \mathbb{U}} c_{i,t} \times \prod_{\mathcal{U}_i^* \in \mathbb{J}} c_{i,t}^*$. Now provided with aux_t and the secret key sk_A, aggregator $\mathcal{A}$ can derive the sum $\sum_{\mathcal{U}_i \in \mathbb{U}} x_{i,t} + \sum_{\mathcal{U}_i^* \in \mathbb{J}} x_{i,t}^*$.

5 Evaluation

Table 1 depicts the theoretical computation and communication cost of our protocol. In each time interval t, aggregator $\mathcal{A}$ first publishes $\mathsf{pk}_{A,t} = H(t)^{\mathsf{sk}_A}$, whereas each user $\mathcal{U}_i$ computes the ciphertext $c_{i,t} = (1 + x_{i,t}N)H(t)^{\mathsf{sk}_i}$ which consists of one exponentiation, one multiplication, one addition and one hash evaluation in $\mathbb{Z}_{N^2}^*$. User $\mathcal{U}_i$ also performs an additional exponentiation to compute the auxiliary information $\mathsf{aux}_{i,t} = \mathsf{pk}_{A,t}^{\mathsf{sk}_i} = H(t)^{\mathsf{sk}_A \mathsf{sk}_i} \in \mathbb{Z}_{N^2}^*$. Then, the collector receives the auxiliary information $\mathsf{aux}_{i,t}$ $(1 \leqslant i \leqslant n)$ and computes the product $\mathsf{aux}_t = \prod_{i=1}^n \mathsf{aux}_{i,t}$ which calls for $n - 1$ multiplications in $\mathbb{Z}_{N^2}^*$. Finally, the aggregator computes the sum $\sum_{i=1}^n x_{i,t}$ by performing $n - 1$ multiplications, one exponentiation, one division in $\mathbb{Z}_{N^2}^*$ and one division in $\mathbb{Z}$. Moreover, if l is the size in bits of N, then each user $\mathcal{U}_i$ sends $2l$ bits for ciphertext $c_{i,t}$ to aggregator $\mathcal{A}$ and $2l$ bits for $\mathsf{aux}_{i,t}$ to collector $\mathcal{C}$. As such, the overall communication cost per user is $4l$ per time interval.

Implementation. We implemented our scheme in Charm [2,1]. Charm is a programming framework that provides cryptographic abstraction in order to build security protocols. We extended the Charm framework with an implementation of the JL encryption using Python 3.2.3. All of our benchmarks are executed on Intel Core i5 CPU M 560 @ 2.67GHz × 4 with 8GB of memory, running Ubuntu 12.04 32bit.

To evaluate our scheme empirically, we generated a synthetic dataset with numbers ranging between 1 and 1000 and we varied the size of the modulus N. Table 2 shows

Table 1. Performance analysis

Algorithm	Computation	Communication
User	2 EXP +1 MULT +1 ADD +1HASH	$4 \cdot l$
Aggregator	2 EXP +2 DIV +$(n - 1)$ MULT +1HASH	$2 \cdot l$
Collector	$(n - 1)$ MULT	$2 \cdot l$

the encryption time for different data ranges and different modulus sizes. As expected, a slight increase in the encryption time (which is in the magnitude of microseconds) occurs as we increase the size of N.

We also assessed the computation cost at the aggregator $\mathcal{A}$. More specifically, we measured the time needed to compute the product $P_t = (\prod_{i=1}^{n} c_{i,t})^{sk_A}$. In table 3 the benchmark results are shown. The multiplication time was measured in seconds and experiments were conducted for different values of N and the number of users n.

Table 2. Computation overhead of encryption with different security levels and possible plaintext range values. The benchmarks were executed 10^6 times in order to eliminate time inconsistencies due to concurrent memory usage.

Values N	[1-10]	[1-100]	[1-1000]
1024	$110.13\,\mu s$	$112.23\,\mu s$	$114.57\,\mu s$
2048	$116.50\,\mu s$	$117.15\,\mu s$	$118.34\,\mu s$
3072	$116.99\,\mu s$	$118.23\,\mu s$	$120.83\,\mu s$

Table 3. Aggregation time as a function of the size of modulus N and the number of users n.

Users N	350	700	1000	2500
1024	$0.26\,s$	$2.40\,s$	$9.65\,s$	$49.92\,s$
2048	$0.65\,s$	$5.82\,s$	$24.16\,s$	$123.19\,s$
3072	$1.01\,s$	$9.37\,s$	$39.34\,s$	$198.12\,s$

6   Related Work

Önen and Molva [11] introduced a scheme to compute aggregate statistics over wireless sensor networks with multilayer encryption by transforming a block cipher into a symmetrically homomorphic encryption. Even if the proposed solution provides generic confidentiality, the sink-aggregator is fully trusted and shares keys with the sensors. In [5], the authors proposed a protocol for secure aggregation of data using a modified version of Paillier homomorphic encryption. The aggregator which is interested in learning the aggregate sum of data is able to decrypt without knowing the decryption key. The idea behind the scheme is a secret sharing mechanism executed between users such that the aggregation of encrypted data reveals the sum if and only if all users' data is aggregated. However, this scheme suffers from an increased communication cost due to secret share exchange between users. A solution that blends multiparty computation with homomorphic encryption is also presented in [8], but contrary to our scheme it does not address the issue of dynamic group management.

The authors in [12,4,6,3] studied privacy preserving data collection protocols with differential privacy. The combination of differential privacy with non conventional encryption schemes can provide an acceptable trade-off between privacy and utility. In

[12], a secret sharing mechanism and additively homomorphic encryption are employed together with the addition of appropriate noise to data by the users. Upon receiving the encrypted values a second round of communication is required between users and aggregator to allow for partial decryption and noise cancellation. At the end of the protocol, the aggregator learns the differential private sum. Jawurek and Kerschbaum [6] eliminate this extra communication round between the users and the aggregator by introducing a key manager which unfortunately can decrypt users' individual data. Barthe *et al.* [3] proposed a solution whereby each smart meter in the protocol establishes an ephemeral DH shared secret with all the aggregators. In their scheme the service provider is willing to learn a noisy weighted sum. Interestingly dynamic leaves and joins are supported with the cost of shared secrets between the smart meter and all the aggregators. Aggregators also, unless they collude they cannot learn individual meterings.

Chan *et al.* [4] devised a privacy preserving aggregation scheme that computes the sum of users' data, and handles user joins and leaves of smart meters and arbitrary user failures. The decrypted sum is perturbed with geometric noise which ensures differential privacy. Nonetheless, this solution calls for a fully trusted dealer that is able to decrypt users' individual data. The authors in [9] presented a solution to tackle the issue of key redistribution after a user joins or leaves. The propounded solution is based on a ring based grouping technique in which users are clustered into disjoint groups, and consequently, whenever a user joins or leaves only a fraction of the users is affected.

The existing work that resembles the most ours is the work of [13,7]. Actually, Song *et al.* [13] employs an additively homomorphic encryption scheme with differential noise to ensure aggregator obliviousness. The proposed solution is based on a linear correlation between the keys which is known to the untrusted aggregator. However the decrypted sum is encoded as an exponent, thus forcing a small plaintext space. Whereas Joye *et al.* [7] designed a solution that addresses the efficiency issues of [13]. Notably, Joye *et al.* [7] introduced a nifty solution to compute discrete logarithms in composite order groups in which the decision composite residuosity problem is intractable. Still, the scheme in [7] depends on a fully trusted key dealer which renders the scheme impractical for a real world application. Moreover, both schemes do not tackle either the issue of dynamic group management or user failures.

7   Concluding Remarks

In this paper, we presented a privacy preserving solution for time-series data aggregation which contrary to existing work supports arbitrary user failures and does not depend on trusted key dealers. The idea is to rely on a semi-trusted collector which plays the role of an intermediary between the users and the aggregator, and which enables the aggregator to compute the aggregate sum of users' private data without undermining users' privacy. An interesting feature of the proposed scheme is that users' joins and leaves do not incur any additional computation or communication cost at either the users or the aggregator. Furthermore, the scheme is provably privacy preserving against honest-but-curious aggregators and collectors.

Acknowledgments. We thank the anonymous reviewers for their suggestions for improving this paper. We are also grateful to Melek Önen for early discussions.

The research leading to these results was partially funded by the FP7-USERCENTRICNETWORKING european ICT project under the grant number 611001.

References

1. Akinyele, J.A., Green, M., Rubin, A.D.: Charm: A tool for rapid cryptographic prototyping, http://www.charm-crypto.com/Main.html
2. Akinyele, J.A., Green, M., Rubin, A.D.: Charm: A framework for rapidly prototyping cryptosystems. IACR Cryptology ePrint Archive, 2011:617 (2011), http://eprint.iacr.org/2011/617.pdf
3. Barthe, G., Danezis, G., Grégoire, B., Kunz, C., Béguelin, S.Z.: Verified computational differential privacy with applications to smart metering. In: CSF, pp. 287–301 (2013)
4. Chan, T.-H.H., Shi, E., Song, D.: Privacy-preserving stream aggregation with fault tolerance. In: Keromytis, A.D. (ed.) FC 2012. LNCS, vol. 7397, pp. 200–214. Springer, Heidelberg (2012)
5. Erkin, Z., Tsudik, G.: Private computation of spatial and temporal power consumption with smart meters. In: Bao, F., Samarati, P., Zhou, J. (eds.) ACNS 2012. LNCS, vol. 7341, pp. 561–577. Springer, Heidelberg (2012)
6. Jawurek, M., Kerschbaum, F.: Fault-tolerant privacy-preserving statistics. In: Fischer-Hübner, S., Wright, M. (eds.) PETS 2012. LNCS, vol. 7384, pp. 221–238. Springer, Heidelberg (2012)
7. Joye, M., Libert, B.: A scalable scheme for privacy-preserving aggregation of time-series data. In: Sadeghi, A.-R. (ed.) FC 2013. LNCS, vol. 7859, pp. 111–125. Springer, Heidelberg (2013)
8. Kursawe, K., Danezis, G., Kohlweiss, M.: Privacy-friendly aggregation for the smart-grid. In: Fischer-Hübner, S., Hopper, N. (eds.) PETS 2011. LNCS, vol. 6794, pp. 175–191. Springer, Heidelberg (2011)
9. Li, Q., Cao, G.: Efficient privacy-preserving stream aggregation in mobile sensing with low aggregation error. In: De Cristofaro, E., Wright, M. (eds.) PETS 2013. LNCS, vol. 7981, pp. 60–81. Springer, Heidelberg (2013)
10. Lisovich, M., Mulligan, D., Wicker, S.: Inferring personal information from demand-response systems. IEEE Security Privacy 8(1), 11–20 (January-February)
11. Önen, M., Molva, R.: Secure data aggregation with multiple encryption. In: Langendoen, K.G., Voigt, T. (eds.) EWSN 2007. LNCS, vol. 4373, pp. 117–132. Springer, Heidelberg (2007)
12. Rastogi, V., Nath, S.: Differentially private aggregation of distributed time-series with transformation and encryption. In: Proceedings of the 2010 ACM SIGMOD International Conference on Management of Data, SIGMOD 2010, pp. 735–746. ACM, New York (2010)
13. Shi, E., Chan, T.-H.H., Rieffel, E.G., Chow, R., Song, D.: Privacy-preserving aggregation of time-series data. In: NDSS (2011)

A   Aggregator Obliviousness

Theorem 1. *The proposed solution ensures aggregator obliviousness under the decisional composite residuosity (DCR) assumption in $\mathbb{Z}_{N^2}^*$.*

Proof. Assume there is an aggregator $\mathcal{A}$ that breaks the aggregator obliviousness of our scheme with a non-negligible advantage ϵ. We show in what follows that there exists an aggregator $\mathcal{B}$ that uses $\mathcal{A}$ to break the aggregator obliviousness of the JL protocol (which is ensured under DCR) with a non-negligible advantage ϵ.

For ease of exposition, we denote $\mathcal{O}_{\text{setup}}^{\text{JL}}$, $\mathcal{O}_{\text{corrupt}}^{\text{JL}}$, $\mathcal{O}_{\text{encrypt}}^{\text{JL}}$ and $\mathcal{O}_{\text{AO}}^{\text{JL}}$ the oracles needed for the aggregator obliviousness game of the JL protocol. We also assume that the aggregation system of the JL scheme involves n users $\mathbb{U} = \{\mathcal{U}_1, ..., \mathcal{U}_n\}$, each is endowed with secret key sk_i.

Now to break the aggregator obliviousness of the JL scheme, aggregator $\mathcal{B}$ simulates the aggregator obliviousness game of our scheme for aggregator $\mathcal{A}$ as follows:

Learning Phase

- To simulate the oracle $\mathcal{O}_{\text{setup},\mathcal{A}}$ for aggregator $\mathcal{A}$, $\mathcal{B}$ first invokes the oracle $\mathcal{O}_{\text{setup}}^{\text{JL}}$ which returns the public parameters $\mathcal{P} = \{N, H\}$ (where N is the product of two safe primes, and $H : \mathbb{Z} \to \mathbb{Z}_{N^2}^*$ is a cryptographic hash function) and the aggregator secret key sk_B. We recall that according to the description of the JL scheme $\text{sk}_B = -\sum_{i=1}^{n} \text{sk}_i$. Then, $\mathcal{B}$ supplies aggregator $\mathcal{A}$ in our scheme with the public parameters $\mathcal{P} = \{N, H\}$. After receiving $\mathcal{P}$, aggregator $\mathcal{A}$ selects a secret key $\text{sk}_A \in \mathbb{Z}_{N^2}^*$ and for each time interval t it publishes $\text{pk}_{A,t} = H(t)^{\text{sk}_A}$.
- Whenever $\mathcal{A}$ submits a corruption query for some user $\mathcal{U}_i$ to the oracle $\mathcal{O}_{\text{corrupt}}$, $\mathcal{B}$ relays this query to the corruption oracle $\mathcal{O}_{\text{corrupt}}^{\text{JL}}$ of the JL scheme which accordingly returns the secret key sk_i of user $\mathcal{U}_i$.
- Whenever $\mathcal{A}$ calls the encryption oracle $\mathcal{O}_{\text{encrypt}}$ with an encryption query $(t, \text{uid}_i, x_{i,t})$, $\mathcal{B}$ forwards this query to $\mathcal{O}_{\text{encrypt}}^{\text{JL}}$ which returns the matching ciphertext $c_{i,t} = (1 + x_{i,t}N)H(t)^{\text{sk}_i}$ to $\mathcal{B}$. Next, $\mathcal{B}$ provides $\mathcal{A}$ with $c_{i,t}$.
- Whenever $\mathcal{A}$ queries the collection oracle $\mathcal{O}_{\text{collect},\mathcal{A}}$ with time interval t, $\mathcal{B}$ computes $\text{aux}_t = \text{pk}_{A,t}^{-\text{sk}_B}$ which it returns to $\mathcal{A}$. Note that $\text{aux}_t = \text{pk}_{A,t}^{-\text{sk}_B} = H(t)^{-\text{sk}_A \text{sk}_B} = H(t)^{\text{sk}_A \sum \text{sk}_i}$ corresponds to the actual auxiliary information that a collector in our scheme could have computed.

Challenge Phase. In the challenge phase, $\mathcal{A}$ chooses a subset $\mathbb{S}^*$ of users that were not compromised and a challenge time interval t^* for which it did not make an encryption query during the learning phase. $\mathcal{A}$ publishes $\text{pk}_{A,t^*} = H(t^*)^{\text{sk}_A}$. $\mathcal{A}$ then submits two time-series $\mathcal{X}_{t^*}^0 = (\mathcal{U}_i, t^*, x_{i,t^*}^0)_{\mathcal{U}_i \in \mathbb{S}^*}$ and $\mathcal{X}_{t^*}^1 = (\mathcal{U}_i, t^*, x_{i,t^*}^1)_{\mathcal{U}_i \in \mathbb{S}^*}$ such that $\sum x_{i,t^*}^0 = \sum x_{i,t^*}^1$ to $\mathcal{B}$ which simulates oracle $\mathcal{O}_{\text{AO}}$ as follows:

- It submits the time-series $\mathcal{X}_{t^*}^0$ and $\mathcal{X}_{t^*}^1$ to the oracle $\mathcal{O}_{\text{AO}}^{\text{JL}}$ which picks randomly $b \in \{0, 1\}$ and returns the encryption $(c_{i,t^*}^b)_{\mathcal{U}_i \in \mathbb{S}^*}$ for the time-serie $\mathcal{X}_{t^*}^b$.
- Then it computes the auxiliary information $\text{aux}_{t^*}^b = \text{pk}_{A,t^*}^{-\text{sk}_B} = H(t^*)^{-\text{sk}_A \text{sk}_B} = H(t^*)^{\text{sk}_A \sum \text{sk}_i}$ matching the time interval t^*.
- Finally, $\mathcal{B}$ returns $(c_{i,t^*}^b)_{\mathcal{U}_i \in \mathbb{S}^*}$ and $\text{aux}_{t^*}^b$ to $\mathcal{A}$.

It is important to notice here that aggregator $\mathcal{A}$ cannot tell whether it is interacting with the actual oracles or with aggregator $\mathcal{B}$ during this simulated game. As a matter of fact, the messages that $\mathcal{A}$ receives during this simulation are correctly computed.

Now at the end of the challenge phase, $\mathcal{A}$ outputs a guess b^* for the bit b. Note that if $\mathcal{A}$ has a non-negligible advantage ϵ in breaking the aggregator obliviousness of our scheme, then this entails that it outputs a correct guess b^* for the bit b with a non-negligible advantage ϵ. Notably, if $\mathcal{A}$ outputs $b^* = 1$, then $(c_{i,t^*}^b)_{\mathcal{U}_i \in \mathbb{S}}$ is an encryption of time-serie $\mathcal{X}_{t^*}^1$; otherwise it is an encryption of time-serie $\mathcal{X}_{t^*}^0$. Now to break the aggregator obliviousness of the JL scheme, it suffices that $\mathcal{B}$ outputs the bit b^*.

To conclude, if there is an aggregator $\mathcal{A}$ which breaks the aggregator obliviousness of our solution, then there exists an aggregator $\mathcal{B}$ which breaks the aggregator obliviousness of the JL scheme with the same non-negligible advantage ϵ. This leads to a contradiction under the decisional composite residuosity assumption in $\mathbb{Z}_{N^2}^*$.   □

B   Collector Obliviousness

Theorem 2. *The proposed scheme assures collector obliviousness in the random oracle model under the decisional composite residuosity (DCR) assumption in $\mathbb{Z}_{N^2}^*$, the quadratic residuosity (QR) assumption in $\mathbb{Z}_N^*$ and the decisional Diffie-Hellman (DDH) assumption in the subgroup of quadratic residues in $\mathbb{Z}_N^*$.*

Proof. Assume there is a collector $\mathcal{C}$ that breaks the collector obliviousness of our scheme with a non-negligible advantage ϵ. We show in what follows that there exists an aggregator $\mathcal{B}$ that uses $\mathcal{C}$ to break the aggregator obliviousness of the JL protocol (which is ensured under DCR) with a non-negligible advantage ϵ'.

To break the aggregator obliviousness of the JL scheme, aggregator $\mathcal{B}$ simulates the collector obliviousness game of our scheme to collector $\mathcal{C}$ as follows:

Learning Phase

- To simulate the oracle $\mathcal{O}_{setup,\mathcal{C}}$ for collector $\mathcal{C}$, $\mathcal{B}$ first queries the oracle $\mathcal{O}_{setup}^{JL}$ which returns the aggregator's secret key sk_B and the public parameters $\mathcal{P} = \{N, H\}$ (where N is the product of two safe primes and $H : \mathbb{Z} \to \mathbb{Z}_{N^2}^*$ is a cryptographic hash function). Then, $\mathcal{B}$ supplies collector $\mathcal{C}$ with the public parameters $\mathcal{P} = \{N, H\}$. Finally, aggregator $\mathcal{B}$ picks randomly $sk_A \in \mathbb{Z}_{N^2}^*$ and for each time interval t, $\mathcal{B}$ simulates aggregator $\mathcal{A}$ by publishing $pk_{A,t} = H(t)^{sk_A}$.
- Whenever $\mathcal{C}$ queries the oracle $\mathcal{O}_{corrupt}$ for some user $\mathcal{U}_i$, $\mathcal{B}$ forwards the query to the corruption oracle of the JL scheme $\mathcal{O}_{corrupt}^{JL}$ which outputs the secret key sk_i of user $\mathcal{U}_i$.
- Whenever $\mathcal{C}$ submits an encryption query $(t, uid_i, x_{i,t})$ to oracle $\mathcal{O}_{encrypt}$, $\mathcal{B}$ sends this query to $\mathcal{O}_{encrypt}^{JL}$ which returns the matching ciphertext $c_{i,t} = (1 + x_{i,t}N)H(t)^{sk_i}$ to $\mathcal{B}$. $\mathcal{B}$ then provides $\mathcal{C}$ with ciphertext $c_{i,t}$.
- Whenever $\mathcal{C}$ queries the collection oracle $\mathcal{O}_{collect,\mathcal{C}}$ with time interval t, user identifier uid and ciphertext $c_{i,t}$, $\mathcal{B}$ simulates $\mathcal{O}_{collect,\mathcal{C}}$ as follows:
  - It submits the encryption query $(t, uid_i, 0)$ to $\mathcal{O}_{encrypt}^{JL}$ which returns accordingly $(1 + 0 \cdot N)H(t)^{sk_i} = H(t)^{sk_i}$.
  - Then using sk_A it computes $aux_{i,t} = H(t)^{sk_i sk_A}$.

It is noteworthy that the messages that $\mathcal{C}$ received so far are correctly computed. This entails that $\mathcal{C}$ cannot detect during the learning phase that it is interacting with aggregator $\mathcal{B}$.

Challenge Phase. In the challenge phase, $\mathcal{C}$ chooses a subset $\mathbb{S}^*$ of users that were not compromised and a challenge time interval t^* for which it did not make an encryption query during the learning phase. Next, $\mathcal{C}$ submits two time-series $\mathcal{X}_{t^*}^0 = (\mathcal{U}_i, t^*, x_{i,t^*}^0)_{\mathcal{U}_i \in \mathbb{S}^*}$ and $\mathcal{X}_{t^*}^1 = (\mathcal{U}_i, t^*, x_{i,t^*}^1)_{\mathcal{U}_i \in \mathbb{S}^*}$ to $\mathcal{B}$ which simulates oracle $\mathcal{O}_{\mathsf{CO}}$ as follows:

- It picks time-serie $\mathcal{X}_{t^*}^0$ and generates a new time serie $\mathcal{X}_{t^*}^{\prime 1} = (\mathcal{U}_i, t^*, x_{i,t^*}^{\prime 1})_{\mathcal{U}_i \in \mathbb{S}^*}$ such that $\sum x_{i,t}^0 = \sum x_{i,t}^{\prime 1}$ and provides oracle $\mathcal{O}_{\mathsf{AO}}^{\mathsf{JL}}$ with the time series $\mathcal{X}_{t^*}^0$ and $\mathcal{X}_{t^*}^{\prime 1}$. $\mathcal{O}_{\mathsf{AO}}^{\mathsf{JL}}$ consequently flips a coin $b \in \{0, 1\}$ and returns the tuple of ciphertexts $(c_{i,t^*}^b)_{\mathcal{U}_i \in \mathbb{S}^*}$ such that $(c_{i,t^*}^b)_{\mathcal{U}_i \in \mathbb{S}^*}$ is an encryption of the time-serie $\mathcal{X}_{t^*}^0$ if $b = 0$; otherwise, it is an encryption of the time-serie $\mathcal{X}_{t^*}^{\prime 1}$.
- Upon receipt of $(c_{i,t^*}^b)_{\mathcal{U}_i \in \mathbb{S}^*}$, $\mathcal{B}$ selects randomly $\mathsf{pk}_{A,t^*} \in \mathbb{Z}_{N^2}^*$, and computes aux_{i,t^*}^b of each user $\mathcal{U}_i \in \mathbb{S}$ by picking a random number $r_{i,t^*}^b \in \mathbb{Z}_{N^2}^*$ and setting $\mathsf{aux}_{i,t^*}^b = r_{i,t^*}^b$.
- Finally, $\mathcal{B}$ gives $(\langle c_{i,t^*}^b, \mathsf{aux}_{i,t^*}^b \rangle)_{\mathcal{U}_i \in \mathbb{S}^*}$ to collector $\mathcal{C}$. It is important to indicate here that under the DDH assumption and the random oracle model, $\mathcal{C}$ cannot detect that pk_{A,t^*} and aux_{i,t^*}^b are generated randomly, instead of being computed as $\mathsf{pk}_{A,t^*} = H(t^*)^{\mathsf{sk}_A}$ and $\mathsf{aux}_{i,t^*} = H(t^*)^{\mathsf{sk}_i \mathsf{sk}_A}$ (cf. Lemma 1).

Now notice that if $b = 0$ and if $\mathcal{C}$ does not detect that $\langle (\mathsf{aux}_{i,t^*})_{\mathcal{U}_i \in \mathbb{S}^*}, \mathsf{pk}_{A,t^*} \rangle$ are generated randomly, then from the point of view of collector $\mathcal{C}$ $(\langle c_{i,t^*}^b, \mathsf{aux}_{i,t^*}^b \rangle)_{\mathcal{U}_i \in \mathbb{S}^*}$ corresponds to a well formed tuple for the time-serie $\mathcal{X}_{t^*}^0$, and as a result, $\mathcal{C}$ will have a non-negligible advantage ϵ in breaking collector obliviousness of our scheme. Notably, $\mathcal{C}$ will output the correct guess $b^* = 0$ for the bit b with a non-negligible advantage ϵ. In this case, if $\mathcal{B}$ outputs the bit $b^* = 0$ then it will break the aggregator obliviousness of the JL scheme with a non-negligible advantage ϵ.

If $b = 1$, then the tuple $(\langle c_{i,t^*}^b, \mathsf{aux}_{i,t^*}^b \rangle)_{\mathcal{U}_i \in \mathbb{S}^*}$ is independent of the time-series $\mathcal{X}_{t^*}^0$ and $\mathcal{X}_{t^*}^1$ submitted by $\mathcal{C}$. Consequently, $\mathcal{C}$ will return with probability $1/2$ either the bit $b^* = 1$ or the bit $b^* = 0$. Therefore, to break the aggregator obliviousness of the JL scheme, all $\mathcal{B}$ needs to do is output b^*. □

Lemma 1. *In the random oracle model, collector $\mathcal{C}$ cannot detect that pk_{A,t^*} and $(\mathsf{aux}_{i,t^*})_{\mathcal{U}_i \in \mathbb{S}^*}$ are generated randomly under the decisional composite residuosity (DCR) assumption in $\mathbb{Z}_{N^2}^*$, the quadratic residuosity (QR) assumption in $\mathbb{Z}_N^*$ and the decisional Diffie-Hellman (DDH) assumption in the subgroup of quadratic residues in $\mathbb{Z}_N^*$.*

Due to space limitation, we omit the proof of lemma 1.

Privacy-Enhanced Participatory Sensing with Collusion Resistance and Data Aggregation

Felix Günther[1], Mark Manulis[2], and Andreas Peter[3]

[1] Cryptoplexity, Technische Universität Darmstadt, Germany
guenther@cs.tu-darmstadt.de
[2] Surrey Centre for Cyber Security, University of Surrey, United Kingdom
mark@manulis.eu
[3] Distributed and Embedded Security Group, University of Twente, The Netherlands
a.peter@utwente.nl

Abstract. Participatory sensing enables new paradigms and markets for information collection based on the ubiquitous availability of smartphones, but also introduces *privacy* challenges for participating users and their data. In this work, we review existing security models for privacy-preserving participatory sensing and propose several improvements that are both of theoretical and practical significance.

We first address an important drawback of prior work, namely the lack of consideration of *collusion attacks* that are highly relevant for such multi-user settings. We explain why existing security models are insufficient and why previous protocols become insecure in the presence of colluding parties. We remedy this problem by providing new security and privacy definitions that guarantee meaningful forms of collusion resistance. We propose new collusion-resistant participatory sensing protocols satisfying our definitions: a generic construction that uses anonymous identity-based encryption (IBE) and its practical instantiation based on the Boneh-Franklin IBE scheme.

We then extend the functionality of participatory sensing by adding the ability to perform *aggregation* on the data submitted by the users, without sacrificing their privacy. We realize this through an *additively-homomorphic IBE* scheme which in turn is constructed by slightly modifying the Boneh-Franklin IBE scheme. From a practical point of view, the resulting scheme is suitable for calculations with small sensor readings/values such as temperature measurements, noise levels, or prices, which is sufficient for many applications of participatory sensing.

Keywords: Privacy, participatory sensing, collusion resistance, data aggregation, cryptographic models, additively homomorphic identity-based encryption.

1 Introduction

Participatory sensing is a novel paradigm for data collection using smartphones or other mobile devices with a multitude of applications (e.g., [18,12,10]). They all leverage the high and increasing distribution of mobile phones, whose number

D. Gritzalis et al. (Eds.): CANS 2014, LNCS 8813, pp. 321–336, 2014.

of subscriptions surpassed 6 billion including a high share of smartphones with sufficient computation power for a variety of sensing tasks.

The employment of people's mobile phones as sensors however also introduces privacy risks. These sensors—now carried around by their owners—reveal sensitive location and behavioral information. In many settings, the sensed data itself is highly privacy-sensitive and requires appropriate protection when published or reported to a central data pool. Participatory sensing hence introduces the challenging task to handle the sensed data in a secure and privacy-preserving manner while offering maximal benefit from the obtained data to its users.

The utility for the above mentioned applications of participatory sensing increases with a growing number of participants. Providing people with an incentive to participate is therefore of crucial importance. From a business point of view, it is reasonable to assume that such an incentive is given by a privacy-preserving version of participatory sensing which may ultimately attract more people to participate. This argument becomes even more striking when the sensors are supposed to read very sensitive data such as data related to the personal health of participants. For instance, in the European Union (cf. European Data Protection Directive [13]), the data collector must prove sound security and stewardship of such sensitive data, which can be done through the use of provably secure cryptographic techniques.

The PEPSI Model. The only provably secure cryptographic treatment of participatory sensing so far is due to De Cristofaro and Soriente [7,9,8], who came up with a clear and concise infrastructural model and formally specified desirable privacy goals. Their model, called *PEPSI*, involves *mobile nodes* that sense and report data such as temperature, noise level, etc., forming the user basis for participatory sensing, *queriers* that represent entities (individuals or organizations) that consume sensed data such as "noise level on Time Square, New York", and an intermediate *service provider* that stores data reports received from mobile nodes and forwards the data to subscribed queriers. The service provider is an indispensable part of the infrastructure, needed to provide adequate efficiency and enable asynchronous communication between (resource-constrained) mobile nodes and queriers. However, its intermediary position, receiving both sensing data reports as well as interest subscriptions of queriers, induces additional privacy challenges, treated in PEPSI's corresponding privacy requirements.

Our Contribution. We show that although PEPSI contains formal definitions of privacy for participatory sensing, it leaves aside a very important security aspect, namely *collusion attacks* across different parties. In an application environment with many interacting mobile nodes and queriers, the possibility that some of them collude (potentially also with the service provider) in order to gain insight into the interests of others constitutes a realistic threat with devastating consequences on privacy. For instance, consider a scenario where a mobile node and a querier, who should be restricted to upload data (or obtain data, in the case of the querier) for registered interests only, follow the protocol honestly, but collude by exchanging their obtained keys. In PEPSI, these colluding parties (even if registered only for a single, identical interest), are able to obtain and decrypt sensor readings for any interest of their choice due to the lack of collusion resistance, thus completely breaching the privacy of all other mobile nodes in the system. Note that this form of collusion is already given when a user is registered as both a mobile node and a querier. This simple example illustrates the high importance of collusion resistance in participatory sensing for the protection of all participants' privacy.

We therefore revisit the PEPSI model and protocols from the perspective of collusion resistance and give more precise definitions for its three main privacy goals, namely *node privacy* that protects the content and nature of data reports, *query privacy* that hides the information for which queriers subscribe, and *report unlinkability* that guarantees untraceability of the reports submitted by mobile nodes. In order to distinguish both models, we refer to our model for a *privacy-enhanced participatory sensing infrastructure with collusion resistance* as PEPSICo. Subsequent to defining our extended security model, we give a generic and provably secure PEPSICo construction using identity-based encryption (IBE) and a concrete instantiation based on the Boneh-Franklin IBE scheme [3]. Our construction offers collusion resistance and enjoys particularly low computation, communication, and storage overhead.

Beyond this, in our model we additionally enable support for *data aggregation* at the service provider that, besides functional benefits for participatory sensing, helps to further reduce the communication overhead and to increase the privacy of individual reports. By sending only one aggregated report (with the size of a single one) instead of several single reports, aggregation reduces the amount of transferred data. Moreover, aggregated values hide the contained accumulated individual values, thus increasing the privacy of individual users.

For the purpose of data aggregation, we construct and analyze an *additively homomorphic* IBE scheme as a variant of the Boneh-Franklin IBE scheme and prove its security under the Decisional Bilinear Diffie-Hellman assumption in the random oracle model. This IBE scheme can be directly used within our generic collusion-resistant participatory sensing protocols to achieve data aggregation. We note that our additively homomorphic IBE scheme is only suitable for calculations with small sensor readings, which however is sufficient for most of the above mentioned applications of participatory sensing. For all our constructions, we analyze the performance and offer comparisons to prior work.

Related Work. One of the first privacy-aware architectures is *AnonySense* [6], later extended [17], which however does not provide confidentiality against the service provider or relies on multiple non-colluding parties. Dimitriou et al. [11] aim at querier privacy only, using blind signatures.

So far, the only framework that aims at cryptographically provable privacy is *PEPSI* by De Cristofaro and Soriente [7,9,8]. It is based on a simple but versatile architecture that involves a trusted setup for the key generation phase and an *untrusted* service provider for all later phases (see Section 2 for more details). In contrast to our work, PEPSI does not allow for data aggregation and, more importantly, does not protect against collusion attacks which has destructive implications on privacy as we show in Section 2.1.

In the context of secure data aggregation, a lot of work has been done in wireless sensor networks (see, e.g., [20]), though often focused on external adversaries. Approaches for aggregation in a participatory sensing scenario [14,21,19] in contrast often require a known set of users or introduce additional communication overhead.

A different approach to match data reports with queries would be to incorporate encryption with keyword search [2], which however inherently allows an owner of a detection trapdoor for a keyword to identify this keyword in a given set, rendering anonymity against the service provider impossible in our setting.

2 The PEPSI Model

In this section we briefly recall the PEPSI model as introduced by De Cristofaro and Soriente [7,9,8]. Their infrastructure considers the following parties: *mobile nodes (MNs)* are the devices that sense and report data, *queriers* are end-users interested in receiving sensor reports, the *network operator (NO)* is the provider of cellular network access for MNs, the *service provider (SP)* is the intermediary party between MNs and queriers that relays matching reports to subscribed queriers, and the *registration authority (RA)* is the trusted party performing system setup and node registration. The following PEPSI construction was proposed in [7,9] using an encryption approach derived from the Boneh-Franklin IBE scheme [3]. It uses groups $\mathbb{G}, \mathbb{G}_T$ of prime order q with a generator $g \in \mathbb{G}$ and an efficient bilinear map $e : \mathbb{G} \times \mathbb{G} \mapsto \mathbb{G}_T$ such that $e(g^a, g^b) = e(g, g)^{ab}$ for all $a, b \in \mathbb{Z}_q$ and $e(g, h) \neq 1_{\mathbb{G}_T}$ whenever $g, h \neq 1_{\mathbb{G}}$.

Setup: The RA generates the bilinear group parameters ($\mathbb{G} = \langle g \rangle, q, e \colon \mathbb{G} \times \mathbb{G} \to \mathbb{G}_T$), picks $s \in_R \mathbb{Z}_q^*$ as the master secret key msk and makes $Q := g^s$ public. Further, RA chooses a "nonce" $z \in_R \mathbb{Z}_q^*$, sets $R := g^z$, and fixes three cryptographic hash functions $H_1 \colon \{0,1\}^* \to \mathbb{G}$, $H_2, H_3 \colon \mathbb{G}_T \to \{0,1\}^n$.

MN Registration: A MN registers for the sensing of certain data at the RA and obtains the pair (z, id) where z is the "nonce" from Setup and id the identifier for the readings MN provides.

Query Registration: A querier registers at the RA for some query identifier id^* (e.g., "temperature in Berlin, Germany") and obtains the pair (sk_{id^*}, R) for $sk_{id^*} := H_1(id^*)^s$. It then subscribes at the SP to receive reports for id^* by sending $T^* := H_2(e(R, sk_{id^*}))$.

Data Report: In order to submit a data reading m, a MN sends the pair $(T, c) := (H_2(e(Q, H_1(id)^z)), \mathsf{Enc}_k(m))$ to the SP (via NO's infrastructure), with $k := H_3(e(Q, H_1(id)^z))$ being the key for some symmetric encryption operation Enc, e.g., AES. T is called a *tag*.

Query Execution: The SP matches received reports with query subscriptions by comparing the tag T of a report with the stored subscriptions T^* and forwards matching reports (T, c) to the according queriers.
   The receiving querier computes $k^* := H_3(e(R, sk_{id^*}))$ and $m := \mathsf{Dec}_{k^*}(c)$.

Nonce Renewal: The RA periodically distributes a fresh z to the MNs and $R = g^z$ to the queriers in order to ban misbehaving MNs.

The PEPSI model identifies three *privacy goals*, stated here informally: *node privacy* requires that NO, SP, unauthorized queriers, and other MNs learn nothing about the data or nature (e.g., query id) of a report submitted by a MN; *query privacy* demands that NO, SP, MNs, and other queriers learn nothing about the query identifier a querier subscribes to; *report unlinkability* is achieved if no party can link multiple data reports as originating from the same MN.

2.1   Limitations of PEPSI

With PEPSI [7,9,8], De Cristofaro and Soriente proposed the first cryptographic framework for a formal analysis of security and privacy in participatory sensing. As mentioned earlier, their model however does not achieve the required *collusion resistance* necessary for a secure and privacy-protected participatory sensing infrastructure and cannot deal with *data aggregation* at the SP.

While PEPSI excludes some forms of collusions by trust assumptions (e.g., between the SP and queriers), two types of collusions remain unmentioned which lead to serious privacy loopholes in their construction:

- **Collusion of SP and MN.** All MNs possess the (same) "nonce" z allowing to compute key k and tag T for any identity. The colluding SP and MN can thus together decrypt all reports and determine the identity behind all query subscriptions the SP receives (breaking *node privacy* and *query privacy*).
- **Collusion of MN and Querier.** The colluding MN and querier can use the "nonce" z to subscribe for any identity (computing the resp. tag) and decrypt all received reports (computing the resp. key), thus breaking *node privacy*.[1]

Concerning data aggregation, De Cristofaro and Soriente acknowledge [8] that performing aggregation at the SP would be an expedient capability in the setting of participatory sensing; their constructions however only allow for single encrypted measurements.

We argue that collusions, especially one person registering both as mobile node and querier but also—though to a lesser extent—between MNs and the SP, are a realistic threat in participatory sensing scenarios with devastating consequences on privacy within PEPSI. Therefore, meaningful forms of collusion resistance must also be reflected in the corresponding privacy definitions. Moreover, it would be desirable—both performance- and privacy-wise—to directly allow for aggregation of data reports in the underlying model. This motivates the following revision of the original PEPSI model.

---

[1] We stress that if no (additional) identity management is implemented to authenticate queriers as such when interacting with the SP, this attack actually constitutes a *total privacy breach* as *every* mobile node can subscribe for *any* query identifier without registering as a querier and decrypt *all* received data reports. The collusion-resistant model we introduce eliminates this attack independent of identity management.

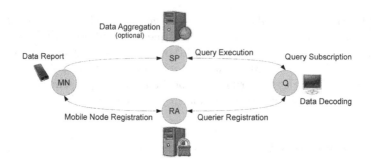

Fig. 1. The PEPSICo infrastructure. Mobile nodes (MNs) and queriers (Qs) register to the registration authority (RA). MNs report data to the service provider (SP), queriers subscribe for reports at the SP. The SP may aggregate multiple reports and sends reports matching with subscriptions to the according querier, which decodes them.

3   PEPSICo: Revised Model for Participatory Sensing

In this section, we propose a revised model for a *privacy-enhanced participatory sensing infrastructure* which captures *collusion resistance* and foresees optional *data aggregation*, denoted as PEPSICo.

The PEPSICo system model (cf. Figure 1) involves mobiles nodes (MNs), queriers, a service provider (SP), and a registration authority (RA) with identical roles as in the PEPSI model. We however drop the network operator, as its attack capabilities in our model are strictly weaker than those of the service provider. Thus, considering the latter only is sufficient.

Definition 1 (PEPSICo Instantiation). *An* instantiation of the privacy-enhanced participatory sensing infrastructure with collusion resistance *(*PEPSICo *instantiation)* PI *consists of the seven algorithms* Setup, RegisterMN, RegisterQ, ReportData, SubscribeQuery, ExecuteQuery, *and* DecodeData *and, potentially, the* optional AggregateData *algorithm defined as follows.*

Setup(1^n): *The setup is executed by the RA to initialize* PI. *On input the security parameter* $n \in \mathbb{N}$, *this probabilistic algorithm outputs the RA's secret key* RAsk *and a master public key* RApk. RApk *contains a description of the query identity space* $\mathcal{I}$ *and the message space* $\mathcal{M}$.

RegisterMN(RApk, RAsk, qid): *The MN registration is executed by the RA to register a new MN for a given query identity* qid. *On input* RApk, RAsk, *and a query identity* $qid \in \mathcal{I}$, *this probabilistic algorithm outputs a mobile node registration value* regMN_{qid} *for* qid, *which the RA sends to the MN.*

RegisterQ(RApk, RAsk, qid): *The querier registration is executed by the RA to register a new querier for a given query identity* $qid \in \mathcal{I}$. *On input* RApk, RAsk, *and* qid, *this probabilistic algorithm outputs a querier registration value* regQ_{qid} *for* qid, *which the RA sends to the querier.*

ReportData(RApk, regMN_{qid}, qid, m): *The data report algorithm is executed by the MN to report a message* $m \in \mathcal{M}$ *under some query identity* $qid \in \mathcal{I}$. *On* input RApk, *a MN registration value* regMN$_{qid}$, *qid, and m, this probabilistic algorithm outputs a data report c, which the MN sends to the SP.*

SubscribeQuery(RApk, regQ$_{qid}$, qid): *The query subscription is executed by the querier to subscribe for a given query identity qid* $\in \mathcal{I}$. *On input* RApk, *a querier registration value* regQ$_{qid}$, *and qid, this probabilistic algorithm outputs a subscription token s, which the querier sends to the SP.*

ExecuteQuery(RApk, c, s): *The query execution is executed by the SP. On input the master public key* RApk, *a data report c, and a subscription token s, this deterministic algorithm outputs either c (indicating that c matches with s) or* $\perp$ *(indicating mismatch) to the querier who provided the token s.*

DecodeData(RApk, regQ$_{qid}$, qid, c): *The data decoding is executed by a querier on a received data report c to obtain the contained message. On input* RApk, *a querier registration value* regQ$_{qid}$, *a query identity qid* $\in \mathcal{I}$, *and c, this deterministic algorithm outputs either a message m or* $\perp$, *indicating failure.*

AggregateData(RApk, c): *The* optional *data aggregation is executed by the SP on a vector of data reports* $\mathbf{c} = (c_1, \ldots, c_k)$ *and, if all match, outputs a single, aggregated data report. On input* RApk *and* $\mathbf{c}$, *this probabilistic algorithm outputs either a single data report c or* $\perp$, *indicating failure.*

If PI *provides the* AggregateData *operation, it is called a* PEPSICo *instantiation with data aggregation.*

3.1 Trust Assumptions and Adversary Model

In our model, we allow collusions between the SP, mobile nodes, and queriers against other mobile nodes or queriers. Particularly, we consider mobile nodes to be arbitrary, unauthenticated users. Since our model aims at the higher-level application of participatory sensing it is assumed that (uncorrupted) parties communicate over confidential yet not necessarily authenticated channels.

In order to define security and privacy of a PEPSICo instantiation PI, we consider a probabilistic polynomial-time (PPT) adversary $\mathcal{A}$ interacting with PI. We allow for corruptions of MNs, queriers, the SP, and (in special cases) the RA. Let $\mathcal{CI}_{MN}$ resp. $\mathcal{CI}_Q$ denote the set of identities $\mathcal{A}$ learned registration values for by corrupting MNs resp. queriers and $\mathcal{CI} := \mathcal{CI}_{MN} \cup \mathcal{CI}_Q$. Corruption of the SP resp. RA is denoted by $\mathcal{C}_{SP} = 1$ resp. $\mathcal{C}_{RA} = 1$; initially both are 0. $\mathcal{A}$ has access to the following oracles:

CorruptMN(qid): On input a query id qid, compute regMN$_{qid} \leftarrow$ RegisterMN(RApk, RAsk, qid), provide $\mathcal{A}$ with regMN$_{qid}$, and add qid to $\mathcal{CI}_{MN}$.

CorruptQ(qid): On input a query id qid, compute regQ$_{qid} \leftarrow$ RegisterQ(RApk, RAsk, qid), provide $\mathcal{A}$ with regQ$_{qid}$, and add qid to $\mathcal{CI}_Q$.

CorruptSP(): Set flag $\mathcal{C}_{SP} := 1$. (This influences subsequent ReportData queries.)

CorruptRA(): Provide $\mathcal{A}$ with RAsk and set flag $\mathcal{C}_{RA} := 1$.

ReportData(qid, m, s): On input a query id qid, a message m, and a vector of subscription tokens $\mathbf{s} = (s_1, \ldots, s_k)$, let regMN$_{qid} \leftarrow$ RegisterMN(RApk, RAsk, qid) and c $\leftarrow$ ReportData(RApk, regMN$_{qid}$, qid, m). If $\mathcal{C}_{SP} = 1$, c is given to

$\mathcal{A}$. Otherwise $\mathcal{A}$ receives $\mathbf{c} := (c_1, \ldots, c_k)$, where $c_i \leftarrow \mathtt{ExecuteQuery}(\mathsf{RApk},$
$c, s_i)$ for $i \in \{1, \ldots, k\}$ (some of the c_i may be $\perp$).[2]

SubscribeQuery(qid): On input a query id qid, compute $\mathsf{regQ}_{qid} \leftarrow \mathtt{RegisterQ}($
$\mathsf{RApk}, \mathsf{RAsk}, qid)$, $s \leftarrow \mathtt{SubscribeQuery}(\mathsf{RApk}, \mathsf{regQ}_{qid}, qid)$, and give s to $\mathcal{A}$.

DecodeData(qid, c): On input a query id qid and a data report c, compute
$\mathsf{regQ}_{qid} \leftarrow \mathtt{RegisterQ}(\mathsf{RApk}, \mathsf{RAsk}, qid)$, $m \leftarrow \mathtt{DecodeData}(\mathsf{RApk}, \mathsf{regQ}_{qid},$
$qid, c)$, and give m to $\mathcal{A}$.

3.2   Privacy and Security Definitions

We proceed by strengthening the definitions of the three central privacy goals
for participatory sensing identified in [7] with collusion resistance.

Node Privacy. Our notion of *node privacy* formalizes confidentiality of data
reports against the SP, unauthorized queriers, and other MNs. More precisely,
node privacy hides both the message and the query identity of a report from
these parties, even if all of them collude. We thus model node privacy as indistinguishability of data reports generated using two query identity-message pairs
freely chosen by an adaptive adversary that can obtain data reports, subscribe
to queries, and corrupt SP as well as MNs and queriers for other query identities.
Similar to classical security notions for encryption, we distinguish between node
privacy under chosen-ciphertext and under chosen-plaintext attacks, where in
the first the adversary has additional access to the decoding oracle.

Definition 2 (Node Privacy). *Let* PI *be a* PEPSICo *instantiation and* $\mathcal{A} = (\mathcal{A}_1, \mathcal{A}_2)$ *a PPT adversary interacting with* PI *via the queries defined in Section 3.1 within the following game* $\mathtt{Game}_{\mathsf{PI}, \mathcal{A}}^{\mathsf{NP\text{-}CCA}}(n)$:

Setup. Setup(1^n) *is executed and outputs* $(\mathsf{RAsk}, \mathsf{RApk})$.
Phase I. $\mathcal{A}_1$ *receives* RApk *and has access to the oracles* CorruptMN, CorruptQ,
CorruptSP, ReportData, SubscribeQuery, *and* DecodeData. *Eventually,* $\mathcal{A}_1$
stops and outputs two challenge query identity-message pairs (qid_0, m_0),
(qid_1, m_1) *and a vector of subscription tokens* $\mathbf{s} = (s_1, \ldots, s_k)$.
Challenge. *A bit* $b \in_R \{0, 1\}$ *is chosen,* $\mathsf{regMN}_{qid_b} \leftarrow \mathtt{RegisterMN}(\mathsf{RApk}, \mathsf{RAsk},$
$qid_b)$ *and* $c \leftarrow \mathtt{ReportData}(\mathsf{RApk}, \mathsf{regMN}_{qid_b}, qid_b, m_b)$ *are executed. If* $\mathcal{C}_{SP} = 1$, *set* $\mathbf{R} := (c)$, *otherwise set* $\mathbf{R} := (c_1, \ldots, c_k)$, *where* $c_i \leftarrow \mathtt{ExecuteQuery}($
$\mathsf{RApk}, c, s_i)$ *for* $i \in \{1, \ldots, k\}$.
Phase II. $\mathcal{A}_2$ *receives* RApk *and* $\mathbf{R}$ *and has access to the oracles from Phase I.*
Guess. *Eventually,* $\mathcal{A}_2$ *outputs a guess* $b' \in \{0, 1\}$ *for* b.

Adversary $\mathcal{A}$ *wins the game, denoted by* $\mathtt{Game}_{\mathsf{PI}, \mathcal{A}}^{\mathsf{NP\text{-}CCA}}(n) = 1$, *if* $b = b'$, $\{qid_0, qid_1\} \cap \mathcal{CI} = \emptyset$, *and all the following conditions hold:*

1. $\mathcal{A}$ *did not query* SubscribeQuery *with* qid_0 *or* qid_1.

---

[2] The intuition of separating the cases $\mathcal{C}_{SP} = 1$ and $\mathcal{C}_{SP} = 0$ (i.e., SP is corrupted or
not) is as follows: If SP is corrupted, $\mathcal{A}$ sees any data report sent to SP. Otherwise,
$\mathcal{A}$ only learns reports for which he can provide a matching subscription token s_i.

2. If $\mathcal{C}_{SP} = 1$, then $\mathcal{A}$ did not query ReportData with qid_0 or qid_1.
3. In Phase II $\mathcal{A}$ did not query DecodeData($qid_0, \mathbf{R}[i]$) or DecodeData($qid_1, \mathbf{R}[i]$) for any element $\mathbf{R}[i]$ of $\mathbf{R}$.

We say PI provides node privacy under chosen-ciphertext attacks (or NP-CCA security) if for all PPT adversaries $\mathcal{A}$ the following advantage function is negligible in n: $\mathrm{Adv}_{\mathsf{PI},\mathcal{A}}^{\mathsf{NP\text{-}CCA}}(n) := \big| \Pr\big[\mathrm{Game}_{\mathsf{PI},\mathcal{A}}^{\mathsf{NP\text{-}CCA}}(n) = 1\big] - \frac{1}{2}\big|$.

Consider the game $\mathrm{Game}_{\mathsf{PI},\mathcal{A}}^{\mathsf{NP\text{-}CPA}}(n)$, which is identical to $\mathrm{Game}_{\mathsf{PI},\mathcal{A}}^{\mathsf{NP\text{-}CCA}}(n)$, except that $\mathcal{A}$ is not given access to the DecodeData oracle. We say PI provides node privacy under chosen-plaintext attacks (or NP-CPA security) if for all PPT adversaries $\mathcal{A}$ the analogously defined advantage $\mathrm{Adv}_{\mathsf{PI},\mathcal{A}}^{\mathsf{NP\text{-}CPA}}(n)$ is negligible in n.

Remark 1. PEPSICo schemes with data aggregation *never* provide NP-CCA security, as an adversary in $\mathrm{Game}_{\mathsf{PI},\mathcal{A}}^{\mathsf{NP\text{-}CCA}}(n)$ can apply the `AggregateData` algorithm on challenge c and a c' for known m' and decode the result using the `DecodeData` oracle. Therefore, the desirable privacy flavor in case of aggregation is NP-CPA.

Query Privacy. By *query privacy* we formalize the privacy of queriers when subscribing for query identities. We require that the query identity of a subscription is hidden from the SP as well as MNs and other queriers, even if all of them collude. Query privacy is thus modeled as indistinguishability of subscription tokens for two query identities freely chosen by an adaptive adversary that can obtain data reports, subscribe to queries, and corrupt SP as well as MNs and queriers for other query identities.

Definition 3 (Query Privacy). Let PI be a PEPSICo instantiation and $\mathcal{A} = (\mathcal{A}_1, \mathcal{A}_2)$ a PPT adversary interacting with PI via the queries defined in Section 3.1 within the following game $\mathrm{Game}_{\mathsf{PI},\mathcal{A}}^{\mathsf{QP}}(n)$:

Setup. Setup(1^n) is executed and outputs (RAsk, RApk); set $\mathcal{C}_{SP} := 1$.
Phase I. $\mathcal{A}_1$ receives RApk and has access to the oracles CorruptMN, CorruptQ, ReportData, SubscribeQuery, and DecodeData. Eventually, $\mathcal{A}_1$ stops and outputs two challenge query identities qid_0 and qid_1.
Challenge. A bit $b \in_R \{0,1\}$ is chosen, $\mathrm{regQ}_{qid_b} \leftarrow$ RegisterQ(RApk, RAsk, qid_b) and $s \leftarrow$ SubscribeQuery(RApk, $\mathrm{regQ}_{qid_b}, qid_b$) are executed.
Phase II. $\mathcal{A}_2$ receives RApk and s and has access to the oracles from Phase I.
Guess. Eventually, $\mathcal{A}_2$ outputs a guess $b' \in \{0,1\}$ for b.

Adversary $\mathcal{A}$ wins the game, denoted by $\mathrm{Game}_{\mathsf{PI},\mathcal{A}}^{\mathsf{QP}}(n) = 1$, if $b = b'$, $\{qid_0, qid_1\} \cap \mathcal{CI} = \emptyset$, and $\mathcal{A}$ did not query ReportData or SubscribeQuery with qid_0 or qid_1. We say PI provides query privacy if for all PPT adversaries $\mathcal{A}$ the following advantage function is negligible in n: $\mathrm{Adv}_{\mathsf{PI},\mathcal{A}}^{\mathsf{QP}}(n) := \big| \Pr\big[\mathrm{Game}_{\mathsf{PI},\mathcal{A}}^{\mathsf{QP}}(n) = 1\big] - \frac{1}{2}\big|$.

Report Unlinkability. *Report unlinkability* prevents the linkage of two reports as originating from the same MN by any other party, *including* the RA. As MNs (as well as queriers) are not distinguished by device identifiers or anything similar in our model, we tie the notion of report unlinkability to the MN registration

ExecuteQuery: If $T = T^*$ output (T, c'), else output $\bot$.
AggregateData: If $T_1 = \cdots = T_\ell$ output $(T, c') = (T_1, c_1 \circ \cdots \circ c_\ell)$, else output $\bot$. (optional)

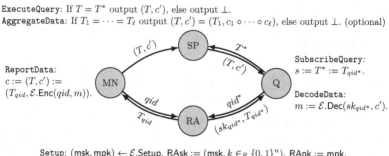

ReportData:
$c := (T, c') :=$
$(T_{qid}, \mathcal{E}.\mathsf{Enc}(qid, m)).$

SubscribeQuery:
$s := T^* := T_{qid^*}.$

DecodeData:
$m := \mathcal{E}.\mathsf{Dec}(sk_{qid^*}, c').$

Setup: $(\mathsf{msk}, \mathsf{mpk}) \leftarrow \mathcal{E}.\mathsf{Setup}$, $\mathsf{RAsk} := (\mathsf{msk}, k \in_R \{0,1\}^n)$, $\mathsf{RApk} := \mathsf{mpk}$.
RegisterMN: $\mathsf{regMN}_{qid} := T_{qid} := f_k(qid)$.
RegisterQ: $\mathsf{regQ}_{qid^*} := (sk_{qid^*} \leftarrow \mathcal{E}.\mathsf{Extract}(\mathsf{msk}, qid^*), T_{qid^*})$.

Fig. 2. Generic PEPSICo instantiation $\mathsf{PI}_{\mathsf{IBE}}$ based on an IBE scheme $\mathcal{E}$ and a PRF f

value used to generate a data report. We model report unlinkability as indistinguishability of the MN registration value used to generate a data report for a query identity-message pair freely chosen by an adaptive adversary that can obtain data reports, subscribe to queries, and corrupt SP, any MN and querier as well as the RA (after setup). Due to space limitations, we give the formal definition of report unlinkability in the full version of this paper [16].

Collusion Attacks against PEPSI. It is easy to see that the original PEPSI scheme [7,9,8] does not fulfill our definitions of node and query privacy due to collusion attacks by leveraging the ability to corrupt mobile nodes.

4   A Generic Solution Using Identity-based Encryption

We build our generic PEPSICo instantiation from an arbitrary IBE scheme $\mathcal{E} = (\mathsf{Setup}, \mathsf{Extract}, \mathsf{Enc}, \mathsf{Dec})$ (where $\mathsf{Extract}$ denotes the algorithm to derive secret keys from identities using the master secret). For a formal definition of IBE schemes as well as the established security notions of anonymity and indistinguishability under chosen-ciphertext (ANO-IND-ID-CCA) resp. chosen-plaintext (ANO-IND-ID-CPA) attacks we refer to the full version of this paper [16] resp. the work of Boneh and Franklin [3] and Abdalla et al. [1].

Our generic PEPSICo scheme, denoted $\mathsf{PI}_{\mathsf{IBE}}$ and specified in Definition 4, incorporates an IBE scheme $\mathcal{E}$ and a pseudorandom function (PRF) $f \colon \{0,1\}^n \times \{0,1\}^* \to \{0,1\}^n$. Figure 2 illustrates its mapping to the PEPSICo infrastructure.

Definition 4 ($\mathsf{PI}_{\mathsf{IBE}}$ Scheme). *Let* $\mathcal{E} = (\mathsf{Setup}, \mathsf{Extract}, \mathsf{Enc}, \mathsf{Dec})$ *be an identity-based encryption scheme and* $f \colon \{0,1\}^n \times \{0,1\}^* \to \{0,1\}^n$ *a pseudorandom function. The* $\mathsf{PI}_{\mathsf{IBE}}$ *scheme is defined as follows:*

$\mathsf{Setup}(1^n)$**:** *Let* $(\mathsf{msk}, \mathsf{mpk}) \leftarrow \mathsf{Setup}(1^n)$ *and* $k \in_R \{0,1\}^n$. *Output* $\mathsf{RAsk} :=$ (msk, k) *and* $\mathsf{RApk} := \mathsf{mpk}$. $\mathcal{M}$ *is the message space of* $\mathcal{E}$, $\mathcal{I} = \{0,1\}^*$.

RegisterMN(RApk, RAsk, qid): *Let* $T_{qid} := f_k(qid)$, *output* regMN$_{qid} := T_{qid}$.
RegisterQ(RApk, RAsk, qid): *Let* $sk_{qid} \leftarrow$ Extract(mpk, msk, qid) *and compute*
    $T_{qid} := f_k(qid)$. *Output* regQ$_{qid} := (sk_{qid}, T_{qid})$.
ReportData(RApk, regMN$_{qid}$, qid, m): *Output* $c := (T_{qid}, \mathsf{Enc}(\mathsf{mpk}, qid, m))$.
SubscribeQuery(RApk, regQ$_{qid}$, qid): *Output* $s := T_{qid}$.
ExecuteQuery(RApk, c, s): *Parse* c *as* (T, c'). *If* $T = s$ *output* c, *else output* $\perp$.
DecodeData(RApk, regQ$_{qid}$, qid, c): *Parse* c *as* (T, c'). *Output* $m :=$ Dec(mpk,
    sk_{qid}, c').

If $\mathcal{E}$ is homomorphic w.r.t. some operation $\circ$, then PI$_{\mathsf{IBE}}$ *supports data aggregation using the following generic algorithm:*

AggregateData(RApk, **c**): *Parse* **c** *as* $((T_1, c_1), \ldots, (T_\ell, c_\ell))$. *If* $T_1 = \cdots = T_\ell$,
    compute $c' = c_1 \circ c_2 \circ \cdots \circ c_\ell$ *and output* $c = (T_1, c')$, *otherwise output* $\perp$.

We obtain the following security result for PI$_{\mathsf{IBE}}$.

Theorem 1 (Privacy and Security of PI$_{\mathsf{IBE}}$). *If f is pseudorandom and $\mathcal{E}$ provides* ANO-IND-ID-CCA *(resp.* ANO-IND-ID-CPA*) security, then* PI$_{\mathsf{IBE}}$ *provides node privacy under chosen-ciphertext (resp. chosen-plaintext) attacks, query privacy, and report unlinkability.*

Proof of Node Privacy. Assume we have an adversary $\mathcal{A} = (\mathcal{A}_1, \mathcal{A}_2)$ against PI$_{\mathsf{IBE}}$ with non-negligible advantage $\mathsf{Adv}^{\mathsf{NP\text{-}CCA}}_{\mathsf{PI}_{\mathsf{IBE}}, \mathcal{A}}(n)$.[3] We first consider the game $\mathsf{Game}^{\mathsf{NP\text{-}CCA}^*}_{\mathsf{PI}_{\mathsf{IBE}}, \mathcal{A}}(n)$, which is like $\mathsf{Game}^{\mathsf{NP\text{-}CCA}}_{\mathsf{PI}_{\mathsf{IBE}}, \mathcal{A}}(n)$, except that instead of f a real random function $g: \{0,1\}^n \times \{0,1\}^* \to \{0,1\}^n$ is used to compute the tags T_{qid}. We argue that $\varepsilon(n) := \left| \mathsf{Adv}^{\mathsf{NP\text{-}CCA}}_{\mathsf{PI}_{\mathsf{IBE}}, \mathcal{A}}(n) - \mathsf{Adv}^{\mathsf{NP\text{-}CCA}^*}_{\mathsf{PI}_{\mathsf{IBE}}, \mathcal{A}}(n) \right|$ is negligible, otherwise $\mathcal{A}$ can be used to construct a distinguisher $\mathcal{D}$ between f and g by relaying evaluations of f in the game to its oracle. If $\mathcal{D}$ is given oracle access to f, then it acts like the challenger in $\mathsf{Game}^{\mathsf{NP\text{-}CCA}}_{\mathsf{PI}_{\mathsf{IBE}}, \mathcal{A}}(n)$, otherwise like in $\mathsf{Game}^{\mathsf{NP\text{-}CCA}^*}_{\mathsf{PI}_{\mathsf{IBE}}, \mathcal{A}}(n)$. $\mathcal{D}$ outputs the game result (i.e., $b = b'$) as its own guess and thus has advantage ε to distinguish f and g. As f by assumption is pseudorandom, ε is negligible.

Thus $\mathcal{A}$'s advantage in the modified game $\mathsf{Game}^{\mathsf{NP\text{-}CCA}^*}_{\mathsf{PI}_{\mathsf{IBE}}, \mathcal{A}}(n)$ is non-negligible, too. We construct an adversary $\mathcal{B}$ with non-negligible advantage in breaking the ANO-IND-ID-CCA security of $\mathcal{E}$ which uses $\mathcal{A}$ as follows.

Setup. $\mathcal{B}$ receives the master public key mpk in the ANO-IND-ID-CCA game.
Phase I. $\mathcal{B}$ provides $\mathcal{A}_1$ with RApk = mpk and answers the oracle queries as
    specified. It uses its Extract oracle to obtain secret keys sk_{qid} for CorruptQ
    queries, chooses tags $T_{qid} \in_R \{0,1\}^n$ at random on first request (reusing the
    value later), and relays DecodeData queries to its own Dec oracle.
    $\mathcal{A}_1$ eventually outputs (qid_0, m_0), (qid_1, m_1), and **s** $= (s_1, \ldots, s_k)$.
Challenge. $\mathcal{B}$ forwards $(qid_0, m_0), (qid_1, m_1)$ as its own challenge and receives
    c^*. $\mathcal{B}$ chooses $T \in_R \{0,1\}^n$ and sets $c := (T, c^*)$. If $\mathcal{C}_{SP} = 1$, $\mathcal{B}$ sets **R** $:= (c)$,
    else **R** $:= (c_1, \ldots, c_k)$ for $c_i \leftarrow$ ExecuteQuery(RApk, c, s_i).

---

[3] We prove the NP-CCA/ANO-IND-ID-CCA case here, the NP-CPA/ANO-IND-ID-CPA
case works identical by removing the DecodeData oracle queries.

Phase II. $\mathcal{B}$ provides $\mathcal{A}_2$ with RApk and $\mathbf{R}$ and answers queries as above.

Guess. $\mathcal{A}_2$ outputs a guess $b' \in \{0, 1\}$, which $\mathcal{B}$ forwards as its own guess.

As $\mathcal{B}$ perfectly simulates $\text{Game}_{\text{PI}_{\text{IBE}},\mathcal{A}}^{\text{NP-CCA}^*}(n)$ for $\mathcal{A}$, we have $\text{Adv}_{\mathcal{E},\mathcal{B}}^{\text{ANO-IND-ID-CCA}}(n) = \text{Adv}_{\text{PI}_{\text{IBE}},\mathcal{A}}^{\text{NP-CCA}^*}(n)$, which is non-negligible. $\qquad \square$

Proof of Query Privacy. Assume we have an adversary $\mathcal{A}$ against PI_{IBE} with non-negligible advantage $\text{Adv}_{\text{PI}_{\text{IBE}},\mathcal{A}}^{\text{QP}}(n)$. Similar to the node privacy proof we consider $\text{Game}_{\text{PI}_{\text{IBE}},\mathcal{A}}^{\text{QP}^*}(n)$, which is identical to $\text{Game}_{\text{PI}_{\text{IBE}},\mathcal{A}}^{\text{QP}}(n)$, except that instead of f a real random function g is used to compute the tags T_{qid}. This is likewise indistinguishable for $\mathcal{A}$, i.e., $\left| \text{Adv}_{\text{PI}_{\text{IBE}},\mathcal{A}}^{\text{QP}}(n) - \text{Adv}_{\text{PI}_{\text{IBE}},\mathcal{A}}^{\text{QP}^*}(n) \right|$ is negligible.

In $\text{Game}_{\text{PI}_{\text{IBE}},\mathcal{A}}^{\text{QP}^*}(n)$, $\mathcal{A}$ now receives a challenge subscription token s chosen at random. As $\mathcal{A}$ is not allowed to corrupt MNs or queriers registered for qid_0 or qid_1 or query ReportData or SubscribeQuery on qid_0 or qid_1, he receives no further evaluation of g under qid_0 or qid_1. Thus, for $\mathcal{A}$, the probabilities $\Pr[g(qid_0) = s]$ and $\Pr[g(qid_1) = s]$ are equal for any value s. Hence $\mathcal{A}$ can guess b no better than with probability $\frac{1}{2}$, so $\text{Adv}_{\text{PI}_{\text{IBE}},\mathcal{A}}^{\text{QP}^*}(n) = 0$ and $\text{Adv}_{\text{PI}_{\text{IBE}},\mathcal{A}}^{\text{QP}}(n)$ is negligible. $\qquad \square$

We give the proof for report unlinkability in the full version of this paper [16].

5   Concrete **PEPSICo** Instantiations

We now show how our generic PI_{IBE} construction (without and with data aggregation) can be instantiated in practice.

5.1   **PEPSICo** Schemes in the Random Oracle and Standard Model

The generic PI_{IBE} construction can directly be instantiated with the IBE scheme proposed by Boneh and Franklin [3], which provides ANO-IND-ID-CPA security (under the Bilinear Diffie-Hellman (BDH) assumption [3] in the random oracle model). The resulting PEPSICo scheme, denoted PI_{BF}, thus by Theorem 1 provides node privacy under chosen-plaintext attacks, query privacy, and report unlinkability. As our comparison in Section 6 shows, PI_{BF} offers the same high practical performance as the original PEPSI scheme.

Since our result in Theorem 1 holds in the standard model, we can easily obtain further PEPSICo schemes whose security does not require random oracles. For instance, the anonymous IBE schemes by Boyen and Waters [5] or Gentry [15] can likewise be used as appropriate building blocks to instantiate PI_{IBE}.

5.2   **PEPSICo** Schemes with Data Aggregation

Additively Homomorphic IBE Scheme. For our PEPSICo scheme with data aggregation we first introduce an *additively homomorphic* IBE scheme AIBE that we developed as a modification of the Boneh-Franklin IBE scheme [3].

Definition 5 (AIBE Scheme). *The additively homomorphic IBE scheme* AIBE *is defined as follows.*

Setup(1^n). *Generate the bilinear group parameters* $(\mathbb{G} = \langle g \rangle, q, e \colon \mathbb{G} \times \mathbb{G} \to \mathbb{G}_T)$ *with* $\mathbb{G}_T = \langle \bar{g} \rangle$ *for* $\bar{g} = e(g, g)$. *Choose* $x \in_R \mathbb{Z}_q^*$, *set* $y := g^x$, *and fix a cryptographic hash function* $H \colon \{0, 1\}^* \to \mathbb{G}^*$. *The message space is* $\mathcal{M} = \mathbb{Z}_M = \{0, \ldots, M - 1\} \subseteq \mathbb{Z}_q$ *with* $M = p(n) < q$ *for some polynomial* p, *the ciphertext space is* $\mathcal{C} = \mathbb{G}^* \times \mathbb{G}_T$. *Output* mpk $= (q, \mathbb{G} = \langle g \rangle, \mathbb{G}_T = \langle \bar{g} \rangle, e, y, H)$ *and* msk $= x$.

Extract(mpk, msk, id). *Compute and output* $sk_{id} := H(id)^x$.

Enc(mpk, id, m). *Choose* $r \in_R \mathbb{Z}_q^*$ *and output* $c = (g^r, \bar{g}^m \cdot e(H(id), y)^r)$.

Dec(mpk, sk_{id}, c). *Parse* c *as* (c_1, c_2). *Compute* $\overline{m} := c_2 / e(sk_{id}, c_1)$ *and* $m = \log_{\bar{g}}(\overline{m})$ *as the discrete logarithm to the base* $\bar{g}$ *of* $\overline{m}$ *in* $\mathbb{G}_T$ *(which takes polynomial time in* n *as* $m < M$ *, cf. the performance discussion below).*

Our AIBE scheme is *additively* homomorphic in the message space $\mathcal{M} = \mathbb{Z}_M$ by element-wise multiplication of ciphertexts: $c \cdot c' = (g^r \cdot g^{r'}, \bar{g}^m \cdot e(H(id), y)^r \cdot \bar{g}^{m'} \cdot e(H(id), y)^{r'}) = (g^{r+r'}, \bar{g}^{m+m'} \cdot e(H(id), y)^{r+r'}) = $ Enc(mpk, id, $m + m' \mod q$).

Theorem 2 (ANO-IND-ID-CPA Security of AIBE). AIBE *provides anonymity and indistinguishability under chosen-plaintext attacks under the DBDH assumption, in the random oracle model.*

Due to space limitations, the proof of Theorem 2 is given in the full version of this paper [16]. We however note that the proof of indistinguishability takes a similar approach as the proof of Theorem 4.1 in [4] and that ANO-IND-ID-CPA-security, using this result, can be directly reduced to the DBDH assumption.

The full version of this paper [16] also includes a performance evaluation of AIBE showing that, based on Pollard's kangaroo method, computation of a discrete logarithm within the decryption algorithm is feasible even for 32-bit integer values on standard desktop hardware.[4] We remark that AIBE's restriction to a polynomial message space is typical for additively homomorphic schemes based on decisional DH assumptions where messages are encrypted in the exponents.

PEPSICo Scheme with Data Aggregation. We now instantiate the generic PI$_{\text{IBE}}$ construction with the AIBE scheme and denote the resulting PEPSICo scheme with data aggregation as PI$_{\text{AIBE}}$. Combining Theorems 1 and 2, the resulting scheme provides node privacy under chosen-plaintext attacks, query privacy, and report unlinkability (under the DBDH assumption in the random oracle model). We evaluate its practical performance in Section 6.

6 Performance Evaluation and Comparisons

We now evaluate the performance of our two concrete PEPSICo schemes: PI$_{\text{BF}}$ from Section 5.1 and PI$_{\text{AIBE}}$ from Section 5.2. In particular, we compare the

---

[4] Note that decryption will *not* be performed by resource-constrained mobile devices.

Table 1. Computation and communication overhead of PEPSI [7], $\mathsf{PI_{BF}}$, and $\mathsf{PI_{AIBE}}$

Algorithm	PEPSI		$\mathsf{PI_{BF}}$		$\mathsf{PI_{AIBE}}$	
	Comp.	Comm.	Comp.	Comm.	Comp.	Comm.
Setup	2E	–	1E	–	1E	–
RegisterMN	–	n	1f	n	1f	n
RegisterQ	1E	2G	1f+1E	1G+n	1f+1E	1G+n
ReportData	1E+1P+2H	2n	2E+1P+2H	1G+2n	3E+1P+1H	2G+n
SubscribeQuery	1P+1H	n	–	n	–	n
ExecuteQuery	–	2n	–	1G+2n	–	2G+n
DecodeData	1P+1H	–	1P+1H	–	1P+1DL	–
AggregateData	n/a	n/a	n/a	n/a	$\approx 0^*$	–

E — modular exponentiation in $\mathbb{G}$ or $\mathbb{G}_T$; P — pairing evaluation; H — hash function evaluation; f — PRF evaluation; DL — computation of discrete logarithm; G — group element in $\mathbb{G}$ or $\mathbb{G}_T$; n — message length, Hash/PRF output length
* The AggregateData algorithm of $\mathsf{PI_{AIBE}}$ requires 2ℓ group multiplications to aggregate ℓ ciphertexts, negligible compared to the other units used.

induced computation, communication, and storage overhead of the two schemes with the original PEPSI scheme [7,9], though keeping in mind that it does not fulfill the requirements of node and query privacy in our model due to collusion attacks.

Table 1 shows the computation and communication overhead introduced by PEPSI, $\mathsf{PI_{BF}}$, and $\mathsf{PI_{AIBE}}$. PEPSI and $\mathsf{PI_{BF}}$ perform similar in computation, except that $\mathsf{PI_{BF}}$ uses a pseudorandom function for tag generation. Computation overhead of $\mathsf{PI_{AIBE}}$ (the only scheme providing data aggregation) is significantly higher only for the DecodeData operation, which requires computation of a discrete logarithm. Note that DecodeData is *not* executed by the (resource-constrained) mobile nodes, but by queriers with a presumable computing power comparable to the machine running our test measurements. In return, $\mathsf{PI_{AIBE}}$ saves decryption time if reports are aggregated, requiring only $2(\ell - 1)$ cheap group multiplications to aggregate ℓ reports.[5]

Concerning communication costs, the only practical difference is in the length of ciphertexts. While ciphertexts in PEPSI have the same length as messages, in $\mathsf{PI_{BF}}$ and $\mathsf{PI_{AIBE}}$ they additionally contain one group element of $\mathbb{G}$. Aggregation in $\mathsf{PI_{AIBE}}$ however allows for huge savings (a factor ℓ for ℓ aggregated reports) in the communication between SP and queriers. More important, $\mathsf{PI_{BF}}$ and $\mathsf{PI_{AIBE}}$ do not require any periodic update operations as opposed to the regular "nonce renewal" of PEPSI, saving further computation and communication resources.

Table 2 shows the (virtually identical) space requirements of all three schemes. Note however that the aggregation of reports possible in $\mathsf{PI_{AIBE}}$ saves additional storage capacity of the SP and queriers.

---

[5] Our measurements for discrete logarithm and pairing computation (discrete logarithm in interval $[0, M]$: $0.18\sqrt{M}$ ms; pairing: 5.99 ms) show that $\mathsf{PI_{AIBE}}$ *outperforms* $\mathsf{PI_{BF}}$ wrt. the decryption overhead if messages are integers between 0 and about 1000—independently of how many messages are aggregated in an arbitrary large message space.

Table 2. Space requirements of PEPSI [7], PI_{BF}, and PI_{AIBE}.

Component	PEPSI	PI_{BF}	PI_{AIBE}
RA Public Key RApk	3G+n	3G+n	3G+n
RA Secret Key RAsk	1G+2n	2n	2n
MN Registration Value $regMN_{qid}$	n	n	n
Querier Registration Value $regQ_{qid}$	2G	1G+n	1G+n
Data Report c	2n	1G+2n	2G+n
Subscription Token s	n	n	n

G — group element in $\mathbb{G}$ or $\mathbb{G}_T$; n — message length, Hash/PRF output length

In summary, PI_{BF} performs similar to PEPSI wrt. computation overhead and key sizes and has only slightly higher communication overhead, while providing stronger node privacy, query privacy, and report unlinkability guarantees in the presence of colluding parties. For small messages, PI_{AIBE} is almost as fast as the PI_{BF} scheme while achieving the same level of security and enabling support for aggregation. The latter property allows for a significant reduction of the communication overhead between service provider and queriers and can offer more stringent privacy guarantees with respect to individual data reports.

7 Conclusion and Outlook

We presented PEPSICo, a refined version of the PEPSI model [7] that protects data confidentiality and user privacy under collusion attacks and additionally allows for data aggregation. Our generic and concrete instantiations leveraging anonymous identity-based encryption (IBE) achieve full privacy as well as equally high practical performance as earlier approaches. For future work, constructing an efficient additively homomorphic IBE scheme with exponential-sized message space remains an open problem of independent interest.

Acknowledgments. Felix Günther is supported by BMBF through EC SPRIDE and by DFG through CRC 1119 CROSSING. Mark Manulis is supported by DFG through PRIMAKE (MA 4957). Andreas Peter is supported by the THeCS project as part of the Dutch national program COMMIT.

References

1. Abdalla, M., Bellare, M., Catalano, D., Kiltz, E., Kohno, T., Lange, T., Malone-Lee, J., Neven, G., Paillier, P., Shi, H.: Searchable Encryption Revisited: Consistency Properties, Relation to Anonymous IBE, and Extensions. In: Shoup, V. (ed.) CRYPTO 2005. LNCS, vol. 3621, pp. 205–222. Springer, Heidelberg (2005)
2. Boneh, D., Di Crescenzo, G., Ostrovsky, R., Persiano, G.: Public Key Encryption with Keyword Search. In: Cachin, C., Camenisch, J.L. (eds.) EUROCRYPT 2004. LNCS, vol. 3027, pp. 506–522. Springer, Heidelberg (2004)
3. Boneh, D., Franklin, M.K.: Identity-Based Encryption from the Weil Pairing. In: Kilian, J. (ed.) CRYPTO 2001. LNCS, vol. 2139, pp. 213–229. Springer, Heidelberg (2001)

4. Boneh, D., Franklin, M.K.: Identity-Based Encryption from the Weil Pairing. SIAM Journal on Computing 32(3), 586–615 (2003)
5. Boyen, X., Waters, B.: Anonymous Hierarchical Identity-Based Encryption (Without Random Oracles). In: Dwork, C. (ed.) CRYPTO 2006. LNCS, vol. 4117, pp. 290–307. Springer, Heidelberg (2006)
6. Cornelius, C., Kapadia, A., Kotz, D., Peebles, D., Shin, M., Triandopoulos, N.: AnonySense: Privacy-Aware People-Centric Sensing. In: Grunwald, D., Han, R., de Lara, E., Ellis, C.S. (eds.) MobiSys 2008, pp. 211–224. ACM, New York (2008)
7. De Cristofaro, E., Soriente, C.: Short Paper: PEPSI: Privacy-Enhanced Participatory Sensing Infrastructure. In: Gollmann, D., Westhoff, D., Tsudik, G., Asokan, N. (eds.) WISEC 2011, pp. 23–28. ACM, New York (2011)
8. De Cristofaro, E., Soriente, C.: Extended Capabilities for a Privacy-Enhanced Participatory Sensing Infrastructure (PEPSI). IEEE Transactions on Information Forensics and Security 8(12), 2021–2033 (2013)
9. De Cristofaro, E., Soriente, C.: Participatory Privacy: Enabling Privacy in Participatory Sensing. IEEE Network 27(1), 32–36 (2013)
10. D'Hondt, E., Stevens, M., Jacobs, A.: Participatory noise mapping works! An evaluation of participatory sensing as an alternative to standard techniques for environmental monitoring. Pervasive and Mobile Computing 9(5), 681–694 (2013)
11. Dimitriou, T., Krontiris, I., Sabouri, A.: PEPPeR: A Querier's Privacy Enhancing Protocol for PaRticipatory Sensing. In: Schmidt, A.U., Russello, G., Krontiris, I., Lian, S. (eds.) MobiSec 2012. LNICST, vol. 107, pp. 93–106. Springer, Heidelberg (2012)
12. Eisenman, S.B., Miluzzo, E., Lane, N.D., Peterson, R.A., Ahn, G.S., Campbell, A.T.: The BikeNet mobile sensing system for cyclist experience mapping. In: Jha, S. (ed.) SenSys 2007, pp. 87–101. ACM, New York (2007)
13. European Parliament and Council: EU Directive 95/46/EC (1995), http://www.dataprotection.ie/viewdoc.asp?docid=89
14. Ganti, R.K., Pham, N., Tsai, Y.E., Abdelzaher, T.F.: PoolView: Stream Privacy for Grassroots Participatory Sensing. In: Abdelzaher, T.F., Martonosi, M., Wolisz, A. (eds.) SenSys 2008, pp. 281–294. ACM, New York (2008)
15. Gentry, C.: Practical Identity-Based Encryption Without Random Oracles. In: Vaudenay, S. (ed.) EUROCRYPT 2006. LNCS, vol. 4004, pp. 445–464. Springer, Heidelberg (2006)
16. Günther, F., Manulis, M., Peter, A.: Privacy-Enhanced Participatory Sensing with Collusion Resistance and Data Aggregation. Cryptology ePrint Archive, Report 2014/382 (2014), http://eprint.iacr.org/
17. Huang, K.L., Kanhere, S.S., Hu, W.: Preserving privacy in participatory sensing systems. Computer Communications 33(11), 1266–1280 (2010)
18. Hull, B., Bychkovsky, V., Zhang, Y., Chen, K., Goraczko, M., Miu, A., Shih, E., Balakrishnan, H., Madden, S.: CarTel: A Distributed Mobile Sensor Computing System. In: Campbell, A.T., Bonnet, P., Heidemann, J.S. (eds.) SenSys 2006, pp. 125–138. ACM, New York (2006)
19. Li, Q., Cao, G.: Efficient Privacy-Preserving Stream Aggregation in Mobile Sensing with Low Aggregation Error. In: De Cristofaro, E., Wright, M. (eds.) PETS 2013. LNCS, vol. 7981, pp. 60–81. Springer, Heidelberg (2013)
20. Özdemir, S., Xiao, Y.: Secure data aggregation in wireless sensor networks: A comprehensive overview. Computer Networks 53(12), 2022–2037 (2009)
21. Shi, J., Zhang, R., Liu, Y., Zhang, Y.: PriSense: Privacy-Preserving Data Aggregation in People-Centric Urban Sensing Systems. In: INFOCOM 2010, pp. 758–766. IEEE (2010)

Short Comparable Encryption

Jun Furukawa

NEC Corporation, Kanagawa 211-8666, Japan
j-furukawa@ay.jp.nec.co.jp

Abstract. The notion of comparable encryption is introduced in Esorics 2013 [18] which overcomes the weakness of order-preserving encryption (OPE). While an OPE enables to compare the numerical order of numbers from their corresponding ciphertexts alone, the comparable encryption enables to compare the numerical order of the pair of numbers from their ciphertexts if either of the ciphertexts is accompanied with the corresponding token. Hence, it significantly reduces the amount of disclosed knowledge with respect to encrypted numbers from their ciphertexts. Since an OPE is considered to be a key primitive for encrypted databases such as CryptDB [31] and Monomi [36], a comparable encryption has a potential to enhance the security of these applications. However, the previous comparable encryption requires large ciphertext length, which so severely spoils the performance of encrypted databases that it is no longer practical. We propose in this paper, a very short comparable encryption. While each bit is encrypted into a string of security parameter length, say 160 bits, in the previous works, ours encrypts each bit into 3-ary. This is even shorter than the ciphertext length of OPEs.

Keywords: token-based, encrypted database, range query, order comparison.

1 Introduction

A database (DB) system has been widely used to store and process a large amount of data and has been an indispensable platform for variety of services. Since many DBs store sensitive information, they have been the primary target for data theft. But it has been extremely difficult to completely prevent such a theft if DBs are persistently attacked or if DBs are on clouds that may have malicious intent. A promising countermeasure is to encrypt data in such a way that keys for decryption are kept by only data owners [12,21,22]. This can be best compared to a current product for transparent database encryption such as [28] that keeps keys along databases.

However, as simply encrypting data makes DBs unable to offer sufficient functionalities, some dedicated encryption mechanisms are necessary. Searchable encryptions [2,4,16,20,23] enable a DB management system (DBMS) to search necessary data without decrypting them, and order-preserving encryptions (OPEs) [1,8,9] enable a DBMS to recognize the numerical order of data without decrypting them. The controlled joining [19] and the adjustable join [31] enable

D. Gritzalis et al. (Eds.): CANS 2014, LNCS 8813, pp. 337–352, 2014.

a management system of relational database (RDB) [15] to join encrypted tables without decrypting them. These mechanism enable DBs to offer various functionalities even if they are encrypted.

CryptDB [31] and MONOMI [36] employed some of these dedicated encryption mechanisms and demonstrated these mechanisms can enable encrypted RDBs to mark practical efficiency in TPC-C [34] and TPC-H [35] measures. It is certain that these encryption mechanisms are weaker than strong cryptographic protocols such as private information retrieval (PIR) introduced in [13, 14, 24], which leaks only few knowledge. However, such an approach as PIR inevitably requires either heavy computational or communicational cost for DBs and is not practical except when DBs are tiny. As it is commonly understood that there is no perfect security with reasonable availability in real services, the trade-off and the level of compromise are critically important. These encrypted databases are now attracting much attention as they are considered to offer beneficial trade-off.

Although these dedicated encryptions are attractive, they often fail to provide not only perfect security but the minimum level of security. Thus, their trade-off needs to be scrutinized. For example, CryptDB and MONOMI use deterministic encryption so as to respond to search queries. However, deterministic encryption reveals whether or not any pair of two encrypted data are the same. This is a fatal vulnerability if data are consists of a single bit that indicates, for example, whether or not each patient is affected with a highly sensitive disease. Such a vulnerability in searchable encryptions is basically solved by the scheme in [16] where relevant data is pointed only when queried with the corresponding token. This token-based searchable encryption is strengthened in [23] to securely update data.

An OPE [8,9] received great attention from the applied community [17,25,26, 31, 33, 38] when introduced. As the order comparison is a fundamental process that are frequently executed (next to searching by simple matching) in databases, OPE is what makes encrypted databases practical. However, it is even worse than deterministic encryption from the security perspective. Indeed, it is easy to see that if a set of numbers that includes the all numbers in a domain D are encrypted by an OPE, an adversary is able to decrypt all the ciphertexts simply by sorting them.

The weakness of OPE demands the development of token-based cryptographic protocols for range query as those for searching. This demands is very natural as an OPE is deterministic encryption and token based approaches are already common in [16,19,20,23,31] when deterministic approaches are no longer appropriate. Furukawa [18] proposed a notion of comparable encryption that overcome this weakness of order-preserving encryption (OPE). The comparable encryption enables to compare the numerical order of the pair of numbers from their ciphertexts if either of the ciphertexts is accompanied with the corresponding token. Hence, it significantly reduces the amount of disclosed knowledge with respect to encrypted numbers from their ciphertexts. This is the first token-based protocol for the range query.

However, the development of the comparable encryption neither open the way nor remove the last hurdle for practical encrypted databases. The previous comparable encryption requires awfully large ciphertext length, which severely spoils the performance of encrypted databases. As it converts each bit into a string of security parameter length, the ciphertext of 4 byte long message can be 640 byte long when the security parameter is 80. This is not an acceptable cost for almost all databases. Therefore, the lack of short comparable encryptions is still the fundamental problem for providing a practical encrypted database service.

We proposed in this paper, a very short comparable encryption to solve this problem. While each bit is encrypted into a string of security parameter length in the previous works, ours encrypts each bit into 3-ary. Its each ciphertext additionally requires an initial vector to ensure its uniqueness. The resulting ciphertext is even shorter than typical OPE in most cases. Our comparable encryption requires twice computational cost when comparing ciphertexts than the previous comparable encryption.

Although [18] introduced the notion of ideal security requirement for comparable encryption, it also introduced a weaker security requirement and presented only a scheme that satisfies this weaker security requirement. The weakness of this weaker notion compared to the ideal notion is evaluated in that paper. The expected ratio between the number of occasions when a token of an ideal scheme distinguishes two ciphertexts and the number of occasions when a token of a weaker scheme distinguishes two ciphertexts are shown to be only at most "2.8". Hence, schemes with the weaker security still have significance. Our scheme inherits the technique of the scheme in [18] and achieves exactly the same level of security in the standard model.

The proposed encryption scheme can encrypt data without loosing the ability of database management systems to handle range queries. The most queries in most RDBs can be handled if searching, inequality test, joining, and summation are possible. Currently searching can be handled by [23], joining can be handled by [31] or [19], and summation can be handled by [29] with a reasonable security. Hence, additionally with our short comparable encryption, an RDB management system now can process most of queries by combining these protocols while data are being encrypted. A small amount of data that cannot be processed by the management system itself can be sent back to the application, and then application who made queries can process them after decrypting them.

If we apply the above strategy to cloud databases, their users can be confident that the data will not be leaked via even cloud service providers. A cloud management system and a database management system have so an extensive privilege for accessing and controlling data that is difficult to audit rigorously. Moreover, cloud users are not allowed to audit cloud management system which includes systems of other users. Hence, encrypting database is most practical solution to make users feel their data safe. If we apply this strategy to on-premise databases, these databases can be managed thorough the network, which is often impossible within the current technology since there is no way to monitor database administrators outside the organization who might to access to confidential data.

The disadvantage of installing comparable encryption to databases is that the cost for evaluating inequality of each ciphertext compared to the query requires much higher than evaluating inequalities of plaintexts. The most database system developers are crazy about speed. In most relational databases, simple comparison between plaintexts are not always executed as is but leverage index technology for high performance. The proposed comparable encryption needs to be in concert with such technology so that its lower performance remain to be acceptable. We show how this is done in Section 2.

Related Works. Several works proposed stronger primitives for range query that can be replaced with OPEs. These are the committed efficiently-orderable encryption (CEOE) [9] that exploits a monotone minimal perfect hash function [3], range, conjunctive, and subset query methods in a public key setting [11,32], and searchable encryptions in a public key setting [4,5,10]. Among these, CEOE is not token based and are still unable to provide enough security when data are densely distributed. Some of range, conjunctive, subset queries or searching in public key settings are token based. As they are public key primitives, an attacker is able to generate ciphertexts and test which key word the token, i.e., the query, includes. Hence, although these primitives exercise heavy public key operations, they do not suit for our purpose. An order-preserving encryption with additional interactions [30] can enhance the security, but most applications assume that an RDB handles a thread of instructions without such additional interactions.

Organization. Section 2 discusses how comparable encryptions are employed by database management system in concert. Section 3 introduces the algorithms of comparable encryption and describes its basic functionality. Section 4 first introduces the security requirement of ideal comparable encryptions and its weaker variant. Then the comparison of ideal and weaker requirements is given. Section 5 presents a concrete scheme of our novel comparable encryption. Section 6 proves that our scheme satisfies the completeness and weak indistinguishability. Then it compares complexity of our scheme with that of the previous one. Section 7 summarizes our paper and poses an open problem.

2   Comparable Encryption for DB Management System

Suppose that every data in a database is encrypted by a comparable encryption. Then, its user is able to make an encrypted range query by sending tokens for the edges of this range. Upon receiving the query, the DB is able to compare these stored encrypted values with the edge values without interacting with the user to select out the required ciphertexts. Here, that the DB needs no more interaction is extremely important since it receives a sequence of requests at one time to avoid heavy communication and incoherent transaction. To implement such a functionality into databases, one can install a comparing protocol of comparable encryption as a user-defined-function. This is how CryptDB [31] install several cryptographic protocols into databases.

A comparable encryption leaks some numerical orders of the data to the DB via issued tokens, but what is leaked to the DB is what the DB needs for processing data with practical efficiency. A use of a protocol such as "private information retrieval" introduced in [13,14,24] may provide security closer to perfect one but requires awfully heavy resources, which spoils the benefit of databases. A huge number of different and varied queries may help DBMS decrypt data. Our approach is no longer effective in such an extreme case.

One may consider that an efficient comparable encryption provides a perfect solution for both range queries and insertion queries in encrypted DBs. However, before concluding, we must consider the fact that logarithmic time (binary) search is obligatory in almost all of current actual DBs requires some ciphertexts to be sorted in order. Then, the numerical order of the ciphertexts is no longer hidden even if comparable encryption is deployed. In such a case, the numerical order is not what we can conceal from the DBs without sacrificing their practicality.

Even when numerical order is revealed, a comparable encryption has an advantage over OPEs and avoids its ciphertexts from being totally decrypted. According to the impossibility result shown in [9] and the extreme case we discussed before, an OPE reveals much more (and even awfully in some cases) than numerical order of encrypted numbers. That is, each number can be almost or even totally decrypted. On the other hand, a comparable encryption reveals only the numerical order from sorted DBs without tokens. Suppose that there are m numbers in a domain of the size n where $m > n$. If these numbers are encrypted by OPE, the resulting values varies less than n. On the other hand, if these numbers are encrypted by comparable encryption, the resulting values are all different (m values appear.). That means, comparable encryptions unlike OPEs do not reveal equality of two encrypted numbers. Hence, the state of duplication is not revealed and thus, unlike OPEs, sorting does not decrypt ciphertexts. This is the main advantage of comparable encryptions over OPEs when applied to DBs that provide fast range querying.

An comparable encryption can insert an encrypted number into an ordered table also in logarithmic time. We summarize how an DB maintains a table of encrypted numbers by deploying comparable encryption. A user first encrypts all numbers in the table by the comparable encryption and sends them to the DB in numerical order of the original numbers. The DB keeps these encrypted numbers in a table in this order. When the user is to insert a new encrypted number into this table, it generates the corresponding token and sends it to the DB with this encrypted number. Since the DB is able to compare this new encrypted number with other stored encrypted numbers (with the help of the token), the DB can successfully insert the new encrypted number into the table in the right numerical order. The number of comparison that this process requires is a logarithm of the size of the stored numbers. For range queries, the DB can again compare the edge numbers to other stored encrypted numbers if the tokens for these edges are given, which requires only logarithmic time also.

3   Model

Now we introduce the model of comparable encryption. Comparable encryption is composed of four algorithms (Gen, Enc, Der, Cmp).

Gen: A probabilistic algorithm that, given a security parameter $\kappa \in \mathbb{N}$ and a range parameter $n \in \mathbb{N}$, outputs a parameter *param* and a master key *mkey*. n is included in *param*.

$$(param, mkey) = \mathsf{Gen}(\kappa, n)$$

Enc: A probabilistic algorithm that, given a parameter *param*, a master key *mkey*, and a number $0 \leq num < 2^n$, outputs a ciphertext *ciph*.

$$ciph = \mathsf{Enc}(param, mkey, num)$$

Der: A possibly probabilistic algorithm that, given a parameter *param*, a master key *mkey*, and a number $0 \leq num < 2^n$, outputs a token *token*.

$$token = \mathsf{Der}(param, mkey, num)$$

Cmp: An algorithm that, given a parameter *param*, two ciphertexts *ciph* and *ciph'*, and a token *token*, outputs 0, 1, or 2.

$$\mathsf{Cmp}(param, ciph, ciph', token) \in \{0, 1, 2\}$$

Although this model provides no decryption algorithm, it can be easily provided by appending an ordinary ciphertext $\widetilde{ciph}$ to each comparable encryption ciphertext *ciph* as $ciph|\widetilde{ciph}$ and preparing an ordinary decryption algorithm for it. Then, decryption is straightforward.

We assume *ciph* and *token* input to Cmp are related so that they satisfy $ciph = \mathsf{Enc}(param, mkey, num)$ and $token = \mathsf{Der}(param, mkey, num)$ for the same *param*, *mkey*, and *num*. The output of Cmp is 0, 1, or 2, respectively, when $num = num'$, $num > num'$, or $num < num'$. This requirement is formalized in the following completeness.

Definition 1. *We say a comparable encryption is* **complete** *if, for every $\kappa \in \mathbb{N}$, $n \in \mathbb{N}$, $0 \leq num, num' < 2^n$, and random tapes input to* Gen, Der, Enc, *and* Cmp, *it holds that*

$$(param, mkey) = \mathsf{Gen}(\kappa, n), token = \mathsf{Der}(param, mkey, num),$$
$$ciph = \mathsf{Enc}(param, mkey, num), ciph' = \mathsf{Enc}(param, mkey, num'),$$
$$\mathsf{Cmp}(param, ciph, ciph', token) = \begin{cases} 0 & \text{if } num = num' \\ 1 & \text{if } num > num' \\ 2 & \text{if } num < num' \end{cases}$$

One may model comparable encryption with Cmp that is fed only *param, ciph,* and *token.* In fact we consider *token* is always used with *ciph* and thus *token* can be redefined as (*token, ciph*). Our definitions of indistinguishability assume such a manner of using *token.* However, we consider the choice is a matter of taste and choose the previous way.

4   Security Requirements

4.1   Ideal and Weaker Requirements

We require comparable encryptions are indistinguishable against chosen plaintext attacks as long as no token is generated. We also require the knowledge that token discloses to DBMS is minimum while the efficiency of DBMS is maintained. Hence, it is considered that, when a token *token* with respect to a number *num* is given, it is best if *token* only enables to compare this *num* with other encrypted numbers. We introduce the notion of ideal indistinguishability and weak indistinguishability which are more simple than those defined in [18]. The simplification is due to the fact that both token and ciphertext are issued when (cmprkey, *num*) is queried in our games. Since the token input to our Cmp always accompanies a ciphertext of plaintext with respect to which the token is generated, this simultaneous issuing is what the usage of comparable encryptions is supposed to. We first introduce ideal security requirement.

Definition 2. *The* **distinguishing game** *is played between challenger C and adversary A^* as in the following. It begins when C receives a security parameter $\kappa \in \mathbb{N}$ and a range parameter $n \in \mathbb{N}$, runs (param, mkey) $\leftarrow$ Gen(κ, n), and gives param to A^*. C responds to queries from A^* in the game as follows;*

- *Upon receiving* (encrypt, *num*) *for any* $0 \leq num < 2^n$, *C returns ciph =* Enc(param, mkey, *num*).
- *Upon receiving* (cmprkey, *num*) *for any* $0 \leq num < 2^n$, *C returns token =* Der(param, mkey, *num*) *and ciph =* Enc(param, mkey, *num*).
- *C receives* (test, num_0^*, num_1^*) *such that* $0 \leq num_0^* < num_1^* < 2^n$ *only once in the game. On receiving this message, C randomly chooses $b \in \{0, 1\}$ and generates and returns* ciph* = Enc(param, mkey, num_b^*).

During the game, A^* is not allowed to make such a query (cmprkey, *num*) *that the following relation holds:*

$$num_0^* \leq num \leq num_1^* \tag{1}$$

At the end of the game, A^* sends $b' \in \{0, 1\}$ to C. The result of the game $\mathsf{Exp}_{C,A^*}^{\kappa}$ *is 1 if $b = b'$; otherwise 0.*

The distinguishing game challenges the adversary's ability to distinguish ciphertexts. However, if a certain set of queries is sent to the challenger, it is inevitable to prevent rational adversaries from distinguishing these ciphertexts. This is because tokens for comparing a pair of encrypted numbers inevitably enable DBMS to compare these numbers as designed. Hence, the cases and only the cases when tokens trivially help distinguishing ciphertexts need to be excluded from the games to measures the strength of the scheme. This trivial distinguishing is captured by the restriction to cmprkey queries.

We do not consider chosen-ciphertext attacks here. This is partly because encrypt-then-MAC [6] generic construction can easily make the scheme resistant for them even when an ordinary ciphertext is concatenated to each ciphertext so as to be decryptable. And this is mostly because preventing chosen-ciphertext attacks has few significance in our scenario. An encrypted database cannot prove the correctness of the response efficiently. For example. it is unrealistic for the encrypted databases to prove so when no matching data exist, that is, responses are malleable.

Definition 3. *We say a comparable encryption is* **indistinguishable (Ind)** *if, for every polynomial time adversary A^*, $\mathrm{Adv}^\kappa_{C,A^*} := |\Pr[\mathrm{Exp}^\kappa_{C,A^*} = 0] - \Pr[\mathrm{Exp}^\kappa_{C,A^*} = 1]|$ is negligible with respect to κ in the distinguishing game.*

We next introduce weaker security requirement. This requirement is defined via weak distinguishing game which is the same with the distinguishing game except that the allowed queries to the adversary is more restricted.

Definition 4. *The* **weak distinguishing game** *is played between challenger C and adversary A^* as in the following. It begins when C receives a security parameter $\kappa \in \mathbb{N}$ and a range parameter $n \in \mathbb{N}$, runs $(\mathrm{param}, \mathrm{mkey}) \leftarrow \mathsf{Gen}(\kappa, n)$, and gives param to A^*. C responds to queries from A^* in the game as follows;*

- *Upon receiving $(\mathsf{encrypt}, \mathrm{num})$ for any $0 \leq \mathrm{num} < 2^n$, C returns $\mathrm{ciph} = \mathsf{Enc}(\mathrm{param}, \mathrm{mkey}, \mathrm{num})$.*
- *Upon receiving $(\mathsf{cmprkey}, \mathrm{num})$ for any $0 \leq \mathrm{num} < 2^n$, C returns $\mathrm{token} = \mathsf{Der}(\mathrm{param}, \mathrm{mkey}, \mathrm{num})$ and $\mathrm{ciph} = \mathsf{Enc}(\mathrm{param}, \mathrm{mkey}, \mathrm{num})$.*
- *C receives $(\mathsf{test}, \mathrm{num}_0^*, \mathrm{num}_1^*)$ such that $0 \leq \mathrm{num}_0^* < \mathrm{num}_1^* < 2^n$ only once in the game. On receiving this message, C randomly chooses $b \in \{0,1\}$ and generates and returns $\mathrm{ciph}^* = \mathsf{Enc}(\mathrm{param}, \mathrm{mkey}, \mathrm{num}_b^*)$. .*

During the game, A^* is not allowed to make such a query $(\mathsf{cmprkey}, \mathrm{num})$ that the following relation holds:

$$\exists \ell (0 < \ell \leq n) \text{ s.t.}$$
$$((\alpha_\ell, \ldots, \alpha_{n-1}) = (\beta_\ell, \ldots, \beta_{n-1}) = (\gamma_\ell, \ldots, \gamma_{n-1})) \quad \wedge \quad (\beta_{\ell-1} < \gamma_{\ell-1}). \ (2)$$

where $\mathrm{num} = \sum_{i=0}^{n-1} \alpha_i 2^i$, $\mathrm{num}_0^* = \sum_{i=0}^{n-1} \beta_i 2^i$, $\mathrm{num}_1^* = \sum_{i=0}^{n-1} \gamma_i 2^i$ such that $\alpha_i, \beta_i, \gamma_i \in \{0,1\}$ for all i.

At the end of the game, A^* sends $b' \in \{0,1\}$ to C. The result of the game $\mathrm{Exp}^\kappa_{C,A^*}$ is 1 if $b = b'$; otherwise 0.

Note that here, if $\mathrm{num}_0^* < \mathrm{num}_1^*$, then there is ℓ such that

$$((\beta_\ell, \ldots, \beta_{n-1}) = (\gamma_\ell, \ldots, \gamma_{n-1})) \wedge (\beta_{\ell-1} < \gamma_{\ell-1}).$$

holds. And $num_0^* \leq num \leq num_1^*$ guarantees that

$$(\alpha_\ell, \ldots, \alpha_{n-1}) = (\beta_\ell, \ldots, \beta_{n-1}) = (\gamma_\ell, \ldots, \gamma_{n-1})$$

holds for this ℓ. Hence, the weak distinguishing game forbids larger class of queries than the distinguishing game.

Definition 5. *We say that a comparable encryption is* **weakly indistinguishable** *if, for every polynomial time adversary A^*, $\mathsf{Adv}_{C,A^*}^\kappa := |\Pr[\mathsf{Exp}_{C,A^*}^\kappa = 0] - \Pr[\mathsf{Exp}_{C,A^*}^\kappa = 1]|$ is negligible w.r.t. κ in the weak distinguishing game.*

As the weak distinguishing game forbids larger class of queries than the distinguishing game, Def. 5 guarantees weaker security than Def. 3 does. However, the difference between these requirement are estimated as moderately small in [18] if the number of leaked queries is small. The intuition of the weakness is sketched in Section A.

4.2   Evaluation of Weaker Indistinguishability

Let $0 \leq num_0^* < num_1^* < 2^n$, $D(num_0^*, num_1^*)$ be the number of num such that $num_0^* \leq num \leq num_1^*$, and $N(num_0^*, num_1^*)$ be the number of num such that Eq. (2) is satisfied. Then $R(num_0^*, num_1^*) = N(num_0^*, num_1^*)/D(num_0^*, num_1^*)$ is the ratio of "the number of occasions when tokens of a weaker scheme distinguishes a pair of ciphertexts" to "the number of occasions when tokens of an ideal scheme distinguishes a pair of ciphertexts", which represents how weaker scheme is weak compared to ideal scheme. When the ratio is one, they guarantee the ideal level of security. A larger ratio signifies the weakness.

As the ratio $R(num_0^*, num_1^*)$ varies over the choice of pair (num_0^*, num_1^*), its expected value over uniformly and randomly chosen (num_0^*, num_1^*) is estimated as a measure of the weakness in [18]. Similarly, the expected value of $D(num_0^*, num_1^*)/N(num_0^*, num_1^*)$ and the expected value of $N(num_0^*, num_1^*)$ are also evaluated. These estimation reported in [18] is given in Table. 1

Table 1. Various comparison measures

Measures	value
Expected Value of "$N(num_0^*, num_1^*)/D(num_0^*, num_1^*)$"	≤ 2.8
Expected Value of "$D(num_0^*, num_1^*)/N(num_0^*, num_1^*)$"	≤ 2
"E.V. of $N(num_0^*, num_1^*)$"/ "E. V. of $D(num_0^*, num_1^*)$"	$\geq 1/2$

5   Proposed Scheme

Now we present the specific construction of our scheme. Suppose a number num is such that $num = \sum_{i=0}^{n-1} b_i 2^i$ with $b_i \in \{0,1\}$ for all $0 \leq i \leq n-1$ for a range parameter $n \in \mathbb{N}$. Then, we let $(b_0, \ldots, b_{n-1})$ represent num and express this relation as $num = (b_0, \ldots, b_{n-1})$.

Intuitively, each number is assigned to a leaf of tree. Each bit in a number corresponds to the node of this tree and the value of this bit indicate which child node the next bit corresponds to. HashA in Der reveals a sequence of hash values, each unique to each of nodes along the route to the leaf. HashB in Enc give a random base to each node which is added to the bit corresponding to this node. Because of this base, the value of this bit is hidden as long as the ciphertexts with the same bit-value of this node are given with their corresponding tokens. HashC encrypts each bit probabilistically.

Gen: Suppose a security parameter $\kappa \in \mathbb{N}$ and the range parameter n are given. Gen first randomly chooses a hash function HashA, HashB, HashC : $\{0,1\}^\kappa \times \{0,1\}^* \to \{0,1\}^\kappa$ and assigns $param = (n, \mathsf{HashA}, \mathsf{HashB}, \mathsf{HashC})$. Next, Gen uniformly and randomly chooses a master key $mkey \in \{0,1\}^\kappa$. Gen outputs $param = (n, \mathsf{HashA}, \mathsf{HashB}, \mathsf{HashC})$ and $mkey$.

Der: Suppose that $param = (n, \mathsf{HashA}, \mathsf{HashB}, \mathsf{HashC})$, $mkey$, and a number $num = (b_0, b_1, \ldots, b_{n-1})$ are given. Der sets $b_n = 0$ and generates

$$d_i = \mathsf{HashA}(mkey, b_n, b_{n-1}, \ldots, b_i)) \qquad \text{for } i = n, \ldots, 1$$

Der outputs the token $token = (d_1, \ldots, d_n)$.

Enc: Suppose that $param = (n, \mathsf{HashA}, \mathsf{HashB}, \mathsf{HashC})$, $mkey$, and a number $num = (b_0, b_1, \ldots, b_{n-1})$ are given. Enc first generates $(d_1, \ldots, d_n) = \mathsf{Der}(param, mkey, num)$ and then randomly chooses random number $I \in \{0,1\}^\kappa$. Next, Enc generates

$$f_i = \mathsf{HashC}(d_{i+1}, I) + \mathsf{HashB}(mkey, d_{i+1}) + b_i \bmod 3$$

for $i = n-1, \ldots, 0$. Enc finally outputs ciphertext $ciph = (I, (f_0, \ldots, f_{n-1}))$. Here, $(f_0, \ldots, f_{n-1})$ can be encoded into an integer $F = \sum_{i=0}^{n-1} f_i 3^i$ to make the ciphertext short.

Cmp: Suppose that $param = (n, \mathsf{HashA}, \mathsf{HashB}, \mathsf{HashC})$, a pair of ciphertexts $ciph = (I, (f_0, \ldots, f_{n-1}))$ and $ciph' = (I', (f'_0, \ldots, f'_{n-1}))$, and a token $token = (d_1, \ldots, d_n)$ are given.
  - Cmp sets $j = n-1$ and keep generating the following c_j by repeatedly decreasing j by 1 at each step.

$$c_j = f_j - f'_j - \mathsf{HashC}(d_{j+1}, I) + \mathsf{HashC}(d_{j+1}, I') \bmod 3$$

This repetition stops when Cmp generated c_j such that $c_j \neq 0$ or when $c_j = 0$ for all $0 \leq j \leq n-1$. In the former case, Cmp outputs this first non zero c_j. In the latter case Cmp outputs 0.

6 Property of the Proposed Comparable Encryption

6.1 Security

Theorem 1. *The proposed comparable encryption is complete.*   □

Definition 6. *We say a function* Hash : $\{0,1\}^\kappa \times \{0,1\}^\ell \to \{0,1\}^L$ *is a* pseudorandom function *if every poly-time distinguisher D has an advantage in distinguishing whether it is accessing* Hash$(K, \cdot)$ *with randomly chosen key $K \in \{0,1\}^\kappa$ or it is accessing a random function $R : \{0,1\}^\ell \to \{0,1\}^L$ with at most negligible probability in κ.*

Theorem 2. *The proposed comparable encryption is* **weakly indistinguishable** *as long as* HashA, HashB, HashC *are a pseudorandom function.*

The structure of ciphertext of our protocol is essentially the same as that of the previous protocol [18] except that our protocol no longer equipped with the largest element in the previous one. This element was use to check whether or not each bit of number *num* to which the token is associated to equals to the bit of the number *num'* to which *num* is compared to. But this check is done by $(f_i)_i$ in our scheme. Although this checking mechanism is quite different from the previous one, the difference in the proofs of indistinguishability depends only on the structure of ciphertexts. Hence, our proof is very similar to that in [18].

The proof is straightforward. We replace some of outputs of hash functions with random variable and then simply prove indistinguishability of them.

Proof. The proof is by contraposition. Suppose that there exists an adversary A^* such that $\mathsf{Adv}^\kappa_{C,A^*}$ is not negligible with respect to κ in the weak distinguishing game. Then, we show that Hash is distinguishable from the random function, which is against the assumption that they are pseudorandom function. In particular, we consider a sequence of games by challengers C, C_1, and C_2 and then prove the theorem by the hybrid argument.

From two lemmas 1 and 2 and the hybrid argument, $|\mathsf{Adv}^\kappa_{C,A^*} - \mathsf{Adv}^\kappa_{C_2,A^*}|$ is negligible in κ as long as Hash is a pseudorandom function. Since $\mathsf{Adv}^\kappa_{C_2,A^*} = 0$ from Lemma 3, $\mathsf{Adv}^\kappa_{C,A^*}$ is negligible in κ. Hence, the theorem is proved.

Definition 7. *Challenger C_1 is the same as C in Definition 2 except the following:*

- *At the beginning of the game, C_1 discards* mkey.
- *C_1 prepares a table for each of hash functions* HashA(mkey, $\cdot$) *and* HashB(mkey, $\cdot$) *and simulate them. That is, whenever C_1 simulates* output = HashA(mkey, input) *or* output = HashB(mkey, input) *for some* input, *C_1 let* output *be* output' *if an entry* (input, output') *is in the corresponding table. Otherwise, C_1 randomly chooses* output $\in \{0,1\}^\kappa$ *and writes* (input, output) *into that table.*

Lemma 1. *Assume that* HashA *and* HashB *are a pseudorandom function. For every polynomial time A^*, $|\mathsf{Adv}^\kappa_{C_1,A^*} - \mathsf{Adv}^\kappa_{C,A^*}|$ is negligible in κ.*

Proof. Since mkey is used for only input to hash functions and is never revealed to A^*, the lemma follows from the indistinguishability of pseudorandom function.

Definition 8. *Challenger C_2 is the same as C_1 except the following:*

- *Let $(\bar{d}_1, \ldots, \bar{d}_n)$ and $(\hat{d}_1, \ldots, \hat{d}_n)$ be $(\bar{d}_1, \ldots, \bar{d}_n) = \mathsf{Der}(\mathrm{param}, \mathrm{mkey}, \mathrm{num}_0^*)$, $(\hat{d}_1, \ldots, \hat{d}_n) = \mathsf{Der}(\mathrm{param}, \mathrm{mkey}, \mathrm{num}_1^*)$. Here, $\bar{d}_i = \hat{d}_i$ for $\ell \le i \le n$ where ℓ is such that $((\beta_\ell, \ldots, \beta_{n-1}) = (\gamma_\ell, \ldots, \gamma_{n-1}))$ $\wedge$ $(\beta_{\ell-1} < \gamma_{\ell-1})$. for $\mathrm{num}_0^* = (\beta_0, \beta_1, \ldots, \beta_{n-1}), \mathrm{num}_1^* = (\gamma_0, \gamma_1, \ldots, \gamma_{n-1})$. C_2 prepares a table and simulate hash function $\mathsf{HashC}(\bar{d}_i, \cdot)$ and $\mathsf{HashC}(\hat{d}_i, \cdot)$ for all $0 \le i \le \ell$. The simulation is as is the before.*

Lemma 2. *Assume that HashC is a pseudorandom function. For every polynomial time A^*, $|\mathsf{Adv}_{C_2, A^*}^\kappa - \mathsf{Adv}_{C_1, A^*}^\kappa|$ is negligible in κ.*

Proof. Suppose that the adversary queries $(\mathrm{cmprkey}, \mathrm{num})$ for $\mathrm{num} = (\alpha_0, \ldots, \alpha_{n-1})$. If $\alpha_i = \beta_i$ for $\ell \le i < n$, then such a query is not allowed in the weak distinguishing game by definition. Hence, this is not the case we consider. Therefore, there exists j such that $\alpha_j \ne \beta_j$ and that $\ell + 1 \le j < n$. In such case, none of $\bar{d}_0, \ldots, \bar{d}_\ell, \hat{d}_0, \ldots, \hat{d}_\ell$ is revealed to the adversary. Since, the values $\bar{d}_0, \ldots, \bar{d}_\ell, \hat{d}_0, \ldots, \hat{d}_\ell$ are randomly chosen and unrevealed, the hardness of distinguishing random values with outputs of $\mathsf{HashC}(\bar{d}_i, \cdot)$ and $\mathsf{HashC}(\hat{d}_i, \cdot)$ for $0 \le i \le \ell$ follows from the indistinguishability of pseudorandom function.

Lemma 3. *For every polynomial time A^*, $\mathsf{Adv}_{C_2, A^*}^\kappa = 0$.*

Proof. The lemma follows from the fact that $ciph^*$ does not depend on b, which can be shown as follows. The difference between ciphertexts of num_0^* and of num_1^* occur only in $(f_i)_i$ for $i = 0, \ldots, \ell - 1$. Since each $\mathsf{HashC}(\bar{d}_i, \cdot)$ (we assume $b = 0$ w.l.g.) for $i = 0, \ldots, \ell$ is randomly chosen, every f_i for $i = 0, \ldots, \ell - 1$ does not depend on b. Therefore, the lemma is proved.

6.2   Performance

We compare complexity of our scheme and the previous comparable encryption in Table 2. Here, n is the maximum length of numbers, Hash is the cost of computing hash function which we consider the dominant cost, and ℓ is such that $(\beta_\ell, \ldots, \beta_{n-1}) = (\gamma_\ell, \ldots, \gamma_{n-1})$ and $\beta_{\ell-1} < \gamma_{\ell-1}$ for $\mathrm{num}_0^* = (\beta_0, \beta_1, \ldots, \beta_{n-1})$, $\mathrm{num}_1^* = (\gamma_0, \gamma_1, \ldots, \gamma_{n-1})$.

Our scheme provide very short ciphertext length and smaller encryption cost compared to those of the previous scheme. But our scheme requires twice cost for comparison. Other complexities are the same.

When our scheme is applied, it is natural to attach ciphertexts so that they can be decrypted when necessary. For these ciphertexts to be both probabilistic and short, we can use format preserving encryptions such as [7] or [27] that maps short messages to short ciphertexts of the same length with randomly chosen initial vector. If this initial vector is reused as the initial vector of our

Table 2. Comparison

	Previous Scheme [18]	Our Scheme
ciphertext(text) length (bits)	$(n+1)\kappa + 2n$	$\kappa + (\ln 3/\ln 2)n$
token length (bits)	$(n+1)\kappa$	$(n+1)\kappa$
encryption cost	$(4n+1) \cdot$ Hash	$3n \cdot$ Hash
token generation cost	$(n+1) \cdot$ Hash	$(n+1) \cdot$ Hash
comparison cost	$(n-\ell+2) \cdot$ Hash	$2(n-\ell+2) \cdot$ Hash

scheme, ciphertexts length of our scheme is shortened to be only $(\ln 3/\ln 2)n$. This is very short.

We have implemented core mechanism. For hash function, we employed AES rather than SHA1 etc. so that AES-NI instructions can be used for higher performance. The performance was evaluated with Intel Core i7 1.9GHz in 1 core by running 10,000 comparisons sequentially. The average number of cycles required for one comparison was roughly 8000, which means 250,000 comparisons are possible in one second.

7   Summary and Open Problem

We greatly improved the length of the comparable encryption in [18] which satisfies the same security level as the original scheme. With this technology as well as searchable encryption in [23], the adjustable join in [31], and homomorphic encryption in [29], a meaningful encrypted relational databases can be provided.

We consider the effect on privacy of the weaker notion needs to be analyzed more. What we consider most important is the comparison of leaked information between two encrypted databases, one uses comparable encryption with the weaker notion and the other with the ideal notion. The comparison is best if data and queries are distributed as those of real.

References

1. Agrawal, R., Kiernan, J., Srikant, R., Xu, Y.: Order-preserving encryption for numeric data. In: Weikum, G., König, A.C., Deßloch, S. (eds.) SIGMOD Conference, pp. 563–574. ACM (2004)
2. Amanatidis, G., Boldyreva, A., O'Neill, A.: Provably-secure schemes for basic query support in outsourced databases. In: Barker, S., Ahn, G.-J. (eds.) Data and Applications Security 2007. LNCS, vol. 4602, pp. 14–30. Springer, Heidelberg (2007)
3. Belazzougui, D., Boldi, P., Pagh, R., Vigna, S.: Monotone minimal perfect hashing: searching a sorted table with $o(1)$ accesses. In: Mathieu, C. (ed.) SODA, pp. 785–794. SIAM (2009)
4. Bellare, M., Boldyreva, A., O'Neill, A.: Deterministic and efficiently searchable encryption. In: Menezes, A. (ed.) CRYPTO 2007. LNCS, vol. 4622, pp. 535–552. Springer, Heidelberg (2007)

5. Bellare, M., Fischlin, M., O'Neill, A., Ristenpart, T.: Deterministic encryption: Definitional equivalences and constructions without random oracles. In: Wagner [37], pp. 360–378

6. Bellare, M., Namprempre, C.: Authenticated encryption: Relations among notions and analysis of the generic composition paradigm. In: Okamoto, T. (ed.) ASI-ACRYPT 2000. LNCS, vol. 1976, pp. 531–545. Springer, Heidelberg (2000)

7. Bellare, M., Ristenpart, T., Rogaway, P., Stegers, T.: Format-preserving encryption. In: Jacobson Jr., M.J., Rijmen, V., Safavi-Naini, R. (eds.) SAC 2009. LNCS, vol. 5867, pp. 295–312. Springer, Heidelberg (2009)

8. Boldyreva, A., Chenette, N., Lee, Y., O'Neill, A.: Order-preserving symmetric encryption. In: Joux, A. (ed.) EUROCRYPT 2009. LNCS, vol. 5479, pp. 224–241. Springer, Heidelberg (2009)

9. Boldyreva, A., Chenette, N., O'Neill, A.: Order-preserving encryption revisited: Improved security analysis and alternative solutions. In: Rogaway, P. (ed.) CRYPTO 2011. LNCS, vol. 6841, pp. 578–595. Springer, Heidelberg (2011)

10. Boldyreva, A., Fehr, S., O'Neill, A.: On notions of security for deterministic encryption, and efficient constructions without random oracles. In: Wagner [37], pp. 335–359

11. Boneh, D., Waters, B.: Conjunctive, subset, and range queries on encrypted data. In: Vadhan, S.P. (ed.) TCC 2007. LNCS, vol. 4392, pp. 535–554. Springer, Heidelberg (2007)

12. Ceselli, A., Damiani, E., di Vimercati, S.D.C., Jajodia, S., Paraboschi, S., Samarati, P.: Modeling and assessing inference exposure in encrypted databases. ACM Trans. Inf. Syst. Secur. 8(1), 119–152 (2005)

13. Chor, B., Goldreich, O., Kushilevitz, E., Sudan, M.: Private information retrieval. In: FOCS, pp. 41–50 (1995)

14. Chor, B., Kushilevitz, E., Goldreich, O., Sudan, M.: Private information retrieval. J. ACM 45(6), 965–981 (1998)

15. Codd, E.F.: A relational model of data for large shared data banks. Commun. ACM 13(6), 377–387 (1970)

16. Curtmola, R., Garay, J.A., Kamara, S., Ostrovsky, R.: Searchable symmetric encryption: improved definitions and efficient constructions. In: Juels, A., Wright, R.N., di Vimercati, S.D.C. (eds.) ACM Conference on Computer and Communications Security, pp. 79–88. ACM (2006)

17. Ding, Y., Klein, K.: 0002. Model-driven application-level encryption for the privacy of e-health data. In: ARES, pp. 341–346. IEEE Computer Society (2010)

18. Furukawa, J.: Request-based comparable encryption. In: Crampton, J., Jajodia, S., Mayes, K. (eds.) ESORICS 2013. LNCS, vol. 8134, pp. 129–146. Springer, Heidelberg (2013)

19. Furukawa, J., Isshiki, T.: Controlled joining on encrypted relational database. In: Abdalla, M., Lange, T. (eds.) Pairing 2012. LNCS, vol. 7708, pp. 46–64. Springer, Heidelberg (2013)

20. Goh, E.-J.: Secure indexes. Cryptology ePrint Archive, Report 2003/216 (2003), http://eprint.iacr.org/

21. Hacigümüs, H., Iyer, B.R., Li, C., Mehrotra, S.: Executing sql over encrypted data in the database-service-provider model. In: Franklin, M.J., Moon, B., Ailamaki, A. (eds.) SIGMOD Conference, pp. 216–227. ACM (2002)

22. Hacigümüs, H., Mehrotra, S., Iyer, B.R.: Providing database as a service. In: ICDE, p. 29. IEEE Computer Society (2002)

23. Kamara, S., Papamanthou, C., Roeder, T.: Dynamic searchable symmetric encryption. In: Yu, T., Danezis, G., Gligor, V.D. (eds.) ACM Conference on Computer and Communications Security, pp. 965–976. ACM (2012)
24. Kushilevitz, E., Ostrovsky, R.: Replication is not needed: Single database, computationally-private information retrieval. In: FOCS, pp. 364–373 (1997)
25. Liu, H., Wang, H., Chen, Y.: Ensuring data storage security against frequency-based attacks in wireless networks. In: Rajaraman, R., Moscibroda, T., Dunkels, A., Scaglione, A. (eds.) DCOSS 2010. LNCS, vol. 6131, pp. 201–215. Springer, Heidelberg (2010)
26. Lu, W., Varna, A.L., Wu, M.: Security analysis for privacy preserving search of multimedia. In: ICIP, pp. 2093–2096. IEEE (2010)
27. Minematsu, K.: Building blockcipher from small-block tweakable blockcipher. In: Designs, Codes and Cryptography, pp. 1–19 (2013)
28. Oracle. Oracle database 11g, oracle advanced security, http://www.oracle.com/technology/global/jp/products/security/db_security/htdocs/aso.html
29. Paillier, P.: Public-key cryptosystems based on composite degree residuosity classes. In: Stern, J. (ed.) EUROCRYPT 1999. LNCS, vol. 1592, pp. 223–238. Springer, Heidelberg (1999)
30. Popa, R.A., Li, F.H., Zeldovich, N.: An ideal-security protocol for order-preserving encoding. Cryptology ePrint Archive, Report 2013/129 (2013), http://eprint.iacr.org/
31. Popa, R.A., Redfield, C.M.S., Zeldovich, N., Balakrishnan, H.: Cryptdb: protecting confidentiality with encrypted query processing. In: Wobber, T., Druschel, P. (eds.) SOSP, pp. 85–100. ACM (2011)
32. Shi, E., Bethencourt, J., Chan, H.T.-H., Song, D.X., Perrig, A.: Multi-dimensional range query over encrypted data. In: IEEE Symposium on Security and Privacy, pp. 350–364. IEEE Computer Society (2007)
33. Tang, Q.: Privacy preserving mapping schemes supporting comparison (2010)
34. TPC-C. Transaction processing performance council, http://www.tpc.org/tpcc/
35. TPC-H. Transaction processing performance council, http://www.tpc.org/tpch/
36. Tu, S., Kaashoek, M.F., Madden, S., Zeldovich, N.: Processing analytical queries over encrypted data. PVLDB 6(5), 289–300 (2013)
37. Wagner, D. (ed.): CRYPTO 2008. LNCS, vol. 5157. Springer, Heidelberg (2008)
38. Wang, C., Cao, N., Li, J., Ren, K., Lou, W.: Secure ranked keyword search over encrypted cloud data. In: ICDCS, pp. 253–262. IEEE Computer Society (2010)

A   Intuition for Weaker Security Requirement

Indistinguishability and weak indistinguishability are different only in that queries of type cmprkey, num are more restricted in weak distinguishing game. The Fig. 1 illustrates the difference between two notions in the case $num_0^* = 9$ and $num_1^* = 13$. The figure consists of nodes of a tree expressed by dots. The leftmost dot is the root and rightmost dots are leaves. Other dots are internal nodes. Each path from the root to a leaf expresses a number in $[0, 2^5)$. Each path consists of five edge and each edge represents a bit. An upward edge represents 1 and downward one represents 0. Hence 13, which is $(b_4, b_3, b_2, b_1, b_0) = (0, 1, 1, 0, 1)$, is expressed as a path that advances from the root to a leaf by choosing directions (down,up,up,down,up) at nodes on the path.

In the case of Fig. 1, the adversary are not allowed to query (cmprkey, *num*) for $m_0^* = 9 \leq num \leq 13 = m_1^*$ in distinguishing game. But in weak distinguishing game, the adversary may not allowed to query (cmprkey, *num*) for $8 \leq num \leq 15$. Note that these numbers $8, 9, 13, 15$ share the same node pointed indicated by "*branch point*$(9, 13)$" in the figure. Here, 8 and 15 are the minimum and the maximum number that share the node where 9 and 13 branch away. The weak distinguishing game forbids numbers in wider range to be queried. If we consider how much this range is widened is how much schemes get weaker, the range $13 - 9 + 1 = 5$ is widened to $15 - 8 + 1 = 8$ by the ratio of $8/5 = 1.6$ in this example. The expected value of this ratio is estimated as smaller than 2.8 in [18].

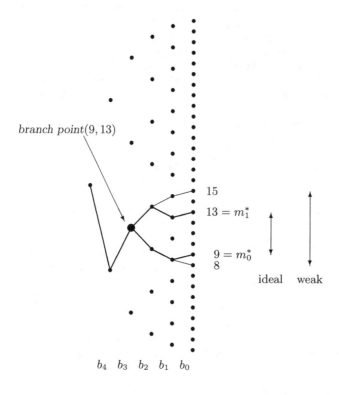

Fig. 1. Tree Representations of 9 and 13, and the ranges forbidden by two games

Decentralized Distributed Data Usage Control

Florian Kelbert and Alexander Pretschner

Technische Universität München, Germany
{kelbert,pretschn}@cs.tum.edu

Abstract. Data usage control provides mechanisms for data owners to remain in control over how their data is used after it is has been shared. Many data usage policies can only be enforced on a global scale, as they refer to data usage events happening within multiple distributed systems: 'not more than three employees may ever read this document', or 'no copy of this document may be modified after it has been archived'. While such global policies can be enforced by a centralized enforcement infrastructure that observes all data usage events in all relevant systems, such a strategy involves heavy communication. We show how the overall coordination overhead can be reduced by deploying a decentralized enforcement infrastructure. Our contributions are: (i) a formal distributed data usage control system model; (ii) formal methods for identifying all systems relevant for evaluating a given policy; (iii) identification of situations in which no coordination between systems is necessary without compromising policy enforcement; (iv) proofs of correctness of (ii, iii).

1   Introduction

Consider a company's financial department in which the CFO and her employees collaborate via email. Business reports, contracts, and transactional information are exchanged via email and edited by multiple employees. Employees also use email to collaborate on documents that are *not* considered sensitive. However, due to the other documents' sensitivity and their decentral sharing, the company deploys usage control [1,2] technologies on the employees' devices with the goal to enforce policies such as 'document D1 must not be edited' (**P1**), or 'there may be at most one ongoing edit process for document D2 at each point in time and no editing is allowed after the CFO archived the final version' (**P2**). What is usually meant by such policies is that not only one particular file pertaining to a document (e.g. D1) must be protected, but all copies and derivations of it: If the document is copied to another file, loaded into a Java application or sent via the network, all of these *representations* of D1 (file, java object, network packet) must be protected [3,4]. We refer to policies P1 and P2 throughout this paper.

Once representations of documents D1 and D2 have been emailed to multiple employees and exist in different systems, each of those systems is in charge of enforcing the corresponding policies P1 and P2 [5]. Intuitively, policy P1 can be enforced locally by denying all edit requests for each local copy of D1. Policy P2, in contrast, refers to events happening within multiple systems and introduces dependencies between them. Thus, enforcement of policy P2 necessitates

D. Gritzalis et al. (Eds.): CANS 2014, LNCS 8813, pp. 353–369, 2014.

coordination between all systems potentially capable of editing and archiving representations of document D2.

Within one single system, usage control enforcement infrastructures are commonly implemented in correspondence with the XACML standard architecture [6]: System-layer specific policy enforcement points (PEPs, e.g. for MS Windows [7], OpenBSD/Linux [4], Mozilla Thunderbird [5]) intercept data usage events (e.g., *save*, *edit*, *send*, *archive*) and signal them to the local policy decision point (PDP) [3, 8, 9]. The PDP evaluates each event against the deployed data usage policies and signals its decision back to the corresponding PEP, which will then enforce it. For taking this decision, the PDP might need additional information about the system's state, such as subject and object attributes, or the data's current representations—also called the *data flow state*. Such information is collected by the policy information point (PIP), which is queried by the PDP.

As indicated earlier, policy P1 can be enforced locally: The system's PEPs signal <u>all</u> *edit* events to their local PDP, which in turn queries the local PIP to learn whether a particular *edit* event takes place on a representation of document D1. If so, the PDP's decision is to disallow the event.

Policy P2, however, can not be enforced by local PDPs/PIPs only: Assume three representations of document D2 on three different systems. Whenever an employee requests to edit a representation of D2, this *edit* event must only be allowed if no other employee is currently editing a representation of D2. Similarly, after the event *archive* has been performed by the CFO on a representation of D2, all future editing requests must be disallowed. Because the representations of D2 are decentrally shared and because *edit* and *archive* events can happen on any of those systems, purely local PDPs are generally unable to decide about this policy. Additional information is needed, e.g. 'how many employees are currently editing D2?', and 'has D2 been archived in the past?'.

Intuitively, policy P2, or, more generally, any policy referring to distributed data and data usage events, can be enforced by a centralized enforcement infrastructure, i.e. a single global PDP/PIP (Fig. 1). However, such a centralized infrastructure imposes the **problem** of heavy communication overhead, as all data usage events from all relevant systems must be signalled to the central PDP/PIP. Such an approach is particularly inappropriate if employees also work on unprotected documents. Moreover, if employees work while travelling, each event must be sent to the central PDP/PIP via a mobile internet connection. This is likely to make the work cumbersome due to large communication delays

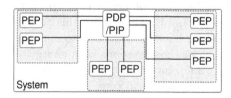

Fig. 1. Naive centralized enforcement.

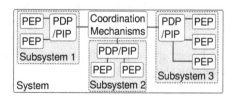

Fig. 2. Decentralized variant (§3-4)

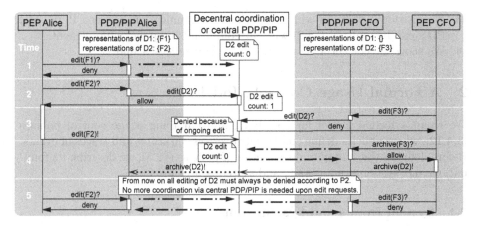

Fig. 3. Enforcement of policies P1 and P2 given the event trace of Table 1

and the fact that PEPs usually block system execution upon each intercepted event until the PDP's decision is available [7, 10, 11].

Our **goal** is to improve on this situation by reducing the amount of communication needed whenever global policies of the kind of P2 ought to be enforced.

Our **solution** is an enforcement infrastructure that is inherently distributed. It deploys a local PDP/PIP on each site, e.g., a physical device or virtual machine (Fig. 2). PEPs signal events to these local PDPs/PIPs using fast inter process communication. While the local components can independently (i.e. without coordination with other PDPs/PIPs) decide P1, some coordination with other PDPs/PIPs is still needed for the enforcement of P2. Fig. 3 depicts the advantages of our proposed solution when enforcing P1 and P2, given the trace of events in Table 1; and assuming F1 to be a representation of document D1, and F2 and F3 representations of document D2. Dash-dotted arrows ($\cdots\!-\!\blacktriangleright$) indicate expensive cross-system communication that is needed in a centralized enforcement infrastructure but not in our approach. Dotted arrows ($\cdots\!\blacktriangleright$) indicate communication that is introduced by our solution. Question marks (?) indicate decision requests from PEPs to PDPs if intended events are intercepted. Exclamation marks (!) indicate to a PDP that an event has actually happened.

Table 1. Event trace

Time	Alice	CFO
1	edit(F1)	
2	edit(F2)	
3		edit(F3)
4		archive(F3)
5	edit(F2)	edit(F3)

This work aims at minimizing the communication overhead for such a decentralized enforcement infrastructure by providing the following **contributions**:

1. We provide a formal distributed data usage control system model (§3).
2. We provide formal methods to identify all systems potentially relevant for evaluating a given data usage policy at any point in time (§4.1).

3. We provide insights in which situations communication between PDPs and PIPs can be omitted (§4.2) without compromising policy enforcement.
4. We show the correctness of 2. and 3. in Appendices A and B.

2   A Formal Usage Control Model

We recap a formal model for specifying and enforcing usage control policies [3,4,12], where policies define constraints over system states and traces of events. Before defining the syntax and semantics of policies (§2.3), we describe its foundations, i.e. system events (§2.1) and system states (§2.2).

2.1   System Events and System Runs

Events $\mathcal{E}$ are defined by a name (set *EName*) and a set of parameters, which are, in turn, defined by a name (set *PName*) and a value (set *PValue*): $\mathcal{E} \subseteq$ *EName* $\times \mathbb{P}(PName \times PValue)$. For an event $e \in \mathcal{E}$, let $e.n$ denote the event's name and $e.p$ the set of its parameters. Furthermore, let $obj \in PName$ denote an event's primary object whose value can be accessed using notation $e.obj$.

Event refinement. When specifying policies, it is not useful to define all possible event parameters. Instead, one would like to specify only relevant parameters, quantifying over all unmentioned ones. In our example, it is irrelevant which particular user edits document D2, but not the fact *that* D2 is edited. Hence, *refines* $\subseteq \mathcal{E} \times \mathcal{E}$ defines a refinement relation on events: event e_1 refines event e_2 iff they have the same event name and the parameters of e_1 are a superset of the parameters of e_2: $\forall e_1, e_2 \in \mathcal{E} : e_1$ *refines* $e_2 \Leftrightarrow e_1.n = e_2.n \wedge e_1.p \supseteq e_2.p$.

System events $\mathcal{S}$, i.e. events intercepted by PEPs at runtime in a real system, are always maximally refined, i.e. all parameters are determined. Hence, $\mathcal{S} = \mathcal{E} \setminus \{e \in \mathcal{E} \mid \exists e' \in \mathcal{E} : e' \neq e \wedge e'$ *refines* $e\}$.

System runs are modeled as traces, mapping each abstract moment in time to the set of system events happening at that time: *Trace* $: \mathbb{N} \to \mathbb{P}(\mathcal{S})$.

2.2   System States

Since the data to be protected may exist in multiple representations (e.g., document D1 might be represented as a file, a java object, or a network packet), a system's state is defined in terms of the distribution of data within that system [3,4]. Hence, we also refer to it as the system's data flow state. We call the data's representations *containers* and $\mathcal{C}$ the global set of containers. The global set of *data* to be protected by usage control policies is denoted $\mathcal{D}$, and $\mathcal{C} \cap \mathcal{D} = \emptyset$.

As motivated earlier, data usage policies are specified in terms of data, implying that the imposed restrictions also apply to all copies and derivations. Thus, only elements $v \in \mathcal{D}$ are possible values for an event's *obj* parameter when specifying policies. In contrast, system events $e \in \mathcal{S}$ operate on containers, which is why elements $v \in \mathcal{C}$ are the only possible values for a system event's *obj* parameter. Taken together, elements $v \in \mathcal{C} \cup \mathcal{D}$ are possible values for an event's *obj* parameter, $(\mathcal{C} \cup \mathcal{D}) \subseteq PValue$. For the remainder of this paper we constrain the set of possible values for event parameter obj to $\mathcal{C} \cup \mathcal{D} \cup \{\epsilon\}$, reflecting the fact that an event operates on a container, a data, or neither of the two, respectively.

System states $\Sigma = \mathcal{C} \to \mathbb{P}(\mathcal{D})$ map containers to data potentially stored in them. In our example, $\sigma \in \Sigma$ records which files, emails, and editing processes are representations of documents D1 and D2. Transition relation $\mathcal{R}$ describes how the execution of system events $\mathcal{S}$ changes the system's state: $\mathcal{R} \subseteq \Sigma \times \mathbb{P}(\mathcal{S}) \to \Sigma$.

Given a system trace $t \in Trace$ and a point in time $i \in \mathbb{N}$, the system's state is computed as $\sigma_t^i = \mathcal{R}(\sigma_t^{i-1}, t(i-1))$; $\sigma_t^0 = \emptyset$ represents the trace's initial state.

Instantiations of this generic data flow model, in particular semantics of $\mathcal{R}$, have been described for various system layers such as MS Windows [7], Open-BSD/Linux [4], X11 [13], Thunderbird [5], as well as distributed systems [10].

Event Refinement in the Presence of States. Extending the earlier event refinement, $refines_\Sigma \subseteq (\mathcal{S} \times \Sigma) \times \mathcal{E}$ describes the refinement between two events in the presence of a given system state. The reason is that policies (§2.3) are specified in terms of data ($\exists e_2 \in \mathcal{E}, d \in \mathcal{D} : e_2.obj = d$), while system events operate on containers ($\exists e_1 \in \mathcal{S}, c \in \mathcal{C} : e_1.obj = c$). Hence, we need to evaluate the system's current state $\sigma \in \Sigma$ in order to decide whether an event refines another. We say that (e_1, σ) refines e_2 iff $d \in \sigma(c)$ and if the parameters of e_1 are a superset of the parameters of e_2 when ignoring the obj parameter:

$$\forall e_1 \in \mathcal{S}, e_2 \in \mathcal{E}, \sigma \in \Sigma : (e_1, \sigma) \ refines_\Sigma \ e_2 \iff \exists c \in \mathcal{C}, d \in \mathcal{D} : e_1.n = e_2.n$$
$$\wedge \ e_1.obj = c \wedge e_2.obj = d \wedge d \in \sigma(c) \wedge e_1.p \setminus \{(obj, c)\} \supseteq e_2.p \setminus \{(obj, d)\}$$

For instance, consider a state $\sigma \in \Sigma$ in which file F1 is a representation of document D1. Then $((edit, \{(obj, F1), \ldots\}), \sigma) \ refines_\Sigma \ (edit, \{(obj, D1)\})$.

2.3 Data Usage Policies

Building upon previous work [3, 14–16], we assume technical policies to be expressed as event-condition-action (ECA) rules: whenever a triggering **E**vent is detected and if it makes the **C**ondition *true*, then (additional) **A**ctions might be performed. Because the policies' conditions are formulated in terms of past temporal logics, this work focuses on the evaluation of such formulas. Based on the above foundations and [3], the syntax of ECA **C**onditions (Φ) is defined as:

$$\Psi \ = false \mid \mathcal{E}$$
$$\Phi^\Sigma = \underline{isNotIn}(\mathcal{D}, \mathbb{P}(\mathcal{C})) \mid \underline{isCombined}(\mathcal{D}, \mathcal{D}, \mathbb{P}(\mathcal{C})) \mid \underline{isMaxIn}(\mathcal{D}, \mathbb{N}, \mathbb{P}(\mathcal{C}))$$
$$\Phi \ = (\Phi) \mid \Psi \mid \Phi^\Sigma \mid \Phi \ \underline{and} \ \Phi \mid \underline{not}(\Phi) \mid \Phi \ \underline{since} \ \Phi \mid \Phi \ \underline{before} \ \mathbb{N} \mid \underline{repmin}(\mathbb{N}, \mathbb{N}, \mathcal{E})$$

Ψ is self-explanatory. Φ^Σ defines state-based operators for constraints on the system's data flow state: $\underline{isNotIn}(d, C)$ is true iff data d is not in any of the containers C; $\underline{isCombined}(d_1, d_2, C)$ is true iff there is at least one container in C that contains both data d_1 and d_2; $\underline{isMaxIn}(d, m, C)$ is true iff data d is contained in at most m containers in C. For Φ, the semantics of $\underline{and}$ and $\underline{not}$ are intuitive; $\alpha \ \underline{since} \ \beta$ is true iff β was true some time earlier and α was true ever since, or if α was always true; $\alpha \ \underline{before} \ j$ is true iff α was true exactly

j timesteps ago; $repmin(j, m, e)$ is true iff event e happened at least m times in the last j timesteps. Further shortcuts include those for $\underline{true}$ and $\underline{or}$; plus $repmax(j, m, e) \equiv \underline{not}(repmin(j, m + 1, e))$; $replim(j, m, n, e) \equiv repmin(j, m, e)$ $\underline{and}\ repmax(j, n, e)$. The formal semantics of policies Φ are:

$$\forall t \in Trace, i \in \mathbb{N}, \varphi \in \Phi \bullet (t, i) \models \varphi \iff (\varphi \neq \underline{false}) \land$$
$$\exists e \in \mathcal{E}, e' \in t(i) \bullet (\varphi = e \land (e', \sigma_t^i)\ refines_\Sigma\ e)$$
$$\lor \exists d \in \mathcal{D}, C \subseteq \mathcal{C} \bullet (\varphi = \underline{isNotIn}(d, C) \land \forall c \in C \bullet d \notin \sigma_t^i(c))$$
$$\lor \exists d_1, d_2 \in \mathcal{D}, C \subseteq \mathcal{C} \bullet (\varphi = \underline{isCombined}(d_1, d_2, C) \land \exists c \in C \bullet \{d_1, d_2\} \subseteq \sigma_t^i(c))$$
$$\lor \exists d \in \mathcal{D}, m \in \mathbb{N}, C \subseteq \mathcal{C} \bullet (\varphi = \underline{isMaxIn}(d, m, C) \land |\{c \in C | d \in \sigma_t^i(c)\}| \leq m)$$
$$\lor \exists \alpha, \beta \in \Phi \bullet ((\varphi = \underline{not}(\alpha) \land \neg((t, i) \models \alpha))$$
$$\lor (\varphi = \alpha\ \underline{and}\ \beta \land (t, i) \models \alpha \land (t, i) \models \beta)$$
$$\lor (\varphi = \alpha\ \underline{or}\ \beta \land (t, i) \models \alpha \lor (t, i) \models \beta)$$
$$\lor (\varphi = \alpha\ \underline{since}\ \beta \land \exists j \in [0, i] \bullet ((t, j) \models \beta \land \forall k \in (j, i] \bullet (t, k) \models \alpha)$$
$$\lor \forall k \in [0, i] \bullet (t, k) \models \alpha))$$
$$\lor \exists \alpha \in \Phi, j \in \mathbb{N} \bullet (\varphi = \alpha\ \underline{before}\ j \land (t, i - j) \models \alpha)$$
$$\lor \exists j, m \in \mathbb{N}, e \in \mathcal{E} \bullet (\varphi = \underline{repmin}(j, m, e)$$
$$\land m \leq \sum_{k=0}^{j-1} |\{e' \in t(i - k) | (e', \sigma_t^{i-k})\ refines_\Sigma\ e\}|)$$

Policy enforcement is usually performed as sketched in §1 [3, 8, 9, 11, 13, 17]. With $C_{EditProc}$ denoting the set of all processes with the capability to edit documents [4], one way of expressing our example policies as ECA rules is:

P1	Event: $(edit, \{(obj, D1)\})$
	Condition: $\varphi = \underline{true}$
	Action: $inhibit$
P2	Event: $(edit, \{(obj, D2)\})$
	Condition: $\varphi = \underline{not}(isMaxIn(D2, 0, C_{EditProc})\ \underline{and}$
	$\underline{not}((archive, \{(obj, D2), (user, CFO)\}))\ \underline{since}\ \underline{false})$
	Action: $inhibit$

3   A Distributed System Model

The model in §2 suggests a monolithic view on policy enforcement: at runtime there is one single global trace and system state at any point in time. Technically, one central PDP/PIP globally observes the entire system. As this is likely impractical in real-world distributed scenarios, we propose an extended model in which multiple PDPs and PIPs observe different parts of the global system.

3.1   Individual and Concurrently Executing Subsystems

Adapting to the terms used in §2, we refer to the distributed system as a whole as the *system*, which is, in turn, composed of a set of *subsystems*. In our terminology, each subsystem is a set of possibly distributed system layers whose PEPs share one single PDP. More technically, a subsystem may be an operating system instance, a physical or virtual machine, a set of applications, or a set of physical or virtual machines. A subsystem thus contains exactly one PDP/PIP and at least one PEP (Fig. 2). We assume each subsystem to be assigned a unique identifier $s \in \mathbb{N}$, which could map to a MAC address or UUID in practice.

For each subsystem $s \in \mathbb{N}$ we define $\mathcal{C}_s \subseteq \mathcal{C}$ as its unique set of containers, $\mathcal{S}_s \subseteq \mathcal{S}$ as its unique set of system events[1], $\Sigma_s : \mathcal{C}_s \to \mathbb{P}(\mathcal{D})$ as its set of states, and $Trace_s : \mathbb{N} \to \mathbb{P}(\mathcal{S}_s)$ as its set of all possible runs, $Trace_s \subseteq Trace$. Because we will 'overlay' traces of different subsystems shortly, we require each system event $e \in \mathcal{S}_s$ to carry parameter sub with value s:

$$\forall s, s' \in \mathbb{N}, e \in \mathcal{S}_s : (sub, s) \in e.p \land s \neq s' \implies \mathcal{S}_s \cap \mathcal{S}_{s'} = \emptyset \land \mathcal{C}_s \cap \mathcal{C}_{s'} = \emptyset.^2$$

Containers and system events for a set of subsystems $M \subseteq \mathbb{N}$ are defined by $\forall M \subseteq \mathbb{N} : \mathcal{S}_M = \bigcup_{s \in M} \mathcal{S}_s \land \mathcal{C}_M = \bigcup_{s \in M} \mathcal{C}_s$.

Concurrent System Runs. In practice, subsystems run in parallel and produce independent system traces: Each subsystem's PDP observes a trace of system events, $t_s \in Trace_s$. Assuming sufficiently synchronized system clocks [18], it is the union of these local observations that one single global PDP would observe. When reasoning about this global behavior, the behavior of individual subsystems or of sets of subsystems, we will use notations t_s^τ and t_M^τ, in order to refer to the trace of a particular subsystem $s \in \mathbb{N}$ or set of subsystems $M \subseteq \mathbb{N}$ given a tuple τ of concurrently executing traces. The intuition is that t_M^τ overlays the concurrently executing traces of all subsystems $m \in M$ by unifying all events happening in all subsystems $m \in M$ at each point in time $i \in N$. Let $\prod$ denote the Cartesian product. Then $\tau \in \prod_{n \in \mathbb{N}} Trace_n$ is a tuple of traces of all subsystems, and the m-th element of τ, i.e. $\tau.m$, is a trace of subsystem $m \in \mathbb{N}$. The overlay of a set of traces of subsystems $M \subseteq \mathbb{N}$, t_M^τ, is $\forall \tau \in \prod_{n \in \mathbb{N}} Trace_n, i, s \in \mathbb{N}, M \subseteq \mathbb{N} : t_s^\tau = \tau.s \land t_M^\tau(i) = \bigcup_{m \in M} (\tau.m)(i)$.

In the following, we will mostly talk about sets of subsystems $M \subseteq \mathbb{N}$. The same considerations apply to the single subsystems $s \in \mathbb{N}$ by letting $M = \{s\}$.

3.2 Policy Projections

When considering a set of subsystems $M \subseteq \mathbb{N}$, it is generally not possible to conclusively evaluate a given policy $\varphi \in \Phi$, since evaluation of φ might depend on information unavailable within M. In our example (Fig. 3, Table 1), Alice's PDP cannot decide about event *edit(F2)* at time 2, since another employee might already be editing D2. However, Alice's PDP *can* evaluate a projection of formula φ of policy P2 by hiding parts that refer to other subsystems: Letting C_A denote all containers within Alice's subsystem, subformula *isMaxIn*$(D2, 0, C_{EditProc} \cap C_A)$ can be evaluated by Alice's PDP. We will make use of these policy projections

---

[1] Events belonging to multiple subsystems (such as *transfer(data,from,to)*) are attributed to the initiating one.

[2] Parameter *sub* makes us redefine relations *refines* and *refines$_\Sigma$*, as this parameter must not influence event refinement: $\forall e_1, e_2 \in \mathcal{E}, s, s' \in \mathbb{N} : e_1$ *refines* $e_2 \Leftrightarrow e_1.n = e_2.n \land e_1.p \setminus \{(sub, s)\} \supseteq e_2.p \setminus \{(sub, s')\}$. We refrain from formally redefining *refines$_\Sigma$*.

in §4.2 with the goal to omit unnecessary coordination between subsystems. In general, the projection $\varphi_M \in \Phi$ of $\varphi \in \Phi$ for subsystems M is defined as:

$$
\begin{aligned}
\forall \varphi \in \Phi, M &\subseteq \mathbb{N}, \exists \varphi_M \in \Phi : (\varphi = \underline{false} \wedge \varphi_M = \underline{false}) \\
&\vee (\exists\, \alpha, \beta \in \Phi \bullet (\varphi = \alpha \ \underline{and}\ \beta \wedge \varphi_M = \alpha_M \ \underline{and}\ \beta_M) \\
&\quad \vee (\varphi = \alpha \ \underline{or}\ \beta \wedge \varphi_M = \alpha_M \ \underline{or}\ \beta_M) \\
&\quad \vee (\varphi = \alpha \ \underline{since}\ \beta \wedge \varphi_M = \alpha_M \ \underline{since}\ \beta_M) \\
&\quad \vee (\varphi = \underline{not}(\alpha) \wedge \varphi_M = \underline{not}(\alpha_M)) \\
&\vee (\exists\, e \in \mathcal{E} \bullet (\varphi = e \wedge \varphi_M = e)) \\
&\vee (\exists\, d_1, d_2 \in \mathcal{D}, C \subseteq \mathcal{C} \bullet \varphi = \underline{isCombined}(d_1, d_2, C) \\
&\quad \wedge \varphi_M = \underline{isCombined}(d_1, d_2, C \cap \mathcal{C}_M)) \\
&\vee (\exists\, d \in \mathcal{D}, C \subseteq \mathcal{C} \bullet \varphi = \underline{isNotIn}(d, C) \wedge \varphi_M = \underline{isNotIn}(d, C \cap \mathcal{C}_M)) \\
&\vee (\exists\, d \in \mathcal{D}, m \in \mathbb{N}, C \subseteq \mathcal{C} \bullet \varphi = \underline{isMaxIn}(d, m, C) \\
&\quad \wedge \varphi_M = \underline{isMaxIn}(d, m, C \cap \mathcal{C}_M)) \\
&\vee (\exists\, \alpha \in \Phi, j \in \mathbb{N} \bullet \varphi = \alpha \ \underline{before}\ j \wedge \varphi_M = \alpha_M \ \underline{before}\ j) \\
&\vee (\exists\, j, m \in \mathbb{N}, e \in \mathcal{E} \bullet \varphi = \underline{repmin}(j, m, e) \wedge \varphi_M = \underline{repmin}(j, m, e))
\end{aligned}
$$

4   Coordinating Subsystems

Deploying one PDP/PIP per subsystem necessitates their coordination for the enforcement of certain policies: a PDP's decision might depend on past decisions and observations of other PDPs and PIPs, because policies might refer to events or system states of multiple subsystems. For enforcing policy P2, all subsystems (1) capable of editing or archiving documents *and* (2) having a representation of D2 stored locally must generally coordinate their decisions and data flow states if a representation of D2 is about to be edited. While naively each PDP/PIP could disclose all of its knowledge to all other PDPs/PIPs or to one central PDP/PIP, we aim at minimizing this coordination overhead. For this, we approximate the set of subsystems relevant for evaluating a formula $\varphi \in \Phi$ (§4.1), and analyze in which cases coordination between PDPs/PIPs can safely be omitted (§4.2).

4.1   Identifying Subsystems Relevant for Evaluating Formulas

Our goal is to approximate the subsystems relevant for evaluating $\varphi \in \Phi$ at time $i \in \mathbb{N}$, given the tuple of concurrently executing traces $\tau \in \prod_{n \in \mathbb{N}} Trace_n$, by function $sys(\varphi, i, \tau)$. In particular, if $|sys(\varphi, i, \tau)| \leq 1$, then no coordination is needed for evaluation of φ. We start by defining three auxiliary functions:

(1) $awareC : \mathbb{P}(\mathcal{C}) \to \mathbb{P}(\mathbb{N})$ returns for a given set of containers the set of subsystems that are aware of at least one of the given containers:

$$\forall C \subseteq \mathcal{C} : awareC(C) = \{s \in \mathbb{N} \mid \mathcal{C}_s \cap C \neq \emptyset\}$$

(2) $awareD : \mathbb{P}(\mathcal{D}) \times \mathbb{N} \times \prod Trace \to \mathbb{P}(\mathbb{N})$ returns for a given set of data items, a point in time, and a tuple of executing traces the set of subsystems in which there exists a container that contains at least one of those data items:

$$
\begin{aligned}
\forall D &\subseteq \mathcal{D}, i \in \mathbb{N}, \tau \in \prod_{n \in \mathbb{N}} Trace_n : \\
awareD(D, i, \tau) &= \{s \in \mathbb{N} \mid \exists c \in \mathcal{C}_s : D \cap \sigma^i_{\tau.s}(c) \neq \emptyset\}
\end{aligned}
$$

(3) $mayHappen : \mathcal{E} \times \mathbb{N} \times \prod Trace \rightarrow \mathbb{P}(\mathbb{N})$ returns for an event $e \in \mathcal{E}$, a point in time, and a tuple of executing traces the set of subsystems in which an event refining e might happen. This set contains all subsystems that are able to perform events with name $e.n$ and that are 'aware of' the data addressed by e:

$$\forall e \in \mathcal{E}, i \in \mathbb{N}, \tau \in \prod_{n \in \mathbb{N}} Trace_n : mayHappen(e, i, \tau) =$$
$$\{s \in \mathbb{N} \mid \exists e' \in \mathcal{S}_s : e.n = e'.n \wedge \exists d \in \mathcal{D} \bullet e.obj = d \wedge s \in awareD(\{d\}, i, \tau)\}$$

$sys(\varphi, i, \tau)$ then returns all subsystems potentially relevant for evaluating φ:

$$\forall \varphi \in \Phi \cup \Phi^{\Sigma} \cup \Psi, i \in \mathbb{N}, \tau \in \prod_{n \in \mathbb{N}} Trace_n :$$
$$sys(\varphi, i, \tau) = \{s \in Y \mid (\varphi = \underline{false} \wedge Y = \{\})$$
$$\vee (\exists \alpha, \beta \in \Phi \cup \Phi^{\Sigma} \cup \Psi \bullet ((\varphi = \alpha \ \underline{and} \ \beta \vee \varphi = \alpha \ \underline{or} \ \beta)$$
$$\wedge Y = sys(\alpha, i, \tau) \cup sys(\beta, i, \tau))$$
$$\vee (\varphi = \alpha \ \underline{since} \ \beta \wedge Y = \bigcup_{j=0}^{i} (sys(\alpha, j, \tau) \cup sys(\beta, j, \tau))))$$
$$\vee (\exists \alpha \in \Phi \cup \Phi^{\Sigma} \cup \Psi \bullet \varphi = \underline{not}(\alpha) \wedge Y = sys(\alpha, i, \tau))$$
$$\vee (\exists e \in \mathcal{E} \bullet \varphi = e \wedge Y = mayHappen(e, i, \tau))$$
$$\vee (\exists d_1, d_2 \in \mathcal{D}, C \subseteq \mathcal{C} \bullet \varphi = \underline{isCombined}(d_1, d_2, C)$$
$$\wedge Y = awareD(\{d_1\}, i, \tau) \cap awareD(\{d_2\}, i, \tau) \cap awareC(C))$$
$$\vee (\exists d \in \mathcal{D}, m \in \mathbb{N}, C \subseteq \mathcal{C} \bullet (\varphi = \underline{isNotIn}(d, C) \vee \varphi = \underline{isMaxIn}(d, m, C))$$
$$\wedge Y = awareD(\{d\}, i, \tau) \cap awareC(C))$$
$$\vee (\exists j, m \in \mathbb{N}, e \in \mathcal{E} \bullet \varphi = \underline{repmin}(j, m, e) \wedge Y = \bigcup_{k=0}^{j-1} mayHappen(e, i-k, \tau))$$
$$\vee (\exists \alpha \in \Phi \cup \Phi^{\Sigma} \cup \Psi, j \in \mathbb{N} \bullet \varphi = \alpha \ \underline{before} \ j \wedge Y = sys(\alpha, i-j, \tau))\}$$

We claim that subsystems $sys(\varphi, i, \tau)$ are sufficient to evaluate φ at time i, given executing traces τ. Subsystems $\mathbb{N} \backslash sys(\varphi, i, \tau)$ do not influence evaluation of φ, and no coordination is needed if $|sys(\varphi, i, \tau)| \leq 1$. We provide proofs of correctness in Appendix A. We will refer to $t^{\tau}_{sys(\varphi, i, \tau)}$ as $t^{\tau}_{\mathbb{N}}$, indicating that the investigated trace is equivalent to what a single global PDP would have observed.

Considering example policy P1 ($\varphi = \underline{true}$), $sys(\varphi, i, \tau)$ returns the empty set, matching the intuition that P1 can always be evaluated locally. Considering policy P2, $sys(\varphi, i, \tau)$ returns both Alice's and the CFO's subsystem, since representations of document D2 exist in both subsystems and both subsystems exhibit editing capabilities. Hence, both subsystems might influence policy evaluation.

4.2   Omitting Unnecessary Coordination

While in general coordination between subsystems is needed if an ECA mechanism's triggering event is observed and $|sys(\varphi, i, \tau)| > 1$, there are situations in which no coordination is required. We have seen that $sys(\varphi, i, \tau)$ returns both Alice's and the CFO's subsystems for policy P2. However, at timestep 5 no coordination takes place (cf. Fig. 3). This is because the CFO archived a representation of D2, in which case all further edit requests must be denied. Once Alice's PDP learns that this archiving event has happened, all further editing request can immediately be denied by Alice's PDP without any further coordination.

Given $\tau \in \prod_{n \in \mathbb{N}} Trace_n$ and a policy $\varphi \in \Phi$, there are special situations in which we can deduce a formula $\varphi' \in \Phi$ such that (i) trace t^{τ}_M satisfies φ' at time $i \in N$, and (ii) this local satisfaction of φ' implies global satisfaction of φ, formally: $(t_M^\tau, i) \models \varphi' \implies (t_N^\tau, i) \models \varphi$. For example, a part of the condition of policy P2 is $\underline{not}(\underline{isMaxIn}(D2, 0, C_{EditProc}))$ when converting P2's condition into disjunctive normal form (DNF). If Alice is already editing a representation of D2, any further concurrent edit requests can be denied without coordination.

We formalize this intuition by predicate $S \subseteq \prod Trace_n \times \mathbb{P}(\mathbb{N}) \times \mathbb{N} \times \Phi$ that holds $true$ iff for the tuple of executing traces $\tau \in \prod_{n \in \mathbb{N}} Trace$ and a set of subsystems $M \subseteq \mathbb{N}$, trace t_M^τ satisfies $\varphi_M \in \Phi$ at time $i \in \mathbb{N}$ $((t_M^\tau, i) \models \varphi_M)$ and if this implies global satisfaction of formula $\varphi \in \Phi$ at the same point in time $((t_N^\tau, i) \models \varphi)$. Similarly, the same argument holds for the violation of formula φ, which can intuitively be expressed by negating formula φ:

$$\forall \tau \in \textstyle\prod_{n \in \mathbb{N}} Trace_n, M \subseteq \mathbb{N}, i \in \mathbb{N}, \varphi \in \Phi :$$
$$(t_M^\tau, i) \models \varphi_M \land S(\tau, M, i, \varphi) \implies (t_N^\tau, i) \models \varphi$$
$$\land\ (t_M^\tau, i) \not\models \varphi_M \land S(\tau, M, i, \neg\varphi) \implies (t_N^\tau, i) \not\models \varphi.$$

Demanding $\varphi \in \Phi$ to be given in DNF, we define $S \subseteq \prod Trace \times \mathbb{P}(\mathbb{N}) \times \mathbb{N} \times \Phi$ as follows. Proofs of correctness are provided in Appendix B.

$$\forall \tau \in \textstyle\prod_{n \in \mathbb{N}} Trace_n, M \subseteq \mathbb{N}, i \in \mathbb{N}, \varphi \in \Phi \cup \Phi^\Sigma \cup \Psi : S(\tau, M, i, \varphi)$$
$$\iff \varphi = \underline{true} \lor sys(\varphi, i, \tau) \subseteq M$$
$$\lor (\exists\, e \in \mathcal{E}, j, m \in \mathbb{N} \bullet (\varphi = e \lor \varphi = \underline{repmin}(j, m, e)))$$
$$\lor (\exists\, d_1, d_2 \in \mathcal{D}, C \subseteq \mathcal{C} \bullet \varphi = \underline{isCombined}(d_1, d_2, C))$$
$$\lor (\exists\, d \in \mathcal{D}, m \in \mathbb{N}, C \subseteq \mathcal{C} \bullet (\varphi = \neg \underline{isNotIn}(d, C) \lor \varphi = \neg\underline{isMaxIn}(d, m, C)))$$
$$\lor (\exists\, \alpha \in \Phi \cup \Phi^\Sigma \cup \Psi, j \in \mathbb{N} \bullet (\varphi = \alpha\ \underline{before}\ j \land S(\tau, M, i - j, \alpha)$$
$$\lor (\varphi = \neg(\alpha\ \underline{before}\ j) \land S(\tau, M, i - j, \neg\alpha)))$$
$$\lor (\exists\, \alpha, \beta \in \Phi \cup \Phi^\Sigma \cup \Psi \bullet (\varphi = \alpha\ \underline{since}\ \beta$$
$$\land (\exists j \in [0, i] : ((t_M^\tau, j) \models \beta_M \land S(\tau, M, j, \beta)$$
$$\land \forall k \in (j, i] : (t_M^\tau, k) \models \alpha_M \land S(\tau, M, k, \alpha)))$$
$$\lor (\forall k \in [0, i] : (t_M^\tau, k) \models \alpha_M \land S(\tau, M, k, \alpha)))$$
$$\lor (\varphi = \neg(\alpha\ \underline{since}\ \beta)$$
$$\land (\forall j \in [0, i] : ((t_M^\tau, j) \not\models \beta_M \land S(\tau, M, j, \neg\beta)$$
$$\lor \exists k \in (j, i] : (t_M^\tau, k) \not\models \alpha_M \land S(\tau, M, k, \neg\alpha)))$$
$$\land (\exists k \in [0, i] : (t_M^\tau, k) \not\models \alpha_M \land S(\tau, M, k, \neg\alpha)))$$
$$\lor (\varphi = \alpha\ \underline{and}\ \beta \land S(\tau, M, i, \alpha) \land S(\tau, M, i, \beta))$$
$$\lor (\varphi = \alpha\ \underline{or}\ \beta \land ((t_M^\tau, i) \models \alpha_M \land S(\tau, M, i, \alpha)$$
$$\lor (t_M^\tau, i) \models \beta_M \land S(\tau, M, i, \beta))))$$

This formalism allows us to identify situations such as in timesteps 4 and 5 of our example: After the CFO's PDP has observed event $archive(F3)$ at time 4, subformula $\underline{not}((archive, \{(obj, D2), (user, CFO)\}))\ \underline{since\ false}$ will always evaluate to $false$, implying that policy P2's overall condition φ will always evaluate to $true$. Consequently, all further $edit$ requests can safely be disallowed by the CFO's PDP despite the fact that $|sys(\varphi, i, \tau)| > 1$. Once Alice's PDP gets informed that $archive(D2)$ happened (Fig. 3, time 4), it is capable of disallowing any further $edit$ requests (time 5) without coordination. In sum, all further coordination for enforcing policy P2 can be omitted. Because of space limitations, we do not detail this additional information exchange between PDPs here.

5   Related Work

Chadwick et al. [9] investigate the coordination of distributed stateless PDPs in the access control context. To synchronize resource access across time and space, PDPs synchronize via central 'coordination objects' holding the coordination attributes. Our work is different in that the distributed components are stateful: even policies of a global scale might be evaluated locally (§4.2). Further, our focus is on usage control rather than on access control and our contributions might be implemented in a purely decentralized fashion. Also, our approach enforces policies on all copies of the protected data rather than on only one instance.

Service Automata [11] realize distributed decisions by delegation: If a local monitor's ('service automaton' in [11]) knowledge is insufficient for taking a decision, the decision process is delegated to another local monitor. However, this delegatee is fixed for any pair of conflicting events, thus effectively being a central enforcement point for all corresponding policies. Our approach, in contrast, can be implemented in a pure decentral fashion. As [11] exclusively discusses 'critical events', it remains unclear to which extent Service Automata are able to enforce policies on all copies and derivations of data across systems.

Basin et al. [19] monitor compliance with data usage policies in distributed systems in a *detective* manner: Locally collected logs are merged and a-posteriori evaluated against data usage policies. While [19] also considers propagation of data through the system, our solution targets preventive enforcement.

Lazouski et al. [8] allow for continuous usage control enforcement of data whose copies are distributed. Among policies, also PDP/PIP allocation policies are embedded into the protected data, and they are used by PEPs to locate the PDPs/PIPs responsible for taking decisions. Different to our approach, the responsible PDP is fixed throughout the data's lifetime and for all its copies

Kelbert et al. [10] enable tracking of usage controlled data across systems, as well as enforcement of *local* usage control policies. While distributed PDPs and PIPs exchange information upon cross-system data flows, policies that are of a global scale can not be enforced due to missing coordination between PDPs.

Complementary to our work, Janicke et al. [20] perform *static* analysis of usage control policies with the goal to identify (in)dependencies between PDPs ('Controllers' in [20]). Their analysis results reveal which concurrent decision processes do (not) require synchronization via a central PIP.

Bauer et al. [21] monitor LTL formulas in distributed systems. By leveraging formula rewriting techniques and exchanging rewritten formulas, local monitors can detect satisfaction or violation. Instead of rewriting formulas, our approach exchanges additional information between local monitors. Further, we leverage peculiarities of data usage control policies to minimize communication overhead.

6   Conclusion, Discussion, and Future Work

We have shown how to reduce overall communication overhead when enforcing global data usage control policies such as "only one employee may be editing document D1 at each point in time". While a naive centralized enforcement infrastructure would impose heavy communication overhead, we provide a distributed data usage control model that supports decentral monitoring of multiple concurrently running systems. Once copies of the protected data, as well as their corresponding usage policies, have been distributed, enforcement of policies that refer to data and data usage events within multiple systems, necessitates the coordination of the decentrally deployed enforcement mechanisms (i.e. PDPs and PIPs). While naively each PDP/PIP could disclose all of its knowledge to all other PDPs/PIPs, our contributions aim at reducing this communication overhead. Hence, we provide formal methods to approximate all systems potentially relevant for evaluating a given policy at each point in time. Subsequently, we can limit coordination to this set of identified systems for enforcement of the given policy. Moreover, we provide insights in which situations coordination between distributed PDPs/PIPs can safely be omitted although the policy to be enforced is of a global scale. Further, we show the correctness of our formal approaches.

We occasionally omitted details for simplicity's sake. The literature [3, 10, 12, 22, 23] discusses more complex data flow states, a slightly more expressive policy language, and the differentiation between intended and actual system events: While intended events can be intercepted, and consequently denied, before their execution, actual events can only be observed thereafter. As our intention was to prevent policy violations, we implicitly assumed events to be intended rather than actual. However, the considerations in §3 and §4 apply to actual events as well. We also tacitly assumed policies to be shipped along with the protected data in case of cross-system data flows. Corresponding mechanisms have been described in the literature [5, 8, 10, 24].

While we have exemplified our general contributions along a running example, the performance of our approach depends on the event traces being observed (predicate S). While in our example no more coordination is needed starting from timestep 5, other formulas might necessitate coordination between subsystems at each point in time. Because of this and because there are usually several ways to technically implement high-level usage policies, we see our contributions as a basis for future work that investigates how policies ought to be specified or transformed to allow for their most efficient enforcement. Along the same lines, our contributions can serve as a basis for building efficient usage control enforcement infrastructures: Given a set of concrete uses cases, i.e. event traces and policies, our contributions can help to answer questions such as where to place PDPs/PIPs in order to minimize communication and performance overhead.

We have not investigated whether the described coordination mechanisms should be implemented in a centralized or decentralized fashion. Since both is possible, we plan to implement both approaches and to compare them for several use cases. Depending on the use case, we expect diverse evaluation results, thus providing further insights into how an efficient enforcement infrastructure can be built. While we have an intuitive understanding which information must be exchanged between PDPs/PIPs (e.g. parts of the data flow state or events happening), the planned implementation will shed further light on this question.

References

1. Park, J., Sandhu, R.: The UCON$_{ABC}$ Usage Control Model. ACM Transactions on Information and System Security 7(1), 128–174 (2004)
2. Pretschner, A., Hilty, M., Basin, D.: Distributed Usage Control. Communications of the ACM 49(9), 39–44 (2006)
3. Pretschner, A., Lovat, E., Büchler, M.: Representation-Independent Data Usage Control. In: Garcia-Alfaro, J., Navarro-Arribas, G., Cuppens-Boulahia, N., de Capitani di Vimercati, S. (eds.) DPM 2011 and SETOP 2011. LNCS, vol. 7122, pp. 122–140. Springer, Heidelberg (2012)
4. Harvan, M., Pretschner, A.: State-Based Usage Control Enforcement with Data Flow Tracking using System Call Interposition. In: 3rd International Conference on Network and System Security, pp. 373–380 (2009)
5. Lörscher, M.: Data Usage Control for the Thunderbird Mail Client. Master's thesis, University of Kaiserslautern, Germany (2012)
6. T. Moses (ed.). eXtensible Access Control Markup Language (XACML) Version 2.0. OASIS Standard, pp. 1–141 (2005)
7. Wüchner, T., Pretschner, A.: Data Loss Prevention Based on Data-Driven Usage Control. In: IEEE 23rd Intl. Symp. Software Reliability Eng., pp. 151–160 (2012)
8. Lazouski, A., Mancini, G., Martinelli, F., Mori, P.: Architecture, Workflows, and Prototype for Stateful Data Usage Control in Cloud. In: IEEE Security and Privacy Workshops (2014)
9. Chadwick, D., Su, L., Otenko, O., Laborde, R.: Coordination between Distributed PDPs. In: 7th IEEE Intl. Works. on Policies for Distr. Systems and Networks (2006)
10. Kelbert, F., Pretschner, A.: Data Usage Control Enforcement in Distributed Systems. In: Proc. 3rd ACM Conference on Data and Application Security and Privacy, pp. 71–82 (2013)
11. Gay, R., Mantel, H., Sprick, B.: Service Automata. In: Barthe, G., Datta, A., Etalle, S. (eds.) FAST 2011. LNCS, vol. 7140, pp. 148–163. Springer, Heidelberg (2012)
12. Hilty, M., Pretschner, A., Basin, D., Schaefer, C., Walter, T.: A Policy Language for Distributed Usage Control. In: Biskup, J., López, J. (eds.) ESORICS 2007. LNCS, vol. 4734, pp. 531–546. Springer, Heidelberg (2007)
13. Pretschner, A., Büchler, M., Harvan, M., Schaefer, C., Walter, T.: Usage Control Enforcement with Data Flow Tracking for X11. In: Proc. 5th International Workshop on Security and Trust Management, pp. 124–137 (2009)
14. Pretschner, A., Hilty, M., Basin, D., Schaefer, C., Walter, T.: Mechanisms for Usage Control. In: Proc. 2008 ACM Symposium on Information, Computer and Communications Security, pp. 240–244 (2008)
15. Kumari, P., Pretschner, A.: Deriving Implementation-level Policies for Usage Control Enforcement. In: Proc. 2nd ACM Conference on Data and Application Security and Privacy, pp. 83–94 (2012)
16. Kumari, P., Pretschner, A.: Model-Based Usage Control Policy Derivation. In: Jürjens, J., Livshits, B., Scandariato, R. (eds.) ESSoS 2013. LNCS, vol. 7781, pp. 58–74. Springer, Heidelberg (2013)

17. Fromm, A., Kelbert, F., Pretschner, A.: Data Protection in a Cloud-Enabled Smart Grid. In: Cuellar, J. (ed.) SmartGridSec 2012. LNCS, vol. 7823, pp. 96–107. Springer, Heidelberg (2013)
18. Kloukinas, C., Spanoudakis, G., Mahbub, K.: Estimating Event Lifetimes for Distributed Runtime Verification. In: Proc. 20th Intl. Conf. on Software Eng. (2008)
19. Basin, D., Harvan, M., Klaedtke, F., Zalinescu, E.: Monitoring Data Usage in Distributed Systems. IEEE Trans. on Software Eng. 39(10), 1403–1426 (2013)
20. Janicke, H., Cau, A., Siewe, F., Zedan, H.: Concurrent Enforcement of Usage Control Policies. In: IEEE Workshop on Policies for Distributed Systems and Networks, pp. 111–118 (2008)
21. Bauer, A., Falcone, Y.: Decentralised LTL Monitoring. In: Giannakopoulou, D., Méry, D. (eds.) FM 2012. LNCS, vol. 7436, pp. 85–100. Springer, Heidelberg (2012)
22. Lovat, E., Oudinet, J., Pretschner, A.: On Quantitative Dynamic Data Flow Tracking. In: Proc. 4th ACM Conference on Data and Application Security and Privacy, pp. 211–222 (2014)
23. Lovat, E., Kelbert, F.: Structure Matters – A new Approach for Data Flow Tracking. In: IEEE Security and Privacy Workshops (May 2014)
24. Kelbert, F., Pretschner, A.: Towards a Policy Enforcement Infrastructure for Distributed Usage Control. In: Proc. 17th ACM Symposium on Access Control Models and Technologies, pp. 119–122 (2012)

A   Proofs: Correctness of Function *sys*

Assuming the formulas to be given in disjunctive normal form (DNF), we show that function *sys* as defined in §4.1 is correct in the following sense: For any tuple of concurrently executing traces $\tau \in \prod_{n \in \mathbb{N}} Trace_n$, point in time $i \in \mathbb{N}$, formula $\varphi \in \Phi$, set of subsystems $M = sys(\varphi, i, \tau)$ and $N \subseteq \mathbb{N} \backslash M$ it holds that

$$(t_M^\tau, i) \models \varphi \iff (t_{M \cup N}^\tau, i) \models \varphi.$$

In other words, the set of subsystems $sys(\varphi, i, \tau)$ is sufficient to evaluate φ at time i given τ. Adding any other set of subsystems to the evaluation process does not change the evaluation's result. For each of the following proofs,
part a) shows $(t_M^\tau, i) \models \varphi \implies (t_{M \cup N}^\tau, i) \models \varphi$, while
part b) shows $(t_M^\tau, i) \models \varphi \impliedby (t_{M \cup N}^\tau, i) \models \varphi$.

Because subsystems' states do not overlap ($\Sigma_s : \mathcal{C}_s \to \mathbb{P}(\mathcal{D})$ and $\mathcal{C}_s \cap \mathcal{C}_{s'} = \emptyset$ for $s \neq s'$), for any tuple of concurrently executing traces $\tau \in \prod_{n \in \mathbb{N}} Trace_n$, any point in time $i \in \mathbb{N}$, and any set of subsystems $M \subseteq \mathbb{N}$ we can define their common state as $\sigma_{t_M^\tau}^i = \{x \in (\mathcal{C} \to \mathbb{P}(\mathcal{D})) \mid \exists m \in M : x \in \sigma_{t_m^\tau}^i \}$. It follows that $\forall M, N \subseteq \mathbb{N}, M \subseteq N : \sigma_{t_M^\tau}^i \subseteq \sigma_{t_N^\tau}^i$. We will make use of this relation between states of sets of subsystems throughout the following proofs.

Proof. For $\varphi = e$.

    a) $\forall \tau \in \prod_{n \in \mathbb{N}} Trace_n, i \in \mathbb{N}, e \in \mathcal{E}, \varphi = e, M = sys(\varphi, i, \tau), N \subseteq \mathbb{N} \backslash M :$
$(t_M^\tau, i) \models \varphi$
$\Longleftrightarrow \exists e' \in t_M^\tau(i) : (e', \sigma_{t_M}^i) refines_\Sigma e$
$\Longrightarrow \exists e' \in t_{M \cup N}^\tau(i) : (e', \sigma_{t_{M \cup N}}^i) refines_\Sigma e$
$\Longleftrightarrow (t_{M \cup N}^\tau, i) \models \varphi \,\square$

    b) Assume: $\exists \tau \in \prod_{n \in \mathbb{N}} Trace_n, i \in \mathbb{N}, e \in \mathcal{E}, \varphi = e, M = sys(\varphi, i, \tau)$
$N \subseteq \mathbb{N} \backslash M : (t_{M \cup N}^\tau, i) \models \varphi \wedge (t_M^\tau, i) \not\models \varphi$
$\Longleftrightarrow \exists e' \in t_{M \cup N}^\tau(i) : (e', \sigma_{t_{M \cup N}}^i) \ refines_\Sigma e$
$\wedge \nexists e'' \in t_M^\tau(i) : (e'', \sigma_{t_M}^i) \ refines_\Sigma e$
$\Longrightarrow \exists e' \in t_N^\tau(i) : (e', \sigma_{t_N}^i) \ refines_\Sigma e$
$\Longrightarrow N \cap mayHappen(e, i, \tau) \neq \emptyset$
Since $M = sys(e, i, \tau) = mayHappen(e, i, \tau)$ and $N \subseteq \mathbb{N} \backslash M$
$\Longrightarrow N \cap M \neq \emptyset \wedge N \cap M = \emptyset.$ **Contradiction.** $\square$

Proof. For $\varphi = isCombined(d_1, d_2, C)$.

    a) $\forall \tau \in \prod_{n \in \mathbb{N}} Trace_n, i \in \mathbb{N}, d_1, d_2 \in \mathcal{D}, C \subseteq \mathcal{C}, \varphi = isCombined(d_1, d_2, C),$
$M = sys(\varphi, i, \tau), N \subseteq \mathbb{N} \backslash M :$
$(t_M^\tau, i) \models \varphi \Longleftrightarrow \exists c \in C : \{d_1, d_2\} \subseteq \sigma_{t_M^\tau}^i(c)$
$\Longrightarrow \exists c \in C : \{d_1, d_2\} \subseteq \sigma_{t_{M \cup N}^\tau}^i(c) \Longleftrightarrow (t_{M \cup N}^\tau, i) \models \varphi \,\square$

    b) Assume $\exists \tau \in \prod_{n \in \mathbb{N}} Trace_n, i \in \mathbb{N}, d_1, d_2 \in \mathcal{D}, C \subseteq \mathcal{C},$
$\varphi = isCombined(d_1, d_2, C), M = sys(\varphi, i, \tau), N \subseteq \mathbb{N} \backslash M :$
$(t_{M \cup N}^\tau, i) \models \varphi \wedge (t_M^\tau, i) \not\models \varphi$
$\Longleftrightarrow \exists c \in C : \{d_1, d_2\} \subseteq \sigma_{t_{M \cup N}^\tau}^i(c) \wedge \nexists c' \in C : \{d_1, d_2\} \subseteq \sigma_{t_M^\tau}^i(c')$
$\Longrightarrow \exists c \in C : \{d_1, d_2\} \subseteq \sigma_{t_N^\tau}^i(c) \Longrightarrow \exists c \in \mathcal{C}_N : \{d_1, d_2\} \subseteq \sigma_{t_N^\tau}^i(c)$
Since $N \subseteq \mathbb{N} \backslash M$ and $M = sys(isCombined(d_1, d_2, C), i, \tau)$
$\quad\quad = awareD(\{d_1\}, i, \tau) \cap awareD(\{d_2\}, i, \tau) \cap awareC(C)$
$\Longrightarrow M \cap N = \emptyset \wedge M \cap N \neq \emptyset.$ **Contradiction.** $\square$

We omit proofs for further operators due to space limitations.

B   Proofs: Correctness of Predicate S

We show that predicate S as defined in §4.2 is correct in the following sense: For any tuple of concurrently executing traces $\tau \in \prod_{n \in \mathbb{N}} Trace_n$, set of subsystems $M \subseteq \mathbb{N}$, point in time $i \in \mathbb{N}$, formula $\varphi \in \Phi$, it holds that

$$(t_M^\tau, i) \models \varphi_M \wedge S(\tau, M, i, \varphi) \Longrightarrow (t_{\mathbb{N}}^\tau, i) \models \varphi.$$

Proof. For $sys(\varphi, i, \tau) \subseteq M$.
Follows immediately with the claims and proofs presented in §4.1 and §A.

Proof. For $\varphi = e$

$\forall \tau \in \prod_{n \in \mathbb{N}} Trace_n, e \in \mathcal{E}, M \subseteq \mathbb{N}, i \in \mathbb{N}, \varphi = e :$
$(t_M^\tau, i) \models \varphi_M \Longleftrightarrow \exists e' \in t_M^\tau(i) : (e', \sigma_{t_M}^i) \ refines_\Sigma e$
$\quad\quad \Longrightarrow \exists e' \in t_{\mathbb{N}}^\tau(i) : (e', \sigma_{t_{\mathbb{N}}^\tau}^i) \ refines_\Sigma e \Longleftrightarrow (t_{\mathbb{N}}^\tau, i) \models \varphi \,\square$

Proof. For $\varphi = \underline{isCombined}(d_1, d_2, C)$

$\forall \tau \in \prod_{n \in \mathbb{N}} Trace_n, d_1, d_2 \in \mathcal{D}, C \subseteq \mathcal{C}, M \subseteq \mathbb{N}, i \in \mathbb{N}, \varphi = \underline{isCombined}(d_1, d_2, C):$
$(t_M^\tau, i) \models \varphi_M \iff (t_M^\tau, i) \models \underline{isCombined}(d_1, d_2, C \cap \mathcal{C}_M)$
$\iff \exists c \in C \cap \mathcal{C}_M : \{d_1, d_2\} \subseteq \sigma_{t_M^\tau}^i(c) \implies \exists c \in C : \{d_1, d_2\} \subseteq \sigma_{t_\mathbb{N}}^i(c)$
$\iff (t_\mathbb{N}^\tau, i) \models \underline{isCombined}(d_1, d_2, C) \iff (t_\mathbb{N}^\tau, i) \models \varphi$ $\square$

Proof. For $\varphi = \neg \underline{isNotIn}(d, C)$

$\forall \tau \in \prod_{n \in \mathbb{N}} Trace_n, d \in \mathcal{D}, C \subseteq \mathcal{C}, M \subseteq \mathbb{N}, i \in \mathbb{N}, \varphi = \neg \underline{isNotIn}(d, C):$
$(t_M^\tau, i) \models \varphi_M \iff (t_M^\tau, i) \models \neg \underline{isNotIn}(d, C \cap \mathcal{C}_M)$
$\iff \neg(\forall c \in C \cap \mathcal{C}_M : d \notin \sigma_{t_M^\tau}^i(c)) \iff \exists c \in C \cap \mathcal{C}_M : d \in \sigma_{t_M^\tau}^i(c)$
$\implies \exists c \in C : d \in \sigma_{t_\mathbb{N}^\tau}^i(c) \iff \neg(\forall c \in C : d \notin \sigma_{t_\mathbb{N}^\tau}^i(c))$
$\iff (t_\mathbb{N}^\tau, i) \models \neg \underline{isNotIn}(d, C) \iff (t_\mathbb{N}^\tau, i) \models \varphi$ $\square$

Proof. For $\varphi = \neg \underline{isMaxIn}(d, m, C)$

$\forall \tau \in \prod_{n \in \mathbb{N}} Trace_n, d \in \mathcal{D}, m \in \mathbb{N}, C \subseteq \mathcal{C}, M \subseteq \mathbb{N}, i \in \mathbb{N}, \varphi = \neg \underline{isMaxIn}(d, m, C):$
$(t_M^\tau, i) \models \varphi_M \iff (t_M^\tau, i) \models \neg \underline{isMaxIn}(d, m, C \cap \mathcal{C}_M)$
$\iff |\{c \in C \cap \mathcal{C}_M \mid d \in \sigma_{t_M^\tau}^i(c)\}| > m \implies |\{c \in C \mid d \in \sigma_{t_\mathbb{N}}^i(c)\}| > m$
$\iff (t_\mathbb{N}^\tau, i) \models \neg \underline{isMaxIn}(d, m, C) \iff (t_\mathbb{N}^\tau, i) \models \varphi$ $\square$

Proof. For $\varphi = \alpha \; \underline{before} \; j$

$\forall \tau \in \prod_{n \in \mathbb{N}} Trace_n, \alpha \in \Phi, j \in \mathbb{N}, M \subseteq \mathbb{N}, i \in \mathbb{N}, \varphi = \alpha \; \underline{before} \; j:$
$(t_M^\tau, i) \models \varphi_M \wedge S(\tau, M, i - j, \alpha) \iff (t_M^\tau, i) \models \alpha_M \; \underline{before} \; j \wedge S(\tau, M, i - j, \alpha)$
$\iff (t_M^\tau, i - j) \models \alpha_M \wedge S(\tau, M, i - j, \alpha) \implies (t_\mathbb{N}^\tau, i - j) \models \alpha$
$\iff (t_\mathbb{N}^\tau, i) \models \alpha \; \underline{before} \; j \iff (t_\mathbb{N}^\tau, i) \models \varphi$ $\square$

Proof. For $\varphi = \alpha \; \underline{since} \; \beta$

$\forall \tau \in \prod_{n \in \mathbb{N}} Trace_n, \alpha, \beta \in \Phi, M \subseteq \mathbb{N}, i \in \mathbb{N}, \varphi = \alpha \; \underline{since} \; \beta:$
$(t_M^\tau, i) \models \varphi_M$
$\quad \wedge(\exists j \in [0, i] : ((t_M^\tau, j) \models \beta_M \wedge S(\tau, M, j, \beta)$
$\quad\quad \wedge \forall k \in (j, i] : (t_M^\tau, k) \models \alpha_M \wedge S(\tau, M, k, \alpha))$
$\quad \vee \forall k \in [0, i] : (t_M^\tau, k) \models \alpha_M \wedge S(\tau, M, k, \alpha))$
$\iff (\exists j \in [0, i] : ((t_M^\tau, j) \models \beta_M \wedge \forall k \in (j, i] : (t_M^\tau, k) \models \alpha_M$
$\quad \vee \forall k \in [0, i] : (t_M^\tau, k) \models \alpha_M))$
$\quad \wedge(\exists j \in [0, i] : ((t_M^\tau, j) \models \beta_M \wedge S(\tau, M, j, \beta)$
$\quad\quad \wedge \forall k \in (j, i] : (t_M^\tau, k) \models \alpha_M \wedge S(\tau, M, k, \alpha))$
$\quad \vee \forall k \in [0, i] : (t_M^\tau, k) \models \alpha_M \wedge S(\tau, M, k, \alpha))$
$\iff \exists j \in [0, i] : ((t_M^\tau, j) \models \beta_M \wedge S(\tau, M, j, \beta)$
$\quad\quad \wedge \forall k \in (j, i] : (t_M^\tau, k) \models \alpha_M \wedge S(\tau, M, k, \alpha))$
$\quad \vee \forall k \in [0, i] : (t_M^\tau, k) \models \alpha_M \wedge S(\tau, M, k, \alpha)$
$\implies \exists j \in [0, i] : ((t_\mathbb{N}, j) \models \beta \wedge \forall k \in (j, i] : (t_\mathbb{N}, k) \models \alpha)$
$\quad \vee \forall k \in [0, i] : (t_\mathbb{N}, k) \models \alpha$
$\iff (t_\mathbb{N}, i) \models \alpha \; \underline{since} \; \beta \iff (t_\mathbb{N}, i) \models \varphi$ $\square$

Proof. For $\varphi = \alpha \ \underline{or} \ \beta$

$\forall \tau \in \prod_{n \in \mathbb{N}} Trace_n, \alpha, \beta \in \Phi, M \subseteq \mathbb{N}, i \in \mathbb{N}, \varphi = \alpha \ \underline{or} \ \beta :$
$(t_M^\tau, i) \models \varphi_M \wedge ((t_M^\tau, i) \models \alpha_M \wedge S(\tau, M, i, \alpha) \vee (t_M^\tau, i) \models \beta_M \wedge S(\tau, M, i, \beta))$
$\iff ((t_M^\tau, i) \models \alpha_M \vee (t_M^\tau, i) \models \beta_M)$
$\qquad \wedge ((t_M^\tau, i) \models \alpha_M \wedge S(\tau, M, i, \alpha) \vee (t_M^\tau, i) \models \beta_M \wedge S(\tau, M, i, \beta))$
$\iff (t_M^\tau, i) \models \alpha_M \wedge S(\tau, M, i, \alpha) \vee (t_M^\tau, i) \models \beta_M \wedge S(\tau, M, i, \beta)$
$\implies (t_{\mathbb{N}}^\tau, i) \models \alpha \vee (t_{\mathbb{N}}^\tau, i) \models \beta \iff (t_{\mathbb{N}}^\tau, i) \models \alpha \ \underline{or} \ \beta \iff (t_{\mathbb{N}}^\tau, i) \models \varphi \ \square$

Proof. For $\varphi = \underline{repmin}(j, m, e)$

$\forall \tau \in \prod_{n \in \mathbb{N}} Trace_n, j, m \in \mathbb{N}, e \in \mathcal{E}, M \subseteq \mathbb{N}, i \in \mathbb{N}, \varphi = \underline{repmin}(j, m, e) :$
$(t_M^\tau, i) \models \varphi_M \iff (t_M^\tau, i) \models \underline{repmin}(j, m, e)$
$\iff m \leq \sum_{k=0}^{j-1} |\{e' \in t_M^\tau(i - k) \mid (e', \sigma_{t_M^\tau}^{i-k}) \ refines_\Sigma \ e\}|$
$\implies m \leq \sum_{k=0}^{j-1} |\{e' \in t_{\mathbb{N}}^\tau(i - k) \mid (e', \sigma_{t_{\mathbb{N}}}^{i-k}) \ refines_\Sigma \ e\}|$
$\iff (t_{\mathbb{N}}^\tau, i) \models \underline{repmin}(j, m, e) \iff (t_{\mathbb{N}}^\tau, i) \models \varphi \ \square$

Again, we omit proofs for further operators due to space limitations.

Efficient Signatures with Tight Real World Security in the Random-Oracle Model

Christoph Bader

Horst Görtz Institute, Ruhr-University Bochum, Germany
`christoph.bader@rub.de`

Abstract. Security for digital signature schemes is most commonly analyzed in an ideal single user setting where the attacker is provided only with a single public key. However, when digital signature schemes are deployed in practice they are often used by many users, each having its own public key, e.g., in authenticated key exchange (AKE) protocols. Common security models for AKE model real world capabilities of an adversary by allowing it (among others) to corrupt secret user keys. For digital signatures it is well known that security in the idealized single user setting implies security in this stronger and more realistic multi user setting with corruptions. However, the security reduction loses a factor which is linear in the number of users. It is not clear how to avoid this loss in general.

In this paper we propose an efficient signature scheme whose security reduction in the above setting is tight. The security reduction loses a factor of about 2. When 80 bits of security are required our signatures are of size roughly 2700 bits.

Keywords: Tight security, digital signatures, Groth-Sahai proofs, Katz-Wang technique, random-oracle heuristic.

1 Introduction

When a new cryptographic scheme is proposed, nowadays the construction comes along with a proof of security. Most commonly, the proof describes an efficient algorithm, the *reduction*, that turns any successful attacker against the scheme (with respect to the considered security notion) into another efficient algorithm that breaks a supposed to be hard problem. The quality of a reduction R is measured in terms of its success probability ϵ_R relative to its running time t_R. Ideally we have $\frac{\epsilon_R}{t_R} = \mathcal{O}(\frac{\epsilon_F}{t_F})$ where ϵ_F and t_F denote the success probability and the running time of the forger. In this case the reduction is said to be *tight* and the cryptographic scheme is said to have tight security. Tight reductions are a desirable goal since the quality of a reduction influences the size of the system parameters when they are selected in a theoretically sound way, cf. table 1. There exist implementations of many cryptographic primitives that come along with an (almost) tight reduction in the standard or the random oracle model, e.g., for digital signatures in the single user setting [8,21,9,28,20], for public key encryption in the multi user setting [5,17] and for AKE [3].

D. Gritzalis et al. (Eds.): CANS 2014, LNCS 8813, pp. 370–383, 2014.

Digital Signatures in the Multi User setting. The standard security notion for digital signatures (in the single user setting) is existential unforgeability under chosen message attacks (EUF-CMA-security) [15]. EUF-CMA-security was later extended to the multi user setting *without* corruptions [25]. Recently, [3] introduced the notion of *existential unforgeability under chosen message attacks in the multi user setting* with *adaptive corruptions* (MU-EUF-CMA^{Corr}-security). Here the attacker is considered successful if it manages to produce a signature for a message m (that was not signed before with respect to the target public key) that verifies under an uncorrupted public key (the target public key). While tightness in the single user setting is mostly considered with respect to the number μ of sign queries issued by the attacker, in the multi user setting tightness is additionally considered relative to the number ℓ of public keys the adversary has access to and that it may corrupt. Hence, for digital signatures in the multi user setting there are two dimensions to consider tightness in.

It is well known [25,3] that standard EUF-CMA security (i.e., $\ell = 1$) implies MU-EUF-CMA^{Corr}-security. However, the generic reduction loses a factor of ℓ, i.e., $\frac{\epsilon_R}{t_R} = \mathcal{O}(\ell \cdot \frac{\epsilon_F}{t_F})$ and it is not clear how to avoid this loss in general. On the bright side this means that the proofs from [9,28,20] give rise to digital signature schemes in the multi user setting with corruptions that come along with a proof that only depends (linearly) on ℓ (the number of public keys) but is independent of μ (the number of sign queries issued by the attacker). Recently, standard model schemes that come along with a reduction that is independent of μ *and* ℓ were proposed [3]. However, as the authors remark due to its large signature size the full tight scheme from [3] is rather a feasability result. While the almost tight scheme from [3] supports very short signatures it has public parameters that are linear in the length of messages.

We stress that common security models for *authenticated* key exchange (AKE) or channel establishment (ACCE), e.g. [7,11,19], allow the adversary to corrupt long-term secret keys which often are secret keys of a signature scheme, e.g., in ephemeral Diffie-Hellman Ciphersuites of the TLS-Handshake [14] or when compilers lift a passively secure protocol to meet stronger security notions [6,22,18,23]. Therefore, the MU-EUF-CMA^{Corr} security notion is implicitly widely used in practice. However, the security proofs for most schemes apply the "polynomial equivalence between EUF-CMA and MU-EUF-CMA^{Corr} security" argument which incurs a loss of ℓ for the reduction and requires larger parameters when the scheme is implemented in practice. Therefore an efficient signature scheme, i.e., small signatures *and* public parameters, that comes along with a tight MU-EUF-CMA^{Corr} security reduction is a desirable goal with practical applications. In particular, plugging in a tightly MU-EUF-CMA^{Corr}-secure signature scheme into the tightness preserving compiler from [3] leads to a tightly secure authenticated key exchange protocol the efficiency of which is roughly determined by the efficiency of the signature scheme.

Our Contribution. In this paper we propose a signature scheme that tightly satisfies MU-EUF-CMA^{Corr} security, i.e., the running time and the success probability of the reduction are roughly the same as the running time and the success

Table 1. Comparison between our scheme and random oracle signature schemes from the literature. We compare public key size and signature size in bits when parameters are selected to obtain 80 bits of security in a theoretically sound way (i.e., parameter selection considers the security loss) following NIST recommendations [4]. Following [8] we assume $\mu = 2^{30}$ sign-queries and $q_h = 2^{60}$ hash-queries per public key. The BLS and ECDSA schemes as well as our scheme do also require common public parameters. These are omitted in our comparison since they have to be stored only once by each user.

| | $\ell = 1$ | | $\ell = 2^{16}$ | | $\ell = 2^{45}$ | | Loss | Assumption |
	$\|vk\|$	$\|\sigma\|$	$\|vk\|$	$\|\sigma\|$	$\|vk\|$	$\|\sigma\|$		
ECDSA [29,1,30]	≈ 280	≈ 560	≈ 312	≈ 624	≈ 370	≈ 740	$\mathcal{O}(q_h \ell)$	DLOG
BLS [10]	≈ 2000	≈ 220	≈ 3000	≈ 256	> 4000	≈ 310	$\mathcal{O}(\mu \ell)$	CDH
RSA PSS [8,12]	> 1024	1024	> 1350	≈ 1350	> 3000	≈ 3000	$\mathcal{O}(\ell)$	RSA
Ours	1024	2688	1024	2688	1024	2688	$\mathcal{O}(1)$	SXDH

probability of the adversary (and in particular independent of μ and ℓ except for a negligible fraction). The security reduction loses roughly a factor of 2. The scheme works over asymmetric bilinear groups $\mathbb{G} = (\mathcal{G}_1, \mathcal{G}_2, \mathcal{G}_T)$ equipped with an efficiently computable pairing $e : \mathcal{G}_1 \times \mathcal{G}_2 \to \mathcal{G}_T$. Public parameters contain a description of the group, one additional element from $\mathcal{G}_1$, two additional elements from $\mathcal{G}_2$ and the description of a Hash-function. A public key is a single group element from $\mathcal{G}_2$ and signatures live in $\mathcal{G}_1^4 \times \mathcal{G}_2^2$. Table 1 compares our signature scheme to random oracle signature schemes from the literature. We observe that if the number of users is 2^{16} then the signature size of our scheme is roughly twice the size of an RSA PSS signature and 10 times the size of a BLS signature. Our scheme outperforms RSA PSS in both, public key size and signature size, if the number of public keys is about 2^{45} which is a very large number. However, even in this case, BLS and ECDSA signatures are shorter than our signatures. Therefore, for most of today's practical applications our scheme is no better than known solutions. However, due to the loss of the generic reduction (see above) and to some problems that occur by natural approaches (see end of this section) we find it interesting in its own right to construct a signature scheme with tight MU-EUF-CMA^{Corr} security.

Technical Approach. When designing an MU-EUF-CMA^{Corr}-secure signature scheme with tight reduction we are faced with the following problem: On the one hand we need to be able to reveal the secret key to any public key (note that guessing the target public key would cause a loss of ℓ) and on the other hand we must be able to extract a solution to a hard problem from (almost) any forgery that is output by the adversary. That is, we must be able to extract a solution from a forgery even if we know the secret key corresponding to the target public key. To face this problem, we apply non-interactive proof systems that provide two computationally indistinguishable modes of common reference strings (CRS), perfectly *binding* ones and perfectly *hiding* ones. A perfectly binding CRS allows to extract knowledge from a given proof while a perfectly hiding

CRS does not. A signature will roughly be a proof (using a suitable proof system) that the signer 'knows' a one time signature. Now, to extract a solution from an adversarially generated signature the proof output by the adversary needs to be binding. Note that we do not know the target public key and message up front. At the same time, to hide all critical information from the adversary all proofs output by the reduction need to be hiding.

To achieve this we apply the random oracle in a way similar to Katz-Wang [21] to the (standard model, DLIN-based) linearly homomorphic signature scheme from [24] converted to the SXDH-setting. Namely, public parameters contain part of a Groth-Sahai CRS [16]. To sign a message m, a bit b is sampled uniformly at random. The message is hashed together with b and the public key of the signer to complete the CRS. Finally, using the secret key, a one time signature over m is computed and correctness of the computed signature is proved with respect to the CRS. During the security reduction the random oracle will be programmed such that for each pair of message m and public key vk one out of two possible CRS (recall that m and vk are hashed together with b) is perfectly hiding and the other one is perfectly binding. Both are indistinguishable under a computational assumption. Now, the reduction will make all proofs on a hiding CRS (and thus leak no information about sk) and with high probability the adversary will output a forgery on a binding CRS from which we can extract a solution to a hard problem with overwhelming probability.

A note on schemes from OR proofs. We note that it might look heavy to use the random oracle heuristic in combination with pairings at all and in particular to additionally use Groth-Sahai proofs. Probably the most natural way to construct a tightly secure scheme in the ROM would be to apply OR proofs as introduced in [13] to Fiat-Shamir like signature schemes that have a tight reduction, e.g. [21]. Similar to the fully tight construction from [3] and following the Naor-Yung paradigm [27], a public key in such MU-EUF-CMA[Corr]-secure scheme would consist of two public keys (vk_0, vk_1) of the underlying signature scheme whereas the secret key would consist only of one of the corresponding secret keys, sk_δ. A signature on message m would be a witness indistinguishable OR proof that the signer 'knows' a signature on m that validates under vk_0 or vk_1. The OR proofs from [13] provide *perfect* witness indistinguishability. Therefore it remains information theoretically hidden from the view of the adversary which secret key is known by the reduction. Unfortunately perfect witness indistinguishability makes the reduction fail to actually extract knowledge from the forgery output by the adversary.

If we are to apply pairings we can resort to Groth-Sahai proofs [16] and could apply a similar technique. However, in this case we need to prove satisfiability of a set of quadratic equations which makes the proofs expensive, i.e., large. Since we are interested in efficient schemes we do not apply this technique. We note however that this technique works even in the standard model [3]. However, it leads to rather long signatures.

2   Preliminaries

Notation. By $[n]$ we denote the set $[n] := \{1, 2, \ldots, n\}$. If A is a set then by $a \xleftarrow{\$} A$ we denote the action of sampling a uniformly from A. If A is an algorithm then $a \leftarrow A(x)$ denotes that A outputs a when run on input x with fresh uniformly random coins. By PPT we will abbreviate probabilistic polynomial time. If an algorithm A has black-box access to an algorithm $\mathcal{O}$, we will write $A^{\mathcal{O}}$.

By $\mathbb{G} = (e, \mathcal{G}_1, \mathcal{G}_2, \mathcal{G}_T, g_1, g_2, p)$ we denote the description of an asymmetric bilinear group. That is, $e : \mathcal{G}_1 \times \mathcal{G}_2 \to \mathcal{G}_T$ is a non-degenerate bilinear map, g_b is a generator of $\mathcal{G}_b$ and $|\mathcal{G}_1| = |\mathcal{G}_2| = |\mathcal{G}_T| = p$ where p is prime. It is well known that there is a PPT algorithm that on input 1^{κ} returns $\mathbb{G}$ such that $2^{\kappa} < p \leq 2^{\kappa+1}$. We denote this algorithm by GEN.asym(1^{κ}). Throughout the paper we reasonably assume the non-existence of efficiently computable homomorphisms between $\mathcal{G}_1$ and $\mathcal{G}_2$. Given elements $h \in \mathcal{G}_2$ and $\vec{g} = (g, k) \in \mathcal{G}_1^2$ we denote by $E(\vec{g}, h)$ the vector $(e(g, h), e(k, h))$.

Complexity Assumptions. Let in the sequel be $b \in \{1, 2\}$. Given $g, h \in \mathcal{G}_b^2$ we denote by $\mathsf{DDH}_b(g, h)$ the set $\mathsf{DDH}_b(g, h) := \left\{ (\hat{g}, \hat{h}) \in \mathcal{G}_b^2 : \log_g(\hat{g}) = \log_h(\hat{h}) \right\}$.

Definition 1. *Let $\mathbb{G} = (e, \mathcal{G}_1, \mathcal{G}_2, \mathcal{G}_T, g_1, g_2, p) \xleftarrow{\$} \mathsf{GEN.asym}(1^{\kappa})$. We say that an adversary (t, ϵ)-breaks the external Diffie-Hellman assumption in $\mathcal{G}_b$ (XDH$_b$ assumption) if it runs in time t and*

$$\left| \Pr \left[\mathcal{A}(\mathbb{G}, g, h, \hat{g}, \hat{h}) = 1 : (g, h) \xleftarrow{\$} \mathcal{G}_b^2 \wedge (\hat{g}, \hat{h}) \xleftarrow{\$} \mathsf{DDH}(g, h) \right] \right.$$
$$\left. - \Pr \left[\mathcal{A}(\mathbb{G}, g, h, \hat{g}, \hat{h}) = 1 : (g, h) \xleftarrow{\$} \mathcal{G}_b^2 \wedge (\hat{g}, \hat{h}) \xleftarrow{\$} \mathcal{G}_b^2 \right] \right| \geq \epsilon$$

where the probability is over the random choices of $g, h, \hat{g}, \hat{h}$ and the random coins of $\mathcal{A}$.

We say that an adversary (t, ϵ)-breaks the symmetric external Diffie-Hellman assumption in $\mathbb{G}$ if it (t, ϵ)-breaks the XDH$_1$ or XDH$_2$ assumption.

A given instance of the XDH$_b$ problem is efficiently re-randomizable [26,5]. That is, there is an efficient algorithm that, on input $(g, h, \hat{g}, \hat{h}, 1^q)$, outputs q tuples $(g_i, h_i), i \in [q]$ such that

$$(g_i, h_i) \xleftarrow{\$} \mathsf{DDH}(g, h) \text{ if } (\hat{g}, \hat{h}) \in \mathsf{DDH}(g, h)$$
$$(g_i, h_i) \xleftarrow{\$} \mathcal{G}_b^2 \text{ if } (\hat{g}, \hat{h}) \notin \mathsf{DDH}(g, h).$$

Definition 2. *Let $\mathbb{G} = (e, \mathcal{G}_1, \mathcal{G}_2, \mathcal{G}_T, g_1, g_2, p) \xleftarrow{\$} \mathsf{GEN.asym}(1^{\kappa})$ and $(g_z, g_r) \xleftarrow{\$} \mathcal{G}_2^2$. We say that an adversary (t, ϵ)-breaks the double pairing assumption in $\mathcal{G}_2$ (DP$_2$ assumption) if it runs in time t and*

$$\Pr \left[(z, r) \neq (1, 1) \wedge e(z, g_z) \cdot e(r, g_r) = 1 : (z, r) \leftarrow \mathcal{A}(\mathbb{G}, g_z, g_r) \right] \geq \epsilon$$

where the probability is over the random choices of g_z and g_r and the random coins of $\mathcal{A}$.

We define the DP$_1$ assumption analogously.

Lemma 1 ([2]). *For any attacker $\mathcal{A}$ that $(t_{\mathsf{DP}_b}, \epsilon_{\mathsf{DP}_b})$-breaks the DP assumption in $\mathcal{G}_b$ (where $b \in \{1, 2\}$) there exists an attacker $\mathcal{B}$ that $(t_{\mathsf{XDH}}, \epsilon_{\mathsf{XDH}})$-breaks the XDH assumtion in $\mathcal{G}_b$ where $t_{\mathsf{DP}_b} \approx t_{\mathsf{XDH}}$ and $\epsilon_{\mathsf{XDH}} \geq \epsilon_{\mathsf{DP}_b}$.*

Proof. Let wlog $b = 2$. Algorithm $\mathcal{B}$, given an XDH_2 instance $(\mathbb{G}, g, h, \hat{g}, \hat{h})$, runs $\mathcal{A}$ as a subroutine on input $(\mathbb{G}, g, \hat{g})$. When $\mathcal{A}$ outputs (z, r) such that $e(z, g) \cdot e(r, \hat{g}) = 1$ we know that $\log_z(r) = -\log_{\hat{g}}(g)$ and thus $e(z, h) \cdot e(r, \hat{h}) = 1 \Leftrightarrow (\hat{g}, \hat{h}) \in \mathsf{DDH}(g, h)$.

3 Digital Signature Schemes in the Multi User Setting

Syntax. A digital signature scheme $\mathsf{SIG} = (\mathsf{Setup}, \mathsf{Gen}, \mathsf{Sign}, \mathsf{Vfy})$ is a four-tuple of PPT algorithms.

Public Parameters. The parameter generation algorithm $\Pi \leftarrow^{\$} \mathsf{Setup}(1^{\kappa})$ on input 1^{κ} returns public parameters. We silently assume that 1^{κ} is contained in Π. We note that while Setup often is omitted in the single user setting it is convenient to define it in the multi user setting. If not explicitly required, it just outputs 1^{κ}.

Key Generation. The key generation algorithm when input Π outputs a key pair, $(vk, sk) \leftarrow^{\$} \mathsf{Gen}(\Pi)$. Even if not explicitly stated we assume that vk contains at least Π and that sk contains vk.

Signature Generation. The signature generation algorithm, given a secret key sk and message m, outputs a signature σ on that message. That is, it returns $\sigma \leftarrow^{\$} \mathsf{Sign}(sk, m)$.

Verification. The verification algorithm accepts or rejects a signature over a message with respect to a given public key, $\mathsf{Vfy}(vk, m, \sigma) \in \{0, 1\}$.

For correctness we require that for all κ, all $\Pi \leftarrow^{\$} \mathsf{Gen}(1^{\kappa})$, all $(vk, sk) \leftarrow^{\$} \mathsf{Gen}(\Pi)$ and any message m that

$$\Pr\left[\mathsf{Vfy}(vk, m, \sigma) = 1 : \sigma \leftarrow^{\$} \mathsf{Sign}(sk, m)\right] = 1.$$

Security Notion. Consider the following security experiment that is played between a challenger $\mathcal{C}$ and an adversary $\mathcal{A}$ and that is parametrized by μ, the number of overall sign queries the adversary may issue and ℓ the number of public keys the adversary has access to and that it may corrupt.

1. On input 1^{κ} the challenger runs $\Pi \leftarrow^{\$} \mathsf{Setup}(1^{\kappa})$ and samples $(vk_i, sk_i) \leftarrow^{\$} \mathsf{Gen}(\Pi), i \in [\ell]$. Next, it initializes a set $\mathcal{S}^{\mathsf{Corrupt}} \leftarrow \emptyset$ to keep track of corrupted keys and sets $\mathcal{S}^i \leftarrow \emptyset$ to keep track of messages that were signed with respect to public key vk_i. It passes $vk_i, i \in [\ell]$ to $\mathcal{A}$.

2. The adversary may now adaptively issue *sign*-queries (m, i) where m is a message and $i \in [\ell]$ and *corrupt*-queries i (where also $i \in [\ell]$). $\mathcal{C}$ responds to the respective queries as follows. When issued a sign query (m, i), $\mathcal{C}$ updates $\mathcal{S}^i$ to $\mathcal{S}^i \leftarrow \mathcal{S}^i \cup \{m\}$. Next, it returns $\sigma \leftarrow^{\$} \mathsf{Sign}(sk_i, m)$. When issued a corrupt query i, $\mathcal{C}$ updates $\mathcal{S}^{\mathsf{Corrupt}}$ to $\mathcal{S}^{\mathsf{Corrupt}} \leftarrow \mathcal{S}^{\mathsf{Corrupt}} \cup \{i\}$ and returns sk_i. $\mathcal{A}$ is restricted to perform no more than μ overall sign-queries.

3. Finally, $\mathcal{A}$ outputs a forgery (i^*, m^*, σ^*).

Definition 3 (MU-EUF-CMA^{Corr}-security). *We say that an adversary* $(t, \mu, \ell,$ $\epsilon)$-breaks the *multi user existential unforgeability under chosen message attacks with adaptive corruptions security of a signature scheme* SIG *if it runs in time* t *in the above security game and*

$$\Pr\left[\mathsf{Vfy}(vk_{i^*}, m^*, \sigma^*) = 1 : i^* \notin \mathcal{S}^{\mathsf{Corrupt}} \wedge m^* \notin \mathcal{S}^{i^*}\right] \geq \epsilon.$$

4   Non-interactive Proof Systems

Given a binary relation $R \subseteq X \times W$ and (x, w) such that $R(x, w)$ we call x the statement and w the witness. A non-interactive proof system NIPS = (Gen, Prove, Vfy) for witness relation R is a three-tuple of PPT algorithms.

- The common reference string generation algorithm, on input 1^κ, returns a *common reference string*, CRS $\leftarrow^\$ \mathsf{Gen}(1^\kappa)$.
- The prove algorithm when input (x, w) such that $R(x, w)$ returns a proof $\pi \leftarrow^\$ \mathsf{Prove}(\mathsf{CRS}, x, w)$ with respect to CRS.
- The verification algorithm verifies a proof, $\mathsf{Vfy}(\mathsf{CRS}, x, \pi) \in \{0, 1\}$.

Definition 4. *We call* NIPS *a witness indistinguishable proof of knowledge (NIWI-PoK) for R, if the following conditions are satisfied:*

Perfect completeness. *For all* $\kappa \in \mathbb{N}$ *it holds that if* $R(x, w)$ *then*

$$\Pr\left[\mathsf{NIPS.Vfy}(\mathsf{CRS}, x, \pi) = 1 : \mathsf{CRS} \leftarrow^\$ \mathsf{NIPS.Gen}(1^\kappa) \wedge \pi \leftarrow^\$ \mathsf{Prove}(\mathsf{CRS}, x, w)\right] = 1$$

Perfect Witness Indistinguishability. *Let* CRS $\leftarrow^\$ \mathsf{Gen}(1^\kappa)$. *For* $b \in \{0, 1\}$ *we denote by* $\mathcal{O}_b$ *an oracle that when input* (x, w_0, w_1) *such that* $R(x, w_b)$ *returns* $\pi \leftarrow^\$ \mathsf{Prove}(\mathsf{CRS}, x, w_b)$. *We require*

$$\Pr\left[\mathcal{A}^{\mathcal{O}_0} = 1\right] = \Pr\left[\mathcal{A}^{\mathcal{O}_1} = 1\right]$$

Simulated CRS. *There exists an algorithm* $(\mathsf{CRS}_{\mathsf{sim}}, \tau) \leftarrow^\$ \mathcal{E}_0$ *that, on input* 1^κ, *outputs a simulated common reference string* $\mathsf{CRS}_{\mathsf{sim}}$ *and a trapdoor* τ.

Perfect Knowledge Extraction on Simulated CRS.   *Let* $(\mathsf{CRS}_{\mathsf{sim}}, \tau) \leftarrow^\$$ $\mathcal{E}_0(1^\kappa)$. *We require the existence of an algorithm* $\mathcal{E}_1$ *such that for all* $(\pi, x) \leftarrow$ $\mathcal{A}$ *that satisfy* $\mathsf{NIPS.Vfy}(\mathsf{CRS}_{\mathsf{sim}}, x, \pi) = 1$ *it holds that*

$$\Pr\left[w \leftarrow^\$ \mathcal{E}_1(\mathsf{CRS}_{\mathsf{sim}}, \pi, x, \tau) : (x, w) \in R\right] = 1$$

Secure NIWI-PoK. *Let* $\mathsf{CRS}_{\mathsf{real}} \leftarrow^\$ \mathsf{NIPS.Gen}(1^\kappa)$ *and* $(\mathsf{CRS}_{\mathsf{sim}}, \tau) \leftarrow^\$ \mathcal{E}_0(1^\kappa)$. *We say that an algorithm* $(t, \epsilon_{\mathsf{CRS}})$-breaks *the security of a NIWI-PoK if it runs in time* t *and it holds that*

$$\Pr\left[\mathcal{A}(\mathsf{CRS}_{\mathsf{real}}) = 1)\right] - \Pr\left[\mathcal{A}(\mathsf{CRS}_{\mathsf{sim}}) = 1\right] \geq \epsilon_{\mathsf{CRS}}$$

If CRS $\leftarrow^\$ \mathsf{Gen}(1^\kappa)$ we call CRS hiding and if $(\mathsf{CRS}_{\mathsf{sim}}, \cdot) \leftarrow^\$ \mathcal{E}_0(1^\kappa)$ we call $\mathsf{CRS}_{\mathsf{sim}}$ binding. It is easy to verify that perfect witness indistinguishability on a hiding CRS is preserved if many statements are proven.

Defining a Relation. Consider the following equation over (z, r)

$$1 = e(z, k_z) \cdot e(r, k_r) \cdot e(m, k) \tag{1}$$

The core of our signature scheme will be the assumption (which we will justify later) that given (k_z, k_r, k, m) it is hard to compute (z, r) that satisfy equation 1. We define a relation as follows:

$$R\left((k_z, k_r, k, m), (z, r)\right) = \begin{cases} 1, \text{ if } 1 = e(z, k_z) \cdot e(r, k_r) \cdot e(m, k) \\ 0, \text{ else} \end{cases}$$

Suitable Proof Systems. The SXDH-based Groth-Sahai proof system [16] is an (efficient) proof system for witness relation R. Note that equation 1 is *linear* where the variables live in $\mathcal{G}_1$. In this case each commitment costs two elements from $\mathcal{G}_1$ and a proof element costs additional two elements from $\mathcal{G}_2$ (instead of four elements from $\mathcal{G}_1$ and $\mathcal{G}_2$ if we had quadratic equations).

Since we need the notation for our signature scheme we recall SXDH-based Groth-Sahai proofs with efficiency improved verification [24] for relation R here.

CRS $\leftarrow^\$$ Gen(1^κ): The common reference string generation algorithm samples $\mathbb{G} = (e, \mathcal{G}_1, \mathcal{G}_2, \mathcal{G}_T, g_1, g_2, p) \leftarrow^\$$ GEN.asym(1^κ), $\vec{v}_1 = (g_1, f_1) \leftarrow^\$ \mathcal{G}_1^2$ and $\vec{v}_2 = (\hat{g}_1, \hat{f}_1) \notin$ DDH(g_1, f_1). It returns $(\mathbb{G}, \vec{v}_1, \vec{v}_2)$.

$\pi \leftarrow^\$$ Prove(CRS, $(k_z, k_r, k, m), (z, r)$): The prove algorithm first commits to z and r via

$$C_z = (1, z) \cdot \vec{v}_1^{\delta_{z,1}} \cdot \vec{v}_2^{\delta_{z,2}}$$
$$C_r = (1, r) \cdot \vec{v}_1^{\delta_{r,1}} \cdot \vec{v}_2^{\delta_{r,2}}$$

where multiplication is done component-wise. Next, it computes proofs that the commitments actually contain a solution to equation 1. These are computed as

$$\pi' = (\pi_1', \pi_2') = \left(k_z^{-\delta_{z,1}} \cdot k_r^{-\delta_{r,1}}, k_z^{-\delta_{z,2}} \cdot k_r^{-\delta_{r,2}}\right)$$

The proof is returned as $\pi = (C_z, C_r, \pi') \in \mathcal{G}_1^4 \times \mathcal{G}_2^2$.

Vfy(CRS, $(k_z, k_r, k, m), \pi$): The verification algorithm outputs 1 iff

$$(E((1, m), k))^{-1} = E(C_z, k_z) \cdot E(C_r, k_r) \cdot E(\vec{v}_1, \pi_1') \cdot E(\vec{v}_2, \pi_2') \tag{2}$$

(CRS$_{\text{sim}}$, td) $\leftarrow^\$ \mathcal{E}_0(1^\kappa)$: The simulated CRS generation algorithm samples $\mathbb{G} = (e, \mathcal{G}_1, \mathcal{G}_2, \mathcal{G}_T, g_1, g_2, p) \leftarrow^\$$ GEN.asym(1^κ), $\vec{v}_1 = (g_1, f_1) \leftarrow^\$ \mathcal{G}_1^2$ and $\vec{v}_2 = (\hat{g}_1, \hat{f}_1) \leftarrow^\$$ DDH(g_1, f_1). It sets $x = \log_{g_1}(f_1)$ and returns $((\mathbb{G}, \vec{v}_1, \vec{v}_2), x)$.

That for any attacker $\mathcal{A}$ that $(t_{\mathcal{A}}, \epsilon_{\mathcal{A}})$-breaks the NIWI-PoK security of this proof system there is an attacker $\mathcal{B}$ that $(t_{\mathcal{B}}, \epsilon_{\mathcal{B}})$-breaks the SXDH-assumption in $\mathbb{G}$ with $t_{\mathcal{A}} \approx t_{\mathcal{B}}$ and $\epsilon_{\mathcal{B}} \geq \epsilon_{\mathcal{A}}$ is proven in [16]. We stress that if $\vec{v}_2 \in$ DDH($\vec{v}_1$) then $(\vec{v}_1, \vec{v}_2)$ is a perfectly binding CRS whereas if $\vec{v}_2 \notin$ DDH($\vec{v}_1$) then $(\vec{v}_1, \vec{v}_2)$ yields a perfectly hiding CRS both of which are computationally indistinguishable under the XDH$_1$ assumption in $\mathbb{G}$.

5   Our New Signature Scheme

Intuition of our scheme. Before we introduce our scheme formally we would like to give some intuition what is behind the scheme. Actually our scheme is similar to the DLIN-based signature scheme from [24] that allows for *linear* OR-proofs. However, we do not need OR-proofs at all.

A signature over m is an SXDH-based Groth-Sahai proof [16] of satisfiability of equation 1 (where (k_z, k_r, k) are given in the public parameters and the public key, respectively). The system parameters contain part of a Groth-Sahai CRS for relation R described in the previous section. The hash of a message, the verification key of the signer and a uniformly random bit completes the CRS. Now, the signer (using sk) computes (z, r) that satisfies equation 1 and generates a proof of this fact using Prove from the proof system of the previous section. We note that there are many possible solutions to equation 1. The secret key of our signature scheme allows to compute exactly one satisfying solution to equation 1. However, two *distinct* solutions yield a solution to the instance (k_z, k_r) of the DP_2 problem.

Description of our scheme. The scheme works as follows.

SIG.Setup(1^κ). The setup algorithm, on input 1^κ, works as follows:
1. Sample $\mathbb{G} = (e, \mathcal{G}_1, \mathcal{G}_2, \mathcal{G}_T, g_1, g_2, p) \leftarrow^\$ \mathsf{GEN.asym}(1^\kappa)$.
2. Sample $f_1 \leftarrow^\$ \mathcal{G}_1$ and $k_z, k_r \leftarrow^\$ \mathcal{G}_2$ and set $\vec{v}_1 = (g_1, f_1)$.
3. Choose a hash-function $H : \{0,1\}^* \to \mathcal{G}_1$. The security analysis will view H as a random oracle.

It returns $\Pi \leftarrow (\mathbb{G}, k_z, k_r, \vec{v}_1, H)$. The message space is $\mathcal{G}_1$.

SIG.Gen(Π). The key generation algorithm samples $\chi, \gamma \leftarrow^\$ \mathbb{Z}_p$ and computes $k = k_z^\chi k_r^\gamma \in \mathcal{G}_2$. The key is returned as $(vk, sk) \leftarrow (k, (\chi, \gamma))$.

SIG.Sign(sk, m). The sign algorithm first checks if m has been already signed. If this is the case it recovers the bit $b_{vk,m}$ that was previously used to sign m [1]. Else it samples $b_{vk,m} \leftarrow^\$ \{0,1\}$. Next, it proceeds as follows (recall that $m \in \mathcal{G}_1$).
1. Compute $z = m^{-\chi}$ and $r = m^{-\gamma}$.
2. Compute $\vec{v}_2 = (H(0||vk||m||b_{vk,m}), H(1|vk|||m||b_{vk,m})) \in \mathcal{G}_1^2$ and set $\mathsf{CRS} = (\vec{v}_1, \vec{v}_2)$.
3. Run the prove algorithm for relation R from the previous section and return $\sigma \leftarrow^\$ \mathsf{Prove}(\mathsf{CRS}, (k_z, k_r, k, m), (z, r)) \in \mathcal{G}_1^4 \times \mathcal{G}_2^2$.

SIG.Vfy(vk, m, σ). The verification algorithm accepts iff $\mathsf{Vfy}(\mathsf{CRS}, (k_z, k_r, k, m), \sigma)$ where $\mathsf{CRS} = (\vec{v}_1, \vec{v}_2)$ and $v_2 = (H(0||vk||m||0), H(1||vk||m||0))$ or $v_2 = (H(0||vk||m||1), H(1||vk||m||1))$.

---

[1] Note that we could also let the signer evaluate a pseudo-random function on m to determine b. According to [21] another very simple solution is to determine b by evaluating another hash function H' on m and vk (which again will be viewed as a random oracle by the analysis). This way the signer does not need to maintain states.

Remark 1 (On the requirement of a trusted setup). We note that if the scheme is implemented the way we describe it here we require Setup to be run by a trusted party. We can get rid of this requirement if we let the public parameters contain only the description of the group. In this case each user needs to choose $H, \vec{v}_1 \leftarrow^\$ \mathcal{G}_1^2$ and $k_z, k_r \leftarrow^\$ \mathcal{G}_2$ itself and publish these as part of its public key. By the random self reducibility of DDH and DP the tightness of the reduction will be preserved. However, this approach leads to longer public keys. Because of this and for ease of readability we chose to describe the scheme as above.

Next, we show that there is a tight reduction from breaking the SXDH-assumption to breaking the unforgeability of the above signature scheme.

Theorem 1. *For any attacker $\mathcal{A}$ that $(t, \mu, \ell, \epsilon_{\text{SIG}})$-breaks the* MU-EUF-CMA^{Corr}-*security of* SIG *there is an attacker* $\mathcal{B} = (\mathcal{B}_{\text{XDH}}, \mathcal{B}_{\text{DP}})$ *such that* $\mathcal{B}_{\text{XDH}}$ $(t_{\text{XDH}}, \epsilon_{\text{XDH}})$-*breaks the* XDH-*assumption in* $\mathcal{G}_1$ *or* $\mathcal{B}_{\text{DP}}$ $(t_{\text{DP}}, \epsilon_{\text{DP}})$-*breaks the double pairing assumption in* $\mathcal{G}_2$ *with* $t \approx t_{\text{XDH}} \approx t_{\text{DP}}$ *and*

$$\epsilon_{\text{SIG}} < \frac{\ell^2}{2 \cdot p} + 2 \cdot \left(\epsilon_{\text{XDH}} + \epsilon_{\text{DP}} + \frac{\mu + 1}{p} \right).$$

The analysis will view H as a random oracle.

Proof. The proof is built on the following fact: Given only the public key, there are many possible secret keys and the actual values of χ and γ are information theoretically hidden. However, given a message and a secret key the pair (z, r) is determined. That is, a given secret key allows to compute exactly one pair that satisfies equation 1. At the same time, even if the secret key is available, any other tuple that satisfies equation 1 allows to solve an instance of the DP$_2$ problem. We argue that since the signer commits to (z, r) via *hiding* commitments the actual values (z, r) are information theoretically hidden from the view of $\mathcal{A}$. Therefore the secret key is also hidden from the adversary. Now, the reduction will manipulate H to produce binding commitment keys for (almost) any adversarially generated signature. From this, we can extract a DP solution with probability $1 - \frac{1}{p}$.

The proof proceeds in a sequence of games. Here, we denote by $\Pr[\chi_i]$ the probability that $\mathcal{A}$ is considered successful in game i. Let us denote by (i^*, m^*, σ^*) the forgery otuput by $\mathcal{A}$ and vk_{i^*} by vk^*.

GAME 0. This game is the real MU-EUF-CMA^{Corr}-security game. When issued a hash-query for the string s the reduction $\mathcal{R}$ first checks if s has already been hashed. If this is the case it returns the previously computed value $H(s)$. Otherwise it samples r uniformly at random from $\mathcal{G}_1$ and sets and returns $H(s) = r$. All other queries are answered according to the MU-EUF-CMA^{Corr}-security experiment. This perfectly simulates the challenger in the random-oracle model. Thus, we have:

$$\Pr[\chi_0] = \epsilon_{\text{SIG}}$$

GAME 1. Let Q_{vkcoll} denote the following event:

$$Q_{\mathsf{vkcoll}} := \{\exists (i,j) \in [\ell]^2 : i \neq j \wedge vk_i = vk_j\}$$

In Game 1 $\mathcal{R}$ aborts (and $\mathcal{A}$ looses) if event Q_{vkcoll} occurs. Since χ and γ are chosen uniformly at random by $\mathcal{R}$, public keys are distributed uniformly random over $\mathcal{G}_2$ which implies $\Pr[Q] = \frac{\ell \cdot (\ell-1)}{2 \cdot p}$. Thus, we have

$$|\Pr[\chi_0] - \Pr[\chi_1]| \leq \frac{\ell^2}{2 \cdot p}$$

GAME 2. Before we introduce the changes made in Game 2 let us fix some notation. Let $b_{vk,m}$ denote the bit that is (lazily) sampled by $\mathcal{R}$ during signing on m under vk. In Game 2, $\mathcal{R}$ aborts if for the forgery (i^*, m^*, σ^*) that is output by $\mathcal{A}$ it holds that $v_2^* = (H(0||vk^*||m^*||b_{vk^*,m^*}), H(1||vk^*||m^*||b_{vk^*,m^*}))$. In other words, $\mathcal{R}$ aborts (and $\mathcal{A}$ looses) if $\mathcal{A}$ chooses for the forgery the same bit b_{vk^*,m^*} that $\mathcal{R}$ would have chosen itself to sign m^* under vk^*. Since $\mathcal{R}$ chooses each bit uniformly at random the actual choice of b_{vk^*,m^*} is information theoretically hidden from the view of $\mathcal{A}$ (recall that all vk are distinct due to Game 1). Thus we have

$$\Pr[\chi_1] \leq 2 \cdot \Pr[\chi_2]$$

GAME 3. In Game 3 the reduction proceeds similarly to Game 2 except for the following: $\mathcal{R}$ lazily programs the hash-oracle such that for every pair of m and vk we have that $(H(0||vk||m||1 - b_{vk,m}), H(1||vk||m||1 - b_{vk,m})) \in \mathsf{DDH}(g_1, f_1)$. By the random self reducibility of DDH we get:

$$|\Pr[\chi_2] - \Pr[\chi_3]| < \epsilon_{\mathsf{XDH}}$$

GAME 4. This game is similar to Game 3, except that $\mathcal{R}$ aborts (and $\mathcal{A}$ looses), if for any sign query (m, i) issued by $\mathcal{A}$ during the security experiment we have that $(H(0||vk_i||m||b_{vk_i,m}), H(1||vk_i||m||b_{vk_i,m})) \in \mathsf{DDH}(g_1, f_1)$. Since images of H are distributed uniformly over $\mathcal{G}$ we have that

$$|\Pr[\chi_3] - \Pr[\chi_4]| \leq \frac{\mu}{p}$$

GAME 5. Game 5 proceeds exactly like Game 4 except for the following. $\mathcal{R}$ aborts if it cannot extract a satisfying assignment for equation 1 from σ^*. Due to Game 3 we know that $(\hat{g}_1, \hat{f}_1) = (H(0||vk^*||m^*||1 - b_{vk^*,m^*}), H(1||vk^*||m^*||1 - b_{vk^*,m^*})) \in \mathsf{DDH}(g_1, f_1)$. Therefore $(\vec{v}_1, \vec{v}_2)$ is in the (first) range of $\mathcal{E}_0(1^\kappa)$ and gives a perfectly binding CRS.

Given the trapdoor $\tau = \log_{g_1}(f_1)$ and using $\mathcal{E}_1$, $\mathcal{R}$ is able to extract (z^*, r^*) that satisfy equation 1 due to the perfect knowledge extraction on simulated CRS [16]. Thus, we have:

$$\Pr[\chi_4] = \Pr[\chi_5]$$

GAME 6. Game 6 proceeds exactly as Game 5 except for the following. The reduction aborts (and $\mathcal{A}$ looses) if for the forgery that $\mathcal{A}$ outputs it holds that the satisfying assignment of equation 1, (z^*, r^*), that is extracted by $\mathcal{R}$ from σ^* is equal to $((m^*)^{-\chi}, (m^*)^{-\gamma})$. Since for all sign queries (m, i) issued by $\mathcal{A}$ it holds that $(H(0||vk_i||m||b_{vk_i,m}), H(1||vk_i||m||b_{vk_i,m})) \notin \mathsf{DDH}(g_1, f_1)$ (which is due to Game 4) the signatures output by $\mathcal{R}$ are perfectly hiding proofs and do not leak any valuable information on (z, r) that are used by $\mathcal{R}$ to compute the respective commitements. From the view of the adversary all (z, r) that satisfy the respective equation 1 are equally likely. In particular the only information that the adversary obtains on χ and γ comes from the public key. However the public key provides the adversary with one linear equation in two unknowns which has p possible solutions. Thus we have:

$$|\Pr[\chi_5] - \Pr[\chi_6]| \leq \frac{1}{p}$$

Lemma 2. $\Pr[\chi_6] < \epsilon_{\mathsf{DP}_2}$.

We will show that any forgery output by the adversary in Game 6 allows $\mathcal{B}_{\mathsf{DP}}$ to solve a given instance of the DP_2 assumption. To this end, assume that $\mathcal{A}$ outputs a valid signature σ^* for m^* that was not signed before under vk. By Game 5 we know that from σ^* we can extract (z^*, r^*) such that $1 = e(k_z, z^*) \cdot e(k_r, r^*) \cdot (k^*, m^*)$. Moreover due to Game 6 we know that $(z^*, r^*) \neq (z, r) = ((m^*)^{-\chi}, (m^*)^{-\gamma})$. However, we do know that (z, r) also satisfies equation 1. Now, $(\frac{z}{z^*}, \frac{r}{r^*}) \neq (1, 1)$ yields a solution to the DP_2 instance $(k_z, k_r) \in \mathcal{G}_2$:

$$
\begin{aligned}
e(\frac{z}{z^*}, k_z) \cdot e(\frac{r}{r^*}, k_r) &= e(z, k_z) \cdot e(r, k_r) \cdot e(z^*, k_z)^{-1} \cdot e(r^*, k_r)^{-1} \\
&= e(z, k_z) \cdot e(r, k_r) \cdot e(m^*, k^*)^{1-1} \cdot e(z^*, k_z)^{-1} \cdot e(r^*, k_r)^{-1} \\
&= 1
\end{aligned}
$$

where the last equation is due to the fact that both, (z, r) and (z^*, r^*), satisfy equation 1. This completes our proof.   □

We stress that the reduction is able to reveal the secret key corresponding to a public key in every single game throughout the proof and is nevertheless able to extract a solution to a hard problem from a forgery. We do not even have to re-randomize publicly available values. That is, we can use k_z and k_r, as well as v_1 from Π for all users.

Acknowledgements. We would like to thank the anonymous reviewers for their valuable comments and suggestions.

References

1. NIST FIPS 186-4. Digital signature standard (dss). Technical report, NIST (2013)
2. Abe, M., Fuchsbauer, G., Groth, J., Haralambiev, K., Ohkubo, M.: Structure-Preserving Signatures and Commitments to Group Elements. In: Rabin, T. (ed.) CRYPTO 2010. LNCS, vol. 6223, pp. 209–236. Springer, Heidelberg (2010)
3. Bader, C., Hofheinz, D., Jager, T., Kiltz, E., Li, Y.: Tightly secure authenticated key exchange (unpublished manuscript, 2014)
4. Barker, E., Barker, W., Burr, W., Polk, W., Smid, M.: Nist sp 800-57, recommendation for key management – part 1: General (revision 3). Technical report (2012)
5. Bellare, M., Boldyreva, A., Micali, S.: Public-Key Encryption in a Multi-user Setting: Security Proofs and Improvements. In: Preneel, B. (ed.) EUROCRYPT 2000. LNCS, vol. 1807, pp. 259–274. Springer, Heidelberg (2000)
6. Bellare, M., Canetti, R., Krawczyk, H.: A modular approach to the design and analysis of authentication and key exchange protocols (extended abstract). In: 30th Annual ACM Symposium on Theory of Computing, Dallas, Texas, USA, May 23–26, pp. 419–428. ACM Press (1998)
7. Bellare, M., Rogaway, P.: Entity Authentication and Key Distribution. In: Stinson, D.R. (ed.) CRYPTO 1993. LNCS, vol. 773, pp. 232–249. Springer, Heidelberg (1994)
8. Bellare, M., Rogaway, P.: The Exact Security of Digital Signatures - How to Sign with RSA and Rabin. In: Maurer, U.M. (ed.) EUROCRYPT 1996. LNCS, vol. 1070, pp. 399–416. Springer, Heidelberg (1996)
9. Bernstein, D.J.: Proving Tight Security for Rabin-Williams Signatures. In: Smart, N.P. (ed.) EUROCRYPT 2008. LNCS, vol. 4965, pp. 70–87. Springer, Heidelberg (2008)
10. Boneh, D., Lynn, B., Shacham, H.: Short Signatures from the Weil Pairing. In: Boyd, C. (ed.) ASIACRYPT 2001. LNCS, vol. 2248, pp. 514–532. Springer, Heidelberg (2001)
11. Canetti, R., Krawczyk, H.: Analysis of Key-Exchange Protocols and Their Use for Building Secure Channels. In: Pfitzmann, B. (ed.) EUROCRYPT 2001. LNCS, vol. 2045, pp. 453–474. Springer, Heidelberg (2001)
12. Coron, J.-S.: Optimal Security Proofs for PSS and Other Signature Schemes. In: Knudsen, L.R. (ed.) EUROCRYPT 2002. LNCS, vol. 2332, pp. 272–287. Springer, Heidelberg (2002)
13. Cramer, R., Damgård, I.B., Schoenmakers, B.: Proof of Partial Knowledge and Simplified Design of Witness Hiding Protocols. In: Desmedt, Y.G. (ed.) CRYPTO 1994. LNCS, vol. 839, pp. 174–187. Springer, Heidelberg (1994)
14. Dierks, T., Rescorla, E.: The Transport Layer Security (TLS) Protocol Version 1.2. RFC 5246 (Proposed Standard), Updated by RFCs 5746, 5878 (August 2008)
15. Goldwasser, S., Micali, S., Rivest, R.L.: A digital signature scheme secure against adaptive chosen-message attacks. SIAM Journal on Computing 17(2), 281–308 (1988)
16. Groth, J., Sahai, A.: Efficient Non-interactive Proof Systems for Bilinear Groups. In: Smart, N.P. (ed.) EUROCRYPT 2008. LNCS, vol. 4965, pp. 415–432. Springer, Heidelberg (2008)
17. Hofheinz, D., Jager, T.: Tightly Secure Signatures and Public-Key Encryption. In: Safavi-Naini, R., Canetti, R. (eds.) CRYPTO 2012. LNCS, vol. 7417, pp. 590–607. Springer, Heidelberg (2012)

18. Jager, T., Kohlar, F., Schäge, S., Schwenk, J.: Generic Compilers for Authenticated Key Exchange. In: Abe, M. (ed.) ASIACRYPT 2010. LNCS, vol. 6477, pp. 232–249. Springer, Heidelberg (2010)
19. Jager, T., Kohlar, F., Schäge, S., Schwenk, J.: On the Security of TLS-DHE in the Standard Model. In: Safavi-Naini, R., Canetti, R. (eds.) CRYPTO 2012. LNCS, vol. 7417, pp. 273–293. Springer, Heidelberg (2012)
20. Kakvi, S.A., Kiltz, E.: Optimal Security Proofs for Full Domain Hash, Revisited. In: Pointcheval, D., Johansson, T. (eds.) EUROCRYPT 2012. LNCS, vol. 7237, pp. 537–553. Springer, Heidelberg (2012)
21. Katz, J., Wang, N.: Efficiency improvements for signature schemes with tight security reductions. In: Jajodia, S., Atluri, V., Jaeger, T. (eds.) ACM CCS 2003: 10th Conference on Computer and Communications Security, October 27-30, pp. 155–164. ACM Press, Washington, D.C. (2003)
22. Katz, J., Yung, M.: Scalable Protocols for Authenticated Group Key Exchange. In: Boneh, D. (ed.) CRYPTO 2003. LNCS, vol. 2729, pp. 110–125. Springer, Heidelberg (2003)
23. Li, Y., Schäge, S., Yang, Z., Bader, C., Schwenk, J.: New Modular Compilers for Authenticated Key Exchange. In: Boureanu, I., Owesarski, P., Vaudenay, S. (eds.) ACNS 2014. LNCS, vol. 8479, pp. 1–18. Springer, Heidelberg (2014)
24. Libert, B., Peters, T., Joye, M., Yung, M.: Non-malleability from Malleability: Simulation-Sound Quasi-Adaptive NIZK Proofs and CCA2-Secure Encryption from Homomorphic Signatures. In: Nguyen, P.Q., Oswald, E. (eds.) EUROCRYPT 2014. LNCS, vol. 8441, pp. 514–532. Springer, Heidelberg (2014)
25. Menezes, A., Smart, N.P.: Security of signature schemes in a multi-user setting. Des. Codes Cryptography 33(3), 261–274 (2004)
26. Naor, M., Reingold, O.: Number-theoretic constructions of efficient pseudo-random functions. In: 38th Annual Symposium on Foundations of Computer Science, Miami Beach, Florida, October 19-22, pp. 458–467. IEEE Computer Society Press (1997)
27. Naor, M., Yung, M.: Public-key cryptosystems provably secure against chosen ciphertext attacks. In: 22nd Annual ACM Symposium on Theory of Computing, Baltimore, Maryland, USA, May 14-16, pp. 427–437. ACM Press (1990)
28. Schäge, S.: Tight Proofs for Signature Schemes without Random Oracles. In: Paterson, K.G. (ed.) EUROCRYPT 2011. LNCS, vol. 6632, pp. 189–206. Springer, Heidelberg (2011)
29. Schnorr, C.-P.: Efficient Identification and Signatures for Smart Cards. In: Brassard, G. (ed.) CRYPTO 1989. LNCS, vol. 435, pp. 239–252. Springer, Heidelberg (1990)
30. Seurin, Y.: On the Exact Security of Schnorr-Type Signatures in the Random Oracle Model. In: Pointcheval, D., Johansson, T. (eds.) EUROCRYPT 2012. LNCS, vol. 7237, pp. 554–571. Springer, Heidelberg (2012)

More Sparse Families
of Pairing-Friendly Elliptic Curves

Georgios Fotiadis and Elisavet Konstantinou

Department of Information and Communication Systems Engineering,
University of the Aegean, 83200 Karlovassi, Samos, Greece
{gfotiadis,ekonstantinou}@aegean.gr

Abstract. Generating pairing-friendly elliptic curves is a crucial step in
the deployment of pairing-based cryptographic applications. The most
efficient method for their construction is based on polynomial families,
namely complete families, complete families with variable discriminant
and sparse families. In this work we further study the case of sparse
families which seem to produce more pairing-friendly elliptic curves than
the other two polynomial families and also can lead to better ρ-values
in many cases. We present two general methods for producing sparse
families and we apply them for four embedding degrees $k \in \{5, 8, 10, 12\}$.
Particularly for $k = 5$ we introduce for the first time the use of Pell
equations by setting a record with $\rho = 3/2$ and we present a family
that has better chances in producing suitable curve parameters than any
other reported family for $k \notin \{3, 4, 6\}$. In addition we generalise some
existing examples of sparse families for $k = 8, 12$ and provide extensive
experimental results for every new sparse family for $k \in \{5, 8, 10, 12\}$
regarding the number of the constructed elliptic curve parameters.

Keywords: Pairing-based cryptography, pairing-friendly elliptic curves,
polynomial families, Pell equations.

1 Introduction

Over the past few years, pairing-based cryptography has gained much attention
and a variety of pairing-based protocols have been developed (e.g. Joux's one-
round tripartite key agreement protocol [11], Boneh and Franklin's identity-
based encryption [3] etc.). All these protocols require the construction of a special
type of elliptic curves that satisfy certain properties and are known as *pairing-
friendly* elliptic curves [9]. Generating these elliptic curves is a crucial step in
pairing-based applications and even though many methods have been proposed,
it is still an active field.

For a large prime q, let $E/\mathbb{F}_q$ be an ordinary elliptic curve of order $\#E(\mathbb{F}_q) =
hr$ where r is a large prime and h is a small integer called the *cofactor*. Let also
$t = q + 1 - \#E(\mathbb{F}_q)$ be the Frobenius trace of the curve. In many pairing-based
protocols, it is required that $h = 1$ (prime order curves). However such curves
are rare and in most applications a small $h > 1$ is acceptable. In this latter

D. Gritzalis et al. (Eds.): CANS 2014, LNCS 8813, pp. 384–399, 2014.

case, we define the security parameter $\rho = \log(q)/\log(r)$ measuring how close to the ideal case is the constructed curve. Clearly, ρ should be as close to 1 as possible. The *embedding degree* of the curve $E/\mathbb{F}_q$, is the smallest positive integer $k > 1$, such that $E[r] \subseteq E(\mathbb{F}_{q^k})$, where $E[r]$ is the group of r-torsion points of $E/\mathbb{F}_q$. Equivalently we can say that k is the smallest positive integer such that $r \mid q^k - 1$ (see [8,9]). The embedding degree k must be carefully chosen to be large enough ensuring the hardness of the DLP in $\mathbb{F}_{q^k}^*$ and simultaneously small enough in order to keep an efficient arithmetic in $\mathbb{F}_{q^k}^*$. Current requirements indicate that a good security level is around 128 bits or more, in which case $3000 < k \log q < 5000$ [9]. Determining suitable integer triples (q, t, r) satisfying the above properties, for a specific $k > 1$, and requiring at the same time that $\rho \approx 1$, is one of the most demanding tasks in pairing-based cryptography. Once these parameters are generated, the Complex Multiplication (CM) method [1] can be used for the construction of the curve equation. The efficiency of the CM method is closely related to the size of an integer D (called the *CM discriminant*) which is the square free positive value satisfying the CM equation $DY^2 = 4q - t^2$ for a given pair (q, t). The value of D must be relatively small (e.g. $D < 10^{10}$ or even smaller) in order to implement the CM method efficiently.

Since 2001 a variety of methods have been proposed for constructing pairing-friendly elliptic curves, most of which are based on parameterizing the curve parameters as *polynomial families* $(q(x), t(x), r(x))$ in $\mathbb{Q}[x]$. There are three types of such polynomial families depending on the form of the polynomial $4q(x) - t^2(x)$ representing the right hand side of the CM equation expressed in polynomial field.

Definition 1 ([5,9]). A polynomial family $(q(x), t(x), r(x))$ is said to be *complete*, if there exists an $s(x) \in \mathbb{Q}[x]$, such that $4q(x) - t^2(x) = Ds^2(x)$, for some positive, square-free integer D representing the CM discriminant. If the polynomials $q(x)$ and $t(x)$ satisfy $4q(x) - t^2(x) = g(x)s^2(x)$ for some $g(x) \in \mathbb{Q}[x]$ with $\deg g = 1$ then the polynomial family is called *complete with variable discriminant*. If $\deg g > 1$, then the family is called *sparse*.

In this paper we further investigate the construction of sparse families of pairing-friendly elliptic curves using the solutions of a generalized Pell equation. We present two methods for generating sparse families for arbitrary k and focus on four embedding degrees $k \in \{5, 8, 10, 12\}$. Especially when $k = 5$ we introduce for the first time the use of Pell equations and set a record with $\rho = 3/2$. Additionally, we produce some new sparse polynomial families for $k \in \{8, 10, 12\}$ achieving $\rho = 3/2$, which is the smallest value reported in the literature for variable discriminant. Furthermore, the proposed methods generate pairing-friendly elliptic curves with smaller CM discriminant than other existing methods, improving the efficiency of the CM method. Finally, we have conducted extensive experimental assessments which show that the proposed new polynomial families lead to the construction of many elliptic curves, achieving at the same time a relatively small value for the CM discriminant.

The paper is organized as follows. In Section 2 we present some background related to pairing-friendly elliptic curves as well as some of the most important methods for generating suitable curve parameters for the three types of families in Definition 1. We analyze our proposed methods in Sections 3 and 4 and proceed by demonstrating our experimental results in Section 5. Finally, we conclude the paper in Section 6.

2   Preliminaries and Previous Work

In this Section, we will give the notion of *polynomial families* of pairing-friendly elliptic curves and proceed by analyzing the existing methods for their construction. Our goal is to find suitable integers (q, t, r) for a fixed embedding degree $k > 0$, such that $\rho \approx 1$. The best ρ-values in the literature are achieved by representing the parameters (q, t, r) as polynomials $q(x), t(x), r(x) \in \mathbb{Q}[x]$ respectively.

Definition 2 ([9]). Let $q(x), t(x), r(x) \in \mathbb{Q}[x]$ be non-zero polynomials. Then the polynomial triple $(q(x), t(x), r(x))$ parameterizes a *family of pairing-friendly ordinary elliptic curves* with embedding degree k and CM discriminant D if the following conditions are satisfied:

1. the polynomial $q(x)$ represents primes,
2. the polynomial $r(x)$ is non-constant, irreducible, integer-valued, with positive leading coefficient,
3. $r(x)$ divides the polynomials $q(x) + 1 - t(x)$ and $\Phi_k(t(x) - 1)$, where $\Phi_k(x)$ is the kth cyclotomic polynomial and
4. there are infinitely many integer solutions (x, Y) for the parameterized CM equation

$$DY^2 = 4q(x) - t^2(x) = 4h(x)r(x) - (t(x) - 2)^2. \tag{1}$$

The ρ-value of a polynomial family can be measured by the ratio $\rho(q, t, r) = \deg q(x)/\deg r(x)$. The condition $r(x) \mid (q(x)+1-t(x))$ implies that $\#E(\mathbb{F}_{q(x)}) = h(x)r(x)$, where $h(x) \in \mathbb{Q}[x]$ is the cofactor. Our problem now reduces in finding a suitable solution (x_0, Y_0) of Equation (1) such that $q(x_0)$ and $r(x_0)$ are prime integers. Then, we can use the CM method to construct an elliptic curve $E/\mathbb{F}_{q(x_0)}$ with Frobenius trace $t(x_0)$ and order $\#E(\mathbb{F}_{q(x_0)}) = h(x_0)r(x_0)$, where $h(x_0) = 1$ is the ideal case. Let $f(x) = 4q(x) - t^2(x) \in \mathbb{Q}[x]$ be the *CM polynomial*. Most methods focus on CM polynomials of the form $f(x) = g(x)s^2(x)$ for some $g(x), s(x) \in \mathbb{Q}[x]$, where $\deg s$ is arbitrary, but $\deg g \leq 2$. By Definition 1, when $\deg g = 0$ the polynomial family $(q(x), t(x), r(x))$ is complete with $f(x) = Ds^2(x)$, for some square-free positive D. When $\deg g = 1$ we have a complete family with variable discriminant and finally when $\deg g = 2$ but $g(x)$ is not a square, the family is sparse.

Complete Families. The most well known method in this case is the Brezing and Weng method [4] and its variants [9,12,17,19]. These methods start by fixing a $k > 1$ and some square-free CM discriminant D. They choose an irreducible polynomial $r(x) \in \mathbb{Q}[x]$, such that $K \cong \mathbb{Q}[x]/(r(x))$, where K is the field containing a primitive k^{th}-root of unity ζ_k. Then, let $t(x)$ and $s(x)$ be the polynomials mapping to $\zeta_k + 1$ and $(\zeta_k - 1)/\sqrt{-D}$ in K respectively. The resulting

CM polynomial will be of the form $f(x) = Ds^2(x)$. The best family in this case is given in [2] for $k = 12$ and $D = 3$, with $\rho(q, t, r) = 1$. Additional examples appear also in [9,12,17,19].

Complete Families with Variable Discriminant. Such families are constructed in the work of Lee and Park [13] and additionally in [5]. The method of Lee and Park sets the polynomial $r(x)$ to be an irreducible factor of the cyclotomic polynomial $\Phi_k(u(x))$, for some $u(x) \in \mathbb{Q}[x]$. The challenging part of the method is to determine a suitable polynomial $u(x)$. This is accomplished by fixing an embedding degree k and an element $\theta = a_0 + a_1\zeta_k + \ldots + a_{\varphi(k)-1}\zeta_k^{\varphi(k)-1}$ in $\mathbb{Q}(\zeta_k)$. Then, the transition matrix P from the set $\mathcal{B}_\theta = \{1, \theta, \ldots, \theta^{\varphi(k)-1}\}$ to the basis $\mathcal{B}_{\zeta_k} = \{1, \zeta_k, \ldots, \zeta_k^{\varphi(k)-1}\}$ is constructed, which is a $\varphi(k) \times \varphi(k)$ matrix with elements P_{ij} obtained by the relation $\theta^j = \sum_{i=0}^{\varphi(k)-1} P_{ij}\zeta_k^i$, for each $j \in \{0, 1, \ldots, \varphi(k) - 1\}$. If $\det(P) \neq 0$ then P has an inverse $P^{-1} = (P'_{ij})$ and the polynomial $u(x)$ will be equal to $u(x) = \sum_{i=0}^{\varphi(k)-1} P'_{i1}x^i$. Finally, they set $t(x) = u(x) + 1$ and $f(x) \equiv -(u(x) - 1)^2 \bmod r(x)$.

Propositions 1 and 2 in [13] guarantee that if $\theta = a_0 - 2a_1\zeta_k + a_1\zeta_k^2$ for some non-zero $a_0, a_1 \in \mathbb{Q}$, then $\deg f = 1$. Several examples of such polynomial families appear in [13]. However, they all lead to large CM discriminants $D > 10^7$. Clearly, the method of Lee and Park gathers all CM polynomials of the form $f(x) = g(x)s^2(x)$ with $\deg s = 0$ and $\deg g = 1$, but misses the cases where $\deg s > 0$. Such cases are studied in greater detail in [5]. Additional examples appear in [9].

Sparse Families. In this case $f(x) = (ax^2 + bx + c)s^2(x)$, where $a, b, c \in \mathbb{Q}$. Substituting into Equation (1) and excluding the perfect square term $s^2(x)$, we get $DY^2 = g(x) = ax^2 + bx + c$. Multiplying by $4a$ and completing the squares yields a generalized Pell equation of the form

$$X^2 - aD(2Y)^2 = b^2 - 4ac, \quad \text{where} \quad X = 2ax + b. \tag{2}$$

If Equation (2) is solvable for some square-free D, then it has an infinite number of integral solutions (X_i, Y_i) (see [15]). In order to generate the elliptic curve, we firstly check if $X_i = 2ax_0 + b$, for some $x_0 \in \mathbb{Z}$. If this is the case, then we check if $q(x_0)$ and $r(x_0)$ are primes and if $t(x_0)$ satisfies the Hasse's bound.

The first method for generating sparse families is due to Miyaji, Nakabayashi and Takano [14] (MNT method) for $k \in \{3, 4, 6\}$. In their method they describe polynomial families $(q(x), t(x), r(x))$ such that $h(x) = 1$ (ideal case) and so $\rho(q, t, r) = 1$. Several generalizations and extensions of the MNT method have been proposed in [6,7,10,18] allowing $h(x) > 1$. Particularly, in [6] and [7] the notion of *effective polynomial families* is introduced. These are sparse polynomial families leading to CM polynomials of the form $f(x) = g(x)s^2(x)$ with $g(x)$ quadratic and factorable. In this case, the constructed Pell equations have the advantage that they are always solvable for every square-free D and so the sparse family has better chances in producing suitable curve parameters.

For $k \notin \{3, 4, 6\}$, the best known result is reported in [8] for $k = 10$ and achieves a value $\rho(q, t, r) = 1$. Another method for constructing sparse families is discussed in [5], where the author starts by fixing an embedding degree $k > 1$ and constructing a number field K containing a primitive k^{th} root of unity. Then, an irreducible polynomial $r(x) \in \mathbb{Q}[x]$ is chosen so that $K = \mathbb{Q}[x]/(r(x))$ and the algorithm searches for a quadratic polynomial $g(x) \in \mathbb{Q}[x]$ so that $-g(x)$ is a square in K. Finally, $t(x)$ and $s(x)$ are set as polynomials mapping to $\zeta_k + 1$ and $(\zeta_k - 1)/\sqrt{-g(x)}$ respectively. The constructed CM polynomial is not necessarily quadratic, but has a perfect square factor $s^2(x)$ with $\deg s > 1$. An alternative method is described in [6] which starts by fixing a $k > 1$ and chooses an irreducible polynomial $r(x) \in \mathbb{Q}[x]$. Then searches for a trace polynomial $t(x)$, such that $r(x) \mid \Phi_k(t(x) - 1)$. Once these polynomials are determined, the CM polynomial is equal to $f(x) \equiv -(t(x) - 2)^2 \bmod r(x)$.

Our Contribution. Summarizing, Brezing-Weng like polynomial families produce the best ρ-values in the literature for $k \notin \{3, 4, 6, 10\}$. However, they work for a fixed and very small discriminant D which according to the German Information Security Agency may lead to vulnerable elliptic curves. On the other hand, polynomial families with variable discriminant provide some flexibility on D, but result in large CM discriminants which make the CM method very inefficient. In this paper, we argue that sparse families using solutions of generalized Pell equations are more attractive in applications that require variable but relatively small CM discriminants.

   We here present two methods for the generation of sparse families of pairing-friendly elliptic curves. The first method is based on [6] and [13]. It extends the ideas in [13] by searching for CM polynomials $f(x) = g(x)s^2(x)$ with $\deg g = 2$ instead of linear polynomials $f(x)$ and it is more efficient compared to the method in [6]. Using the new method, we obtained for the first time sparse families based on Pell equations for $k = 5$, setting at the same time a record with $\rho = 3/2$. Among these families, we found an effective polynomial family for $k = 5$ leading to a generalized Pell equation that is always solvable for every positive and square-free D. Based on our new method, we also obtained some sparse families for $k = 10$ with $\rho = 3/2$. The second method is more general and can be implemented for any $k > 1$ and arbitrary CM polynomials $f(x) = g(x)s^2(x)$, with $g(x) \in \mathbb{Q}[x]$ quadratic and not a perfect square. Using this method, we give a generalization of the examples presented in [5] for $k = 8, 12$ and $\rho = 3/2$. Finally, we provide experimental results on the number of suitable curve parameters obtained from our newly proposed polynomial families. Our experiments indicate that our effective family for $k = 5$ produces more curve parameters than any other polynomial family for $k \notin \{3, 4, 6\}$.

3   Sparse Families with $\deg f < \deg r$

In this section we present a method for constructing sparse families of pairing-friendly elliptic curves with embedding degree $k > 1$, such that the CM polynomial is of the form $f(x) = g(x)s^2(x)$ with $\deg g = 2$ and $g(x)$ not a perfect square.

Our method starts by choosing an arbitrary embedding degree $k > 1$ and fixing an element $\theta \in \mathbb{Q}(\zeta_k)$ of the form

$$\theta = a_0 + a_1\zeta_k + a_2\zeta_k^2 + \ldots + a_{\varphi(k)-1}\zeta_k^{\varphi(k)-1} \tag{3}$$

such that $u(\theta) = \zeta_k$ in $\mathbb{Q}(\zeta_k)$ for some $u(x) \in \mathbb{Q}[x]$. We then construct the transition matrix P from the set $\mathcal{B}(\theta)$ to the basis $\mathcal{B}(\zeta_k)$ using the relation

$$\theta^j = \sum_{i=0}^{\varphi(k)-1} P_{ij}\zeta_k^i, \quad \text{for} \quad j = 0, 1, \ldots, \varphi(k) - 1. \tag{4}$$

Since $\Phi_k(u(x))$ should contain an irreducible factor of degree $\varphi(k)$, we need to ensure that $a_0, a_1, \ldots, a_{\varphi(k)-1}$ are chosen so that $\det(P) \neq 0$. Then, the coefficients of the polynomial $u(x)$ are given by the second column of the inverse matrix $P^{-1} = (P'_{ij})$ of P using the relation:

$$u(x) = \sum_{i=0}^{\varphi(k)-1} P'_{i1}x^i. \tag{5}$$

Setting the polynomial $u(x)$ as

$$u(x) = u_{\varphi(k)-1}x^{\varphi(k)-1} + \ldots + u_2x^2 + u_1x + u_0 \in \mathbb{Q}[x] \tag{6}$$

Equation (5) implies that the coefficients of $u(x)$ are actually multivariate polynomials in $\mathbb{Q}[a_0, a_1, \ldots, a_{\varphi(k)-1}]$. Once the polynomial $u(x)$ is created, then we set $t(x) = u(x) + 1$ to find the polynomial representing the Frobenius trace. The polynomial $r(x)$ is set to be the irreducible factor of $\Phi_k(u(x))$ with $\deg r = \varphi(k)$ and it is the minimal polynomial of θ over $\mathbb{Q}(\zeta_k)$. Thus, we set

$$r(x) = r_{\varphi(k)}x^{\varphi(k)} + \ldots + r_2x^2 + r_1x + r_0 \in \mathbb{Q}[x]. \tag{7}$$

The coefficients of $r(x)$ are multivariate polynomials in $\mathbb{Q}[a_0, a_1, \ldots, a_{\varphi(k)-1}]$ and can be obtained by solving the system $r(\theta) = 0$.

Algorithm 1.   Families of Pairing-Friendly Elliptic Curves with $\deg g = 2$

Input: The embedding degree k
Output: Suitable polynomials $q(x), t(x), r(x), h(x), f(x) \in \mathbb{Q}[x]$

Step 1: For each $a_0, a_1, a_2, \ldots, a_{\varphi(k)-1} \in \mathbb{Q}$ do
Step 2: Calculate the transition matrix P from $\mathcal{B}(\theta)$ to $\mathcal{B}(\zeta_k)$ by Equation (4)
Step 3: If $\det(P) \neq 0$ compute the coefficients of the polynomials $u(x)$ and $r(x)$ using the Equation (5) and $r(\theta) = 0$ respectively; else return to Step 1
Step 4: Set the CM polynomial to $f(x) \equiv -(u(x) - 1)^2 \bmod r(x)$
Step 5: If $f(x) = g(x)s^2(x)$ with $g(x)$ quadratic and not a perfect square, with positive leading coefficient, then set $h(x) = (f(x) + (u(x) - 1)^2)/4r(x)$, $q(x) = h(x)r(x) + u(x)$ and $t(x) = u(x) + 1$; else return to Step 1
Step 6: If $q(x)$ is irreducible over $\mathbb{Q}[x]$ and $q(x_0) \in \mathbb{Z}$ for some $x_0 \in \mathbb{Z}$, output the polynomials $(t(x), r(x), q(x), h(x), f(x))$; else return to Step 1

After obtaining $u(x)$ and $r(x)$, we set the CM polynomial as $f(x) \equiv -(u(x) - 1)^2 \bmod r(x)$ and we also require that $\deg g = 2$. Additionally, we must also ensure that the leading coefficient of $g(x)$ is positive and that $g(x)$ is not a perfect square. The corresponding generalized Pell equation can be constructed by setting $DY^2 = g(x)$ and following the procedure described in Section 2.

The above method is summarized in Algorithm 1. The proposed algorithm differs from the work of Lee and Park [13] in that we are actually searching for CM polynomials of the form $f(x) = g(x)s^2(x)$, for some quadratic and non-square polynomial $g(x)$. On the other hand, our method is faster than the one proposed in [6], since in this work the authors start by randomly choosing an irreducible polynomial $r(x)$ and then search for a trace polynomial $t(x)$, such that $r(x) \mid \Phi_k(t(x) - 1)$. Clearly, this is a very demanding and time consuming step.

3.1   Families with Embedding Degree k = 5

The 5th-cyclotomic polynomial is represented by $\Phi_5(x) = x^4 + x^3 + x^2 + x + 1$. Set the element $\theta \in \mathbb{Q}(\zeta_5)$ to be of the general form in Equation (3), for some $a_0, a_1, a_2, a_3 \in \mathbb{Q}$ such that $\det(P) \neq 0$, where P is the 4×4 transition matrix from $\mathcal{B}_\theta$ to $\mathcal{B}_{\zeta_5}$. This choice will ensure that $\Phi_5(u(x))$ has a quartic irreducible factor $r(x) \in \mathbb{Q}[x]$. Based on Algorithm 1 and setting $f(x) \equiv -(u(x) - 1)^2 \bmod r(x)$, we will get a CM polynomial $f(x)$ of degree 3. Since we are searching for sparse families we add the condition $\deg f = 2$. Based on our extensive experimental assessments, we realized that θ can be of a special form that leads to quadratic CM polynomials. This special form depends only on the choice of a_0 and a_1 (in an analogy to Proposition 1 of Lee and Park [13]). Randomly choosing integer pairs $(a_0, a_1) \in \mathbb{Q}^2$ we can produce different polynomial families.

Family 1. Let $\theta = a_0 + 7a_1\zeta_5 - 2a_1\zeta_5^2 + 4a_1\zeta_5^3$, for $a_0, a_1 \in \mathbb{Q}$ and $a_1 \neq 0$. The transition matrix has $\det(P) = 55^3 a_1^6$. We then obtain the polynomials:

$$
\begin{aligned}
u(x) &= (4x^3 - (12a_0 - 62a_1)x^2 - (124a_0a_1 - 12a_0^2 - 887a_1^2)x \\
&\quad - (4a_0^3 - 62a_0^2a_1 + 887a_0a_1^2 - 1104a_1^3))/55^2a_1^3 \\
r(x) &= x^4 + (9a_1 - 4a_0)x^3 + (6a_0^2 - 27a_0a_1 + 121a_1^2)x^2 \\
&\quad + (27a_0^2a_1 - 4a_0^3 - 242a_0a_1^2 - 31a_1^3)x \\
&\quad + (a_0^4 - 9a_0^3a_1 + 121a_0^2a_1^2 + 31a_0a_1^3 + 1231a_1^4) \\
f(x) &= ((-x + a_0 - 21a_1)(-x + a_0 - a_1))/55a_1^2
\end{aligned}
$$

with $\rho(q, t, r) = 3/2$. This is an effective polynomial family, since the polynomial $f(x)$ factorizes in $\mathbb{Q}[x]$. Therefore, this family will lead to a larger number of suitable curve parameters compared to other sparse families.

Family 2. Let $\theta = a_0 + a_1\zeta_5 - 8a_1\zeta_5^2 + 20a_1\zeta_5^3$, with $a_0, a_1 \in \mathbb{Q}$ and $a_1 \neq 0$. The transition matrix has $\det(P) = -5^2151^3a_1^6$ and we obtain the following polynomials $\rho(q, t, r) = 3/2$:

$$u(x) = (-4x^3 + (12a_0 + 264a_1)x^2 - (12a_0^2 + 528a_0a_1 + 1931a_1^2)x$$
$$+ (4a_0^3 + 264a_0^2a_1 + 1931a_0a_1^2 + 81040a_1^3))/5 \cdot 151^2 a_1^3$$
$$r(x) = x^4 + (13a_1 - 4a_0)x^3 + (6a_0^2 - 39a_0a_1 + 969a_1^2)x^2$$
$$+ (12177a_1^3 - 4a_0^3 + 39a_0^2a_1 - 1938a_0a_1^2)x$$
$$+ (a_0^4 - 13a_0^3a_1 + 969a_0^2a_1^2 - 12177a_0a_1^3 + 246341a_1^4)$$
$$f(x) = (x^2 + (6a_1 - 2a_0)x + (a_0^2 - 6a_0a_1 + 273a_1^2))/151a_1^2$$

3.2   Families with Embedding Degree k = 10

For embedding degree $k = 10$ we have an ideal polynomial family given by David Freeman [8] with $\rho(q, t, r) = 1$. It may be useful in applications that do not require $\rho = 1$, to use families that provide larger ρ-value. Such examples are obtained by our method with $\rho(q, t, r) = 3/2$. When $k = 10$, the 10th-cyclotomic polynomial is given by $\Phi_{10}(x) = x^4 - x^3 + x^2 - x + 1$. We set $\theta \in \mathbb{Q}(\zeta_{10})$ to be of the form in Equation (3), for some $(a_0, a_1, a_2, a_3) \in \mathbb{Q}^4$, such that $\det(P) \neq 0$. As in the case $k = 5$ we obtained certain special forms for θ depending only on $a_0, a_1 \in \mathbb{Q}$, that lead to quadratic CM polynomials.

Family 3 (Freeman [8]). Let $\theta = a_0 + a_1\zeta_{10} - 2a_1\zeta_{10}^2$, for some $a_0, a_1 \in \mathbb{Q}$, with $a_1 \neq 0$. The transition matrix has $\det(P) = -25a_1^6$ and we obtain the following polynomials with $\rho(q, t, r) = 1$:

$$u(x) = (2x^2 - (4a_0 + 3a_1)x + (2a_0^2 + 3a_0a_1 + 8a_1^2))/5a_1^2$$
$$r(x) = x^4 - (4a_0 + 3a_1)x^3 + (6a_0^2 + 9a_0a_1 + 9a_1^2)x^2$$
$$- (4a_0^3 - 9a_0^2a_1 - 18a_0a_1^2 - 7a_1^3)x + (a_0^4 + 3a_0^3a_1 + 9a_0^2a_1^2 + 7a_1a_1^3 + 11a_1^4)$$
$$f(x) = (3x^2 - (6a_0 + 2a_1)x + (3a_0^2 + 2a_0a_1 + 7a_1^2))/5a_1^2$$

Family 4. Let $\theta = a_0 + 7a_1\zeta_{10} - 6a_1\zeta_{10}^2 + 4a_1\zeta_{10}^3$, with $a_0, a_1 \in \mathbb{Q}$ and $a_1 \neq 0$. The transition matrix has $\det(P) = 31^3 a_1^6$ and we obtain the following polynomial family with $\rho(q, t, r) = 3/2$:

$$u(x) = (4x^3 - (12a_0 + 38a_1)x^2 + (12a_0^2 + 76a_0a_1 + 391a_1^2)x$$
$$- (4a_0^3 + 38a_0^2a_1 + 391a_0a_1^2 + 80a_1^3))/31^2 a_1^3$$
$$r(x) = x^4 - (4a_0 + 17a_1)x^3 + (6a_0^2 + 51a_0a_1 + 169a_1^2)x^2$$
$$- (4a_0^3 + 51a_0^2a_1 + 338a_0a_1^2 + 633a_1^3)x + (a_0^4 + 17a_0^3a_1 + 169a_0^2a_1^2 + 1111a_1^4)$$
$$f(x) = (4x^2 - 2(a_0 + a_1)x + (a_0^2 + 2a_0a_1 + 13a_1^2))/31a_1^2$$

4   Sparse Families for Arbitrary CM Polynomials

In this section we present a more general method for the construction of polynomial families of pairing-friendly elliptic curves. This approach can be applied for

CM polynomials of any form, but as in the previous section we focus on cases where $f(x) = g(x)s^2(x)$ for some quadratic, non-square polynomial $g(x)$ (sparse families). The proposed method is based on the remarks in [10,13].

We start by fixing an element $\theta \in \mathbb{Q}(\zeta_k)$ such that $\det(P) \neq 0$, where P is the transition matrix form $\mathcal{B}(\theta)$ to the basis $\mathcal{B}(\zeta_k)$. The polynomials $u(x)$ and $r(x)$ are determined in the same way as described in Algorithm 1 where the coefficients of $u(x)$ and $r(x)$ are all multivariate polynomials in $\mathbb{Q}[a_0, a_1, \ldots, a_{\varphi(k)-1}]$. We compute these polynomials according to Equations (6) and (7) and we set the trace polynomial to $t(x) = u(x) + 1$. The next step is to construct the cofactor $h(x)$ by setting

$$h(x) = h_{\varphi(k)-2}x^{\varphi(k)-2} + \ldots + h_2x^2 + h_1x + h_0 \in \mathbb{Q}[x]. \tag{8}$$

We require that $\deg h = \varphi(k) - 2$ or smaller, because in this case $\rho = (2\varphi(k) - 2)/\varphi(k) < 2$ (since $\deg(u-1)^2 = 2\varphi(k) - 2$, while $\deg r = \varphi(k)$). Substituting the polynomials $h(x), r(x)$ and $t(x)$ into the parameterized CM equation (1) we will get a degree $2\varphi(k) - 2$ CM polynomial of the form

$$f(x) = f_{2\varphi(k)-2}x^{2\varphi(k)-2} + f_{2\varphi(k)-3}x^{2\varphi(k)-3} + \ldots + f_2x^2 + f_1x + f_0. \tag{9}$$

The only unknown values are the coefficients of the cofactor which must be determined. Suppose that we are searching for CM polynomials with $\deg f = i$, for some even $i = 2, 4, \ldots 2\varphi(k) - 2$. Then the first $2\varphi(k) - i - 2$ coefficients of $f(x)$ in Equation (9) must satisfy $f_{2\varphi(k)-2} = f_{2\varphi(k)-3} = \ldots = f_{i+1} = 0$. Using this system we can calculate some, or all the coefficients of the cofactor $h(x)$. If we set $\deg f < \deg r = \varphi(k)$, then all coefficients of $h(x)$ can be determined by the above system. Otherwise, for the remaining coefficients of $h(x)$ we will have to do some additional search.

For example, when $\varphi(k) = 4$, (i.e. $k \in \{5, 8, 10, 12\}$) the polynomials $f(x)$ and $h(x)$ will have $\deg f = 6$ and $\deg h = 2$ respectively. For CM polynomials of the form $f(x) = g(x)s^2(x)$, with $g(x)$ quadratic and non-square, the possible values for the degree of $f(x)$ are $\deg f \in \{2, 4, 6\}$. Setting $\deg f = 2$, we have $f_6 = f_5 = f_4 = f_3 = 0$. From $f_6 = f_5 = f_4 = 0$ we determine $h(x)$ and we must also guarantee that $f_3 = 0$. When $\deg f = 4$, we require some search for h_0, while when $\deg f = 6$ we need to search for all coefficients of $h(x)$. We applied this idea for $k = 8, 12$ and we obtained a generalization of Drylo's examples given in [5], by representing θ in two variables $a_0, a_1 \in \mathbb{Q}$.

Family 5. Let $\theta = a_0 + a_1\zeta_8 + a_1\zeta_8^2 - a_1\zeta_8^3$, with $a_0, a_1 \in \mathbb{Q}$ and $a_1 \neq 0$. The transition matrix has $\det(P) = -24a_1^6$ and setting $h(x) = (x-a_0-3a_1)^2/(576a_1^6)$ we obtain the next polynomial family with $\rho(q, t, r) = 3/2$:

$$u(x) = (-x^3 + 3(a_0 + a_1)x^2 - (3a_0^2 + 6a_0a_1 - 5a_1^2)x$$
$$+ (a_0^3 + 3a_0^2a_1 - 5a_0a_1^2 - 3a_1^3))/12a_1^3$$
$$r(x) = x^4 - 4a_0x^3 + (6a_0^2 - 2a_1^2)x^2 - (4a_0^3 - 4a_0a_1^2)x + (a_0^4 - 2a_0^2a_1^2 + 9a_1^4)$$
$$f(x) = (x^2 - 2a_0x + a_0^2 - a_1^2)(x - a_0 - 3a_1)^2/18a_1^4$$

Family 6. Let $\theta = a_0 + 2a_1\zeta_{12} + a_1\zeta_{12}^2 - a_1\zeta_{12}^3$, with $a_0, a_1 \in \mathbb{Q}$ and $a_1 \neq 0$. The transition matrix has $\det(P) = -45a_1^6$ and setting $h(x) = (x - a_0 - 3a_1)^2/(900a_1^6)$ we obtain the next polynomials with $\rho(q, t, r) = 3/2$:

$$u(x) = (-x^3 + (3a_0 + 4a_1)x^2 - (3a_0^2 + 8a_0a_1 - 5a_1^2)x$$
$$+ (a_0^3 + 4a_0^2a_1 - 5a_0a_1^2 - 9a_1^3))/15a_1^3$$
$$r(x) = x^4 - (4a_0 - 2a_1)x^3 + (6a_0^2 + 6a_0a_1 - 3a_1^2)x^2$$
$$- (4a_0^3 + 6a_0^2a_1 - 6a_0a_1^2 - 4a_1^3)x + (a_0^4 + 2a_0^3a_1 - 3a_0^2a_1^2 - 4a_0a_1^3 + 13a_1^4)$$
$$f(x) = (4x^2 - 4(2a_0 + a_1)x + 4a_0^2 + 4a_0a_1 + 17a_1^2)(x - a_0 - 3a_1)^2/75a_1^4$$

5   Experimental Results

We demonstrate some experimental results obtained by every polynomial family described in Sections 3 and 4. Recall that each representative comes of a random choice $a_0, a_1 \in \mathbb{Q}$. For each polynomial family, different a_0, a_1 will result in different polynomials $q(x), t(x), r(x)$, producing the same curve parameters. Before constructing the generalized Pell equation, we need to apply a linear transformation on each family in order to make the polynomials integer valued (See [12,13]). Furthermore, evaluating Families 5, 6 at $(a_0, a_1) = (0, 1)$ we get Drylo's examples [5].

Example 1 (k = 5). Set $(a_0, a_1) = (1, 1)$ in Family 1 and apply the transformation $x \to (55x - 20)$ to obtain the next polynomial family with $\rho(q, t, r) = 3/2$:

$$t(x) = 220x^3 + 470x^2 + 345x + 87$$
$$r(x) = 55x^4 + 145x^3 + 145x^2 + 65x + 11$$
$$q(x) = 12100x^6 + 51700x^5 + 93175x^4 + 90645x^3 + 50215x^2 + 15030x + 1901$$

with CM polynomial $f(x) = 5(x + 1)(11x + 7)$ and generalized Pell equation:

$$(55x - 10)^2 - 55DY^2 = 100 \tag{10}$$

Example 2 (k = 5). Set $(a_0, a_1) = (0, 1)$ in Family 2 and apply the transformation $x \to (755x + 223)$ to get the polynomial family with $\rho(q, t, r) = 3/2$:

$$t(x) = -15100x^3 - 12060x^2 - 3185x - 276$$
$$r(x) = 3775x^4 + 4525x^3 + 2040x^2 + 410x + 31$$
$$q(x) = 57002500x^6 + 91053000x^5 + 60407650x^4 + 21289350x^3 + 4201280x^2$$
$$+ 440095x + 19129$$

with CM polynomial is $f(x) = 3775x^2 + 2260x + 340$ and generalized Pell equation:

$$(755x + 226)^2 - 151DY^2 = -264. \tag{11}$$

Example 3 (Freeman for k = 10). Set $(a_0, a_1) = (0, 1)$ in Family 3 and apply the transformation $x \rightarrow (5x + 2)$ to obtain the following polynomial family with $\rho(q, t, r) = 1$:

$$t(x) = 10x^2 + 5x + 3$$
$$r(x) = 25x^4 + 25x^3 + 15x^2 + 5x + 1$$
$$q(x) = 25x^4 + 25x^3 + 25x^2 + 10x + 3$$

with CM polynomial $f(x) = 15x^2 + 10x + 3$ and generalized Pell equation:

$$(15x + 5)^2 - 15DY^2 = -20. \tag{12}$$

Example 4 (k = 10). Set $(a_0, a_1) = (0, 1)$ in Family 4 and apply the transformation $x \rightarrow (31x - 8)$ to obtain the next polynomial family with $\rho(q, t, r) = 3/2$:

$$t(x) = 124x^3 - 134x^2 + 57x - 7$$
$$r(x) = 31x^4 - 49x^3 + 31x^2 - 9x + 1$$
$$q(x) = 3844x^6 - 8308x^5 + 8023x^4 - 4253x^3 + 1289x^2 - 204x + 13$$

with CM polynomial $f(x) = 31x^2 - 18x + 3$ and generalized Pell equation:

$$(31x - 9)^2 - 31DY^2 = -12 \tag{13}$$

Example 5 (k = 8). Set $(a_0, a_1) = (1, 1)$ in Family 5 and apply the transformation $x \rightarrow (12x + 4)$ to conclude to the polynomial family with $\rho(q, t, r) = 3/2$:

$$t(x) = -144x^3 - 72x^2 - 4x + 2$$
$$r(x) = 288x^4 + 288x^3 + 104x^2 + 16x + 1$$
$$q(x) = 5184x^6 + 5184x^5 + 1872x^4 + 144x^3 - 54x^2 - 4x + 1$$

Setting $h(x) = 18x^2$ we get the CM polynomial $f(x) = 8x^2(144x^2 + 72x + 7)$ and the generalized Pell equation:

$$(24x + 6)^2 - 2DY^2 = 8 \tag{14}$$

Example 6 (k = 12). Set $(a_0, a_1) = (1, 1)$ in Family 6 and apply the transformation $x \rightarrow (30x + 24)$ to conclude to the polynomial family with $\rho(q, t, r) = 3/2$:

$$t(x) = -1800x^3 - 3900x^2 - 2796x - 662$$
$$r(x) = 3600x^4 + 10800x^3 + 12132x^2 + 6048x + 1129$$
$$q(x) = 810000x^6 + 3510000x^5 + 6329700x^4 + 6078600x^3 + 3277725x^2$$
$$+ 940704x + 112237$$

Setting $h(x) = 25(3x + 2)^2$ we get the CM polynomial $f(x) = 12(400x^2 + 600x + 223)(3x + 2)^2$ and the generalized Pell equation:

$$(60x + 45)^2 - 3DY^2 = 18 \tag{15}$$

A different transformation in each example may result in some different curve parameters. Recall that we are searching for $x_0 \in \mathbb{Z}$ such that $q(x_0)$ and $r(x_0)$ are both primes. However, this condition can be further loosened if we allow $r(x_0)$ to contain a small cofactor s [18]. Pell Equation (10) is considered as special because it is always solvable, for any positive and square free integer D. This is because the standard Pell equation $U^2 - 55DV^2 = 1$ is always solvable (see Theorem 4.1 [16]) and if (U_i, V_i) is a solution of this equation, then $(10U_i, 10V_i)$ is a solution for (10). Thus we expect that Family 1 will produce more curve parameters compared to the other sparse families (see [7] for details). In Table 1

Table 1. Suitable parameters for $k \in \{5, 8, 10, 12\}$ ($128 \leq \log q \leq 960$)

Construction	k	$D < 10^5$	$D < 10^6$	$\rho(q, t, r)$
Example 1	5	12	47	3/2
Example 2	5	0	1	3/2
Example 3	10	2	4	1
Example 4	10	2	5	3/2
Example 5	8	1	5	3/2
Example 6	12	0	1	3/2

we present the number of suitable parameters obtained from Examples 1 to 6. The field size is between 128 and 960 bits, while for D we set a limit up to 10^6 which is a reasonable value in order to keep CM method efficient. For Examples 2 and 6, increasing the bound for D will result in more suitable triples (q, t, r). The table justifies our earlier claim that Family 1 has better chances in generating suitable curve parameters than any other family reported for $k \notin \{3, 4, 6\}$. We also found several examples for $k = 5$ that improve the examples appeared in [13] where a 252-bit prime q is constructed using a CM discriminant D with 7 decimal digits. Some examples of suitable parameters (q, t, r) are given in the Appendix A.

6   Conclusion

We presented two different methods for producing sparse families of pairing-friendly elliptic curves. We focus on the cases $k \in \{5, 8, 10, 12\}$, but our methods can be applied for every embedding degree. Particularly for $k = 5$, we introduce for the first time the use of Pell equations and presented an effective polynomial family leading to a Pell equation that produces more curve parameters than others. Furthermore our ρ-value 3/2 sets a record on sparse families with $k = 5$. We also presented experimental results for the number of suitable triples (q, t, r) obtained by every family of Section 5 for $k \in \{5, 8, 10, 12\}$.

References

1. Atkin, A.O.L., Morain, F.: Elliptic Curves and Primality Proving. Mathematics of Computation 61, 29–68 (1993)
2. Barreto, P.S.L.M., Naehrig, M.: Pairing-Friendly Elliptic Curves of Prime Order. In: Preneel, B., Tavares, S. (eds.) SAC 2005. LNCS, vol. 3897, pp. 319–331. Springer, Heidelberg (2006)
3. Boneh, D., Franklin, M.: Identity-Based Encryption from the Weil Pairing. SIAM Journal of Computing 32(3), 586–615 (2003)
4. Brezing, F., Weng, A.: Elliptic Curves Suitable for Pairing Based Cryptography. Designs, Codes and Cryptography 37, 133–141 (2005)
5. Dryło, R.: On Constructing Families of Pairing-Friendly Elliptic Curves with Variable Discriminant. In: Bernstein, D.J., Chatterjee, S. (eds.) INDOCRYPT 2011. LNCS, vol. 7107, pp. 310–319. Springer, Heidelberg (2011)
6. Duan, P., Cui, S., Chan, C.W.: Finding More Non-Supersingular Elliptic Curves for Pairing-Based Cryptosystems. International Journal of Information Technology 2(2), 157–163 (2005)
7. Fotiadis, G., Konstantinou, E.: On the Efficient Generation of Generalized MNT Elliptic Curves. In: Muntean, T., Poulakis, D., Rolland, R. (eds.) CAI 2013. LNCS, vol. 8080, pp. 147–159. Springer, Heidelberg (2013)
8. Freeman, D.: Constructing Pairing-Friendly Elliptic Curves with Embedding Degree 10. In: Hess, F., Pauli, S., Pohst, M. (eds.) ANTS 2006. LNCS, vol. 4076, pp. 452–465. Springer, Heidelberg (2006)
9. Freeman, D., Scott, M., Teske, E.: A Taxonomy of Pairing-Friendly Elliptic Curves. Journal of Cryptology 23, 224–280 (2010)
10. Galbraith, S.D., McKee, J., Valença, P.: Ordinary Abelian Varieties Having Small Embedding Degree. Finite Fields and Their Applications 13(4), 800–814 (2007)
11. Joux, A.: A One Round Protocol for Tripartite Diffie-Hellman. In: Bosma, W. (ed.) ANTS 2000. LNCS, vol. 1838, pp. 385–394. Springer, Heidelberg (2000)
12. Kachisa, E.J., Schaefer, E.F., Scott, M.: Constructing Brezing-Weng Pairing-Friendly Elliptic Curves Using Elements in the Cyclotomic Field. In: Galbraith, S.D., Paterson, K.G. (eds.) Pairing 2008. LNCS, vol. 5209, pp. 126–135. Springer, Heidelberg (2008)
13. Lee, H.-S., Park, C.-M.: Generating Pairing-Friendly Curves with the CM Equation of Degree 1. In: Shacham, H., Waters, B. (eds.) Pairing 2009. LNCS, vol. 5671, pp. 66–77. Springer, Heidelberg (2009)
14. Miyaji, A., Nakabayashi, M., Takano, S.: New Explicit Conditions of Elliptic Curve Traces for FR-Reduction. IEICE Transactions Fundamentals E84-A(5), 1234–1243 (2001)
15. Mollin, R.A.: Fundamental Number Theory with Applications. CRC Press, Boca Raton (1998)
16. Mollin, R.A.: Simple Continued Fraction Solutions for Diophantine Equations. Expositines Mathematicae 19, 55–73 (2001)
17. Murphy, A., Fitzpatrick, N.: Elliptic Curves for Pairing Applications. IACR Eprint archive (2005), http://eprint.iacr.org/2005/302/
18. Scott, M., Barreto, P.S.L.M.: Generating more MNT Elliptic Curves. Designs, Codes and Cryptography 38, 209–217 (2006)
19. Tanaka, S., Nakamula, K.: Constructing Pairing-Friendly Elliptic Curves Using Factorization of Cyclotomic Polynomials. In: Galbraith, S.D., Paterson, K.G. (eds.) Pairing 2008. LNCS, vol. 5209, pp. 136–145. Springer, Heidelberg (2008)

A   Additional Polynomial Families and Parameters of Proper Cryptographic Size

A.1   Additional Polynomial Families for k ∈ {5, 10}

We present two additional examples of sparse families for $k = 5, 10$. The following families are constructed from elements θ which depend only on $a_0, a_1 \in \mathbb{Q}$.

Family 7. Let $\theta = a_0 + a_1\zeta_5 + 2a_1\zeta_5^2 + 6a_1\zeta_5^3$, with $a_0, a_1 \in \mathbb{Q}$ and $a_1 \neq 0$. The transition matrix has $\det(P) = -11^3 a_1^6$ and we obtain the polynomials:

$$
\begin{aligned}
u(x) &= (-6x^3 + (18a_0 + 22a_1)x^2 + (39a_1^2 - 18a_0^2 - 44a_0a_1)x \\
&\quad + (6a_0^3 + 22a_0^2a_1 - 39a_0a_1^2 - 1328a_1^3))/(11a_1)^3 \\
r(x) &= x^4 + (9a_1 - 4a_0)x^3 + (6a_0^2 - 27a_0a_1 + 21a_1^2)x^2 \\
&\quad + (27a_0^2a_1 - 4a_0^3 - 42a_0a_1^2 + 139a_1^3)x \\
&\quad + (a_0^4 - 9a_0^3a_1 + 21a_0^2a_1^2 - 139a_0a_1^3 + 881a_1^4) \\
f(x) &= (x^2 + (2a_1 - 2a_0)x + (a_0^2 - 2a_0a_1 - 19a_1^2))/11a_1^2
\end{aligned}
$$

with $\rho(q, t, r) = 3/2$.

Family 8. Let $\theta = a_0 + 4a_1\zeta_{10} - 9a_1\zeta_{10}^2 + 6a_1\zeta_{10}^3$, with $a_0, a_1 \in \mathbb{Q}$ and $a_1 \neq 0$. The transition matrix has $\det(P) = 5^2 11^3 a_1^6$ and we obtain the polynomials:

$$
\begin{aligned}
u(x) &= (-3x^3 + (9a_0 + 72a_1)x^2 - (9a_0^2 + 144a_0a_1 + 490a_1^2)x \\
&\quad + (3a_0^3 + 72a_0^2a_1 + 490a_0a_1^2 - 324a_1^3))/605b^3 \\
r(x) &= x^4 - (4a_0 + 19a_1)x^3 + (6a_0^2 + 57a_0a_1 + 91a_1^2)x^2 \\
&\quad - (4a_0^3 + 57a_0^2a_1 + 182a_0a_1^2 - 371a_1^3)x \\
&\quad + (a_0^4 + 19a_0^3a_1 + 91a_0^2a_1^2 - 371a_0a_1^3 + 331a_1^4) \\
f(x) &= (2x^2 - (4a_0 + 19a_1)x + (2a_0^2 + 19a_0a_1 - 13a_1^2))/55a_1^2
\end{aligned}
$$

with $\rho(q, t, r) = 3/2$.

A.2   Curve Parameters of Proper Cryptographic Size

We give some examples of suitable integer triples (q, t, r) obtained from the polynomial families described in Section 5. Recall that we considered cases where the order r is not necessarily prime but it may contain a small cofactor s, in which case $r = s \cdot \tilde{r}$ for some large prime $\tilde{r}$. We also give some examples obtained by Freeman's family again considering r as a nearly prime integer.

Family of Example 1   (k = 5)

$D = 107$

$x_0 = 1170622244439162529$

$q = 31137662343827744551142706385896615302997261945942170125424854062898211567553375827328090$
$44143203492336457053214$1 (374 bits)

$t = 3529173407121148789366133507929632648094593506564547701$67

$\bar{r} = 1539243254418467024087909893002579533613676471213037240276601779369022$61 (237 bits)

$s = 671$

$\rho = 1.5802$

$D = 141811$

$x_0 = -11994919643295$

$q = 360387258071796328461219822648940205060151162806445544212956339551492448899191689$41 (275 bits)

$t = -37967736728532888596979964823118201071433$

$r = 1138549877741377933395022094278669277536945192203801451$ (180 bits)

$\rho = 1.5272$

$D = 227715$

$x_0 = -6451333850566315667727$

$q = 87233333991933520436364492086029196902705342851777194616867647955622986668808024860010894$
$03487387153091586524941357188961198673506951$81 (449 bits)

$t = -590705794763970536881010335173602186528078248153386214994783435510$33

$r = 952710072371620457893849236339552861390318069913935779737394327278004087802884034273884$11
(296 bits)

$\rho = 1.5165$

$D = 383259$

$x_0 = -4133570859843463005$

$q = 60358396257221629182345603319603709624185200112850740092554000742162689307714418757327712$
$558715354305776137285883341$ (385 bits)

$t = -1553813325431618625135528907637686836809814054831735432758$3

$\bar{r} = 5179675390032747099609975684233738625865444473148777038574010932848279596$71 (249 bits)

$s = 31$

$\rho = 1.5496$

$D = 584915$

$x_0 = 923586152635579344325$

$q = 75101713820205889762723839841611970090249093111475504738731273047109345166689007527938953$
$2690347512935567729431524623380740598514$1 (432 bits)

$t = 17332248996619670045112689321580235563044249767647964847796549986$7

$\bar{r} = 629525458436623677361367527688019566219283592204259776270209146137288982600232581$ (269 bits)

$s = 63571$

$\rho = 1.6074$

$D = 879515$

$x_0 = -44614321100137293687$

$q = 95418174239059772134251115900324243294147299645849145168155742349228224690584734518526584$
$4699020517433440788818779116438$1 (406 bits)

$t = -1953644535109289241903492054048903458344975439049065329295843$3

$r = 217901311512235692233368368115403359841826330176190408953014913308137507745536211$ (267 bits)

$\rho = 1.5183$

Family of Example 3   (k = 10)

$D = 35707$

$x_0 = 18496897600565332717798$

$q = 2926412733580100992307561873039833220827733137936969076285307797490604260428897294595498283$ (301 bits)

$t = 342135220845799562782407456500213155772327033$

$\bar{r} = 57260607882184639852175799183316565623469177348339331566461603130898144603670340016$1 (279 bits)

$s = 5110691$

$\rho = 1.08$

Family of Example 4   (k = 10)

$D = 203547$

$x_0 = 22135059892867860$

$q = 4521344380948830909026966456233867832092140208088819075816094157320371410316681666082765648 27307572973$ (338 bits)

$t = 13448188548572377759346650184620835875675923835456 13$

$\bar{r} = 95031432439416827668770468044372610003540028857393005182963713$1 (210 bits)

$s = 7831$

$\rho = 1.6141$

Family of Example 5   (k = 8)

$D = 123998$

$x_0 = -4905703988594849146021$

$q = 72255852307496602190358838372039620872388857865993606551782283905685268613721698290007633 18637304350092946396263846666831004992439879$9 (445 bits)

$t = 13448188548572377759346650184620835875675923835456 13$

$r = 166800690696195508912807274002584741056682578896316371026683908097448317598808893213388889$ (279 bits)

$\rho = 1.5003$

$D = 249614$

$x_0 = -12121921090938970$

$q = 16447265702239232230524893751417864688297201974229296032271581948519955327250225227613898 691712275281$ (333 bits)

$t = 256493787076718349353650951939281473598462227483082$

$\bar{r} = 1048633203123130337276405407401273934255676169285600920328669201$7 (213 bits)

$s = 593$

$\rho = 1.5654$

Author Index